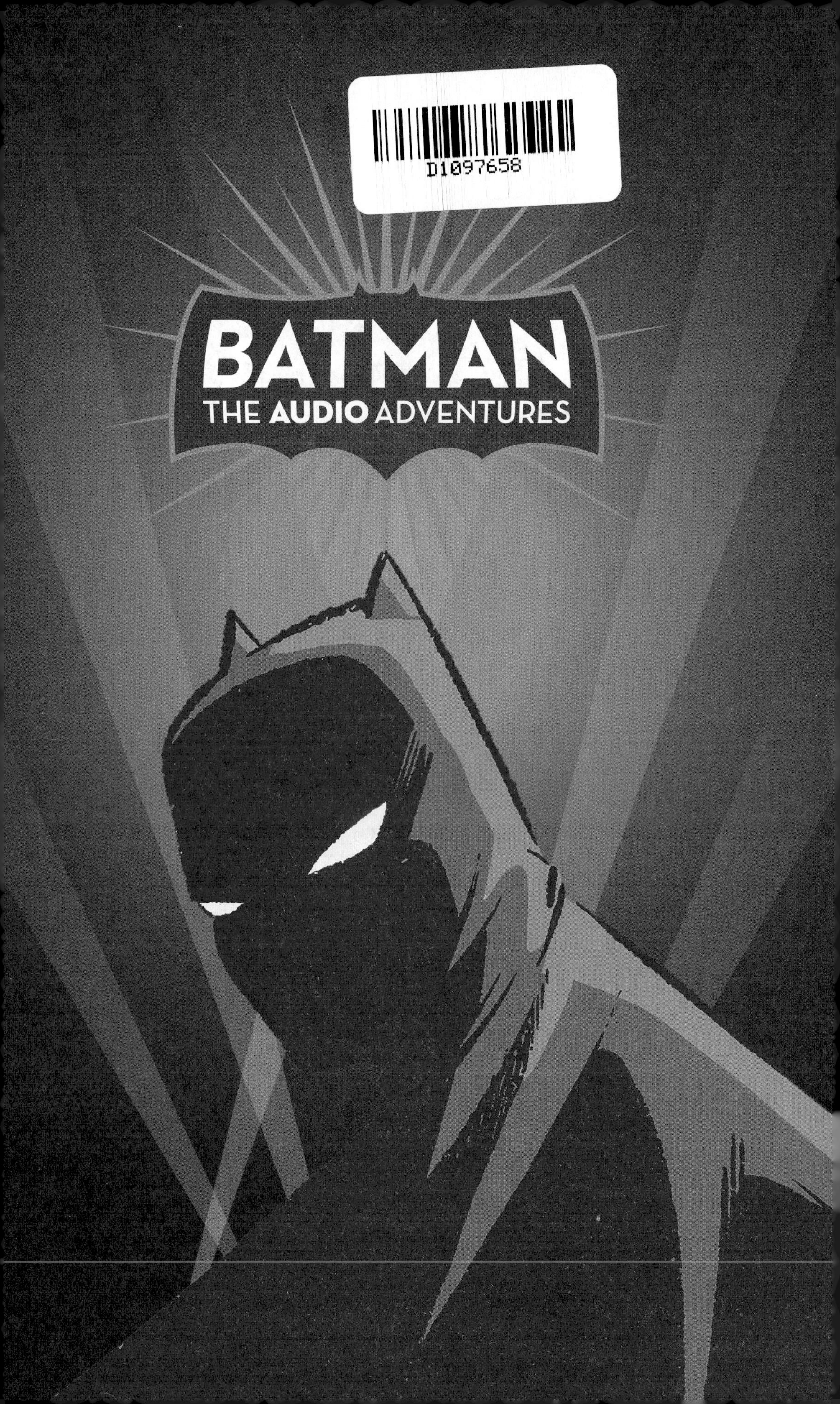
BATMAN
THE AUDIO ADVENTURES

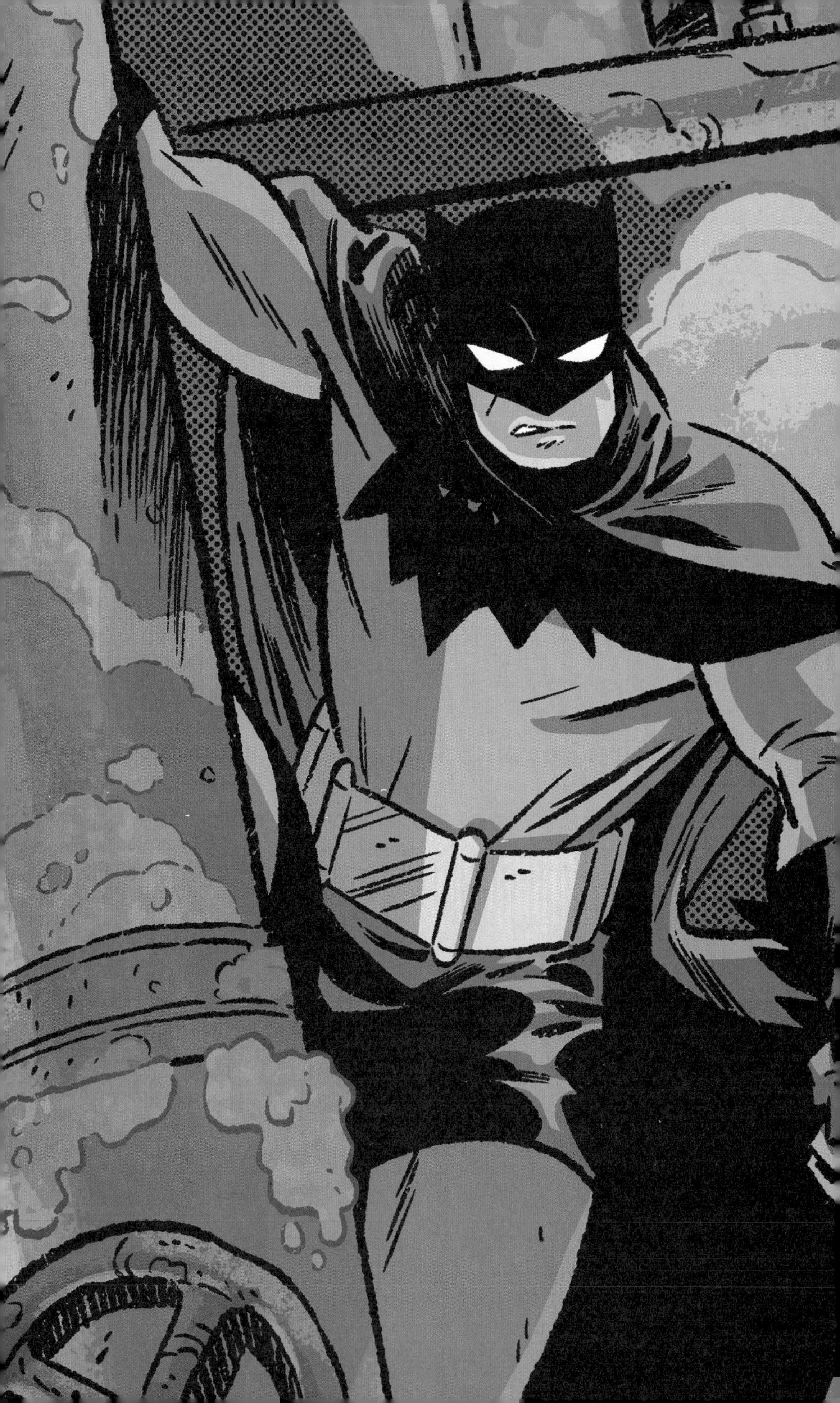

McNicholas, Dennis,
Batman, the Audio Adventures /
[2023]
33305256792114
ca   10/23/23

BATMAN
THE AUDIO ADVENTURES

DENNIS McNICHOLAS
IKE BARINHOLTZ
HEIDI GARDNER
BOBBY MOYNIHAN
PAUL SCHEER
writers

ANTHONY MARQUES
J. BONE
JUNI BA
DEREC DONOVAN
JACOB EDGAR
RICH ELLIS
JESÚS HERVÁS
EMMA KUBERT
JON MIKEL
GERMAN PERALTA
LEONARDO ROMERO
pencillers

J. BONE
JUNI BA
DEREC DONOVAN
JACOB EDGAR
RICH ELLIS
ROBERTO POGGI
JESÚS HERVÁS
JON MIKEL
GERMAN PERALTA
inkers

DAVE STEWART
NICK FILARDI
DAVID BARON
HI-FI
REX LOKUS
KRISTIAN ROSSI
MIKE SPICER
colorists

FERRAN DELGADO
CARLOS M. MANGUAL
PAT BROSSEAU
ANDWORLD DESIGN
JOSH REED
letterers

DAVE JOHNSON
collection and
series cover **artist**

BATMAN
created by BOB KANE
with BILL FINGER

*Experience the complete story by following *Batman: The Audio Adventures* across the comics and audio show in this chronology:

1) *Batman: The Audio Adventures Special #1*
2) *Batman: The Audio Adventures: Season 1* (on Max)
3) *Batman: The Audio Adventures #1-7*
4) *Batman: The Audio Adventures: Season 2* (on Max)

BATMAN
THE **AUDIO** ADVENTURES

ANDREW MARINO
KATIE KUBERT Editors – Original Series
BEN MEARES Associate Editor – Original Series
ALEX GALER Assistant Editor – Original Series
& Editor – Collected Edition
STEVE COOK Design Director – Books
& Publication Design
SUZANNAH ROWNTREE Publication Production

MARIE JAVINS VP – Editor-in-Chief

JIM LEE President, Publisher & Chief Creative Officer
ANNE DePIES Senior VP & General Manager
LARRY BERRY VP – Brand Design & Creative Services
DON FALLETTI VP – Manufacturing & Production
LAWRENCE GANEM VP – Editorial Programming & Talent Strategy
ALISON GILL Senior VP – Manufacturing & Operations
NICK J. NAPOLITANO VP – Publishing & Business Operations
NANCY SPEARS VP – Sales & Marketing

BATMAN: THE AUDIO ADVENTURES

Published by DC Comics. Compilation and all new material Copyright © 2023 DC Comics.
All Rights Reserved. Originally published in single magazine form in *Batman: The Audio
Adventures Special* I, *Batman: The Audio Adventures* I-7. Copyright © 2021, 2022, 2023
DC Comics. All Rights Reserved. All characters, their distinctive likenesses, and related
elements featured in this publication are trademarks of DC Comics. The stories, characters,
and incidents featured in this publication are entirely fictional. DC Comics does not read or
accept unsolicited submissions of ideas, stories, or artwork.

DC Comics, 4000 Warner Blvd., Bldg. 700, 2nd Floor, Burbank, CA 91522
Printed by Solisco Printers, Scott, QC, Canada. 8/4/23. First Printing.
ISBN: 978-1-77952-066-1

Library of Congress Cataloging-in-Publication Data is available.

PEFC Certified
This product is from
sustainably managed
forests and controlled
sources
PEFC
PEFC/26-31-02   www.pefc.org

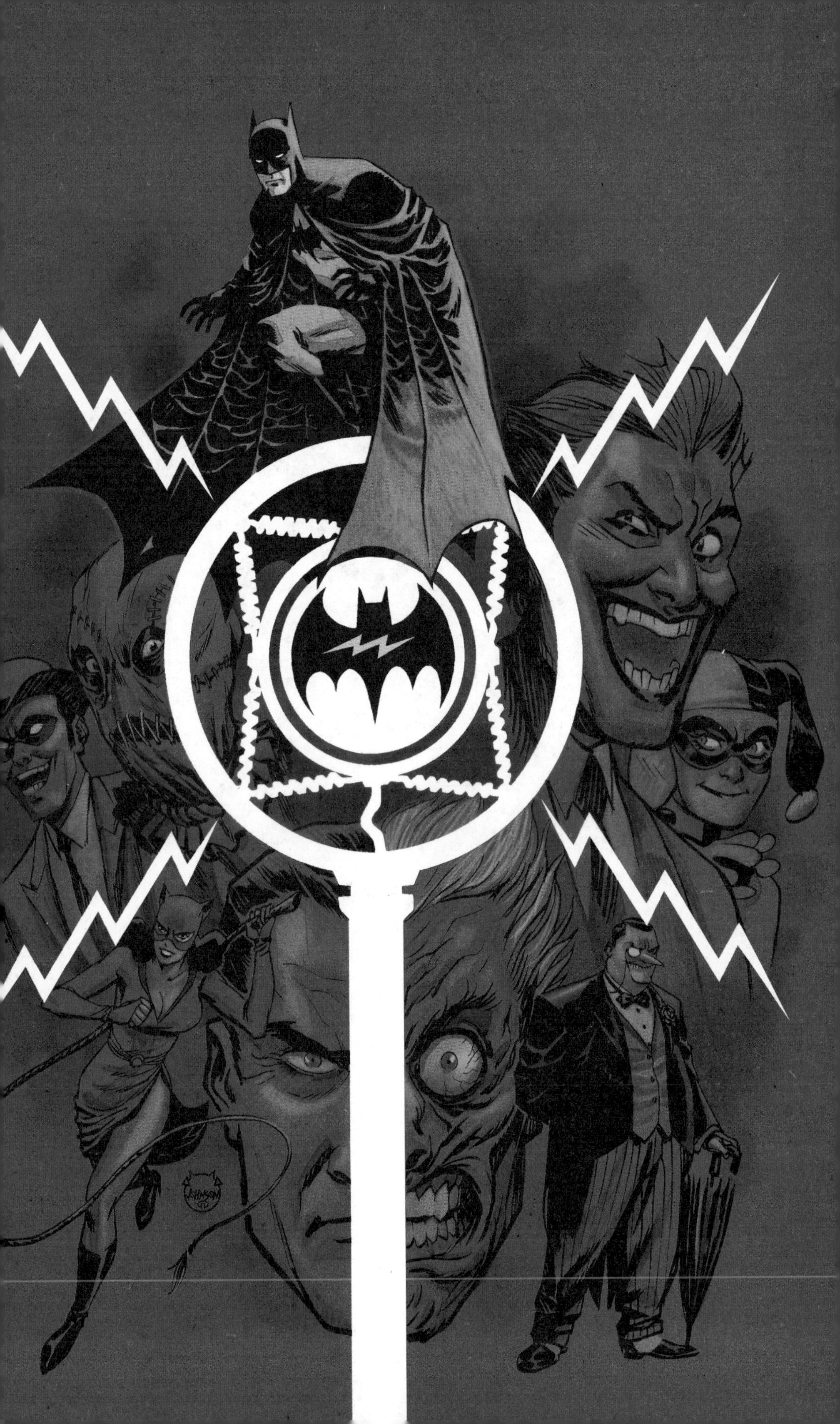

Batman: The Audio Adventures Special #1
variant cover by Francis Manapul

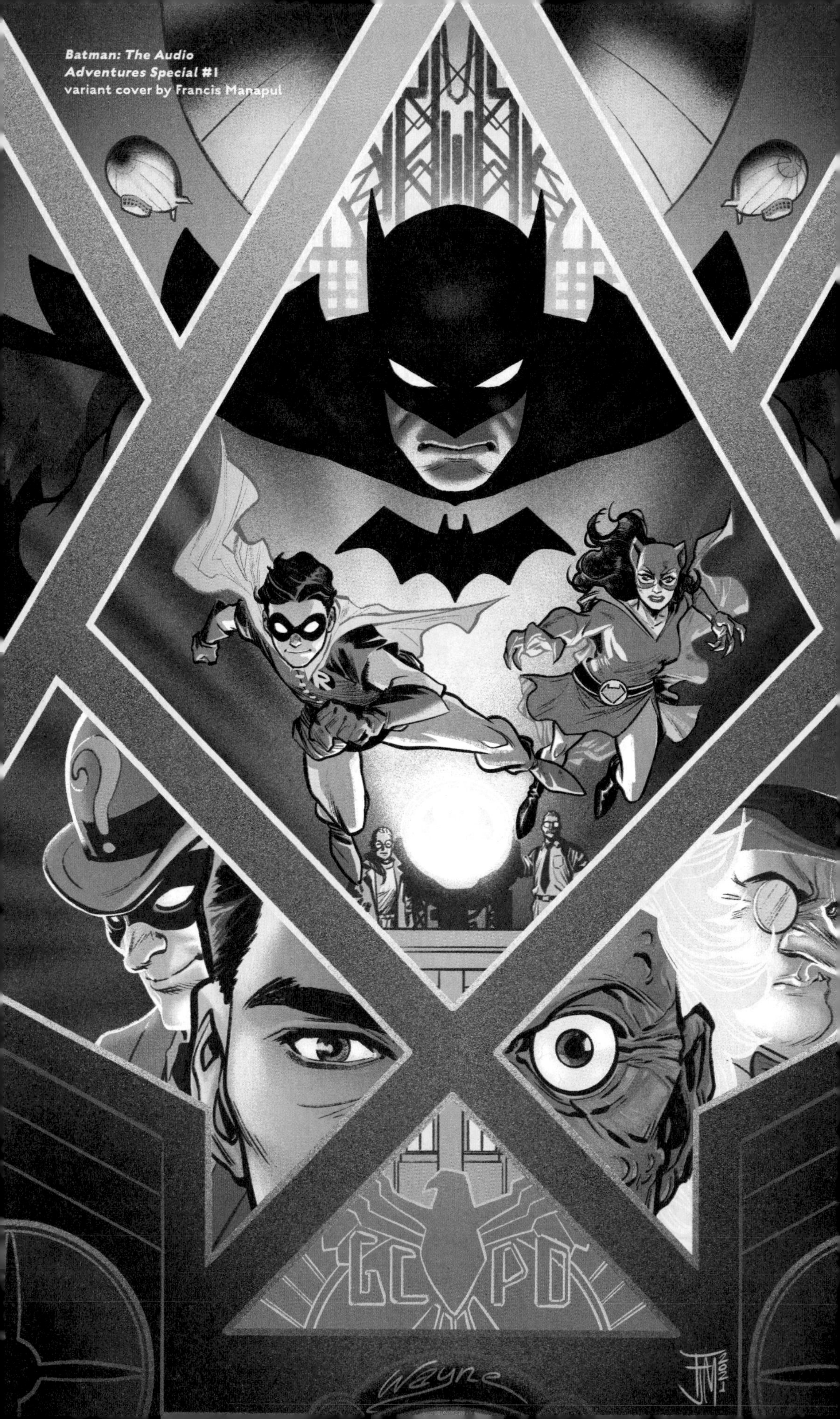
GCPD
Wayne

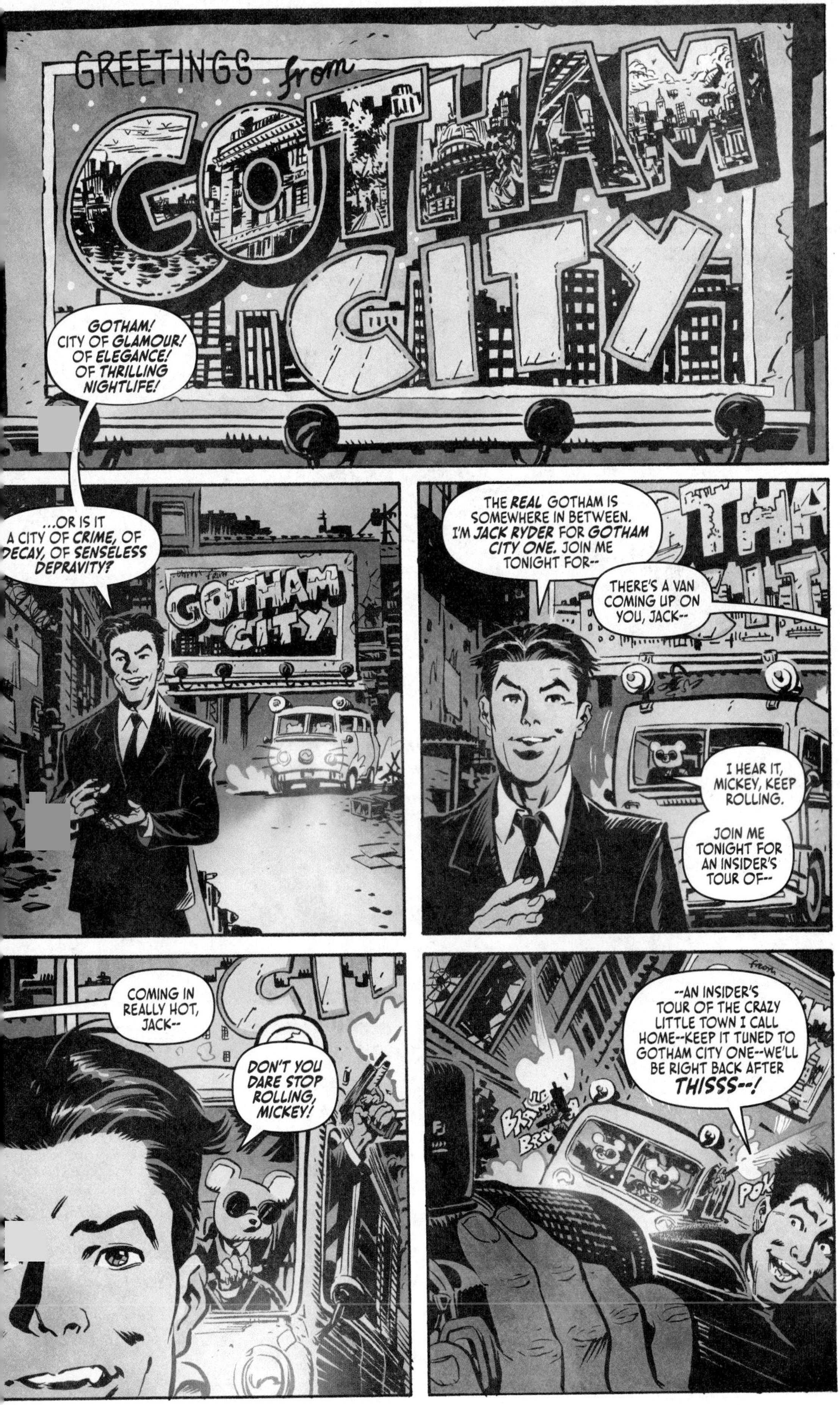
GREETINGS from GOTHAM CITY
GOTHAM! CITY OF GLAMOUR! OF ELEGANCE! OF THRILLING NIGHTLIFE!
...OR IS IT A CITY OF CRIME, OF DECAY, OF SENSELESS DEPRAVITY?
GOTHAM CITY
THE REAL GOTHAM IS SOMEWHERE IN BETWEEN. I'M JACK RYDER FOR GOTHAM CITY ONE. JOIN ME TONIGHT FOR--
THERE'S A VAN COMING UP ON YOU, JACK--
I HEAR IT, MICKEY, KEEP ROLLING.
JOIN ME TONIGHT FOR AN INSIDER'S TOUR OF--
COMING IN REALLY HOT, JACK--
DON'T YOU DARE STOP ROLLING, MICKEY!
--AN INSIDER'S TOUR OF THE CRAZY LITTLE TOWN I CALL HOME--KEEP IT TUNED TO GOTHAM CITY ONE--WE'LL BE RIGHT BACK AFTER THISSS--!
POK

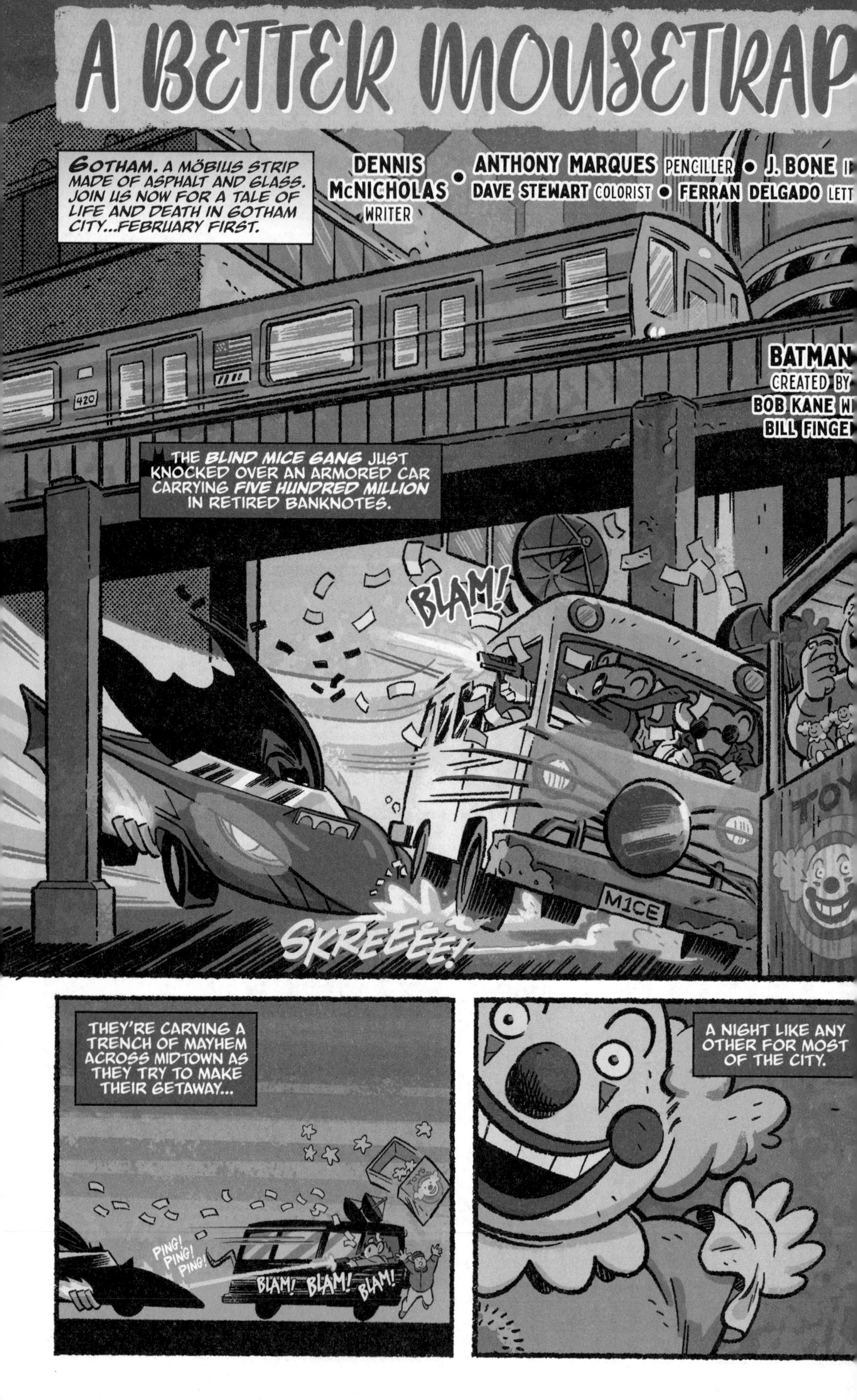
A BETTER MOUSETRAP
GOTHAM. A MÖBIUS STRIP MADE OF ASPHALT AND GLASS. JOIN US NOW FOR A TALE OF LIFE AND DEATH IN GOTHAM CITY...FEBRUARY FIRST.
DENNIS McNICHOLAS WRITER • ANTHONY MARQUES PENCILLER • J. BONE I
DAVE STEWART COLORIST • FERRAN DELGADO LETT
BATMAN CREATED BY BOB KANE W
BILL FINGE
THE BLIND MICE GANG JUST KNOCKED OVER AN ARMORED CAR CARRYING FIVE HUNDRED MILLION IN RETIRED BANKNOTES.
BLAM!
M1CE
SKREEEEE!
THEY'RE CARVING A TRENCH OF MAYHEM ACROSS MIDTOWN AS THEY TRY TO MAKE THEIR GETAWAY...
PING! PING! PING!
BLAM! BLAM! BLAM!
A NIGHT LIKE ANY OTHER FOR MOST OF THE CITY.

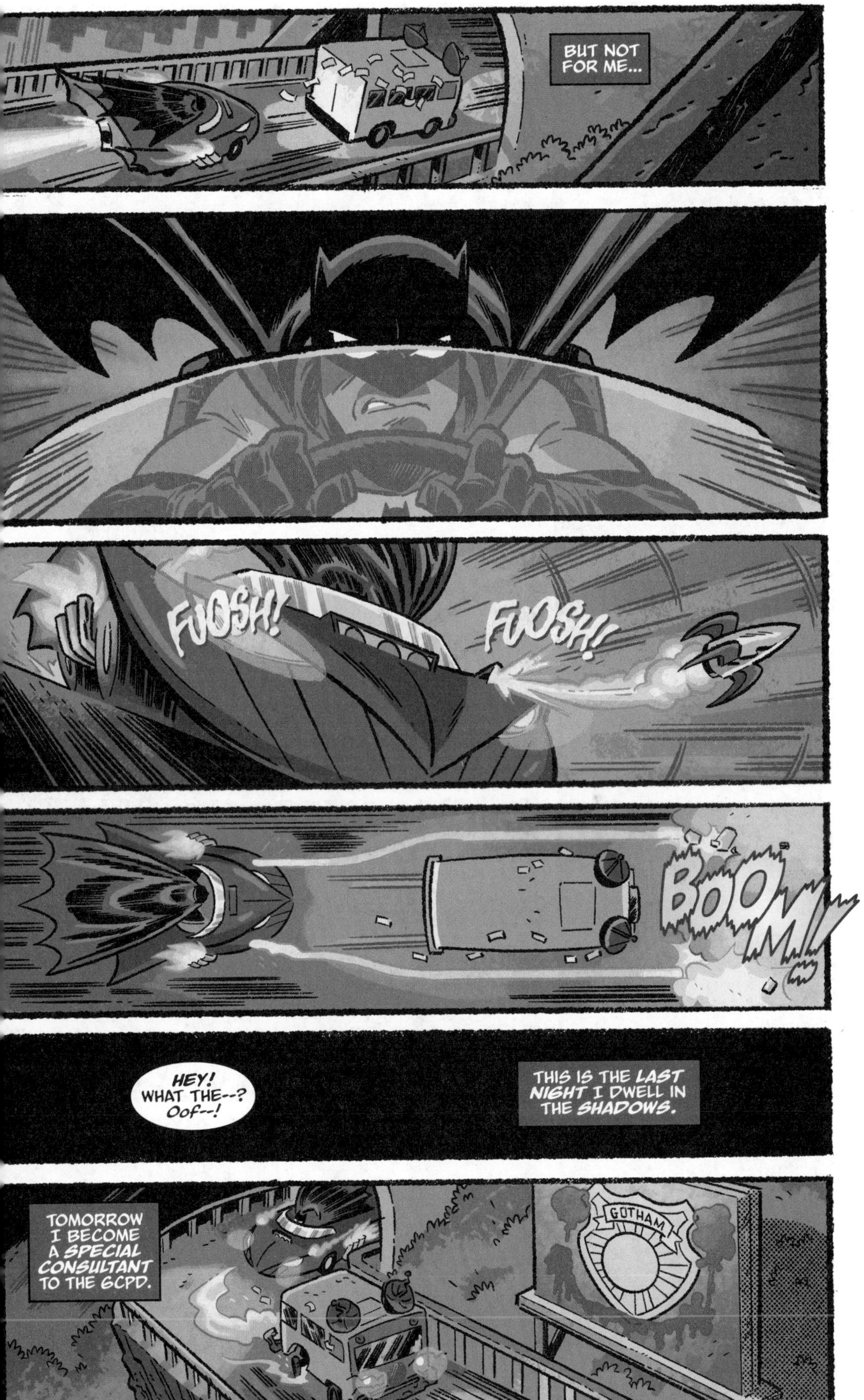
BUT NOT FOR ME...
FUOSH!
FUOSH!
BOOM!!
HEY! WHAT THE--? Oof--!
THIS IS THE LAST NIGHT I DWELL IN THE SHADOWS.
TOMORROW I BECOME A SPECIAL CONSULTANT TO THE GCPD.
GOTHAM

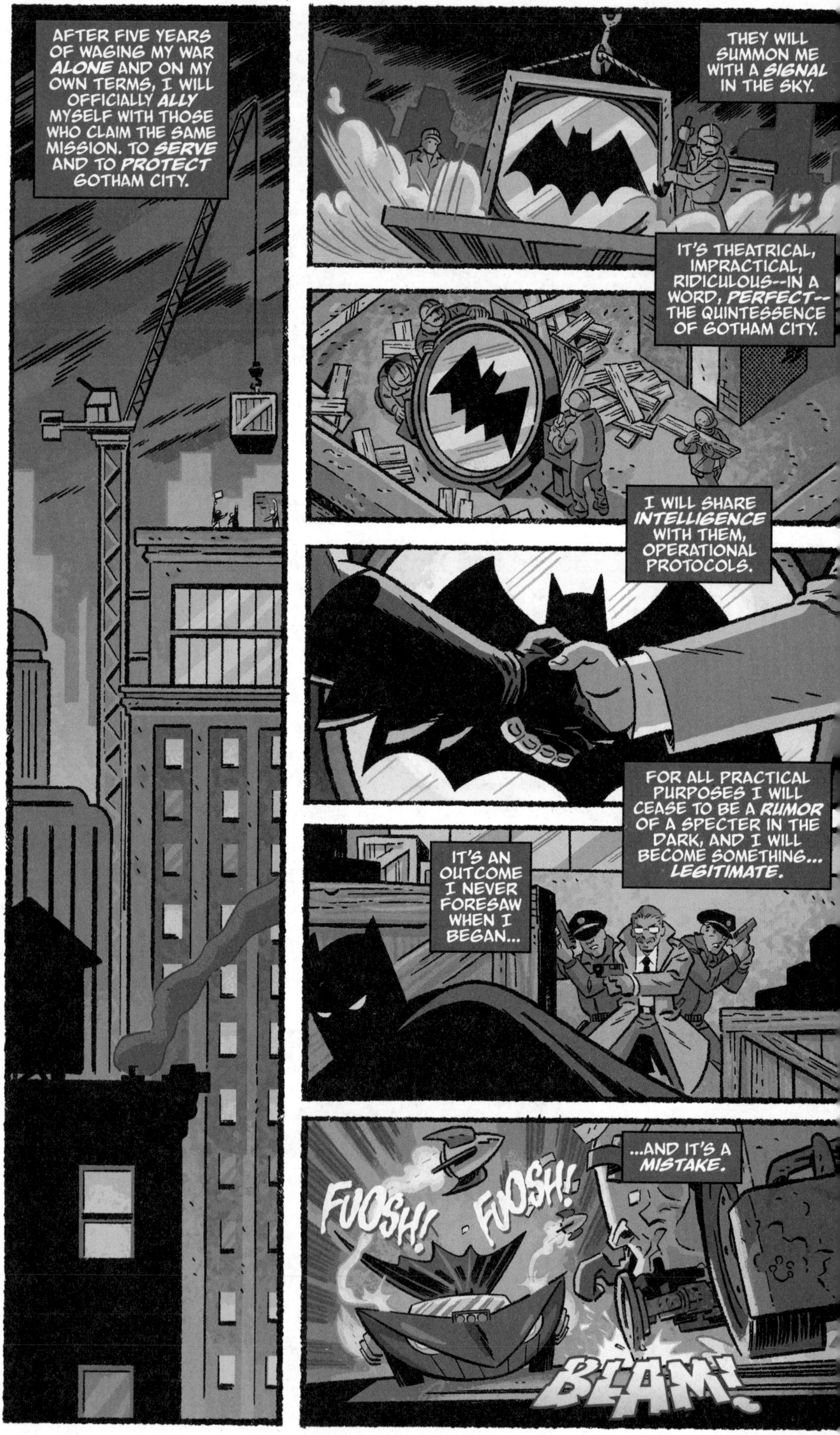
AFTER FIVE YEARS OF WAGING MY WAR ALONE AND ON MY OWN TERMS, I WILL OFFICIALLY ALLY MYSELF WITH THOSE WHO CLAIM THE SAME MISSION. TO SERVE AND TO PROTECT GOTHAM CITY.
THEY WILL SUMMON ME WITH A SIGNAL IN THE SKY.
IT'S THEATRICAL, IMPRACTICAL, RIDICULOUS--IN A WORD, PERFECT-- THE QUINTESSENCE OF GOTHAM CITY.
I WILL SHARE INTELLIGENCE WITH THEM, OPERATIONAL PROTOCOLS.
FOR ALL PRACTICAL PURPOSES I WILL CEASE TO BE A RUMOR OF A SPECTER IN THE DARK, AND I WILL BECOME SOMETHING... LEGITIMATE.
IT'S AN OUTCOME I NEVER FORESAW WHEN I BEGAN...
...AND IT'S A MISTAKE.
FUOSH!
FUOSH!
BLAM!

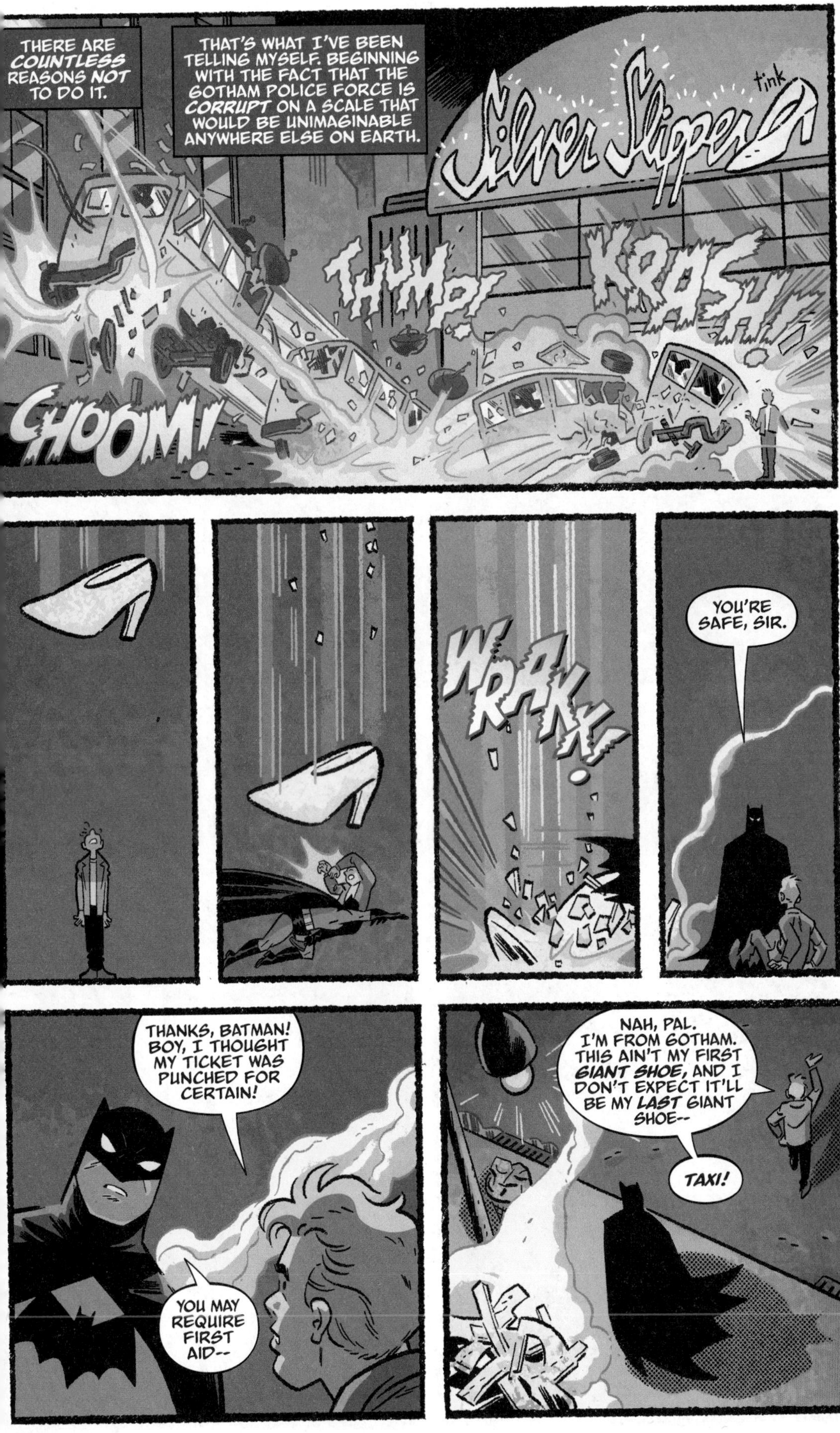

THERE ARE COUNTLESS REASONS NOT TO DO IT.
THAT'S WHAT I'VE BEEN TELLING MYSELF. BEGINNING WITH THE FACT THAT THE GOTHAM POLICE FORCE IS CORRUPT ON A SCALE THAT WOULD BE UNIMAGINABLE ANYWHERE ELSE ON EARTH.
Silver Slipper
tink
THUMP!
KRASH!
CHOOM!
WRAKK!
YOU'RE SAFE, SIR.
THANKS, BATMAN! BOY, I THOUGHT MY TICKET WAS PUNCHED FOR CERTAIN!
YOU MAY REQUIRE FIRST AID--
NAH, PAL. I'M FROM GOTHAM. THIS AIN'T MY FIRST GIANT SHOE, AND I DON'T EXPECT IT'LL BE MY LAST GIANT SHOE--
TAXI!

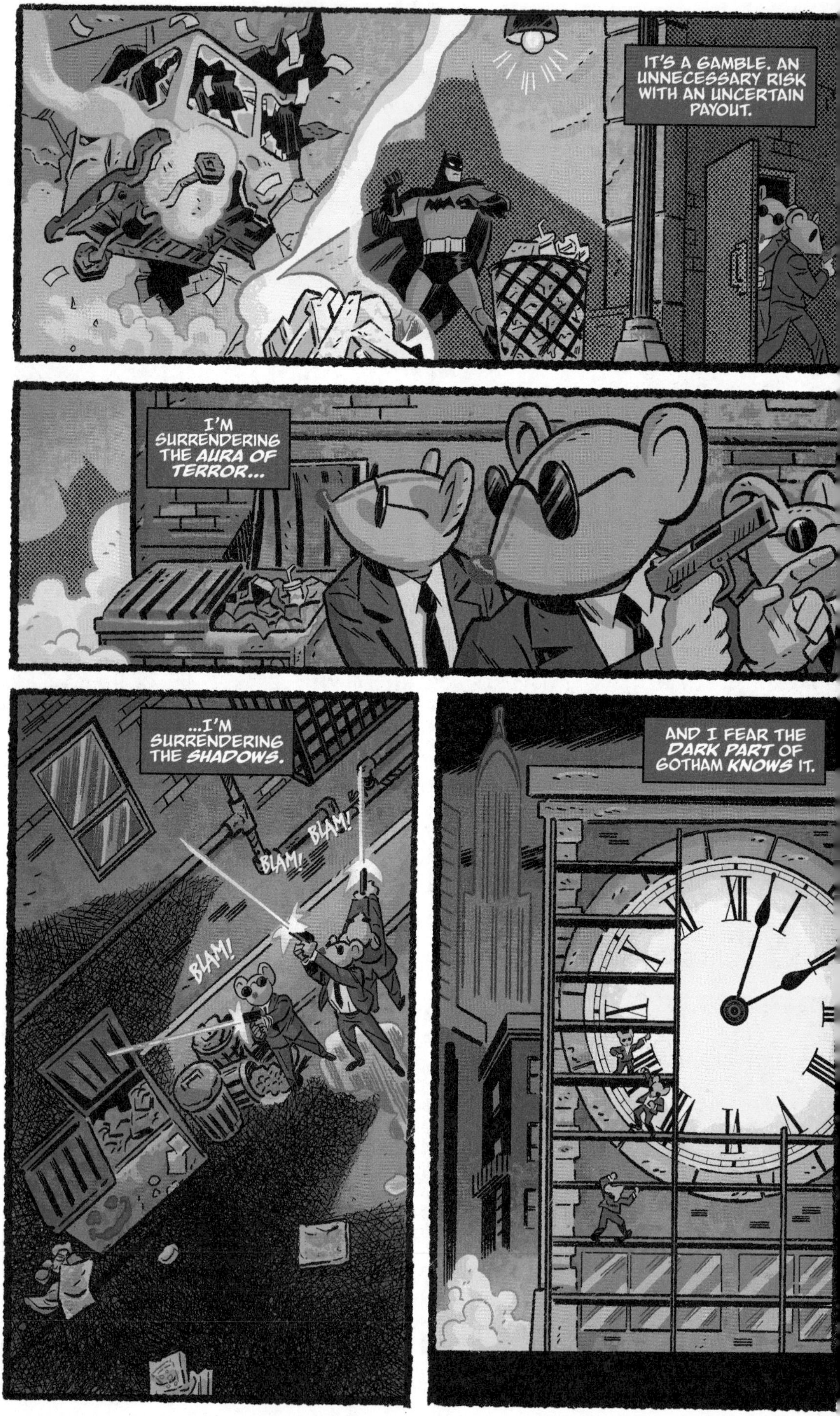
IT'S A GAMBLE. AN UNNECESSARY RISK WITH AN UNCERTAIN PAYOUT.
I'M SURRENDERING THE AURA OF TERROR...
...I'M SURRENDERING THE SHADOWS.
BLAM!
BLAM!
BLAM!
AND I FEAR THE DARK PART OF GOTHAM KNOWS IT.

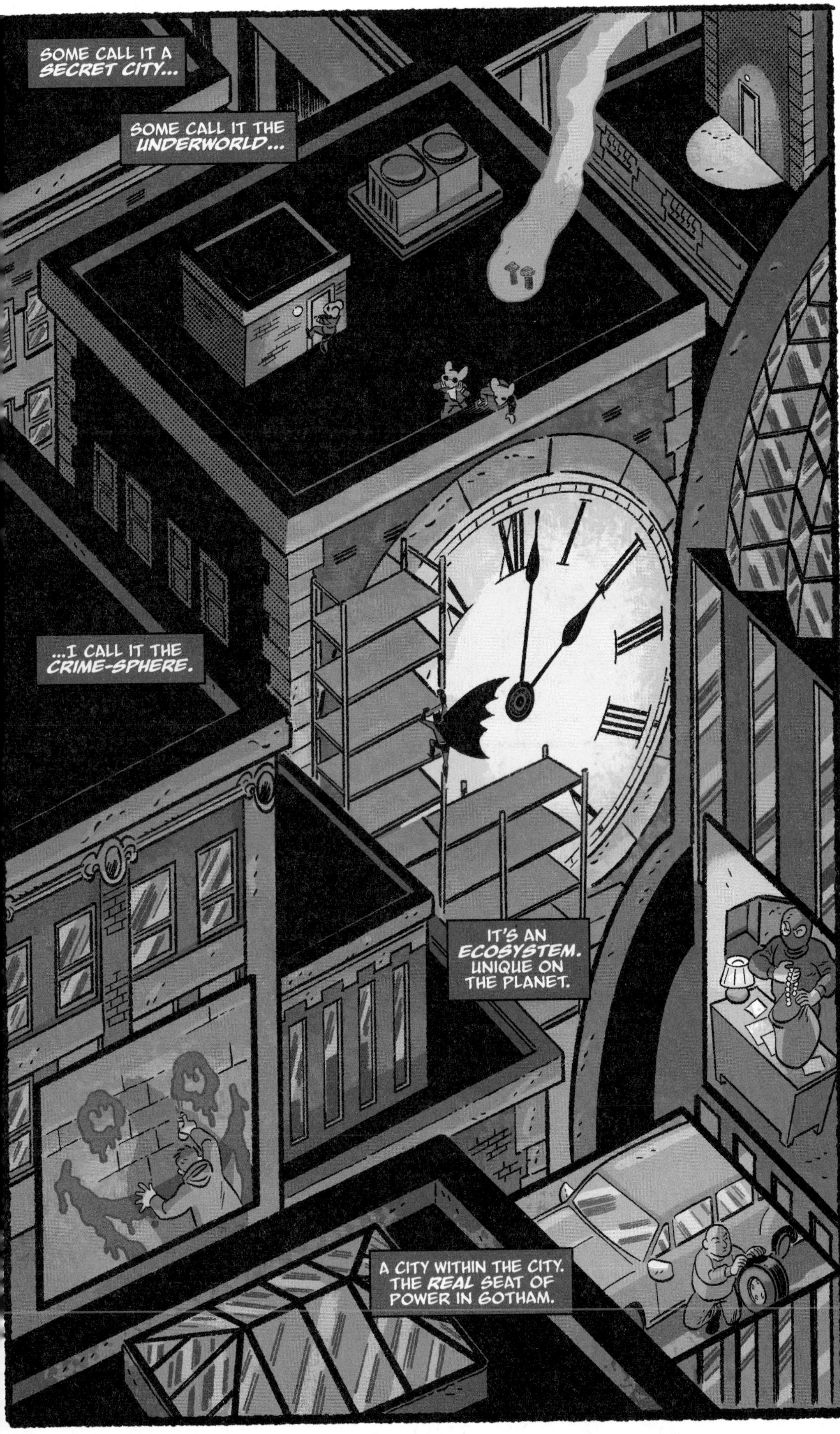
SOME CALL IT A SECRET CITY...
SOME CALL IT THE UNDERWORLD...
...I CALL IT THE CRIME-SPHERE.
IT'S AN ECOSYSTEM. UNIQUE ON THE PLANET.
A CITY WITHIN THE CITY. THE REAL SEAT OF POWER IN GOTHAM.

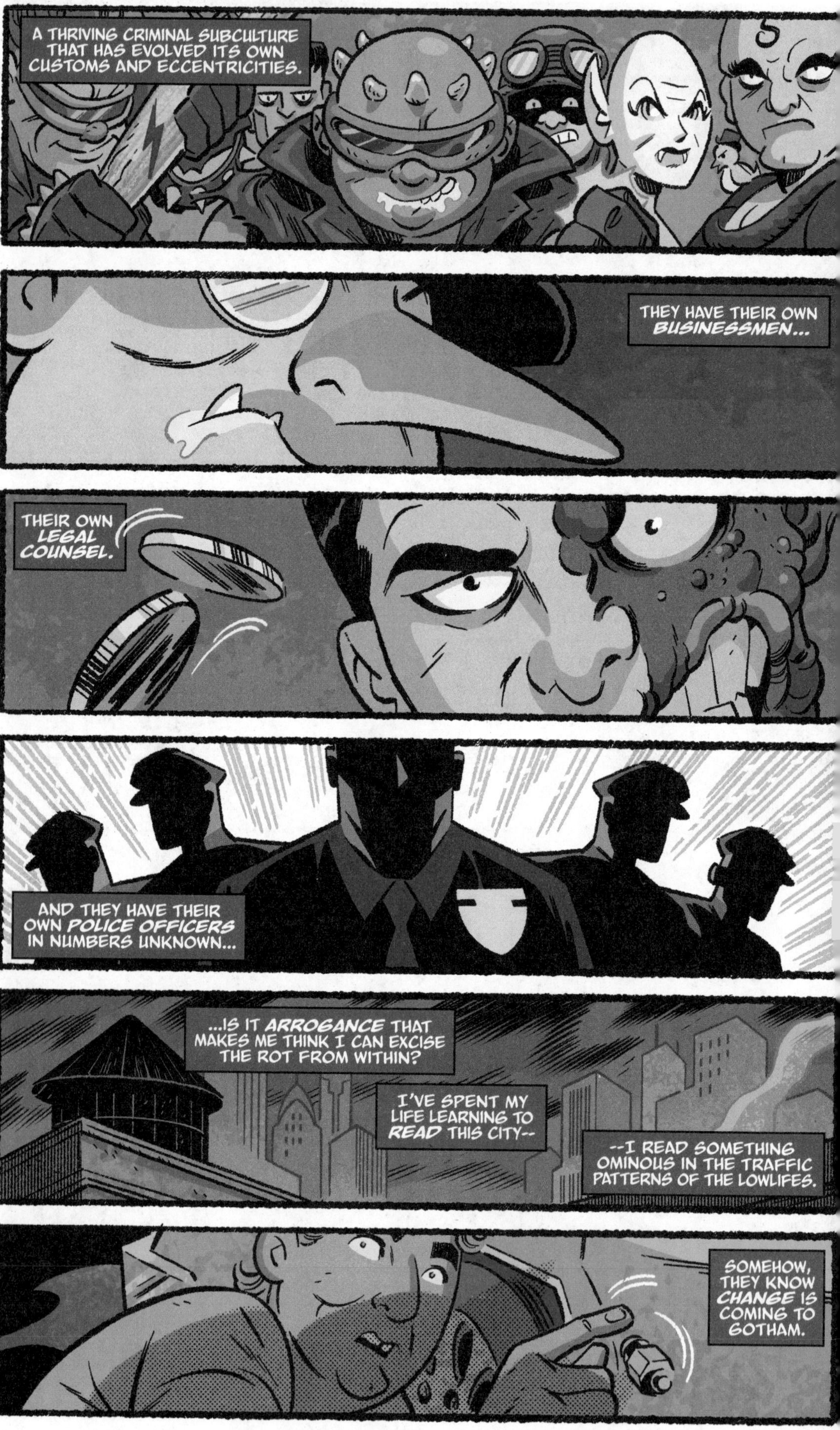
A THRIVING CRIMINAL SUBCULTURE THAT HAS EVOLVED ITS OWN CUSTOMS AND ECCENTRICITIES.
THEY HAVE THEIR OWN *BUSINESSMEN...*
THEIR OWN *LEGAL COUNSEL.*
AND THEY HAVE THEIR OWN *POLICE OFFICERS* IN NUMBERS UNKNOWN...
...IS IT *ARROGANCE* THAT MAKES ME THINK I CAN EXCISE THE ROT FROM WITHIN?
I'VE SPENT MY LIFE LEARNING TO *READ* THIS CITY--
--I READ SOMETHING OMINOUS IN THE TRAFFIC PATTERNS OF THE LOWLIFES.
SOMEHOW, THEY KNOW *CHANGE* IS COMING TO GOTHAM.

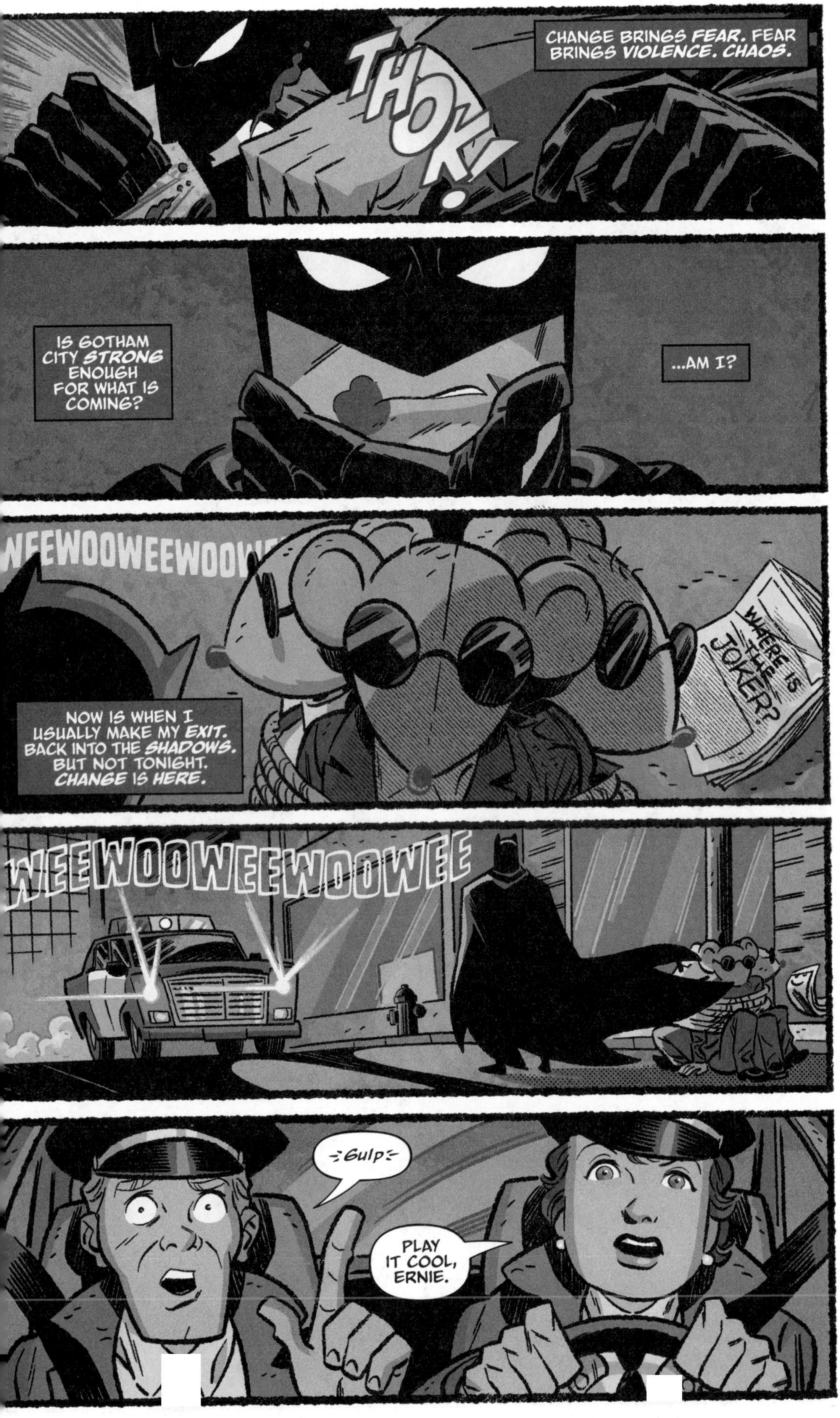
CHANGE BRINGS FEAR. FEAR BRINGS VIOLENCE. CHAOS.
THOK!
IS GOTHAM CITY STRONG ENOUGH FOR WHAT IS COMING?
...AM I?
WEEWOOWEEWOOW
WHERE IS THE JOKER?
NOW IS WHEN I USUALLY MAKE MY EXIT. BACK INTO THE SHADOWS. BUT NOT TONIGHT. CHANGE IS HERE.
WEEWOOWEEWOOWEE
Gulp
PLAY IT COOL, ERNIE.

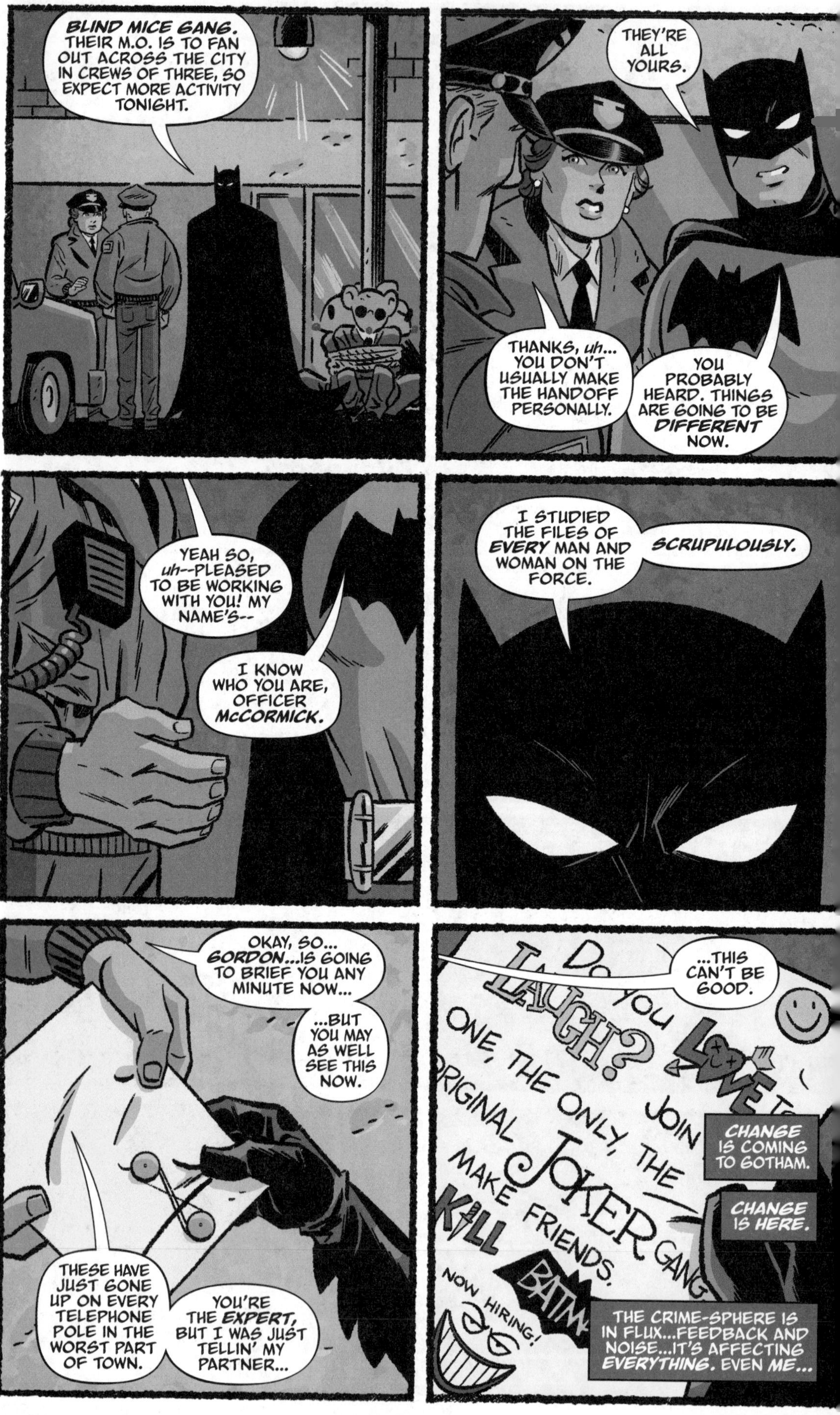
BLIND MICE GANG. THEIR M.O. IS TO FAN OUT ACROSS THE CITY IN CREWS OF THREE, SO EXPECT MORE ACTIVITY TONIGHT.
THEY'RE ALL YOURS.
THANKS, uh... YOU DON'T USUALLY MAKE THE HANDOFF PERSONALLY.
YOU PROBABLY HEARD. THINGS ARE GOING TO BE DIFFERENT NOW.
YEAH SO, uh--PLEASED TO BE WORKING WITH YOU! MY NAME'S--
I KNOW WHO YOU ARE, OFFICER McCORMICK.
I STUDIED THE FILES OF EVERY MAN AND WOMAN ON THE FORCE.
SCRUPULOUSLY.
OKAY, SO... GORDON...IS GOING TO BRIEF YOU ANY MINUTE NOW...
...BUT YOU MAY AS WELL SEE THIS NOW.
THESE HAVE JUST GONE UP ON EVERY TELEPHONE POLE IN THE WORST PART OF TOWN.
YOU'RE THE EXPERT, BUT I WAS JUST TELLIN' MY PARTNER...
...THIS CAN'T BE GOOD.
DO YOU LAUGH?
JOIN
ONE, THE ONLY, THE
ORIGINAL
JOKER
GANG
MAKE FRIENDS.
KILL
NOW HIRING!
CHANGE IS COMING TO GOTHAM.
CHANGE IS HERE.
THE CRIME-SPHERE IS IN FLUX...FEEDBACK AND NOISE...IT'S AFFECTING EVERYTHING. EVEN ME...

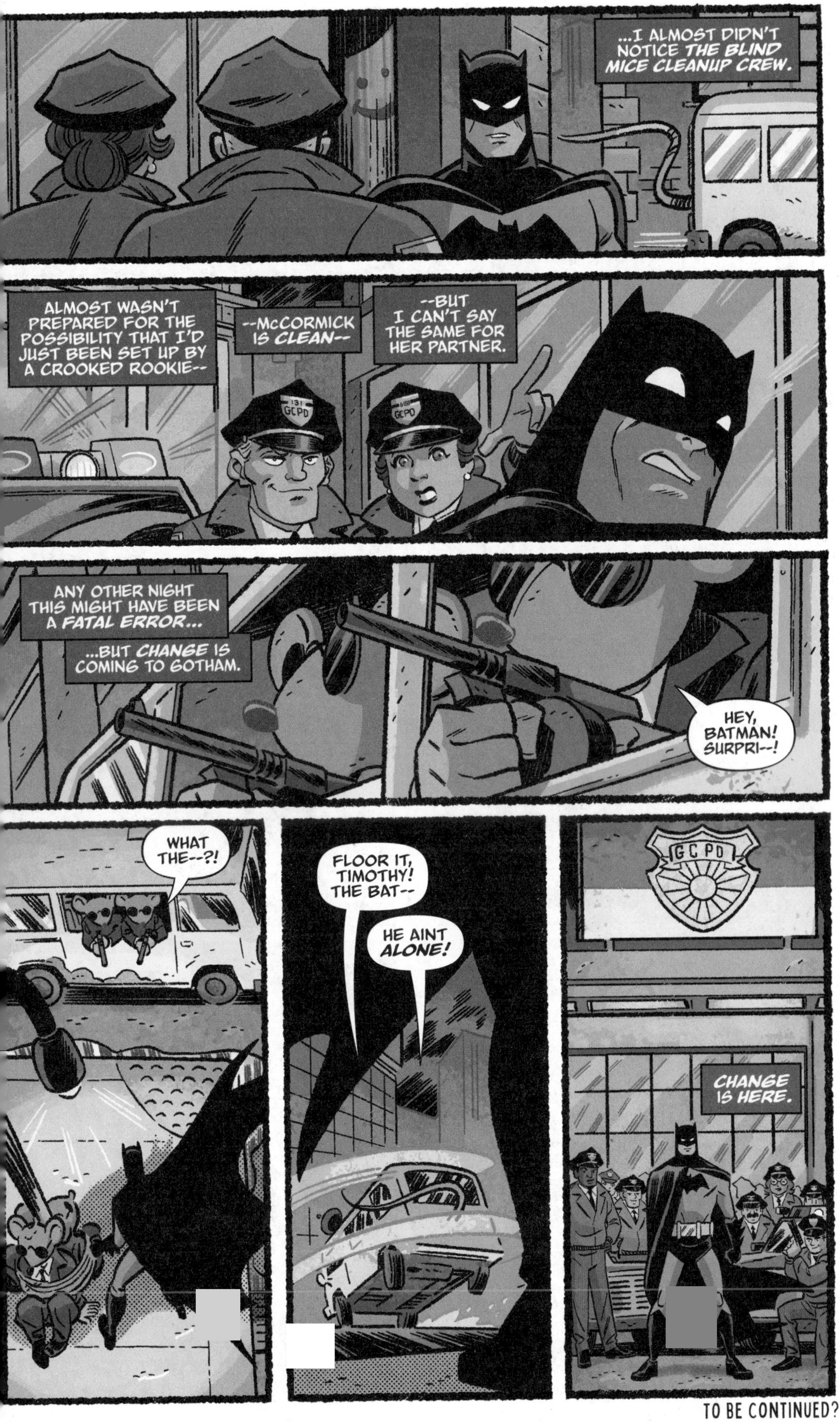
...I ALMOST DIDN'T NOTICE THE BLIND MICE CLEANUP CREW.
ALMOST WASN'T PREPARED FOR THE POSSIBILITY THAT I'D JUST BEEN SET UP BY A CROOKED ROOKIE--
--McCORMICK IS CLEAN--
--BUT I CAN'T SAY THE SAME FOR HER PARTNER.
GCPD
GCPD
ANY OTHER NIGHT THIS MIGHT HAVE BEEN A FATAL ERROR...
...BUT CHANGE IS COMING TO GOTHAM.
HEY, BATMAN! SURPRI--!
WHAT THE--?!
FLOOR IT, TIMOTHY! THE BAT--
HE AINT ALONE!
GCPD
CHANGE IS HERE.

TO BE CONTINUED?

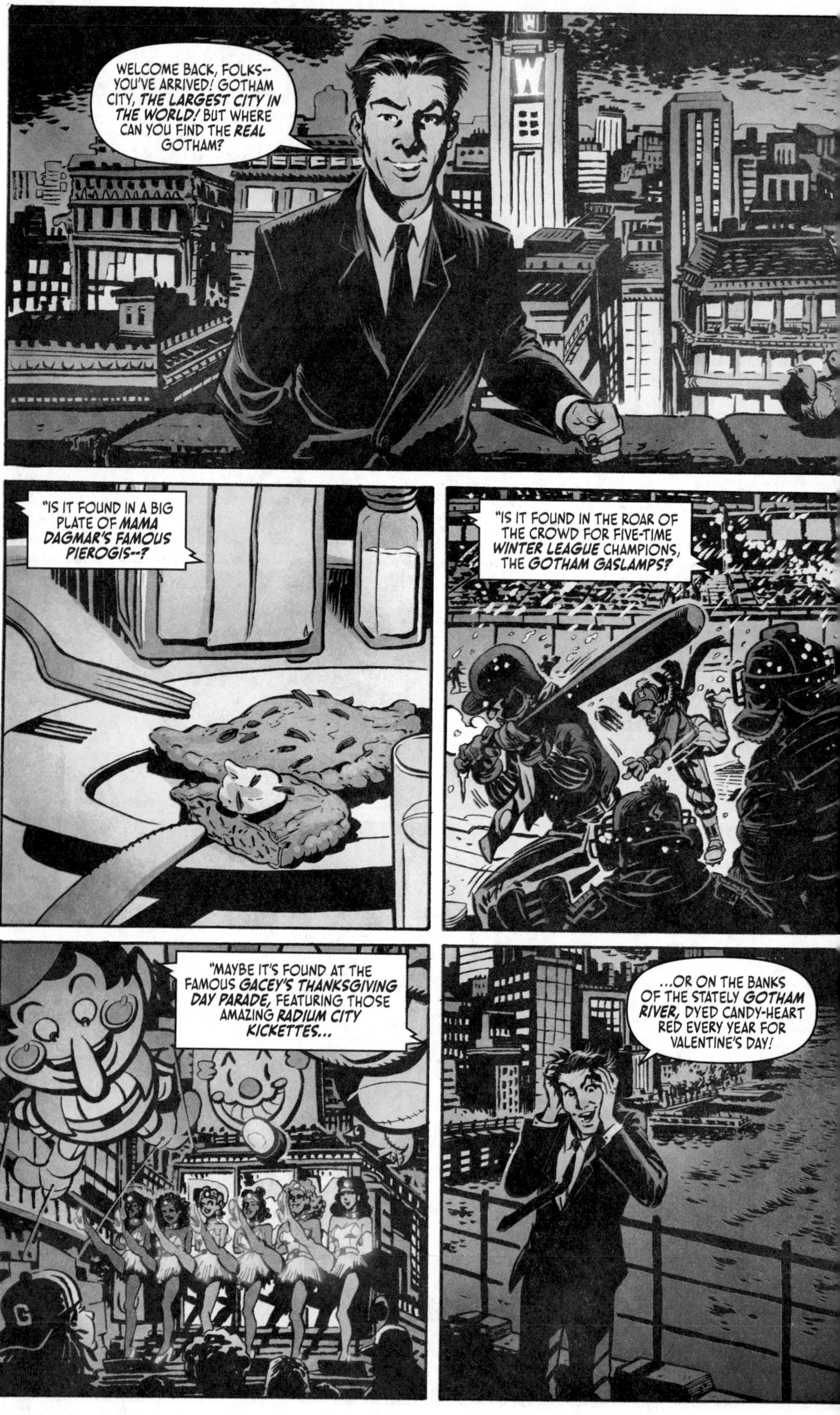
WELCOME BACK, FOLKS-- YOU'VE ARRIVED! GOTHAM CITY, THE LARGEST CITY IN THE WORLD! BUT WHERE CAN YOU FIND THE REAL GOTHAM?
"IS IT FOUND IN A BIG PLATE OF MAMA DAGMAR'S FAMOUS PIEROGIS--?
"IS IT FOUND IN THE ROAR OF THE CROWD FOR FIVE-TIME WINTER LEAGUE CHAMPIONS, THE GOTHAM GASLAMPS?
"MAYBE IT'S FOUND AT THE FAMOUS GACEY'S THANKSGIVING DAY PARADE, FEATURING THOSE AMAZING RADIUM CITY KICKETTES...
...OR ON THE BANKS OF THE STATELY GOTHAM RIVER, DYED CANDY-HEART RED EVERY YEAR FOR VALENTINE'S DAY!
W
G

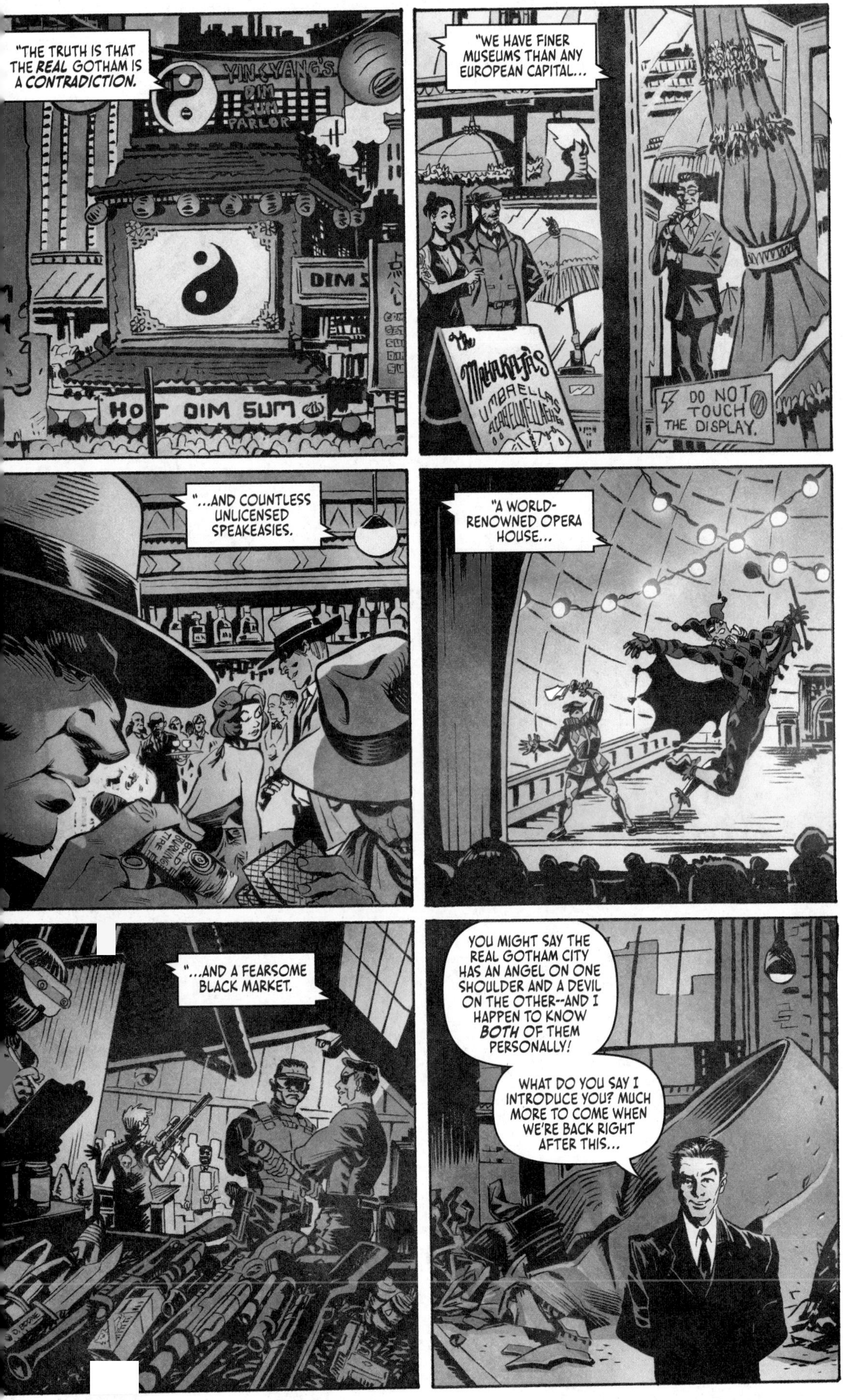
"THE TRUTH IS THAT THE *REAL* GOTHAM IS A *CONTRADICTION.*
YIN & YANG'S DIM SUM PARLOR
DIM S
HOT DIM SUM
"WE HAVE FINER MUSEUMS THAN ANY EUROPEAN CAPITAL...
The MAHARAJA'S UMBRELLAS
DO NOT TOUCH THE DISPLAY.
"...AND COUNTLESS UNLICENSED SPEAKEASIES.
"A WORLD-RENOWNED OPERA HOUSE...
"...AND A FEARSOME BLACK MARKET.
YOU MIGHT SAY THE REAL GOTHAM CITY HAS AN ANGEL ON ONE SHOULDER AND A DEVIL ON THE OTHER--AND I HAPPEN TO KNOW *BOTH* OF THEM PERSONALLY!
WHAT DO YOU SAY I INTRODUCE YOU? MUCH MORE TO COME WHEN WE'RE BACK RIGHT AFTER THIS...

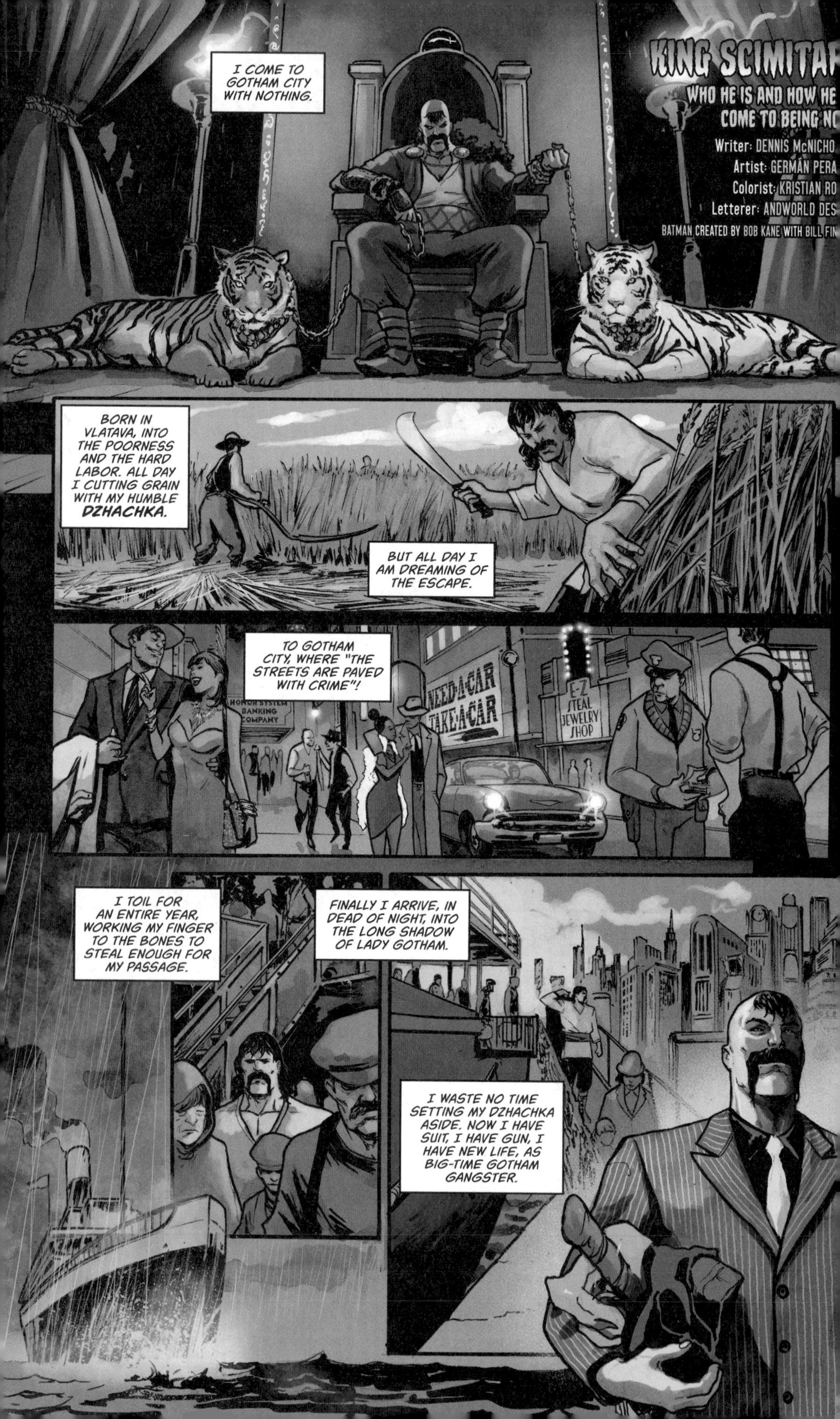
KING SCIMITA
WHO HE IS AND HOW HE
COME TO BEING NO
Writer: DENNIS McNICHO
Artist: GERMÁN PERA
Colorist: KRISTIAN RO
Letterer: ANDWORLD DES
BATMAN CREATED BY BOB KANE WITH BILL FIN
I COME TO GOTHAM CITY WITH NOTHING.
BORN IN VLATAVA, INTO THE POORNESS AND THE HARD LABOR. ALL DAY I CUTTING GRAIN WITH MY HUMBLE DZHACHKA.
BUT ALL DAY I AM DREAMING OF THE ESCAPE.
TO GOTHAM CITY, WHERE "THE STREETS ARE PAVED WITH CRIME"!
HONOR SYSTEM BANKING COMPANY
NEED A CAR TAKE A CAR
E-Z STEAL JEWELRY SHOP
I TOIL FOR AN ENTIRE YEAR, WORKING MY FINGER TO THE BONES TO STEAL ENOUGH FOR MY PASSAGE.
FINALLY I ARRIVE, IN DEAD OF NIGHT, INTO THE LONG SHADOW OF LADY GOTHAM.
I WASTE NO TIME SETTING MY DZHACHKA ASIDE. NOW I HAVE SUIT, I HAVE GUN, I HAVE NEW LIFE, AS BIG-TIME GOTHAM GANGSTER.

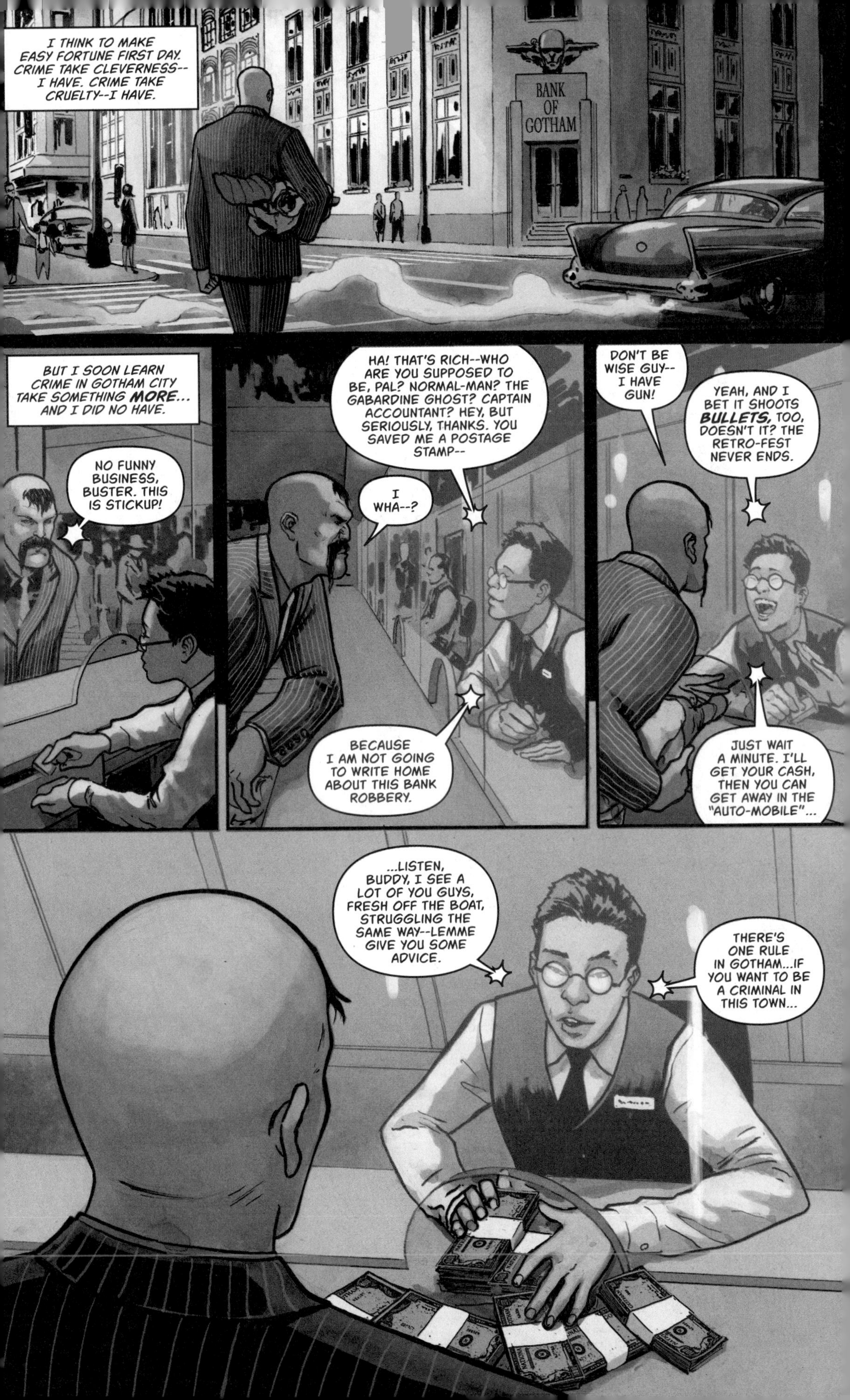
I THINK TO MAKE EASY FORTUNE FIRST DAY. CRIME TAKE CLEVERNESS-- I HAVE. CRIME TAKE CRUELTY--I HAVE.
BANK OF GOTHAM
BUT I SOON LEARN CRIME IN GOTHAM CITY TAKE SOMETHING MORE... AND I DID NO HAVE.
NO FUNNY BUSINESS, BUSTER. THIS IS STICKUP!
I WHA--?
HA! THAT'S RICH--WHO ARE YOU SUPPOSED TO BE, PAL? NORMAL-MAN? THE GABARDINE GHOST? CAPTAIN ACCOUNTANT? HEY, BUT SERIOUSLY, THANKS. YOU SAVED ME A POSTAGE STAMP--
BECAUSE I AM NOT GOING TO WRITE HOME ABOUT THIS BANK ROBBERY.
DON'T BE WISE GUY-- I HAVE GUN!
YEAH, AND I BET IT SHOOTS BULLETS, TOO, DOESN'T IT? THE RETRO-FEST NEVER ENDS.
JUST WAIT A MINUTE. I'LL GET YOUR CASH, THEN YOU CAN GET AWAY IN THE "AUTO-MOBILE"...
...LISTEN, BUDDY, I SEE A LOT OF YOU GUYS, FRESH OFF THE BOAT, STRUGGLING THE SAME WAY--LEMME GIVE YOU SOME ADVICE.
THERE'S ONE RULE IN GOTHAM...IF YOU WANT TO BE A CRIMINAL IN THIS TOWN...

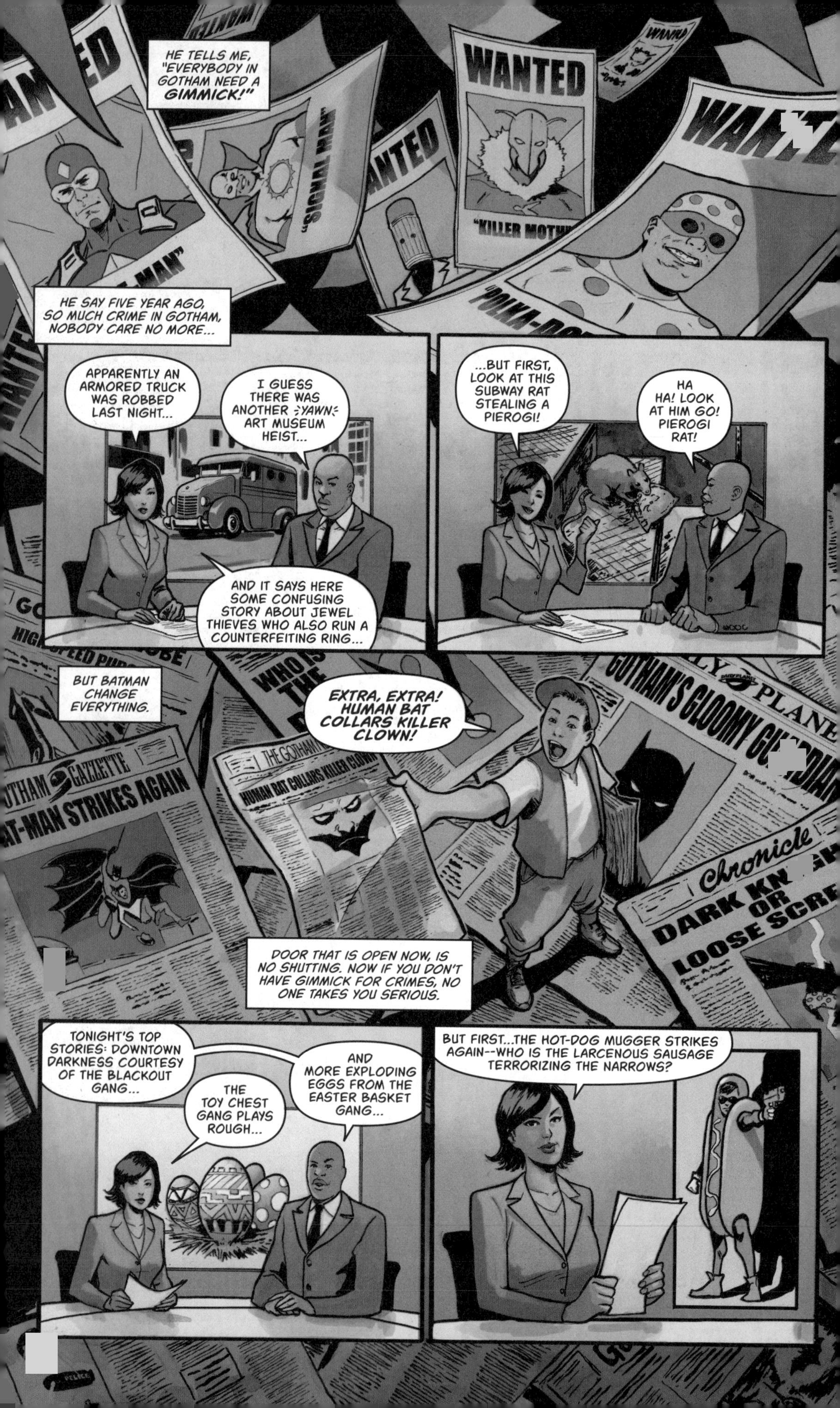
HE TELLS ME, "EVERYBODY IN GOTHAM NEED A GIMMICK!"
WANTED
"KILLER MOTH"
HE SAY FIVE YEAR AGO, SO MUCH CRIME IN GOTHAM, NOBODY CARE NO MORE...
APPARENTLY AN ARMORED TRUCK WAS ROBBED LAST NIGHT...
I GUESS THERE WAS ANOTHER *YAWN* ART MUSEUM HEIST...
AND IT SAYS HERE SOME CONFUSING STORY ABOUT JEWEL THIEVES WHO ALSO RUN A COUNTERFEITING RING...
...BUT FIRST, LOOK AT THIS SUBWAY RAT STEALING A PIEROGI!
HA HA! LOOK AT HIM GO! PIEROGI RAT!
BUT BATMAN CHANGE EVERYTHING.
EXTRA, EXTRA! HUMAN BAT COLLARS KILLER CLOWN!
HUMAN BAT COLLARS KILLER CLOWN
GOTHAM'S GLOOMY GUARDIAN
GOTHAM GAZZETTE
BAT-MAN STRIKES AGAIN
Chronicle
DARK KN OR LOOSE SCRE
DOOR THAT IS OPEN NOW, IS NO SHUTTING. NOW IF YOU DON'T HAVE GIMMICK FOR CRIMES, NO ONE TAKES YOU SERIOUS.
TONIGHT'S TOP STORIES: DOWNTOWN DARKNESS COURTESY OF THE BLACKOUT GANG...
THE TOY CHEST GANG PLAYS ROUGH...
AND MORE EXPLODING EGGS FROM THE EASTER BASKET GANG...
BUT FIRST...THE HOT-DOG MUGGER STRIKES AGAIN--WHO IS THE LARCENOUS SAUSAGE TERRORIZING THE NARROWS?

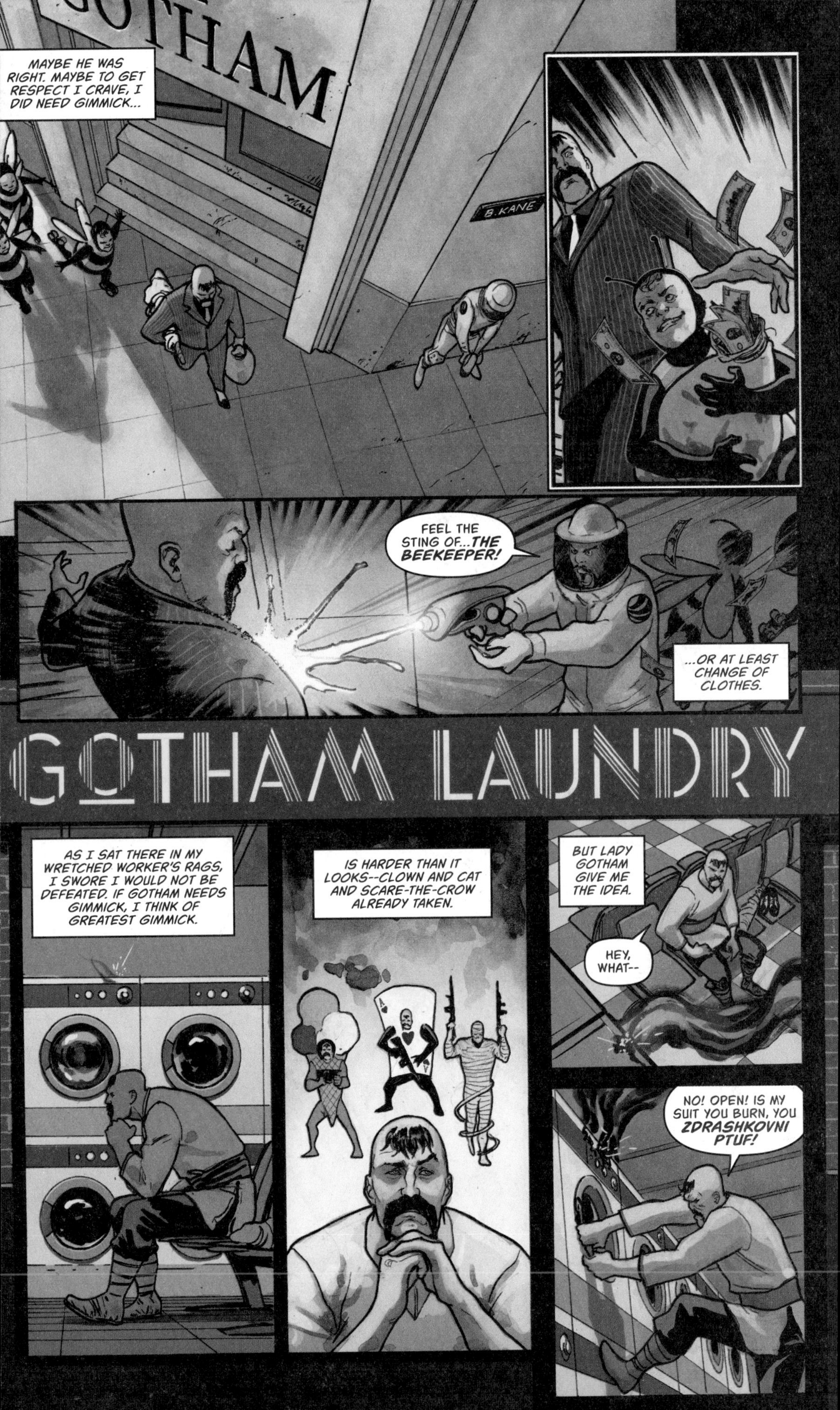

GOTHAM
MAYBE HE WAS RIGHT. MAYBE TO GET RESPECT I CRAVE, I DID NEED GIMMICK...
B.KANE
FEEL THE STING OF...THE BEEKEEPER!
...OR AT LEAST CHANGE OF CLOTHES.
GOTHAM LAUNDRY
AS I SAT THERE IN MY WRETCHED WORKER'S RAGS, I SWORE I WOULD NOT BE DEFEATED. IF GOTHAM NEEDS GIMMICK, I THINK OF GREATEST GIMMICK.
IS HARDER THAN IT LOOKS--CLOWN AND CAT AND SCARE-THE-CROW ALREADY TAKEN.
BUT LADY GOTHAM GIVE ME THE IDEA.
HEY, WHAT--
NO! OPEN! IS MY SUIT YOU BURN, YOU ZDRASHKOVNI PTUF!

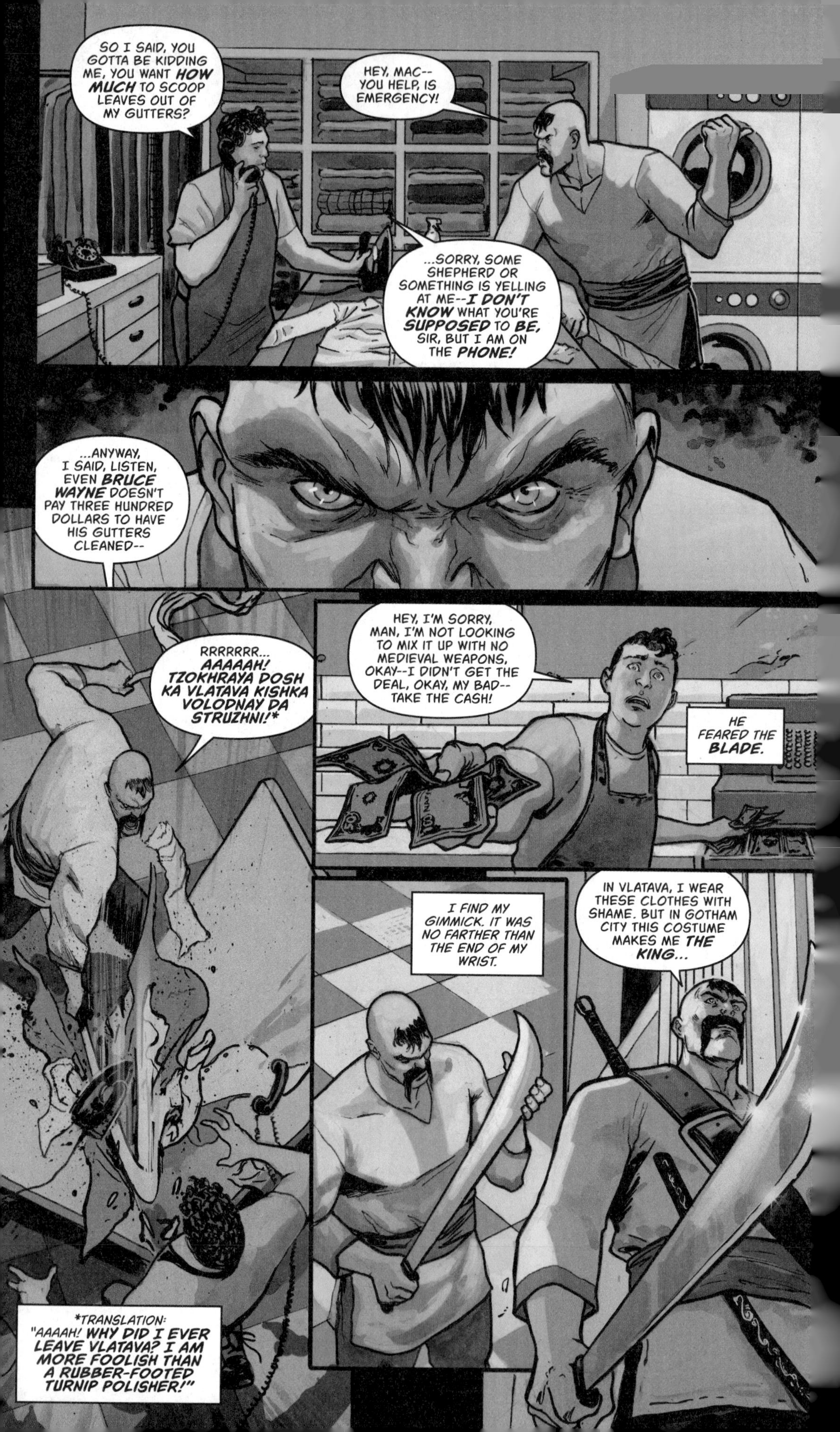
SO I SAID, YOU GOTTA BE KIDDING ME, YOU WANT HOW MUCH TO SCOOP LEAVES OUT OF MY GUTTERS?
HEY, MAC-- YOU HELP, IS EMERGENCY!
...SORRY, SOME SHEPHERD OR SOMETHING IS YELLING AT ME--I DON'T KNOW WHAT YOU'RE SUPPOSED TO BE, SIR, BUT I AM ON THE PHONE!
...ANYWAY, I SAID, LISTEN, EVEN BRUCE WAYNE DOESN'T PAY THREE HUNDRED DOLLARS TO HAVE HIS GUTTERS CLEANED--
RRRRRRR... AAAAAH! TZOKHRAYA DOSH KA VLATAVA KISHKA VOLODNAY DA STRUZHNI!*
HEY, I'M SORRY, MAN, I'M NOT LOOKING TO MIX IT UP WITH NO MEDIEVAL WEAPONS, OKAY--I DIDN'T GET THE DEAL, OKAY, MY BAD-- TAKE THE CASH!
HE FEARED THE BLADE.
I FIND MY GIMMICK. IT WAS NO FARTHER THAN THE END OF MY WRIST.
IN VLATAVA, I WEAR THESE CLOTHES WITH SHAME. BUT IN GOTHAM CITY THIS COSTUME MAKES ME THE KING...
*TRANSLATION: "AAAAH! WHY DID I EVER LEAVE VLATAVA? I AM MORE FOOLISH THAN A RUBBER-FOOTED TURNIP POLISHER!"

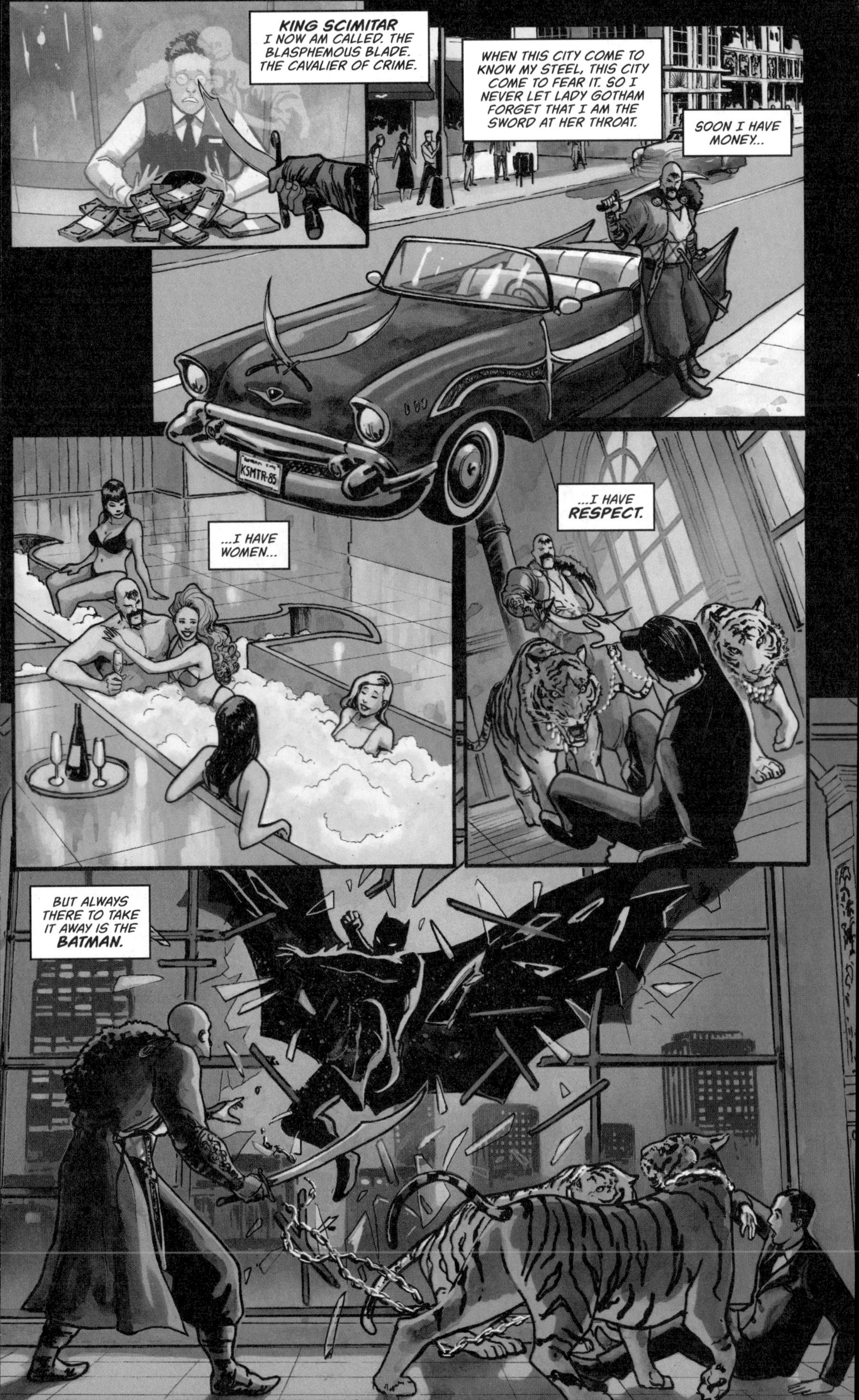

KING SCIMITAR I NOW AM CALLED. THE BLASPHEMOUS BLADE. THE CAVALIER OF CRIME.
WHEN THIS CITY COME TO KNOW MY STEEL, THIS CITY COME TO FEAR IT. SO I NEVER LET LADY GOTHAM FORGET THAT I AM THE SWORD AT HER THROAT.
SOON I HAVE MONEY...
KSMTR-85
...I HAVE WOMEN...
...I HAVE RESPECT.
BUT ALWAYS THERE TO TAKE IT AWAY IS THE BATMAN.

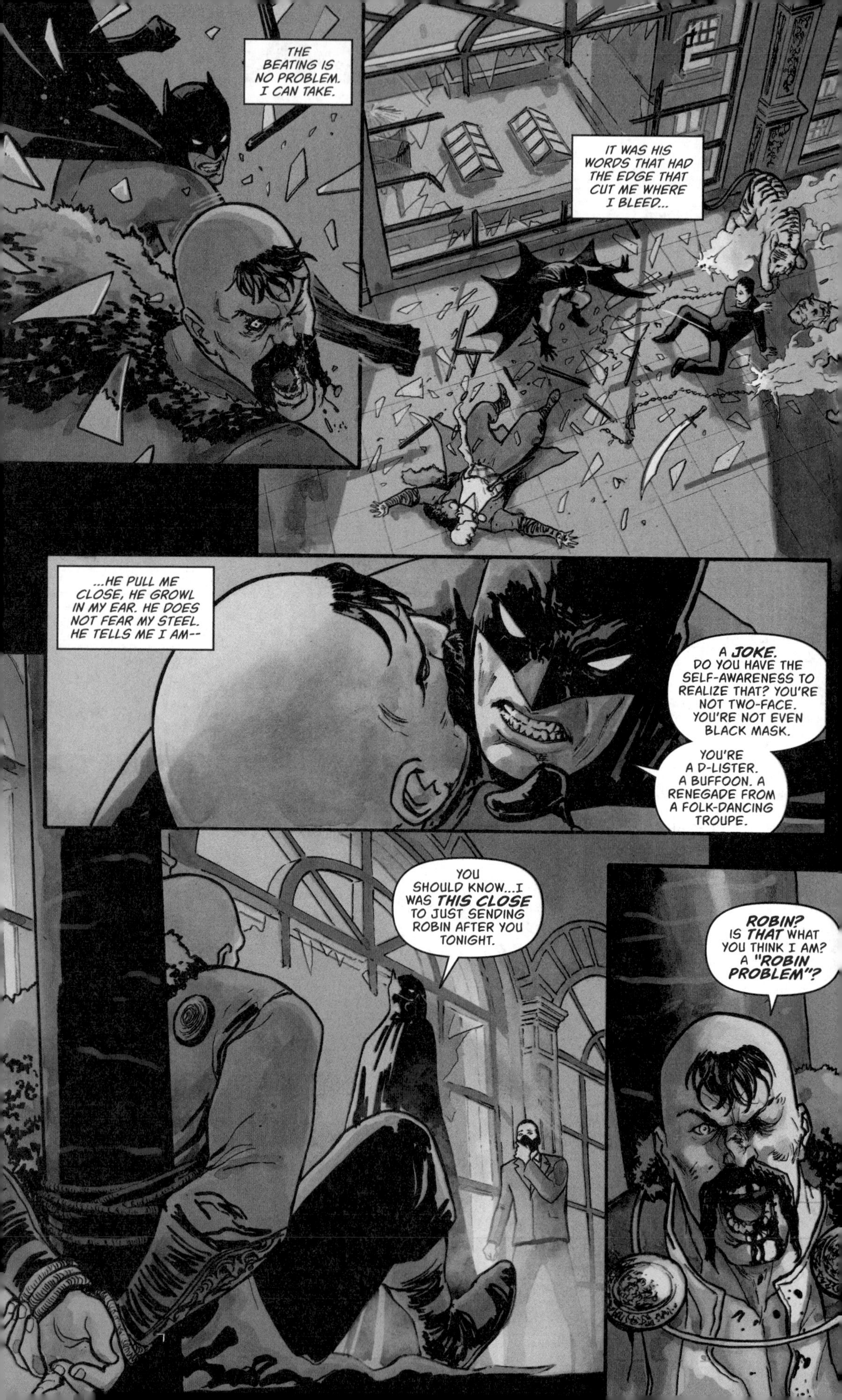
THE BEATING IS NO PROBLEM. I CAN TAKE.
IT WAS HIS WORDS THAT HAD THE EDGE THAT CUT ME WHERE I BLEED...
...HE PULL ME CLOSE, HE GROWL IN MY EAR. HE DOES NOT FEAR MY STEEL. HE TELLS ME I AM--
A JOKE. DO YOU HAVE THE SELF-AWARENESS TO REALIZE THAT? YOU'RE NOT TWO-FACE. YOU'RE NOT EVEN BLACK MASK.
YOU'RE A D-LISTER. A BUFFOON. A RENEGADE FROM A FOLK-DANCING TROUPE.
YOU SHOULD KNOW...I WAS THIS CLOSE TO JUST SENDING ROBIN AFTER YOU TONIGHT.
ROBIN? IS THAT WHAT YOU THINK I AM? A "ROBIN PROBLEM"?

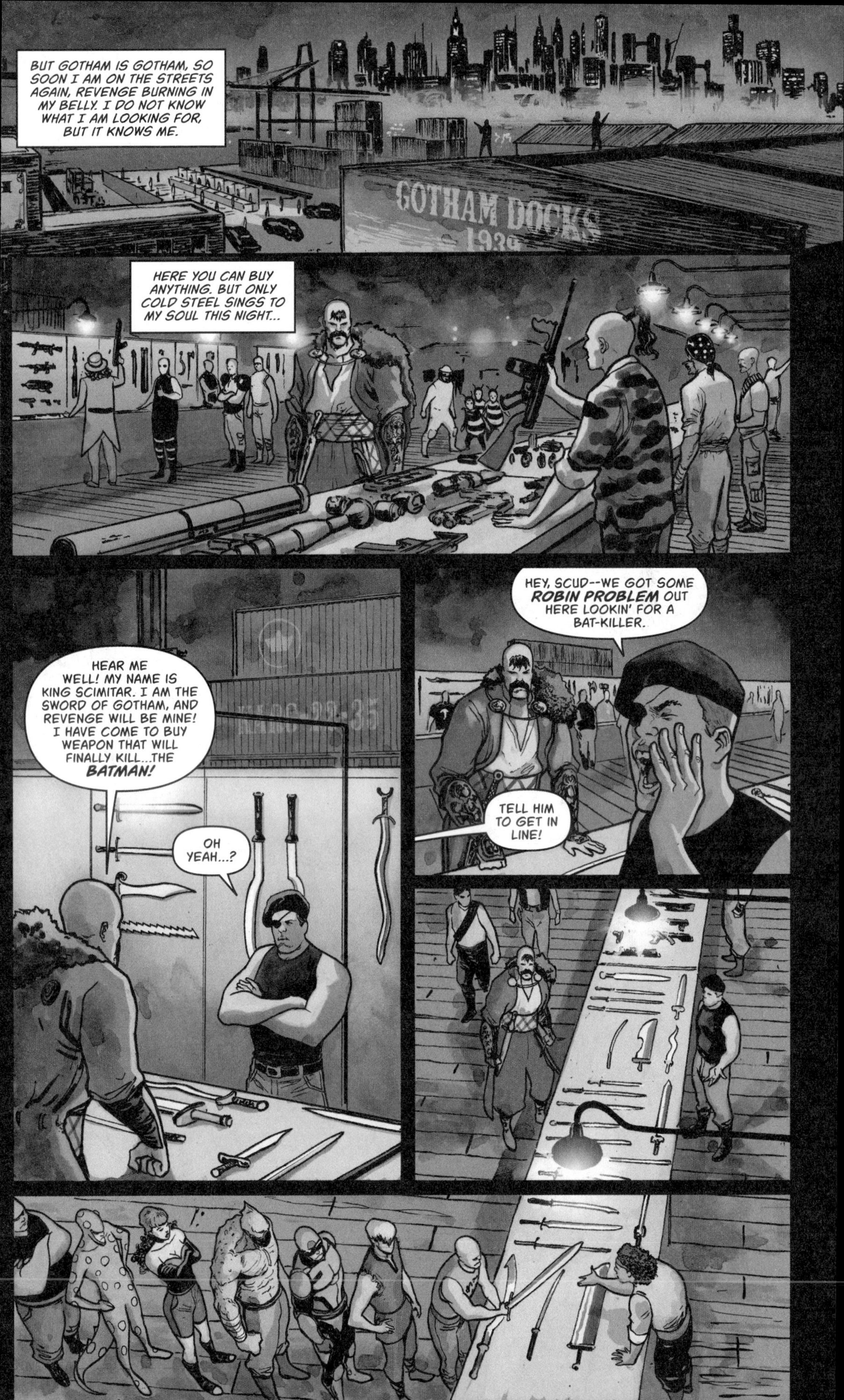
BUT GOTHAM IS GOTHAM, SO SOON I AM ON THE STREETS AGAIN, REVENGE BURNING IN MY BELLY. I DO NOT KNOW WHAT I AM LOOKING FOR, BUT IT KNOWS ME.
GOTHAM DOCKS 1939
HERE YOU CAN BUY ANYTHING. BUT ONLY COLD STEEL SINGS TO MY SOUL THIS NIGHT...
HEAR ME WELL! MY NAME IS KING SCIMITAR. I AM THE SWORD OF GOTHAM, AND REVENGE WILL BE MINE! I HAVE COME TO BUY WEAPON THAT WILL FINALLY KILL...THE BATMAN!
OH YEAH...?
HEY, SCUD--WE GOT SOME ROBIN PROBLEM OUT HERE LOOKIN' FOR A BAT-KILLER.
TELL HIM TO GET IN LINE!

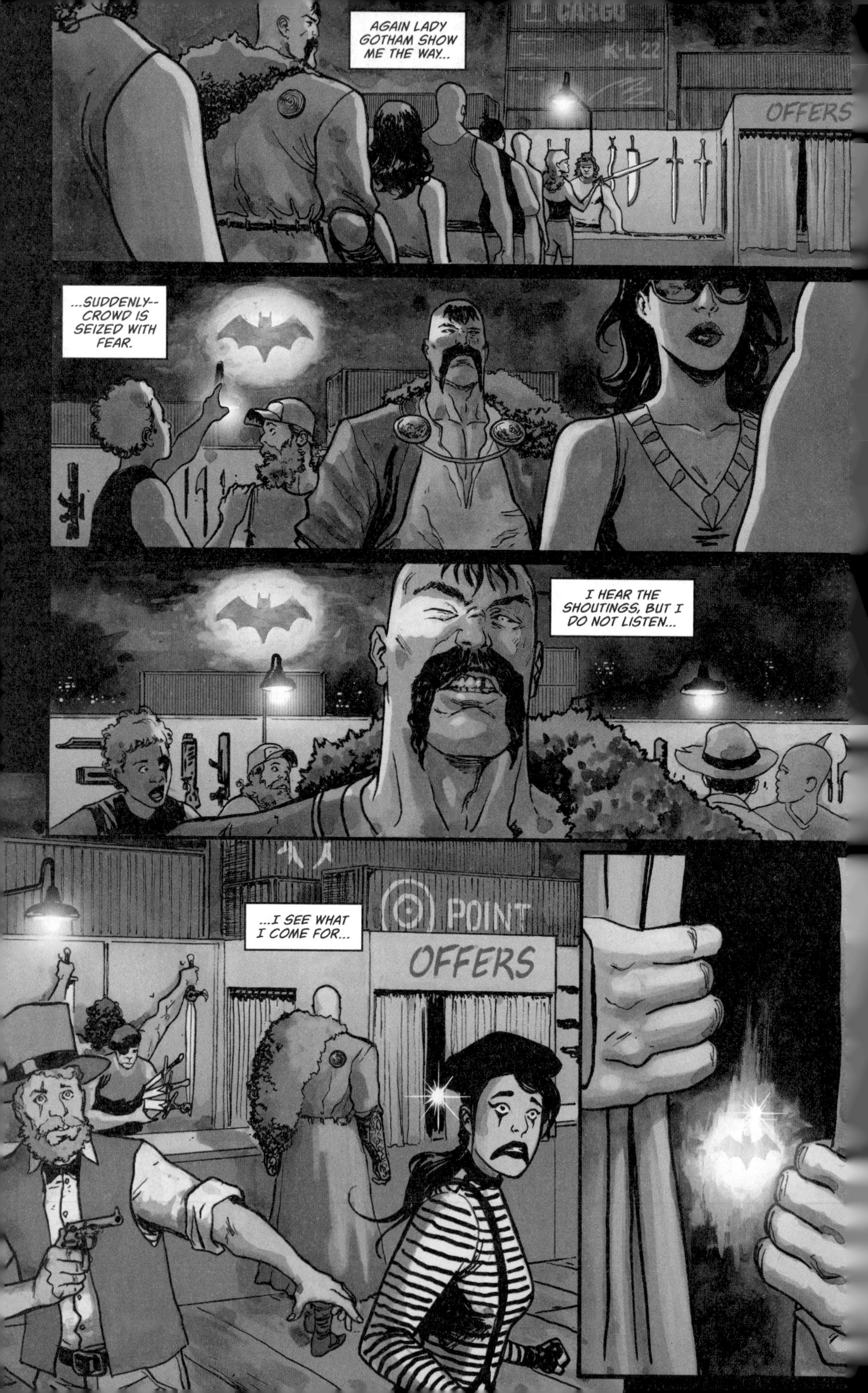
AGAIN LADY GOTHAM SHOW ME THE WAY...
OFFERS
...SUDDENLY--CROWD IS SEIZED WITH FEAR.
I HEAR THE SHOUTINGS, BUT I DO NOT LISTEN...
POINT
OFFERS
...I SEE WHAT I COME FOR...

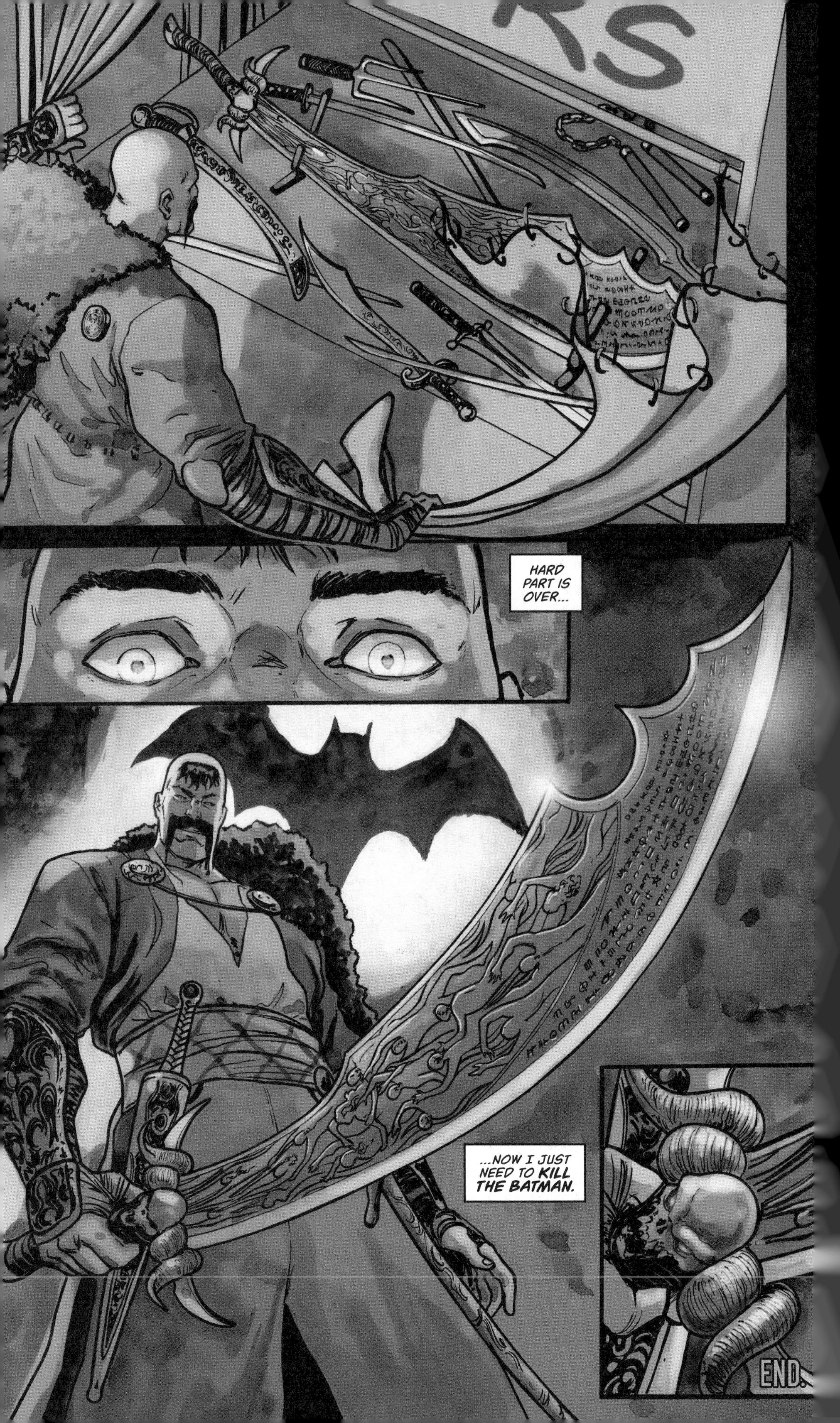
HARD PART IS OVER...
...NOW I JUST NEED TO KILL THE BATMAN.
END.

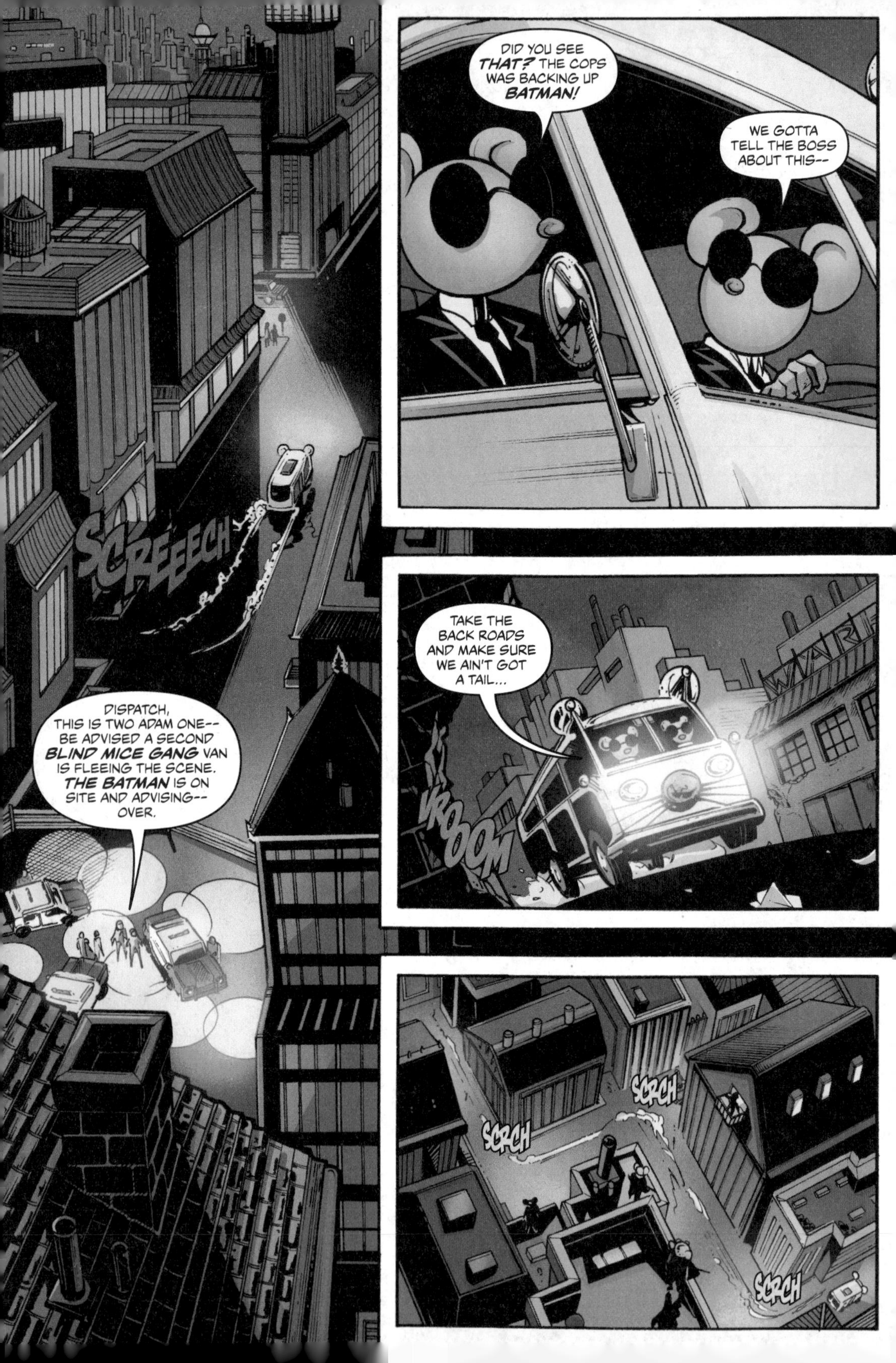
SCREEECH
DISPATCH, THIS IS TWO ADAM ONE-- BE ADVISED A SECOND BLIND MICE GANG VAN IS FLEEING THE SCENE. THE BATMAN IS ON SITE AND ADVISING-- OVER.
DID YOU SEE THAT? THE COPS WAS BACKING UP BATMAN!
WE GOTTA TELL THE BOSS ABOUT THIS--
TAKE THE BACK ROADS AND MAKE SURE WE AIN'T GOT A TAIL...
VROOOM
SCRCH
SCRCH
SCRCH

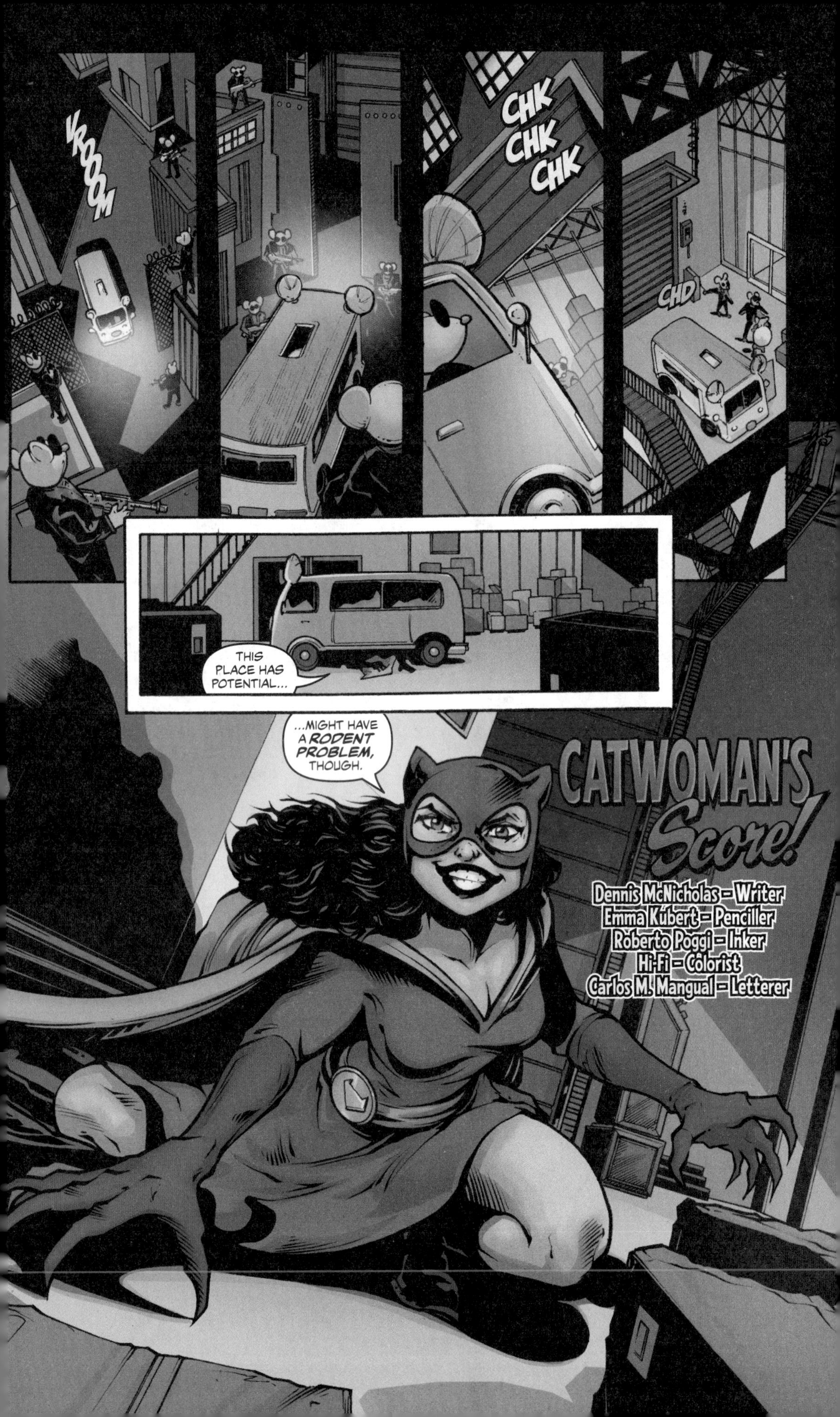
VROOOM
CHK
CHK
CHK
CHD
THIS PLACE HAS POTENTIAL...
...MIGHT HAVE A *RODENT PROBLEM,* THOUGH.
CATWOMAN'S Score!
Dennis McNicholas - Writer
Emma Kubert - Penciller
Roberto Poggi - Inker
Hi-Fi - Colorist
Carlos M. Mangual - Letterer

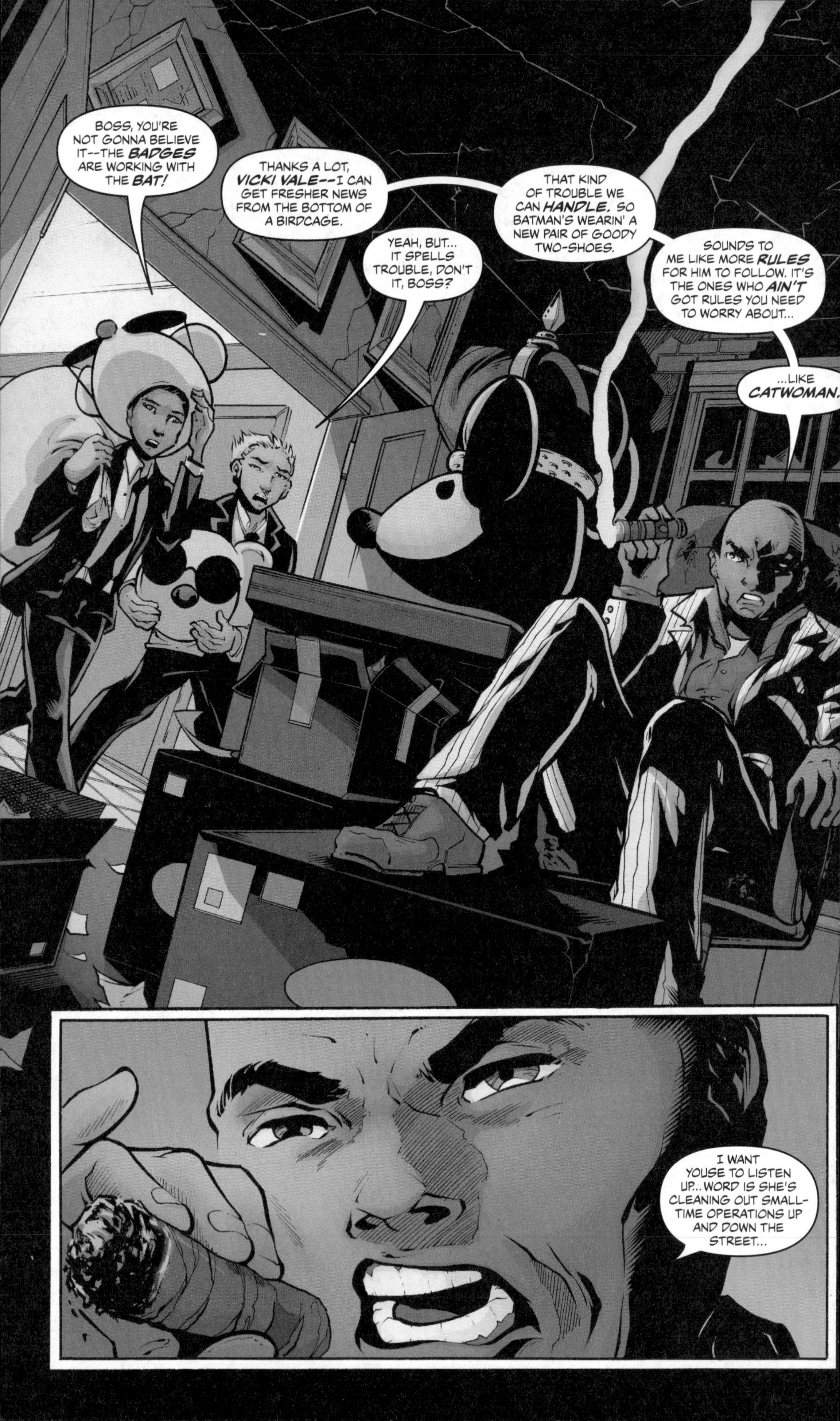
BOSS, YOU'RE NOT GONNA BELIEVE IT--THE BADGES ARE WORKING WITH THE BAT!
THANKS A LOT, VICKI VALE--I CAN GET FRESHER NEWS FROM THE BOTTOM OF A BIRDCAGE.
YEAH, BUT... IT SPELLS TROUBLE, DON'T IT, BOSS?
THAT KIND OF TROUBLE WE CAN HANDLE. SO BATMAN'S WEARIN' A NEW PAIR OF GOODY TWO-SHOES.
SOUNDS TO ME LIKE MORE RULES FOR HIM TO FOLLOW. IT'S THE ONES WHO AIN'T GOT RULES YOU NEED TO WORRY ABOUT...
...LIKE CATWOMAN.
I WANT YOUSE TO LISTEN UP... WORD IS SHE'S CLEANING OUT SMALL-TIME OPERATIONS UP AND DOWN THE STREET...

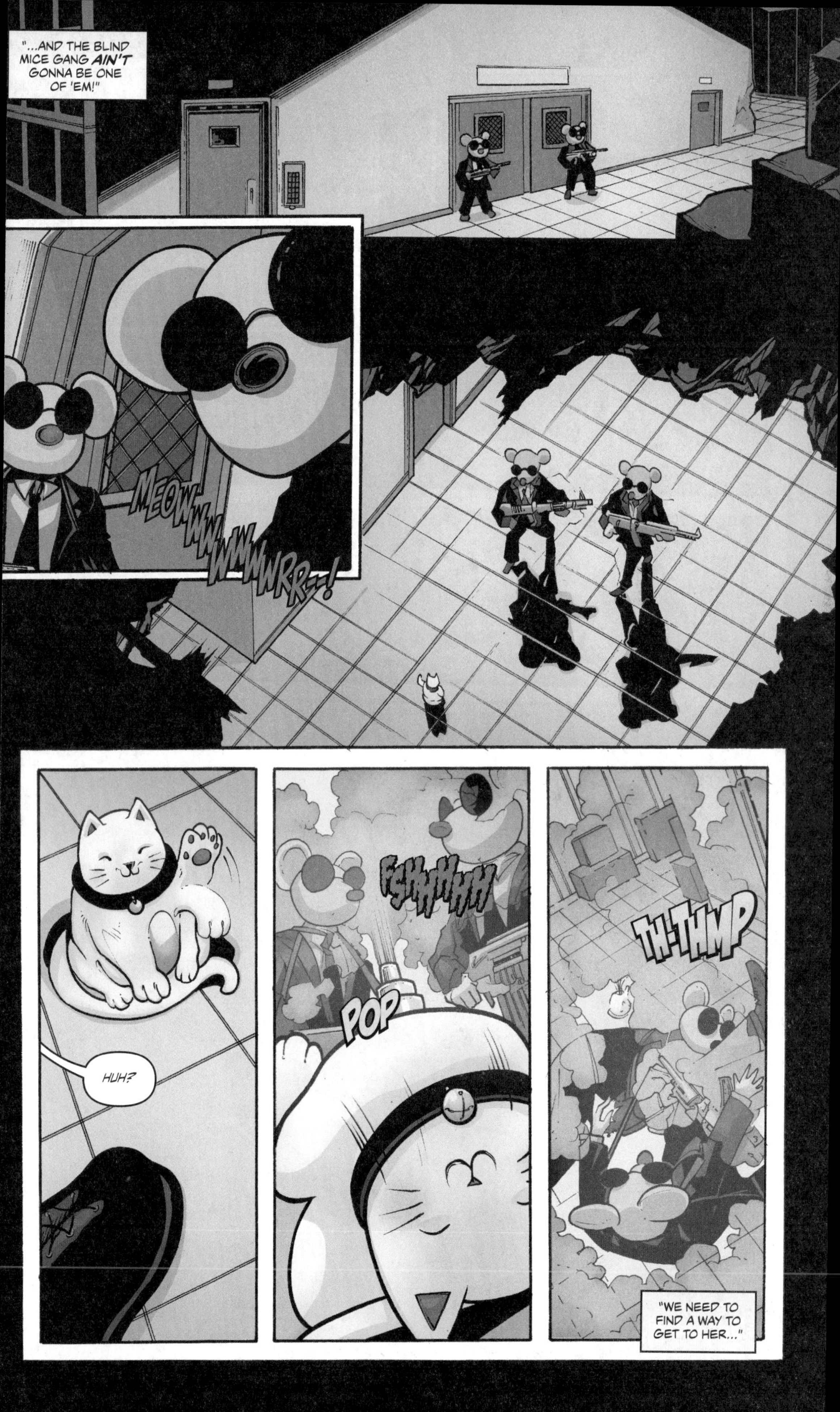
"...AND THE BLIND MICE GANG AIN'T GONNA BE ONE OF 'EM!"
MEOWWWWWWWWRR...!
HUH?
FSHHHHHH
POP
TH-THMP
"WE NEED TO FIND A WAY TO GET TO HER..."

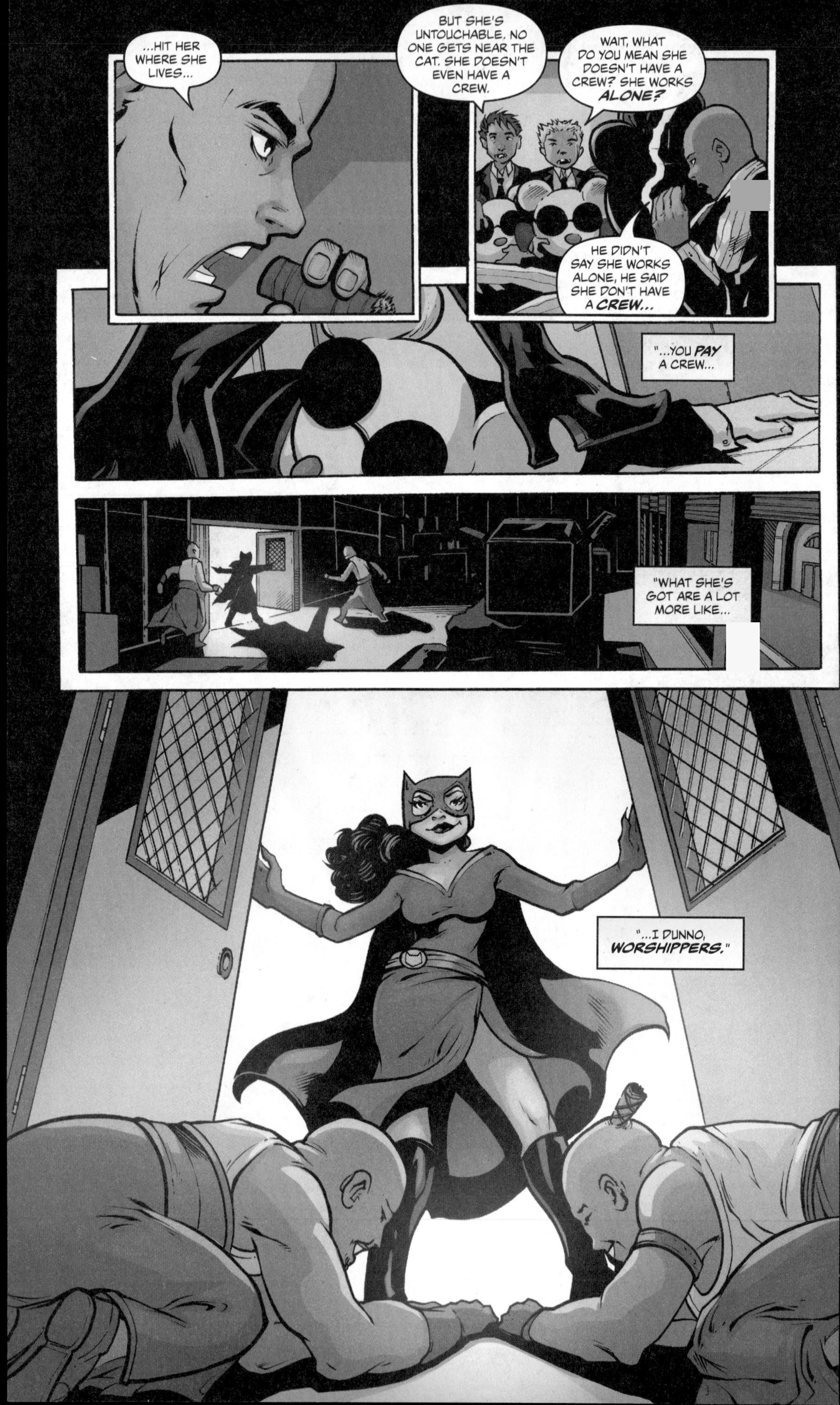

...HIT HER WHERE SHE LIVES...
BUT SHE'S UNTOUCHABLE. NO ONE GETS NEAR THE CAT. SHE DOESN'T EVEN HAVE A CREW.
WAIT, WHAT DO YOU MEAN SHE DOESN'T HAVE A CREW? SHE WORKS ALONE?
HE DIDN'T SAY SHE WORKS ALONE, HE SAID SHE DON'T HAVE A CREW...
"...YOU PAY A CREW...
"WHAT SHE'S GOT ARE A LOT MORE LIKE...
"...I DUNNO, WORSHIPPERS."

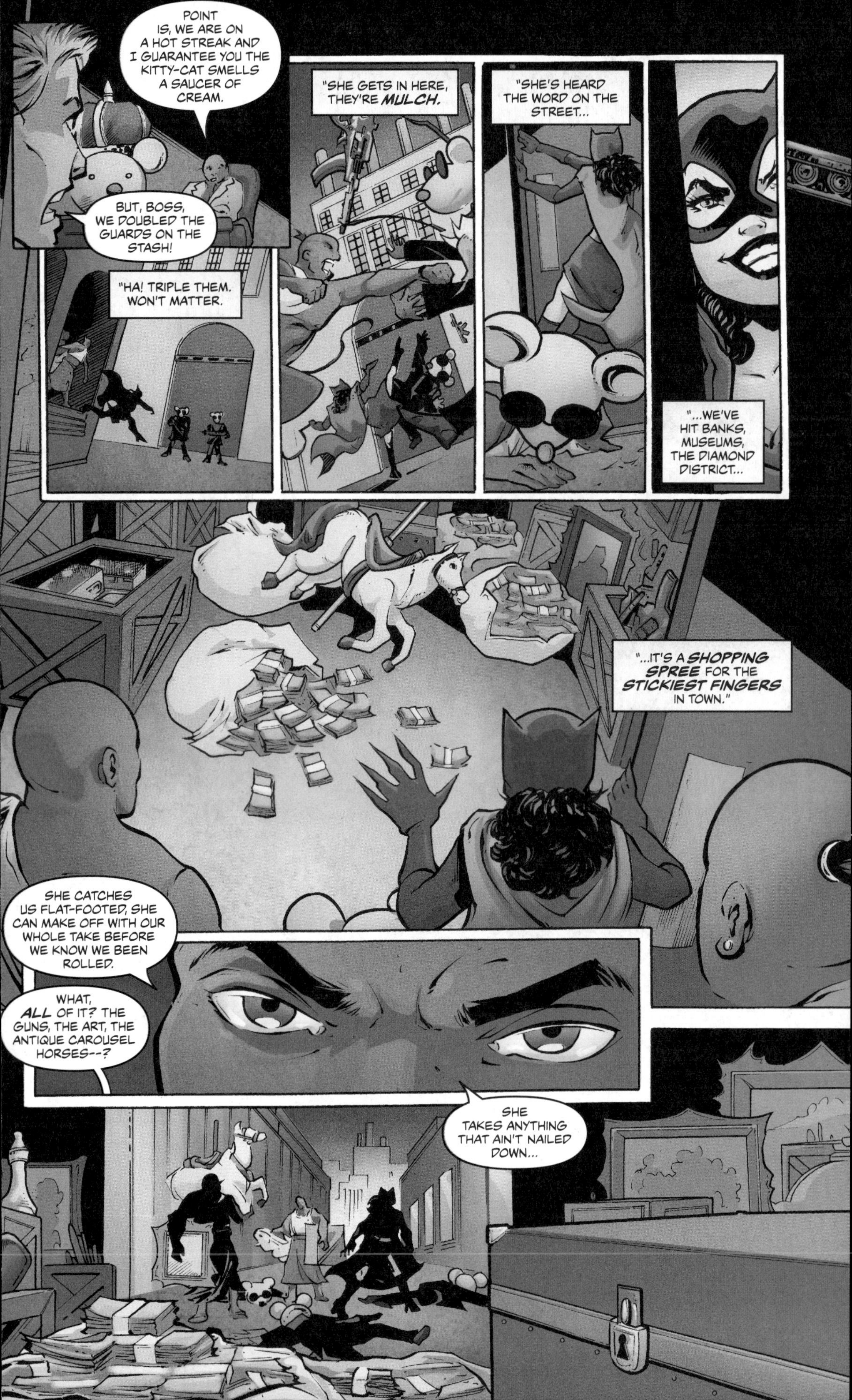
POINT IS, WE ARE ON A HOT STREAK AND I GUARANTEE YOU THE KITTY-CAT SMELLS A SAUCER OF CREAM.
BUT, BOSS, WE DOUBLED THE GUARDS ON THE STASH!
"HA! TRIPLE THEM. WON'T MATTER.
"SHE GETS IN HERE, THEY'RE MULCH.
"SHE'S HEARD THE WORD ON THE STREET...
"...WE'VE HIT BANKS, MUSEUMS, THE DIAMOND DISTRICT...
"...IT'S A SHOPPING SPREE FOR THE STICKIEST FINGERS IN TOWN."
SHE CATCHES US FLAT-FOOTED, SHE CAN MAKE OFF WITH OUR WHOLE TAKE BEFORE WE KNOW WE BEEN ROLLED.
WHAT, ALL OF IT? THE GUNS, THE ART, THE ANTIQUE CAROUSEL HORSES--?
SHE TAKES ANYTHING THAT AIN'T NAILED DOWN...

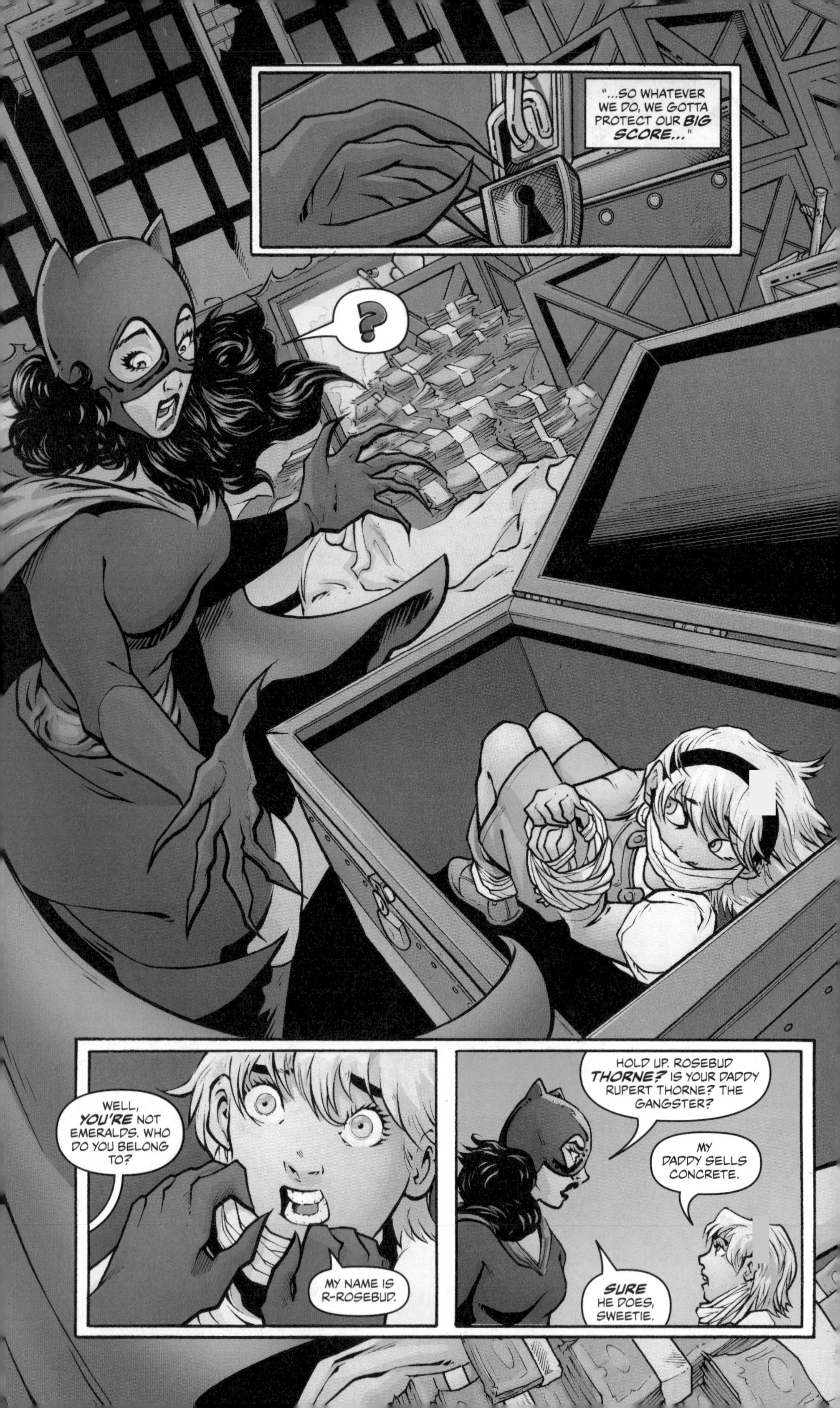

"...SO WHATEVER WE DO, WE GOTTA PROTECT OUR BIG SCORE..."
?
WELL, YOU'RE NOT EMERALDS. WHO DO YOU BELONG TO?
MY NAME IS R-ROSEBUD.
HOLD UP. ROSEBUD THORNE? IS YOUR DADDY RUPERT THORNE? THE GANGSTER?
MY DADDY SELLS CONCRETE.
SURE HE DOES, SWEETIE.

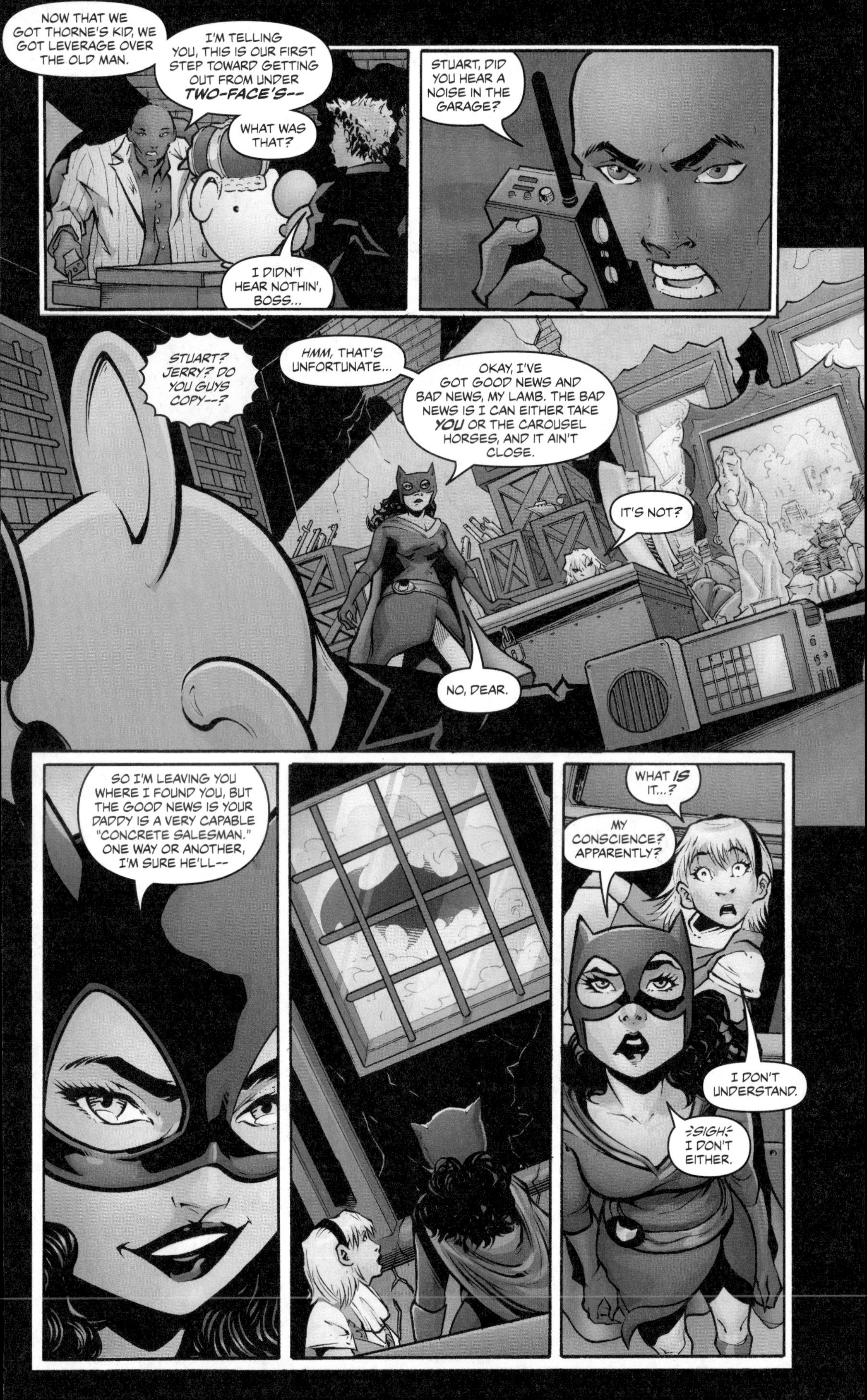
NOW THAT WE GOT THORNE'S KID, WE GOT LEVERAGE OVER THE OLD MAN.
I'M TELLING YOU, THIS IS OUR FIRST STEP TOWARD GETTING OUT FROM UNDER TWO-FACE'S--
WHAT WAS THAT?
I DIDN'T HEAR NOTHIN', BOSS...
STUART, DID YOU HEAR A NOISE IN THE GARAGE?
STUART? JERRY? DO YOU GUYS COPY--?
HMM, THAT'S UNFORTUNATE...
OKAY, I'VE GOT GOOD NEWS AND BAD NEWS, MY LAMB. THE BAD NEWS IS I CAN EITHER TAKE YOU OR THE CAROUSEL HORSES, AND IT AIN'T CLOSE.
IT'S NOT?
NO, DEAR.
SO I'M LEAVING YOU WHERE I FOUND YOU, BUT THE GOOD NEWS IS YOUR DADDY IS A VERY CAPABLE "CONCRETE SALESMAN." ONE WAY OR ANOTHER, I'M SURE HE'LL--
WHAT IS IT...?
MY CONSCIENCE? APPARENTLY?
I DON'T UNDERSTAND.
SIGH I DON'T EITHER.

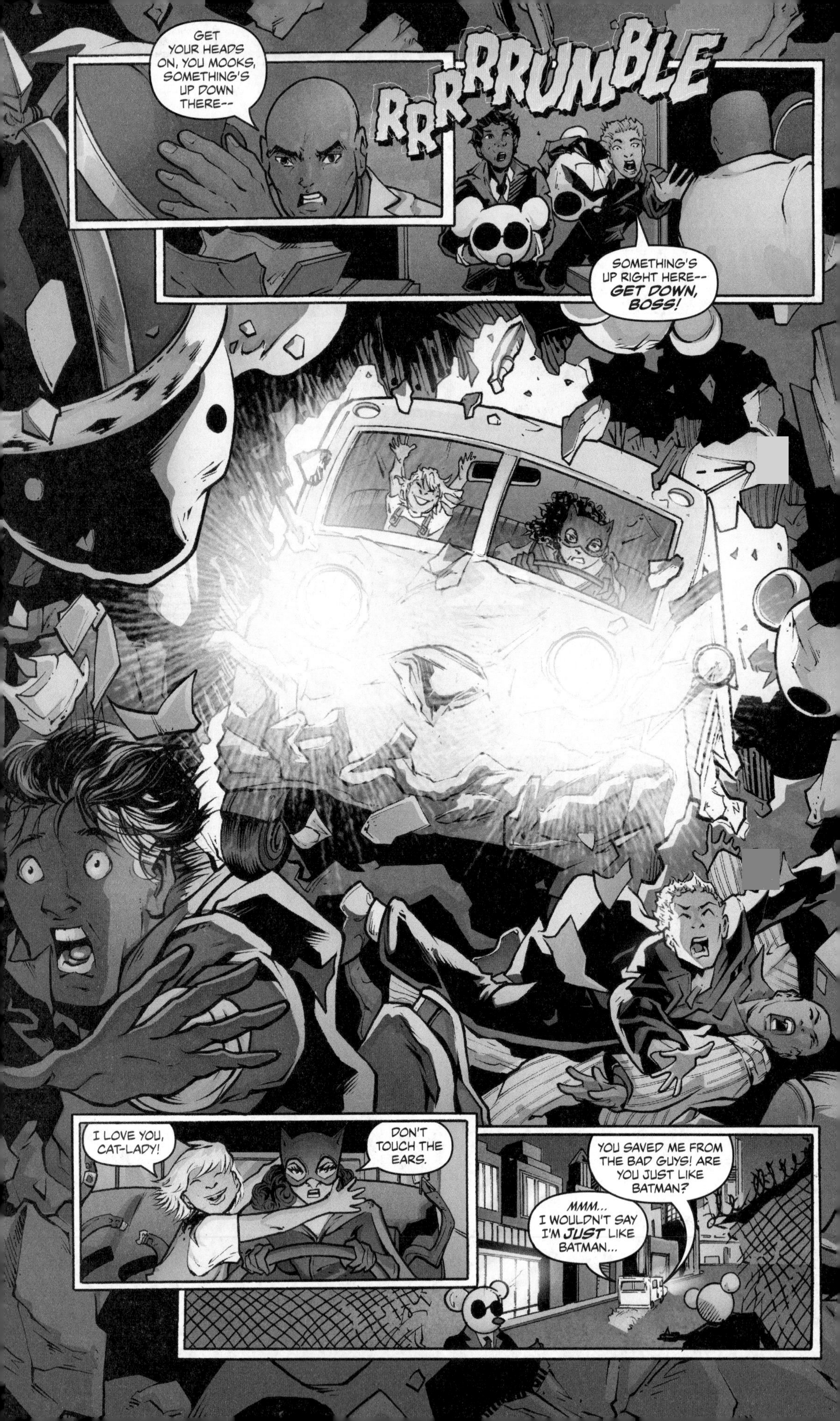
GET YOUR HEADS ON, YOU MOOKS, SOMETHING'S UP DOWN THERE--
RRRRRUMBLE
SOMETHING'S UP RIGHT HERE-- GET DOWN, BOSS!
I LOVE YOU, CAT-LADY!
DON'T TOUCH THE EARS.
YOU SAVED ME FROM THE BAD GUYS! ARE YOU JUST LIKE BATMAN?
MMM... I WOULDN'T SAY I'M JUST LIKE BATMAN...

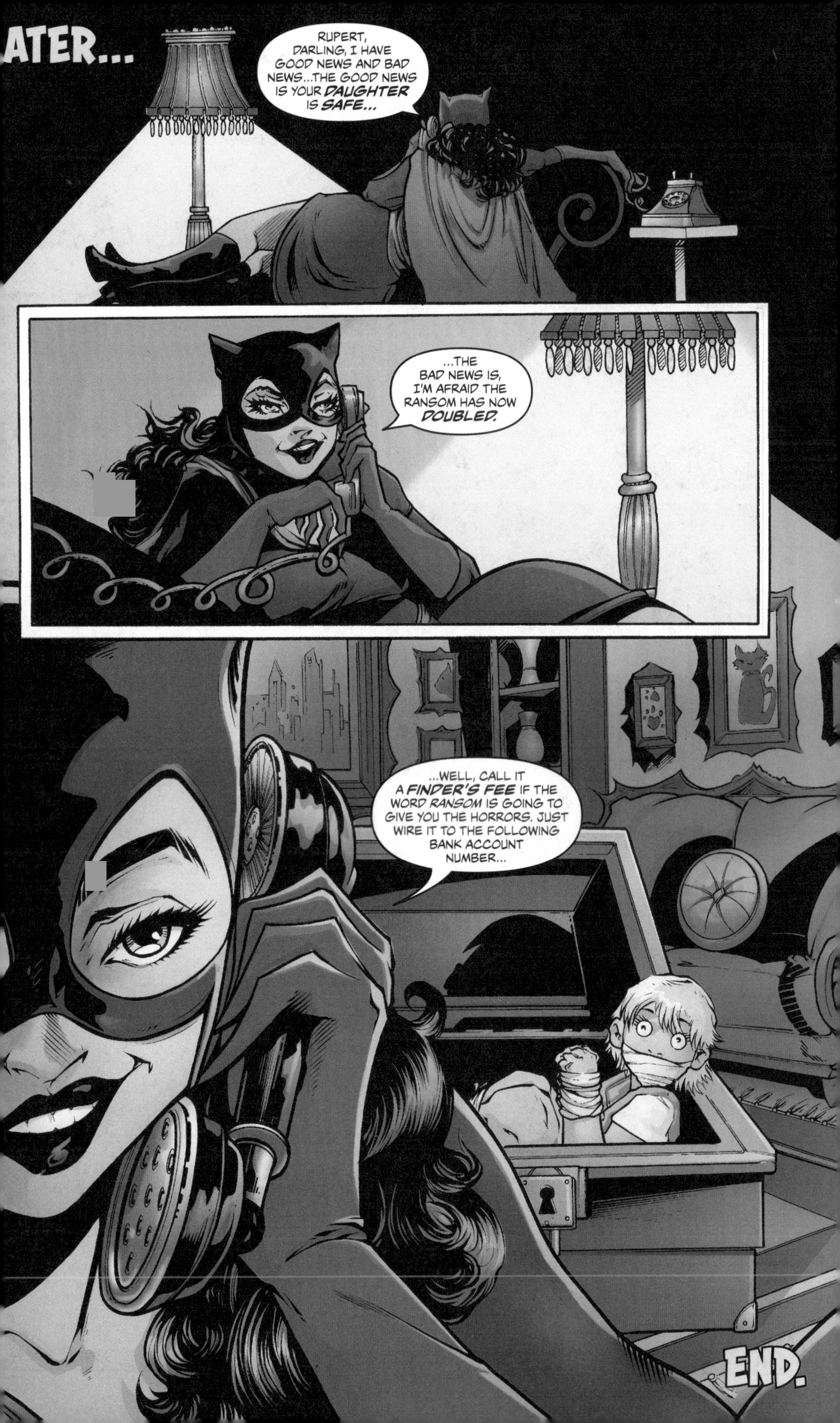

ATER...
RUPERT, DARLING, I HAVE GOOD NEWS AND BAD NEWS...THE GOOD NEWS IS YOUR DAUGHTER IS SAFE...
...THE BAD NEWS IS, I'M AFRAID THE RANSOM HAS NOW DOUBLED.
...WELL, CALL IT A FINDER'S FEE IF THE WORD RANSOM IS GOING TO GIVE YOU THE HORRORS. JUST WIRE IT TO THE FOLLOWING BANK ACCOUNT NUMBER...
END.

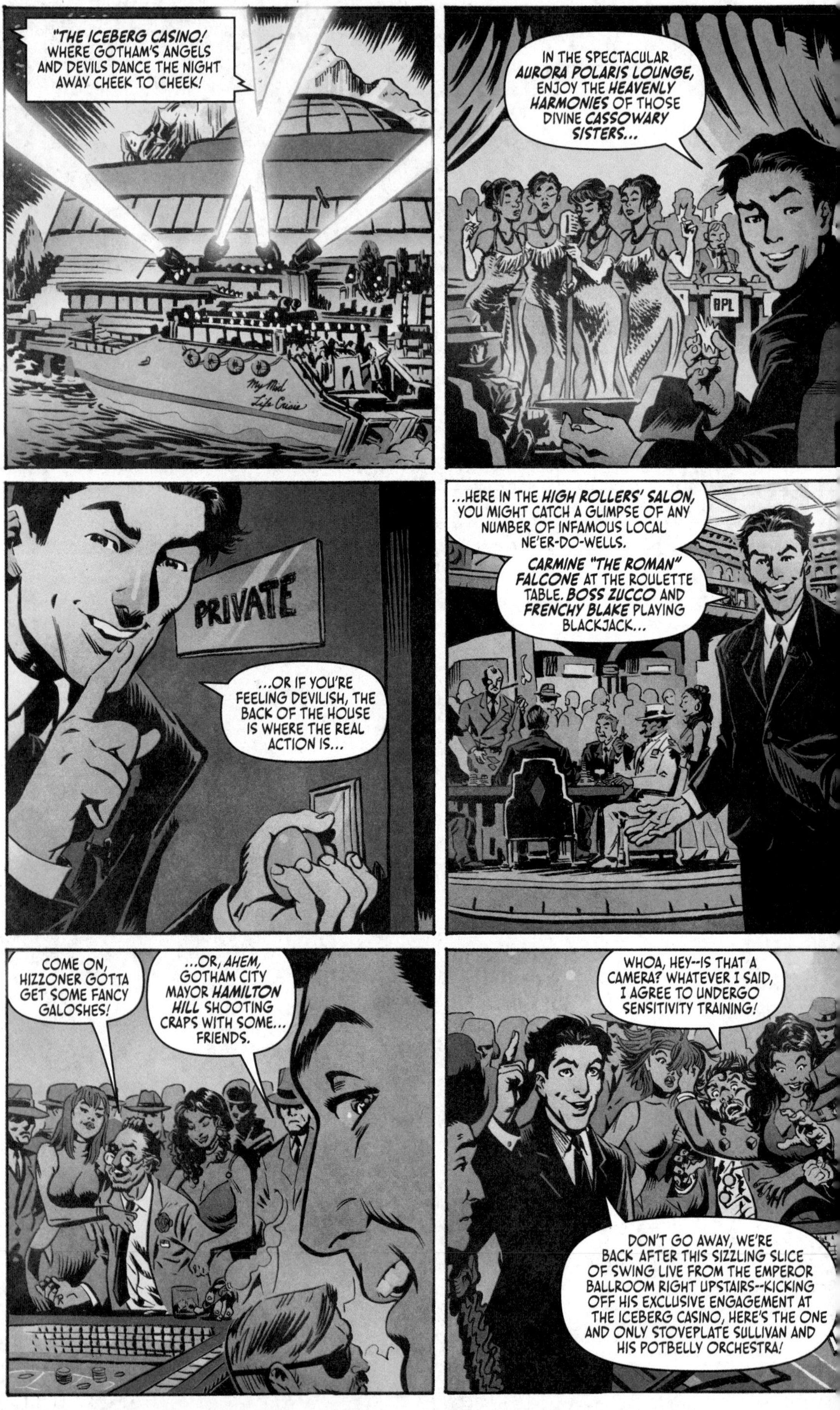
"THE ICEBERG CASINO! WHERE GOTHAM'S ANGELS AND DEVILS DANCE THE NIGHT AWAY CHEEK TO CHEEK!
My Mid Life Crisis
IN THE SPECTACULAR AURORA POLARIS LOUNGE, ENJOY THE HEAVENLY HARMONIES OF THOSE DIVINE CASSOWARY SISTERS...
GPL
PRIVATE
...OR IF YOU'RE FEELING DEVILISH, THE BACK OF THE HOUSE IS WHERE THE REAL ACTION IS...
...HERE IN THE HIGH ROLLERS' SALON, YOU MIGHT CATCH A GLIMPSE OF ANY NUMBER OF INFAMOUS LOCAL NE'ER-DO-WELLS.
CARMINE "THE ROMAN" FALCONE AT THE ROULETTE TABLE. BOSS ZUCCO AND FRENCHY BLAKE PLAYING BLACKJACK...
COME ON, HIZZONER GOTTA GET SOME FANCY GALOSHES!
...OR, AHEM, GOTHAM CITY MAYOR HAMILTON HILL SHOOTING CRAPS WITH SOME... FRIENDS.
WHOA, HEY--IS THAT A CAMERA? WHATEVER I SAID, I AGREE TO UNDERGO SENSITIVITY TRAINING!
DON'T GO AWAY, WE'RE BACK AFTER THIS SIZZLING SLICE OF SWING LIVE FROM THE EMPEROR BALLROOM RIGHT UPSTAIRS--KICKING OFF HIS EXCLUSIVE ENGAGEMENT AT THE ICEBERG CASINO, HERE'S THE ONE AND ONLY STOVEPLATE SULLIVAN AND HIS POTBELLY ORCHESTRA!

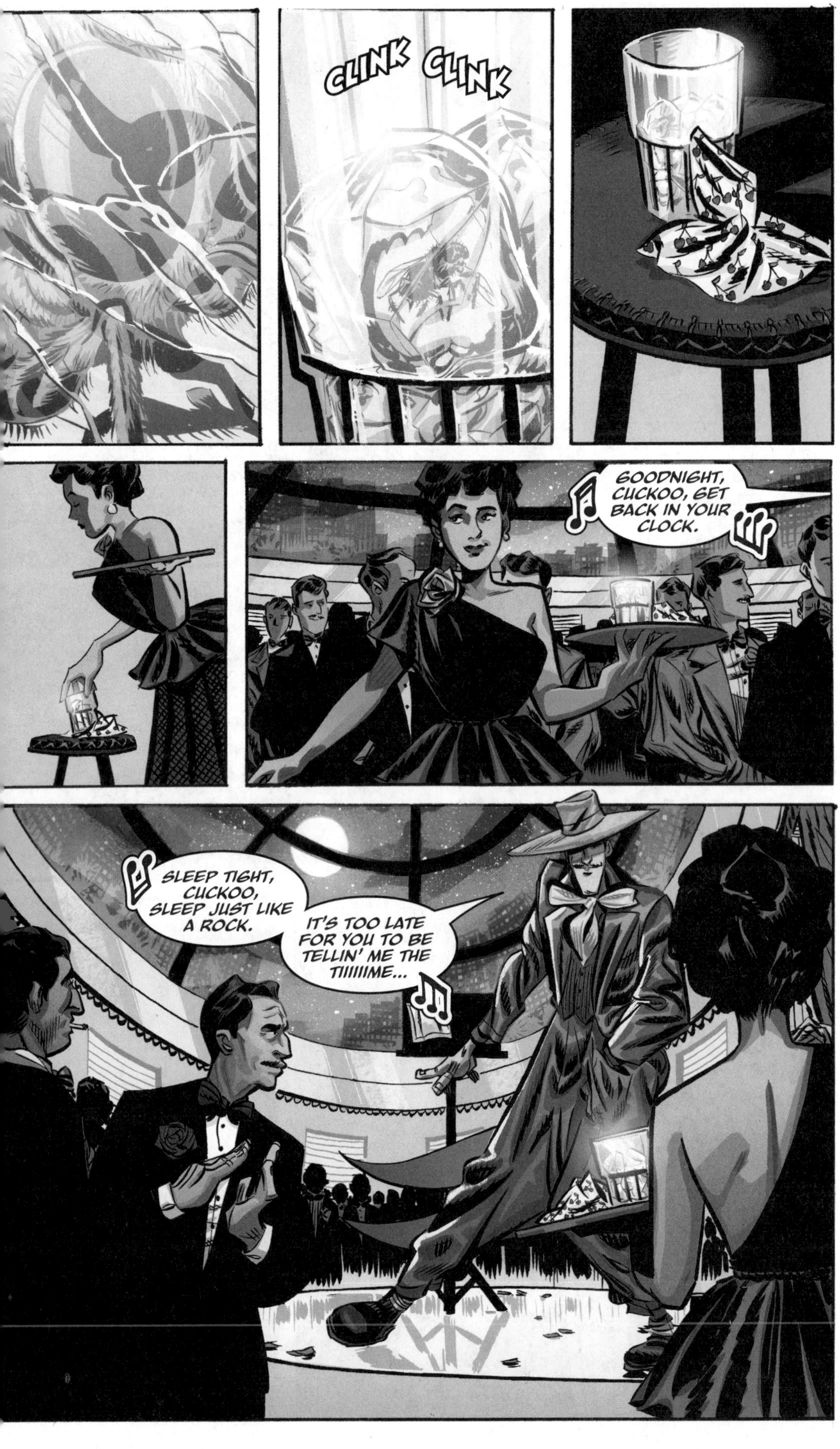
CLINK CLINK
GOODNIGHT, CUCKOO, GET BACK IN YOUR CLOCK.
SLEEP TIGHT, CUCKOO, SLEEP JUST LIKE A ROCK.
IT'S TOO LATE FOR YOU TO BE TELLIN' ME THE TIIIIIIME...

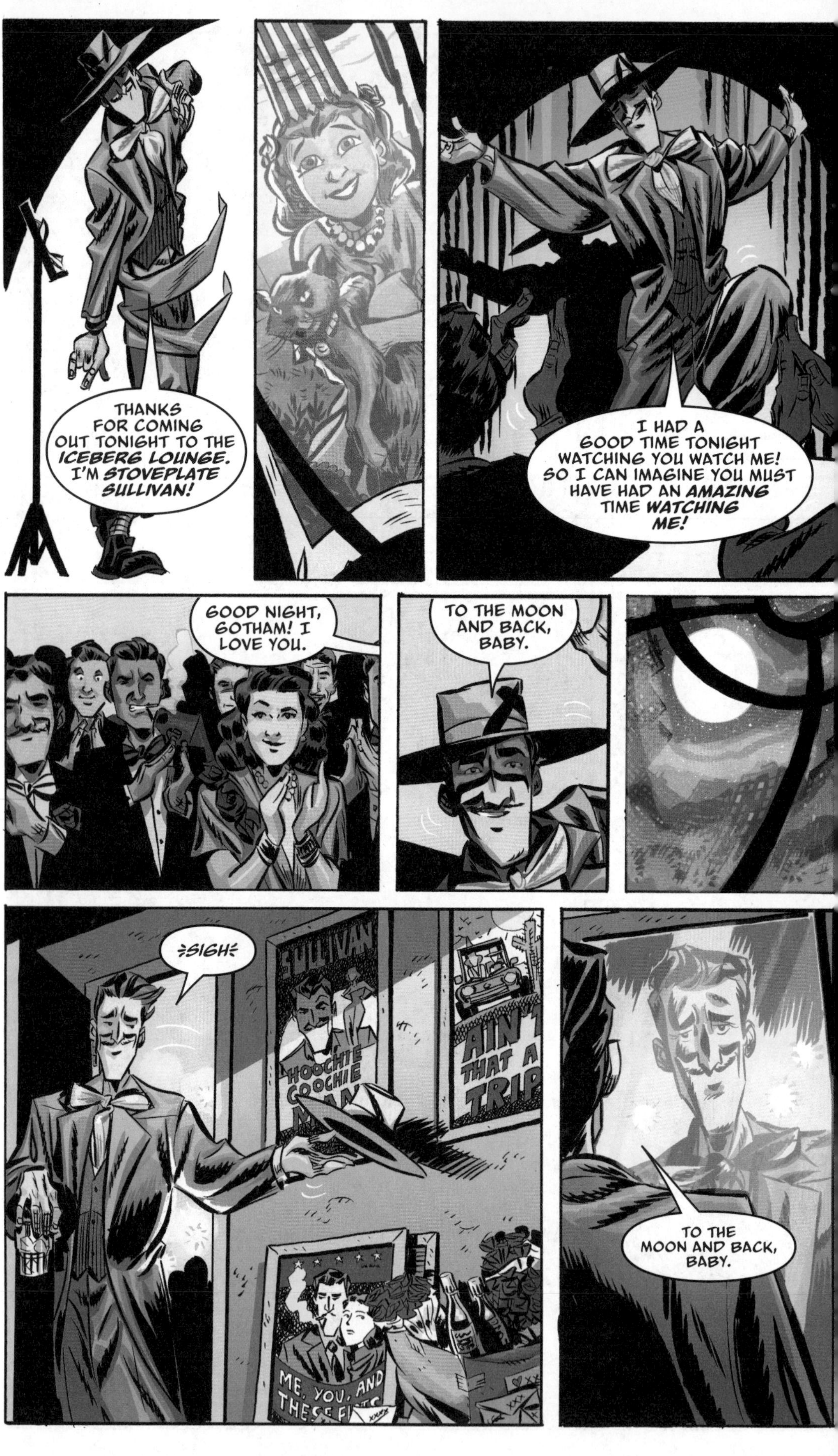
THANKS FOR COMING OUT TONIGHT TO THE ICEBERG LOUNGE. I'M STOVEPLATE SULLIVAN!
I HAD A GOOD TIME TONIGHT WATCHING YOU WATCH ME! SO I CAN IMAGINE YOU MUST HAVE HAD AN AMAZING TIME WATCHING ME!
GOOD NIGHT, GOTHAM! I LOVE YOU.
TO THE MOON AND BACK, BABY.
SIGH
SULLIVAN
HOOCHIE COOCHIE MAN
AIN'T THAT A TRIP
ME, YOU, AND THESE FISTS
TO THE MOON AND BACK, BABY.

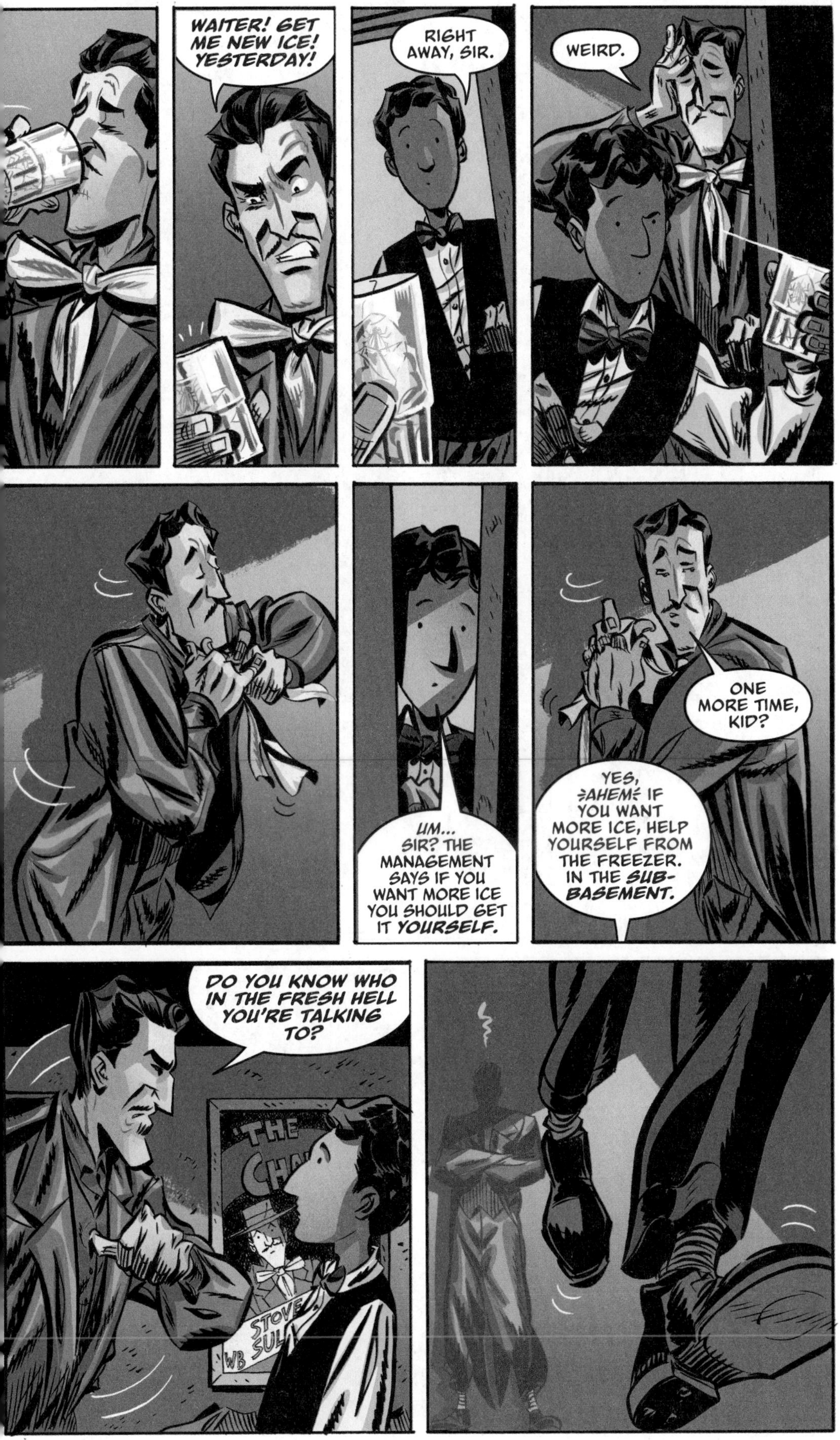
WAITER! GET ME NEW ICE! YESTERDAY!
RIGHT AWAY, SIR.
WEIRD.
UM... SIR? THE MANAGEMENT SAYS IF YOU WANT MORE ICE YOU SHOULD GET IT YOURSELF.
ONE MORE TIME, KID?
YES, AHEM IF YOU WANT MORE ICE, HELP YOURSELF FROM THE FREEZER. IN THE SUB-BASEMENT.
DO YOU KNOW WHO IN THE FRESH HELL YOU'RE TALKING TO?
THE
STOVE
WB

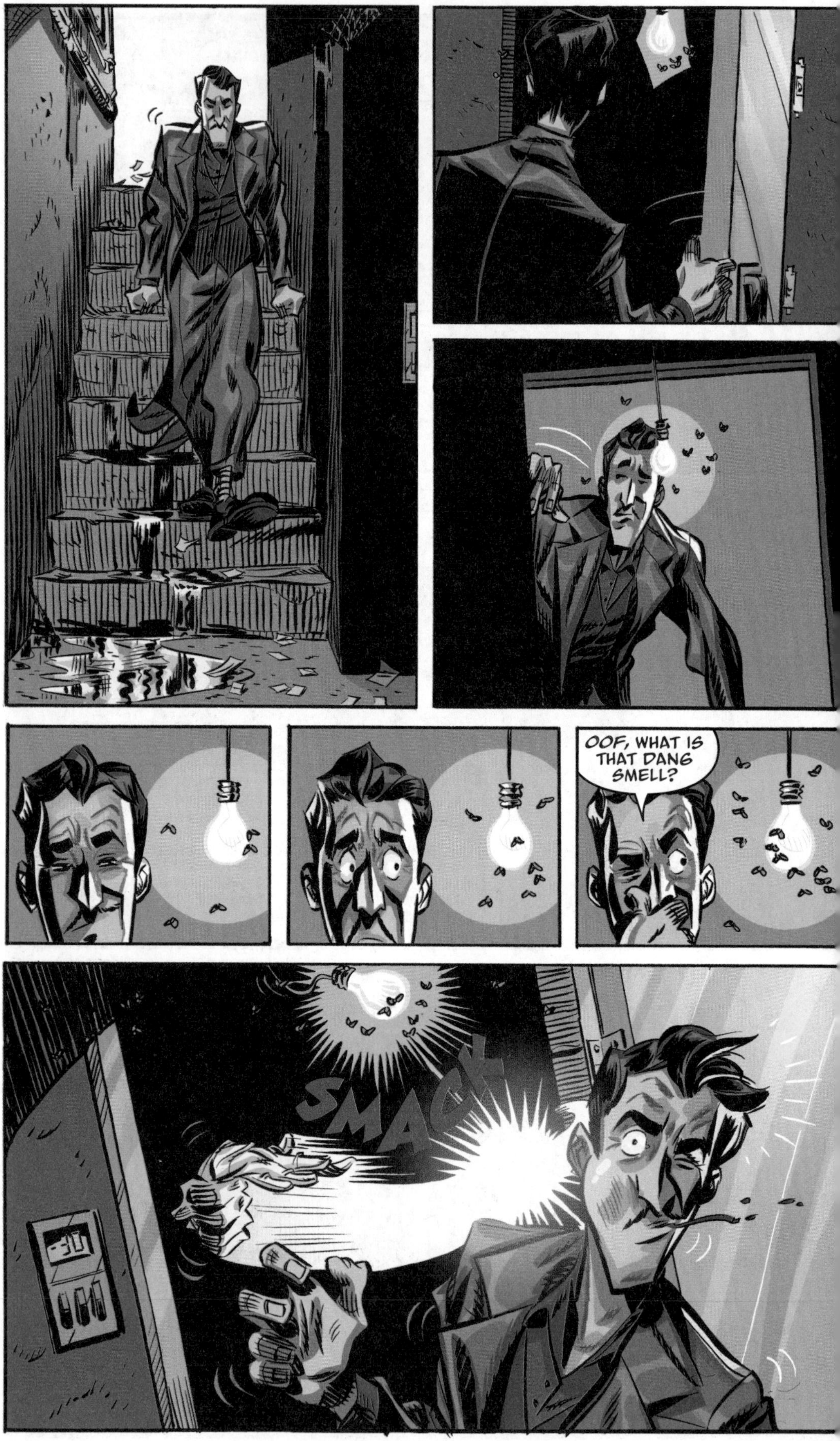
OOF, WHAT IS THAT DANG SMELL?
SMACK

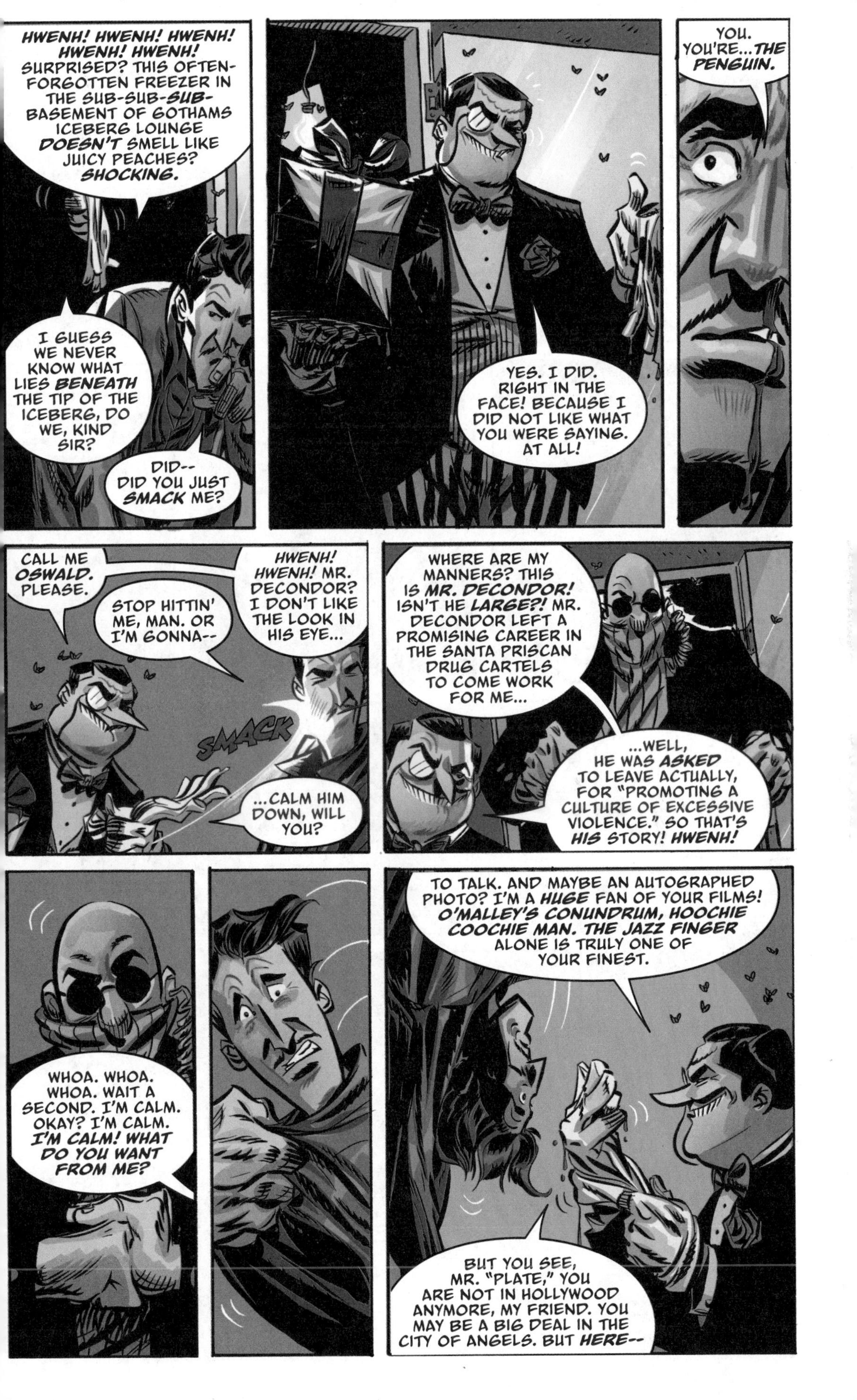
HWENH! HWENH! HWENH! HWENH! HWENH! SURPRISED? THIS OFTEN-FORGOTTEN FREEZER IN THE SUB-SUB-SUB-BASEMENT OF GOTHAMS ICEBERG LOUNGE DOESN'T SMELL LIKE JUICY PEACHES? SHOCKING.
I GUESS WE NEVER KNOW WHAT LIES BENEATH THE TIP OF THE ICEBERG, DO WE, KIND SIR?
DID-- DID YOU JUST SMACK ME?
YES. I DID. RIGHT IN THE FACE! BECAUSE I DID NOT LIKE WHAT YOU WERE SAYING. AT ALL!
YOU. YOU'RE...THE PENGUIN.
CALL ME OSWALD. PLEASE.
STOP HITTIN' ME, MAN. OR I'M GONNA--
HWENH! HWENH! MR. DECONDOR? I DON'T LIKE THE LOOK IN HIS EYE...
SMACK
...CALM HIM DOWN, WILL YOU?
WHERE ARE MY MANNERS? THIS IS MR. DECONDOR! ISN'T HE LARGE?! MR. DECONDOR LEFT A PROMISING CAREER IN THE SANTA PRISCAN DRUG CARTELS TO COME WORK FOR ME...
...WELL, HE WAS ASKED TO LEAVE ACTUALLY, FOR "PROMOTING A CULTURE OF EXCESSIVE VIOLENCE." SO THAT'S HIS STORY! HWENH!
WHOA. WHOA. WHOA. WAIT A SECOND. I'M CALM. OKAY? I'M CALM. I'M CALM! WHAT DO YOU WANT FROM ME?
TO TALK. AND MAYBE AN AUTOGRAPHED PHOTO? I'M A HUGE FAN OF YOUR FILMS! O'MALLEY'S CONUNDRUM, HOOCHIE COOCHIE MAN. THE JAZZ FINGER ALONE IS TRULY ONE OF YOUR FINEST.
BUT YOU SEE, MR. "PLATE," YOU ARE NOT IN HOLLYWOOD ANYMORE, MY FRIEND. YOU MAY BE A BIG DEAL IN THE CITY OF ANGELS. BUT HERE--

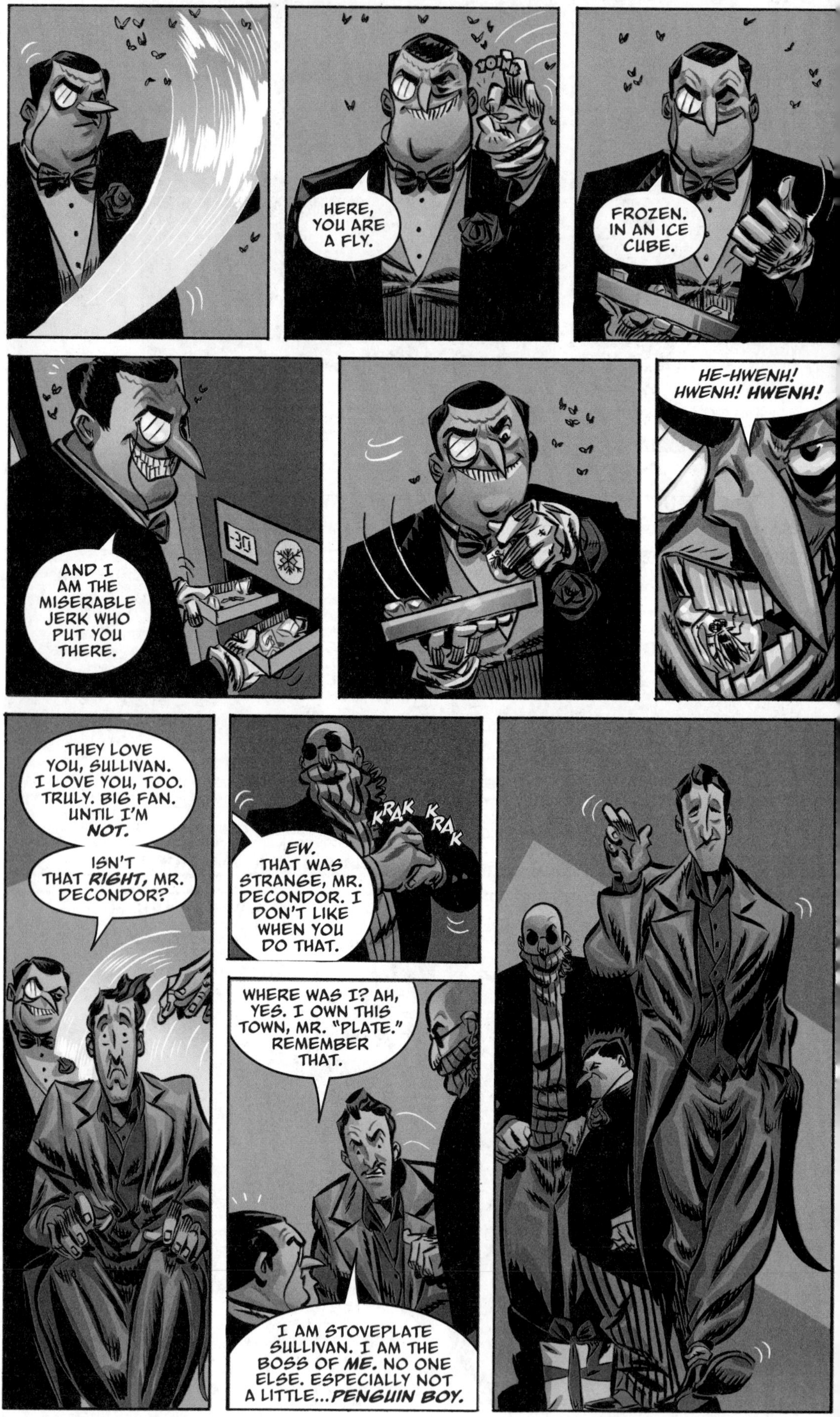
YOINK
HERE, YOU ARE A FLY.
FROZEN. IN AN ICE CUBE.
AND I AM THE MISERABLE JERK WHO PUT YOU THERE.
HE-HWENH! HWENH! HWENH!
THEY LOVE YOU, SULLIVAN. I LOVE YOU, TOO. TRULY. BIG FAN. UNTIL I'M NOT.
ISN'T THAT RIGHT, MR. DECONDOR?
KRAK KRAK
EW. THAT WAS STRANGE, MR. DECONDOR. I DON'T LIKE WHEN YOU DO THAT.
WHERE WAS I? AH, YES. I OWN THIS TOWN, MR. "PLATE." REMEMBER THAT.
I AM STOVEPLATE SULLIVAN. I AM THE BOSS OF ME. NO ONE ELSE. ESPECIALLY NOT A LITTLE...PENGUIN BOY.

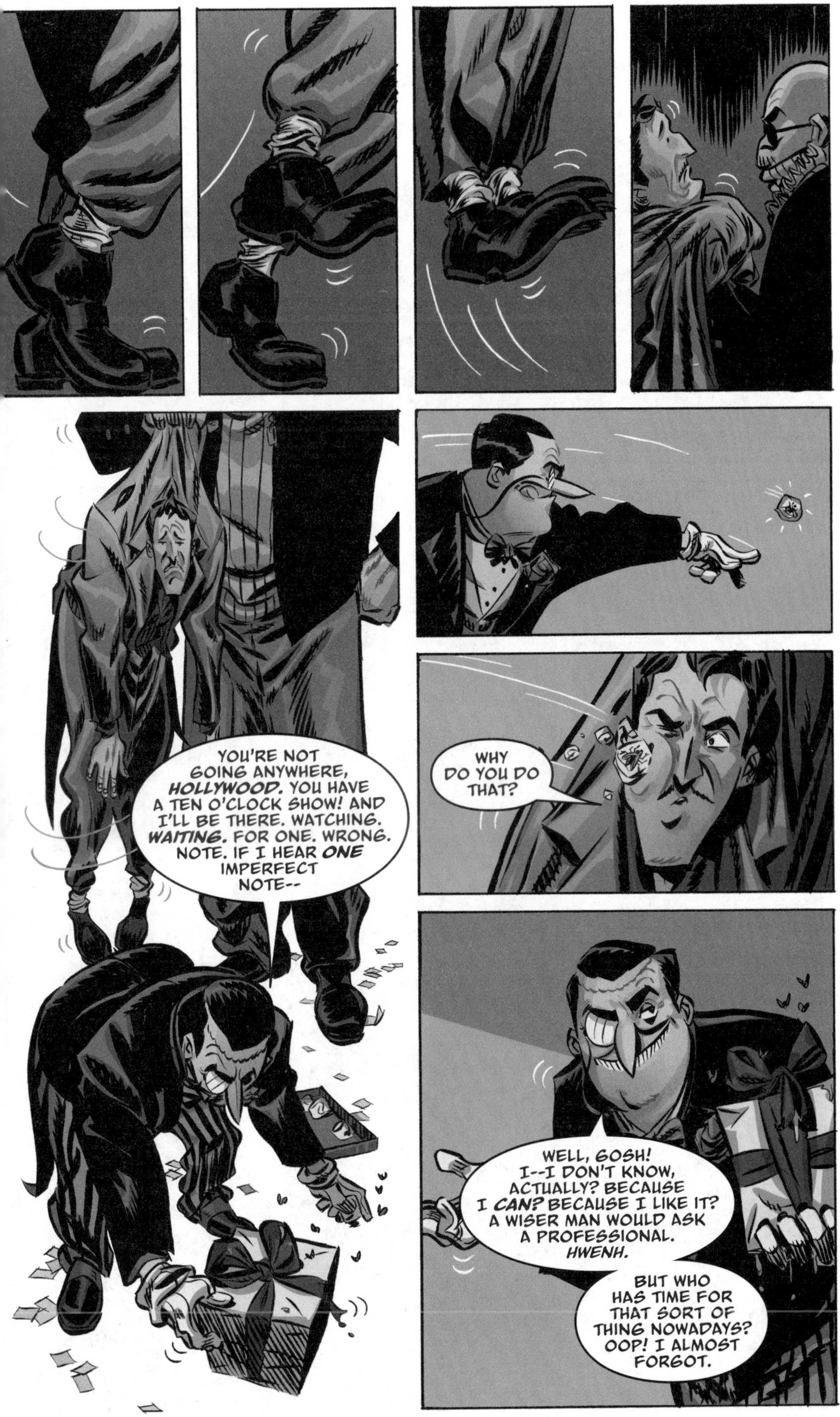
YOU'RE NOT GOING ANYWHERE, HOLLYWOOD. YOU HAVE A TEN O'CLOCK SHOW! AND I'LL BE THERE. WATCHING. WAITING. FOR ONE. WRONG. NOTE. IF I HEAR ONE IMPERFECT NOTE--
WHY DO YOU DO THAT?
WELL, GOSH! I--I DON'T KNOW, ACTUALLY? BECAUSE I CAN? BECAUSE I LIKE IT? A WISER MAN WOULD ASK A PROFESSIONAL. HWENH.
BUT WHO HAS TIME FOR THAT SORT OF THING NOWADAYS? OOP! I ALMOST FORGOT.

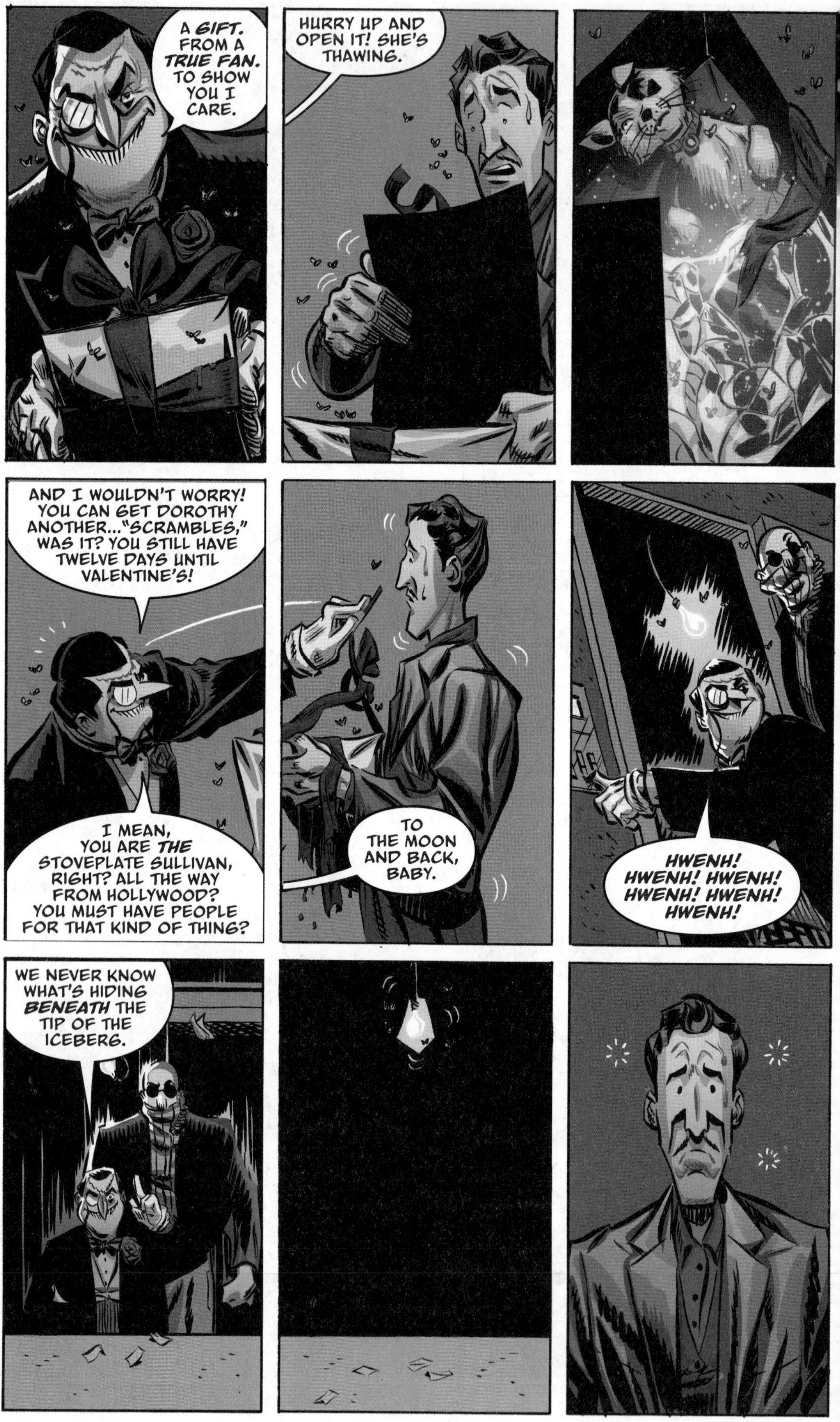
A GIFT. FROM A TRUE FAN. TO SHOW YOU I CARE.
HURRY UP AND OPEN IT! SHE'S THAWING.
AND I WOULDN'T WORRY! YOU CAN GET DOROTHY ANOTHER..."SCRAMBLES," WAS IT? YOU STILL HAVE TWELVE DAYS UNTIL VALENTINE'S!
I MEAN, YOU ARE THE STOVEPLATE SULLIVAN, RIGHT? ALL THE WAY FROM HOLLYWOOD? YOU MUST HAVE PEOPLE FOR THAT KIND OF THING?
TO THE MOON AND BACK, BABY.
HWENH! HWENH! HWENH! HWENH! HWENH! HWENH!
WE NEVER KNOW WHAT'S HIDING BENEATH THE TIP OF THE ICEBERG.

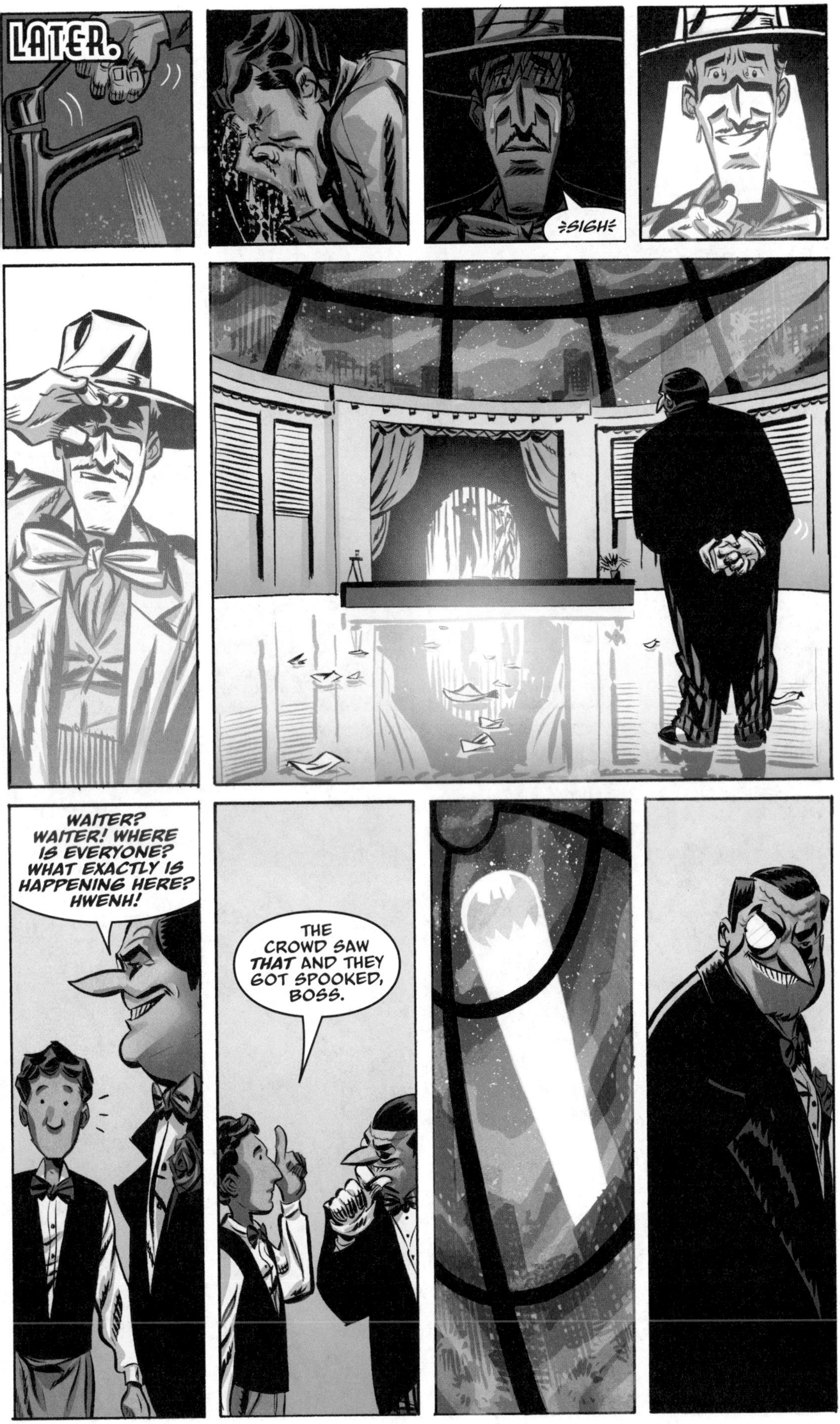
LATER.
SIGH
WAITER? WAITER! WHERE IS EVERYONE? WHAT EXACTLY IS HAPPENING HERE? HWENH!
THE CROWD SAW THAT AND THEY GOT SPOOKED, BOSS.

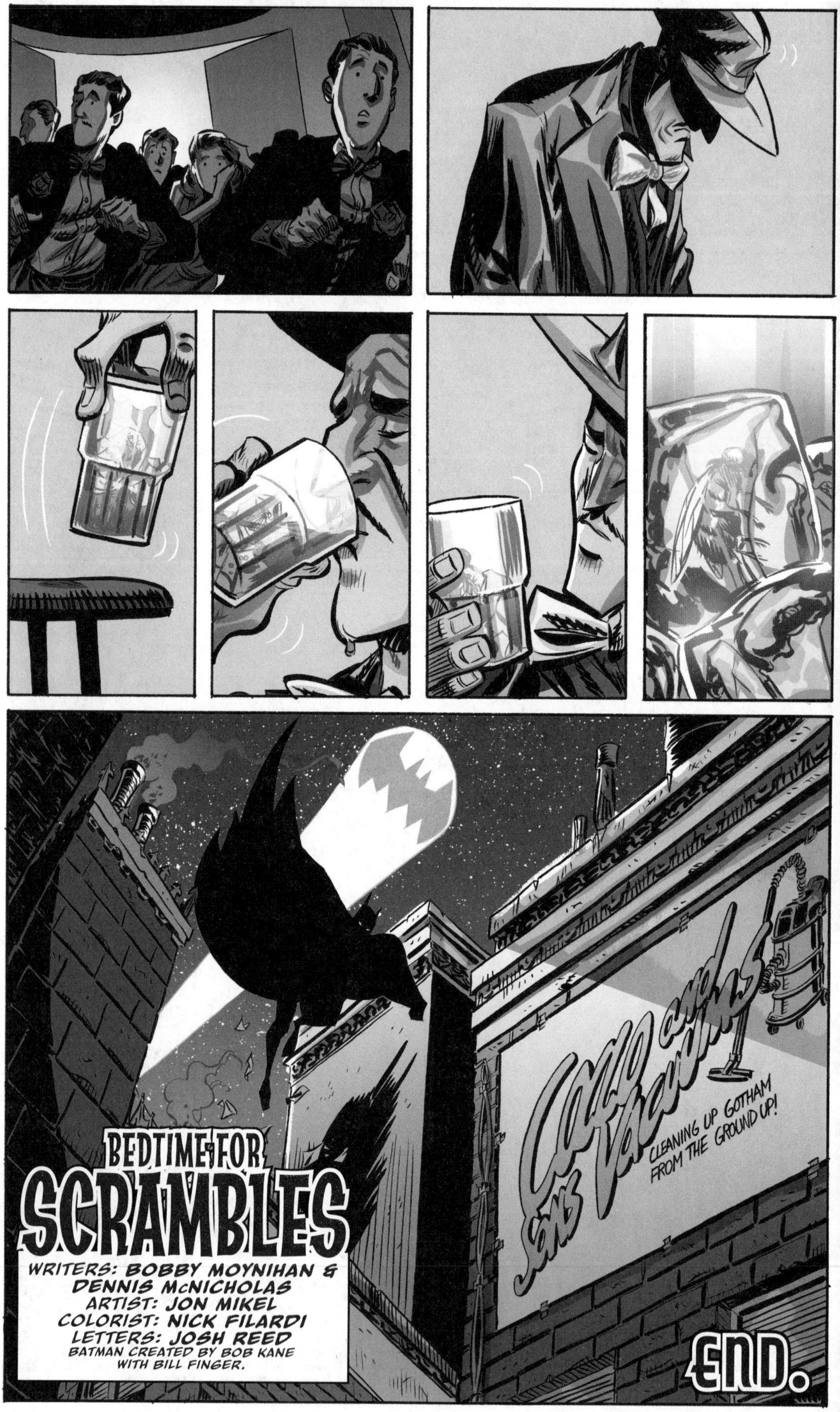
CLEANING UP GOTHAM FROM THE GROUND UP!
BEDTIME FOR SCRAMBLES
WRITERS: BOBBY MOYNIHAN & DENNIS McNICHOLAS
ARTIST: JON MIKEL
COLORIST: NICK FILARDI
LETTERS: JOSH REED
BATMAN CREATED BY BOB KANE WITH BILL FINGER.
END.

STATELY WAYNE MANOR IN THE GOTHAM PALISADES, WHERE THE HOUSES ARE SO FANCY THEY HAVE THEIR OWN CEMETERIES! *OOH LA LA!*

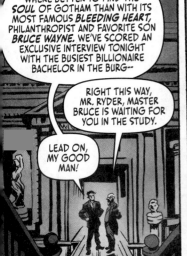

WHERE BETTER TO FIND THE *SOUL* OF GOTHAM THAN WITH ITS MOST FAMOUS *BLEEDING HEART*, PHILANTHROPIST AND FAVORITE SON *BRUCE WAYNE.* WE'VE SCORED AN EXCLUSIVE INTERVIEW TONIGHT WITH THE BUSIEST BILLIONAIRE BACHELOR IN THE BURG--

RIGHT THIS WAY, MR. RYDER, MASTER BRUCE IS WAITING FOR YOU IN THE STUDY.

LEAD ON, MY GOOD MAN!

OH DEAR, PERHAPS HE SAID HE WOULD BE IN THE GARAGE.

WELL, HE DOES SOMETIMES ENJOY BOWLING TEN FRAMES AFTER SUPPER...

I SUPPOSE IT'S POSSIBLE HE'S FEEDING THE ZEBRAS--

HE'S NOT HOME, IS HE?

I HOPE HE HASN'T GOT LOST IN THE HEDGE MAZE AGAIN.

HE BLEW IT OFF, DIDN'T HE? THIS ALWAYS HAPPENS. THE MAN IS LITERALLY *NEVER* HOME. BIGGEST, NICEST HOUSE EVER CONSTRUCTED AND THE MAN IS NEVER HERE. I WAS TOLD HE WOULD BE AT HOME ALL FRIDAY EVENING--

HOLD A MOMENT, IS IT FRIDAY?

AH, WELL, THEN THAT EXPLAINS IT. MASTER BRUCE SPENDS FRIDAY EVENINGS AT THE PENTHOUSE IN THE CITY PLAYING CHARADES WITH VISITING ROYALTY. THAT'S ENTIRELY MY ERROR. SO TERRIBLY SORRY, SIR.

TOUGH TO GET GOOD HELP THESE DAYS.

AS YOU SAY, SIR.

WELL, I CAN'T PROMISE YOU AS GOOD A TIME AS BRUCE WAYNE IS HAVING TONIGHT, BUT WE STILL HAVE SWELL SIGHTS TO SEE WHEN WE'RE BACK AFTER THIS...

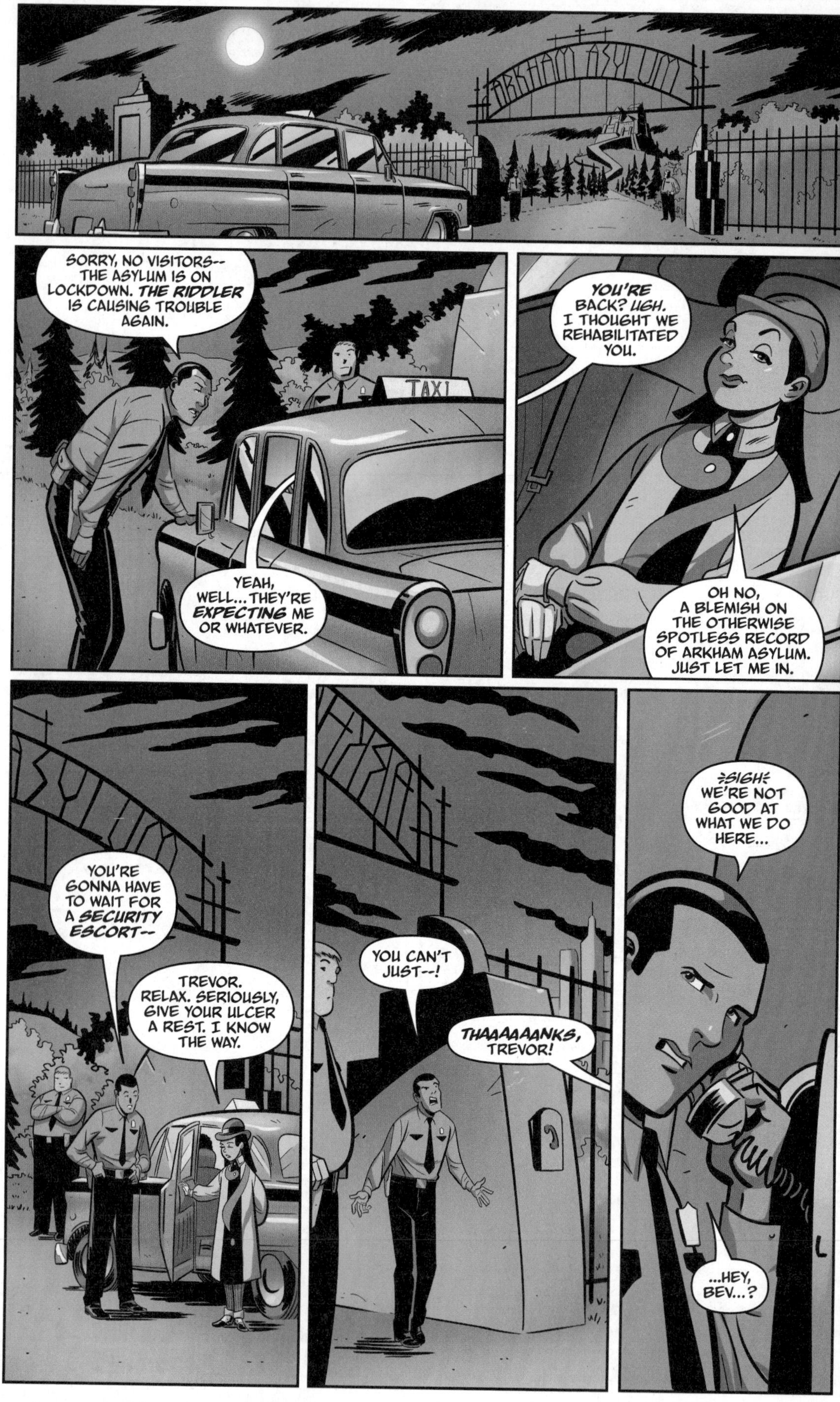
ARKHAM ASYLUM
SORRY, NO VISITORS--THE ASYLUM IS ON LOCKDOWN. THE RIDDLER IS CAUSING TROUBLE AGAIN.
TAXI
YEAH, WELL...THEY'RE EXPECTING ME OR WHATEVER.
YOU'RE BACK? UGH. I THOUGHT WE REHABILITATED YOU.
OH NO, A BLEMISH ON THE OTHERWISE SPOTLESS RECORD OF ARKHAM ASYLUM. JUST LET ME IN.
YOU'RE GONNA HAVE TO WAIT FOR A SECURITY ESCORT--
TREVOR. RELAX. SERIOUSLY, GIVE YOUR ULCER A REST. I KNOW THE WAY.
YOU CAN'T JUST--!
THAAAAAANKS, TREVOR!
SIGH WE'RE NOT GOOD AT WHAT WE DO HERE...
...HEY, BEV...?

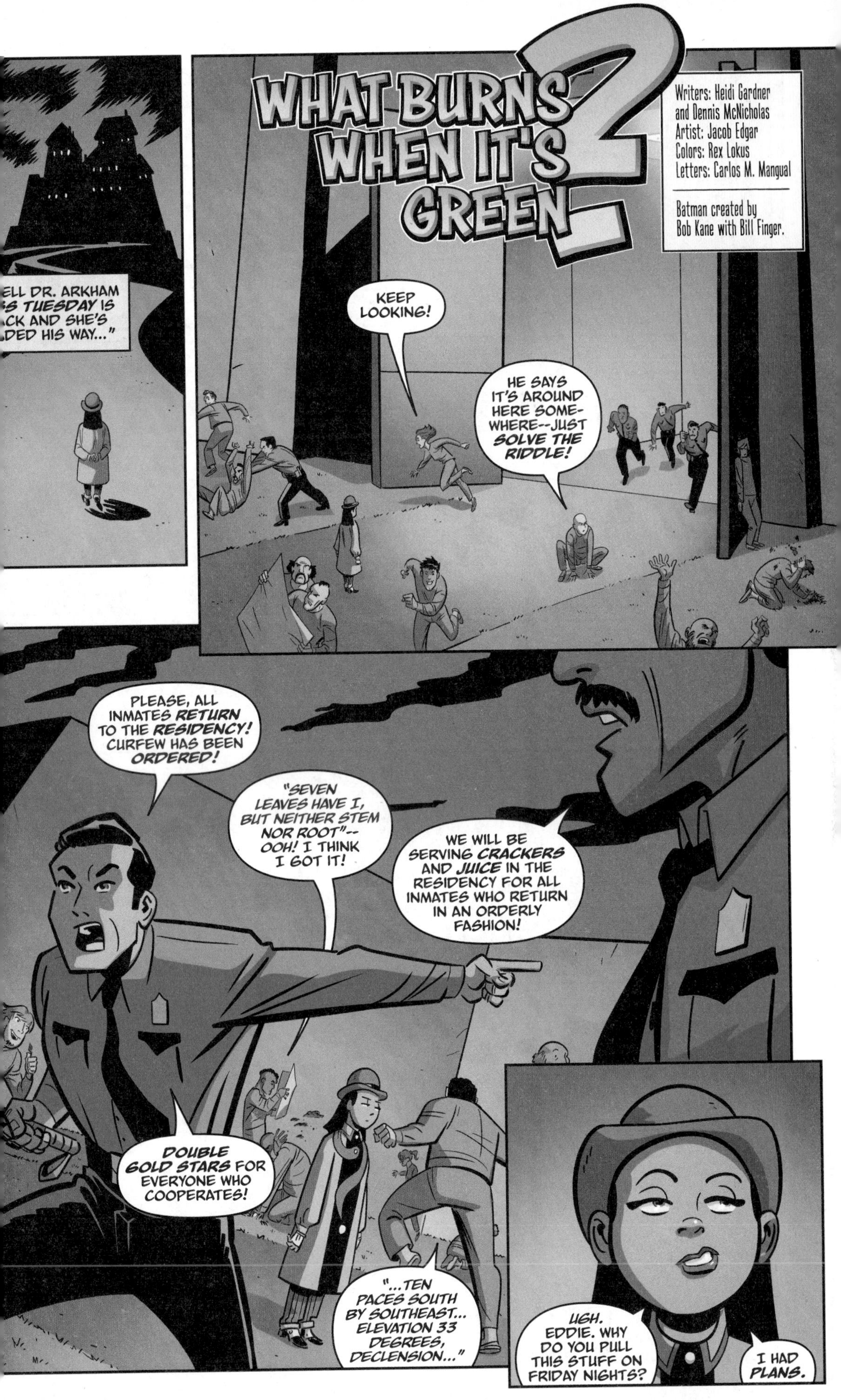

ELL DR. ARKHAM
S TUESDAY IS
CK AND SHE'S
DED HIS WAY..."
WHAT BURNS WHEN IT'S GREEN 2
Writers: Heidi Gardner and Dennis McNicholas
Artist: Jacob Edgar
Colors: Rex Lokus
Letters: Carlos M. Mangual
Batman created by Bob Kane with Bill Finger.
KEEP LOOKING!
HE SAYS IT'S AROUND HERE SOME-WHERE--JUST SOLVE THE RIDDLE!
PLEASE, ALL INMATES RETURN TO THE RESIDENCY! CURFEW HAS BEEN ORDERED!
"SEVEN LEAVES HAVE I, BUT NEITHER STEM NOR ROOT"-- OOH! I THINK I GOT IT!
WE WILL BE SERVING CRACKERS AND JUICE IN THE RESIDENCY FOR ALL INMATES WHO RETURN IN AN ORDERLY FASHION!
DOUBLE GOLD STARS FOR EVERYONE WHO COOPERATES!
"...TEN PACES SOUTH BY SOUTHEAST... ELEVATION 33 DEGREES, DECLENSION..."
UGH. EDDIE. WHY DO YOU PULL THIS STUFF ON FRIDAY NIGHTS?
I HAD PLANS.

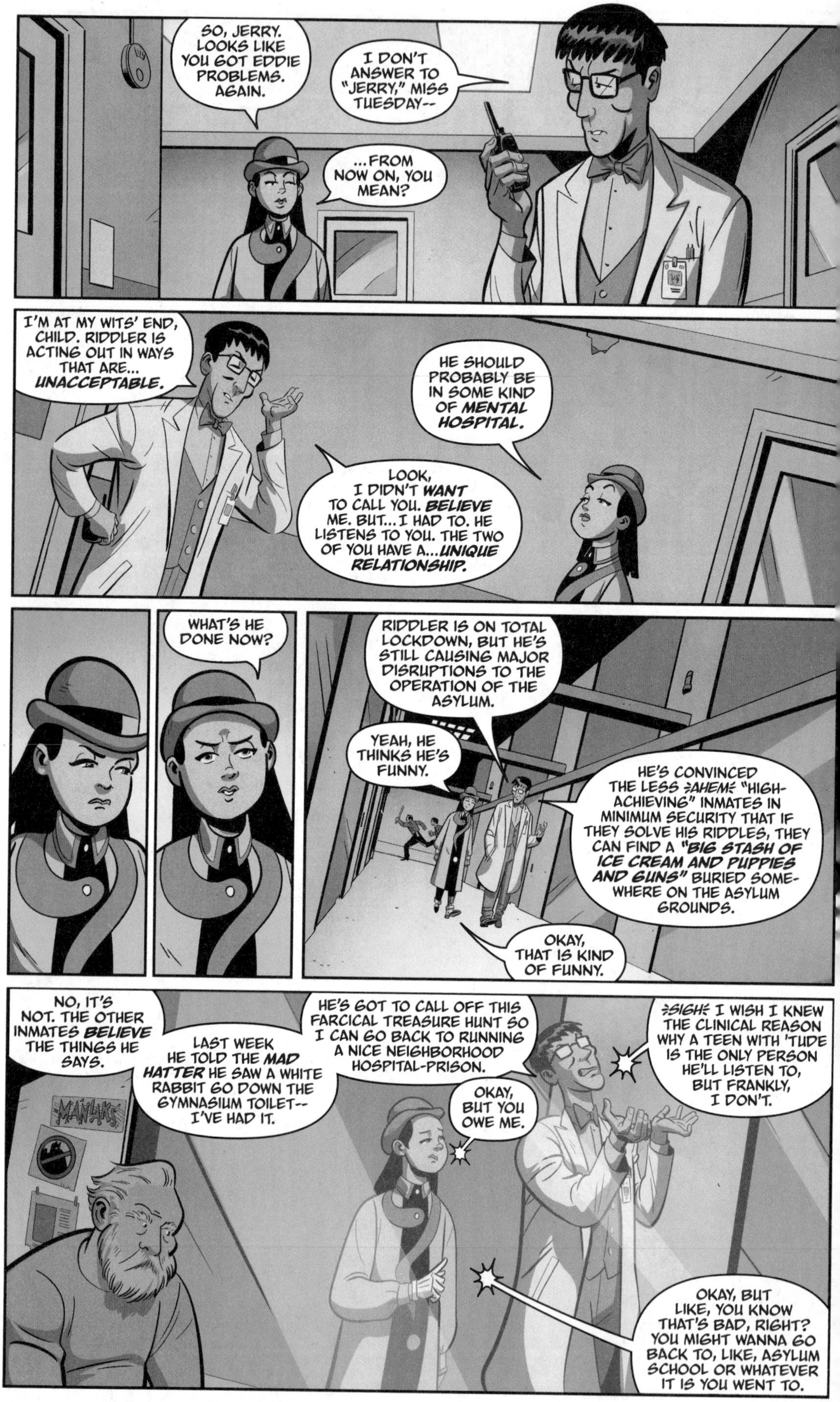
SO, JERRY. LOOKS LIKE YOU GOT EDDIE PROBLEMS. AGAIN.
I DON'T ANSWER TO "JERRY," MISS TUESDAY--
...FROM NOW ON, YOU MEAN?
I'M AT MY WITS' END, CHILD. RIDDLER IS ACTING OUT IN WAYS THAT ARE... UNACCEPTABLE.
HE SHOULD PROBABLY BE IN SOME KIND OF MENTAL HOSPITAL.
LOOK, I DIDN'T WANT TO CALL YOU. BELIEVE ME. BUT... I HAD TO. HE LISTENS TO YOU. THE TWO OF YOU HAVE A...UNIQUE RELATIONSHIP.
WHAT'S HE DONE NOW?
RIDDLER IS ON TOTAL LOCKDOWN, BUT HE'S STILL CAUSING MAJOR DISRUPTIONS TO THE OPERATION OF THE ASYLUM.
YEAH, HE THINKS HE'S FUNNY.
HE'S CONVINCED THE LESS AHEM "HIGH-ACHIEVING" INMATES IN MINIMUM SECURITY THAT IF THEY SOLVE HIS RIDDLES, THEY CAN FIND A "BIG STASH OF ICE CREAM AND PUPPIES AND GUNS" BURIED SOMEWHERE ON THE ASYLUM GROUNDS.
OKAY, THAT IS KIND OF FUNNY.
NO, IT'S NOT. THE OTHER INMATES BELIEVE THE THINGS HE SAYS.
LAST WEEK HE TOLD THE MAD HATTER HE SAW A WHITE RABBIT GO DOWN THE GYMNASIUM TOILET-- I'VE HAD IT.
HE'S GOT TO CALL OFF THIS FARCICAL TREASURE HUNT SO I CAN GO BACK TO RUNNING A NICE NEIGHBORHOOD HOSPITAL-PRISON.
OKAY, BUT YOU OWE ME.
SIGH I WISH I KNEW THE CLINICAL REASON WHY A TEEN WITH 'TUDE IS THE ONLY PERSON HE'LL LISTEN TO, BUT FRANKLY, I DON'T.
MANIAKS
OKAY, BUT LIKE, YOU KNOW THAT'S BAD, RIGHT? YOU MIGHT WANNA GO BACK TO, LIKE, ASYLUM SCHOOL OR WHATEVER IT IS YOU WENT TO.

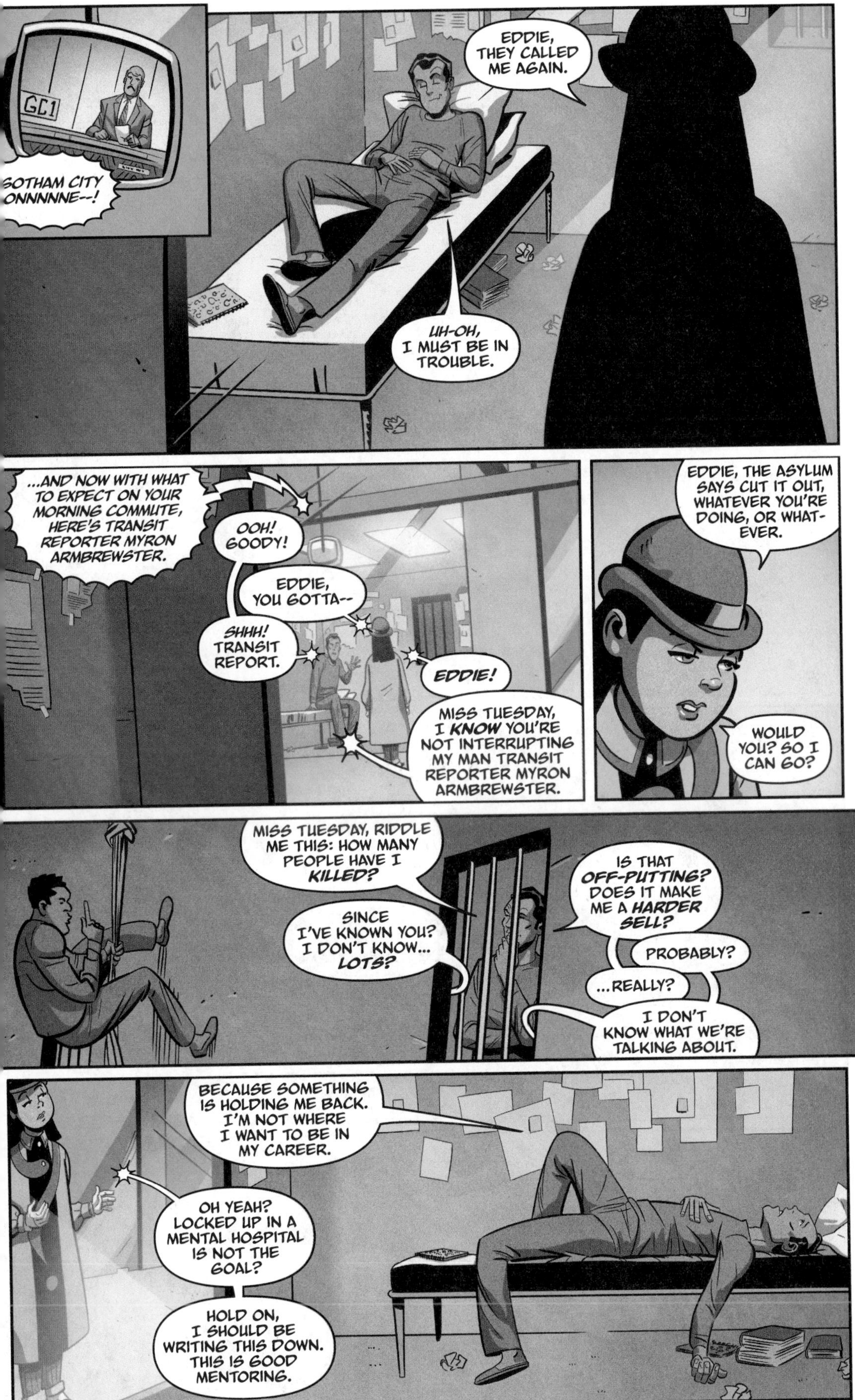
GC1
GOTHAM CITY ONNNNNE--!
EDDIE, THEY CALLED ME AGAIN.
UH-OH, I MUST BE IN TROUBLE.
...AND NOW WITH WHAT TO EXPECT ON YOUR MORNING COMMUTE, HERE'S TRANSIT REPORTER MYRON ARMBREWSTER.
OOH! GOODY!
EDDIE, YOU GOTTA--
SHHH! TRANSIT REPORT.
EDDIE!
MISS TUESDAY, I KNOW YOU'RE NOT INTERRUPTING MY MAN TRANSIT REPORTER MYRON ARMBREWSTER.
EDDIE, THE ASYLUM SAYS CUT IT OUT, WHATEVER YOU'RE DOING, OR WHAT-EVER.
WOULD YOU? SO I CAN GO?
MISS TUESDAY, RIDDLE ME THIS: HOW MANY PEOPLE HAVE I KILLED?
SINCE I'VE KNOWN YOU? I DON'T KNOW... LOTS?
IS THAT OFF-PUTTING? DOES IT MAKE ME A HARDER SELL?
PROBABLY?
...REALLY?
I DON'T KNOW WHAT WE'RE TALKING ABOUT.
BECAUSE SOMETHING IS HOLDING ME BACK. I'M NOT WHERE I WANT TO BE IN MY CAREER.
OH YEAH? LOCKED UP IN A MENTAL HOSPITAL IS NOT THE GOAL?
HOLD ON, I SHOULD BE WRITING THIS DOWN. THIS IS GOOD MENTORING.

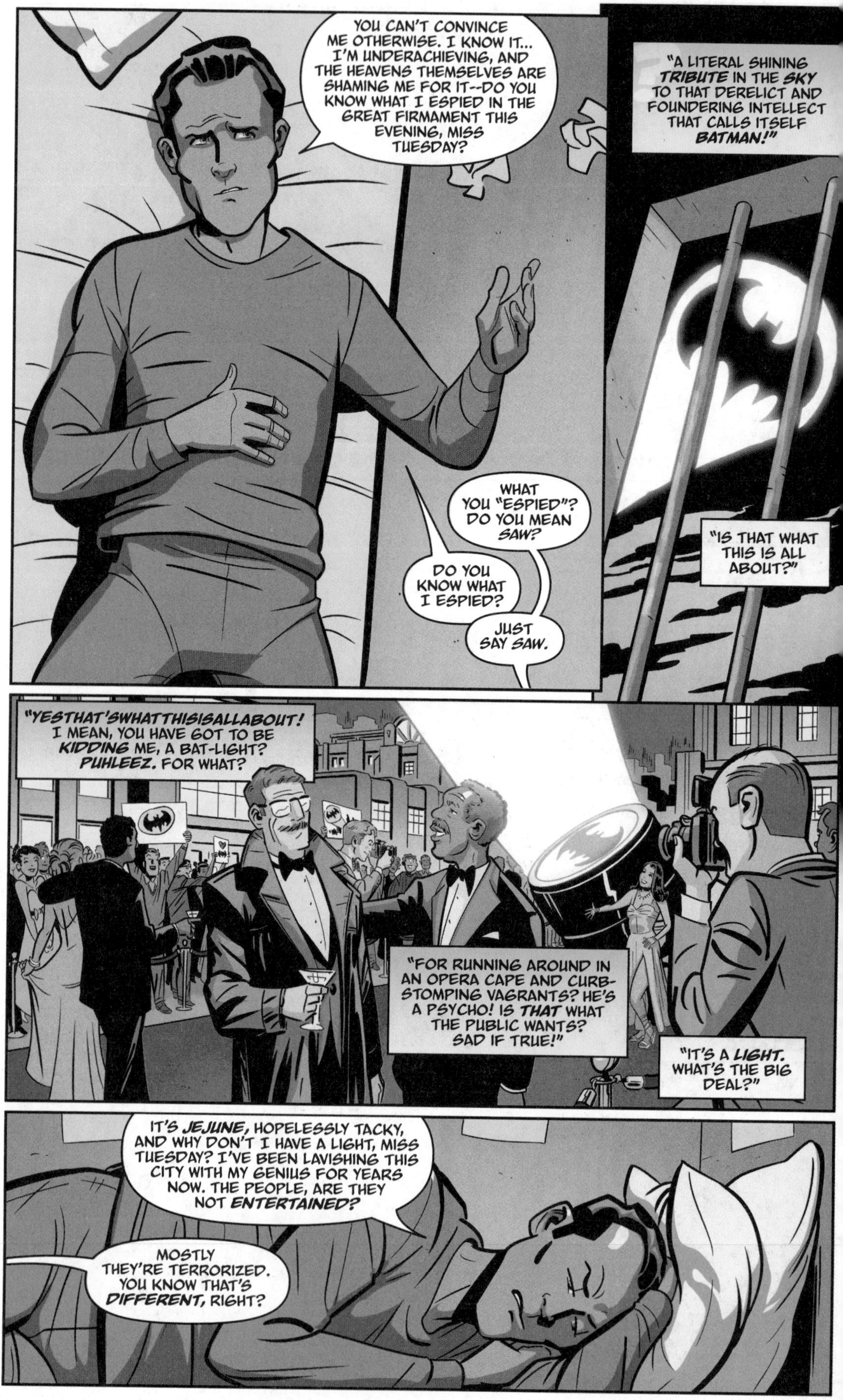

YOU CAN'T CONVINCE ME OTHERWISE. I KNOW IT... I'M UNDERACHIEVING, AND THE HEAVENS THEMSELVES ARE SHAMING ME FOR IT--DO YOU KNOW WHAT I ESPIED IN THE GREAT FIRMAMENT THIS EVENING, MISS TUESDAY?
WHAT YOU "ESPIED"? DO YOU MEAN *SAW?*
DO YOU KNOW WHAT I ESPIED?
JUST SAY *SAW.*
"A LITERAL SHINING ***TRIBUTE*** IN THE ***SKY*** TO THAT DERELICT AND FOUNDERING INTELLECT THAT CALLS ITSELF ***BATMAN!***"
"IS THAT WHAT THIS IS ALL ABOUT?"
"***YESTHAT'SWHATTHISISALLABOUT!*** I MEAN, YOU HAVE GOT TO BE ***KIDDING*** ME, A BAT-LIGHT? ***PUHLEEZ.*** FOR WHAT?
"FOR RUNNING AROUND IN AN OPERA CAPE AND CURB-STOMPING VAGRANTS? HE'S A PSYCHO! IS ***THAT*** WHAT THE PUBLIC WANTS? SAD IF TRUE!"
"IT'S A ***LIGHT.*** WHAT'S THE BIG DEAL?"
IT'S ***JEJUNE,*** HOPELESSLY TACKY, AND WHY DON'T I HAVE A LIGHT, MISS TUESDAY? I'VE BEEN LAVISHING THIS CITY WITH MY GENIUS FOR YEARS NOW. THE PEOPLE, ARE THEY NOT ***ENTERTAINED?***
MOSTLY THEY'RE TERRORIZED. YOU KNOW THAT'S ***DIFFERENT,*** RIGHT?

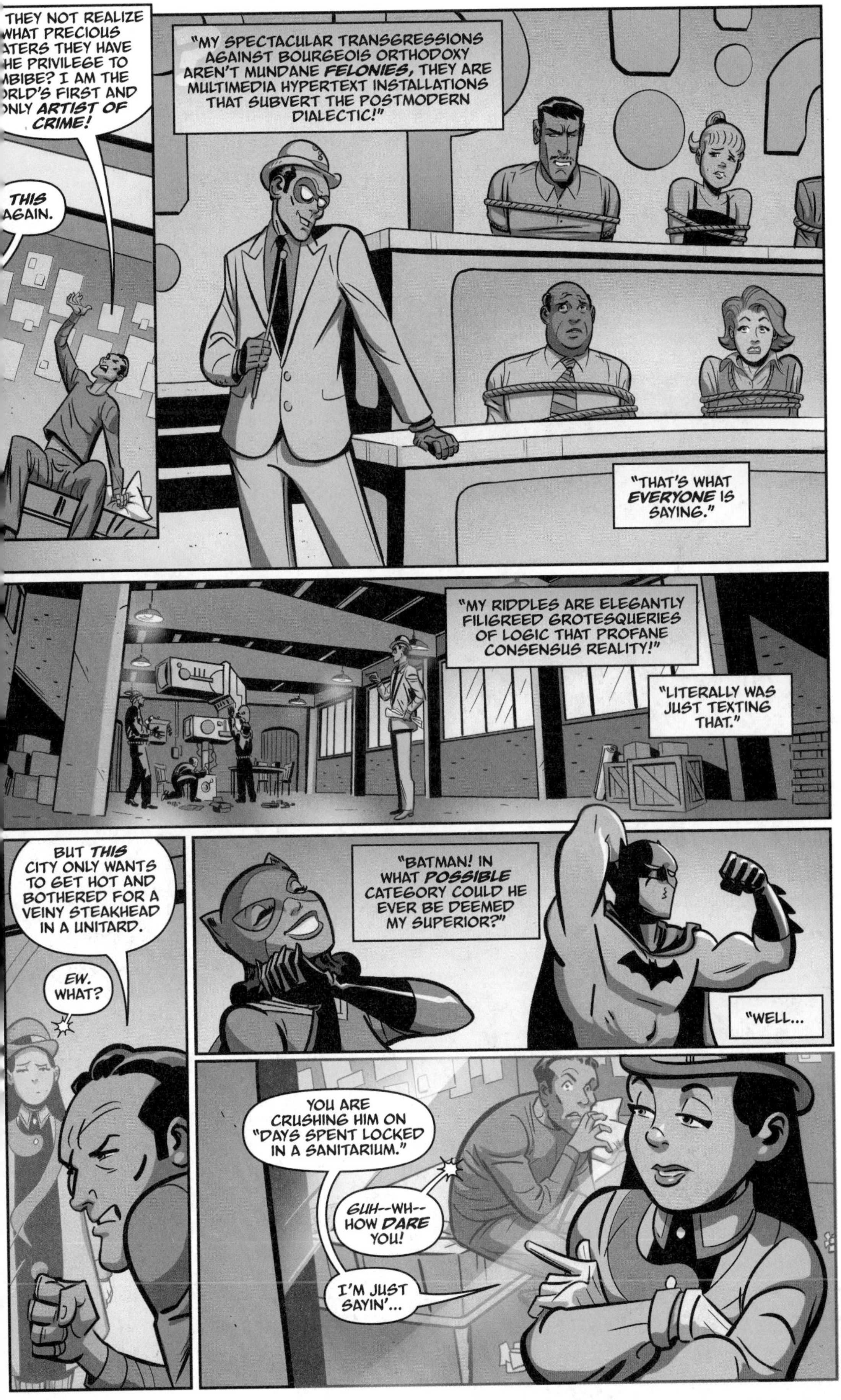
THEY NOT REALIZE WHAT PRECIOUS ATERS THEY HAVE HE PRIVILEGE TO MBIBE? I AM THE ORLD'S FIRST AND ONLY ARTIST OF CRIME!
THIS AGAIN.
"MY SPECTACULAR TRANSGRESSIONS AGAINST BOURGEOIS ORTHODOXY AREN'T MUNDANE FELONIES, THEY ARE MULTIMEDIA HYPERTEXT INSTALLATIONS THAT SUBVERT THE POSTMODERN DIALECTIC!"
"THAT'S WHAT EVERYONE IS SAYING."
"MY RIDDLES ARE ELEGANTLY FILIGREED GROTESQUERIES OF LOGIC THAT PROFANE CONSENSUS REALITY!"
"LITERALLY WAS JUST TEXTING THAT."
BUT THIS CITY ONLY WANTS TO GET HOT AND BOTHERED FOR A VEINY STEAKHEAD IN A UNITARD.
EW. WHAT?
"BATMAN! IN WHAT POSSIBLE CATEGORY COULD HE EVER BE DEEMED MY SUPERIOR?"
"WELL...
YOU ARE CRUSHING HIM ON "DAYS SPENT LOCKED IN A SANITARIUM."
GUH--WH-- HOW DARE YOU!
I'M JUST SAYIN'...

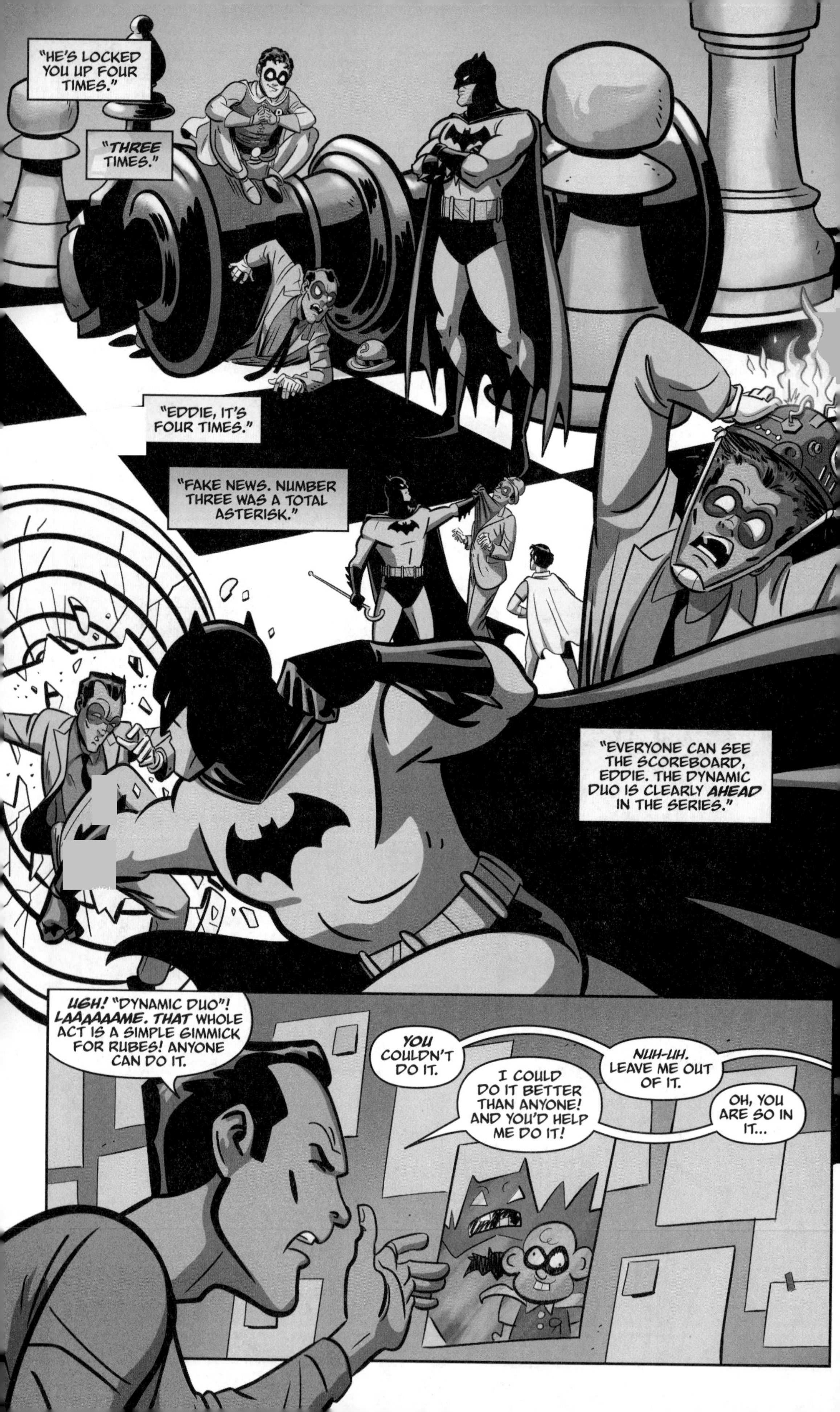
"HE'S LOCKED YOU UP FOUR TIMES."
"THREE TIMES."
"EDDIE, IT'S FOUR TIMES."
"FAKE NEWS. NUMBER THREE WAS A TOTAL ASTERISK."
"EVERYONE CAN SEE THE SCOREBOARD, EDDIE. THE DYNAMIC DUO IS CLEARLY AHEAD IN THE SERIES."
UGH! "DYNAMIC DUO"! LAAAAAAME. THAT WHOLE ACT IS A SIMPLE GIMMICK FOR RUBES! ANYONE CAN DO IT.
YOU COULDN'T DO IT.
I COULD DO IT BETTER THAN ANYONE! AND YOU'D HELP ME DO IT!
NUH-UH. LEAVE ME OUT OF IT.
OH, YOU ARE SO IN IT...

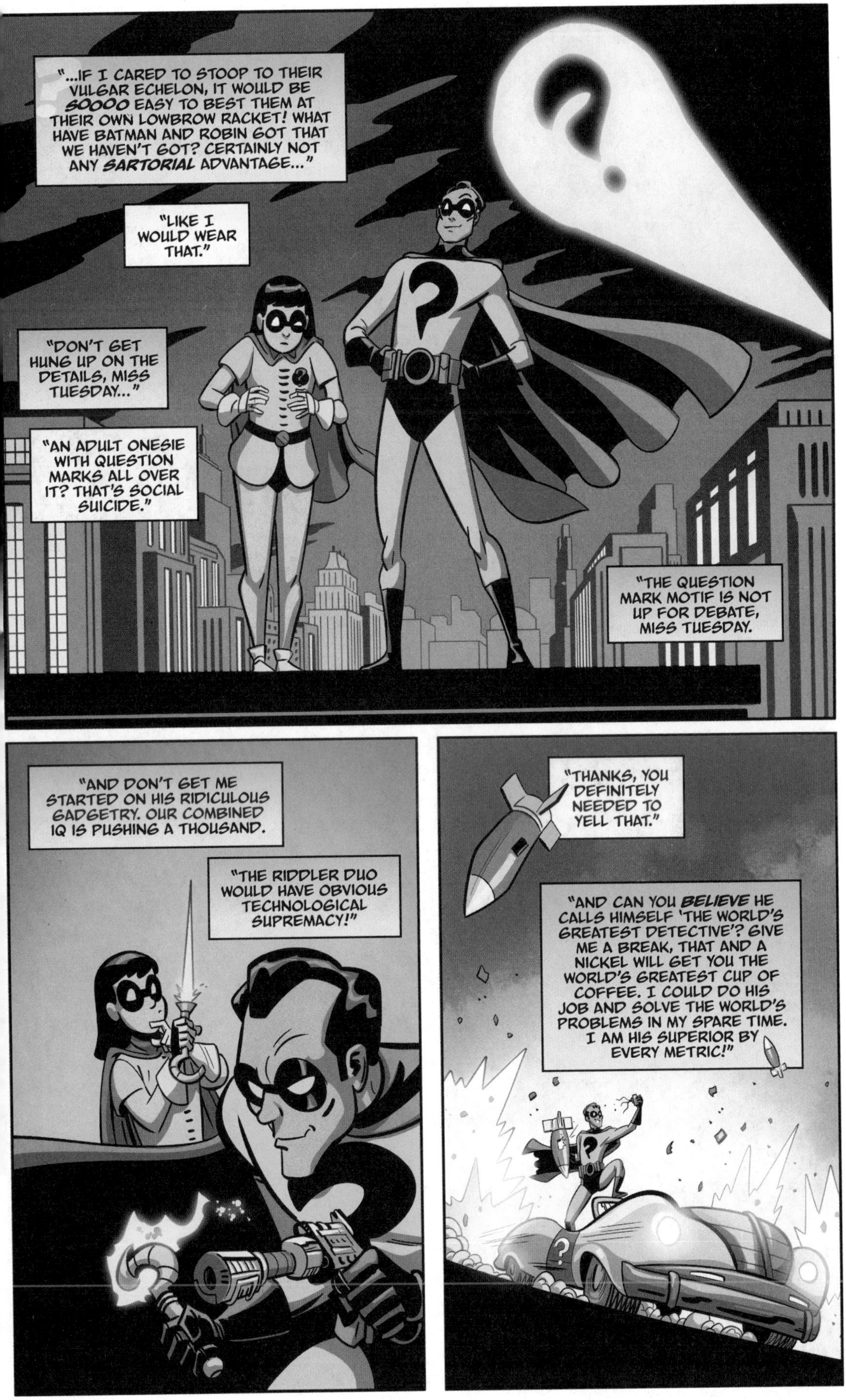
"...IF I CARED TO STOOP TO THEIR VULGAR ECHELON, IT WOULD BE SOOOO EASY TO BEST THEM AT THEIR OWN LOWBROW RACKET! WHAT HAVE BATMAN AND ROBIN GOT THAT WE HAVEN'T GOT? CERTAINLY NOT ANY SARTORIAL ADVANTAGE..."
"LIKE I WOULD WEAR THAT."
"DON'T GET HUNG UP ON THE DETAILS, MISS TUESDAY..."
"AN ADULT ONESIE WITH QUESTION MARKS ALL OVER IT? THAT'S SOCIAL SUICIDE."
"THE QUESTION MARK MOTIF IS NOT UP FOR DEBATE, MISS TUESDAY.
"AND DON'T GET ME STARTED ON HIS RIDICULOUS GADGETRY. OUR COMBINED IQ IS PUSHING A THOUSAND.
"THE RIDDLER DUO WOULD HAVE OBVIOUS TECHNOLOGICAL SUPREMACY!"
"THANKS, YOU DEFINITELY NEEDED TO YELL THAT."
"AND CAN YOU BELIEVE HE CALLS HIMSELF 'THE WORLD'S GREATEST DETECTIVE'? GIVE ME A BREAK, THAT AND A NICKEL WILL GET YOU THE WORLD'S GREATEST CUP OF COFFEE. I COULD DO HIS JOB AND SOLVE THE WORLD'S PROBLEMS IN MY SPARE TIME. I AM HIS SUPERIOR BY EVERY METRIC!"

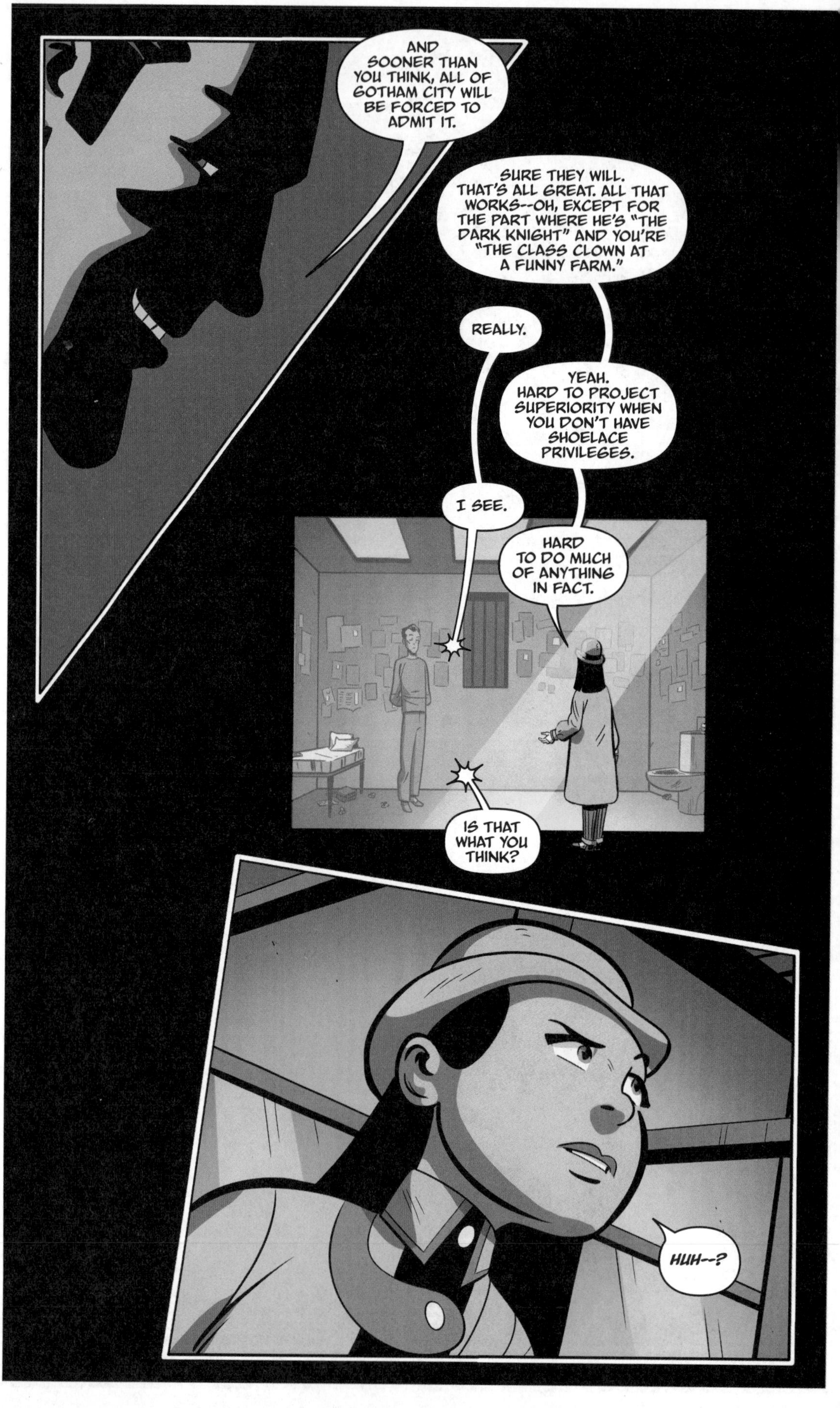

AND SOONER THAN YOU THINK, ALL OF GOTHAM CITY WILL BE FORCED TO ADMIT IT.
SURE THEY WILL. THAT'S ALL GREAT. ALL THAT WORKS--OH, EXCEPT FOR THE PART WHERE HE'S "THE DARK KNIGHT" AND YOU'RE "THE CLASS CLOWN AT A FUNNY FARM."
REALLY.
YEAH. HARD TO PROJECT SUPERIORITY WHEN YOU DON'T HAVE SHOELACE PRIVILEGES.
I SEE.
HARD TO DO MUCH OF ANYTHING IN FACT.
IS THAT WHAT YOU THINK?
HUH--?

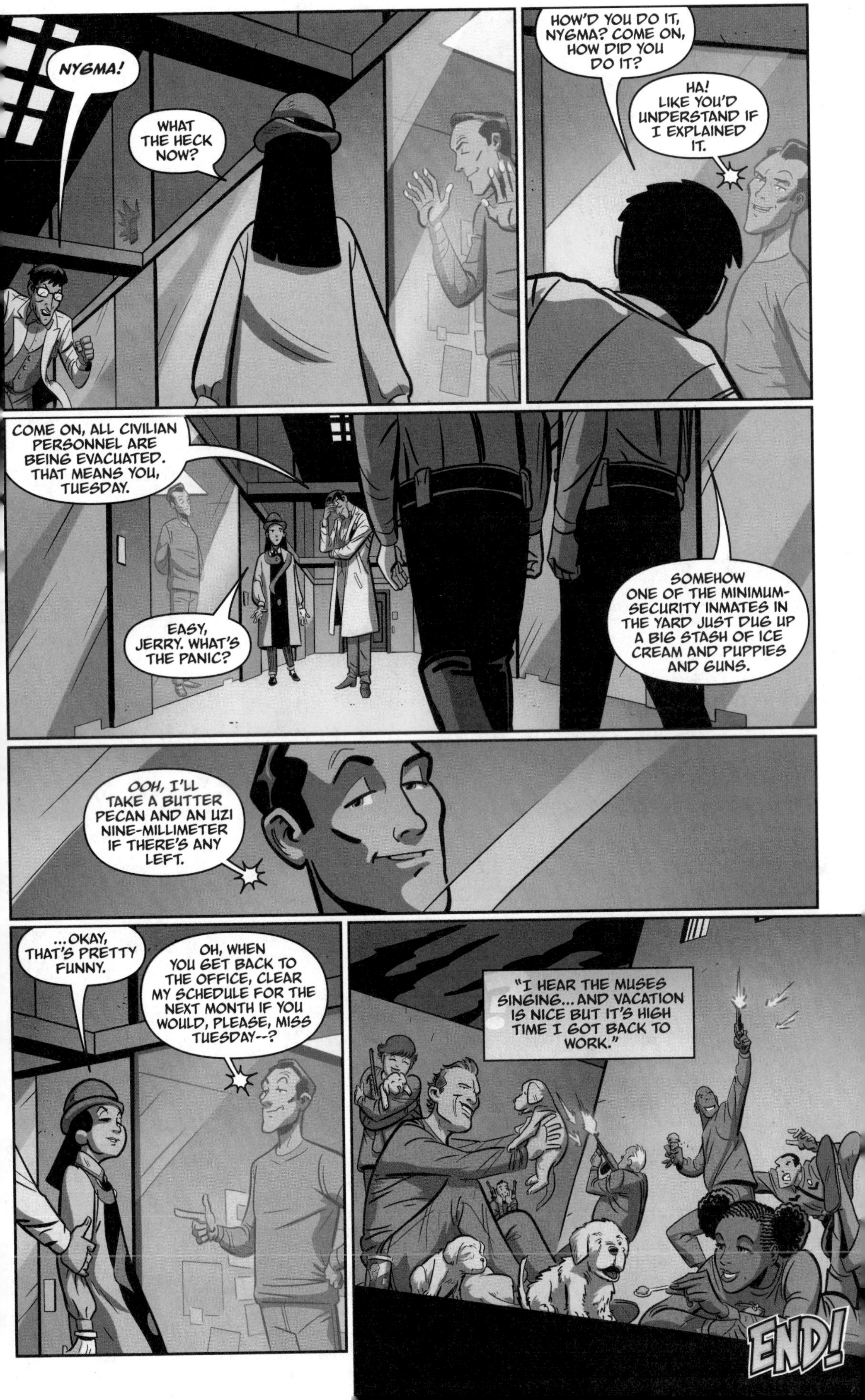
NYGMA!
WHAT THE HECK NOW?
HOW'D YOU DO IT, NYGMA? COME ON, HOW DID YOU DO IT?
HA! LIKE YOU'D UNDERSTAND IF I EXPLAINED IT.
COME ON, ALL CIVILIAN PERSONNEL ARE BEING EVACUATED. THAT MEANS YOU, TUESDAY.
EASY, JERRY. WHAT'S THE PANIC?
SOMEHOW ONE OF THE MINIMUM-SECURITY INMATES IN THE YARD JUST DUG UP A BIG STASH OF ICE CREAM AND PUPPIES AND GUNS.
OOH, I'LL TAKE A BUTTER PECAN AND AN UZI NINE-MILLIMETER IF THERE'S ANY LEFT.
...OKAY, THAT'S PRETTY FUNNY.
OH, WHEN YOU GET BACK TO THE OFFICE, CLEAR MY SCHEDULE FOR THE NEXT MONTH IF YOU WOULD, PLEASE, MISS TUESDAY--?
"I HEAR THE MUSES SINGING... AND VACATION IS NICE BUT IT'S HIGH TIME I GOT BACK TO WORK."
END!

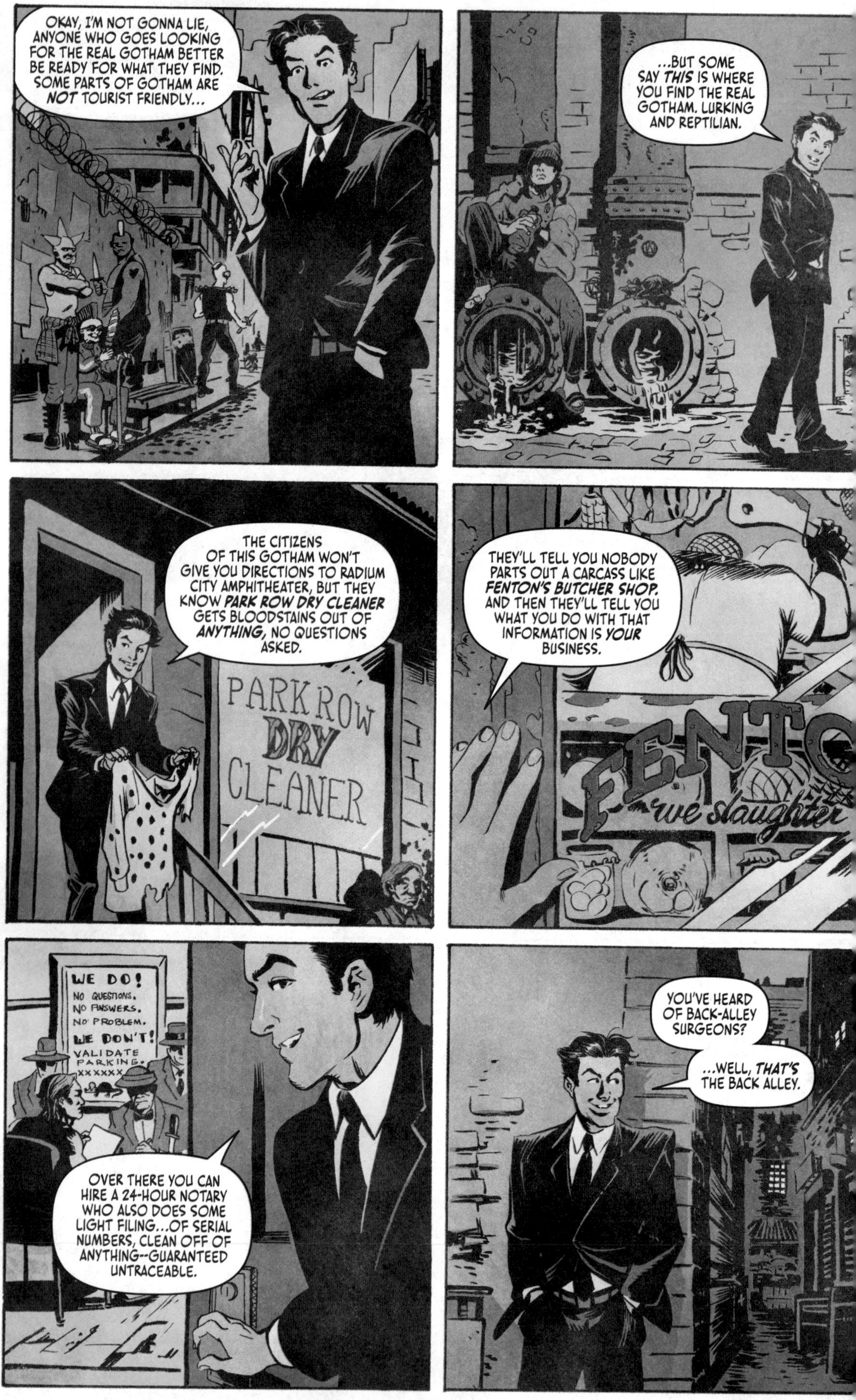

OKAY, I'M NOT GONNA LIE, ANYONE WHO GOES LOOKING FOR THE REAL GOTHAM BETTER BE READY FOR WHAT THEY FIND. SOME PARTS OF GOTHAM ARE *NOT* TOURIST FRIENDLY...
...BUT SOME SAY *THIS* IS WHERE YOU FIND THE REAL GOTHAM. LURKING AND REPTILIAN.
THE CITIZENS OF THIS GOTHAM WON'T GIVE YOU DIRECTIONS TO RADIUM CITY AMPHITHEATER, BUT THEY KNOW *PARK ROW DRY CLEANER* GETS BLOODSTAINS OUT OF *ANYTHING,* NO QUESTIONS ASKED.
PARK ROW DRY CLEANER
THEY'LL TELL YOU NOBODY PARTS OUT A CARCASS LIKE *FENTON'S BUTCHER SHOP,* AND THEN THEY'LL TELL YOU WHAT YOU DO WITH THAT INFORMATION IS *YOUR* BUSINESS.
FENTO
we slaughter
WE DO! NO QUESTIONS. NO ANSWERS. NO PROBLEM. WE DON'T! VALIDATE PARKING. XXXXXX
OVER THERE YOU CAN HIRE A 24-HOUR NOTARY WHO ALSO DOES SOME LIGHT FILING...OF SERIAL NUMBERS, CLEAN OFF OF ANYTHING--GUARANTEED UNTRACEABLE.
YOU'VE HEARD OF BACK-ALLEY SURGEONS?
...WELL, *THAT'S* THE BACK ALLEY.

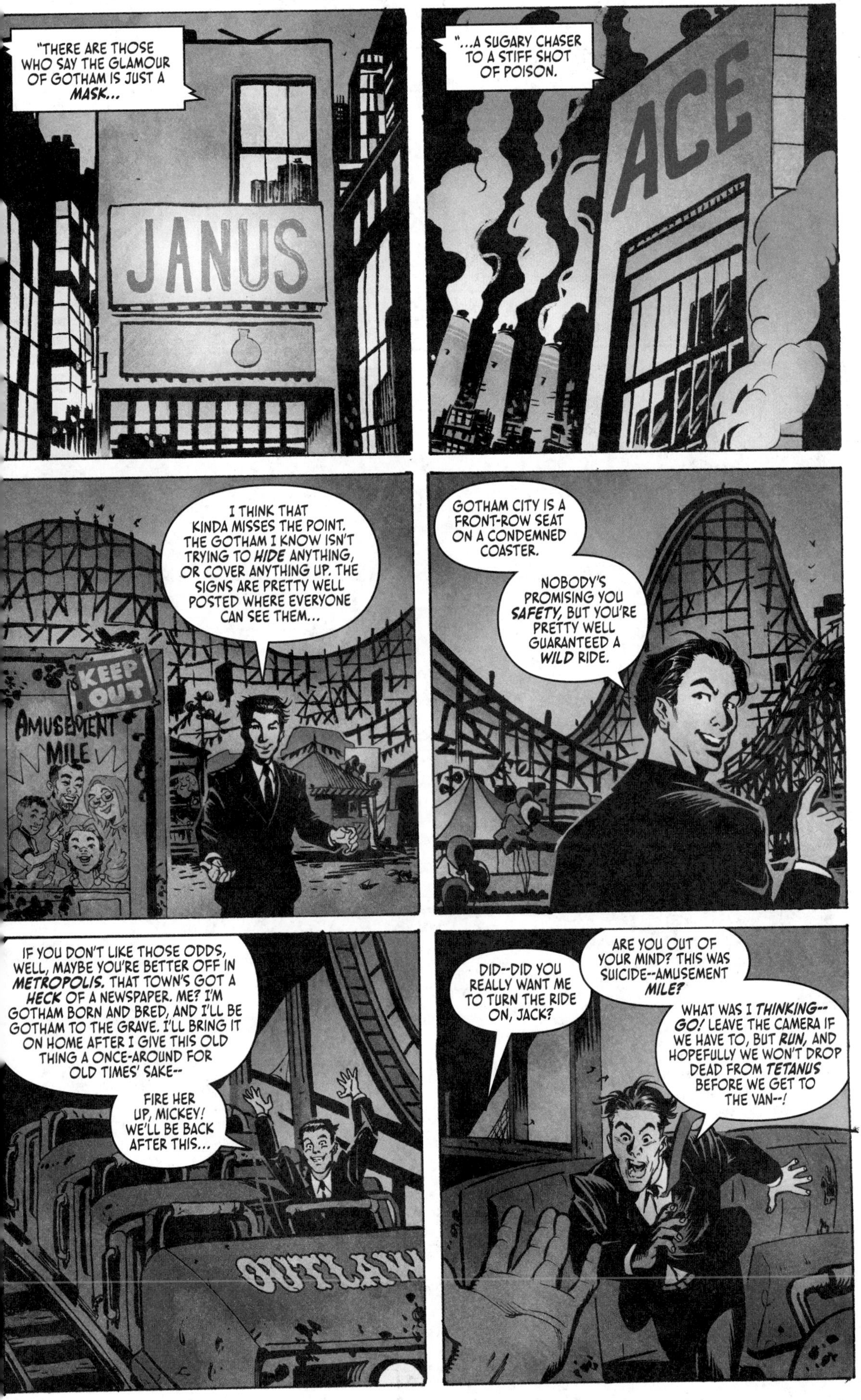
"THERE ARE THOSE WHO SAY THE GLAMOUR OF GOTHAM IS JUST A MASK...
JANUS
"...A SUGARY CHASER TO A STIFF SHOT OF POISON.
ACE
I THINK THAT KINDA MISSES THE POINT. THE GOTHAM I KNOW ISN'T TRYING TO HIDE ANYTHING, OR COVER ANYTHING UP. THE SIGNS ARE PRETTY WELL POSTED WHERE EVERYONE CAN SEE THEM...
KEEP OUT
AMUSEMENT MILE
GOTHAM CITY IS A FRONT-ROW SEAT ON A CONDEMNED COASTER.
NOBODY'S PROMISING YOU SAFETY, BUT YOU'RE PRETTY WELL GUARANTEED A WILD RIDE.
IF YOU DON'T LIKE THOSE ODDS, WELL, MAYBE YOU'RE BETTER OFF IN METROPOLIS. THAT TOWN'S GOT A HECK OF A NEWSPAPER. ME? I'M GOTHAM BORN AND BRED, AND I'LL BE GOTHAM TO THE GRAVE. I'LL BRING IT ON HOME AFTER I GIVE THIS OLD THING A ONCE-AROUND FOR OLD TIMES' SAKE--
FIRE HER UP, MICKEY! WE'LL BE BACK AFTER THIS...
OUTLAW
DID--DID YOU REALLY WANT ME TO TURN THE RIDE ON, JACK?
ARE YOU OUT OF YOUR MIND? THIS WAS SUICIDE--AMUSEMENT MILE?
WHAT WAS I THINKING--GO! LEAVE THE CAMERA IF WE HAVE TO, BUT RUN, AND HOPEFULLY WE WON'T DROP DEAD FROM TETANUS BEFORE WE GET TO THE VAN--!

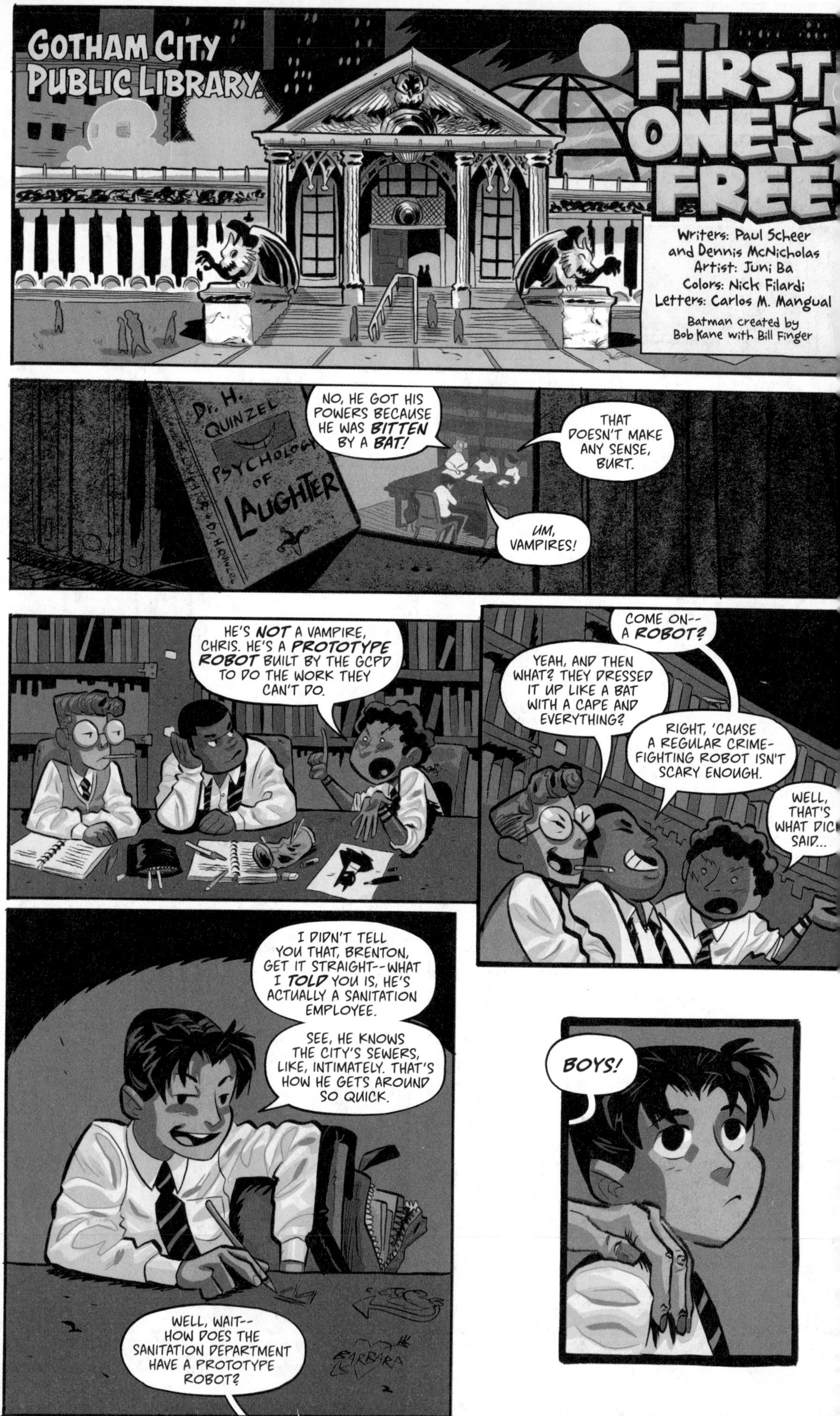
GOTHAM CITY PUBLIC LIBRARY.
FIRST ONE'S FREE
Writers: Paul Scheer and Dennis McNicholas
Artist: Juni Ba
Colors: Nick Filardi
Letters: Carlos M. Mangual
Batman created by Bob Kane with Bill Finger
Dr. H. QUINZEL PSYCHOLOGY OF LAUGHTER
NO, HE GOT HIS POWERS BECAUSE HE WAS BITTEN BY A BAT!
THAT DOESN'T MAKE ANY SENSE, BURT.
UM, VAMPIRES!
HE'S NOT A VAMPIRE, CHRIS. HE'S A PROTOTYPE ROBOT BUILT BY THE GCPD TO DO THE WORK THEY CAN'T DO.
COME ON-- A ROBOT?
YEAH, AND THEN WHAT? THEY DRESSED IT UP LIKE A BAT WITH A CAPE AND EVERYTHING?
RIGHT, 'CAUSE A REGULAR CRIME-FIGHTING ROBOT ISN'T SCARY ENOUGH.
WELL, THAT'S WHAT DIC SAID...
I DIDN'T TELL YOU THAT, BRENTON, GET IT STRAIGHT--WHAT I TOLD YOU IS, HE'S ACTUALLY A SANITATION EMPLOYEE.
SEE, HE KNOWS THE CITY'S SEWERS, LIKE, INTIMATELY. THAT'S HOW HE GETS AROUND SO QUICK.
WELL, WAIT-- HOW DOES THE SANITATION DEPARTMENT HAVE A PROTOTYPE ROBOT?
BARBARA
BOYS!

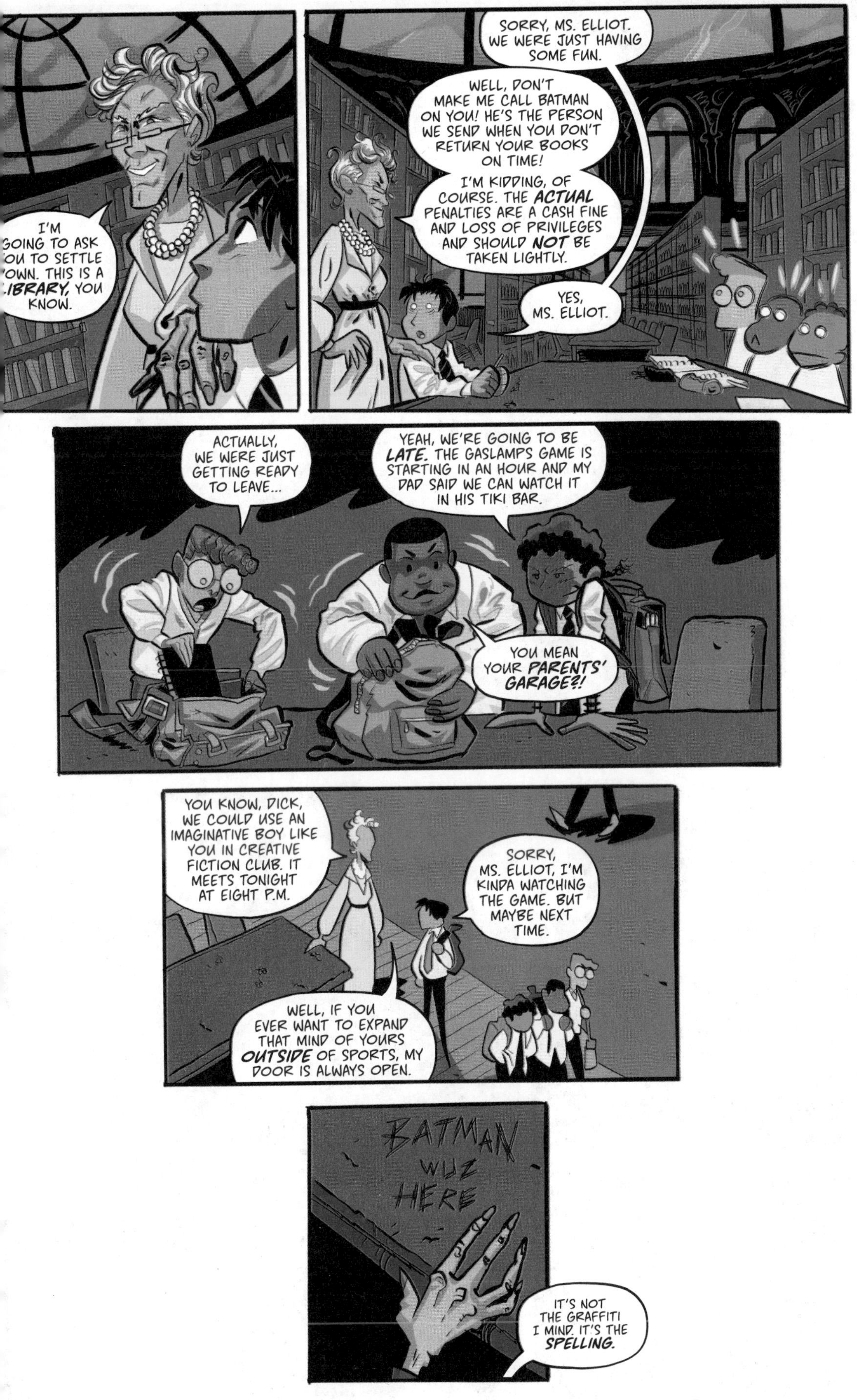

I'M GOING TO ASK OU TO SETTLE OWN. THIS IS A IBRARY, YOU KNOW.
SORRY, MS. ELLIOT. WE WERE JUST HAVING SOME FUN.
WELL, DON'T MAKE ME CALL BATMAN ON YOU! HE'S THE PERSON WE SEND WHEN YOU DON'T RETURN YOUR BOOKS ON TIME!
I'M KIDDING, OF COURSE. THE ACTUAL PENALTIES ARE A CASH FINE AND LOSS OF PRIVILEGES AND SHOULD NOT BE TAKEN LIGHTLY.
YES, MS. ELLIOT.
ACTUALLY, WE WERE JUST GETTING READY TO LEAVE...
YEAH, WE'RE GOING TO BE LATE. THE GASLAMPS GAME IS STARTING IN AN HOUR AND MY DAD SAID WE CAN WATCH IT IN HIS TIKI BAR.
YOU MEAN YOUR PARENTS' GARAGE?!
YOU KNOW, DICK, WE COULD USE AN IMAGINATIVE BOY LIKE YOU IN CREATIVE FICTION CLUB. IT MEETS TONIGHT AT EIGHT P.M.
SORRY, MS. ELLIOT, I'M KINDA WATCHING THE GAME. BUT MAYBE NEXT TIME.
WELL, IF YOU EVER WANT TO EXPAND THAT MIND OF YOURS OUTSIDE OF SPORTS, MY DOOR IS ALWAYS OPEN.
BATMAN WUZ HERE
IT'S NOT THE GRAFFITI I MIND. IT'S THE SPELLING.

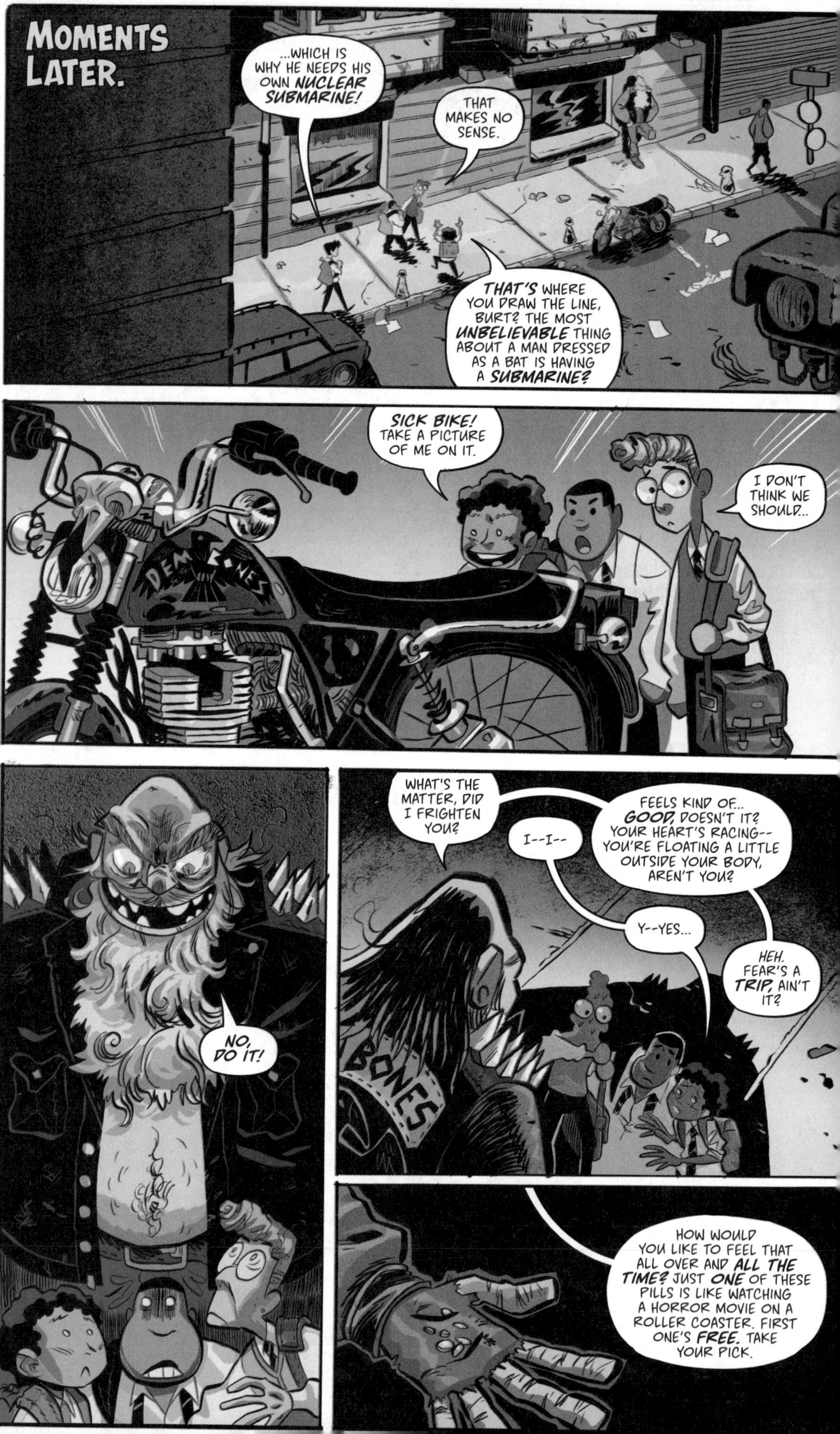

MOMENTS LATER.
...WHICH IS WHY HE NEEDS HIS OWN NUCLEAR SUBMARINE!
THAT MAKES NO SENSE.
THAT'S WHERE YOU DRAW THE LINE, BURT? THE MOST UNBELIEVABLE THING ABOUT A MAN DRESSED AS A BAT IS HAVING A SUBMARINE?
SICK BIKE! TAKE A PICTURE OF ME ON IT.
I DON'T THINK WE SHOULD...
DEMONS
NO, DO IT!
WHAT'S THE MATTER, DID I FRIGHTEN YOU?
I--I--
FEELS KIND OF... GOOD, DOESN'T IT? YOUR HEART'S RACING-- YOU'RE FLOATING A LITTLE OUTSIDE YOUR BODY, AREN'T YOU?
Y--YES...
HEH. FEAR'S A TRIP, AIN'T IT?
BONES
HOW WOULD YOU LIKE TO FEEL THAT ALL OVER AND ALL THE TIME? JUST ONE OF THESE PILLS IS LIKE WATCHING A HORROR MOVIE ON A ROLLER COASTER. FIRST ONE'S FREE. TAKE YOUR PICK.

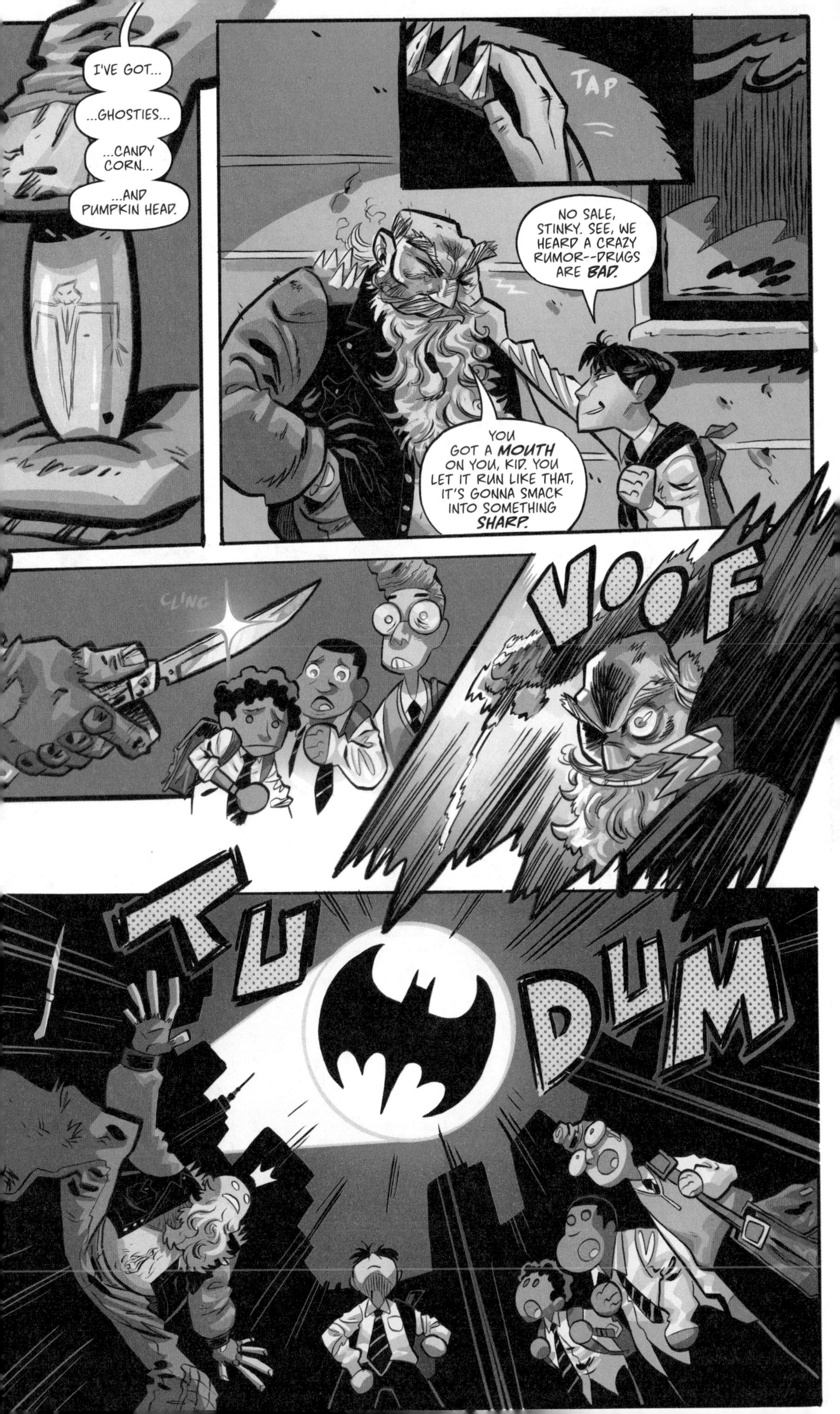
I'VE GOT...
...GHOSTIES...
...CANDY CORN...
...AND PUMPKIN HEAD.
TAP
NO SALE, STINKY. SEE, WE HEARD A CRAZY RUMOR--DRUGS ARE **BAD.**
YOU GOT A **MOUTH** ON YOU, KID. YOU LET IT RUN LIKE THAT, IT'S GONNA SMACK INTO SOMETHING **SHARP.**
CLING
VOOF
TU
DUM

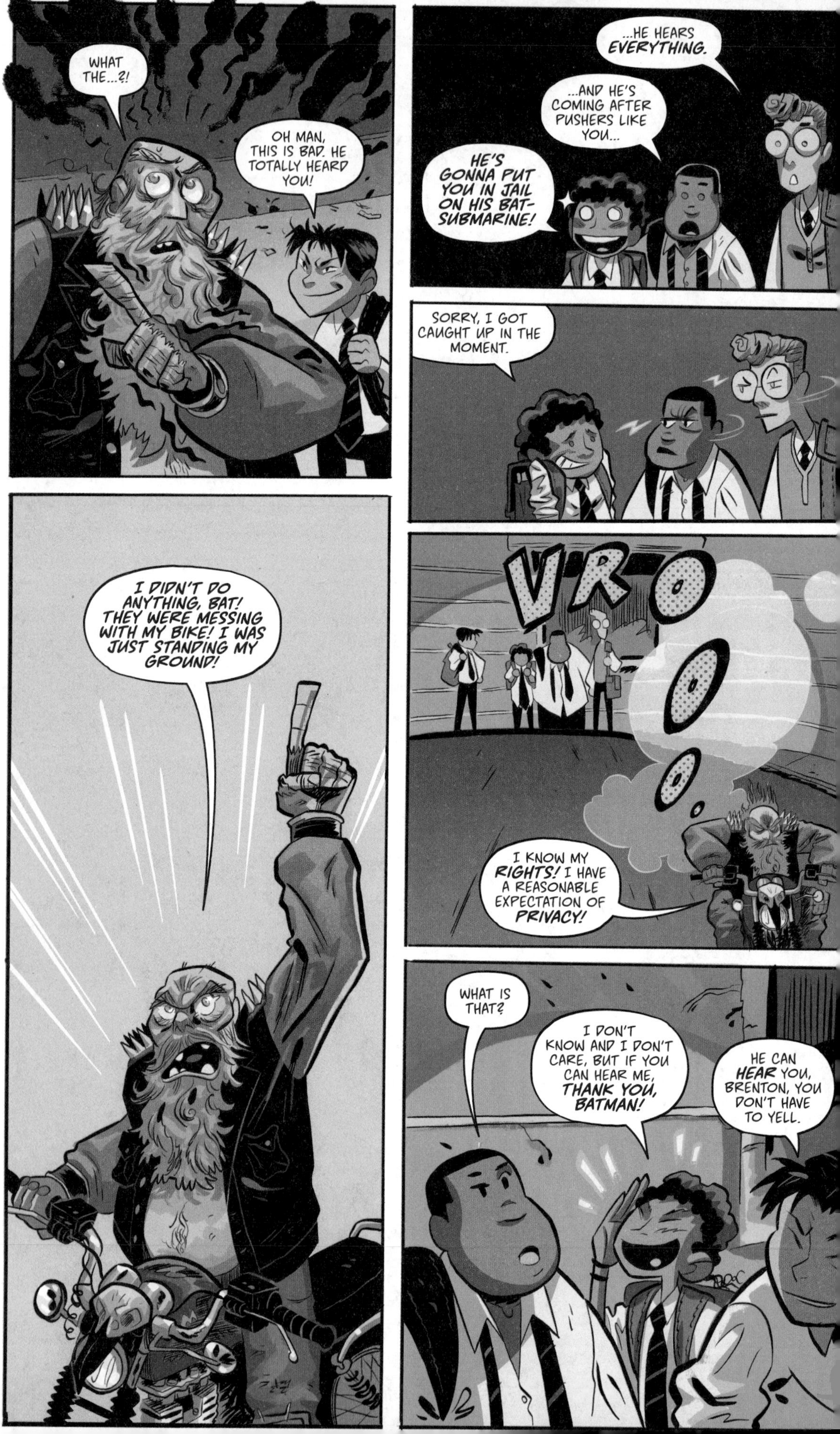
WHAT THE...?!
OH MAN, THIS IS BAD. HE TOTALLY HEARD YOU!
...HE HEARS EVERYTHING.
...AND HE'S COMING AFTER PUSHERS LIKE YOU...
HE'S GONNA PUT YOU IN JAIL ON HIS BAT-SUBMARINE!
SORRY, I GOT CAUGHT UP IN THE MOMENT.
I DIDN'T DO ANYTHING, BAT! THEY WERE MESSING WITH MY BIKE! I WAS JUST STANDING MY GROUND!
VROOOO
I KNOW MY RIGHTS! I HAVE A REASONABLE EXPECTATION OF PRIVACY!
WHAT IS THAT?
I DON'T KNOW AND I DON'T CARE, BUT IF YOU CAN HEAR ME, THANK YOU, BATMAN!
HE CAN HEAR YOU, BRENTON, YOU DON'T HAVE TO YELL.

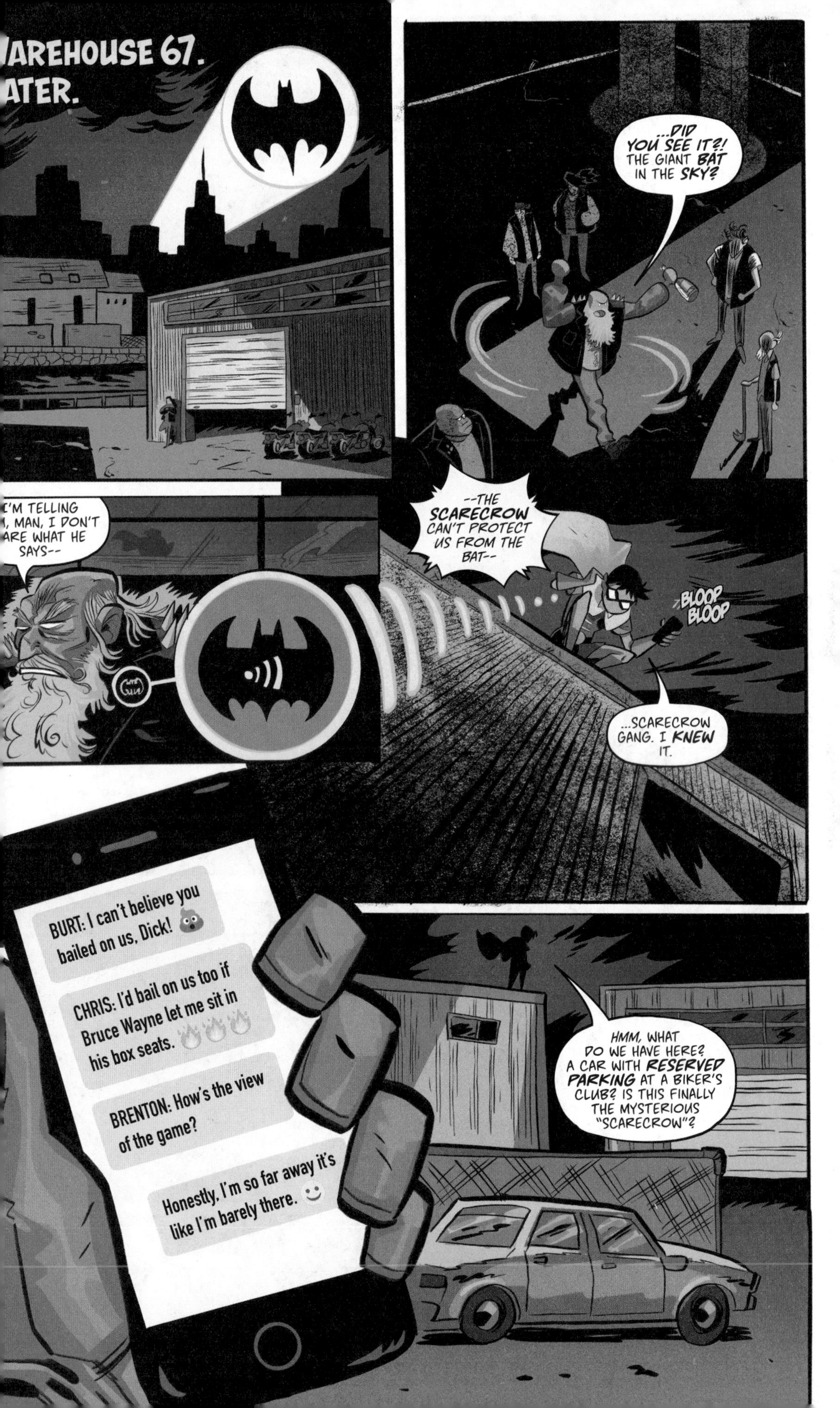

AREHOUSE 67.
ATER.
...DID YOU SEE IT?! THE GIANT BAT IN THE SKY?
I'M TELLING , MAN, I DON'T ARE WHAT HE SAYS--
--THE SCARECROW CAN'T PROTECT US FROM THE BAT--
BLOOP BLOOP
...SCARECROW GANG. I KNEW IT.
BURT: I can't believe you bailed on us, Dick! 💩
CHRIS: I'd bail on us too if Bruce Wayne let me sit in his box seats. 🔥🔥🔥
BRENTON: How's the view of the game?
Honestly, I'm so far away it's like I'm barely there. 🙂
HMM, WHAT DO WE HAVE HERE? A CAR WITH RESERVED PARKING AT A BIKER'S CLUB? IS THIS FINALLY THE MYSTERIOUS "SCARECROW"?

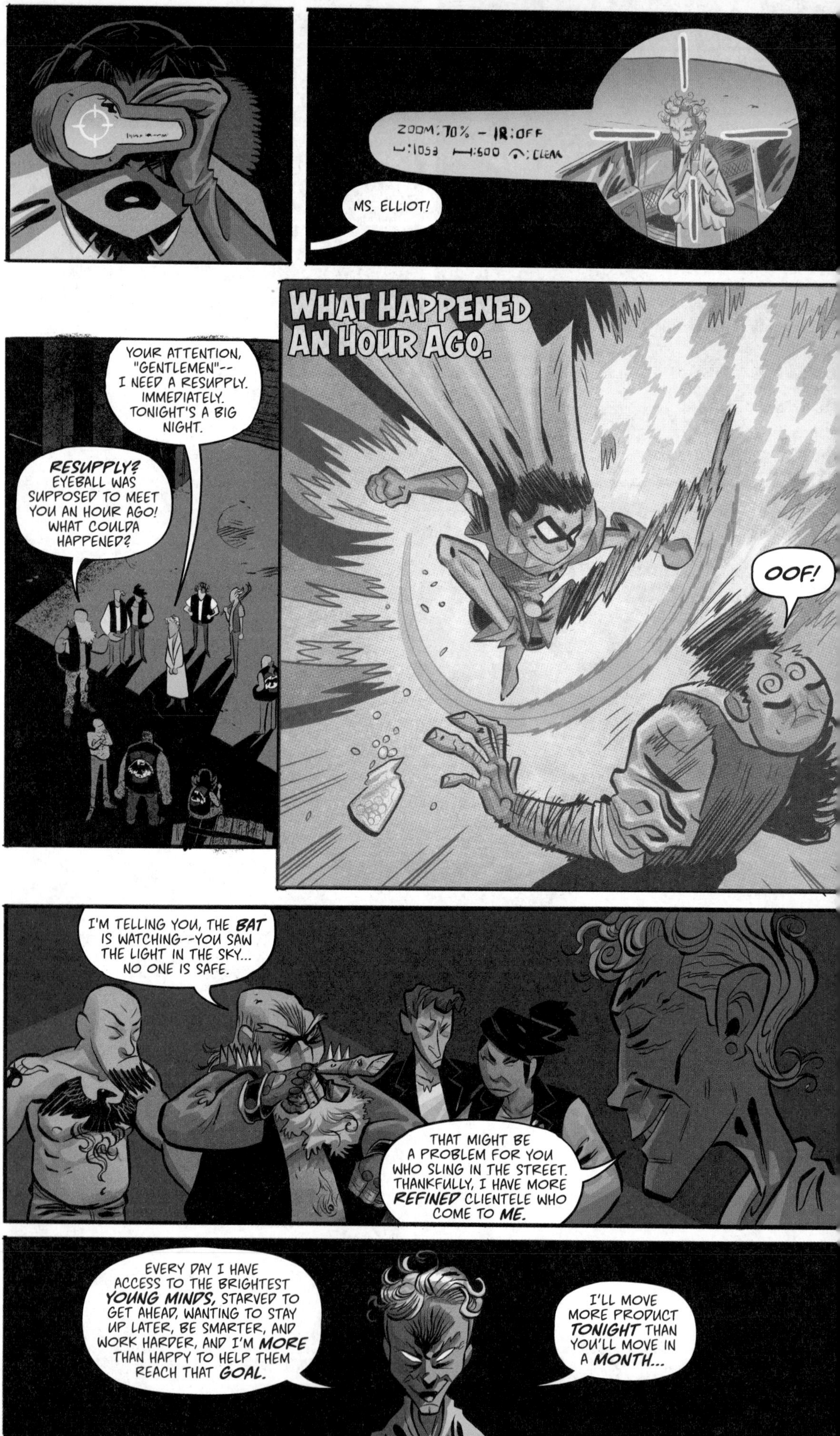

ZOOM: 70% - IR: OFF
MS. ELLIOT!
WHAT HAPPENED AN HOUR AGO.
YOUR ATTENTION, "GENTLEMEN"-- I NEED A RESUPPLY. IMMEDIATELY. TONIGHT'S A BIG NIGHT.
RESUPPLY? EYEBALL WAS SUPPOSED TO MEET YOU AN HOUR AGO! WHAT COULDA HAPPENED?
OOF!
I'M TELLING YOU, THE BAT IS WATCHING--YOU SAW THE LIGHT IN THE SKY... NO ONE IS SAFE.
THAT MIGHT BE A PROBLEM FOR YOU WHO SLING IN THE STREET. THANKFULLY, I HAVE MORE REFINED CLIENTELE WHO COME TO ME.
EVERY DAY I HAVE ACCESS TO THE BRIGHTEST YOUNG MINDS, STARVED TO GET AHEAD, WANTING TO STAY UP LATER, BE SMARTER, AND WORK HARDER, AND I'M MORE THAN HAPPY TO HELP THEM REACH THAT GOAL.
I'LL MOVE MORE PRODUCT TONIGHT THAN YOU'LL MOVE IN A MONTH...

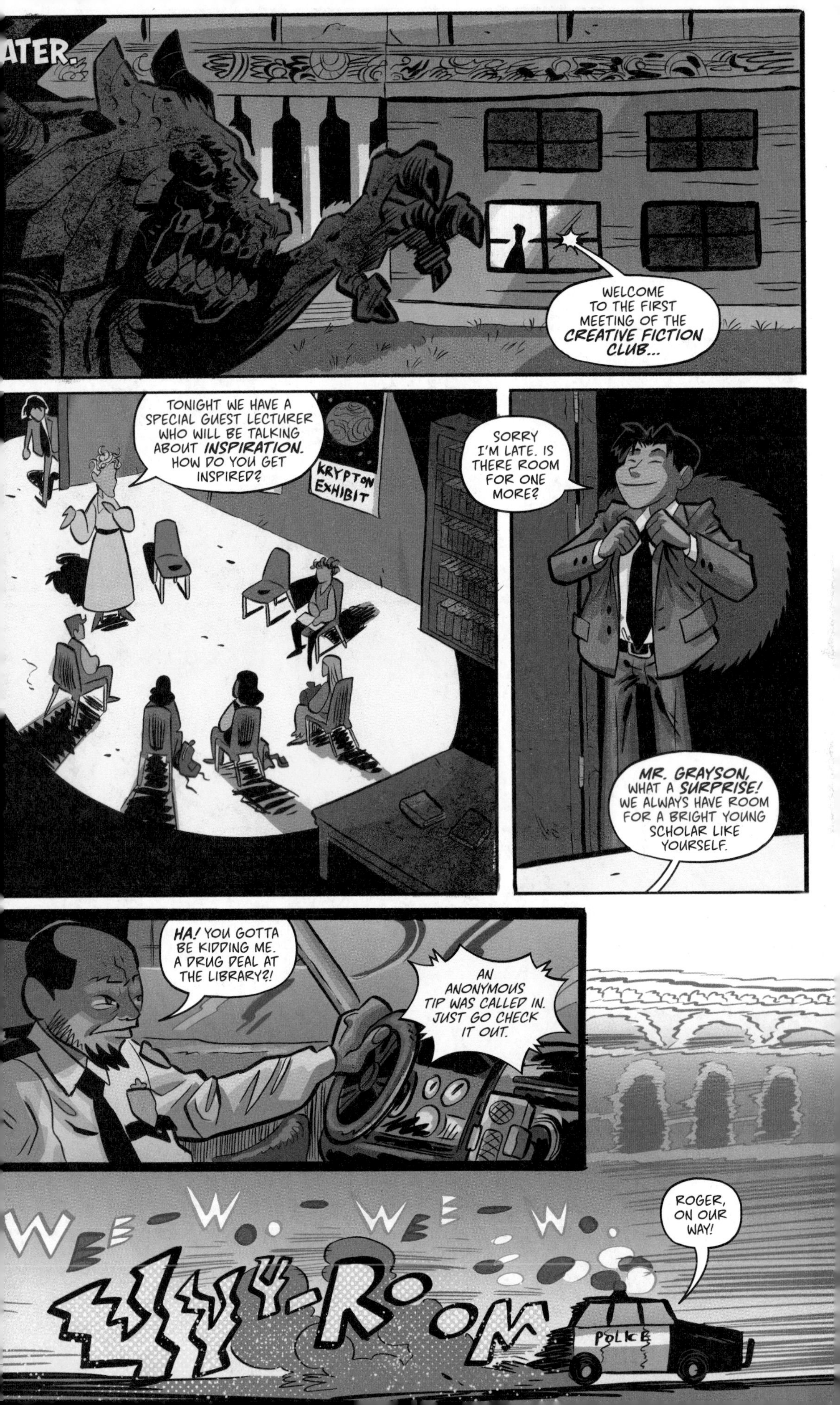
ATER.
WELCOME TO THE FIRST MEETING OF THE CREATIVE FICTION CLUB...
TONIGHT WE HAVE A SPECIAL GUEST LECTURER WHO WILL BE TALKING ABOUT INSPIRATION. HOW DO YOU GET INSPIRED?
KRYPTON EXHIBIT
SORRY I'M LATE. IS THERE ROOM FOR ONE MORE?
MR. GRAYSON, WHAT A SURPRISE! WE ALWAYS HAVE ROOM FOR A BRIGHT YOUNG SCHOLAR LIKE YOURSELF.
HA! YOU GOTTA BE KIDDING ME. A DRUG DEAL AT THE LIBRARY?!
AN ANONYMOUS TIP WAS CALLED IN. JUST GO CHECK IT OUT.
WEE-W. WEE-W.
VVVV-ROOOM
ROGER, ON OUR WAY!
POLICE

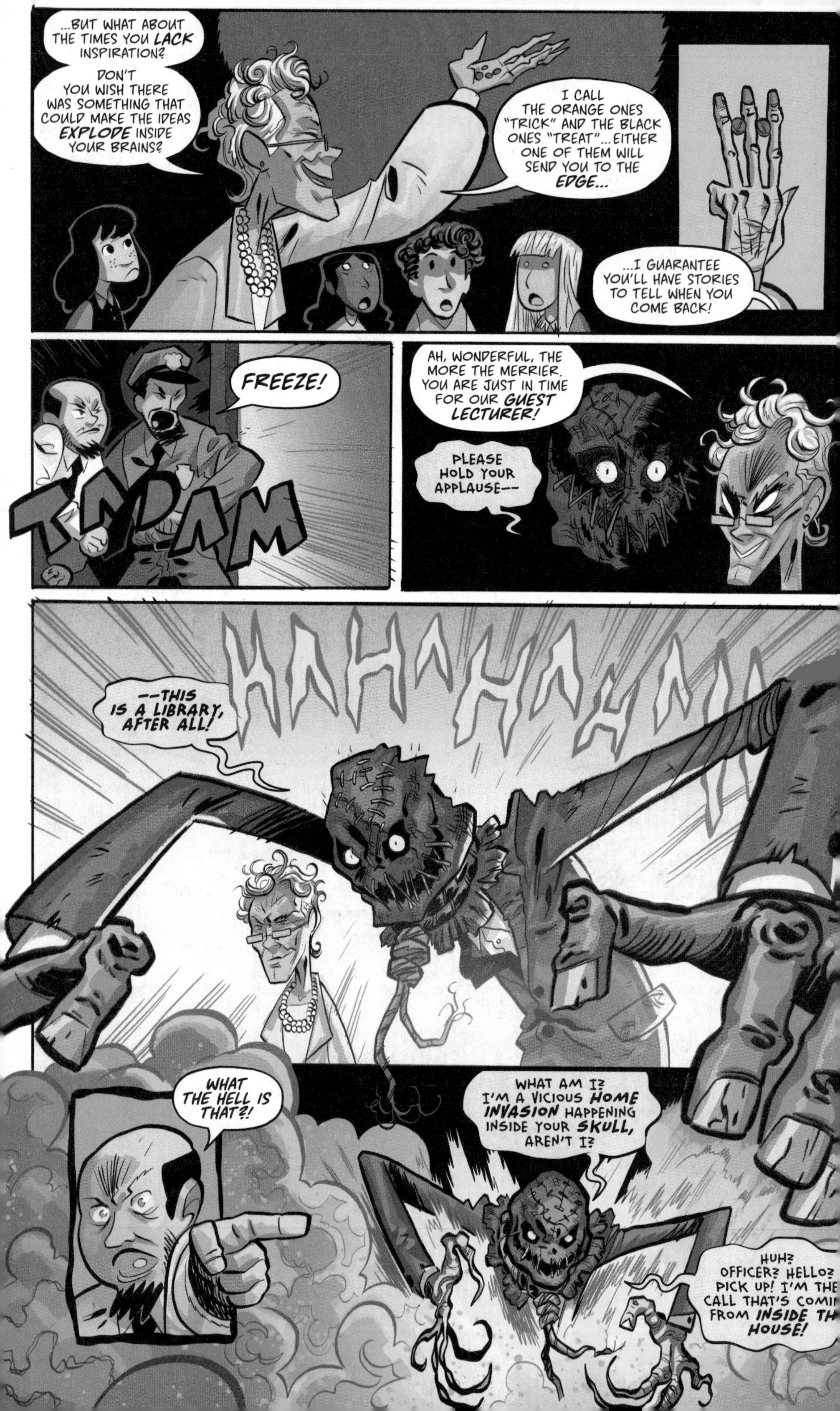
...BUT WHAT ABOUT THE TIMES YOU LACK INSPIRATION?
DON'T YOU WISH THERE WAS SOMETHING THAT COULD MAKE THE IDEAS EXPLODE INSIDE YOUR BRAINS?
I CALL THE ORANGE ONES "TRICK" AND THE BLACK ONES "TREAT"... EITHER ONE OF THEM WILL SEND YOU TO THE EDGE...
...I GUARANTEE YOU'LL HAVE STORIES TO TELL WHEN YOU COME BACK!
FREEZE!
TMDAM
AH, WONDERFUL, THE MORE THE MERRIER. YOU ARE JUST IN TIME FOR OUR GUEST LECTURER!
PLEASE HOLD YOUR APPLAUSE--
--THIS IS A LIBRARY, AFTER ALL!
WHAT THE HELL IS THAT?!
WHAT AM I? I'M A VICIOUS HOME INVASION HAPPENING INSIDE YOUR SKULL, AREN'T I?
HUH? OFFICER? HELLO? PICK UP! I'M THE CALL THAT'S COMIN FROM INSIDE TH HOUSE!

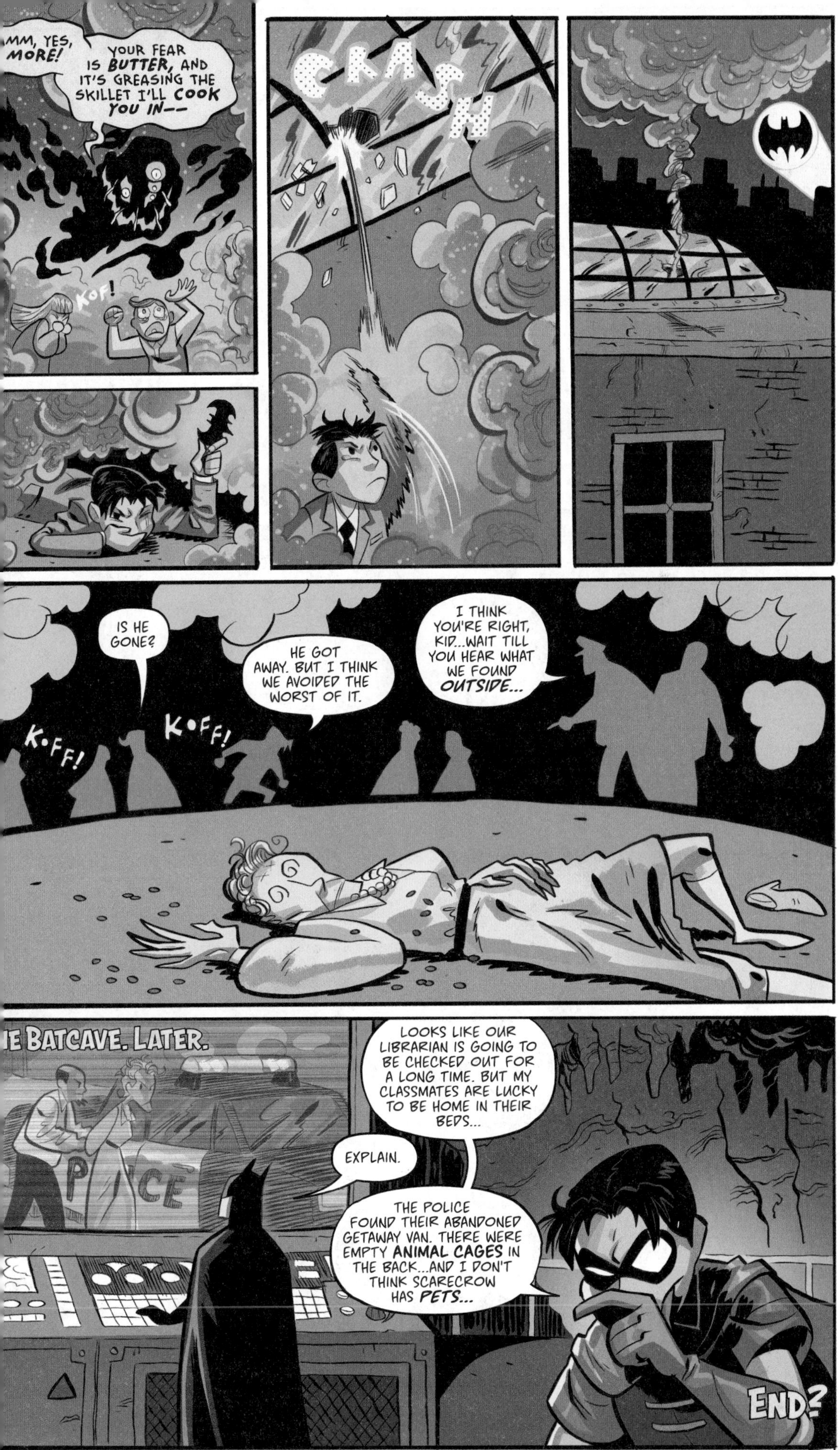
MM, YES, MORE!
YOUR FEAR IS BUTTER, AND IT'S GREASING THE SKILLET I'LL COOK YOU IN--
KOF!
CRASH
IS HE GONE?
HE GOT AWAY. BUT I THINK WE AVOIDED THE WORST OF IT.
I THINK YOU'RE RIGHT, KID...WAIT TILL YOU HEAR WHAT WE FOUND OUTSIDE...
K.FF!
K.FF!
E BATCAVE. LATER.
LOOKS LIKE OUR LIBRARIAN IS GOING TO BE CHECKED OUT FOR A LONG TIME. BUT MY CLASSMATES ARE LUCKY TO BE HOME IN THEIR BEDS...
EXPLAIN.
THE POLICE FOUND THEIR ABANDONED GETAWAY VAN. THERE WERE EMPTY ANIMAL CAGES IN THE BACK...AND I DON'T THINK SCARECROW HAS PETS...
END?

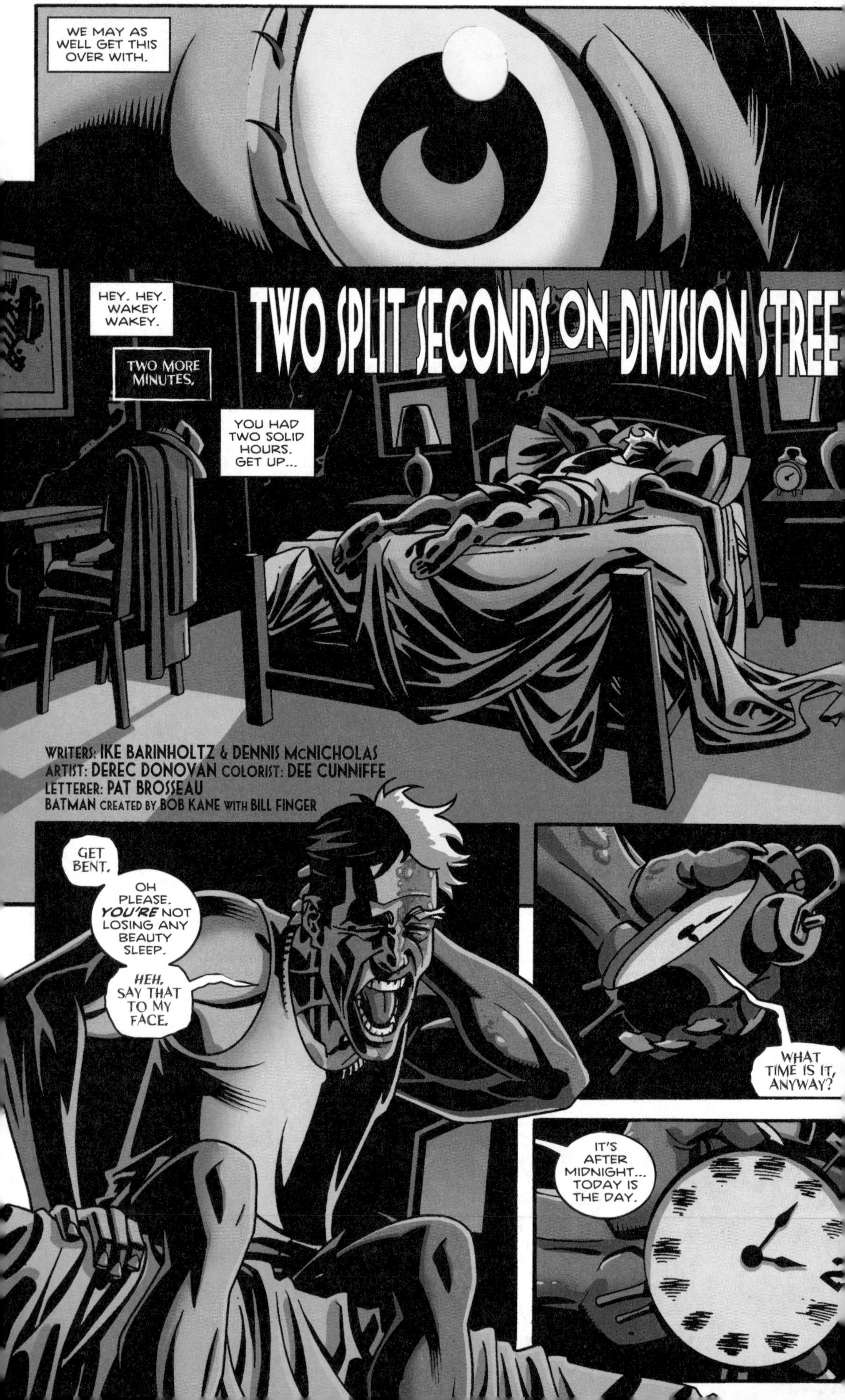
WE MAY AS WELL GET THIS OVER WITH.
HEY. HEY. WAKEY WAKEY.
TWO MORE MINUTES.
YOU HAD TWO SOLID HOURS. GET UP...
TWO SPLIT SECONDS ON DIVISION STREE
WRITERS: IKE BARINHOLTZ & DENNIS McNICHOLAS
ARTIST: DEREC DONOVAN COLORIST: DEE CUNNIFFE
LETTERER: PAT BROSSEAU
BATMAN CREATED BY BOB KANE WITH BILL FINGER
GET BENT.
OH PLEASE. YOU'RE NOT LOSING ANY BEAUTY SLEEP.
HEH. SAY THAT TO MY FACE.
WHAT TIME IS IT, ANYWAY?
IT'S AFTER MIDNIGHT... TODAY IS THE DAY.

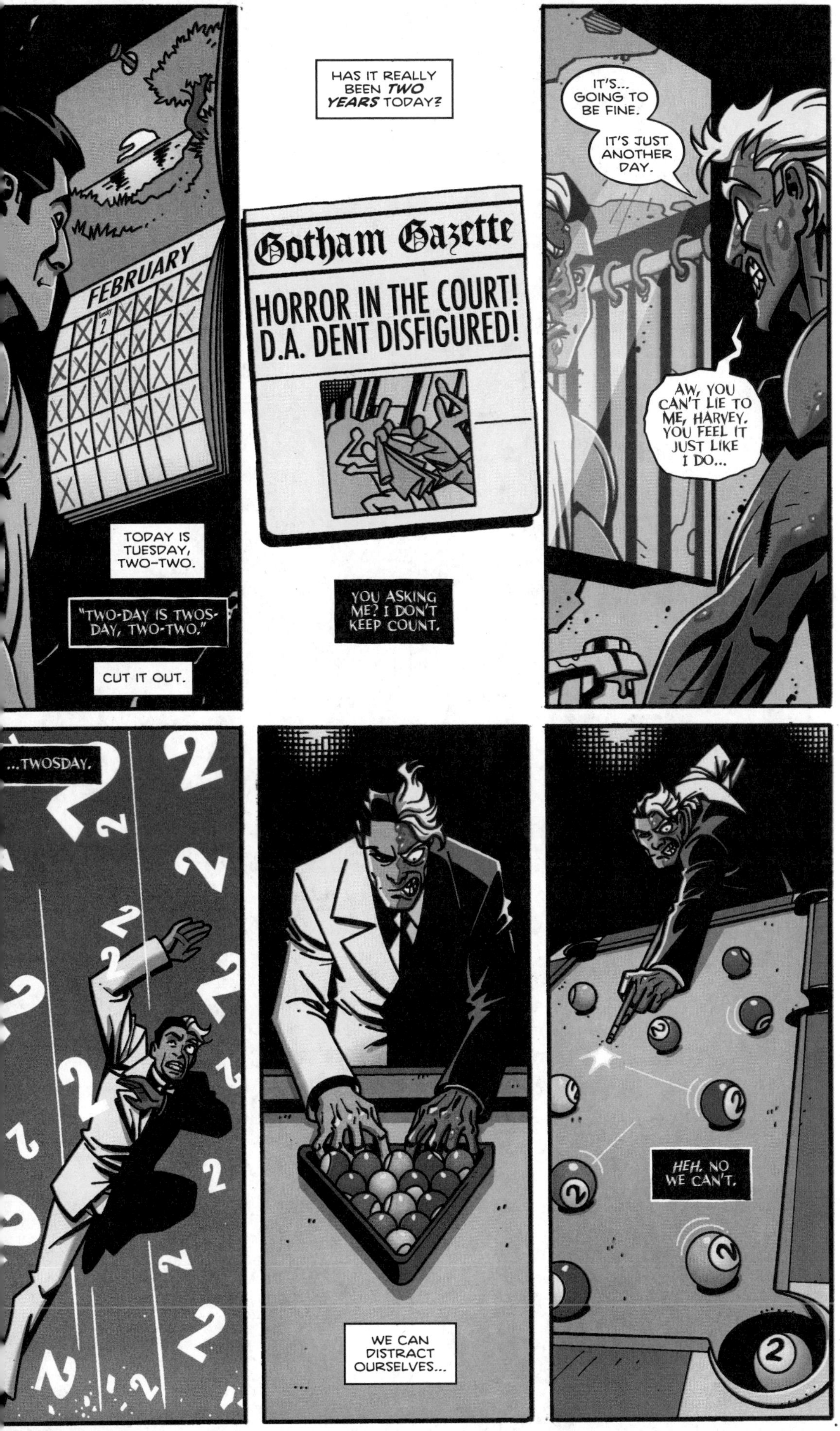
FEBRUARY
Tuesday
2
TODAY IS TUESDAY, TWO-TWO.
"TWO-DAY IS TWOS-DAY, TWO-TWO."
CUT IT OUT.
HAS IT REALLY BEEN TWO YEARS TODAY?
Gotham Gazette
HORROR IN THE COURT! D.A. DENT DISFIGURED!
YOU ASKING ME? I DON'T KEEP COUNT.
IT'S... GOING TO BE FINE.
IT'S JUST ANOTHER DAY.
AW, YOU CAN'T LIE TO ME, HARVEY. YOU FEEL IT JUST LIKE I DO...
...TWOSDAY.
WE CAN DISTRACT OURSELVES...
HEH. NO WE CAN'T.

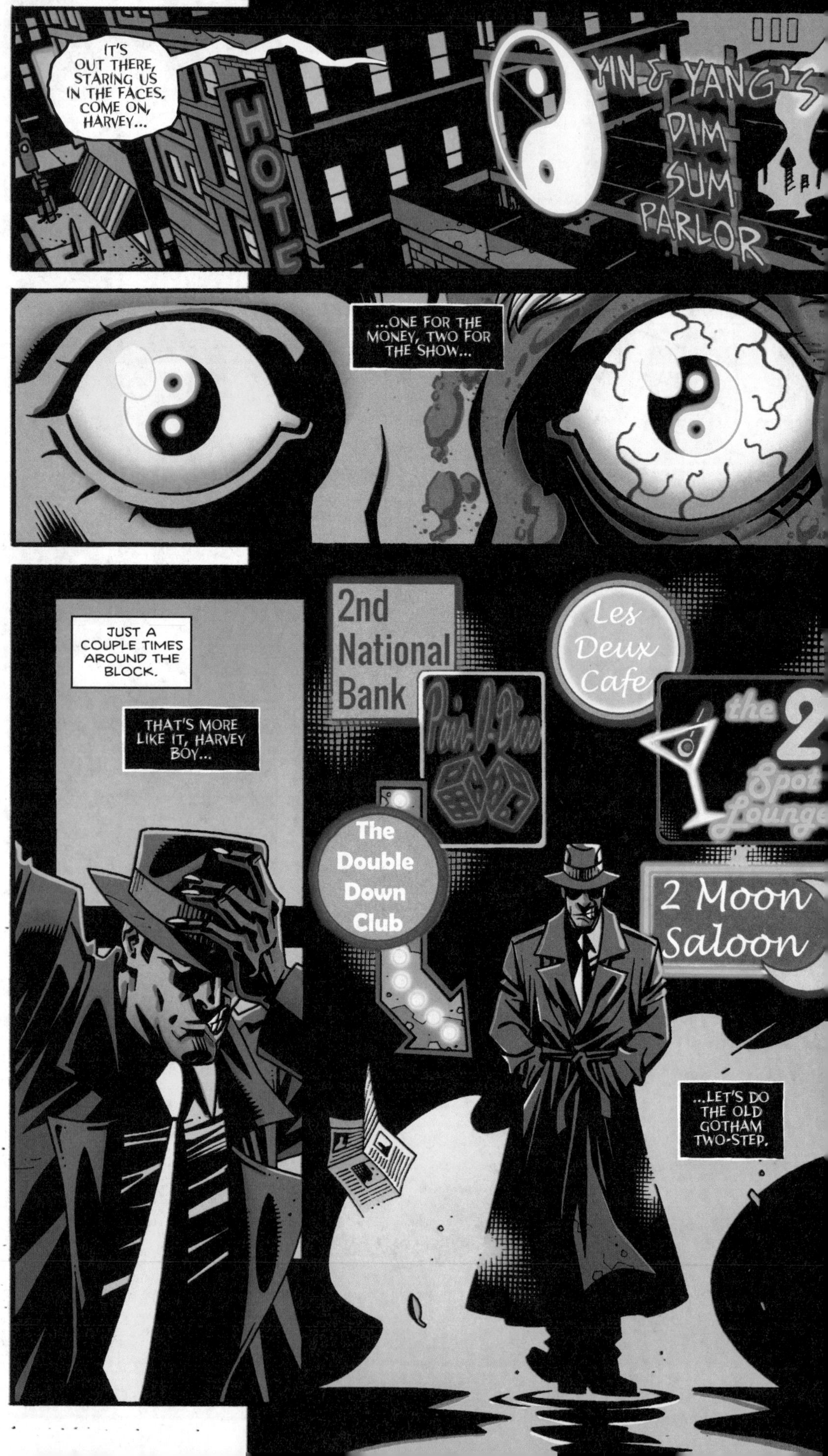
IT'S OUT THERE, STARING US IN THE FACES. COME ON, HARVEY...
HOTE
YIN & YANG'S DIM SUM PARLOR
...ONE FOR THE MONEY, TWO FOR THE SHOW...
JUST A COUPLE TIMES AROUND THE BLOCK.
THAT'S MORE LIKE IT, HARVEY BOY...
2nd National Bank
Les Deux Cafe
Pair-A-Dice
the 2 Spot Lounge
The Double Down Club
2 Moon Saloon
...LET'S DO THE OLD GOTHAM TWO-STEP.

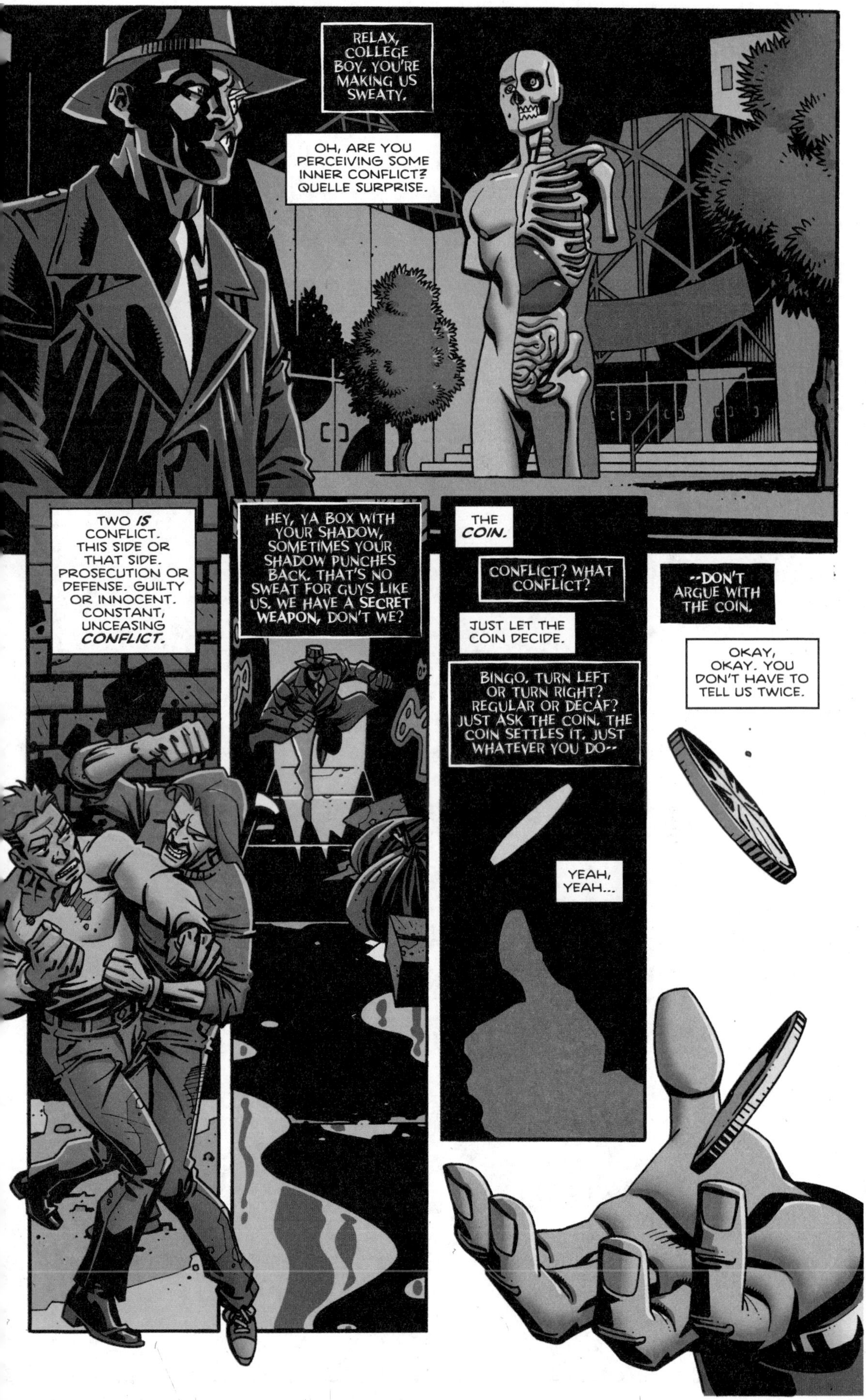

RELAX, COLLEGE BOY. YOU'RE MAKING US SWEATY.
OH, ARE YOU PERCEIVING SOME INNER CONFLICT? QUELLE SURPRISE.
TWO *IS* CONFLICT. THIS SIDE OR THAT SIDE. PROSECUTION OR DEFENSE. GUILTY OR INNOCENT. CONSTANT, UNCEASING *CONFLICT.*
HEY, YA BOX WITH YOUR SHADOW, SOMETIMES YOUR SHADOW PUNCHES BACK. THAT'S NO SWEAT FOR GUYS LIKE US. WE HAVE A SECRET WEAPON, DON'T WE?
THE *COIN.*
CONFLICT? WHAT CONFLICT?
JUST LET THE COIN DECIDE.
BINGO. TURN LEFT OR TURN RIGHT? REGULAR OR DECAF? JUST ASK THE COIN. THE COIN SETTLES IT. JUST WHATEVER YOU DO--
YEAH, YEAH...
--DON'T ARGUE WITH THE COIN.
OKAY, OKAY. YOU DON'T HAVE TO TELL US TWICE.

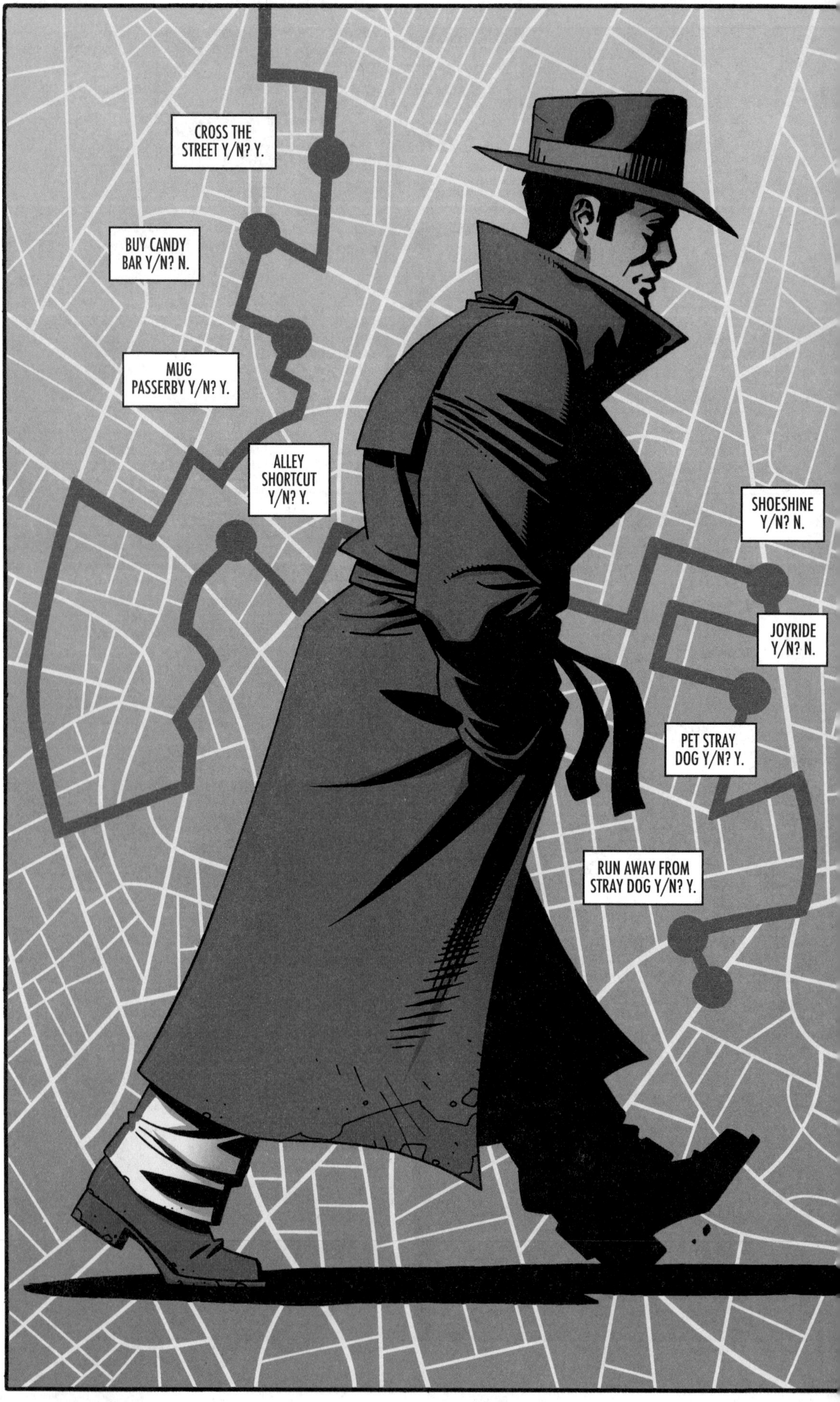
CROSS THE STREET Y/N? Y.
BUY CANDY BAR Y/N? N.
MUG PASSERBY Y/N? Y.
ALLEY SHORTCUT Y/N? Y.
SHOESHINE Y/N? N.
JOYRIDE Y/N? N.
PET STRAY DOG Y/N? Y.
RUN AWAY FROM STRAY DOG Y/N? Y.

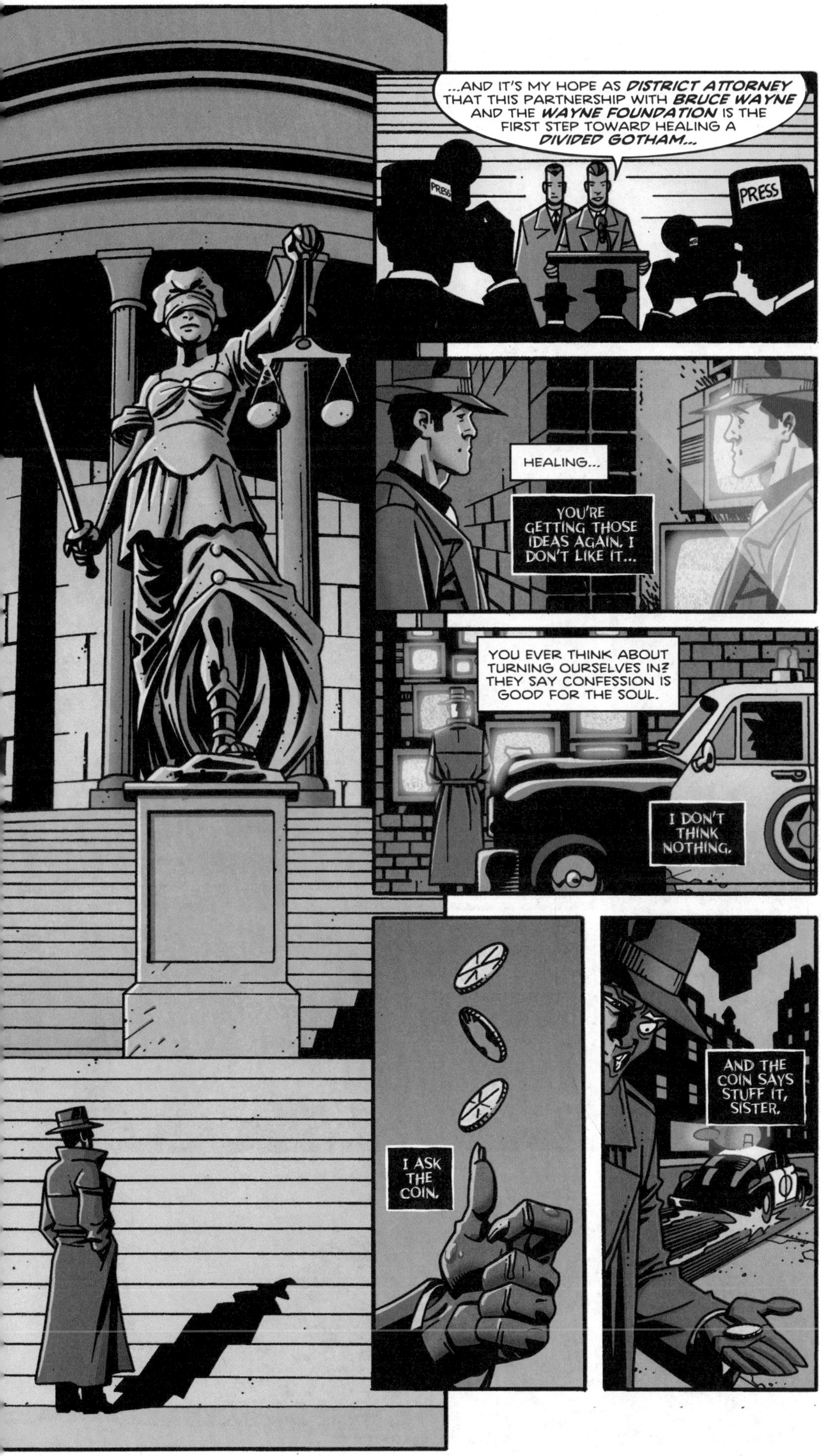
...AND IT'S MY HOPE AS DISTRICT ATTORNEY THAT THIS PARTNERSHIP WITH BRUCE WAYNE AND THE WAYNE FOUNDATION IS THE FIRST STEP TOWARD HEALING A DIVIDED GOTHAM...
PRESS
PRESS
HEALING...
YOU'RE GETTING THOSE IDEAS AGAIN. I DON'T LIKE IT...
YOU EVER THINK ABOUT TURNING OURSELVES IN? THEY SAY CONFESSION IS GOOD FOR THE SOUL.
I DON'T THINK NOTHING.
I ASK THE COIN.
AND THE COIN SAYS STUFF IT, SISTER.

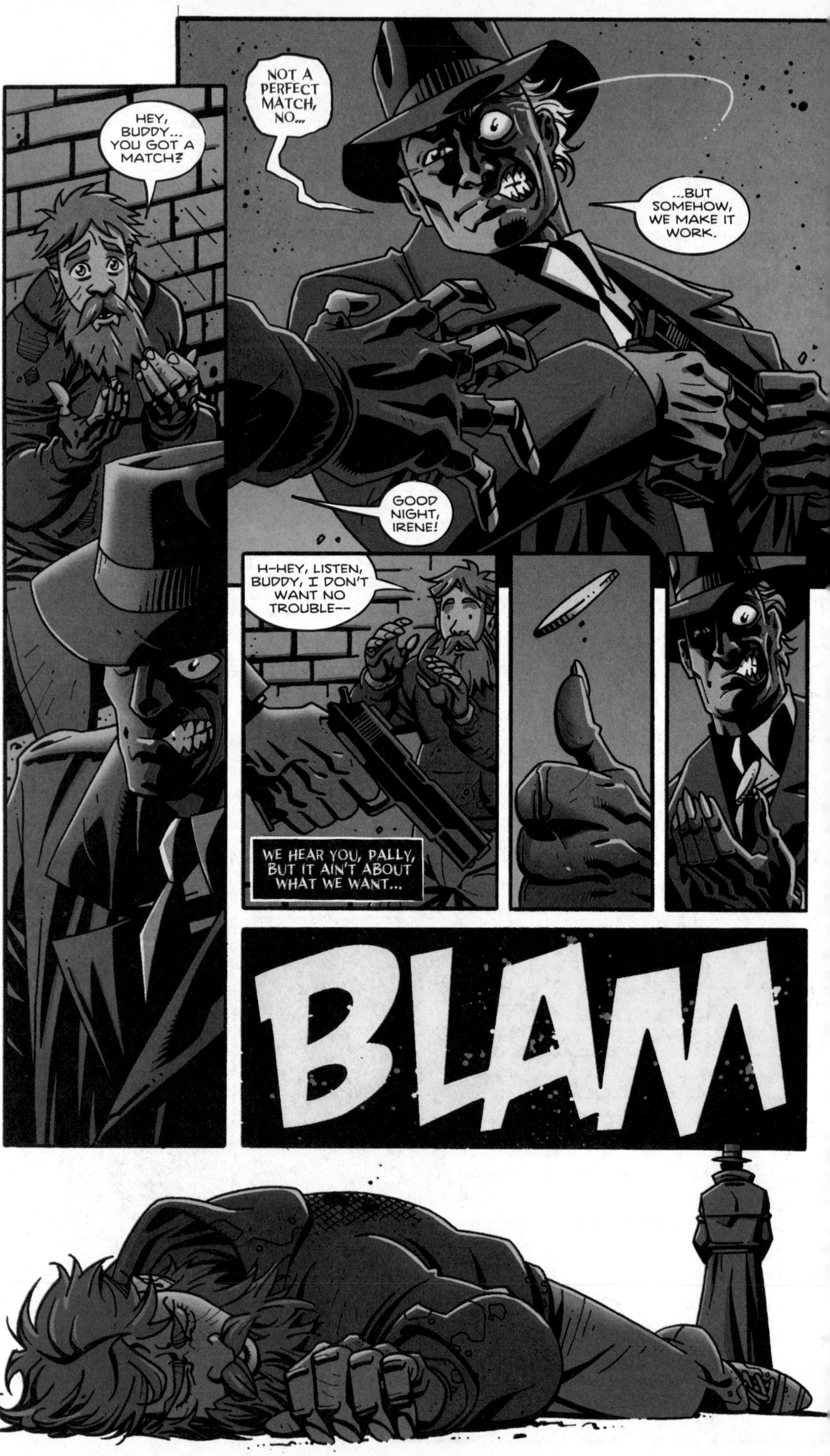
HEY, BUDDY... YOU GOT A MATCH?
NOT A PERFECT MATCH, NO...
...BUT SOMEHOW, WE MAKE IT WORK.
GOOD NIGHT, IRENE!
H-HEY, LISTEN, BUDDY, I DON'T WANT NO TROUBLE--
WE HEAR YOU, PALLY, BUT IT AIN'T ABOUT WHAT WE WANT...
BLAM

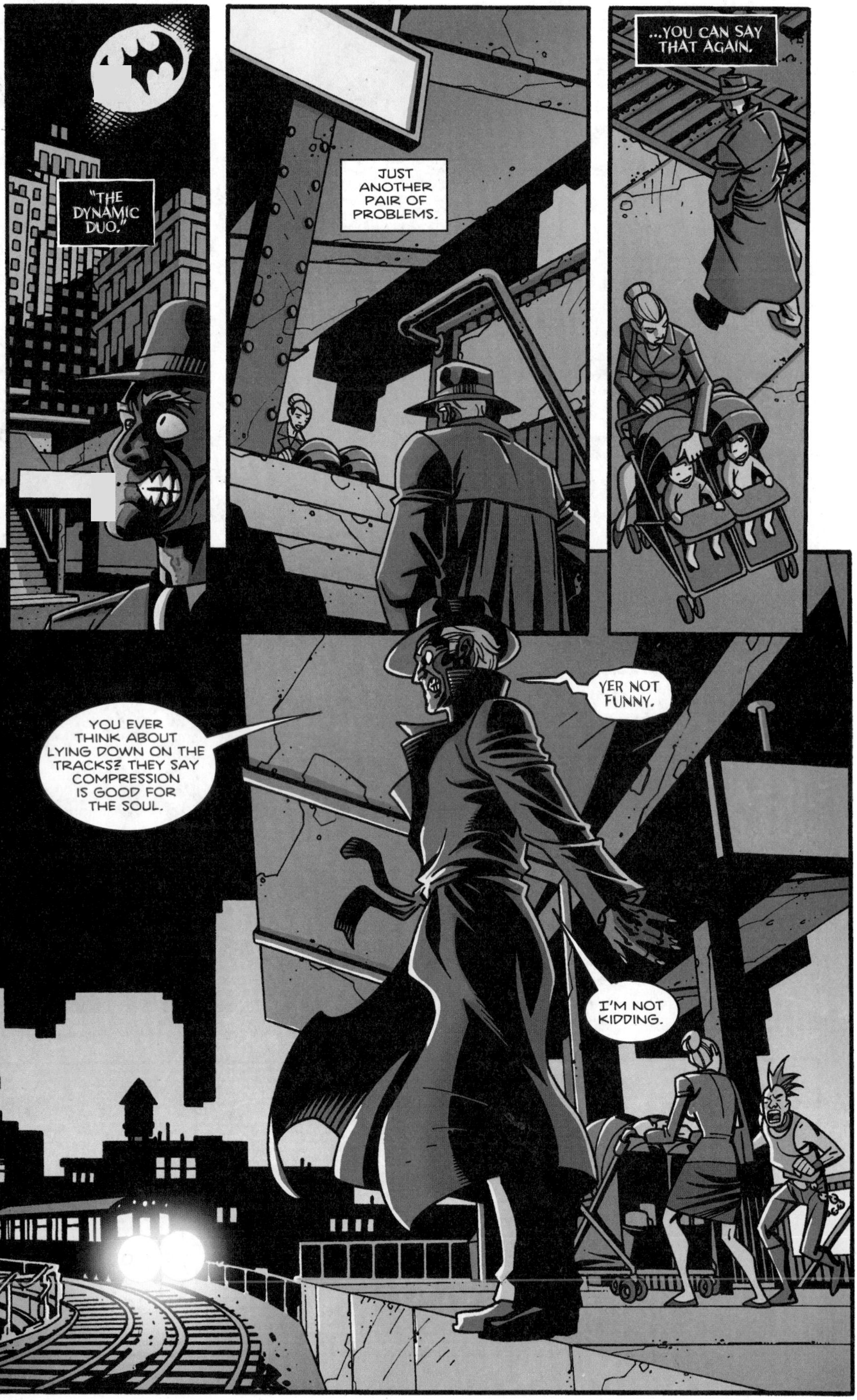
"THE DYNAMIC DUO."
JUST ANOTHER PAIR OF PROBLEMS.
...YOU CAN SAY THAT AGAIN.
YOU EVER THINK ABOUT LYING DOWN ON THE TRACKS? THEY SAY COMPRESSION IS GOOD FOR THE SOUL.
YER NOT FUNNY.
I'M NOT KIDDING.

AAAAAH!

CHK CHK CHK CHK

THE WAYNE FOUNDATION

FOR ONE AND FOR ALL

FOR ONE

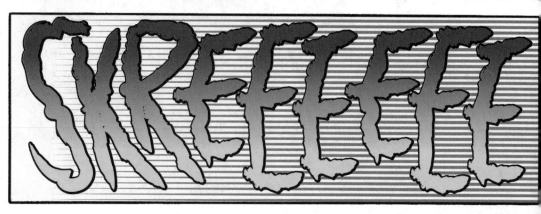

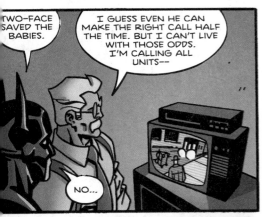

TWO-FACE SAVED THE BABIES.

I GUESS EVEN HE CAN MAKE THE RIGHT CALL HALF THE TIME. BUT I CAN'T LIVE WITH THOSE ODDS. I'M CALLING ALL UNITS--

NO...

...WAIT A NIGHT. I'LL FIND HIM. I CAN *HELP* HIM.

BATMAN, IF YOU SEE SOME REASON FOR HOPE IN THIS LOST CAUSE, I WISH YOU'D CLUE ME IN.

WATCH THE TAPE AGAIN, COMMISSIONER. SEE WHAT ISN'T THERE...HE MADE A SELFLESS DECISION, AT RISK TO HIMSELF...

...BUT HE NEVER FLIPPED THE COIN.

BY GUM, HE DIDN'T. DOES THAT MEAN--?

--HE'S REALLY GOING TO DO THAT *EVERY TIME,* ISN'T HE?

END.

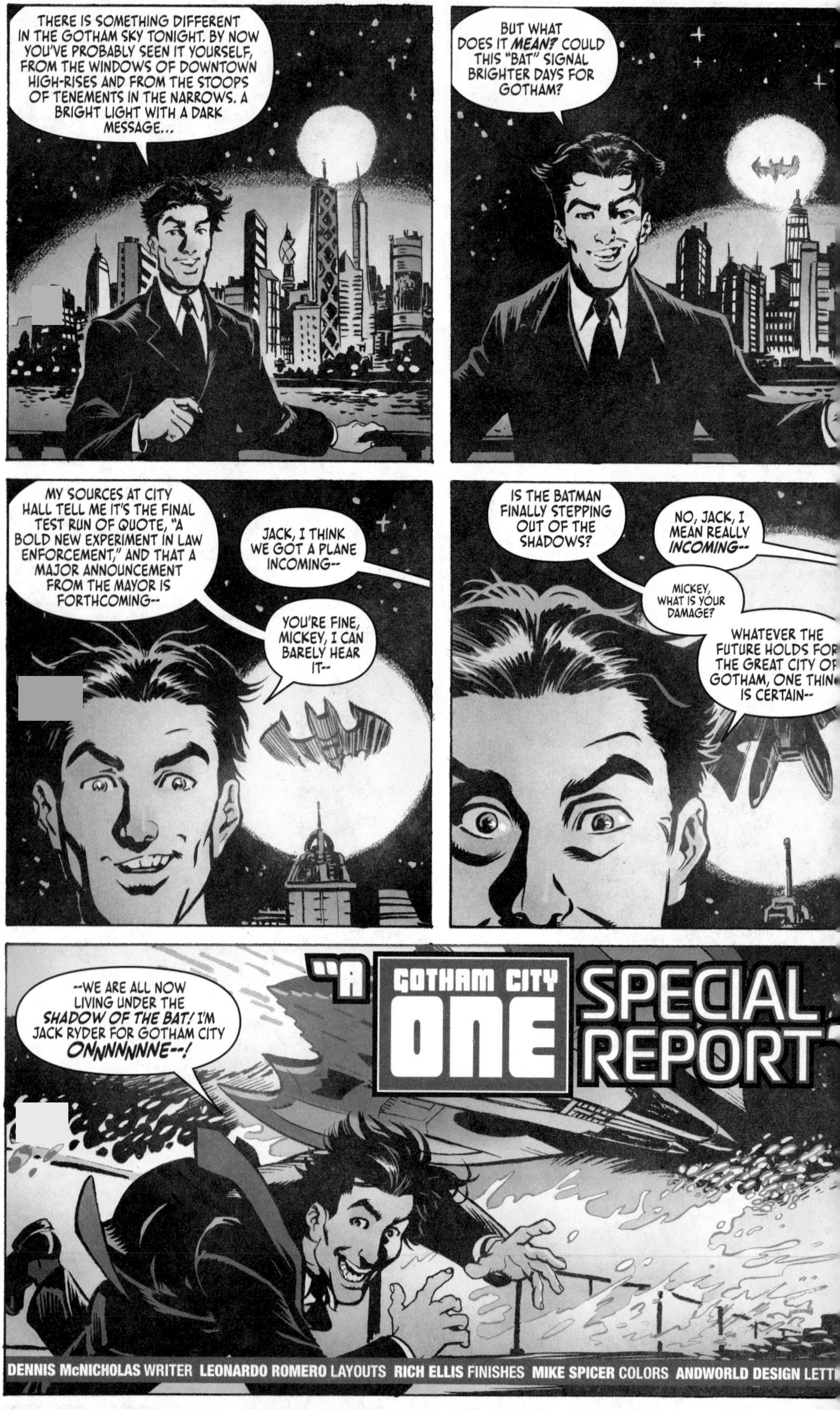
THERE IS SOMETHING DIFFERENT IN THE GOTHAM SKY TONIGHT. BY NOW YOU'VE PROBABLY SEEN IT YOURSELF, FROM THE WINDOWS OF DOWNTOWN HIGH-RISES AND FROM THE STOOPS OF TENEMENTS IN THE NARROWS. A BRIGHT LIGHT WITH A DARK MESSAGE...
BUT WHAT DOES IT MEAN? COULD THIS "BAT" SIGNAL BRIGHTER DAYS FOR GOTHAM?
MY SOURCES AT CITY HALL TELL ME IT'S THE FINAL TEST RUN OF QUOTE, "A BOLD NEW EXPERIMENT IN LAW ENFORCEMENT," AND THAT A MAJOR ANNOUNCEMENT FROM THE MAYOR IS FORTHCOMING--
JACK, I THINK WE GOT A PLANE INCOMING--
YOU'RE FINE, MICKEY, I CAN BARELY HEAR IT--
IS THE BATMAN FINALLY STEPPING OUT OF THE SHADOWS?
NO, JACK, I MEAN REALLY INCOMING--
MICKEY, WHAT IS YOUR DAMAGE?
WHATEVER THE FUTURE HOLDS FOR THE GREAT CITY OF GOTHAM, ONE THIN IS CERTAIN--
--WE ARE ALL NOW LIVING UNDER THE SHADOW OF THE BAT! I'M JACK RYDER FOR GOTHAM CITY ONNNNNNNE--!
"A GOTHAM CITY ONE SPECIAL REPORT"
DENNIS McNICHOLAS WRITER LEONARDO ROMERO LAYOUTS RICH ELLIS FINISHES MIKE SPICER COLORS ANDWORLD DESIGN LETT

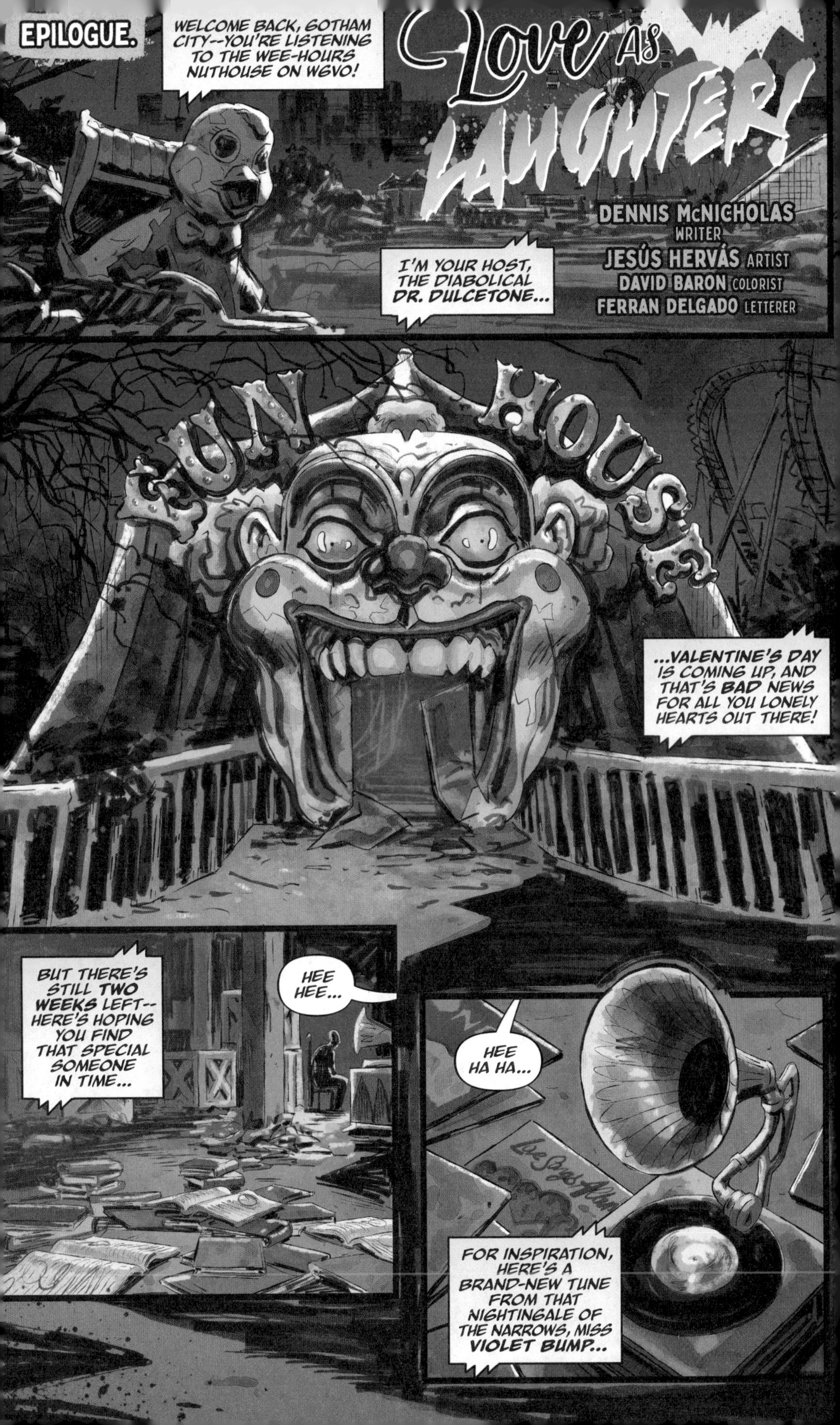
EPILOGUE.
WELCOME BACK, GOTHAM CITY--YOU'RE LISTENING TO THE WEE-HOURS NUTHOUSE ON WGVO!
Love as LAUGHTER!
DENNIS McNICHOLAS WRITER
JESÚS HERVÁS ARTIST
DAVID BARON COLORIST
FERRAN DELGADO LETTERER
I'M YOUR HOST, THE DIABOLICAL DR. DULCETONE...
FUN HOUSE
...VALENTINE'S DAY IS COMING UP, AND THAT'S BAD NEWS FOR ALL YOU LONELY HEARTS OUT THERE!
BUT THERE'S STILL TWO WEEKS LEFT--HERE'S HOPING YOU FIND THAT SPECIAL SOMEONE IN TIME...
HEE HEE...
HEE HA HA...
FOR INSPIRATION, HERE'S A BRAND-NEW TUNE FROM THAT NIGHTINGALE OF THE NARROWS, MISS VIOLET BUMP...

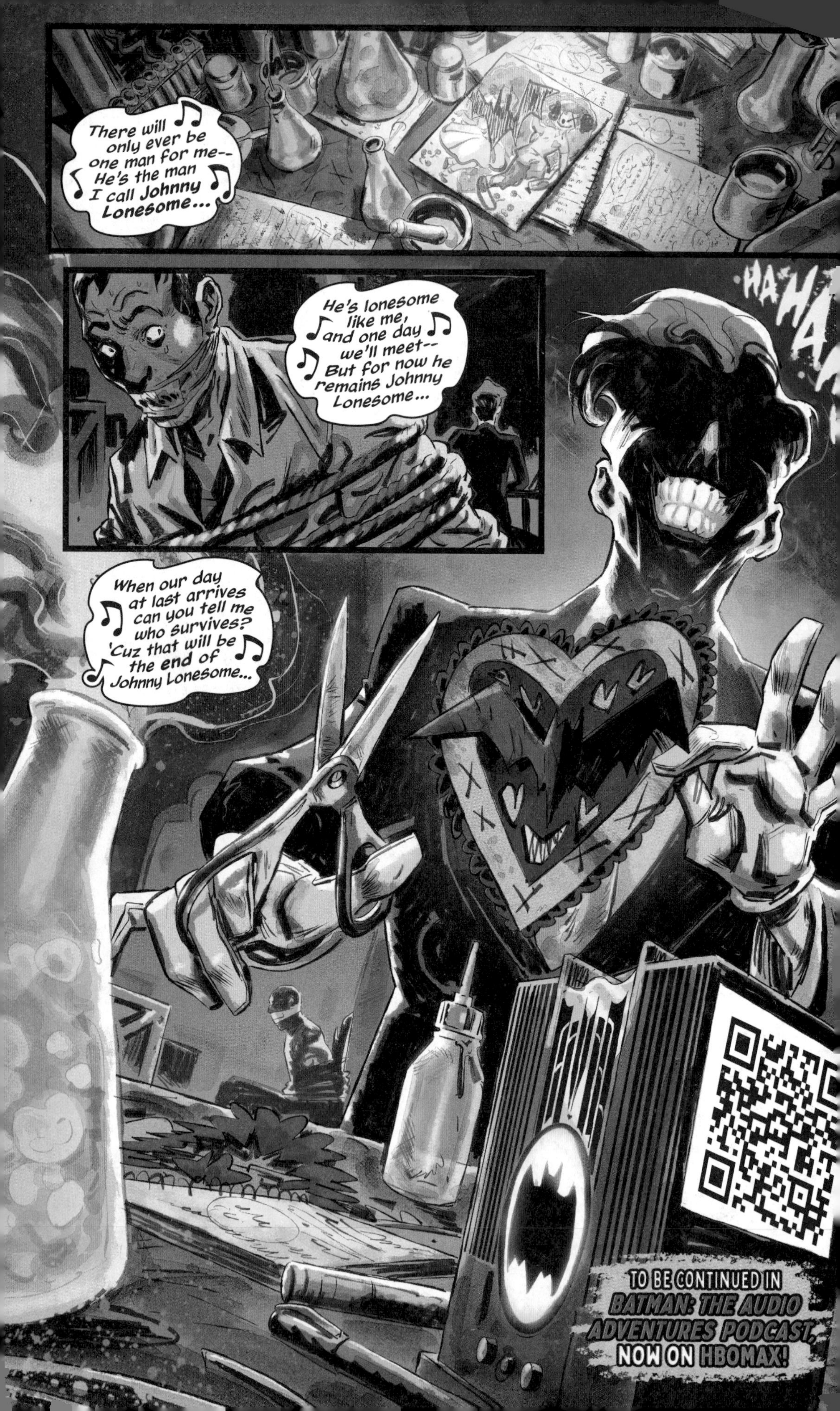

There will only ever be one man for me-- He's the man I call Johnny Lonesome...
He's lonesome like me, and one day we'll meet-- But for now he remains Johnny Lonesome...
HA HA
When our day at last arrives can you tell me who survives? 'Cuz that will be the end of Johnny Lonesome...
TO BE CONTINUED IN BATMAN: THE AUDIO ADVENTURES PODCAST, NOW ON HBOMAX!

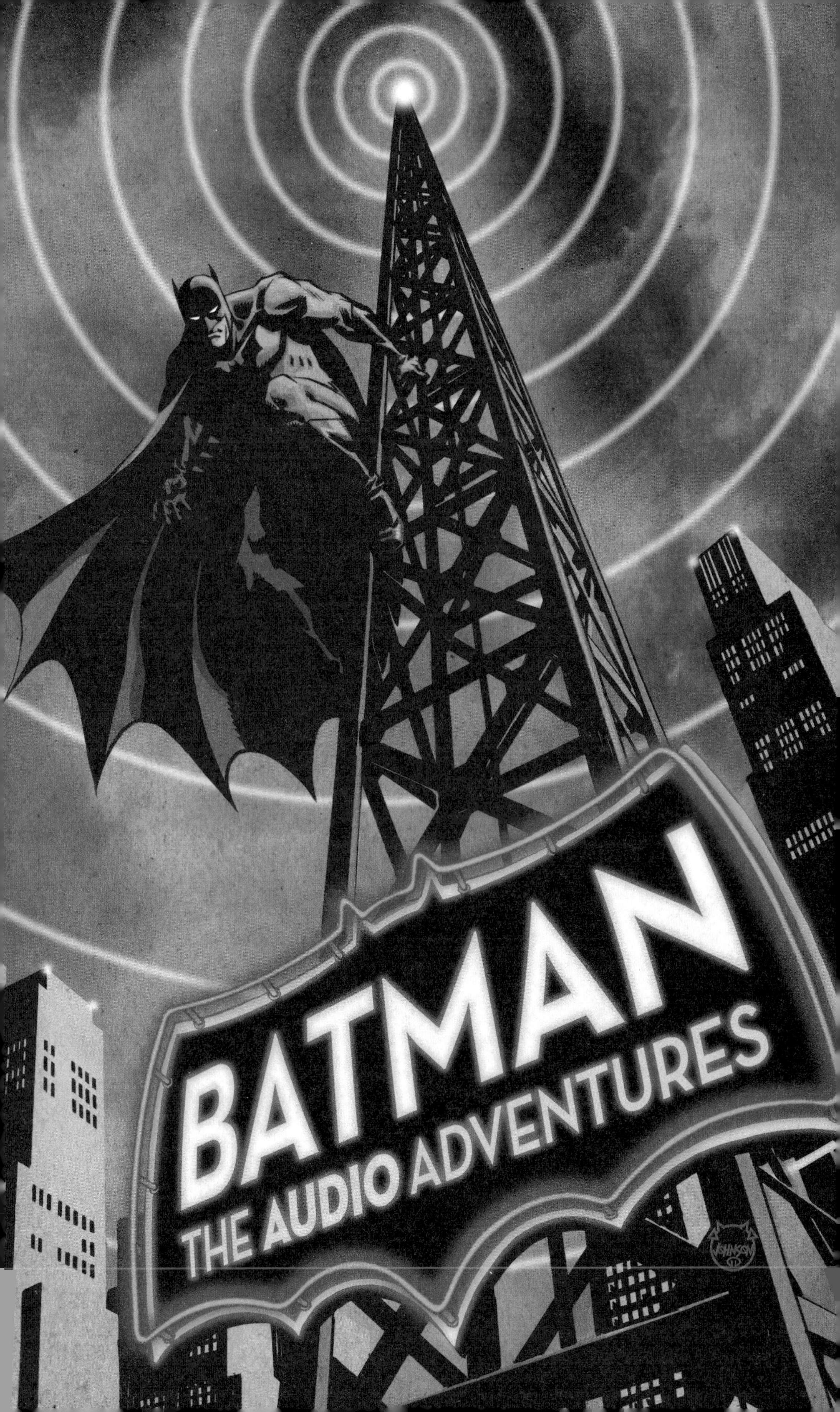
BATMAN
THE AUDIO ADVENTURES
JOHNSON

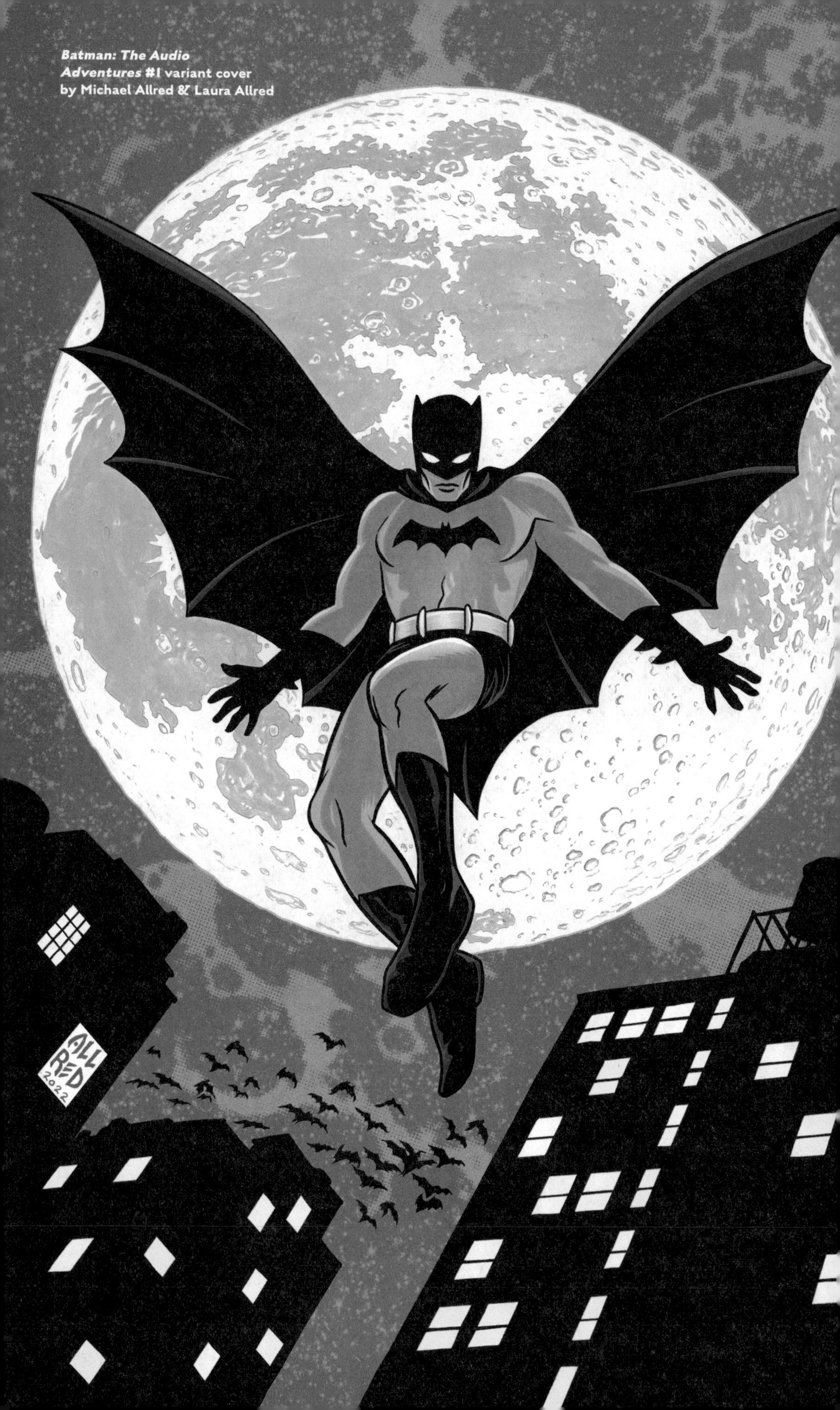
ALL RED 2022

Batman: The Audio Adventures #1 variant cover by Michael Allred & Laura Allred

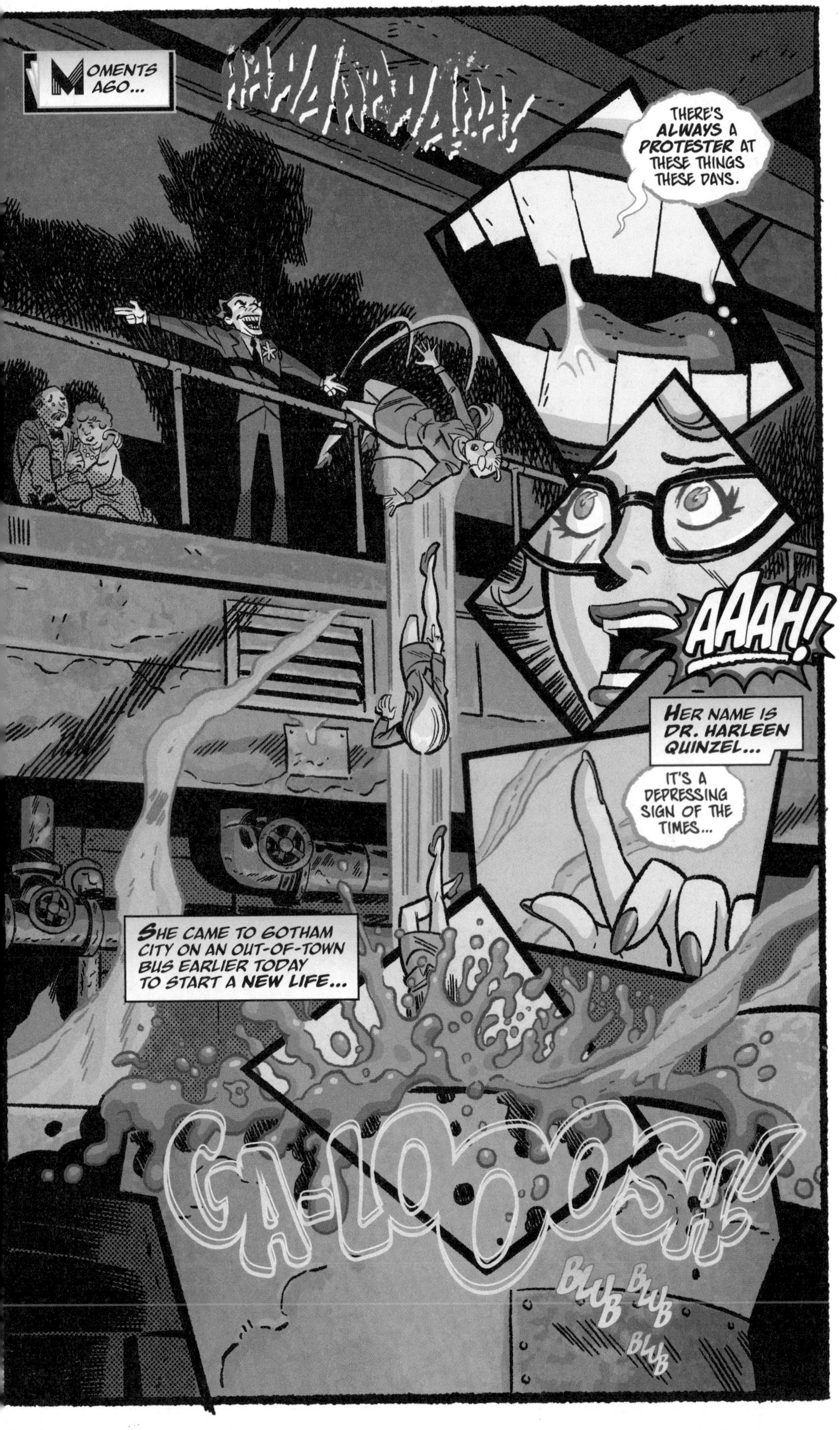
MOMENTS AGO...
THERE'S ALWAYS A PROTESTER AT THESE THINGS THESE DAYS.
AAAH!
HER NAME IS DR. HARLEEN QUINZEL...
IT'S A DEPRESSING SIGN OF THE TIMES...
SHE CAME TO GOTHAM CITY ON AN OUT-OF-TOWN BUS EARLIER TODAY TO START A NEW LIFE...
GA-LOOOOSH!
BLUB BLUB BLUB

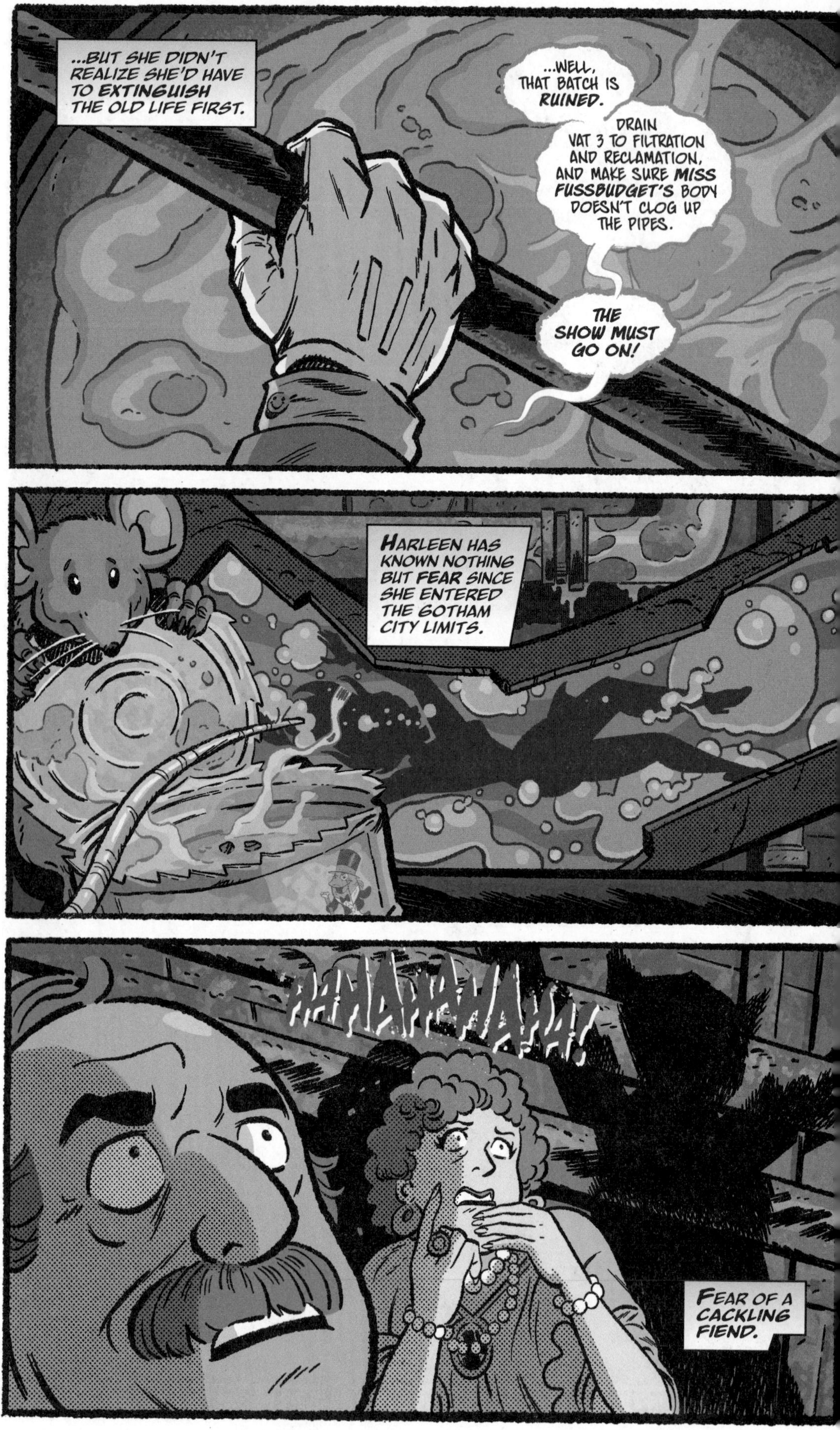
...BUT SHE DIDN'T REALIZE SHE'D HAVE TO EXTINGUISH THE OLD LIFE FIRST.
...WELL, THAT BATCH IS RUINED.
DRAIN VAT 3 TO FILTRATION AND RECLAMATION, AND MAKE SURE MISS FUSSBUDGET'S BODY DOESN'T CLOG UP THE PIPES.
THE SHOW MUST GO ON!
HARLEEN HAS KNOWN NOTHING BUT FEAR SINCE SHE ENTERED THE GOTHAM CITY LIMITS.
HAHAHAHAHAHA!
FEAR OF A CACKLING FIEND.

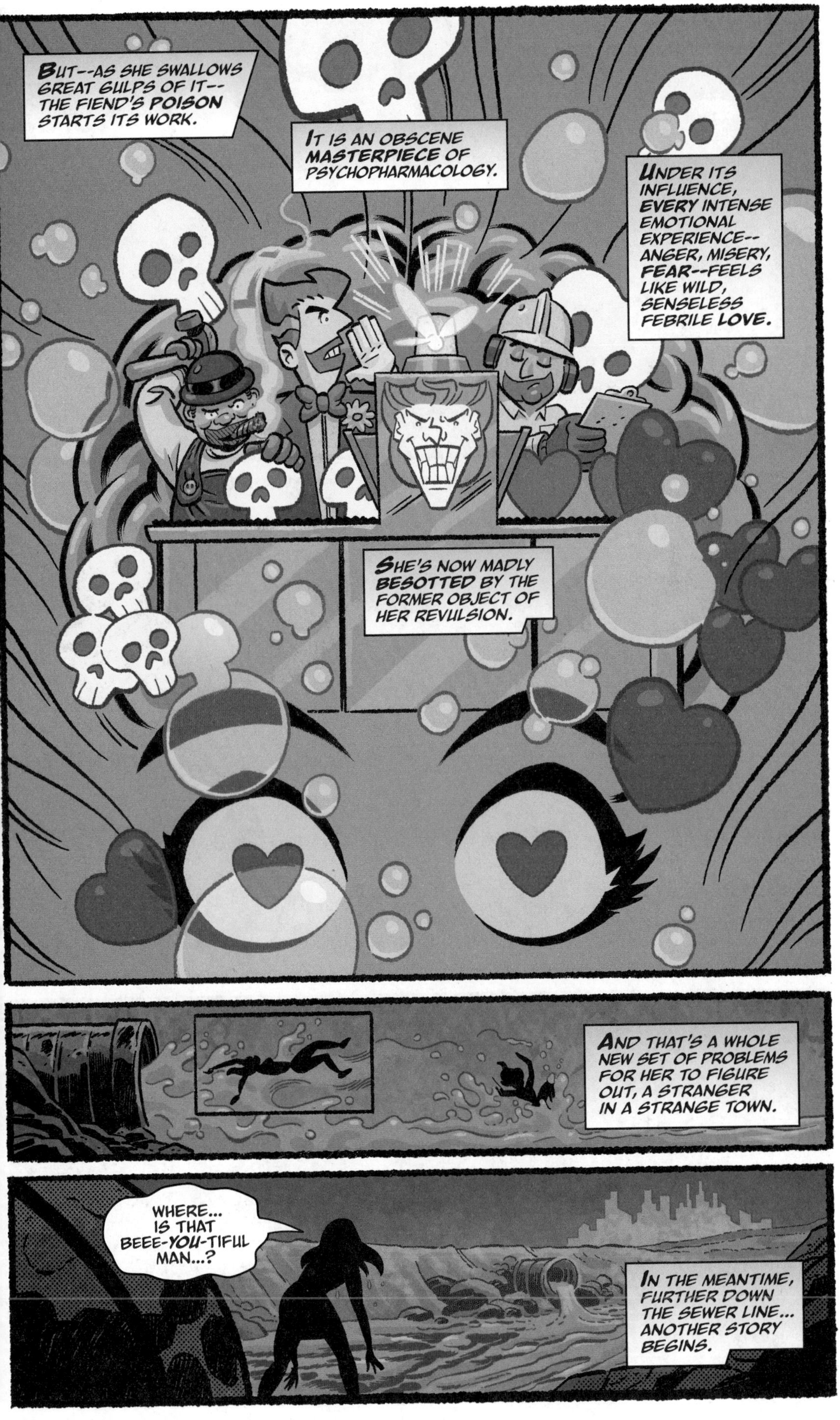
BUT--AS SHE SWALLOWS GREAT GULPS OF IT--THE FIEND'S POISON STARTS ITS WORK.
IT IS AN OBSCENE MASTERPIECE OF PSYCHOPHARMACOLOGY.
UNDER ITS INFLUENCE, EVERY INTENSE EMOTIONAL EXPERIENCE--ANGER, MISERY, FEAR--FEELS LIKE WILD, SENSELESS FEBRILE LOVE.
SHE'S NOW MADLY BESOTTED BY THE FORMER OBJECT OF HER REVULSION.
AND THAT'S A WHOLE NEW SET OF PROBLEMS FOR HER TO FIGURE OUT, A STRANGER IN A STRANGE TOWN.
WHERE... IS THAT BEEE-YOU-TIFUL MAN...?
IN THE MEANTIME, FURTHER DOWN THE SEWER LINE... ANOTHER STORY BEGINS.

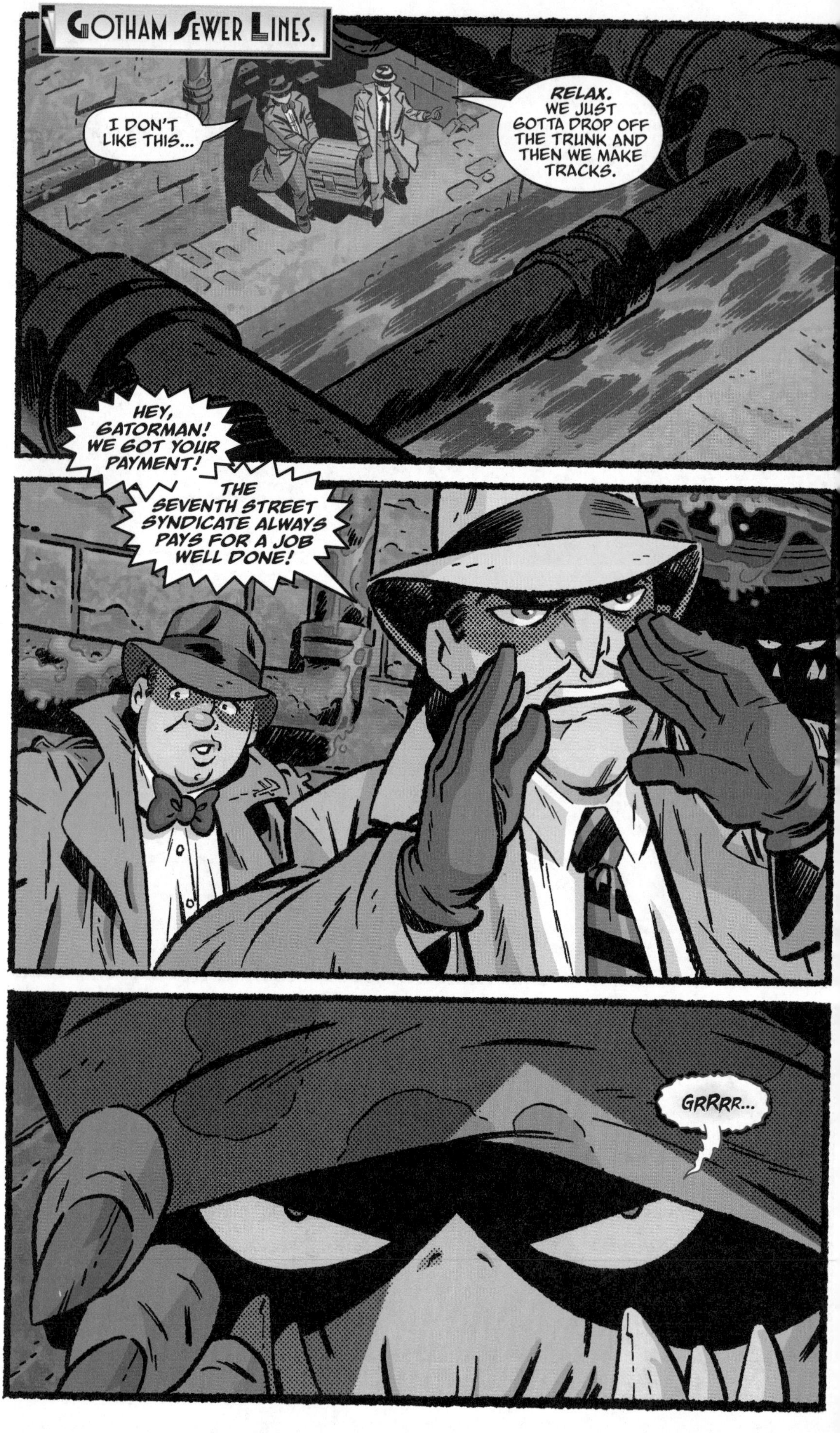
GOTHAM SEWER LINES.
I DON'T LIKE THIS...
RELAX. WE JUST GOTTA DROP OFF THE TRUNK AND THEN WE MAKE TRACKS.
HEY, GATORMAN! WE GOT YOUR PAYMENT!
THE SEVENTH STREET SYNDICATE ALWAYS PAYS FOR A JOB WELL DONE!
GRRRR...

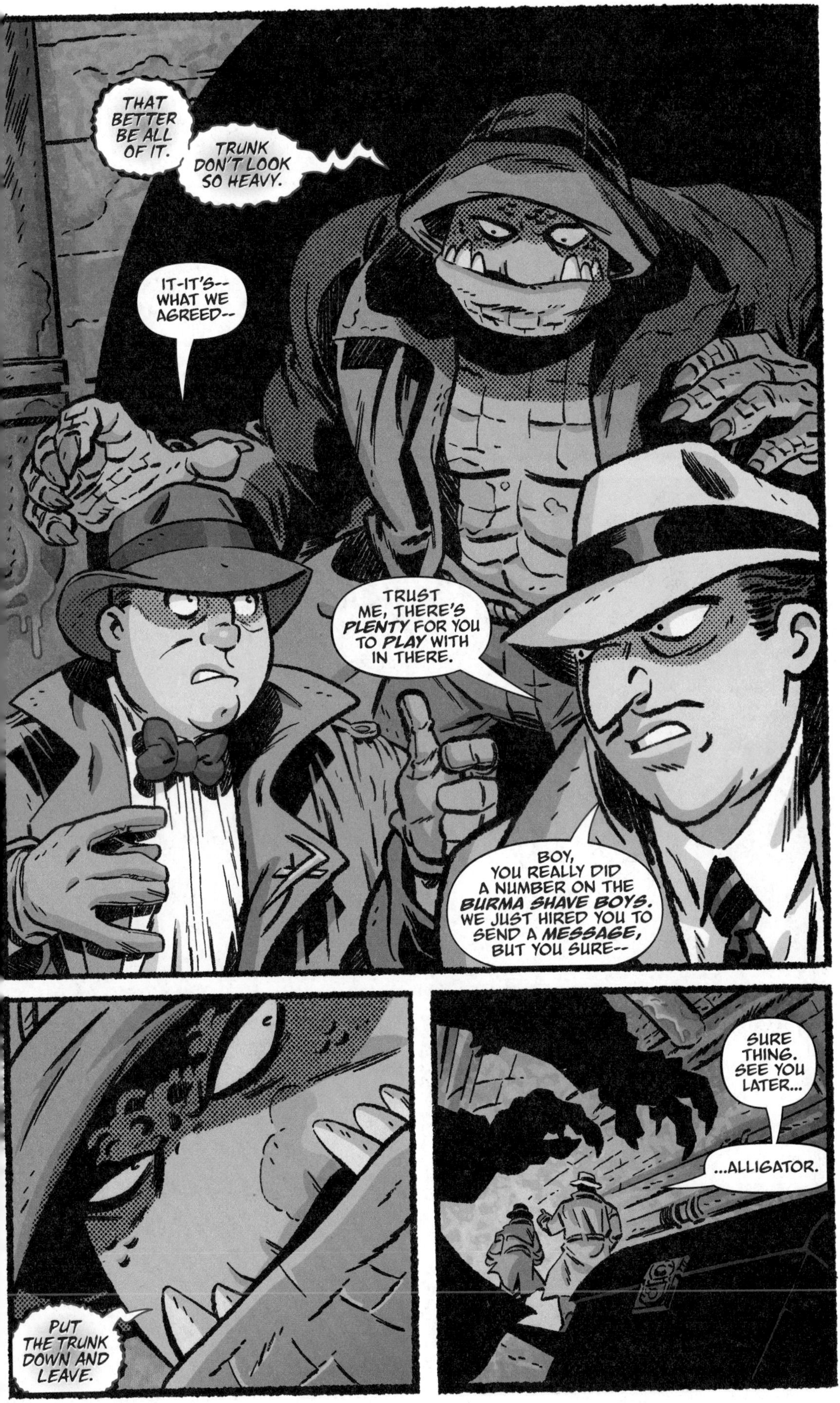

THAT BETTER BE ALL OF IT.
TRUNK DON'T LOOK SO HEAVY.
IT-IT'S-- WHAT WE AGREED--
TRUST ME, THERE'S PLENTY FOR YOU TO PLAY WITH IN THERE.
BOY, YOU REALLY DID A NUMBER ON THE BURMA SHAVE BOYS. WE JUST HIRED YOU TO SEND A MESSAGE, BUT YOU SURE--
PUT THE TRUNK DOWN AND LEAVE.
SURE THING. SEE YOU LATER...
...ALLIGATOR.

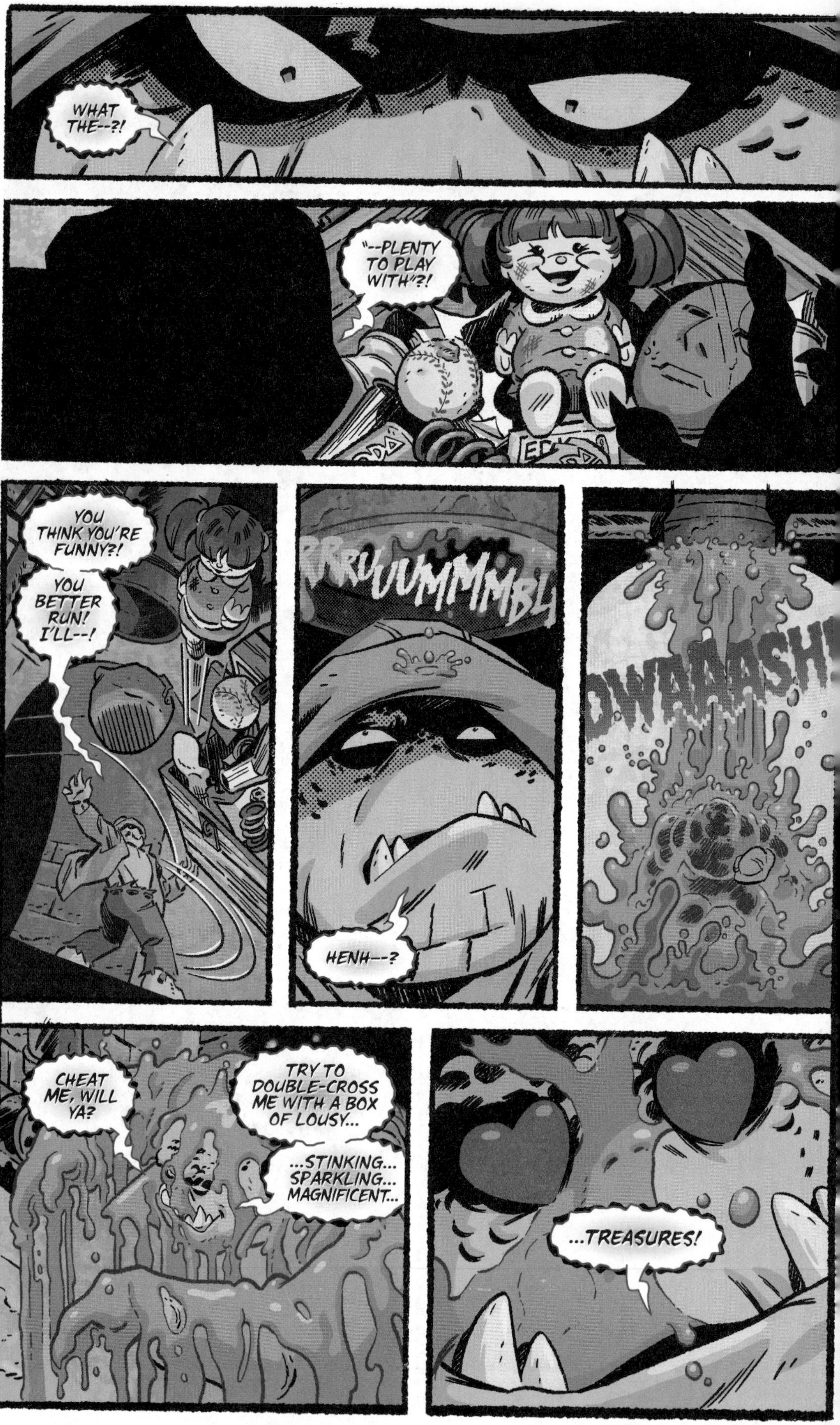
WHAT THE--?!
"--PLENTY TO PLAY WITH"?!
YOU THINK YOU'RE FUNNY?!
YOU BETTER RUN! I'LL--!
RRRUUUMMMBL
HENH--?
DWAAASH
CHEAT ME, WILL YA?
TRY TO DOUBLE-CROSS ME WITH A BOX OF LOUSY...
...STINKING... SPARKLING... MAGNIFICENT...
...TREASURES!

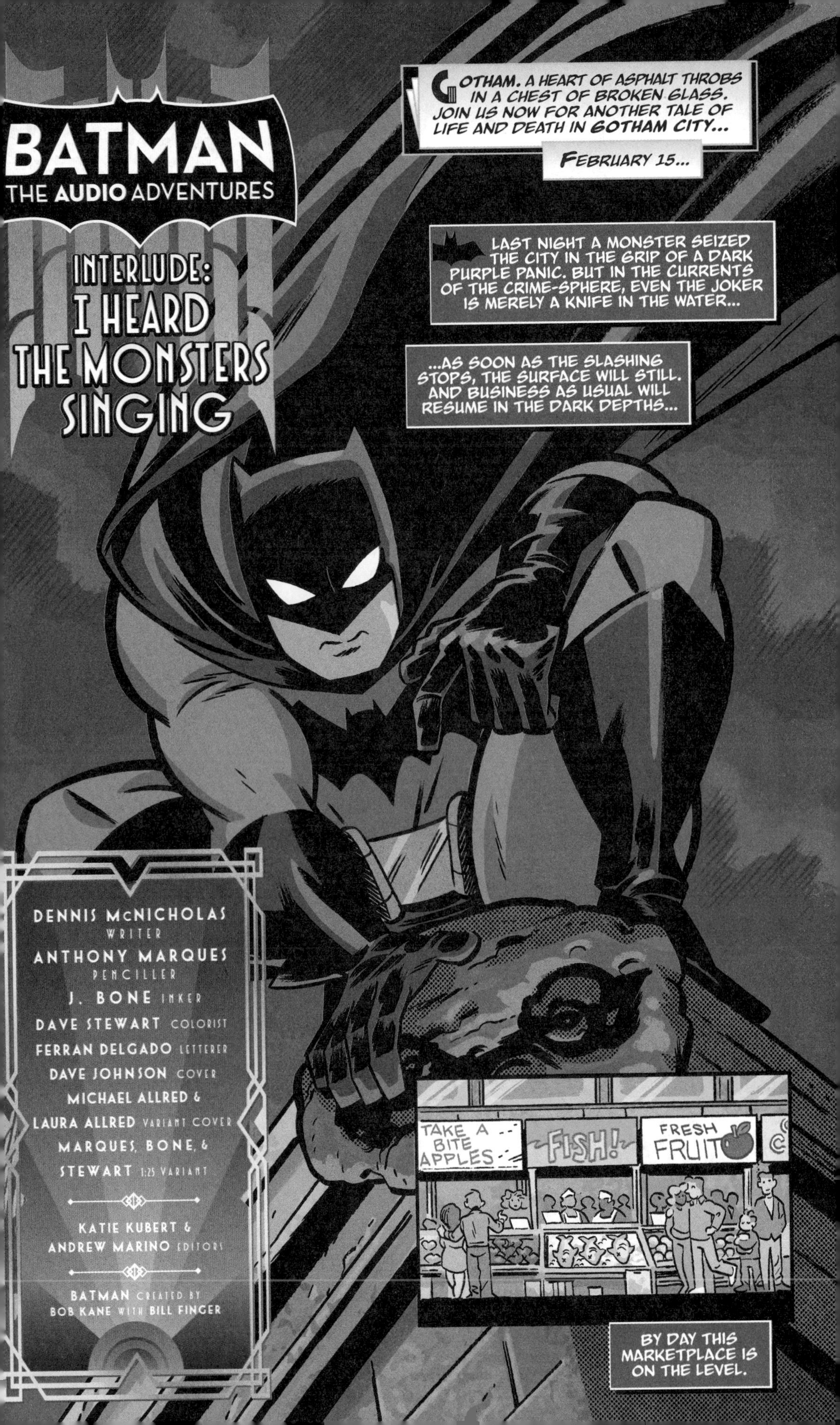

BATMAN
THE AUDIO ADVENTURES
INTERLUDE:
I HEARD THE MONSTERS SINGING
GOTHAM. A HEART OF ASPHALT THROBS IN A CHEST OF BROKEN GLASS. JOIN US NOW FOR ANOTHER TALE OF LIFE AND DEATH IN GOTHAM CITY...
FEBRUARY 15...
LAST NIGHT A MONSTER SEIZED THE CITY IN THE GRIP OF A DARK PURPLE PANIC. BUT IN THE CURRENTS OF THE CRIME-SPHERE, EVEN THE JOKER IS MERELY A KNIFE IN THE WATER...
...AS SOON AS THE SLASHING STOPS, THE SURFACE WILL STILL. AND BUSINESS AS USUAL WILL RESUME IN THE DARK DEPTHS...
DENNIS McNICHOLAS WRITER
ANTHONY MARQUES PENCILLER
J. BONE INKER
DAVE STEWART COLORIST
FERRAN DELGADO LETTERER
DAVE JOHNSON COVER
MICHAEL ALLRED & LAURA ALLRED VARIANT COVER
MARQUES, BONE, & STEWART 1:25 VARIANT
KATIE KUBERT & ANDREW MARINO EDITORS
BATMAN CREATED BY BOB KANE WITH BILL FINGER
TAKE A BITE APPLES
FISH!
FRESH FRUIT
BY DAY THIS MARKETPLACE IS ON THE LEVEL.

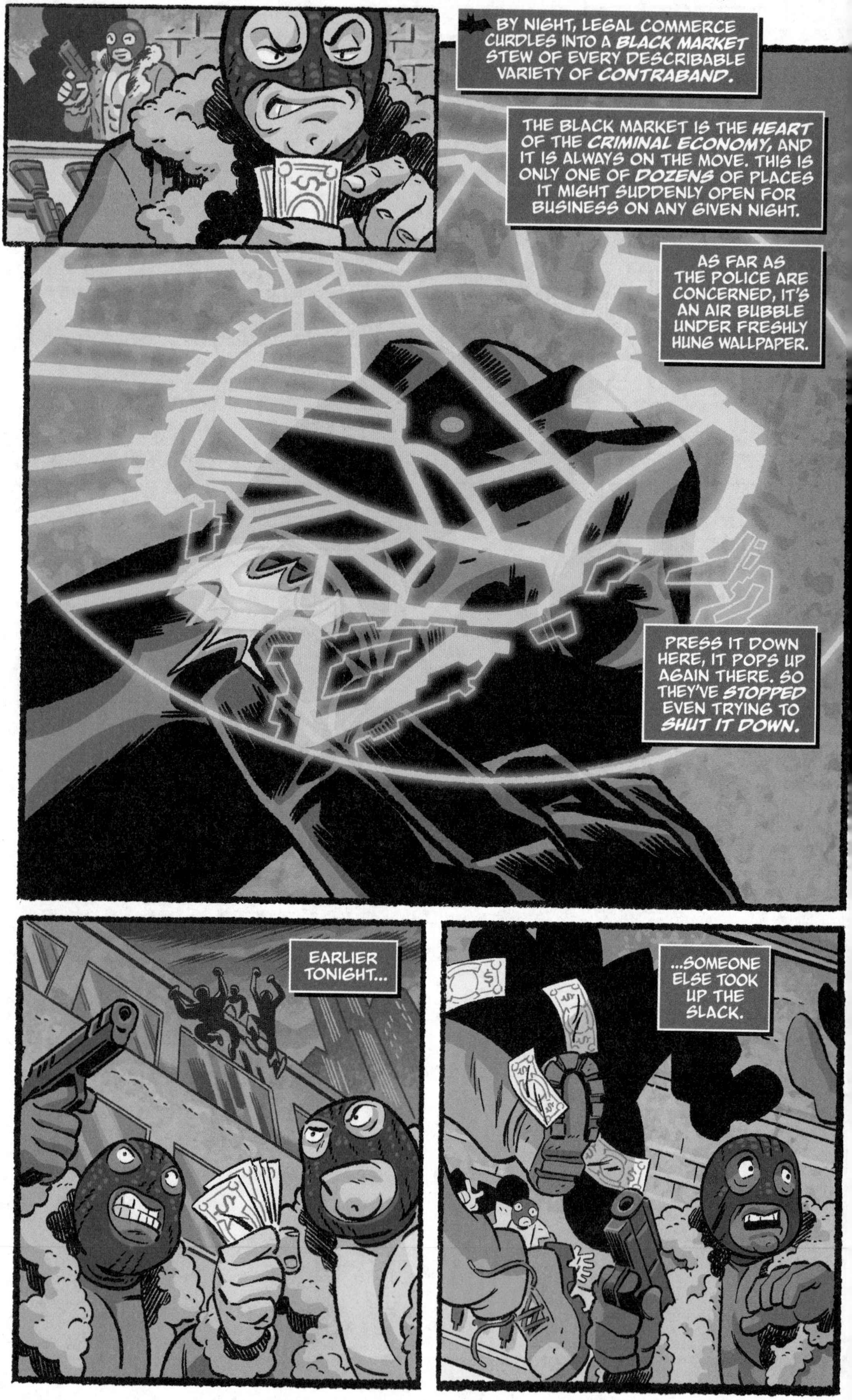
BY NIGHT, LEGAL COMMERCE CURDLES INTO A *BLACK MARKET* STEW OF EVERY DESCRIBABLE VARIETY OF *CONTRABAND.*
THE BLACK MARKET IS THE *HEART* OF THE *CRIMINAL ECONOMY,* AND IT IS ALWAYS ON THE MOVE. THIS IS ONLY ONE OF *DOZENS* OF PLACES IT MIGHT SUDDENLY OPEN FOR BUSINESS ON ANY GIVEN NIGHT.
AS FAR AS THE POLICE ARE CONCERNED, IT'S AN AIR BUBBLE UNDER FRESHLY HUNG WALLPAPER.
PRESS IT DOWN HERE, IT POPS UP AGAIN THERE. SO THEY'VE *STOPPED* EVEN TRYING TO *SHUT IT DOWN.*
EARLIER TONIGHT...
...SOMEONE ELSE TOOK UP THE SLACK.

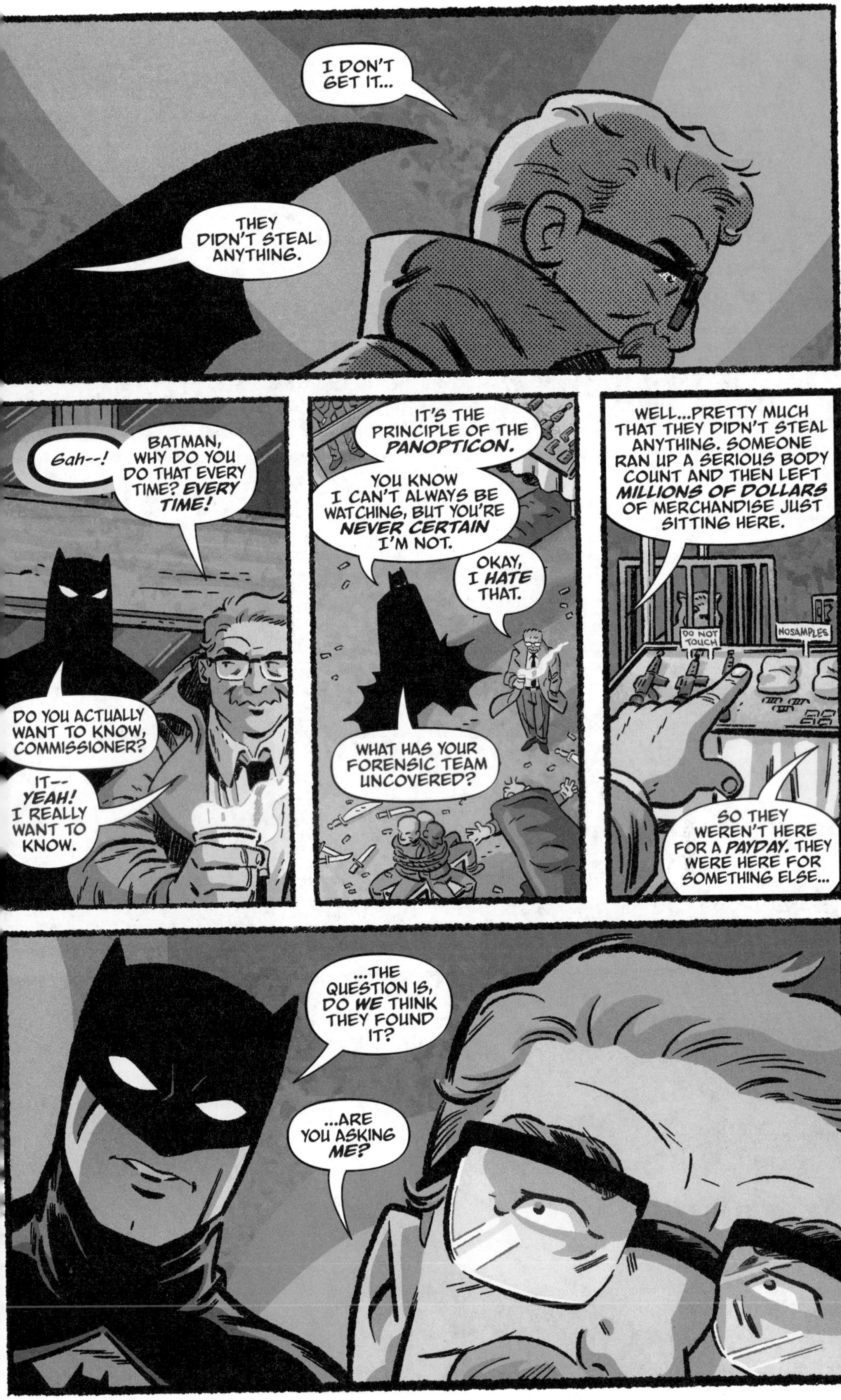
I DON'T GET IT...
THEY DIDN'T STEAL ANYTHING.
Gah--!
BATMAN, WHY DO YOU DO THAT EVERY TIME? EVERY TIME!
DO YOU ACTUALLY WANT TO KNOW, COMMISSIONER?
IT-- YEAH! I REALLY WANT TO KNOW.
IT'S THE PRINCIPLE OF THE PANOPTICON.
YOU KNOW I CAN'T ALWAYS BE WATCHING, BUT YOU'RE NEVER CERTAIN I'M NOT.
OKAY, I HATE THAT.
WHAT HAS YOUR FORENSIC TEAM UNCOVERED?
WELL...PRETTY MUCH THAT THEY DIDN'T STEAL ANYTHING. SOMEONE RAN UP A SERIOUS BODY COUNT AND THEN LEFT MILLIONS OF DOLLARS OF MERCHANDISE JUST SITTING HERE.
DO NOT TOUCH
NO SAMPLES
SO THEY WEREN'T HERE FOR A PAYDAY. THEY WERE HERE FOR SOMETHING ELSE...
...THE QUESTION IS, DO WE THINK THEY FOUND IT?
...ARE YOU ASKING ME?

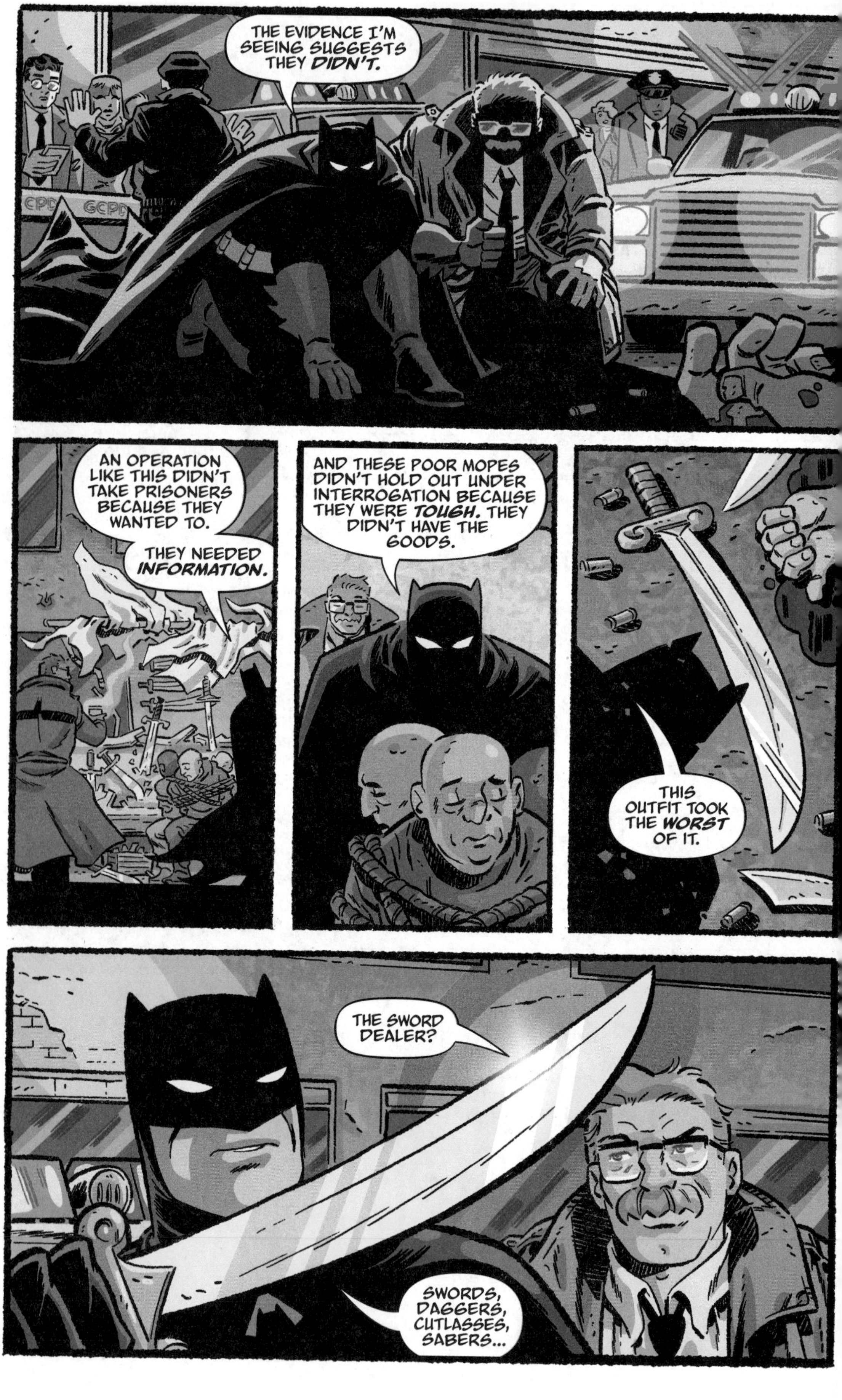

THE EVIDENCE I'M SEEING SUGGESTS THEY *DIDN'T.*
CPD
GCPD
AN OPERATION LIKE THIS DIDN'T TAKE PRISONERS BECAUSE THEY WANTED TO.
THEY NEEDED ***INFORMATION.***
AND THESE POOR MOPES DIDN'T HOLD OUT UNDER INTERROGATION BECAUSE THEY WERE *TOUGH.* THEY DIDN'T HAVE THE GOODS.
THIS OUTFIT TOOK THE *WORST* OF IT.
THE SWORD DEALER?
SWORDS, DAGGERS, CUTLASSES, SABERS...

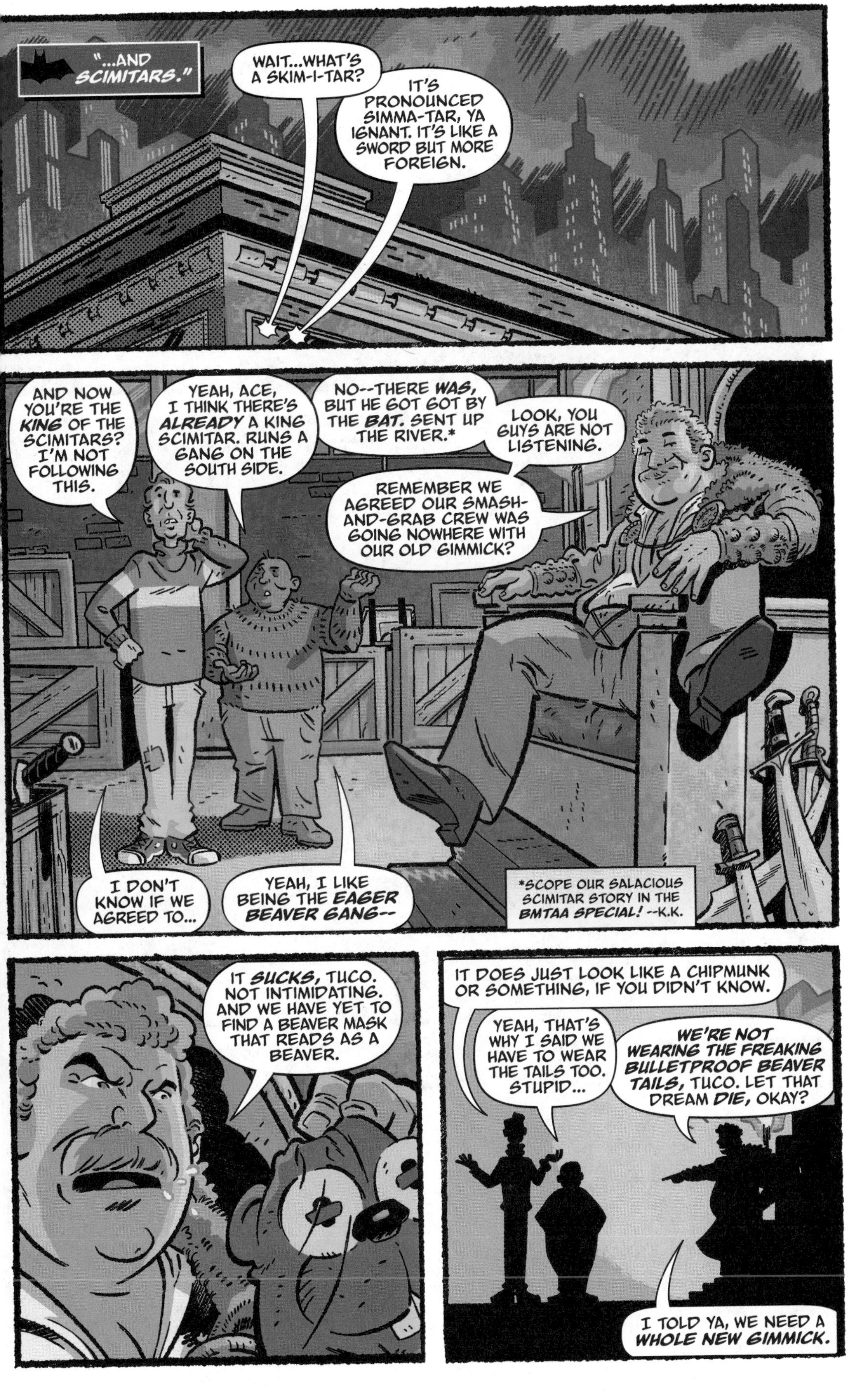

"...AND SCIMITARS."
WAIT...WHAT'S A SKIM-I-TAR?
IT'S PRONOUNCED SIMMA-TAR, YA IGNANT. IT'S LIKE A SWORD BUT MORE FOREIGN.
AND NOW YOU'RE THE KING OF THE SCIMITARS? I'M NOT FOLLOWING THIS.
YEAH, ACE, I THINK THERE'S ALREADY A KING SCIMITAR. RUNS A GANG ON THE SOUTH SIDE.
NO--THERE WAS, BUT HE GOT GOT BY THE BAT. SENT UP THE RIVER.*
LOOK, YOU GUYS ARE NOT LISTENING.
REMEMBER WE AGREED OUR SMASH-AND-GRAB CREW WAS GOING NOWHERE WITH OUR OLD GIMMICK?
I DON'T KNOW IF WE AGREED TO...
YEAH, I LIKE BEING THE EAGER BEAVER GANG--
*SCOPE OUR SALACIOUS SCIMITAR STORY IN THE BMTAA SPECIAL! --K.K.
IT SUCKS, TUCO. NOT INTIMIDATING. AND WE HAVE YET TO FIND A BEAVER MASK THAT READS AS A BEAVER.
IT DOES JUST LOOK LIKE A CHIPMUNK OR SOMETHING, IF YOU DIDN'T KNOW.
YEAH, THAT'S WHY I SAID WE HAVE TO WEAR THE TAILS TOO. STUPID...
WE'RE NOT WEARING THE FREAKING BULLETPROOF BEAVER TAILS, TUCO. LET THAT DREAM DIE, OKAY?
I TOLD YA, WE NEED A WHOLE NEW GIMMICK.

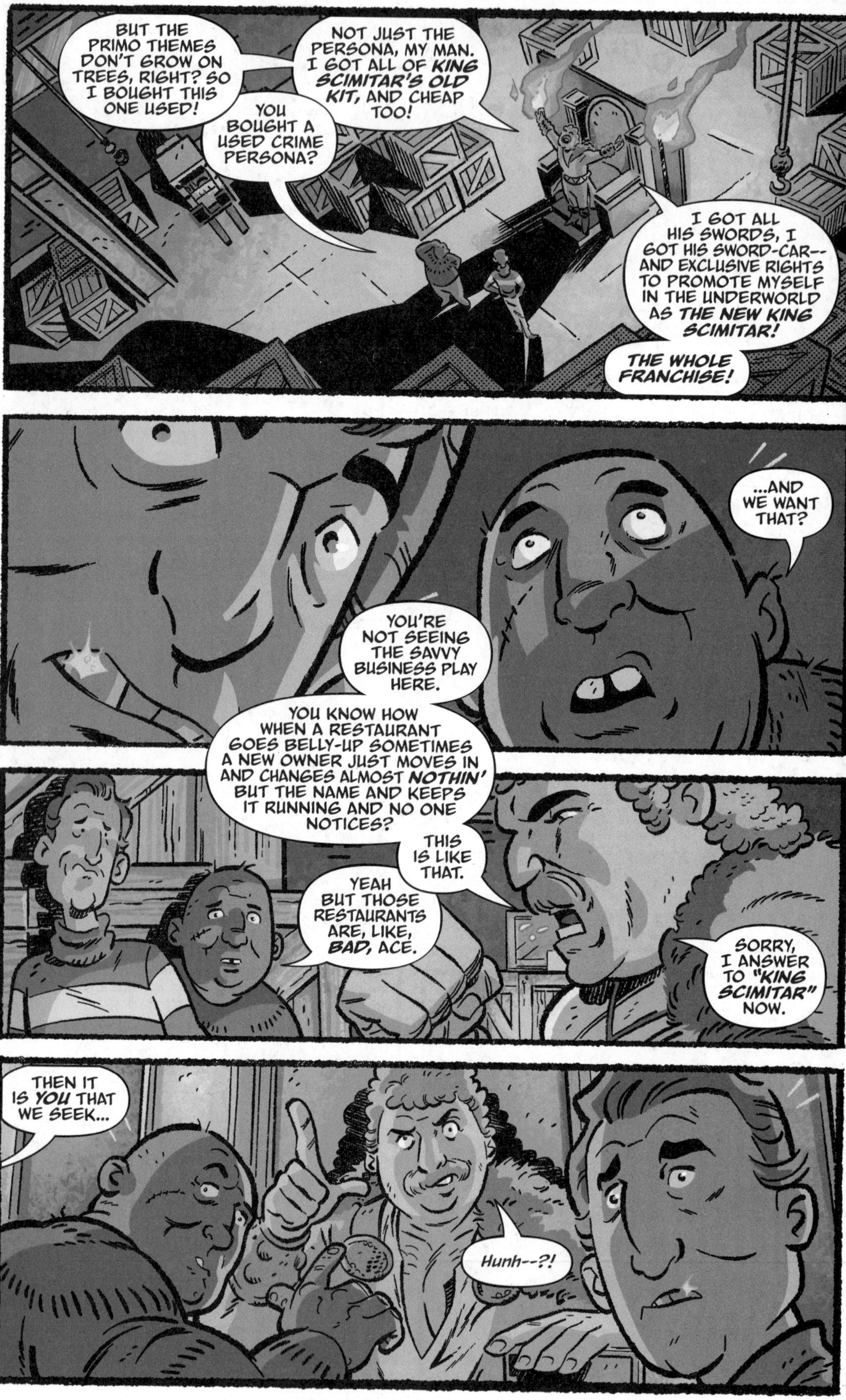

BUT THE PRIMO THEMES DON'T GROW ON TREES, RIGHT? SO I BOUGHT THIS ONE USED!
NOT JUST THE PERSONA, MY MAN. I GOT ALL OF KING SCIMITAR'S OLD KIT, AND CHEAP TOO!
YOU BOUGHT A USED CRIME PERSONA?
I GOT ALL HIS SWORDS, I GOT HIS SWORD-CAR-- AND EXCLUSIVE RIGHTS TO PROMOTE MYSELF IN THE UNDERWORLD AS THE NEW KING SCIMITAR!
THE WHOLE FRANCHISE!
...AND WE WANT THAT?
YOU'RE NOT SEEING THE SAVVY BUSINESS PLAY HERE.
YOU KNOW HOW WHEN A RESTAURANT GOES BELLY-UP SOMETIMES A NEW OWNER JUST MOVES IN AND CHANGES ALMOST NOTHIN' BUT THE NAME AND KEEPS IT RUNNING AND NO ONE NOTICES?
THIS IS LIKE THAT.
YEAH BUT THOSE RESTAURANTS ARE, LIKE, BAD, ACE.
SORRY, I ANSWER TO "KING SCIMITAR" NOW.
THEN IT IS YOU THAT WE SEEK...
Hunh--?!

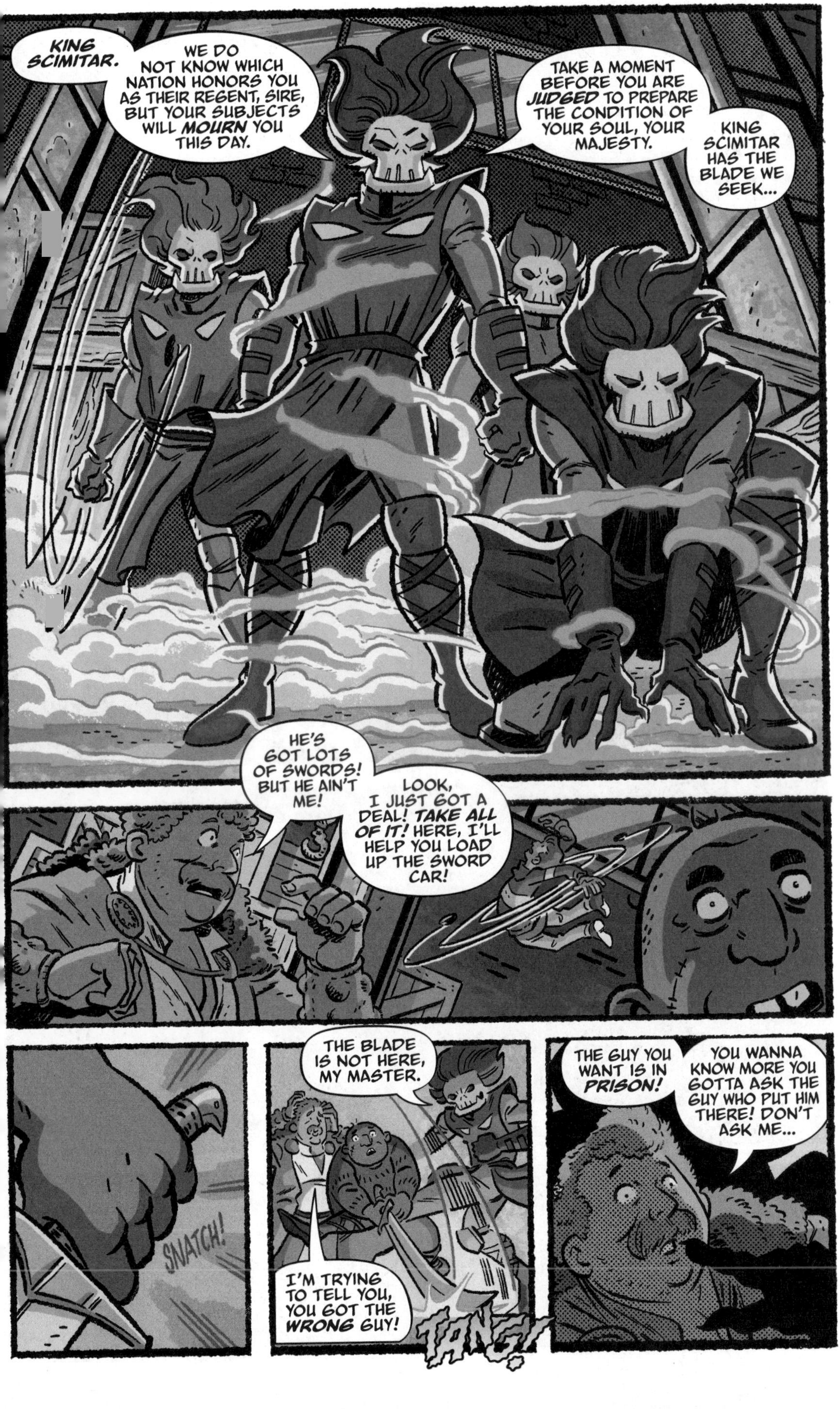
KING SCIMITAR.
WE DO NOT KNOW WHICH NATION HONORS YOU AS THEIR REGENT, SIRE, BUT YOUR SUBJECTS WILL MOURN YOU THIS DAY.
TAKE A MOMENT BEFORE YOU ARE JUDGED TO PREPARE THE CONDITION OF YOUR SOUL, YOUR MAJESTY.
KING SCIMITAR HAS THE BLADE WE SEEK...
HE'S GOT LOTS OF SWORDS! BUT HE AIN'T ME!
LOOK, I JUST GOT A DEAL! TAKE ALL OF IT! HERE, I'LL HELP YOU LOAD UP THE SWORD CAR!
SNATCH!
THE BLADE IS NOT HERE, MY MASTER.
I'M TRYING TO TELL YOU, YOU GOT THE WRONG GUY!
TANG!!
THE GUY YOU WANT IS IN PRISON!
YOU WANNA KNOW MORE YOU GOTTA ASK THE GUY WHO PUT HIM THERE! DON'T ASK ME...

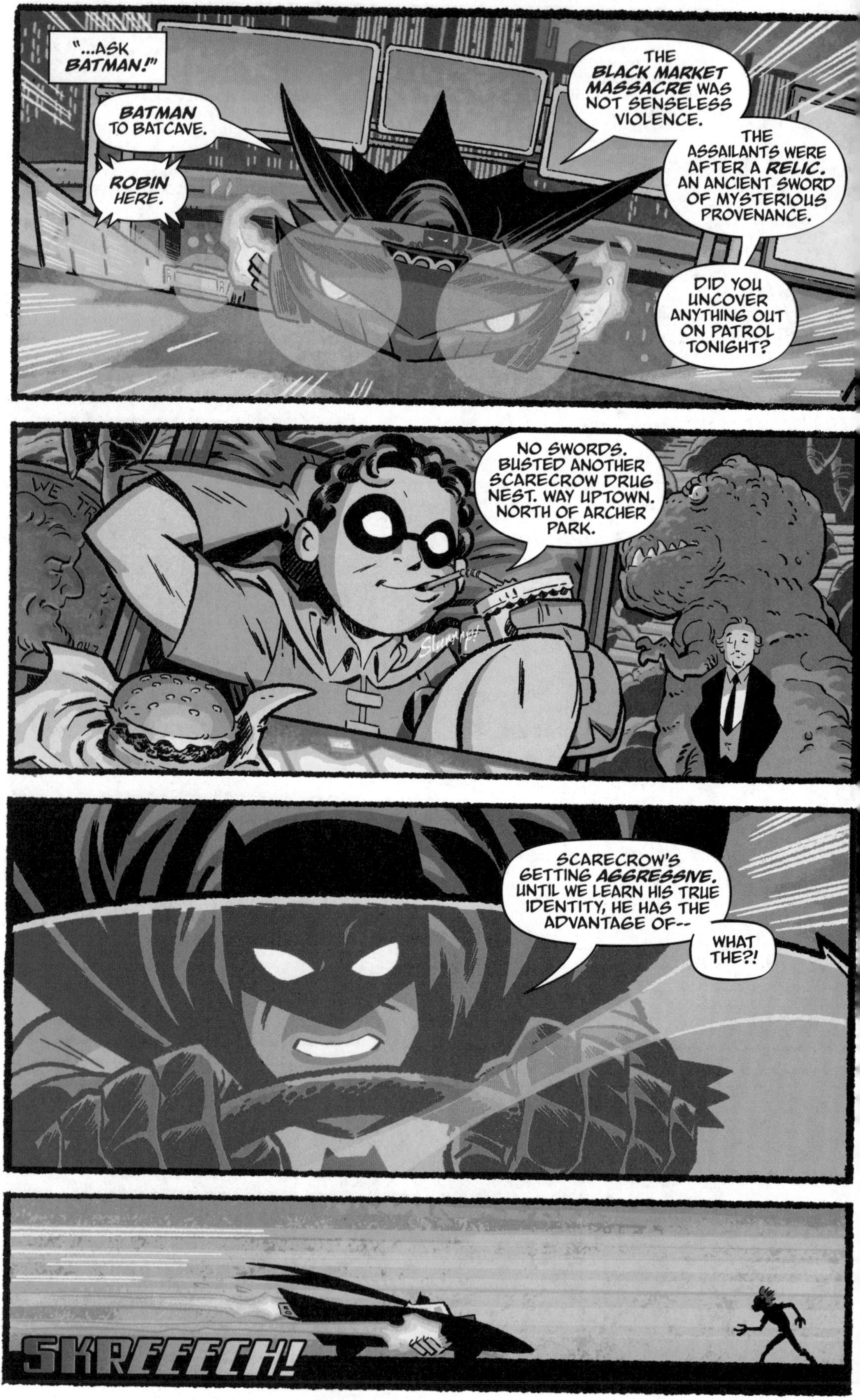
"...ASK BATMAN!"
BATMAN TO BATCAVE.
ROBIN HERE.
THE BLACK MARKET MASSACRE WAS NOT SENSELESS VIOLENCE.
THE ASSAILANTS WERE AFTER A RELIC. AN ANCIENT SWORD OF MYSTERIOUS PROVENANCE.
DID YOU UNCOVER ANYTHING OUT ON PATROL TONIGHT?
NO SWORDS. BUSTED ANOTHER SCARECROW DRUG NEST. WAY UPTOWN. NORTH OF ARCHER PARK.
SCARECROW'S GETTING AGGRESSIVE. UNTIL WE LEARN HIS TRUE IDENTITY, HE HAS THE ADVANTAGE OF--
WHAT THE?!
SKREEECH!

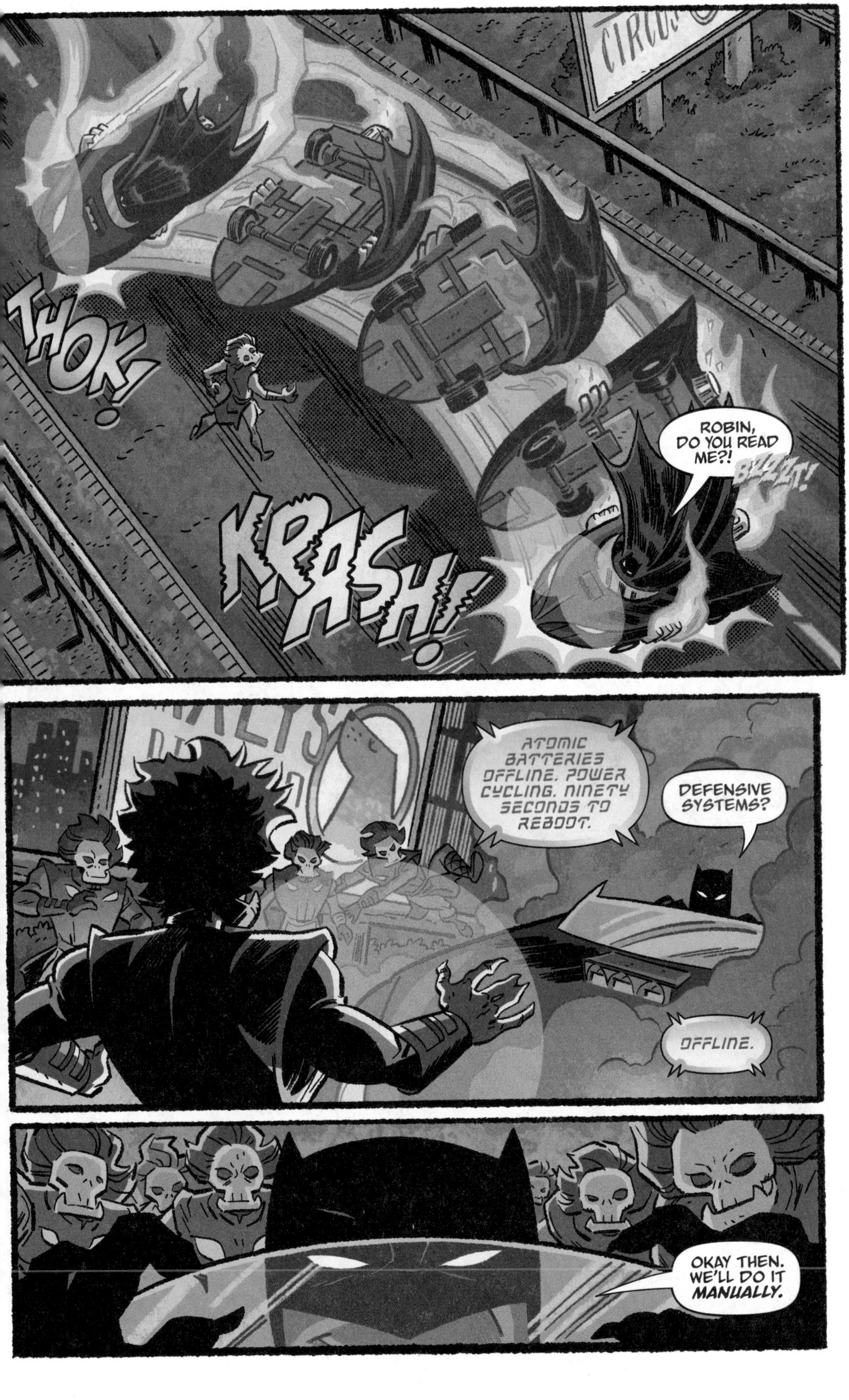
THOK!
KRASH!
ROBIN, DO YOU READ ME?!
BZZZT!
ATOMIC BATTERIES OFFLINE. POWER CYCLING. NINETY SECONDS TO REBOOT.
DEFENSIVE SYSTEMS?
OFFLINE.
OKAY THEN. WE'LL DO IT *MANUALLY.*

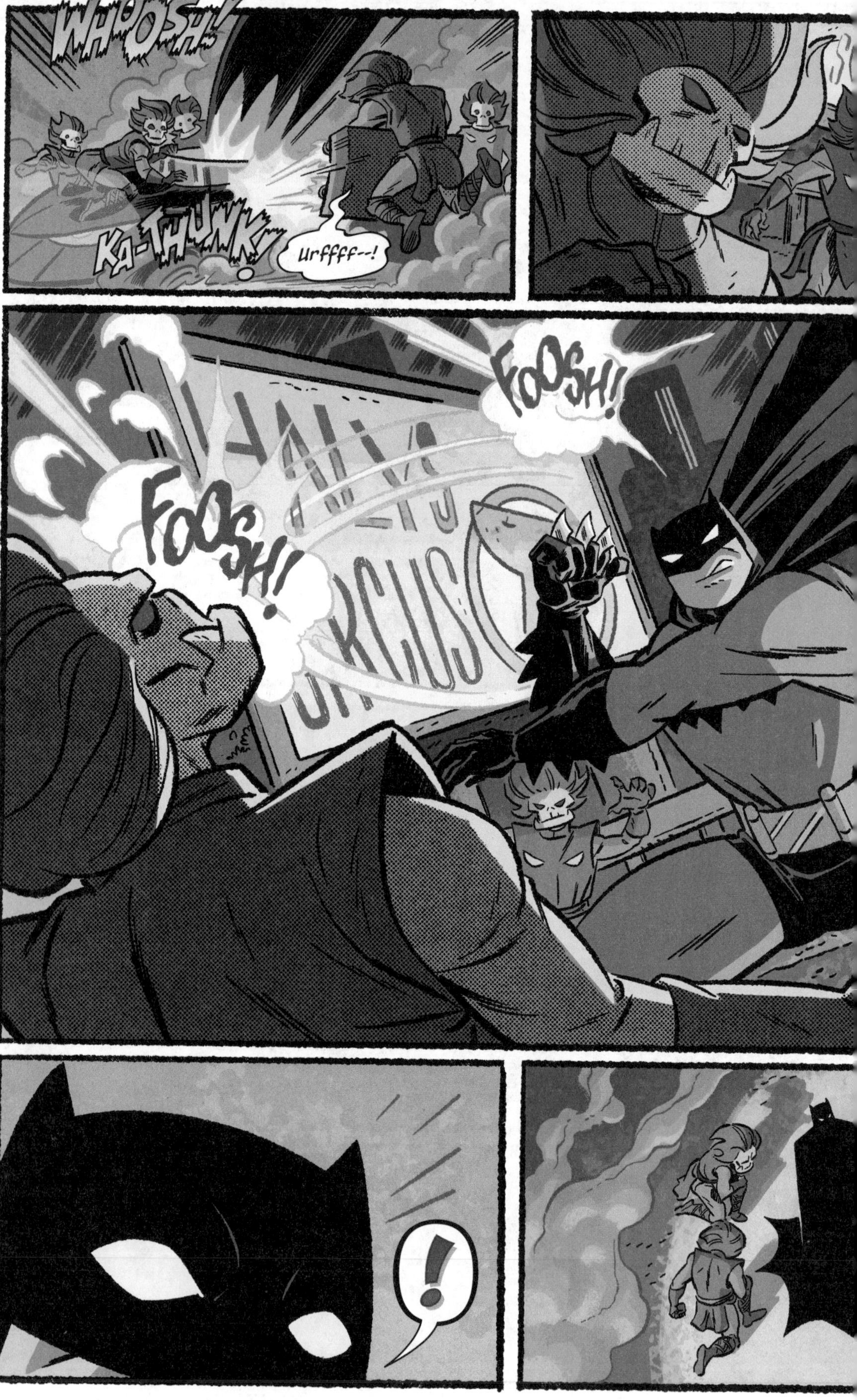
WHOOSH!
KA-THUNK!
Urffff--!
FOOSH!!
FOOSH!!
!

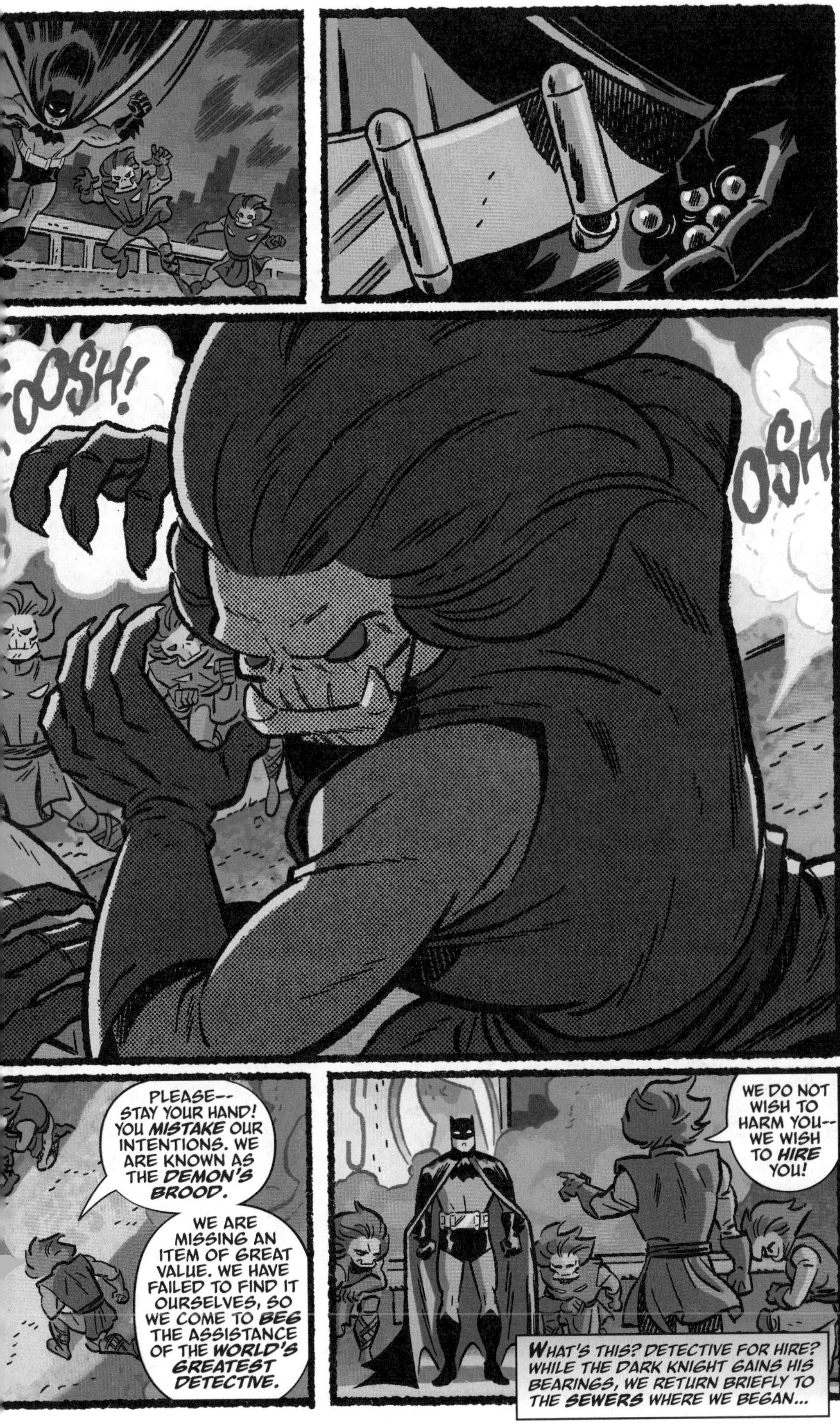
OOSH!
OOSH
PLEASE-- STAY YOUR HAND! YOU MISTAKE OUR INTENTIONS. WE ARE KNOWN AS THE DEMON'S BROOD.
WE ARE MISSING AN ITEM OF GREAT VALUE. WE HAVE FAILED TO FIND IT OURSELVES, SO WE COME TO BEG THE ASSISTANCE OF THE WORLD'S GREATEST DETECTIVE.
WE DO NOT WISH TO HARM YOU-- WE WISH TO HIRE YOU!
WHAT'S THIS? DETECTIVE FOR HIRE? WHILE THE DARK KNIGHT GAINS HIS BEARINGS, WE RETURN BRIEFLY TO THE SEWERS WHERE WE BEGAN...

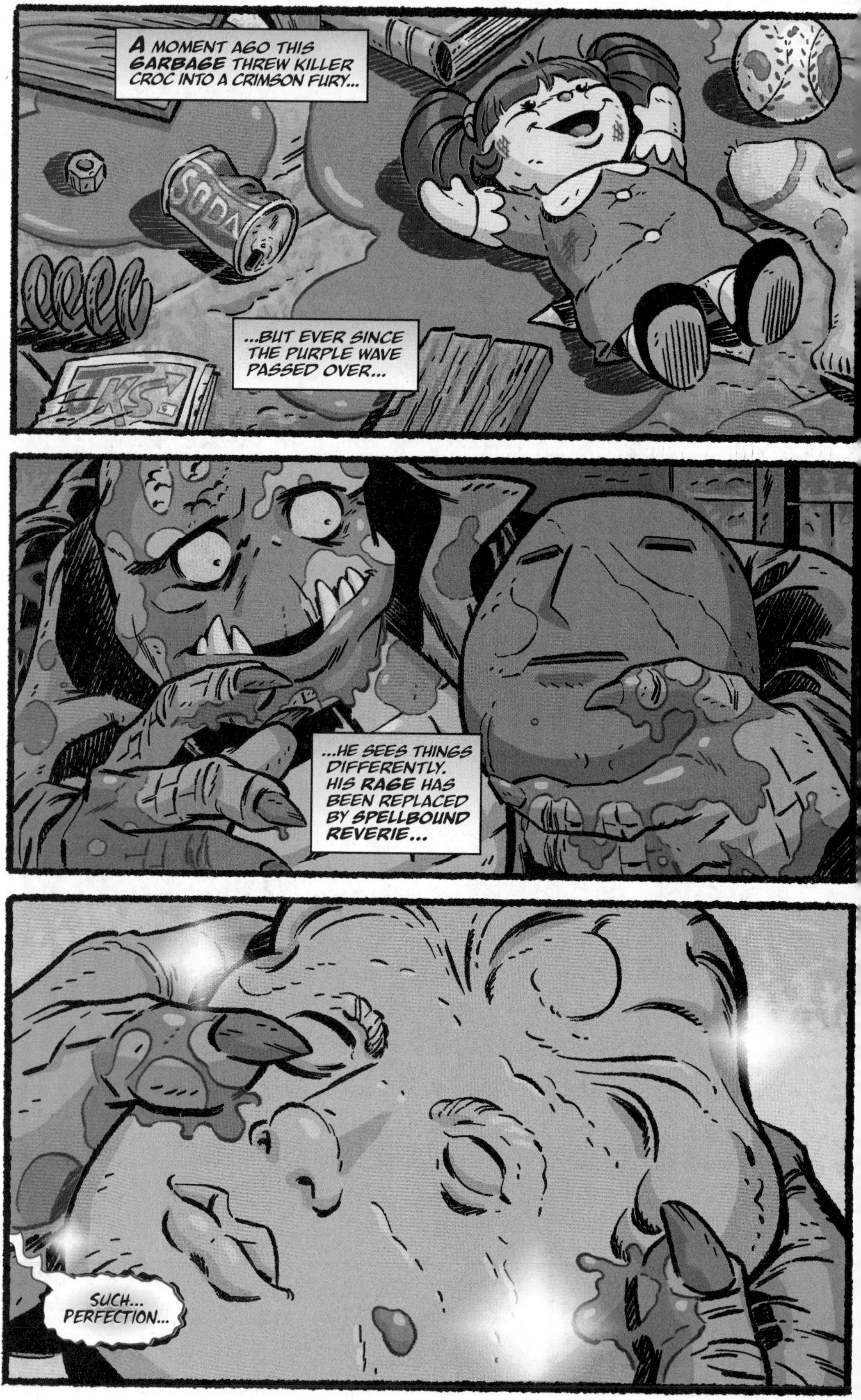

A MOMENT AGO THIS GARBAGE THREW KILLER CROC INTO A CRIMSON FURY...
SODA
...BUT EVER SINCE THE PURPLE WAVE PASSED OVER...
...HE SEES THINGS DIFFERENTLY. HIS RAGE HAS BEEN REPLACED BY SPELLBOUND REVERIE...
SUCH... PERFECTION...

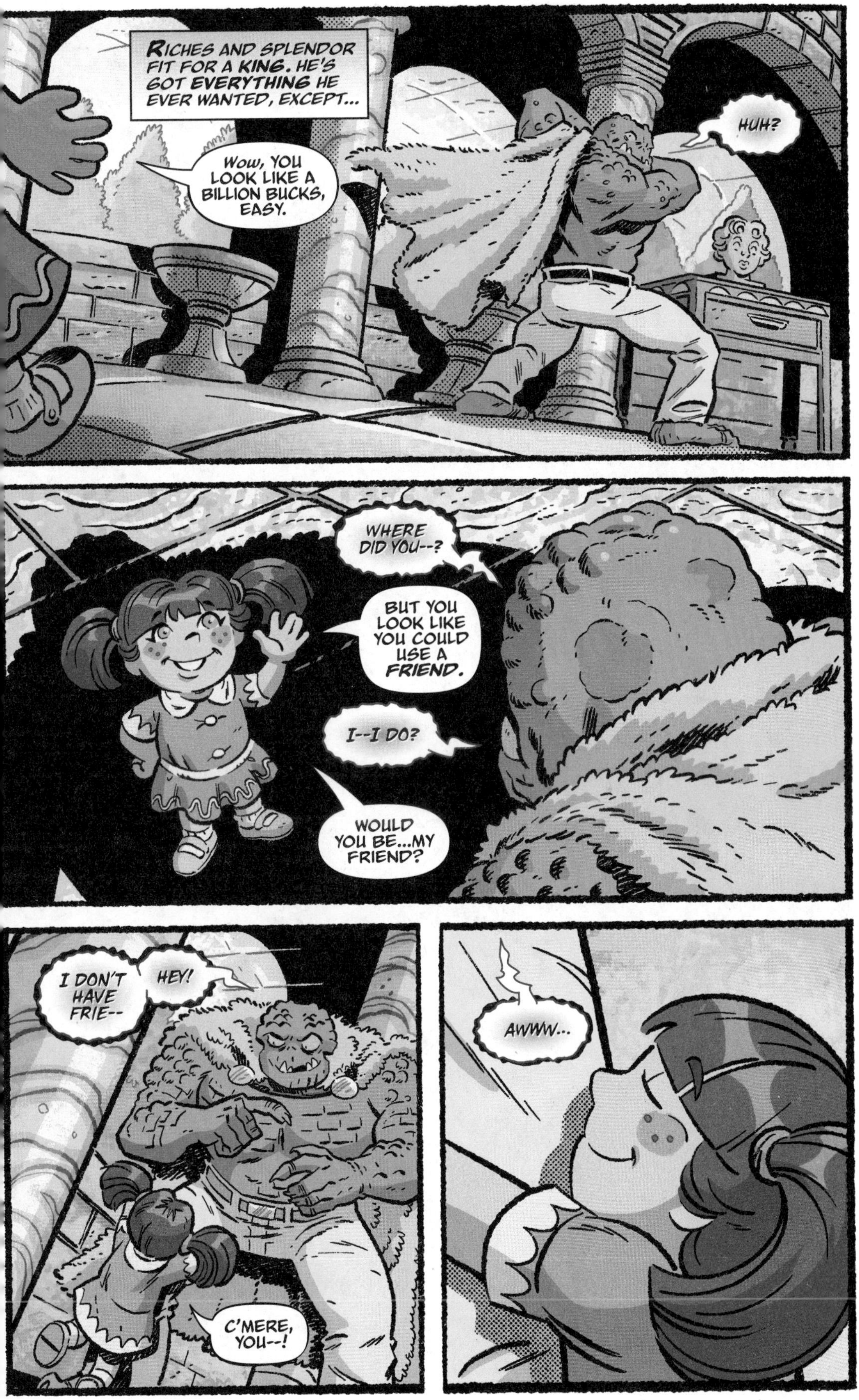
RICHES AND SPLENDOR FIT FOR A KING. HE'S GOT EVERYTHING HE EVER WANTED, EXCEPT...
WOW, YOU LOOK LIKE A BILLION BUCKS, EASY.
HUH?
WHERE DID YOU--?
BUT YOU LOOK LIKE YOU COULD USE A FRIEND.
I--I DO?
WOULD YOU BE...MY FRIEND?
I DON'T HAVE FRIE--
HEY!
C'MERE, YOU--!
AWWW...

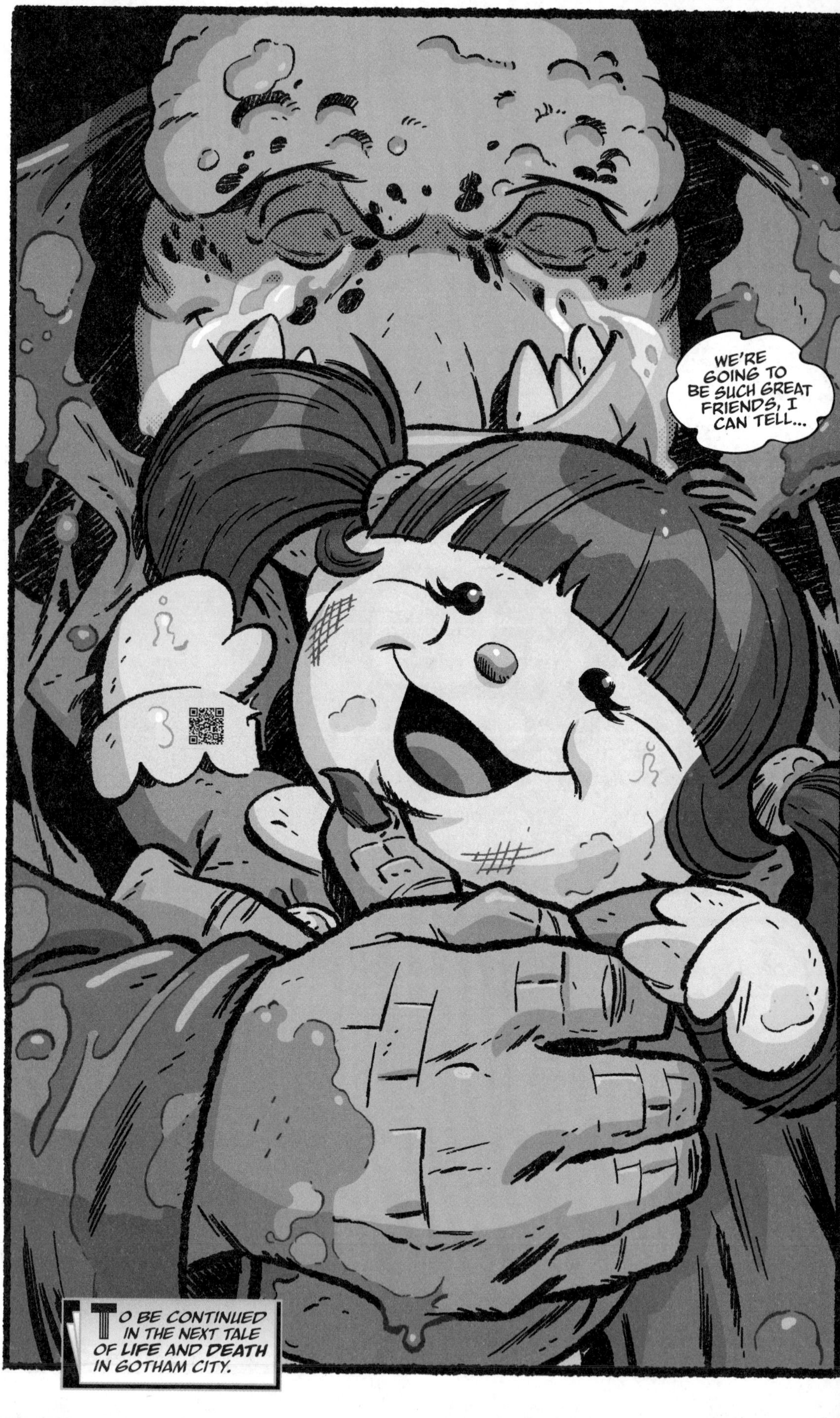
WE'RE GOING TO BE SUCH GREAT FRIENDS, I CAN TELL...
TO BE CONTINUED IN THE NEXT TALE OF LIFE AND DEATH IN GOTHAM CITY.

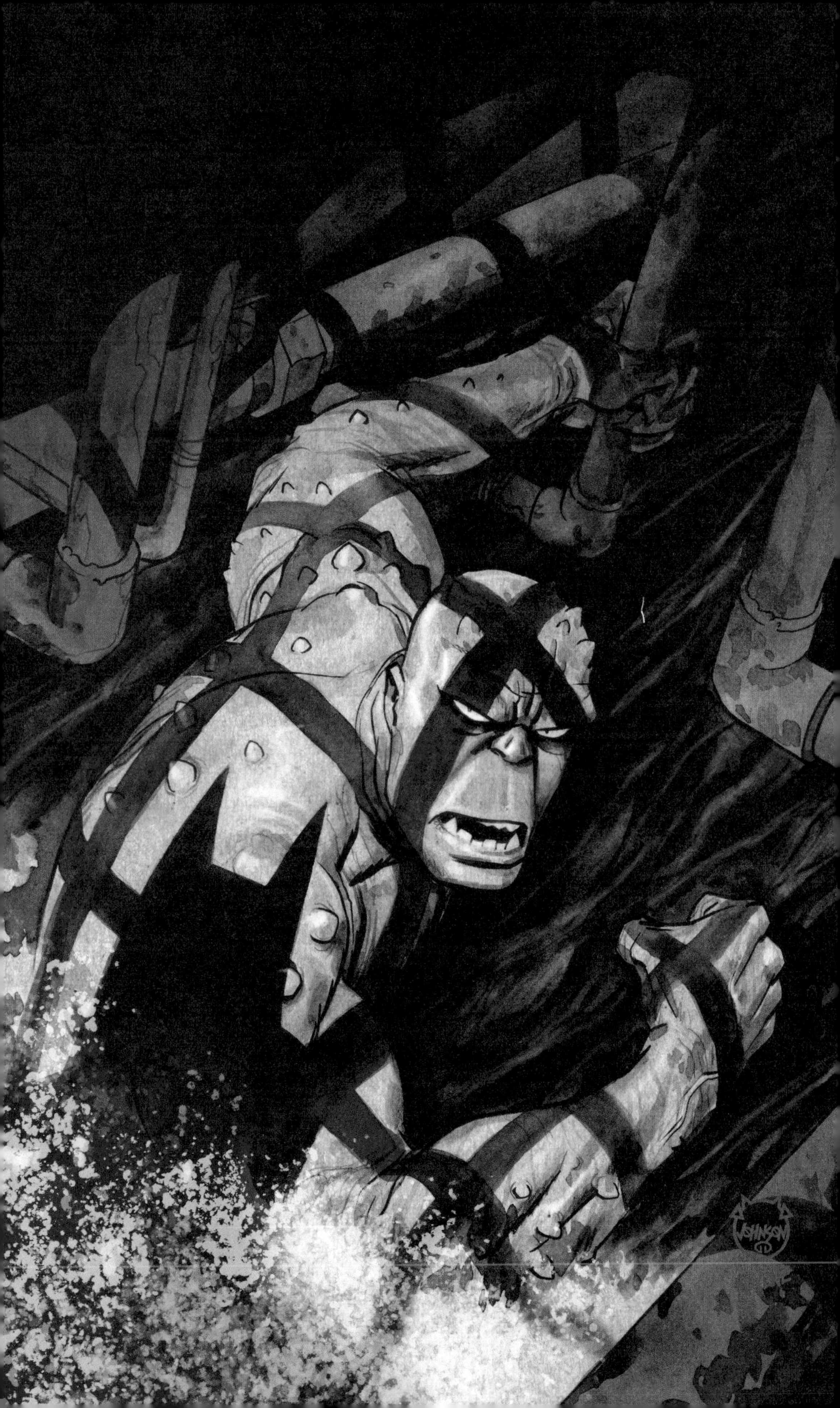

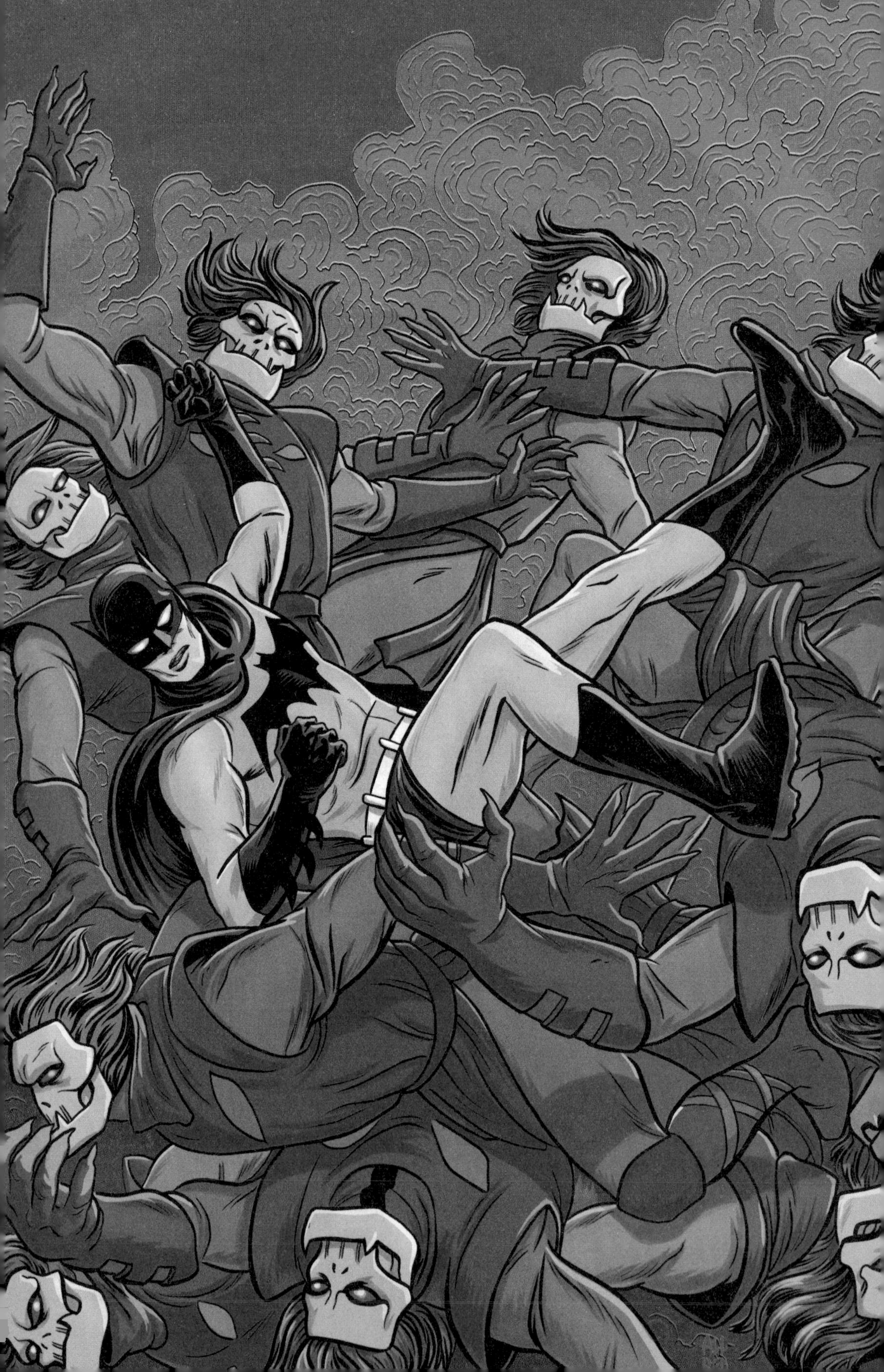

***Batman: The Audio Adventures* #2 variant cover by Michael Allred & Laura Allred**

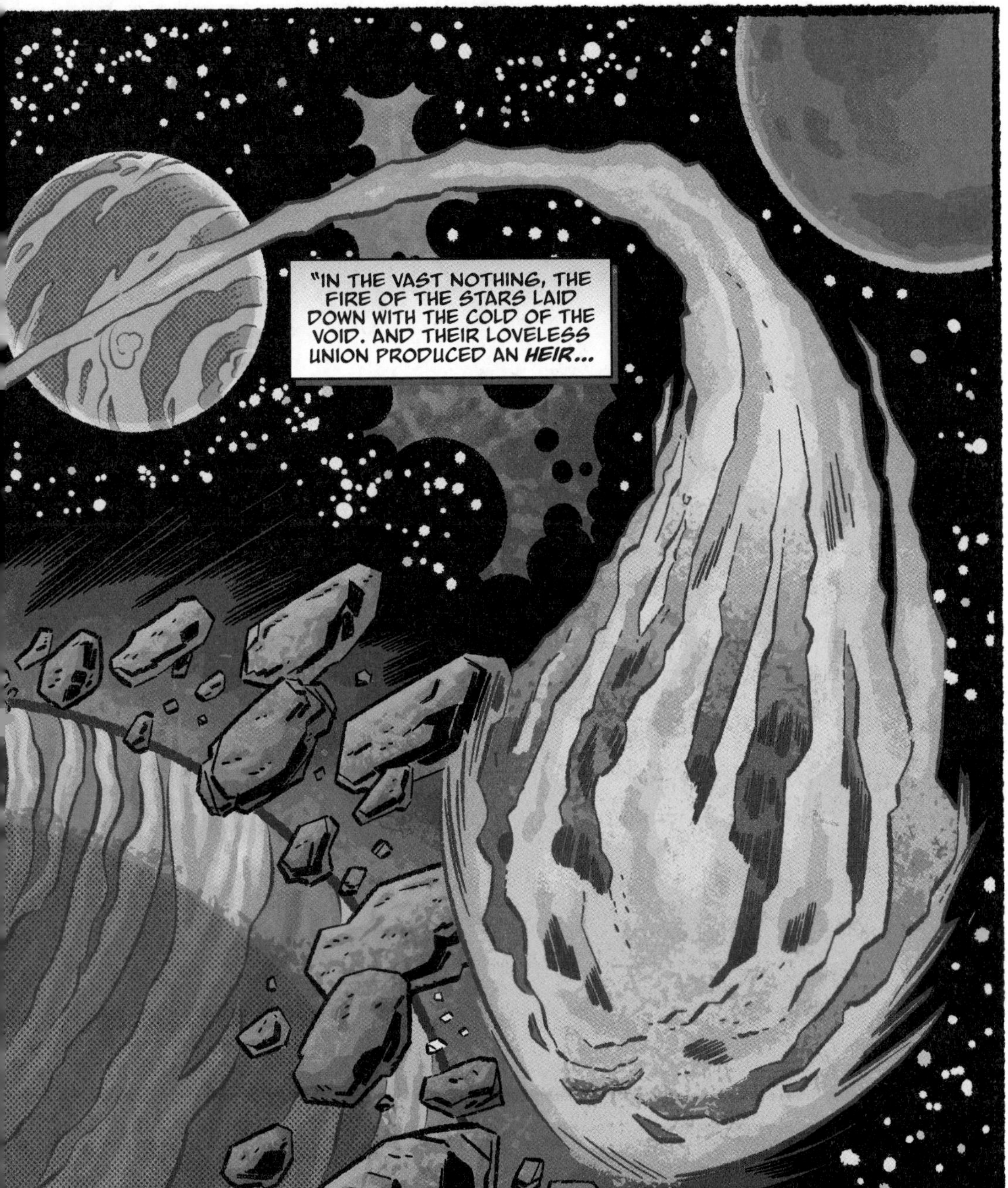
"IN THE VAST NOTHING, THE FIRE OF THE STARS LAID DOWN WITH THE COLD OF THE VOID. AND THEIR LOVELESS UNION PRODUCED AN *HEIR*...
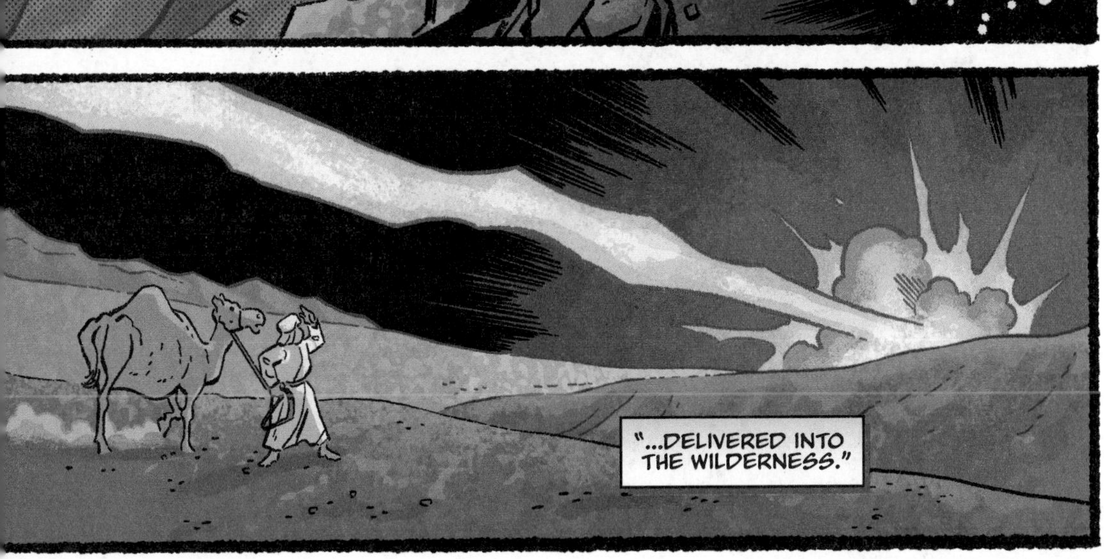
"...DELIVERED INTO THE WILDERNESS."

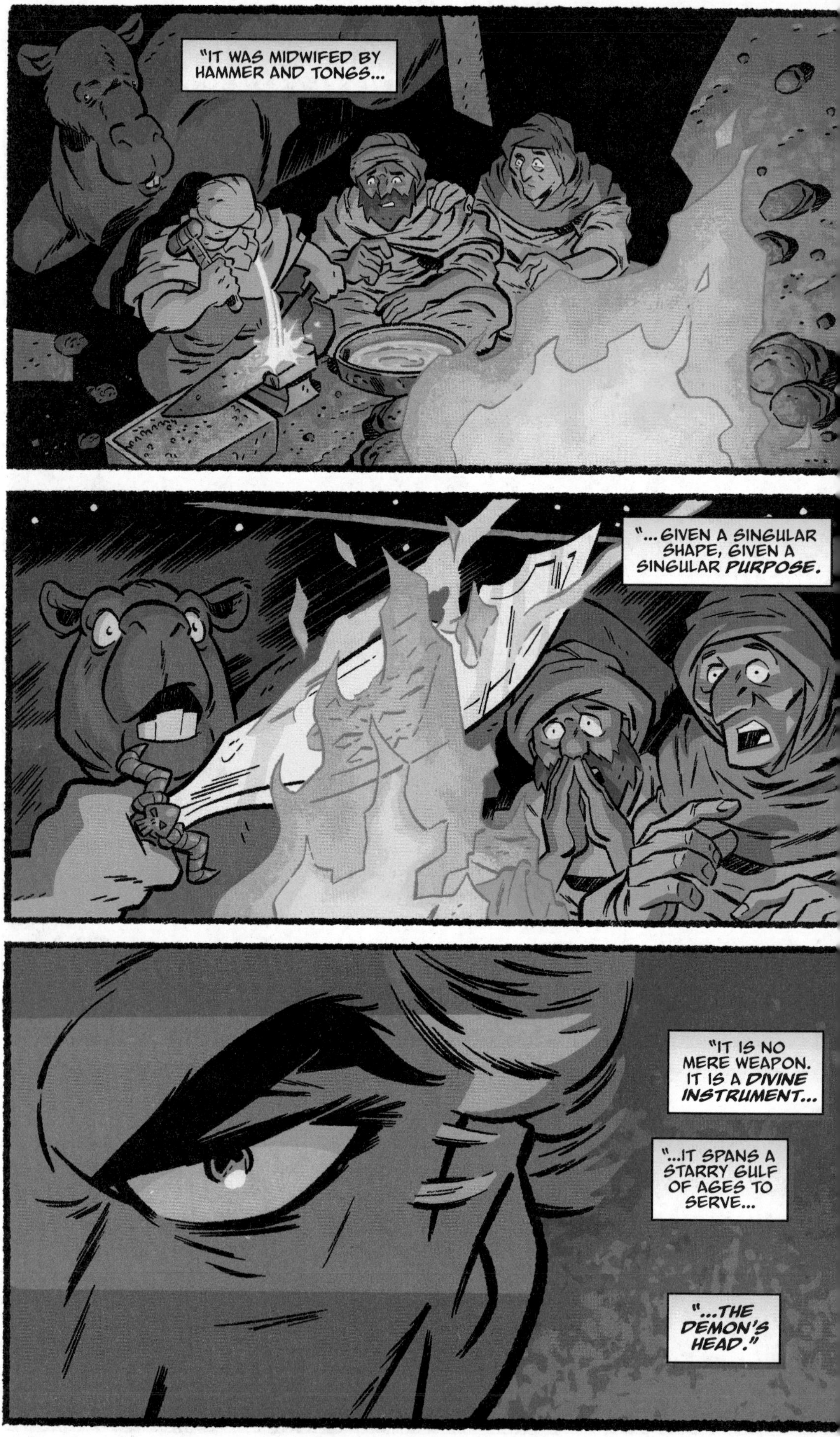
"IT WAS MIDWIFED BY HAMMER AND TONGS...
"...GIVEN A SINGULAR SHAPE, GIVEN A SINGULAR *PURPOSE*.
"IT IS NO MERE WEAPON. IT IS A *DIVINE INSTRUMENT*...
"...IT SPANS A STARRY GULF OF AGES TO SERVE...
"*...THE DEMON'S HEAD.*"

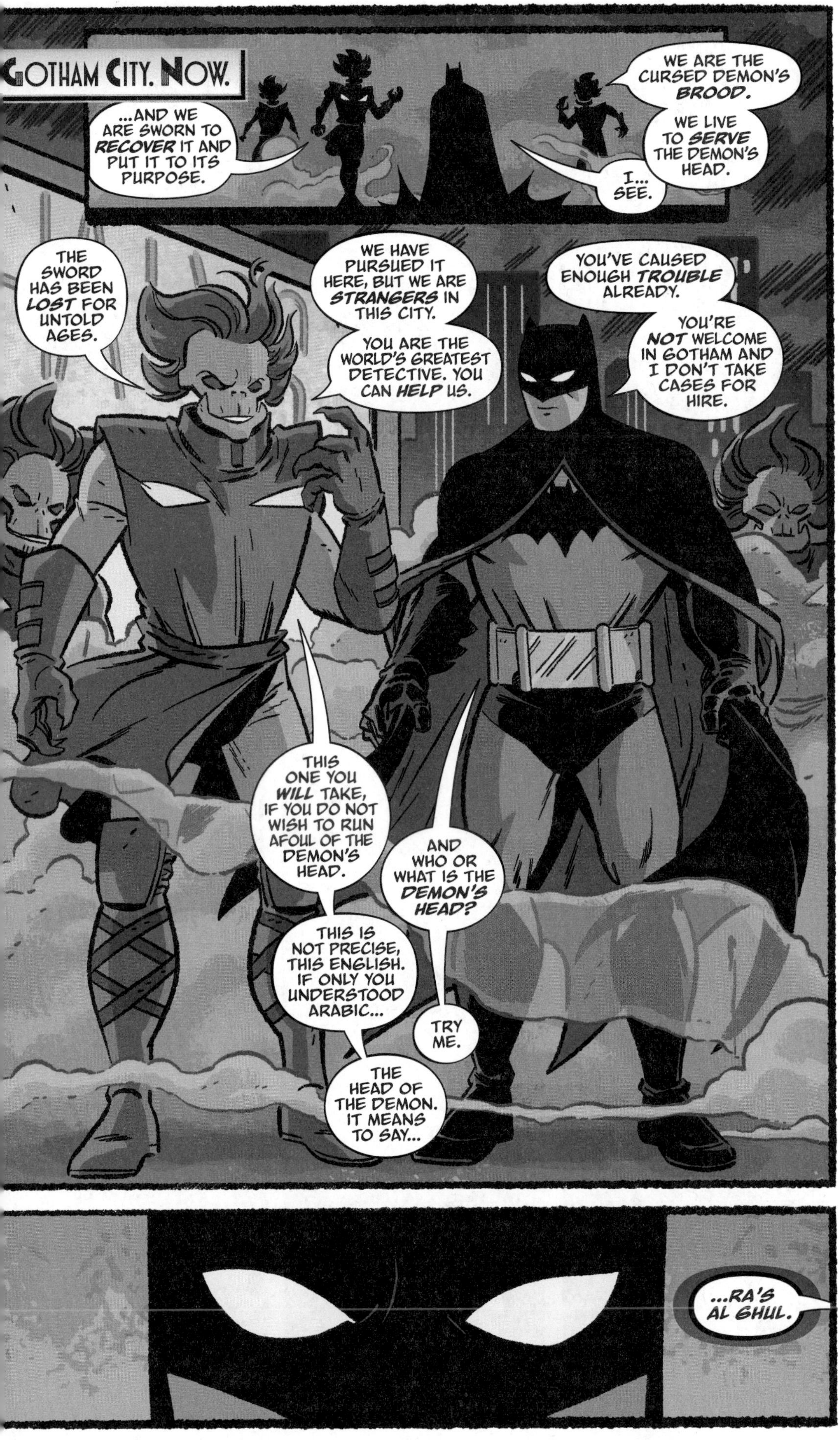

GOTHAM CITY. NOW.
...AND WE ARE SWORN TO RECOVER IT AND PUT IT TO ITS PURPOSE.
WE ARE THE CURSED DEMON'S BROOD.
WE LIVE TO SERVE THE DEMON'S HEAD.
I... SEE.
THE SWORD HAS BEEN LOST FOR UNTOLD AGES.
WE HAVE PURSUED IT HERE, BUT WE ARE STRANGERS IN THIS CITY.
YOU ARE THE WORLD'S GREATEST DETECTIVE. YOU CAN HELP US.
YOU'VE CAUSED ENOUGH TROUBLE ALREADY.
YOU'RE NOT WELCOME IN GOTHAM AND I DON'T TAKE CASES FOR HIRE.
THIS ONE YOU WILL TAKE, IF YOU DO NOT WISH TO RUN AFOUL OF THE DEMON'S HEAD.
AND WHO OR WHAT IS THE DEMON'S HEAD?
THIS IS NOT PRECISE, THIS ENGLISH. IF ONLY YOU UNDERSTOOD ARABIC...
TRY ME.
THE HEAD OF THE DEMON. IT MEANS TO SAY...
...RA'S AL GHUL.

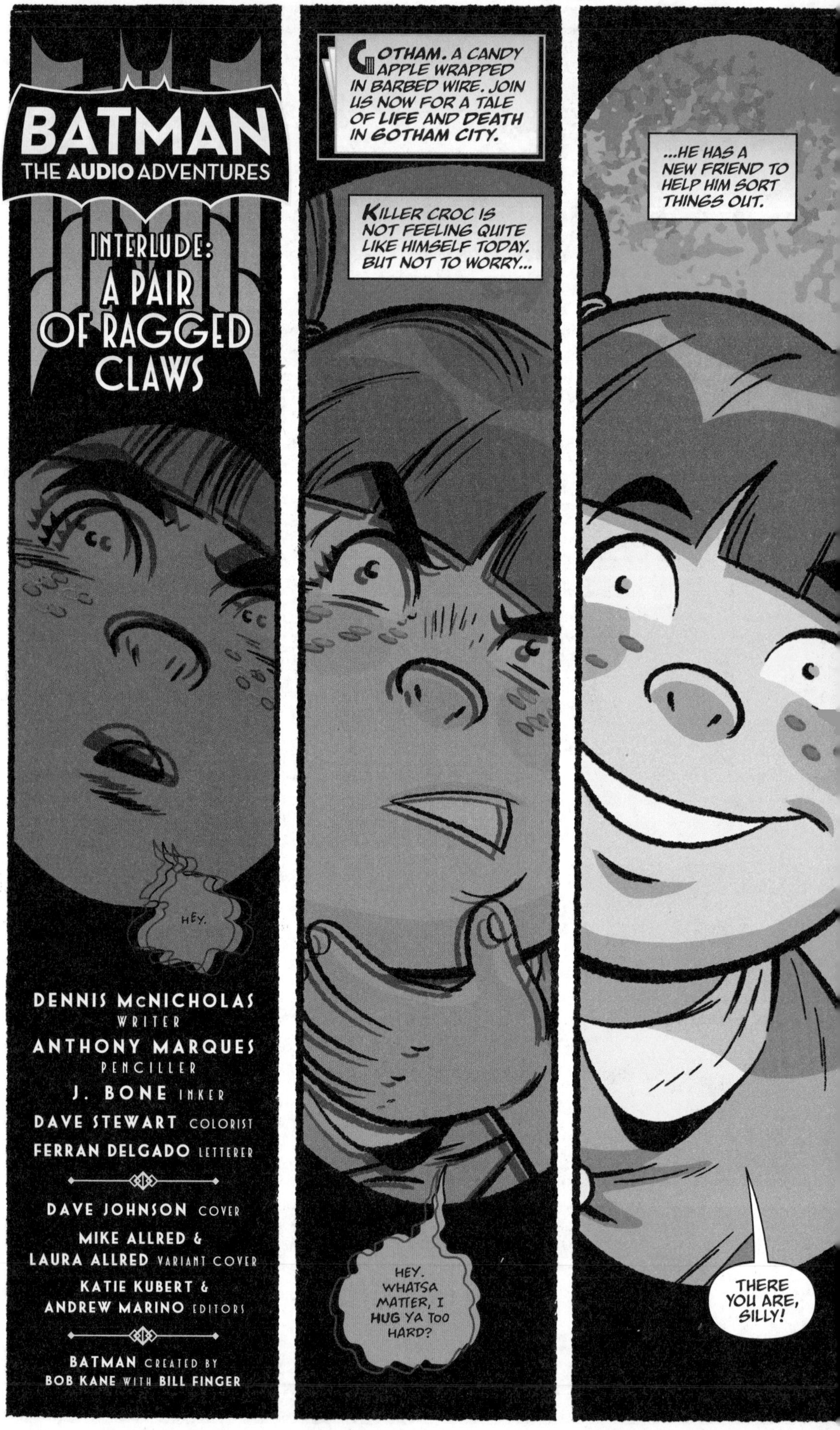
BATMAN
THE AUDIO ADVENTURES
INTERLUDE:
A PAIR OF RAGGED CLAWS
HEY.
DENNIS McNICHOLAS WRITER
ANTHONY MARQUES PENCILLER
J. BONE INKER
DAVE STEWART COLORIST
FERRAN DELGADO LETTERER
DAVE JOHNSON COVER
MIKE ALLRED & LAURA ALLRED VARIANT COVER
KATIE KUBERT & ANDREW MARINO EDITORS
BATMAN CREATED BY BOB KANE WITH BILL FINGER
GOTHAM. A CANDY APPLE WRAPPED IN BARBED WIRE. JOIN US NOW FOR A TALE OF LIFE AND DEATH IN GOTHAM CITY.
KILLER CROC IS NOT FEELING QUITE LIKE HIMSELF TODAY. BUT NOT TO WORRY...
HEY. WHATSA MATTER, I HUG YA TOO HARD?
...HE HAS A NEW FRIEND TO HELP HIM SORT THINGS OUT.
THERE YOU ARE, SILLY!

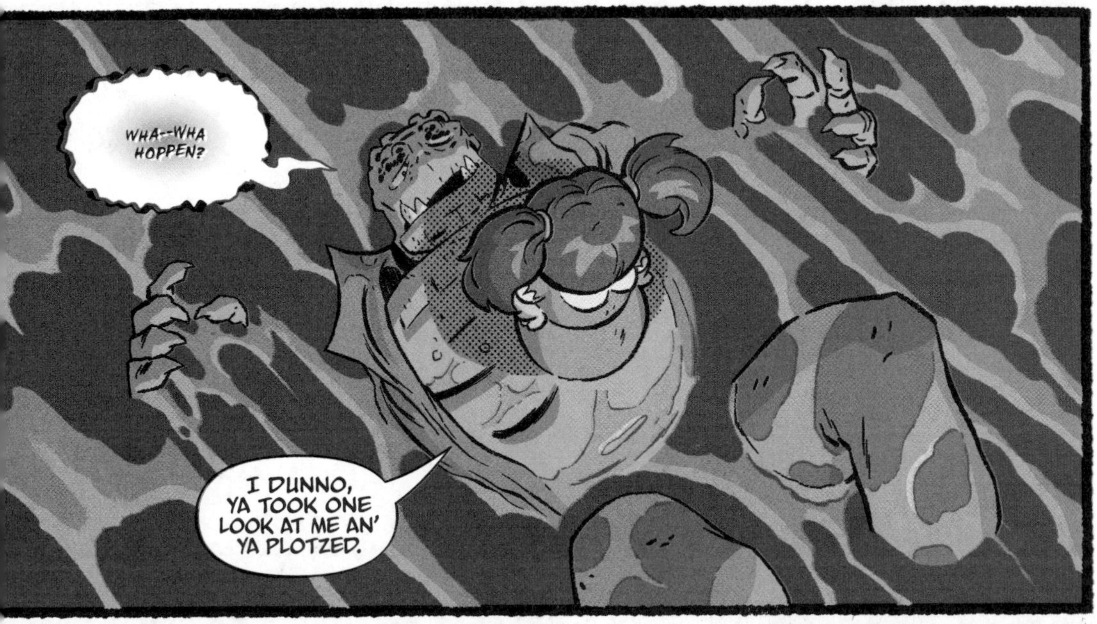
WHA--WHA HOPPEN?
I DUNNO, YA TOOK ONE LOOK AT ME AN' YA PLOTZED.

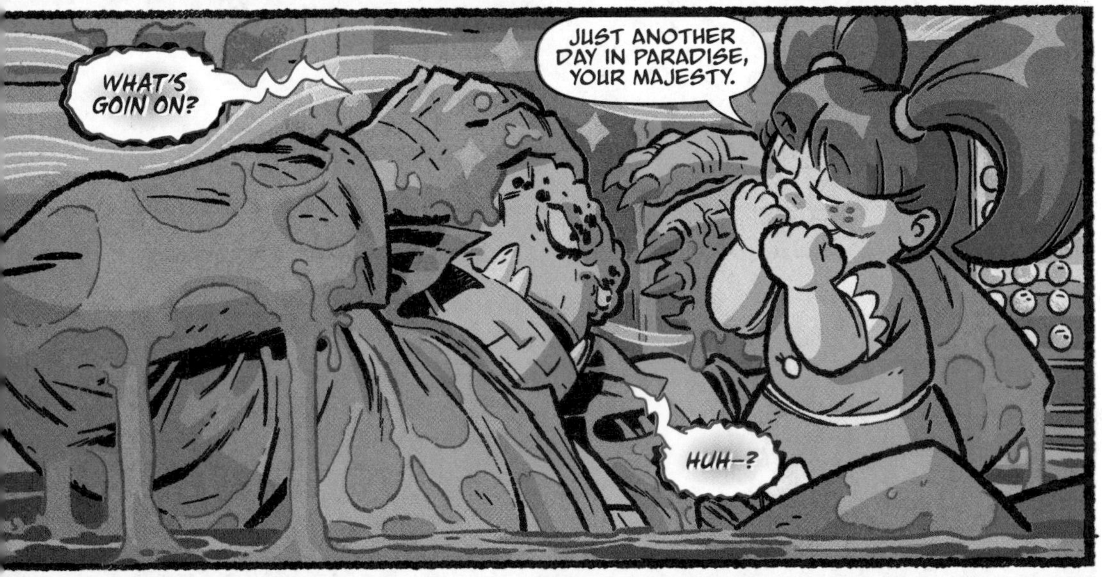
WHAT'S GOIN ON?
JUST ANOTHER DAY IN PARADISE, YOUR MAJESTY.
HUH--?

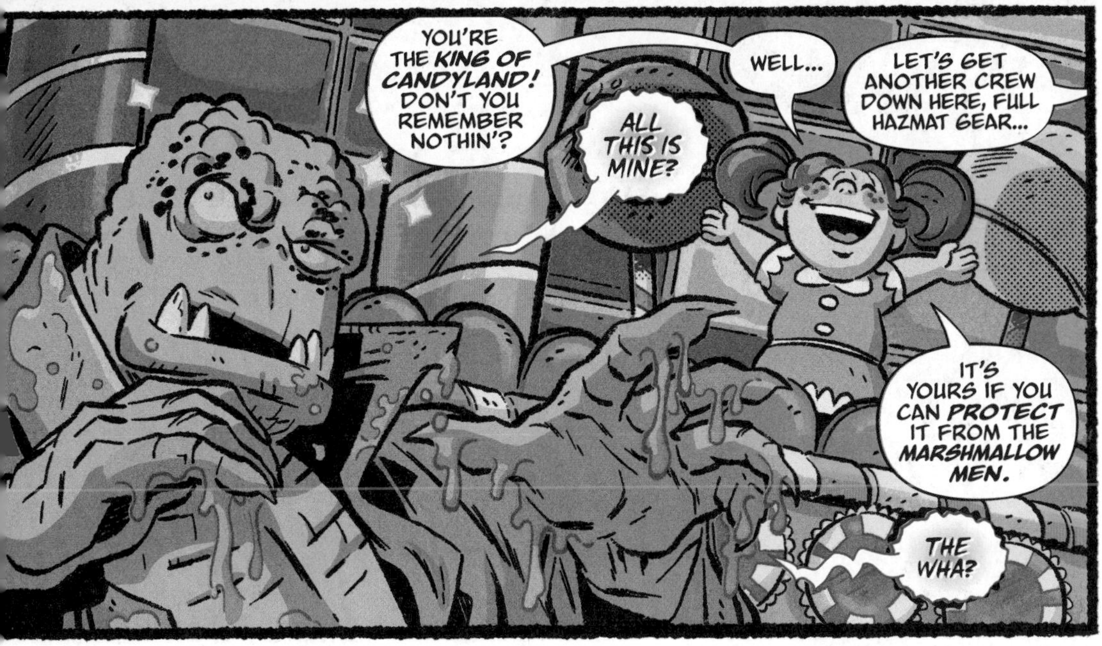
YOU'RE THE *KING OF CANDYLAND!* DON'T YOU REMEMBER NOTHIN'?
WELL...
LET'S GET ANOTHER CREW DOWN HERE, FULL HAZMAT GEAR...
ALL THIS IS MINE?
IT'S YOURS IF YOU CAN *PROTECT* IT FROM THE *MARSHMALLOW MEN.*
THE WHA?

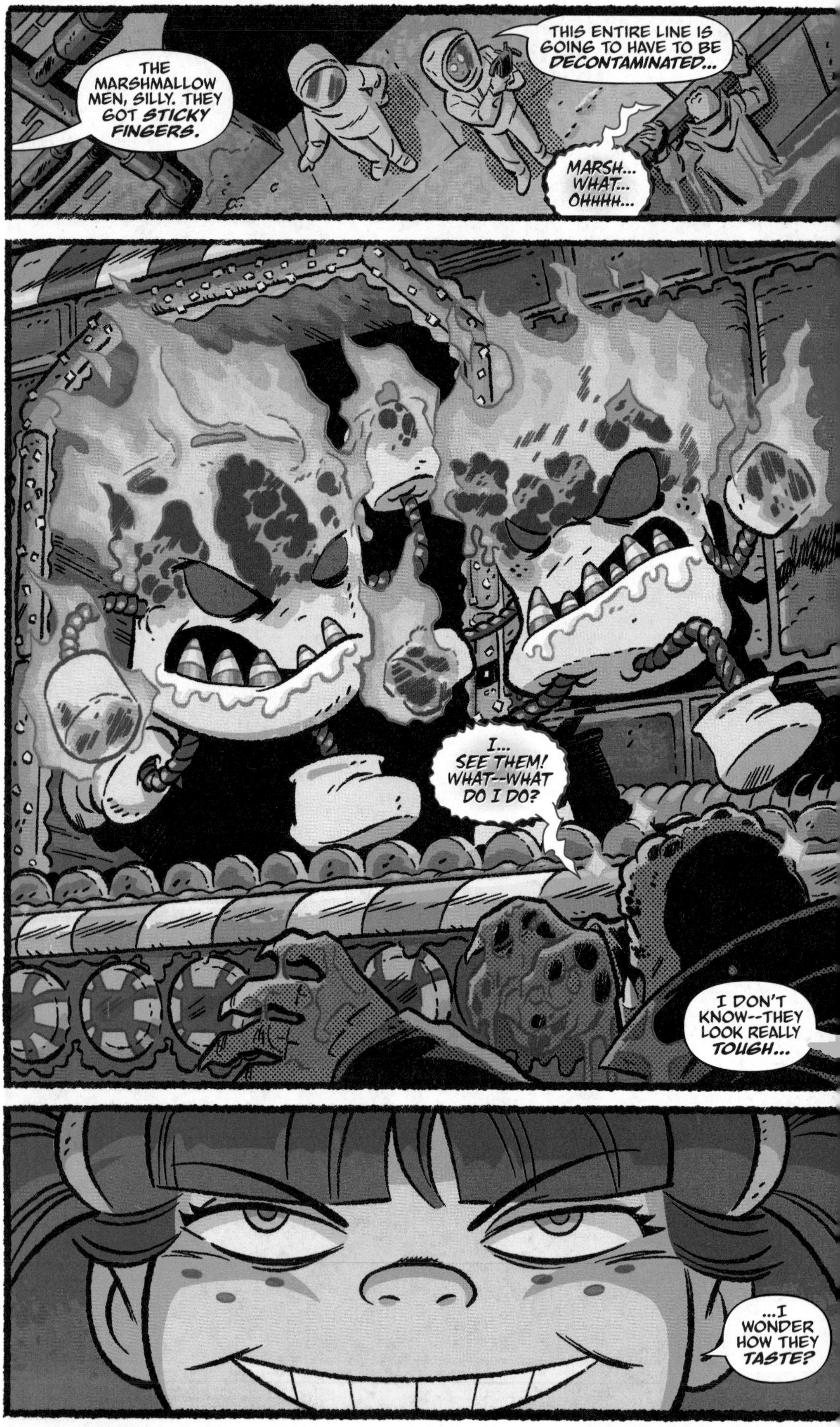
THE MARSHMALLOW MEN, SILLY. THEY GOT *STICKY FINGERS*.
THIS ENTIRE LINE IS GOING TO HAVE TO BE *DECONTAMINATED*...
MARSH... WHAT... OHHHH...
I... SEE THEM! WHAT--WHAT DO I DO?
I DON'T KNOW--THEY LOOK REALLY *TOUGH*...
...I WONDER HOW THEY *TASTE*?

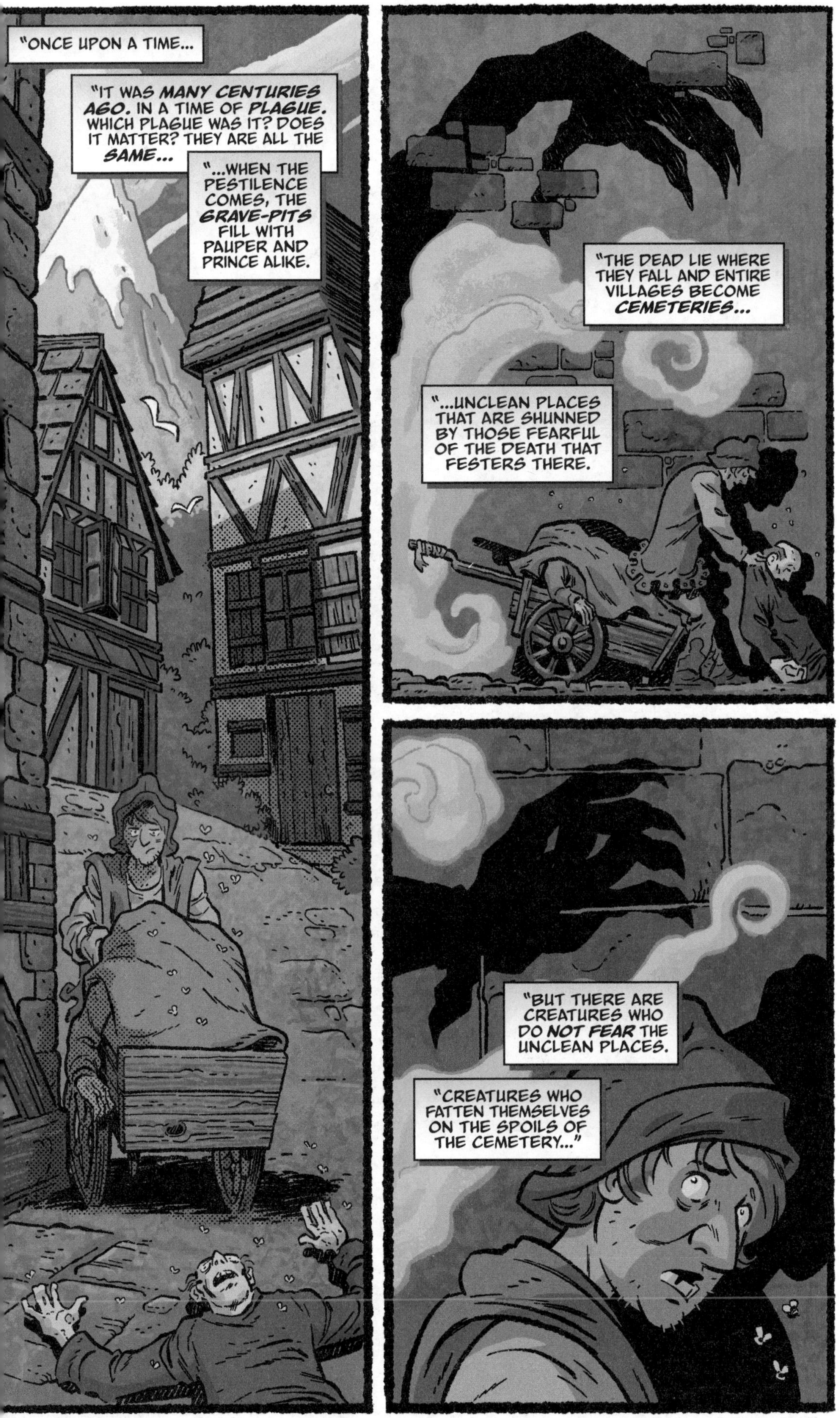
"ONCE UPON A TIME...
"IT WAS MANY CENTURIES AGO. IN A TIME OF PLAGUE. WHICH PLAGUE WAS IT? DOES IT MATTER? THEY ARE ALL THE SAME...
"...WHEN THE PESTILENCE COMES, THE GRAVE-PITS FILL WITH PAUPER AND PRINCE ALIKE.
"THE DEAD LIE WHERE THEY FALL AND ENTIRE VILLAGES BECOME CEMETERIES...
"...UNCLEAN PLACES THAT ARE SHUNNED BY THOSE FEARFUL OF THE DEATH THAT FESTERS THERE.
"BUT THERE ARE CREATURES WHO DO NOT FEAR THE UNCLEAN PLACES.
"CREATURES WHO FATTEN THEMSELVES ON THE SPOILS OF THE CEMETERY..."

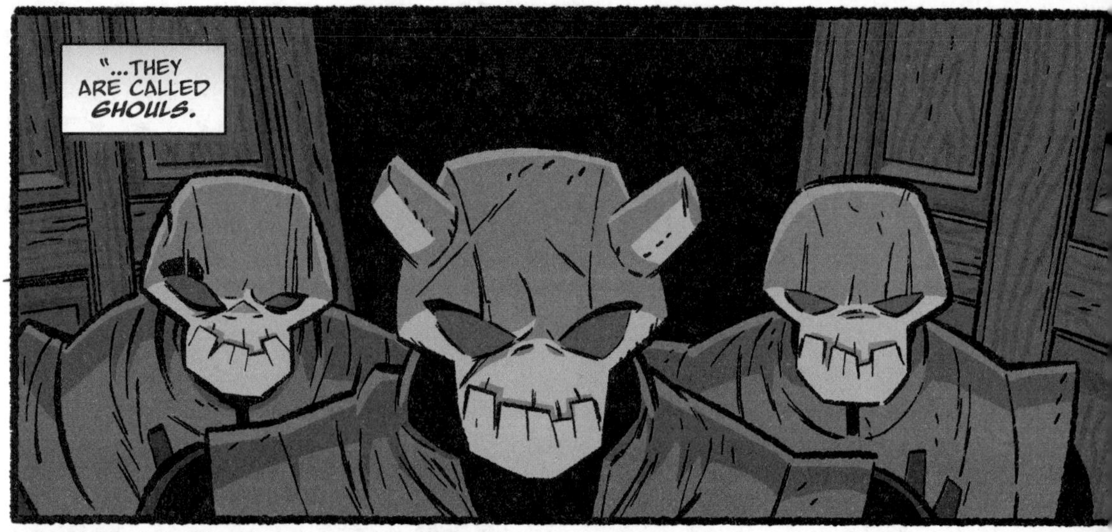
"...THEY ARE CALLED GHOULS.

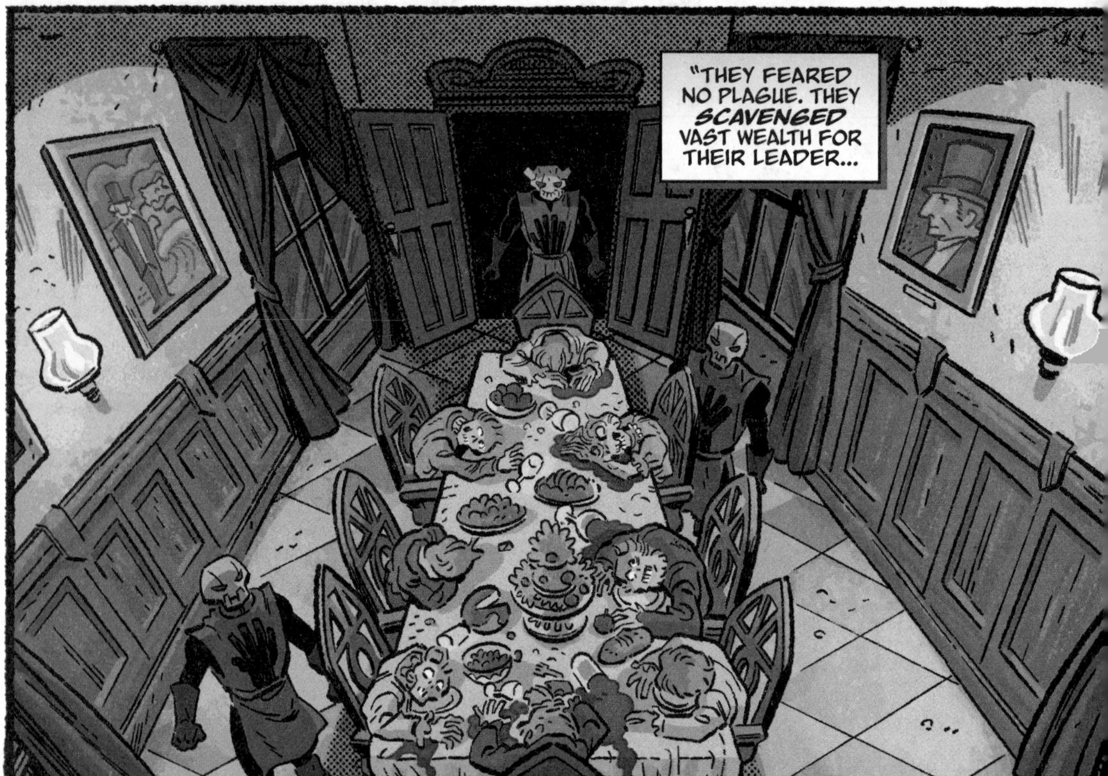
"THEY FEARED NO PLAGUE. THEY SCAVENGED VAST WEALTH FOR THEIR LEADER...

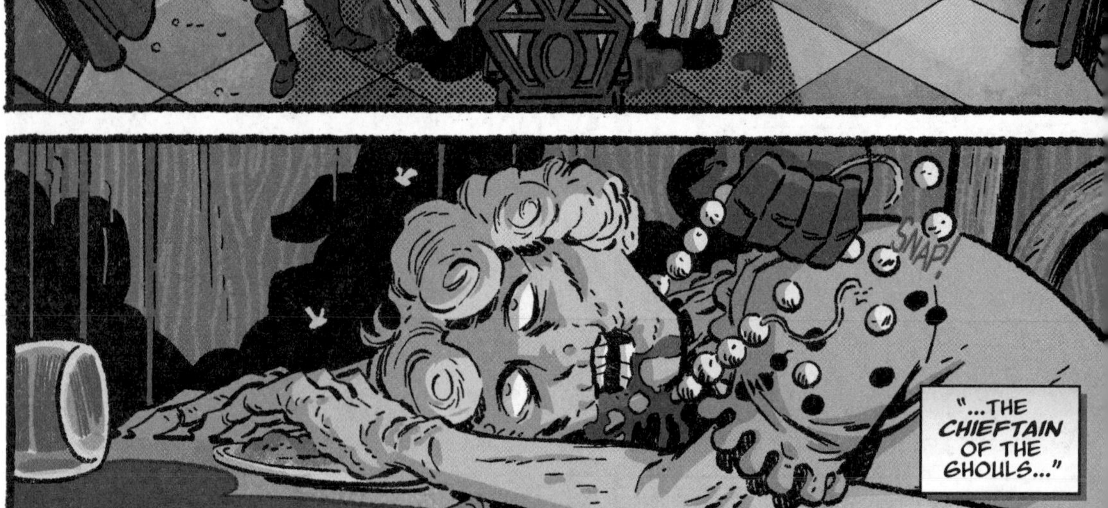
SNAP!
"...THE CHIEFTAIN OF THE GHOULS..."

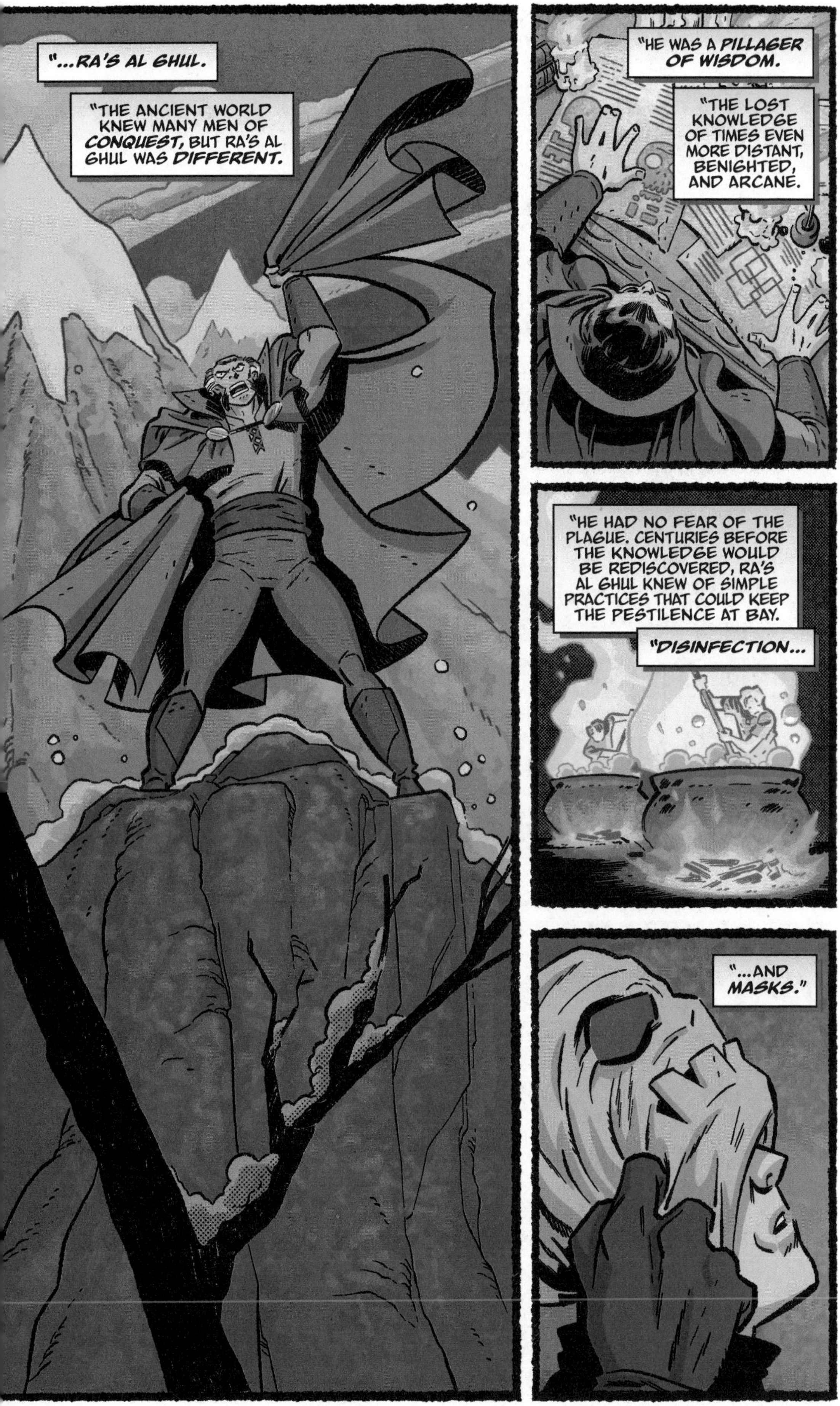
"...RA'S AL GHUL.
"THE ANCIENT WORLD KNEW MANY MEN OF CONQUEST, BUT RA'S AL GHUL WAS DIFFERENT.
"HE WAS A PILLAGER OF WISDOM.
"THE LOST KNOWLEDGE OF TIMES EVEN MORE DISTANT, BENIGHTED, AND ARCANE.
"HE HAD NO FEAR OF THE PLAGUE. CENTURIES BEFORE THE KNOWLEDGE WOULD BE REDISCOVERED, RA'S AL GHUL KNEW OF SIMPLE PRACTICES THAT COULD KEEP THE PESTILENCE AT BAY.
"DISINFECTION...
"...AND MASKS."

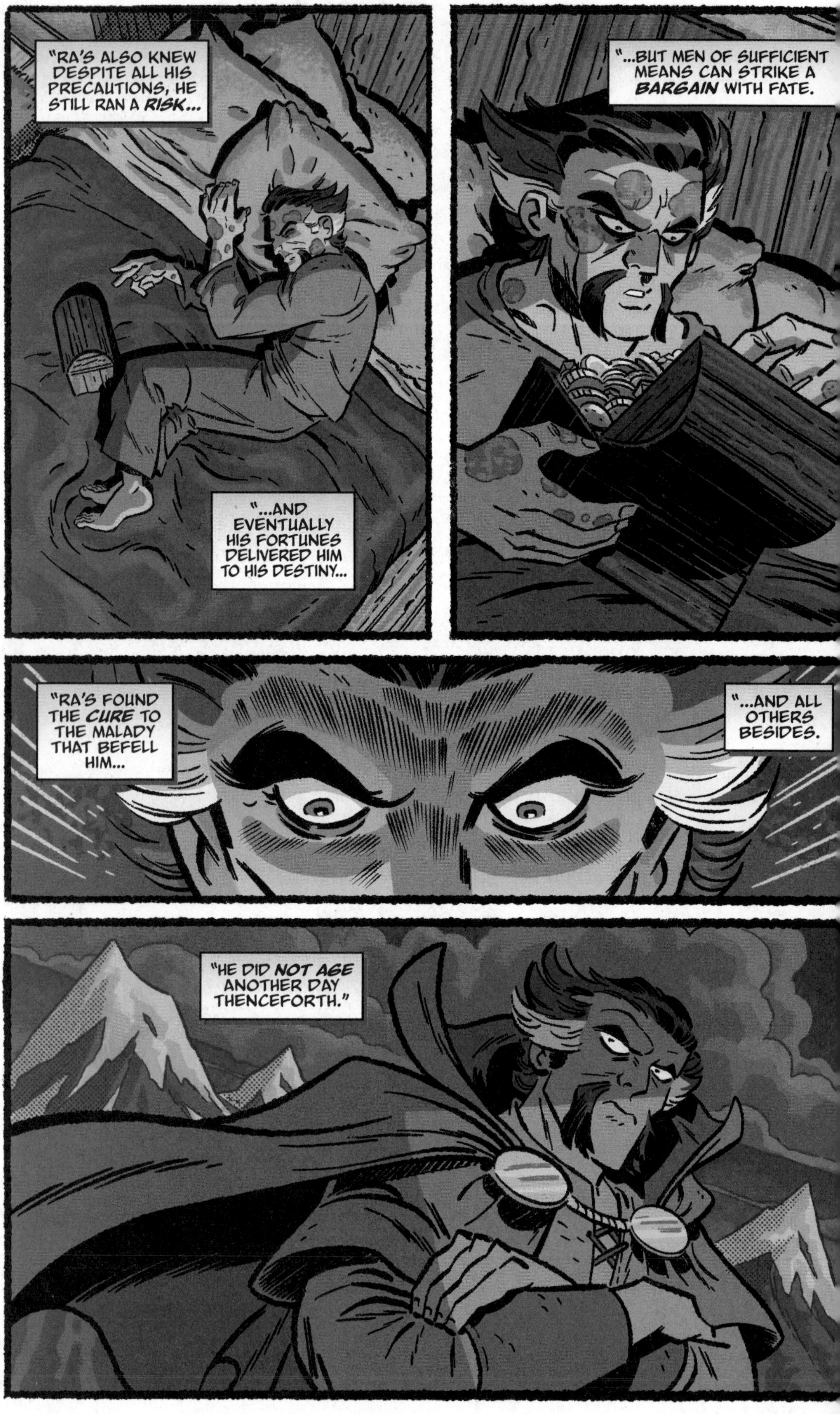
"RA'S ALSO KNEW DESPITE ALL HIS PRECAUTIONS, HE STILL RAN A *RISK*...
"...AND EVENTUALLY HIS FORTUNES DELIVERED HIM TO HIS DESTINY...
"...BUT MEN OF SUFFICIENT MEANS CAN STRIKE A *BARGAIN* WITH FATE.
"RA'S FOUND THE *CURE* TO THE MALADY THAT BEFELL HIM...
"...AND ALL OTHERS BESIDES.
"HE DID *NOT AGE* ANOTHER DAY THENCEFORTH."

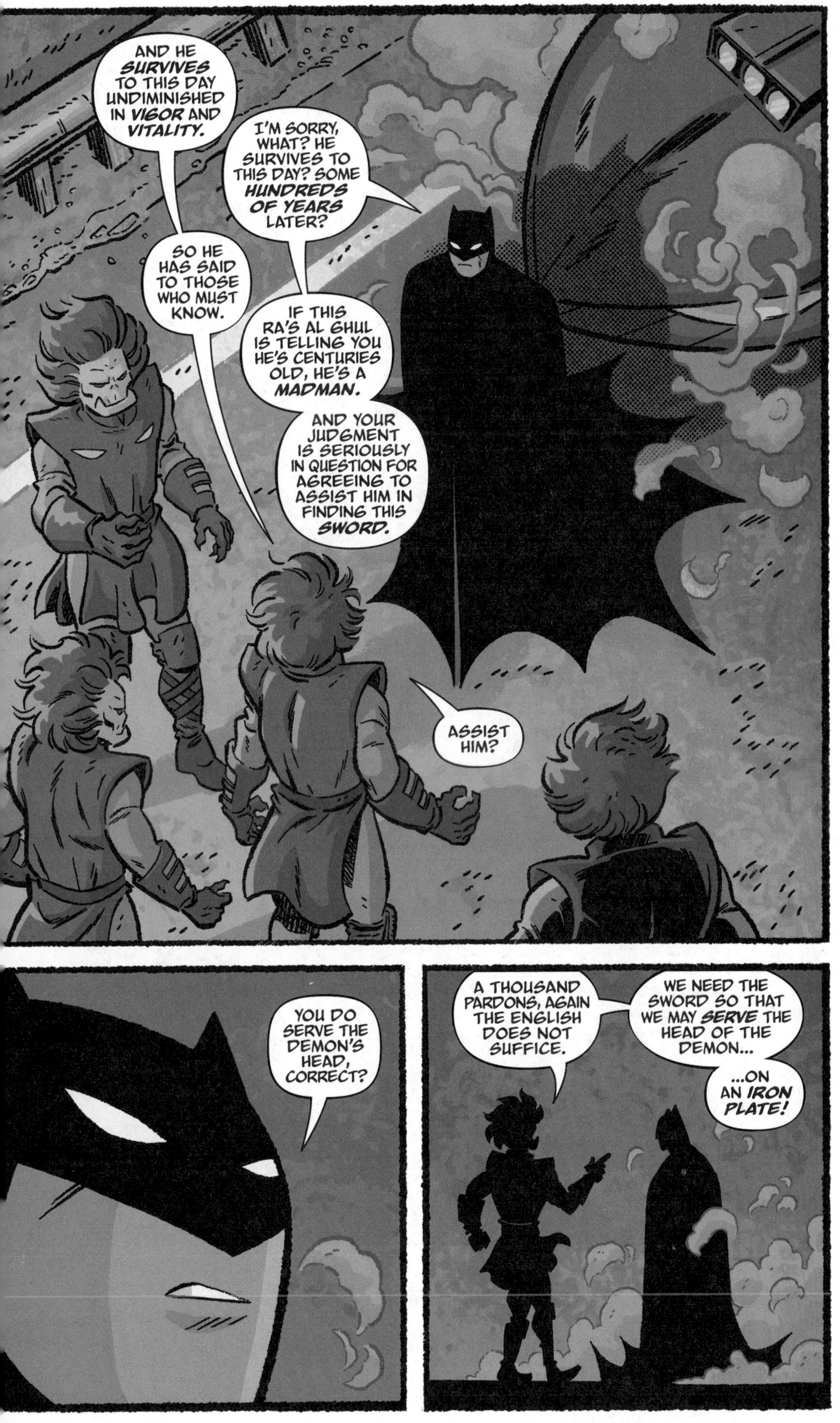
AND HE SURVIVES TO THIS DAY UNDIMINISHED IN VIGOR AND VITALITY.
I'M SORRY, WHAT? HE SURVIVES TO THIS DAY? SOME HUNDREDS OF YEARS LATER?
SO HE HAS SAID TO THOSE WHO MUST KNOW.
IF THIS RA'S AL GHUL IS TELLING YOU HE'S CENTURIES OLD, HE'S A MADMAN.
AND YOUR JUDGMENT IS SERIOUSLY IN QUESTION FOR AGREEING TO ASSIST HIM IN FINDING THIS SWORD.
ASSIST HIM?
YOU DO SERVE THE DEMON'S HEAD, CORRECT?
A THOUSAND PARDONS, AGAIN THE ENGLISH DOES NOT SUFFICE.
WE NEED THE SWORD SO THAT WE MAY SERVE THE HEAD OF THE DEMON...
...ON AN IRON PLATE!

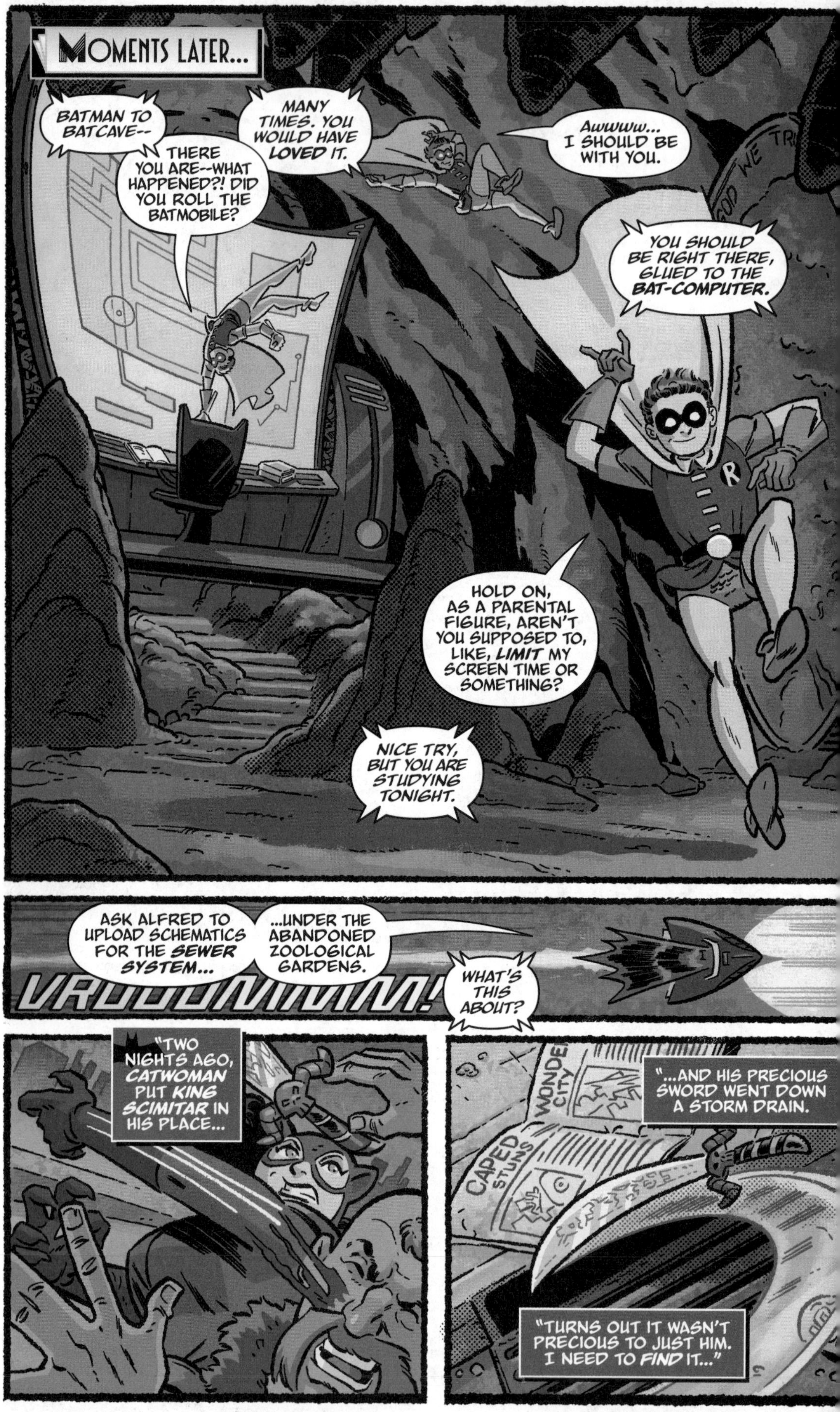
MOMENTS LATER...
BATMAN TO BATCAVE--
THERE YOU ARE--WHAT HAPPENED?! DID YOU ROLL THE BATMOBILE?
MANY TIMES. YOU WOULD HAVE *LOVED* IT.
Awwww... I SHOULD BE WITH YOU.
YOU SHOULD BE RIGHT THERE, GLUED TO THE *BAT-COMPUTER*.
HOLD ON, AS A PARENTAL FIGURE, AREN'T YOU SUPPOSED TO, LIKE, *LIMIT* MY SCREEN TIME OR SOMETHING?
NICE TRY, BUT YOU ARE STUDYING TONIGHT.
ASK ALFRED TO UPLOAD SCHEMATICS FOR THE *SEWER SYSTEM*...
...UNDER THE ABANDONED ZOOLOGICAL GARDENS.
VROOOMMM!
WHAT'S THIS ABOUT?
"TWO NIGHTS AGO, *CATWOMAN* PUT *KING SCIMITAR* IN HIS PLACE...
"...AND HIS PRECIOUS SWORD WENT DOWN A STORM DRAIN.
"TURNS OUT IT WASN'T PRECIOUS TO JUST HIM. I NEED TO *FIND* IT..."

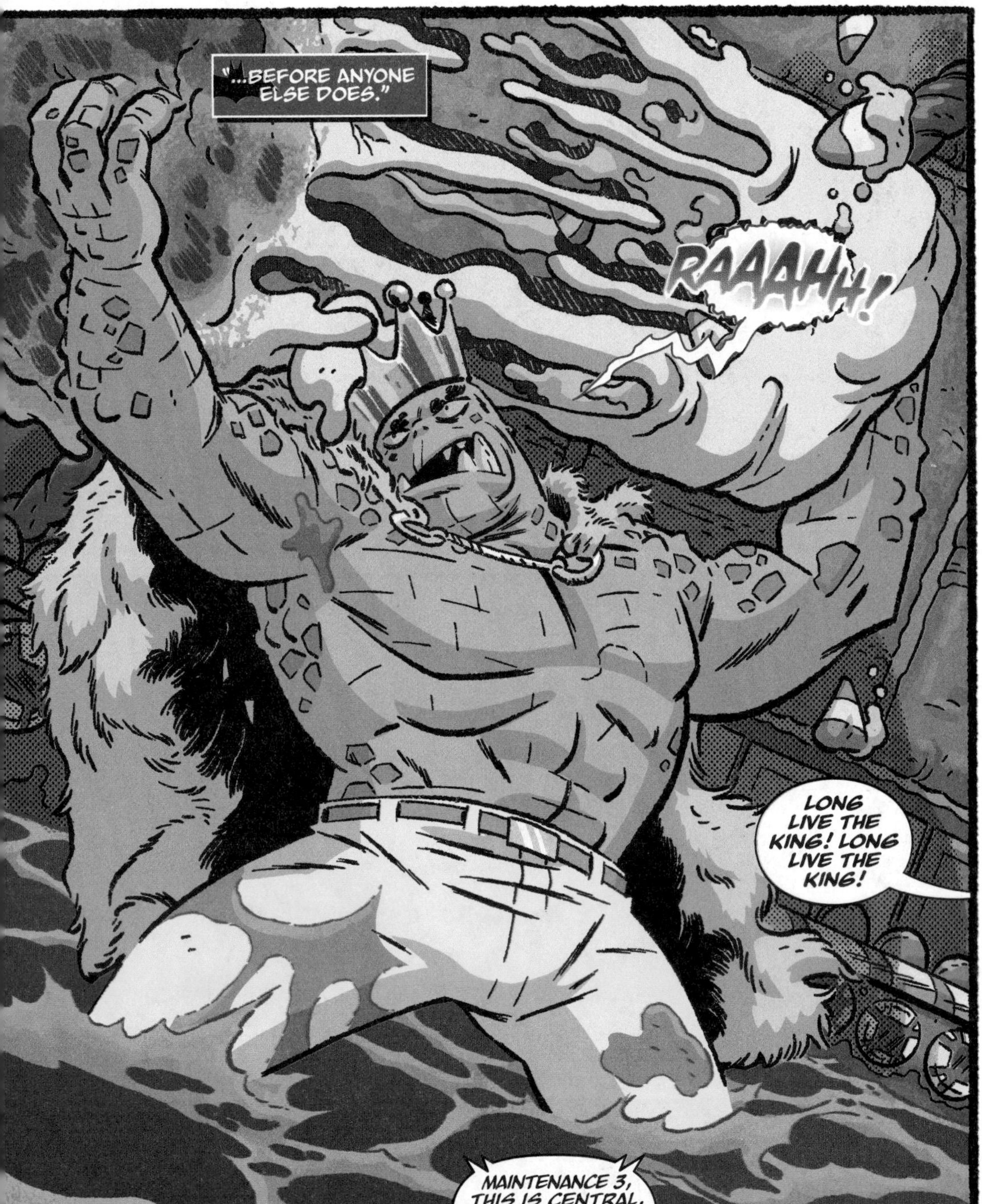
"...BEFORE ANYONE ELSE DOES."
RAAAHH!
LONG LIVE THE KING! LONG LIVE THE KING!
MAINTENANCE 3, THIS IS CENTRAL, WHERE THE HELL ARE THOSE pH READINGS?

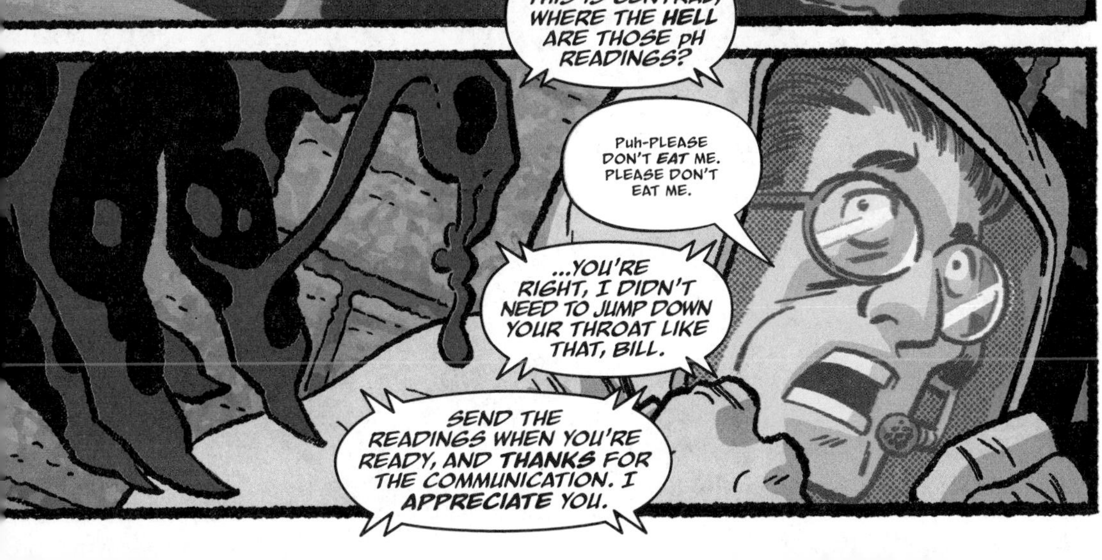
Puh-PLEASE DON'T EAT ME. PLEASE DON'T EAT ME.
...YOU'RE RIGHT, I DIDN'T NEED TO JUMP DOWN YOUR THROAT LIKE THAT, BILL.
SEND THE READINGS WHEN YOU'RE READY, AND THANKS FOR THE COMMUNICATION. I APPRECIATE YOU.

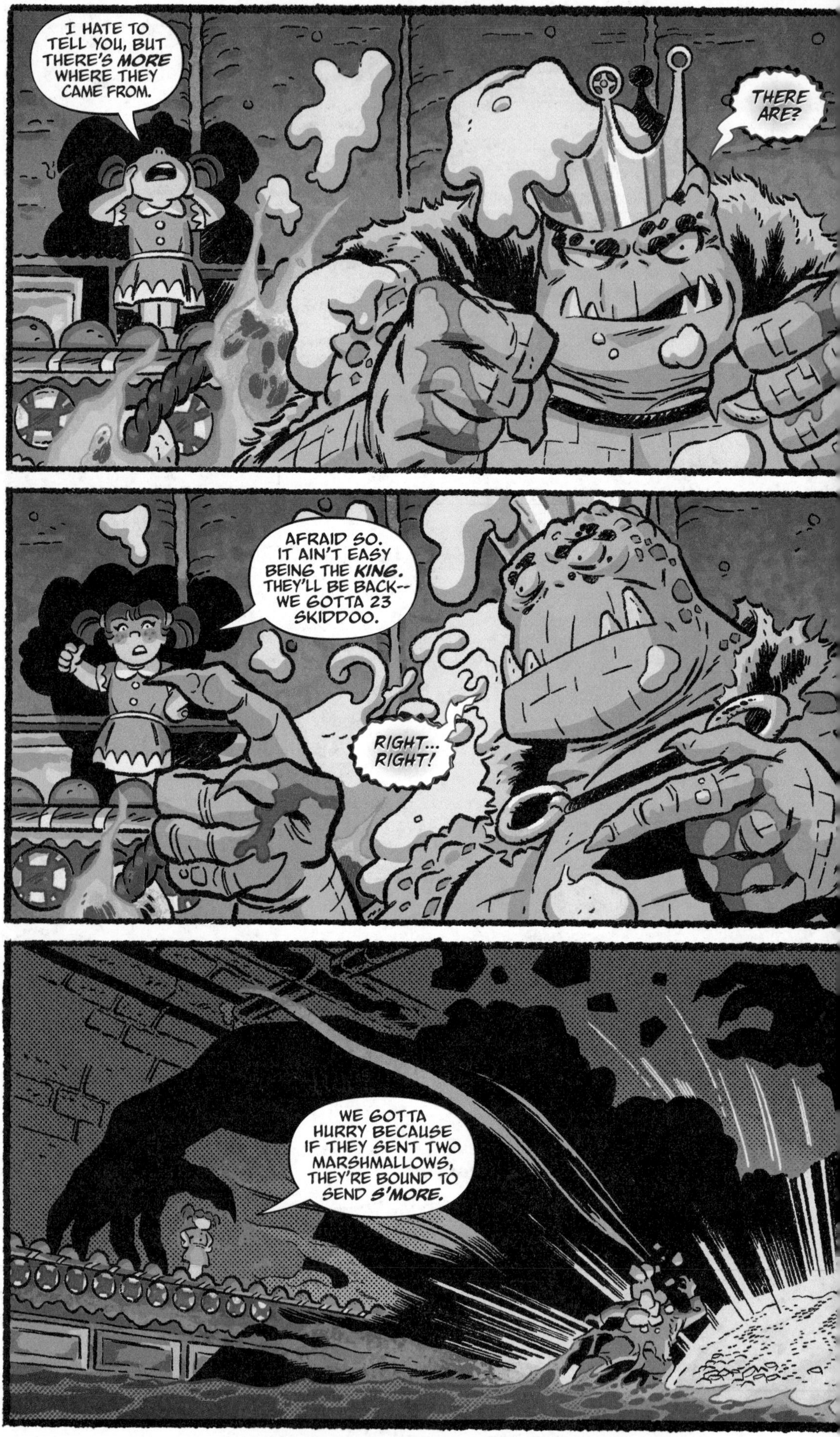
I HATE TO TELL YOU, BUT THERE'S *MORE* WHERE THEY CAME FROM.
THERE ARE?
AFRAID SO. IT AIN'T EASY BEING THE *KING*. THEY'LL BE BACK-- WE GOTTA 23 SKIDDOO.
RIGHT... RIGHT!
WE GOTTA HURRY BECAUSE IF THEY SENT TWO MARSHMALLOWS, THEY'RE BOUND TO SEND *S'MORE.*

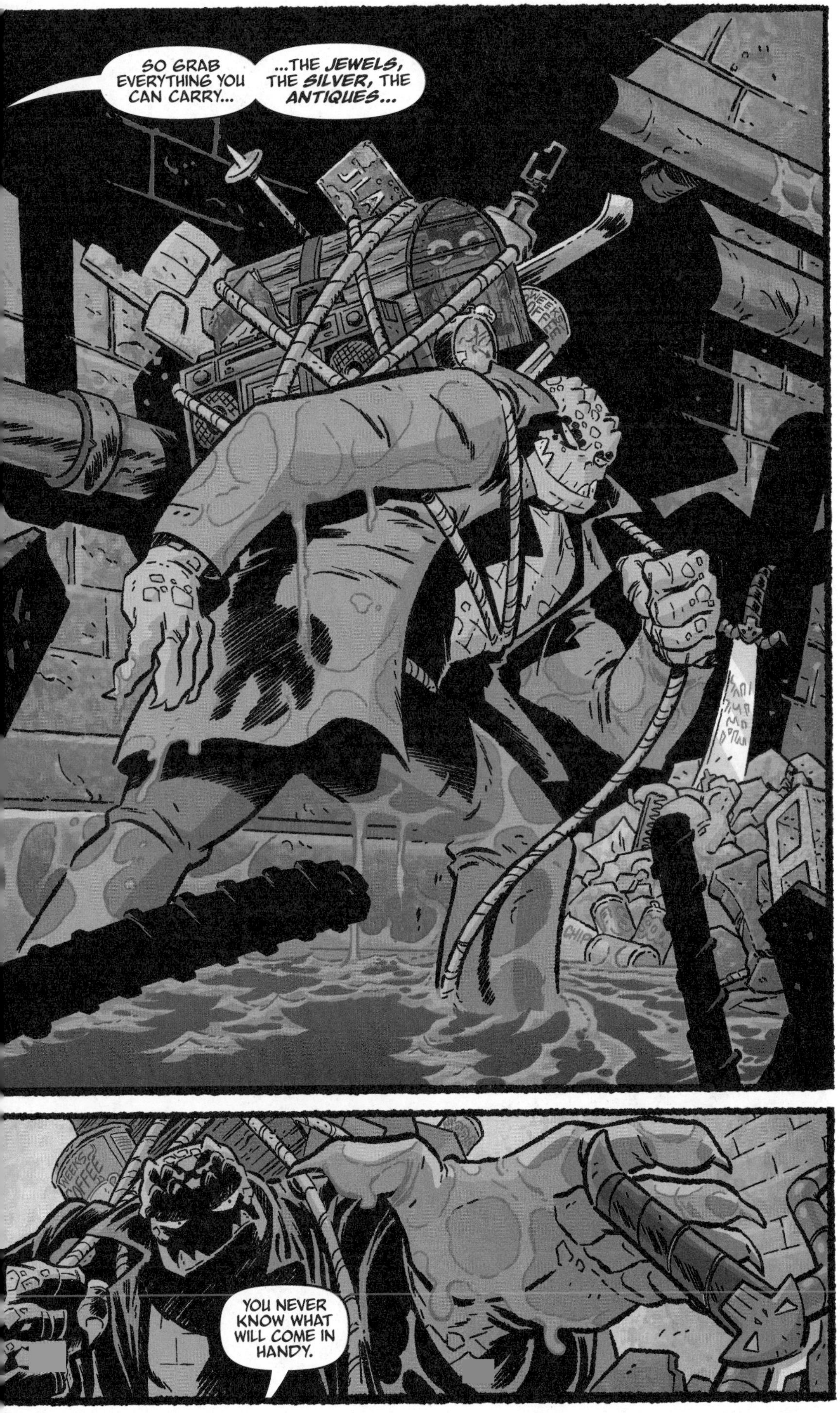
SO GRAB EVERYTHING YOU CAN CARRY...
...THE JEWELS, THE SILVER, THE ANTIQUES...
YOU NEVER KNOW WHAT WILL COME IN HANDY.

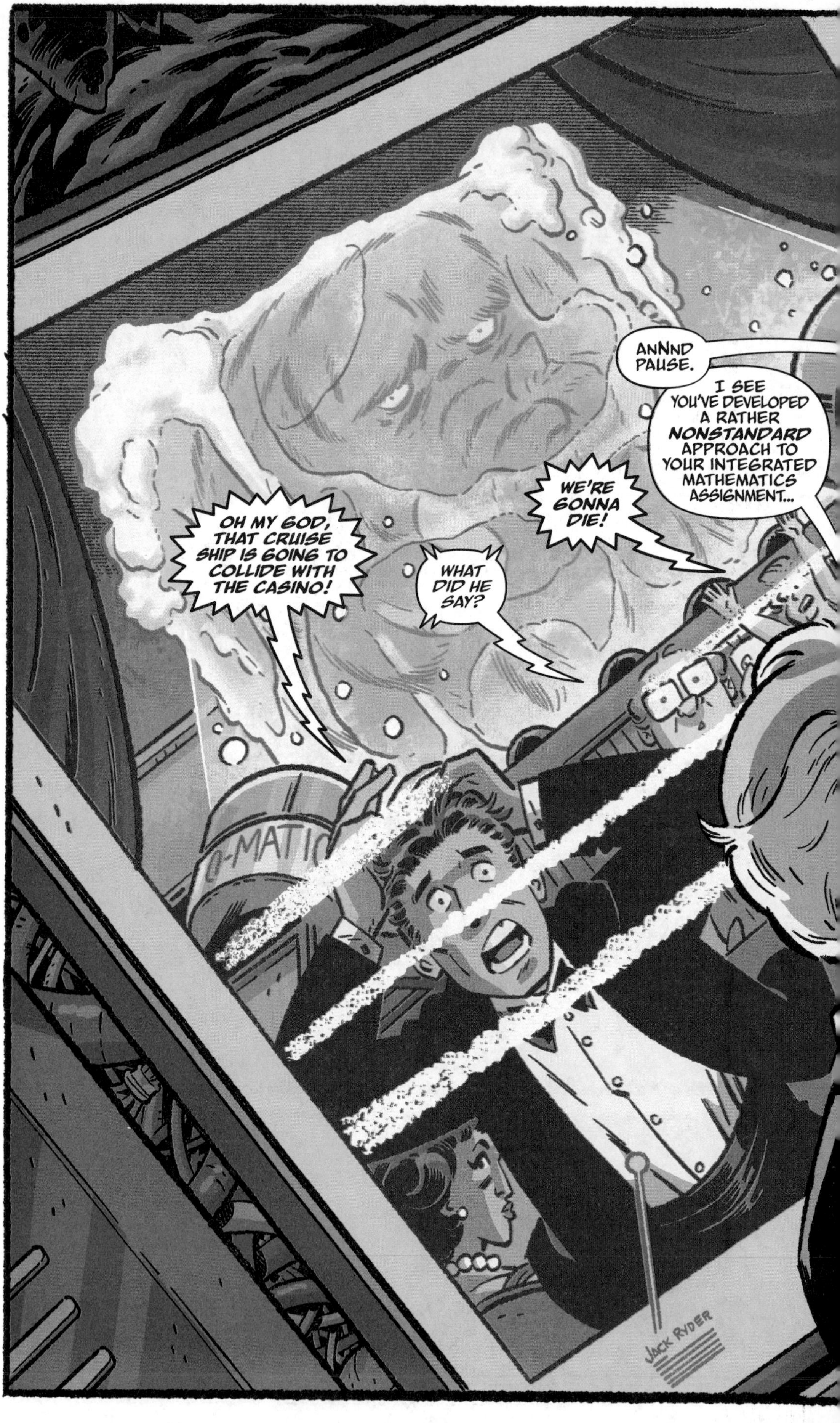
ANNND PAUSE.
I SEE YOU'VE DEVELOPED A RATHER NONSTANDARD APPROACH TO YOUR INTEGRATED MATHEMATICS ASSIGNMENT...
WE'RE GONNA DIE!
OH MY GOD, THAT CRUISE SHIP IS GOING TO COLLIDE WITH THE CASINO!
WHAT DID HE SAY?
-MATIC
JACK RYDER

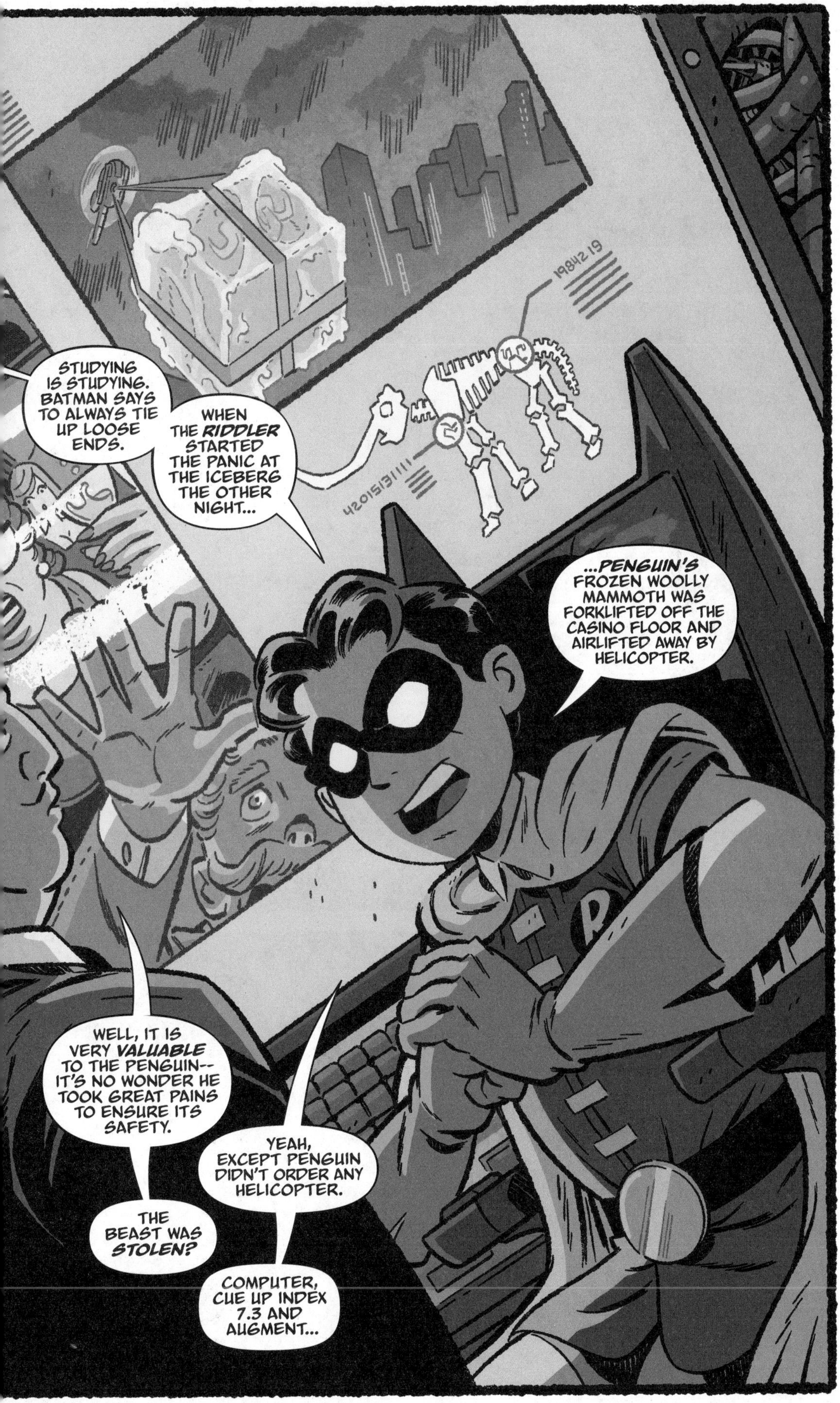
1984219
42015131111
STUDYING IS STUDYING. BATMAN SAYS TO ALWAYS TIE UP LOOSE ENDS.
WHEN THE RIDDLER STARTED THE PANIC AT THE ICEBERG THE OTHER NIGHT...
...PENGUIN'S FROZEN WOOLLY MAMMOTH WAS FORKLIFTED OFF THE CASINO FLOOR AND AIRLIFTED AWAY BY HELICOPTER.
WELL, IT IS VERY VALUABLE TO THE PENGUIN-- IT'S NO WONDER HE TOOK GREAT PAINS TO ENSURE ITS SAFETY.
YEAH, EXCEPT PENGUIN DIDN'T ORDER ANY HELICOPTER.
THE BEAST WAS STOLEN?
COMPUTER, CUE UP INDEX 7.3 AND AUGMENT...

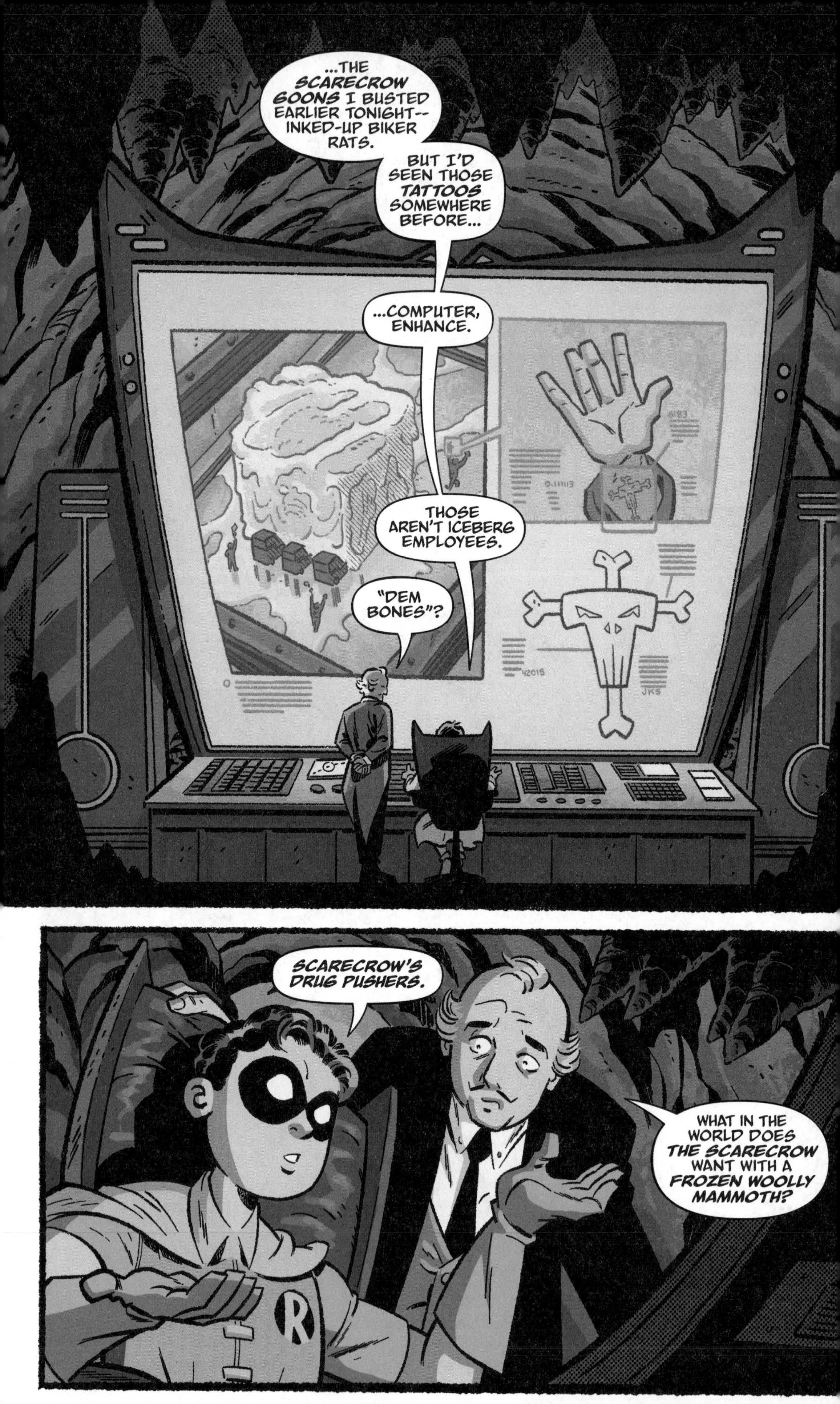
...THE SCARECROW GOONS I BUSTED EARLIER TONIGHT-- INKED-UP BIKER RATS.
BUT I'D SEEN THOSE TATTOOS SOMEWHERE BEFORE...
...COMPUTER, ENHANCE.
THOSE AREN'T ICEBERG EMPLOYEES.
"DEM BONES"?
6183
42015
JKS
SCARECROW'S DRUG PUSHERS.
WHAT IN THE WORLD DOES THE SCARECROW WANT WITH A FROZEN WOOLLY MAMMOTH?

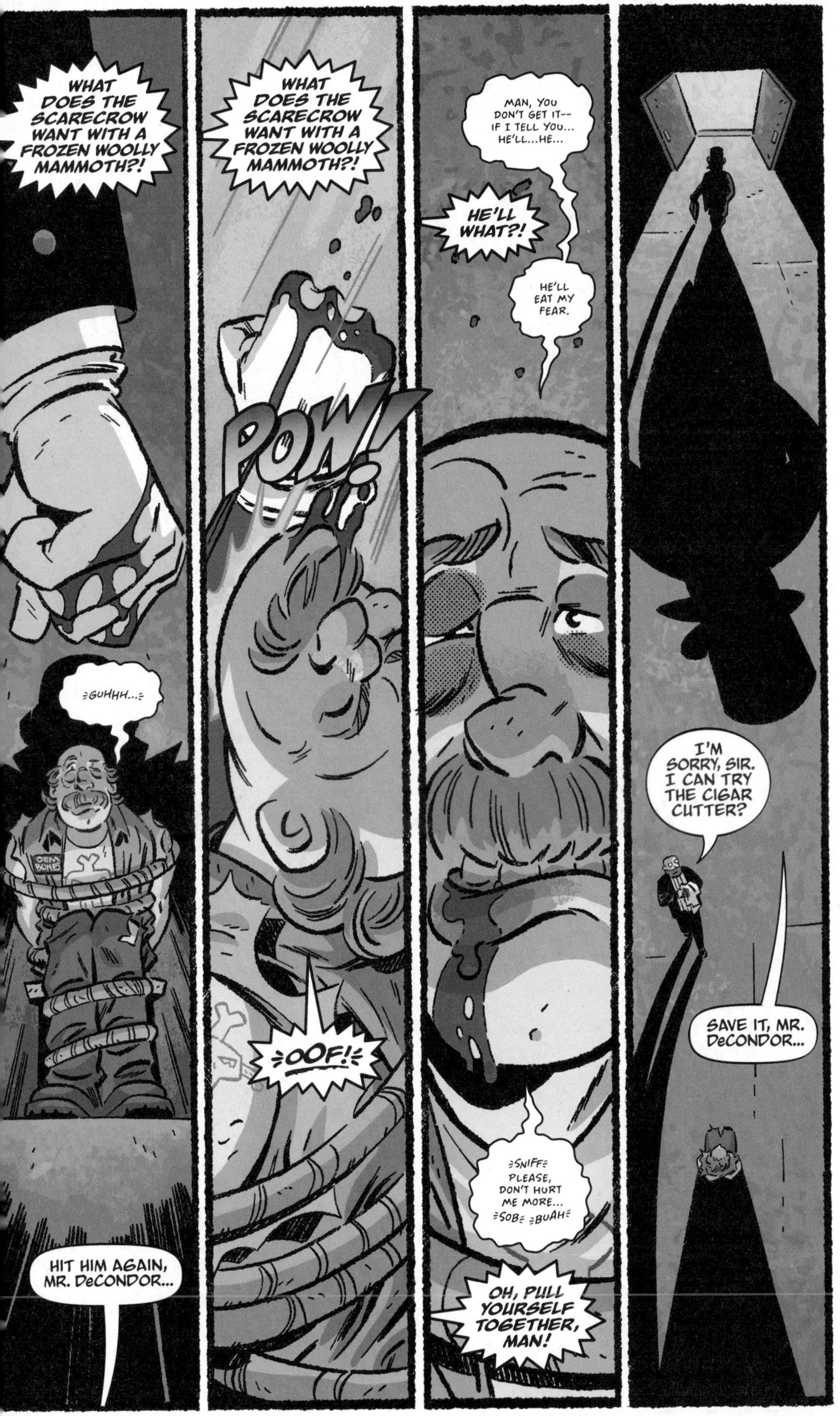
WHAT DOES THE SCARECROW WANT WITH A FROZEN WOOLLY MAMMOTH?!
GUHHH...
HIT HIM AGAIN, MR. DeCONDOR...
WHAT DOES THE SCARECROW WANT WITH A FROZEN WOOLLY MAMMOTH?!
POW!
OOF!
MAN, YOU DON'T GET IT-- IF I TELL YOU... HE'LL...HE...
HE'LL WHAT?!
HE'LL EAT MY FEAR.
SNIFF PLEASE, DON'T HURT ME MORE... SOB BUAH
OH, PULL YOURSELF TOGETHER, MAN!
I'M SORRY, SIR. I CAN TRY THE CIGAR CUTTER?
SAVE IT, MR. DeCONDOR...

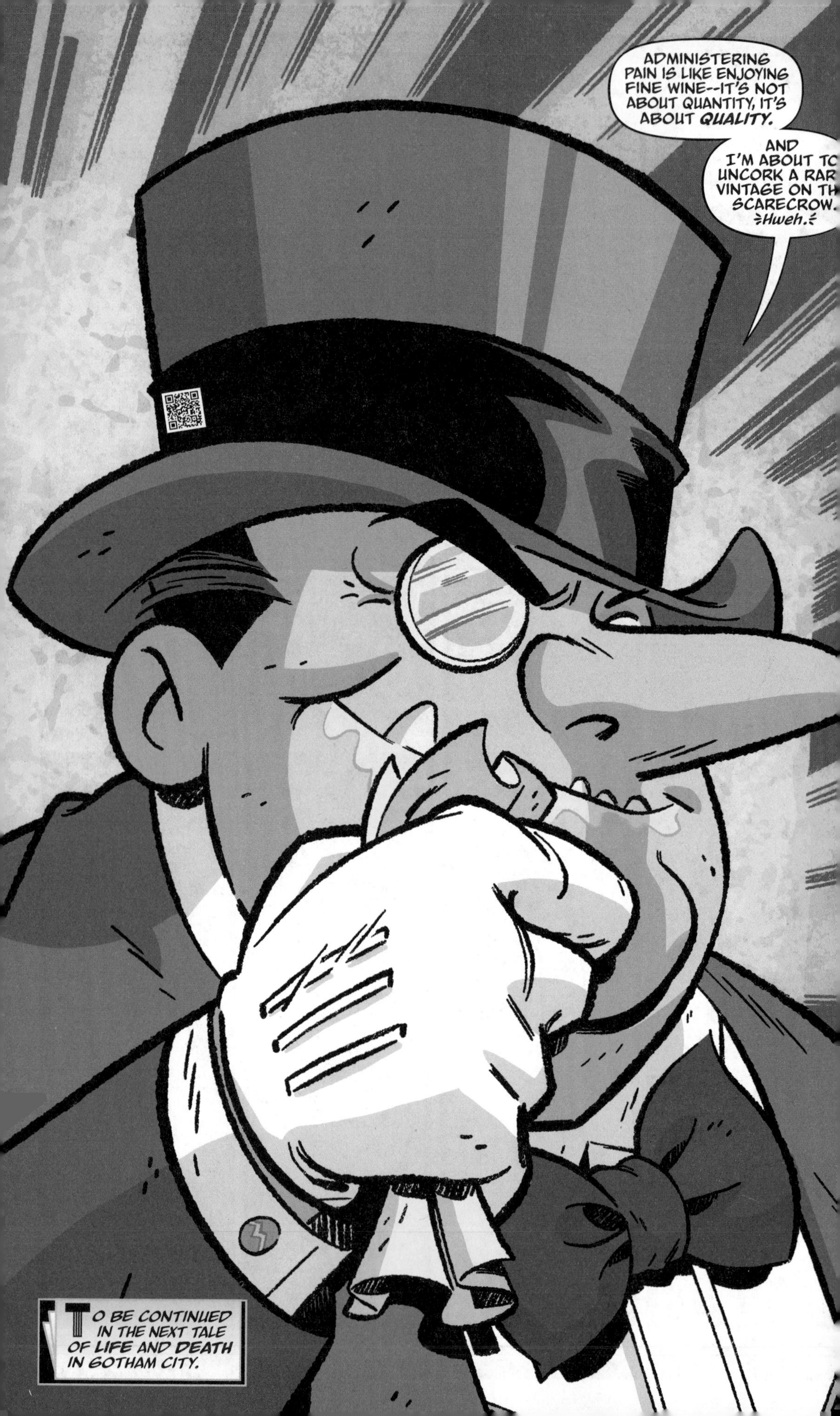
ADMINISTERING PAIN IS LIKE ENJOYING FINE WINE--IT'S NOT ABOUT QUANTITY, IT'S ABOUT *QUALITY.*
AND I'M ABOUT TO UNCORK A RAR VINTAGE ON TH SCARECROW. *Hweh.*
TO BE CONTINUED IN THE NEXT TALE OF *LIFE* AND *DEATH* IN GOTHAM CITY.

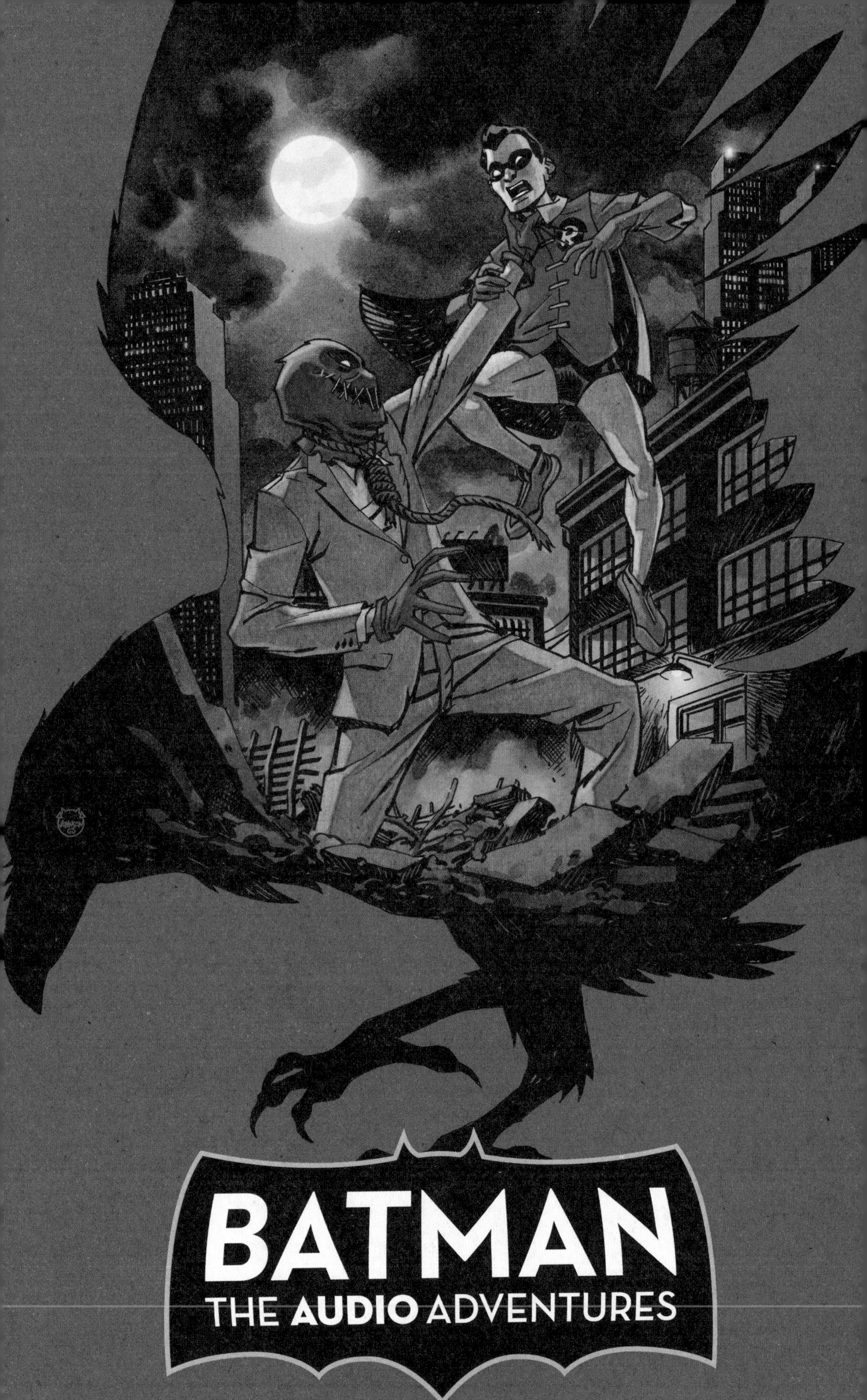

BATMAN
THE AUDIO ADVENTURES

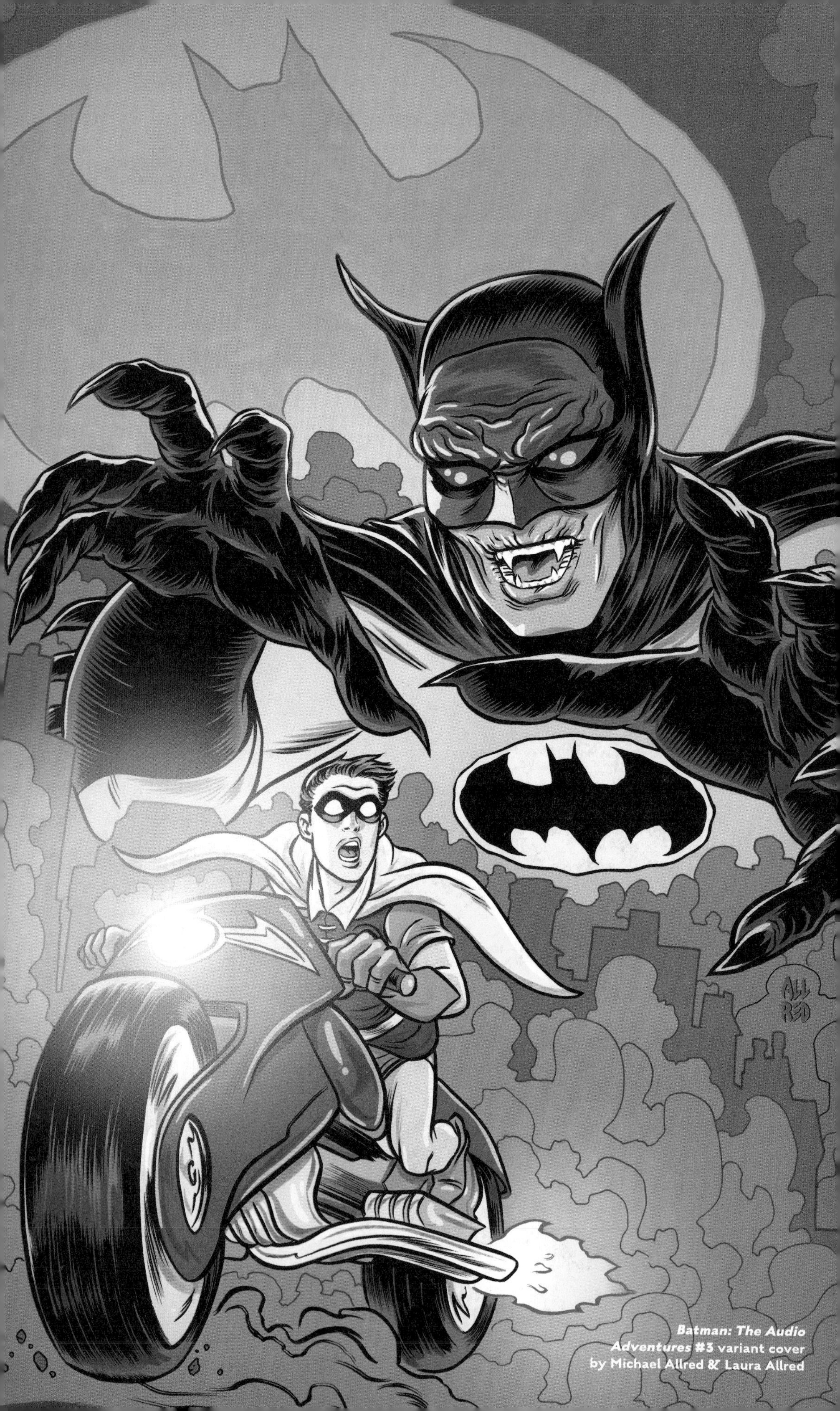

Batman: The Audio Adventures #3 variant cover
by Michael Allred & Laura Allred

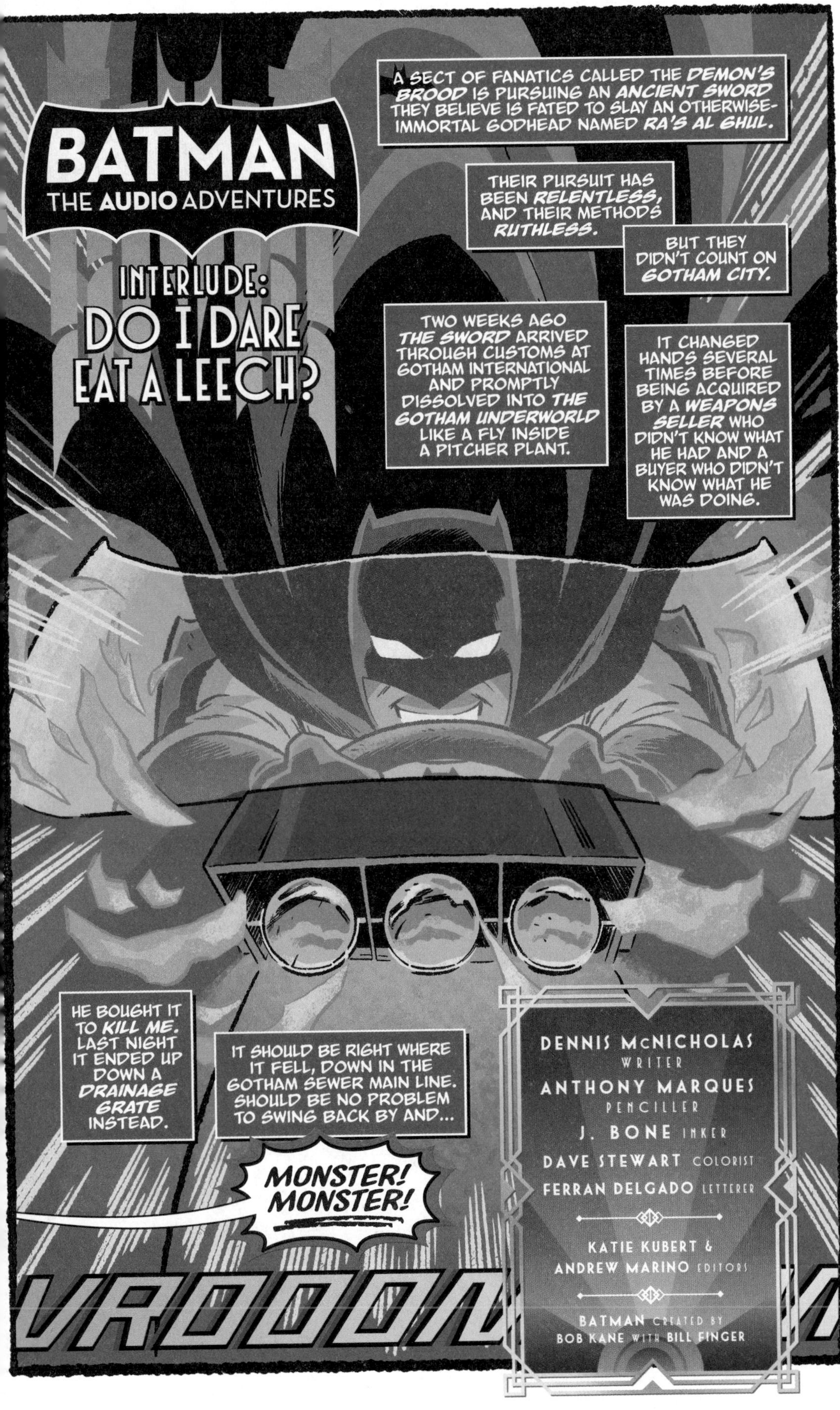

BATMAN THE AUDIO ADVENTURES
INTERLUDE: DO I DARE EAT A LEECH?
A SECT OF FANATICS CALLED THE DEMON'S BROOD IS PURSUING AN ANCIENT SWORD THEY BELIEVE IS FATED TO SLAY AN OTHERWISE-IMMORTAL GODHEAD NAMED RA'S AL GHUL.
THEIR PURSUIT HAS BEEN RELENTLESS, AND THEIR METHODS RUTHLESS.
BUT THEY DIDN'T COUNT ON GOTHAM CITY.
TWO WEEKS AGO THE SWORD ARRIVED THROUGH CUSTOMS AT GOTHAM INTERNATIONAL AND PROMPTLY DISSOLVED INTO THE GOTHAM UNDERWORLD LIKE A FLY INSIDE A PITCHER PLANT.
IT CHANGED HANDS SEVERAL TIMES BEFORE BEING ACQUIRED BY A WEAPONS SELLER WHO DIDN'T KNOW WHAT HE HAD AND A BUYER WHO DIDN'T KNOW WHAT HE WAS DOING.
HE BOUGHT IT TO KILL ME. LAST NIGHT IT ENDED UP DOWN A DRAINAGE GRATE INSTEAD.
IT SHOULD BE RIGHT WHERE IT FELL, DOWN IN THE GOTHAM SEWER MAIN LINE. SHOULD BE NO PROBLEM TO SWING BACK BY AND...
MONSTER! MONSTER!
VROOOM
DENNIS McNICHOLAS WRITER
ANTHONY MARQUES PENCILLER
J. BONE INKER
DAVE STEWART COLORIST
FERRAN DELGADO LETTERER
KATIE KUBERT & ANDREW MARINO EDITORS
BATMAN CREATED BY BOB KANE WITH BILL FINGER

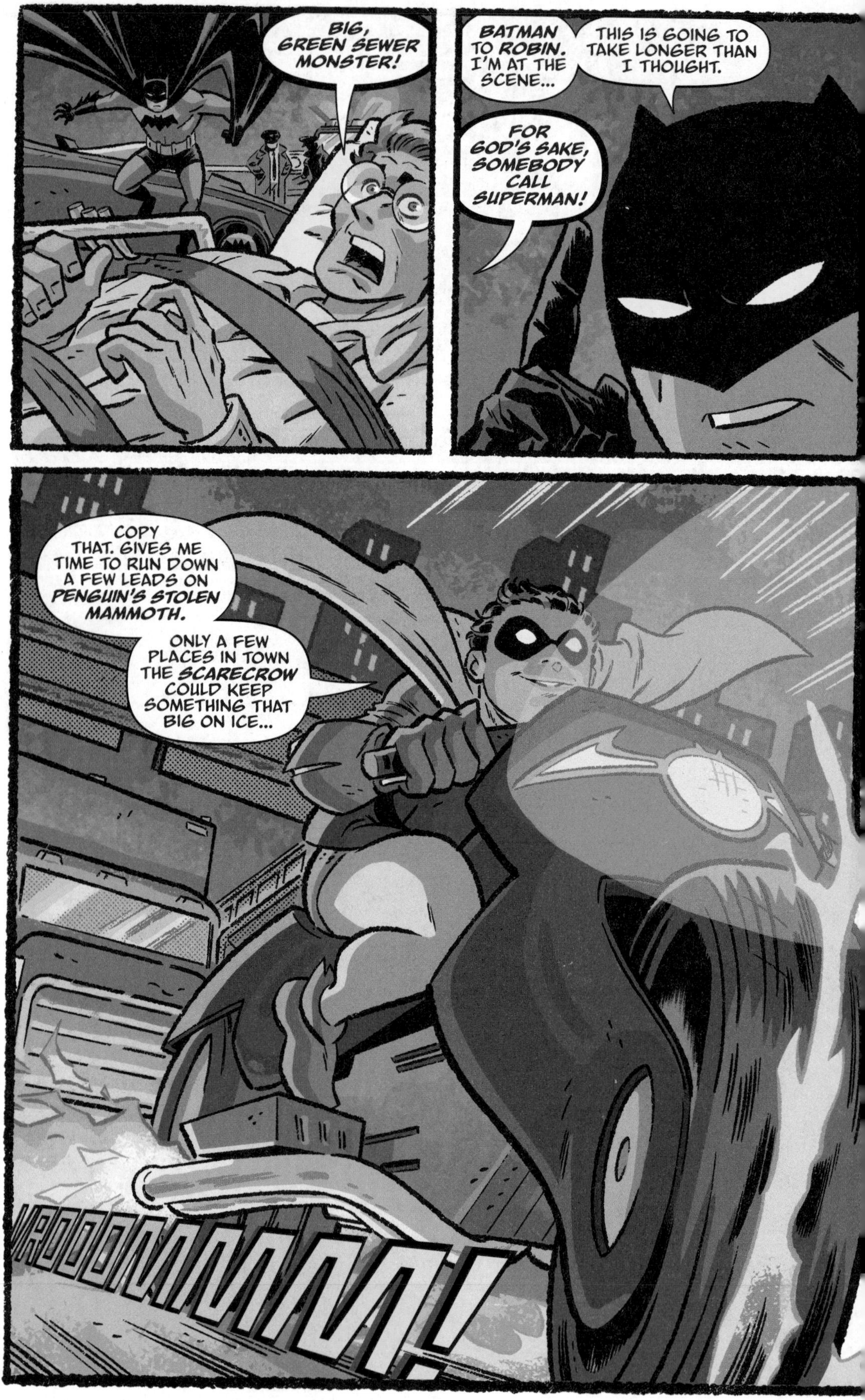
BIG, GREEN SEWER MONSTER!
BATMAN TO ROBIN. I'M AT THE SCENE...
THIS IS GOING TO TAKE LONGER THAN I THOUGHT.
FOR GOD'S SAKE, SOMEBODY CALL SUPERMAN!
COPY THAT. GIVES ME TIME TO RUN DOWN A FEW LEADS ON PENGUIN'S STOLEN MAMMOTH.
ONLY A FEW PLACES IN TOWN THE SCARECROW COULD KEEP SOMETHING THAT BIG ON ICE...
VROOOOMMMMM!

YOU'RE GOING TO BE OKAY, SIR.
PLEASE DON'T EAT ME. I'M N-NOT A M-MARSHMALLOW. I'M NOT A M-M-MUH--
WHAT HAPPENED HERE?
KILLER CROC HAPPENED.
THAT'S GONNA COST A FORTUNE IN THERAPY RIGHT THERE. YOU HATE TO SEE IT.
ATTACKED THE GUY ON THE STRETCHER AND HIS PARTNER...
...WHILE THEY WERE DOING ROUTINE MAINTENANCE.
THAT DOESN'T TRACK. WHAT DOES CROC WANT WITH THAT KIND OF TROUBLE?
SOUNDS LIKE CROC HAS FLIPPED HIS BURGERS, BATMAN.
POOR GUY IN THE AMBULANCE SAID THE WHOLE TIME HE WAS TEARING HIS PARTNER TO PIECES...
...CROC WAS HAVING A CONVERSATION WITH SOMEONE ELSE...
SOMEONE ELSE?
...SAID IT SEEMED LIKE HE WAS TALKING TO A LITTLE GIRL?

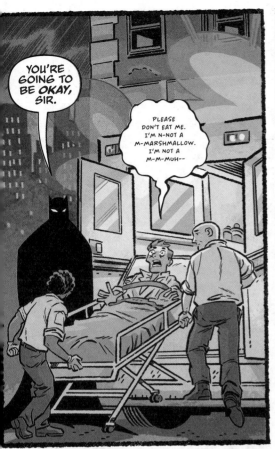

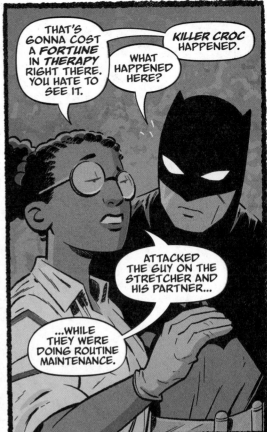

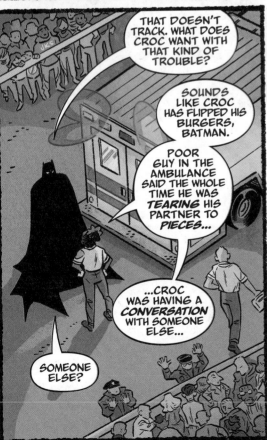

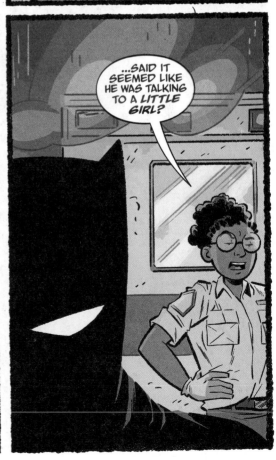

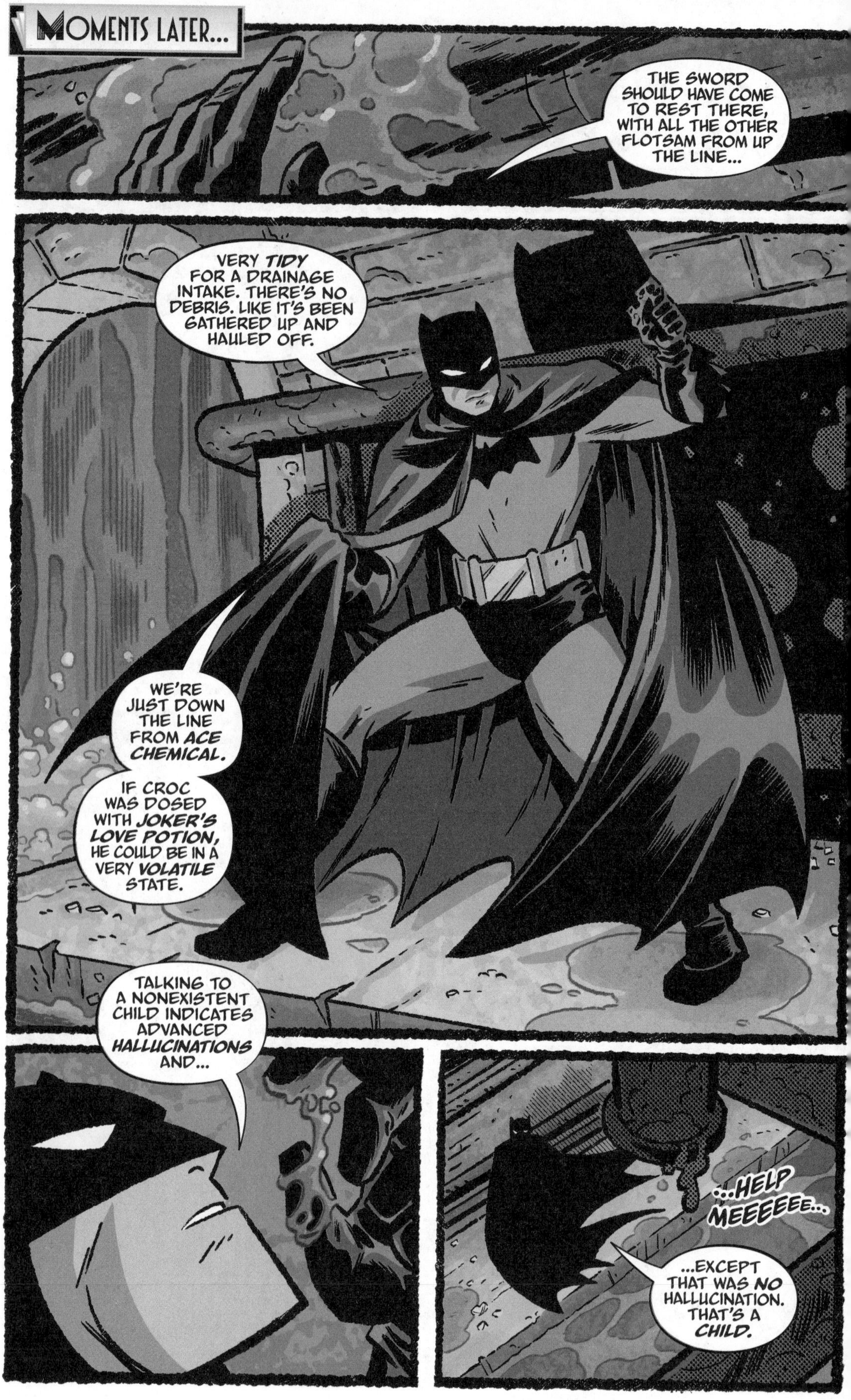
MOMENTS LATER...
THE SWORD SHOULD HAVE COME TO REST THERE, WITH ALL THE OTHER FLOTSAM FROM UP THE LINE...
VERY TIDY FOR A DRAINAGE INTAKE. THERE'S NO DEBRIS. LIKE IT'S BEEN GATHERED UP AND HAULED OFF.
WE'RE JUST DOWN THE LINE FROM ACE CHEMICAL.
IF CROC WAS DOSED WITH JOKER'S LOVE POTION, HE COULD BE IN A VERY VOLATILE STATE.
TALKING TO A NONEXISTENT CHILD INDICATES ADVANCED HALLUCINATIONS AND...
...HELP MEEEEEEE...
...EXCEPT THAT WAS NO HALLUCINATION. THAT'S A CHILD.

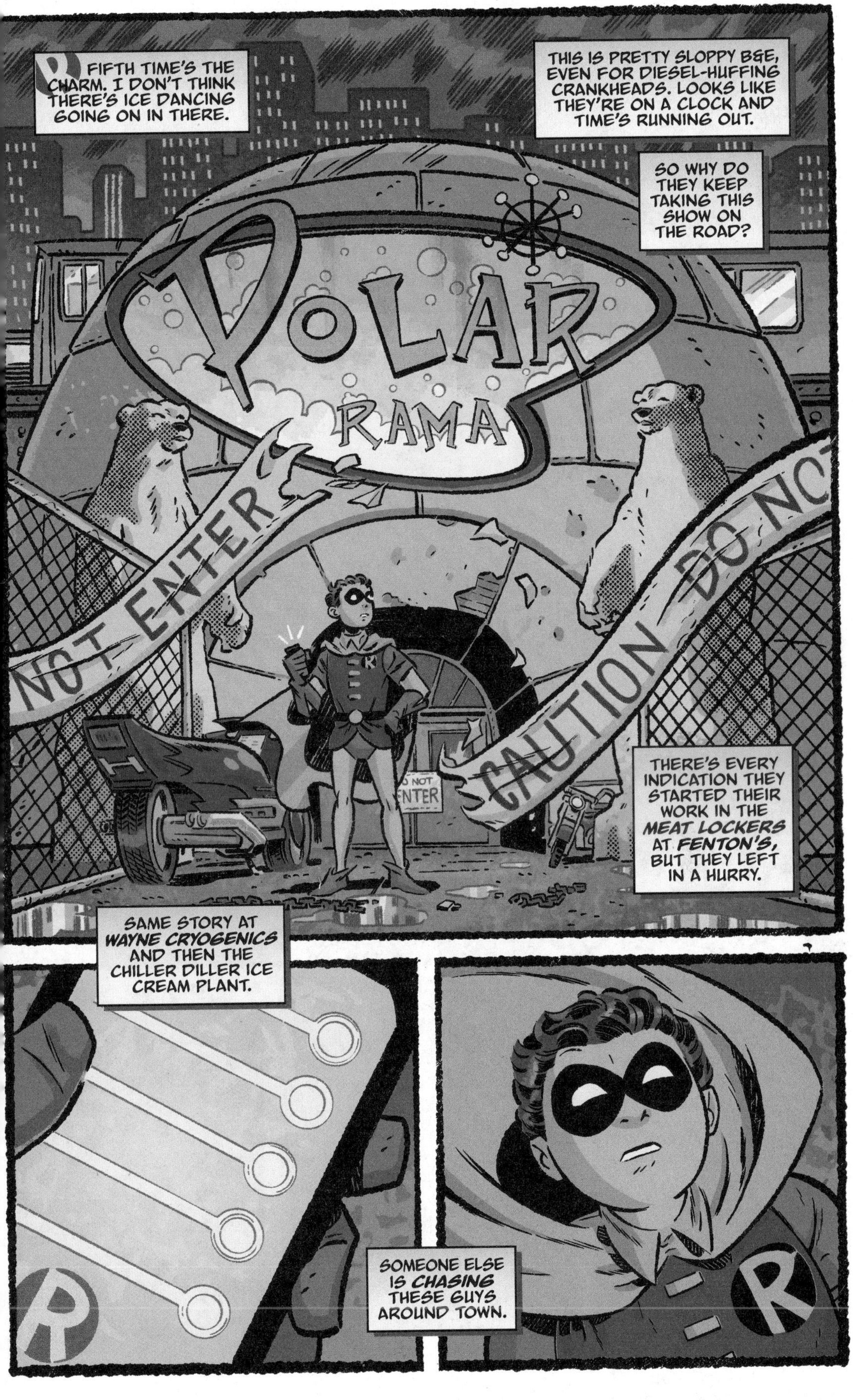
FIFTH TIME'S THE CHARM. I DON'T THINK THERE'S ICE DANCING GOING ON IN THERE.
THIS IS PRETTY SLOPPY B&E, EVEN FOR DIESEL-HUFFING CRANKHEADS. LOOKS LIKE THEY'RE ON A CLOCK AND TIME'S RUNNING OUT.
SO WHY DO THEY KEEP TAKING THIS SHOW ON THE ROAD?
POLAR RAMA
NOT ENTER
CAUTION DO NOT
DO NOT ENTER
THERE'S EVERY INDICATION THEY STARTED THEIR WORK IN THE *MEAT LOCKERS* AT *FENTON'S,* BUT THEY LEFT IN A HURRY.
SAME STORY AT *WAYNE CRYOGENICS* AND THEN THE CHILLER DILLER ICE CREAM PLANT.
SOMEONE ELSE IS *CHASING* THESE GUYS AROUND TOWN.

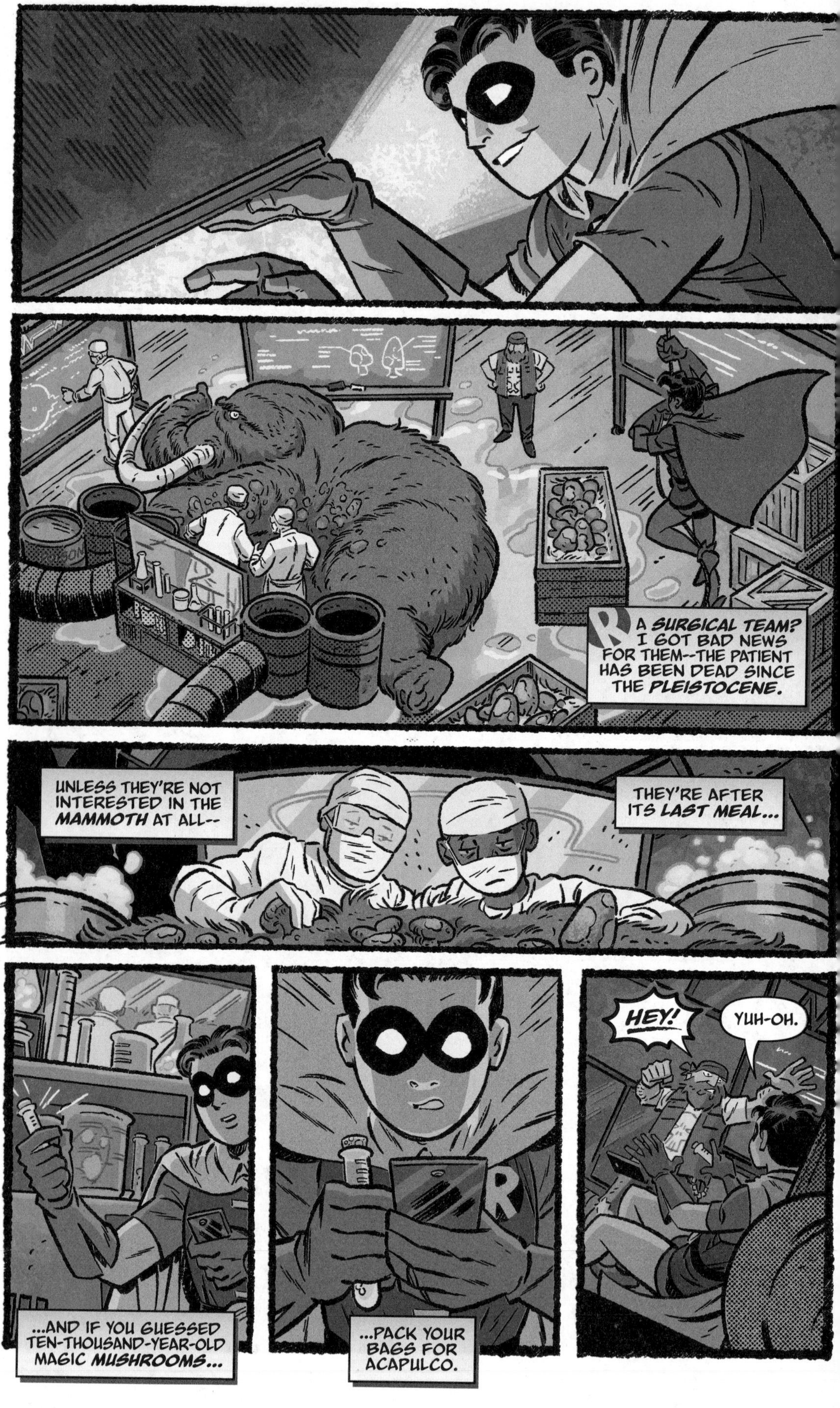
A SURGICAL TEAM? I GOT BAD NEWS FOR THEM--THE PATIENT HAS BEEN DEAD SINCE THE PLEISTOCENE.
UNLESS THEY'RE NOT INTERESTED IN THE MAMMOTH AT ALL--
THEY'RE AFTER ITS LAST MEAL...
...AND IF YOU GUESSED TEN-THOUSAND-YEAR-OLD MAGIC MUSHROOMS...
...PACK YOUR BAGS FOR ACAPULCO.
HEY!
YUH-OH.

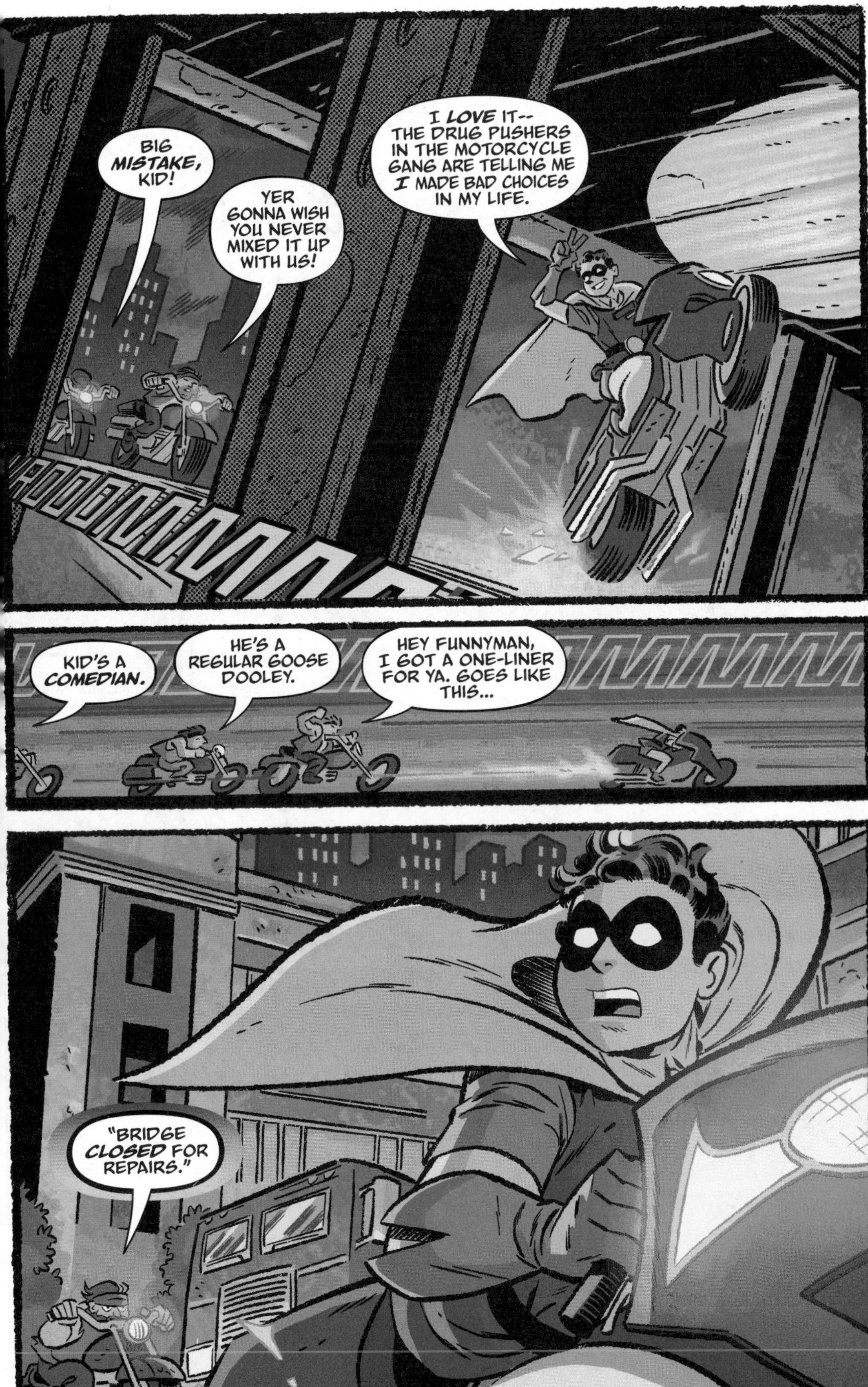
BIG MISTAKE, KID!
YER GONNA WISH YOU NEVER MIXED IT UP WITH US!
I LOVE IT-- THE DRUG PUSHERS IN THE MOTORCYCLE GANG ARE TELLING ME I MADE BAD CHOICES IN MY LIFE.
KID'S A COMEDIAN.
HE'S A REGULAR GOOSE DOOLEY.
HEY FUNNYMAN, I GOT A ONE-LINER FOR YA. GOES LIKE THIS...
"BRIDGE CLOSED FOR REPAIRS."

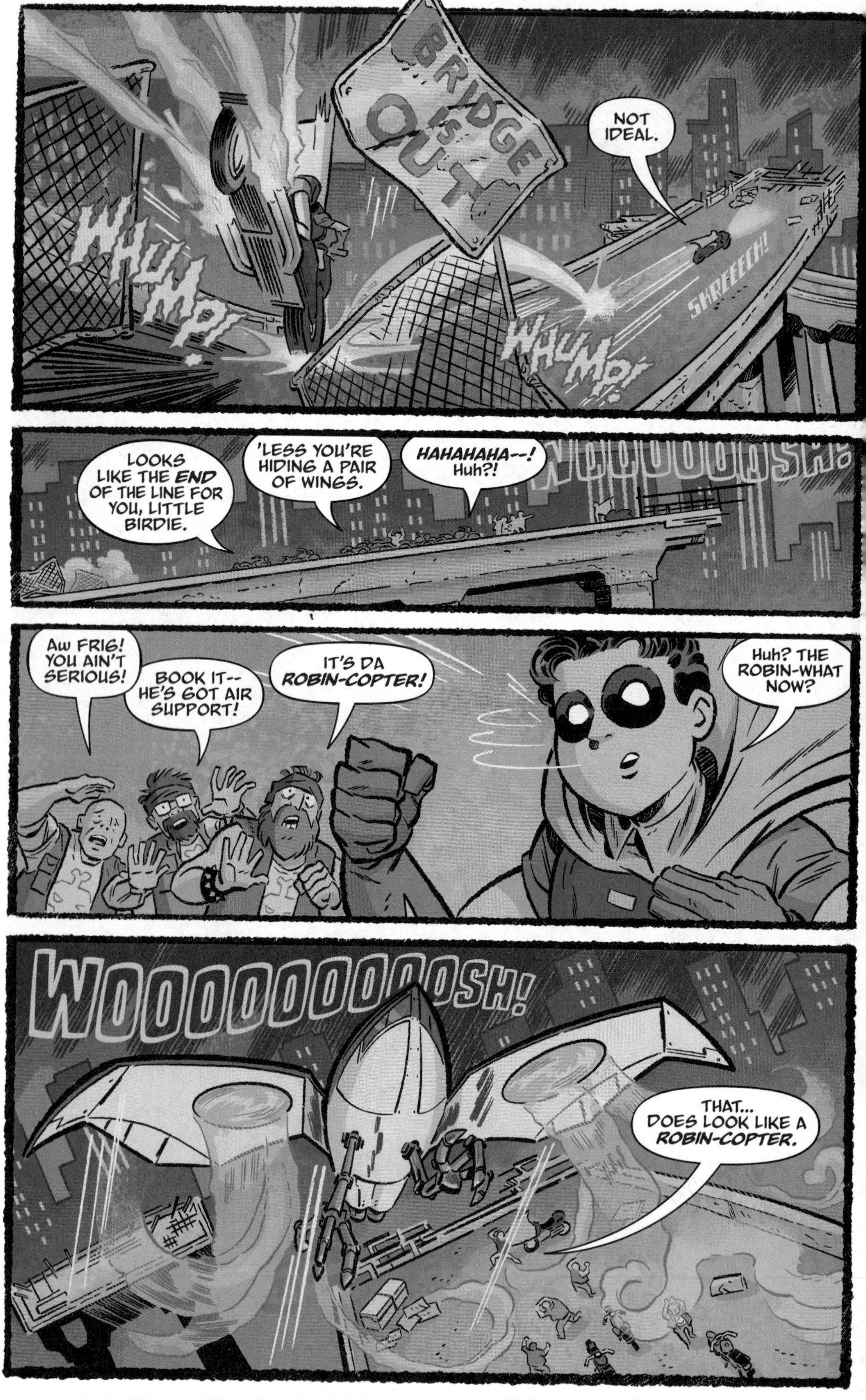
BRIDGE IS OUT
NOT IDEAL.
WHUMP!
SKREEECH!
WHUMP!
LOOKS LIKE THE END OF THE LINE FOR YOU, LITTLE BIRDIE.
'LESS YOU'RE HIDING A PAIR OF WINGS.
HAHAHAHA--! Huh?!
WOOOOOOOOSH!
Aw FRIG! YOU AIN'T SERIOUS!
BOOK IT-- HE'S GOT AIR SUPPORT!
IT'S DA ROBIN-COPTER!
Huh? THE ROBIN-WHAT NOW?
WOOOOOOOOOOSH!
THAT... DOES LOOK LIKE A ROBIN-COPTER.

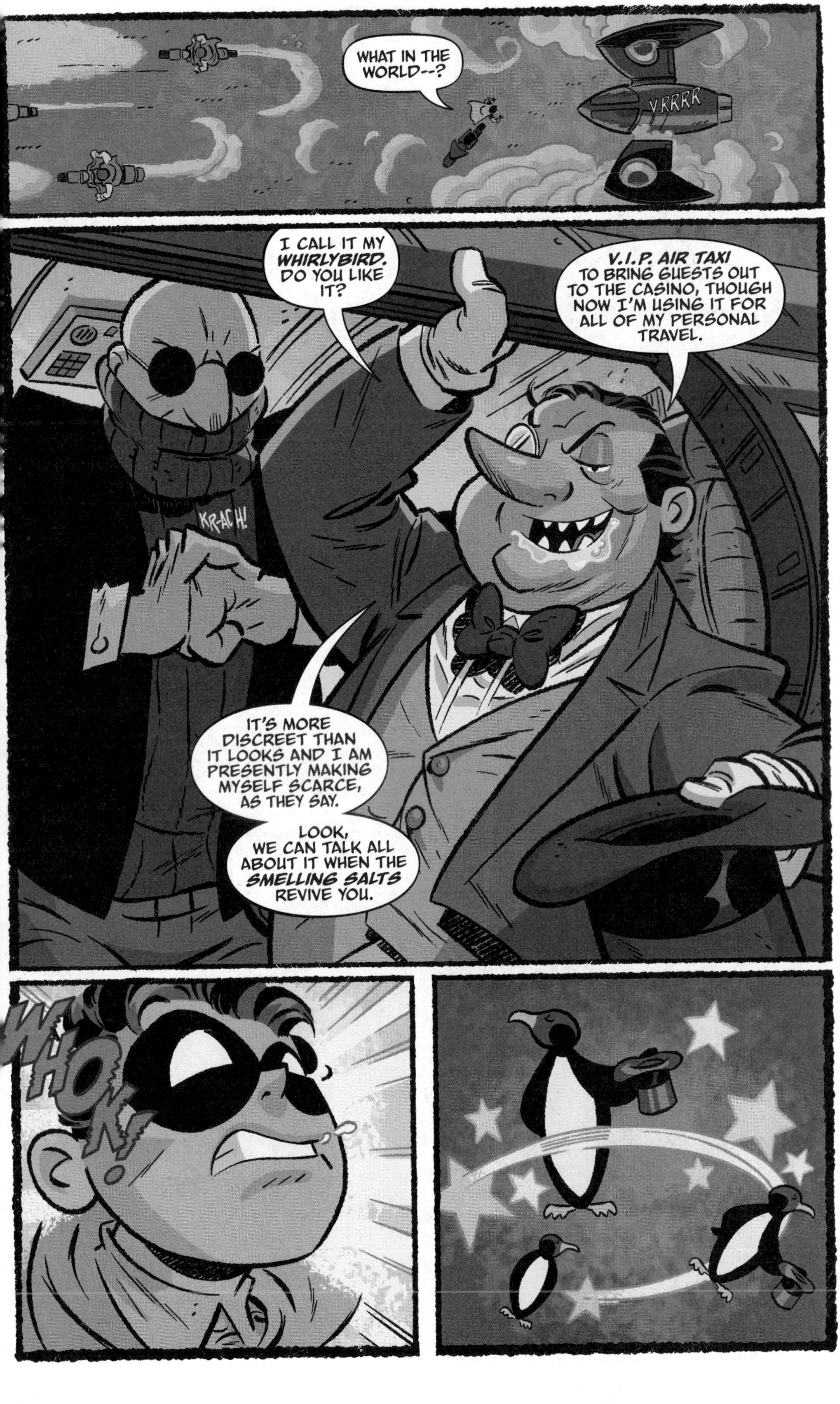
WHAT IN THE WORLD--?
VRRRR
I CALL IT MY *WHIRLYBIRD.* DO YOU LIKE IT?
V.I.P. AIR TAXI TO BRING GUESTS OUT TO THE CASINO, THOUGH NOW I'M USING IT FOR ALL OF MY PERSONAL TRAVEL.
KR-ACH!
IT'S MORE DISCREET THAN IT LOOKS AND I AM PRESENTLY MAKING MYSELF SCARCE, AS THEY SAY.
LOOK, WE CAN TALK ALL ABOUT IT WHEN THE *SMELLING SALTS* REVIVE YOU.
WHOK!

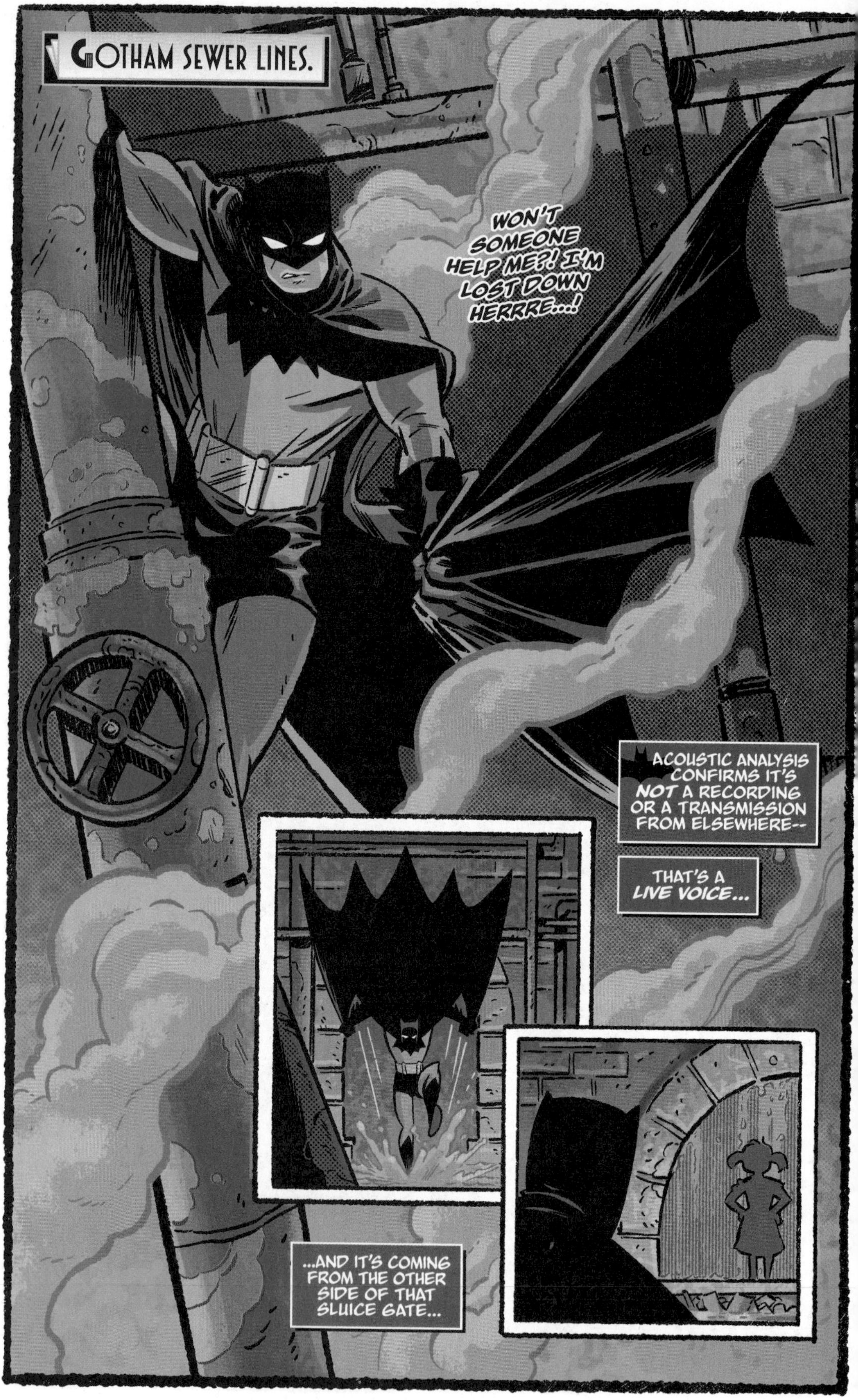
GOTHAM SEWER LINES.
WON'T SOMEONE HELP ME?! I'M LOST DOWN HERRRE...!
ACOUSTIC ANALYSIS CONFIRMS IT'S NOT A RECORDING OR A TRANSMISSION FROM ELSEWHERE--
THAT'S A LIVE VOICE...
...AND IT'S COMING FROM THE OTHER SIDE OF THAT SLUICE GATE...

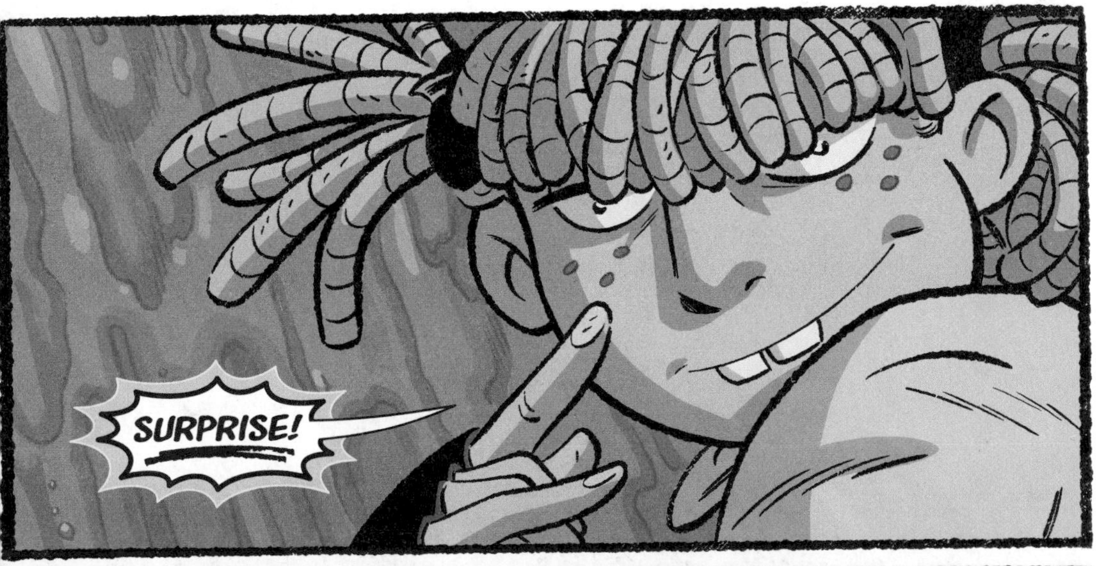
SURPRISE!

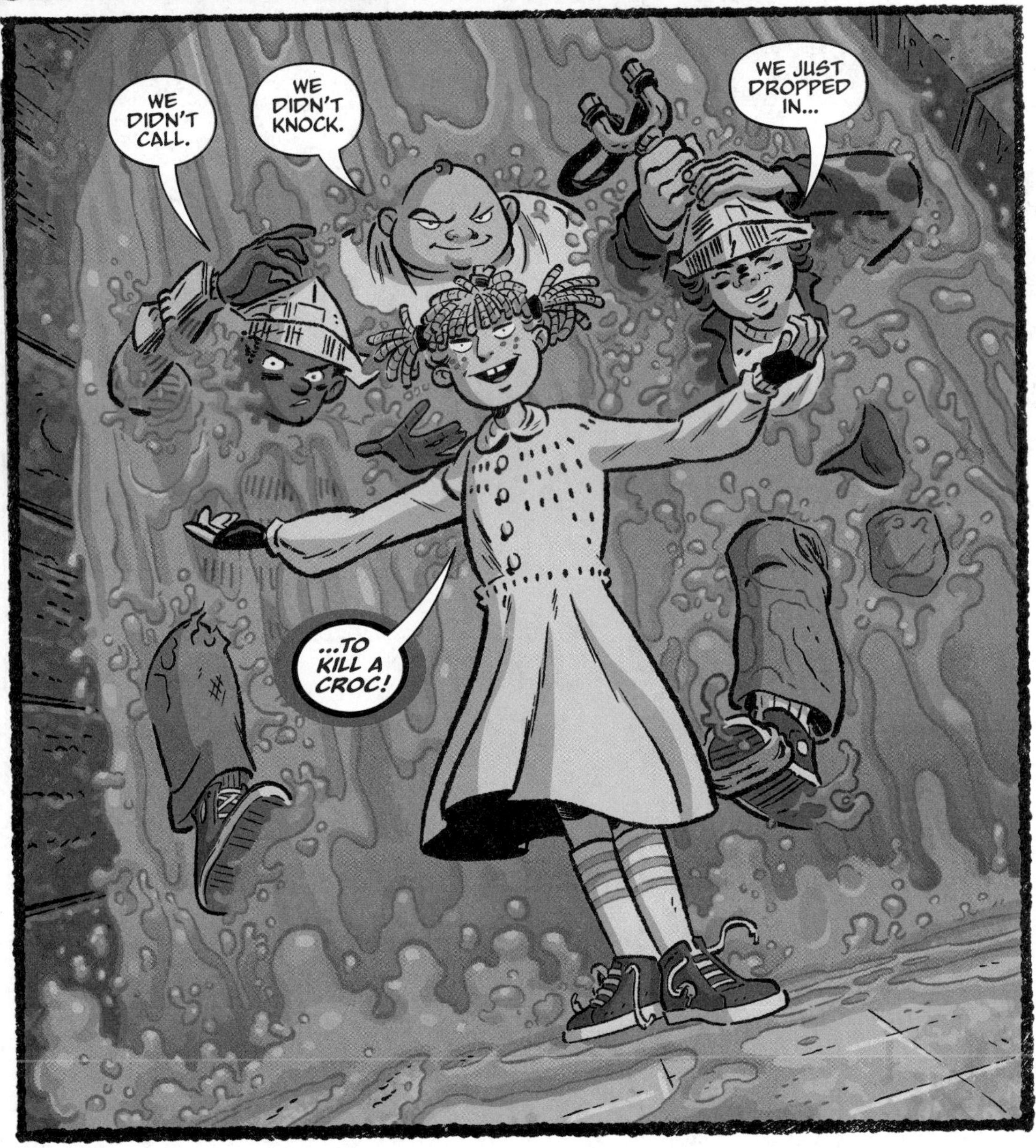
WE DIDN'T CALL.
WE DIDN'T KNOCK.
WE JUST DROPPED IN...
...TO KILL A CROC!

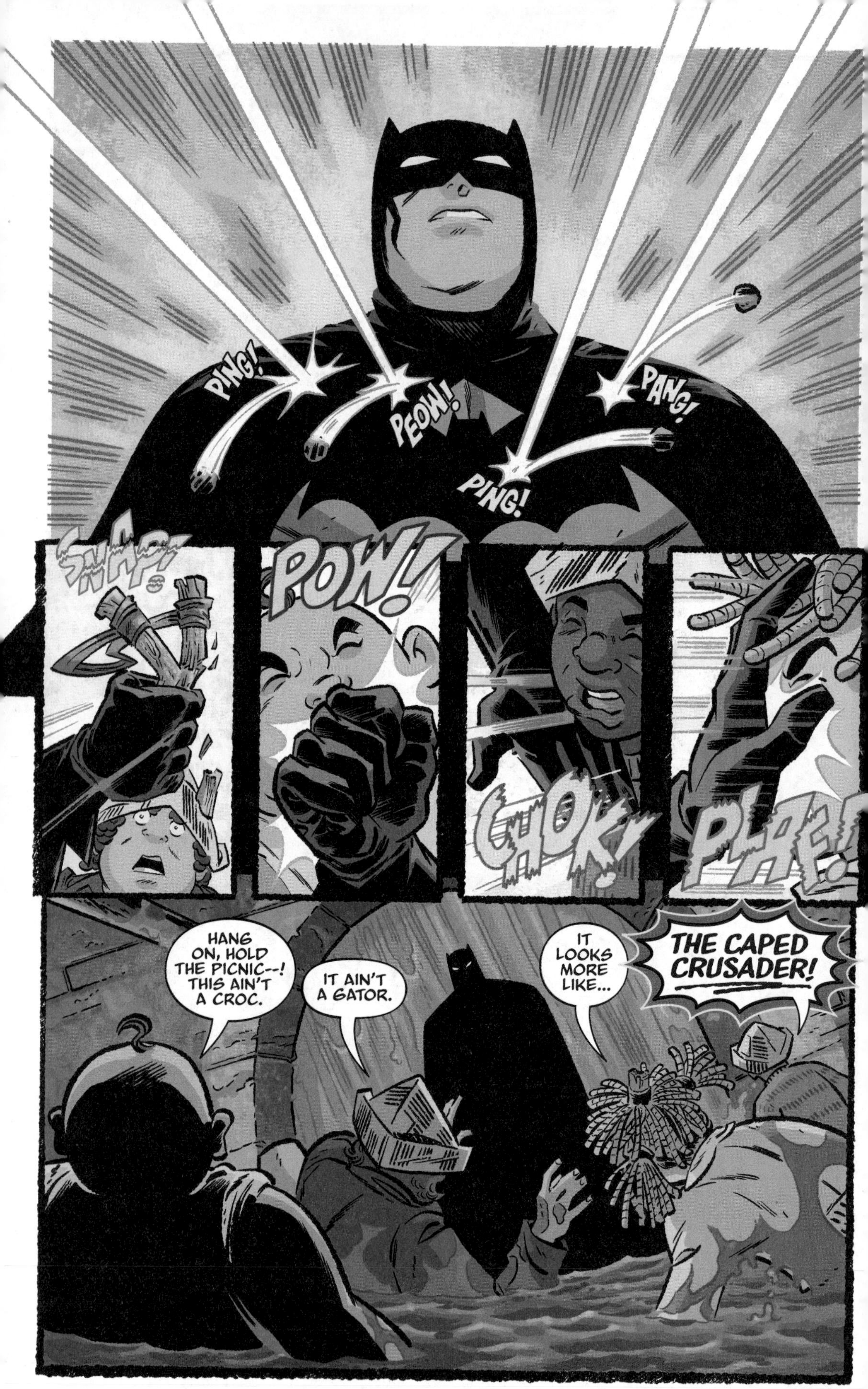
PING!
PEOW!
PANG!
PING!
SNAP!
POW!
CHOK!
HANG ON, HOLD THE PICNIC--! THIS AIN'T A CROC.
IT AIN'T A GATOR.
IT LOOKS MORE LIKE...
THE CAPED CRUSADER!

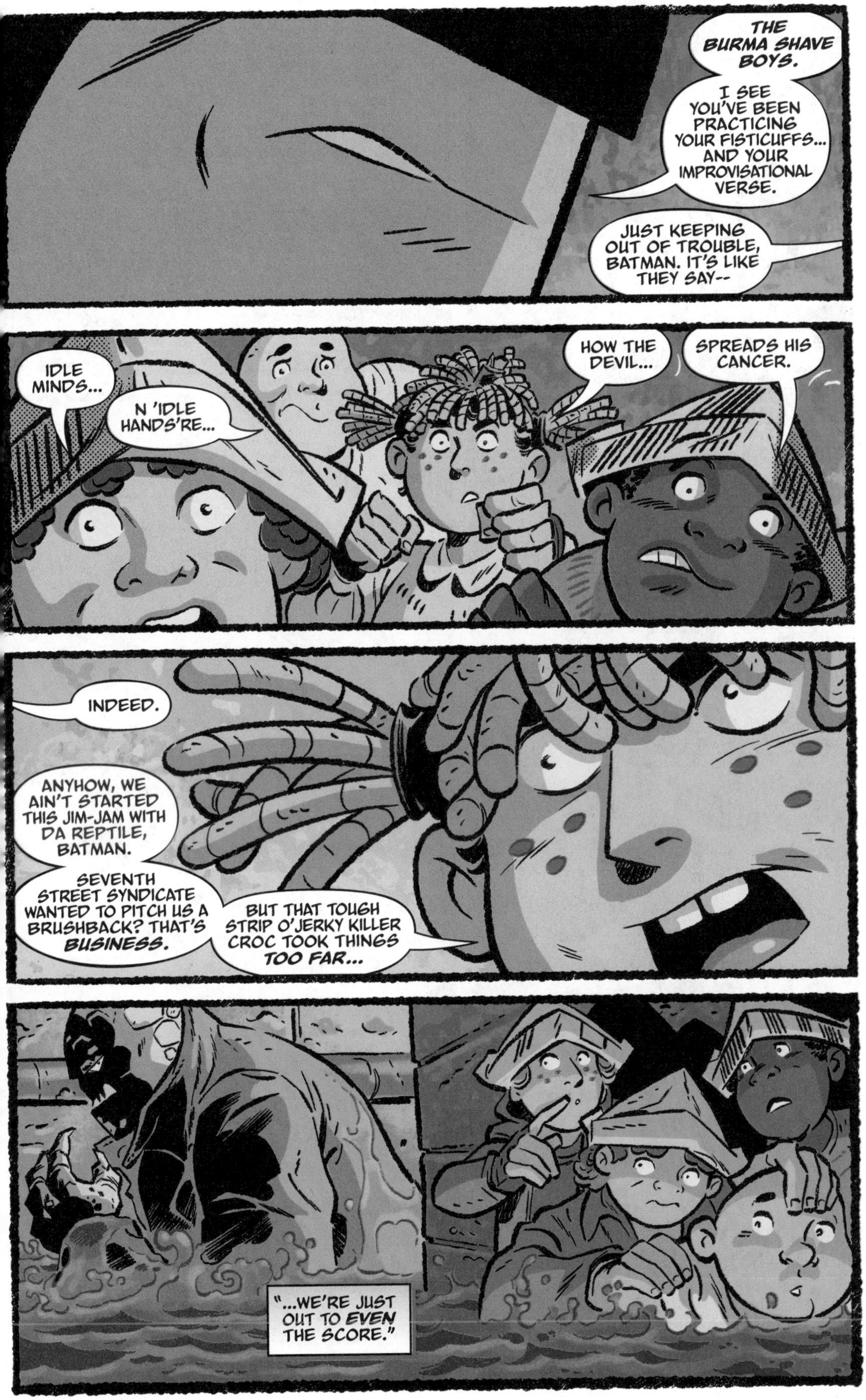
THE BURMA SHAVE BOYS.
I SEE YOU'VE BEEN PRACTICING YOUR FISTICUFFS... AND YOUR IMPROVISATIONAL VERSE.
JUST KEEPING OUT OF TROUBLE, BATMAN. IT'S LIKE THEY SAY--
IDLE MINDS...
N 'IDLE HANDS'RE...
HOW THE DEVIL...
SPREADS HIS CANCER.
INDEED.
ANYHOW, WE AIN'T STARTED THIS JIM-JAM WITH DA REPTILE, BATMAN.
SEVENTH STREET SYNDICATE WANTED TO PITCH US A BRUSHBACK? THAT'S BUSINESS.
BUT THAT TOUGH STRIP O'JERKY KILLER CROC TOOK THINGS TOO FAR...
"...WE'RE JUST OUT TO EVEN THE SCORE."

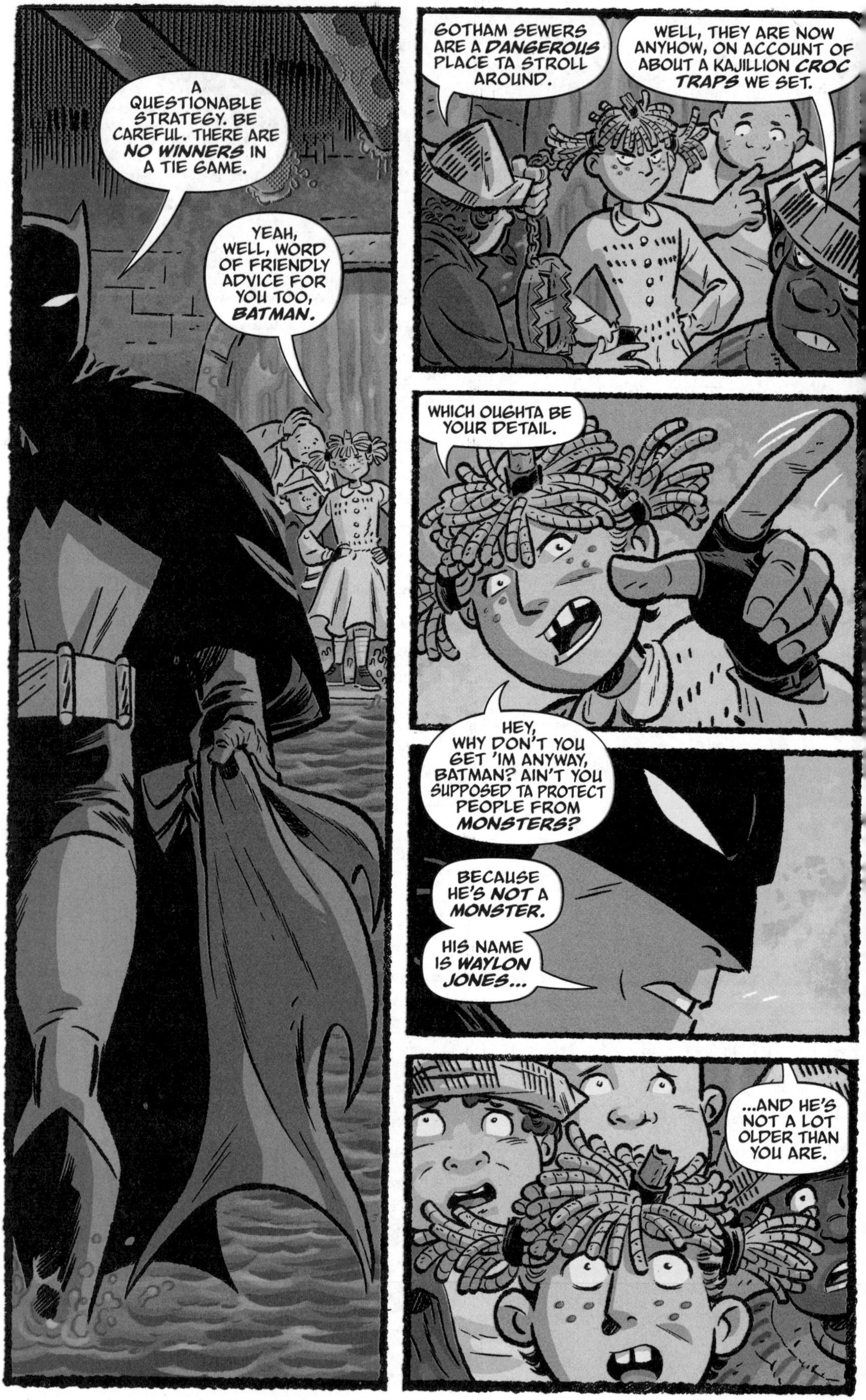
A QUESTIONABLE STRATEGY. BE CAREFUL. THERE ARE NO WINNERS IN A TIE GAME.
YEAH, WELL, WORD OF FRIENDLY ADVICE FOR YOU TOO, BATMAN.
GOTHAM SEWERS ARE A DANGEROUS PLACE TA STROLL AROUND.
WELL, THEY ARE NOW ANYHOW, ON ACCOUNT OF ABOUT A KAJILLION CROC TRAPS WE SET.
WHICH OUGHTA BE YOUR DETAIL.
HEY, WHY DON'T YOU GET 'IM ANYWAY, BATMAN? AIN'T YOU SUPPOSED TA PROTECT PEOPLE FROM MONSTERS?
BECAUSE HE'S NOT A MONSTER.
HIS NAME IS WAYLON JONES...
...AND HE'S NOT A LOT OLDER THAN YOU ARE.

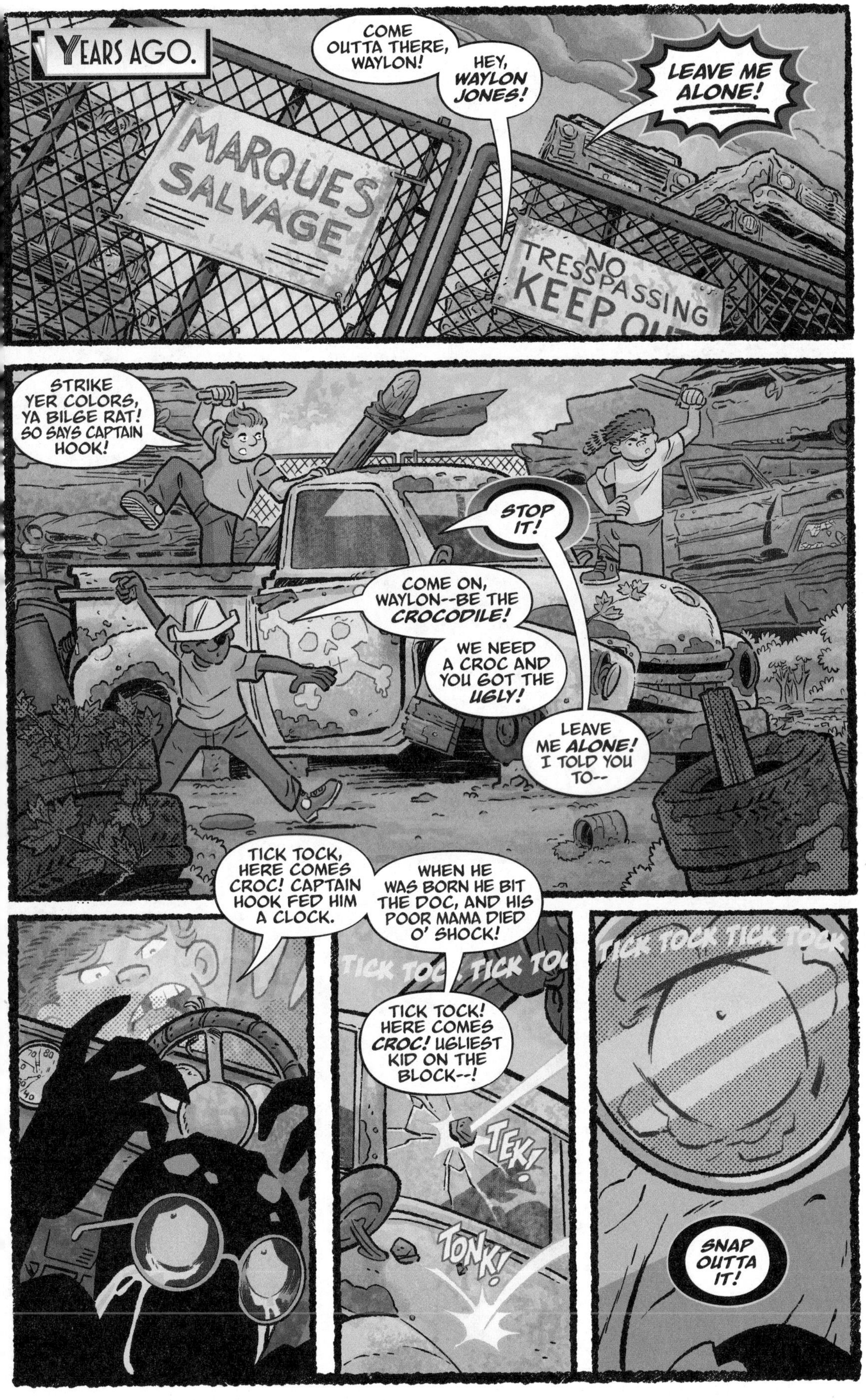
YEARS AGO.
COME OUTTA THERE, WAYLON!
HEY, WAYLON JONES!
LEAVE ME ALONE!
MARQUES SALVAGE
NO TRESSPASSING KEEP OU
STRIKE YER COLORS, YA BILGE RAT! SO SAYS CAPTAIN HOOK!
STOP IT!
COME ON, WAYLON--BE THE CROCODILE!
WE NEED A CROC AND YOU GOT THE UGLY!
LEAVE ME ALONE! I TOLD YOU TO--
TICK TOCK, HERE COMES CROC! CAPTAIN HOOK FED HIM A CLOCK.
WHEN HE WAS BORN HE BIT THE DOC, AND HIS POOR MAMA DIED O' SHOCK!
TICK TOCK, TICK TOC
TICK TOCK! HERE COMES CROC! UGLIEST KID ON THE BLOCK--!
TEK!
TONK!
TICK TOCK TICK TOCK
SNAP OUTTA IT!

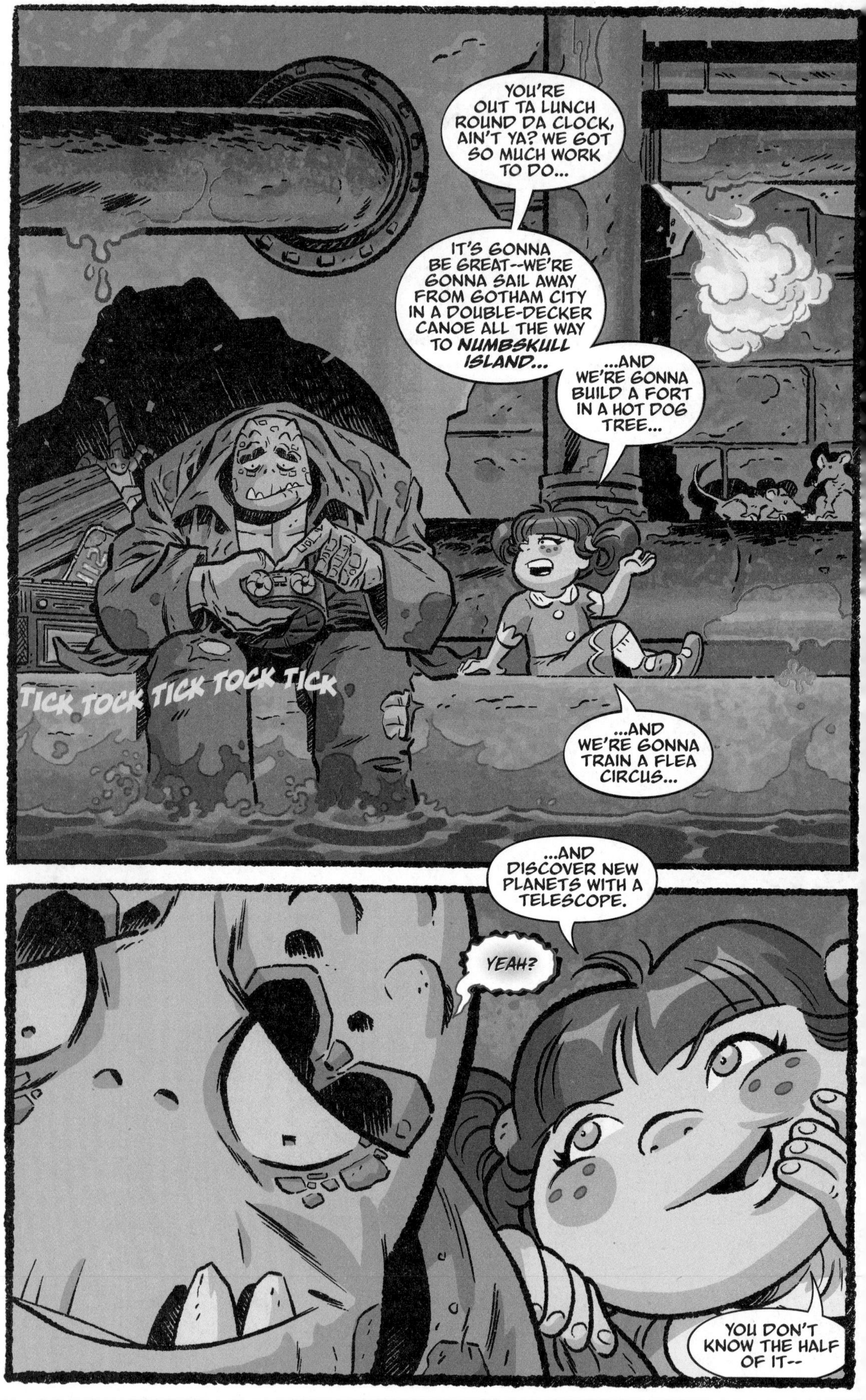
YOU'RE OUT TA LUNCH ROUND DA CLOCK, AIN'T YA? WE GOT SO MUCH WORK TO DO...
IT'S GONNA BE GREAT--WE'RE GONNA SAIL AWAY FROM GOTHAM CITY IN A DOUBLE-DECKER CANOE ALL THE WAY TO *NUMBSKULL ISLAND*...
...AND WE'RE GONNA BUILD A FORT IN A HOT DOG TREE...
TICK TOCK TICK TOCK TICK
...AND WE'RE GONNA TRAIN A FLEA CIRCUS...
...AND DISCOVER NEW PLANETS WITH A TELESCOPE.
YEAH?
YOU DON'T KNOW THE HALF OF IT--

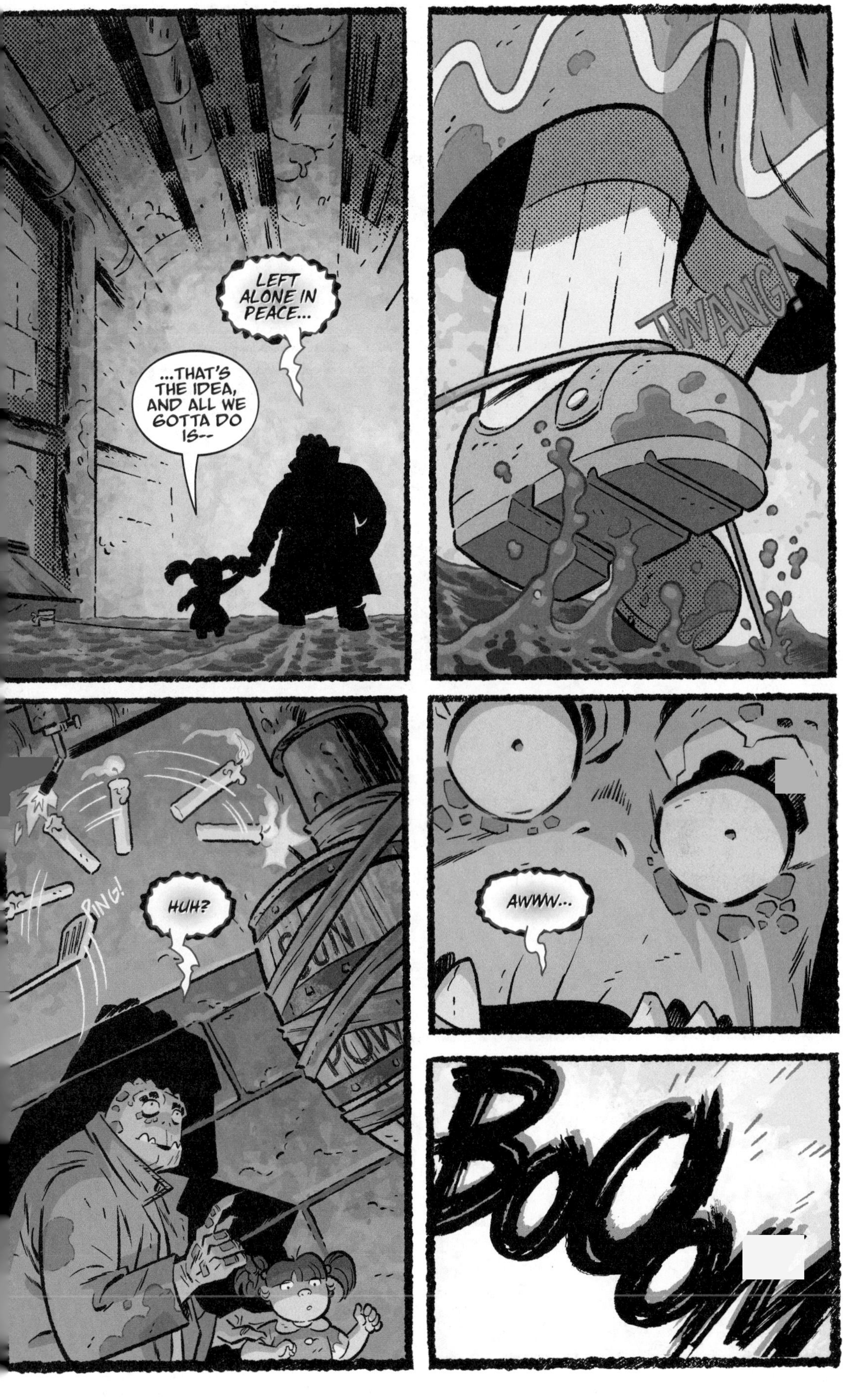
LEFT ALONE IN PEACE...
...THAT'S THE IDEA, AND ALL WE GOTTA DO IS--
TWANG!
PING!
HUH?
AWWW...
BOOOM

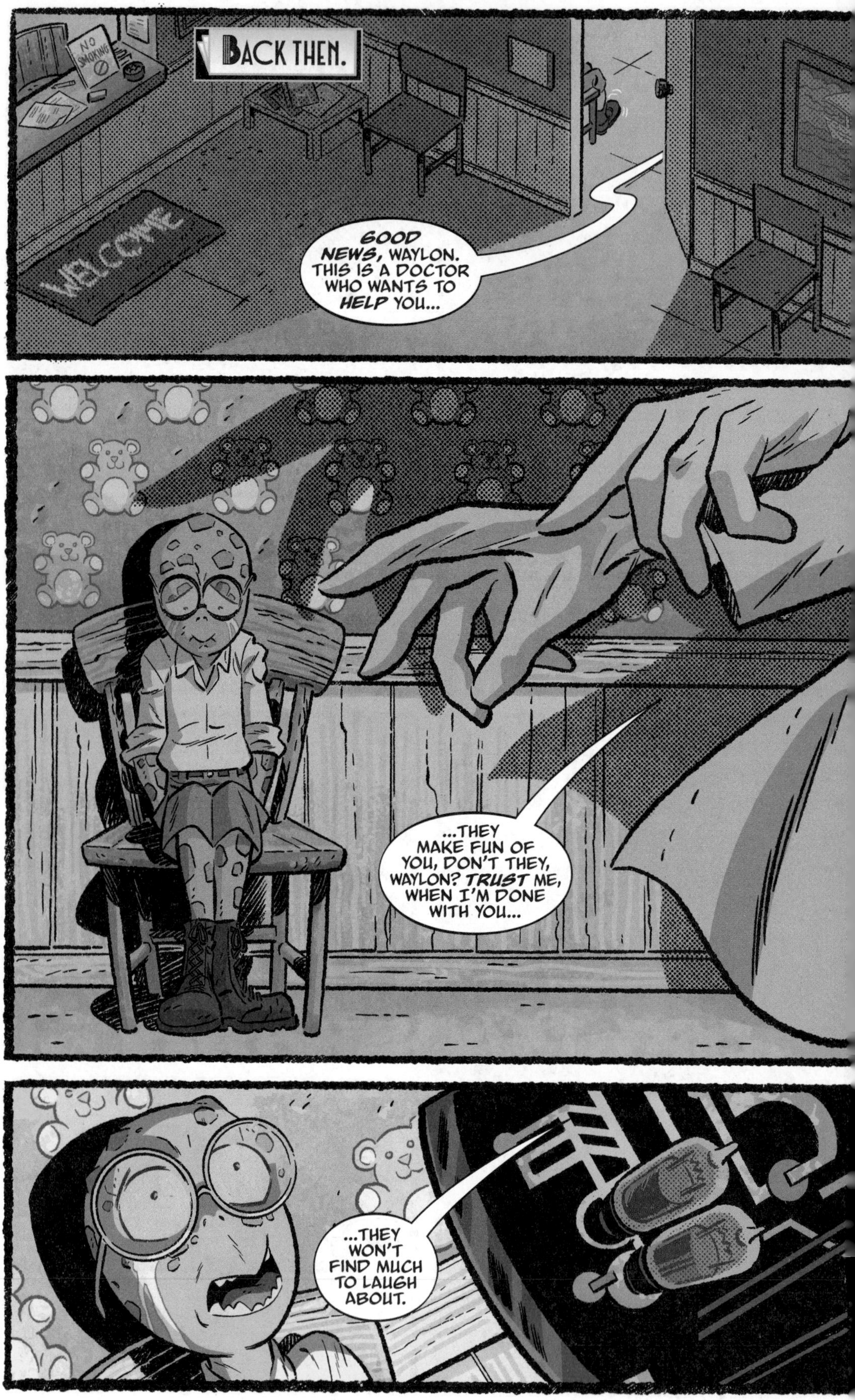

BACK THEN.
NO SMOKING
WELCOME
GOOD NEWS, WAYLON. THIS IS A DOCTOR WHO WANTS TO HELP YOU...
...THEY MAKE FUN OF YOU, DON'T THEY, WAYLON? TRUST ME, WHEN I'M DONE WITH YOU...
...THEY WON'T FIND MUCH TO LAUGH ABOUT.

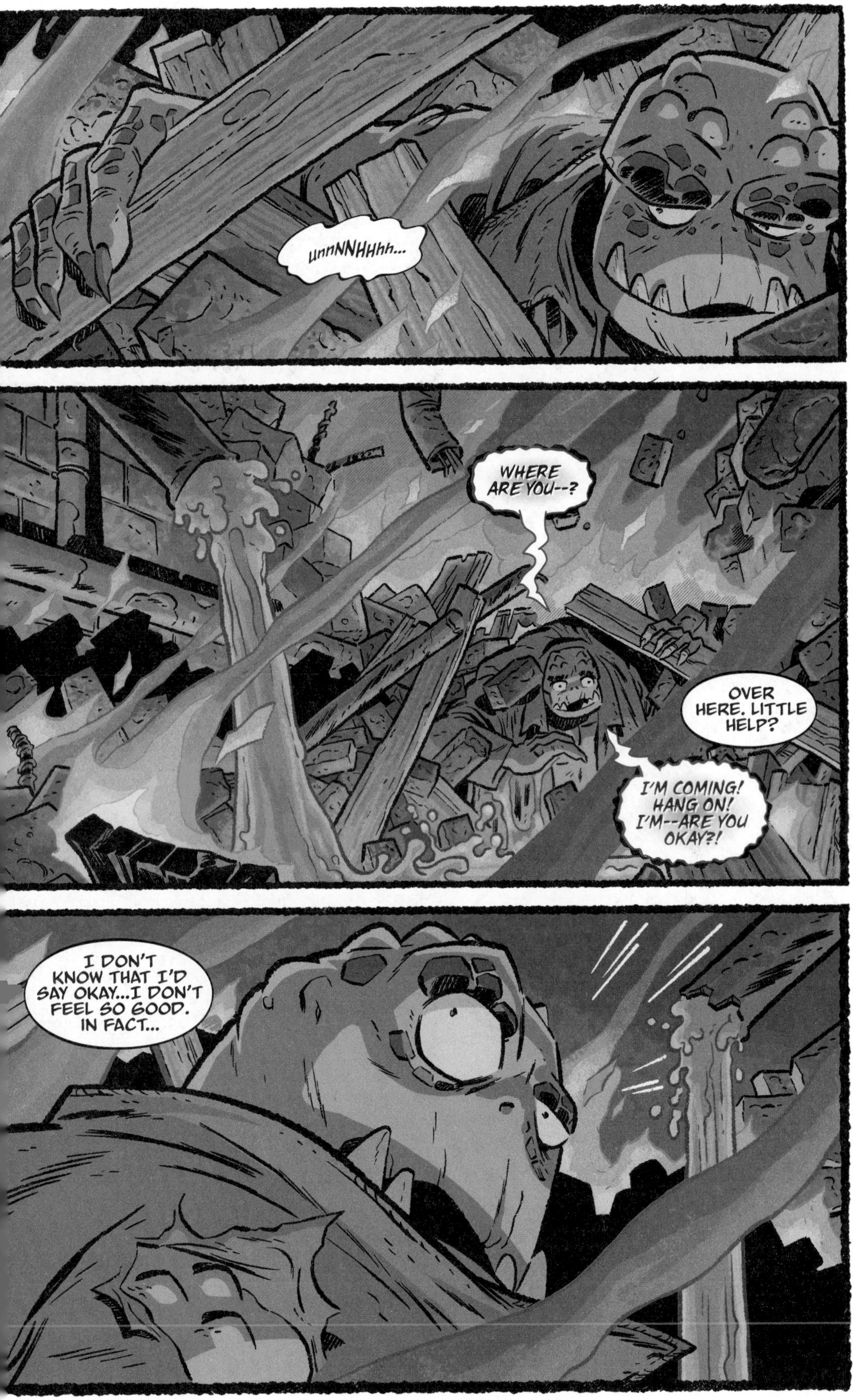
unnNNHhhh...
WHERE ARE YOU--?
OVER HERE. LITTLE HELP?
I'M COMING! HANG ON! I'M--ARE YOU OKAY?!
I DON'T KNOW THAT I'D SAY OKAY...I DON'T FEEL SO GOOD. IN FACT...

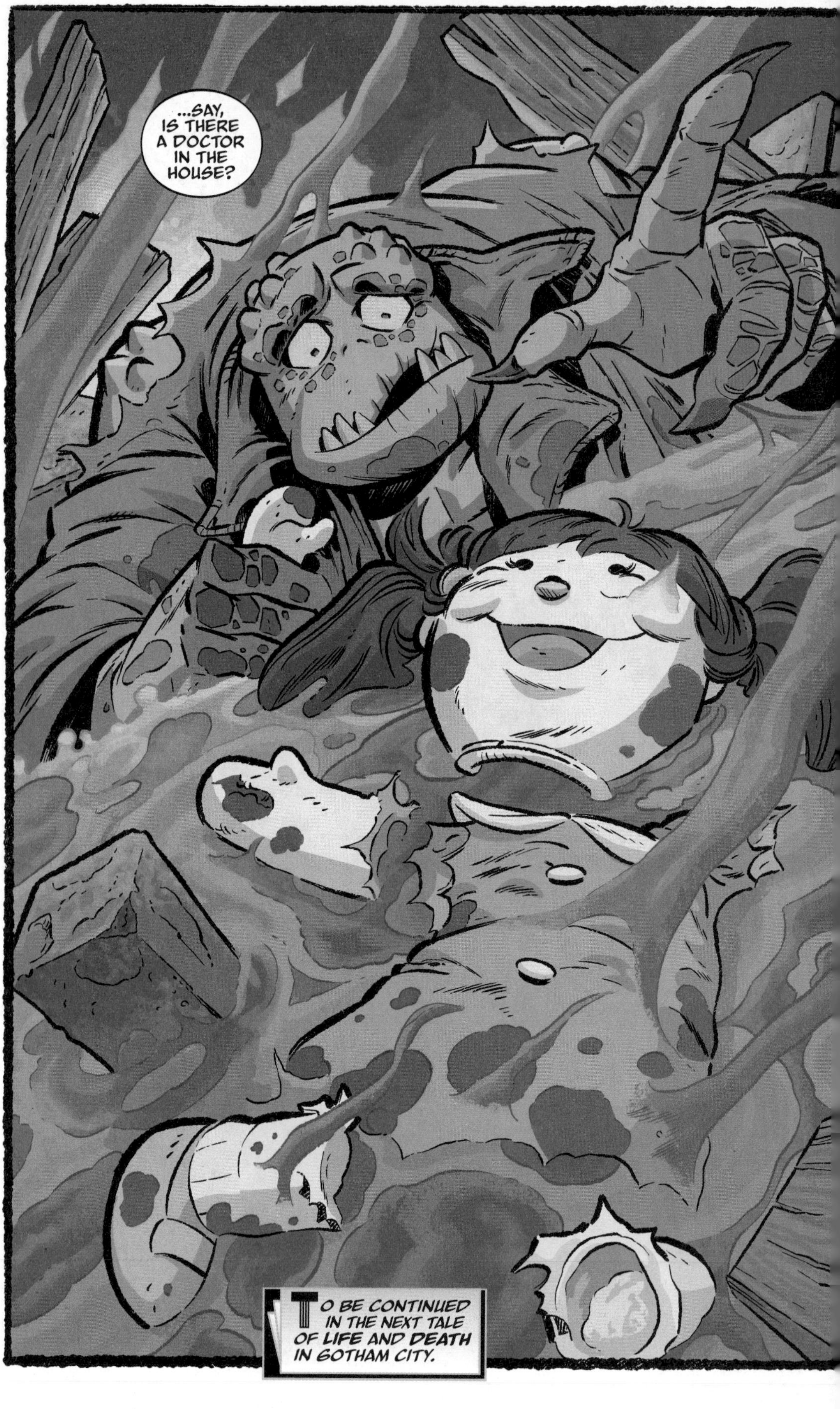
...SAY, IS THERE A DOCTOR IN THE HOUSE?
TO BE CONTINUED IN THE NEXT TALE OF LIFE AND DEATH IN GOTHAM CITY.

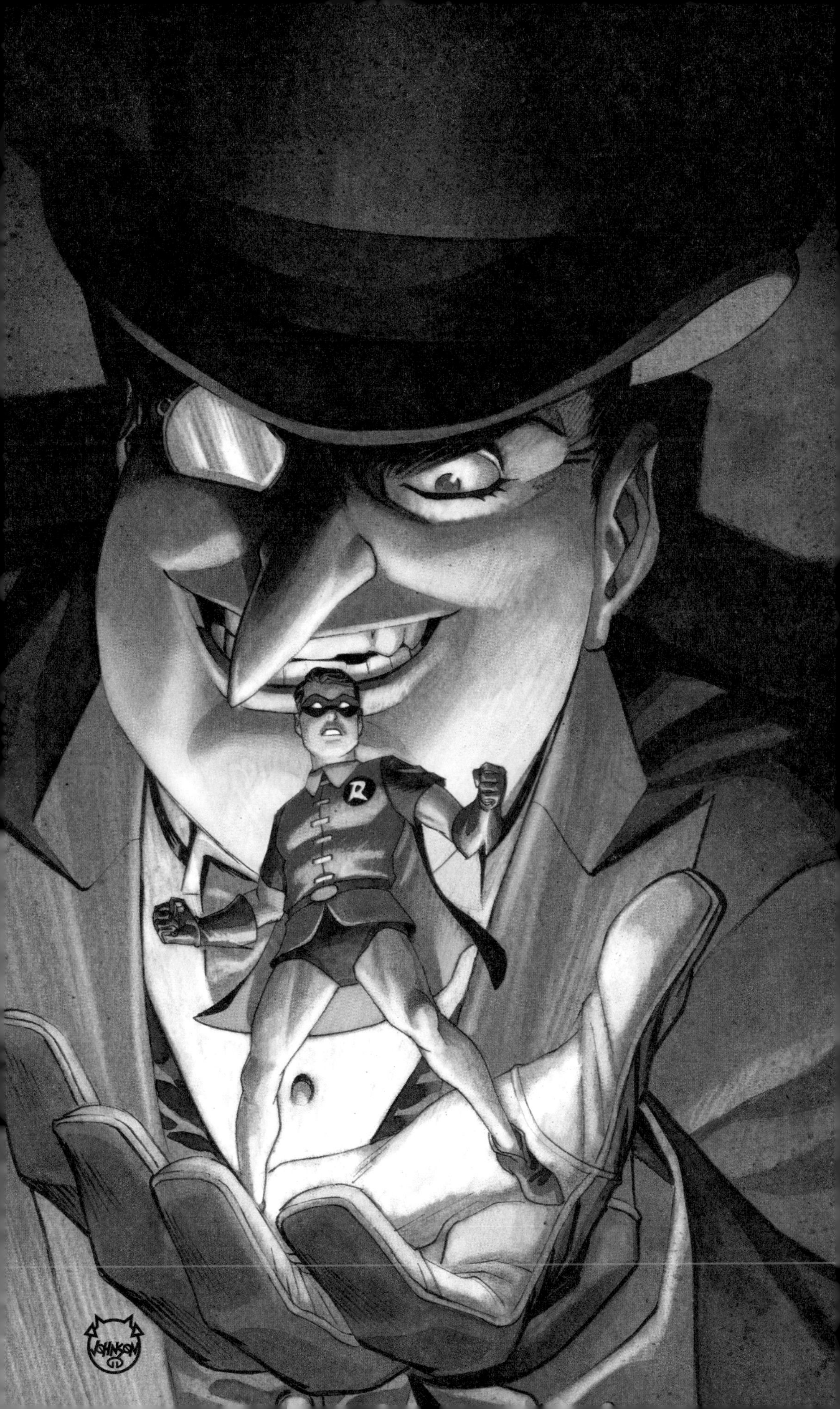
JOHNSON

***Batman: The Audio Adventures* #4 variant cover by Michael Allred & Laura Allred**

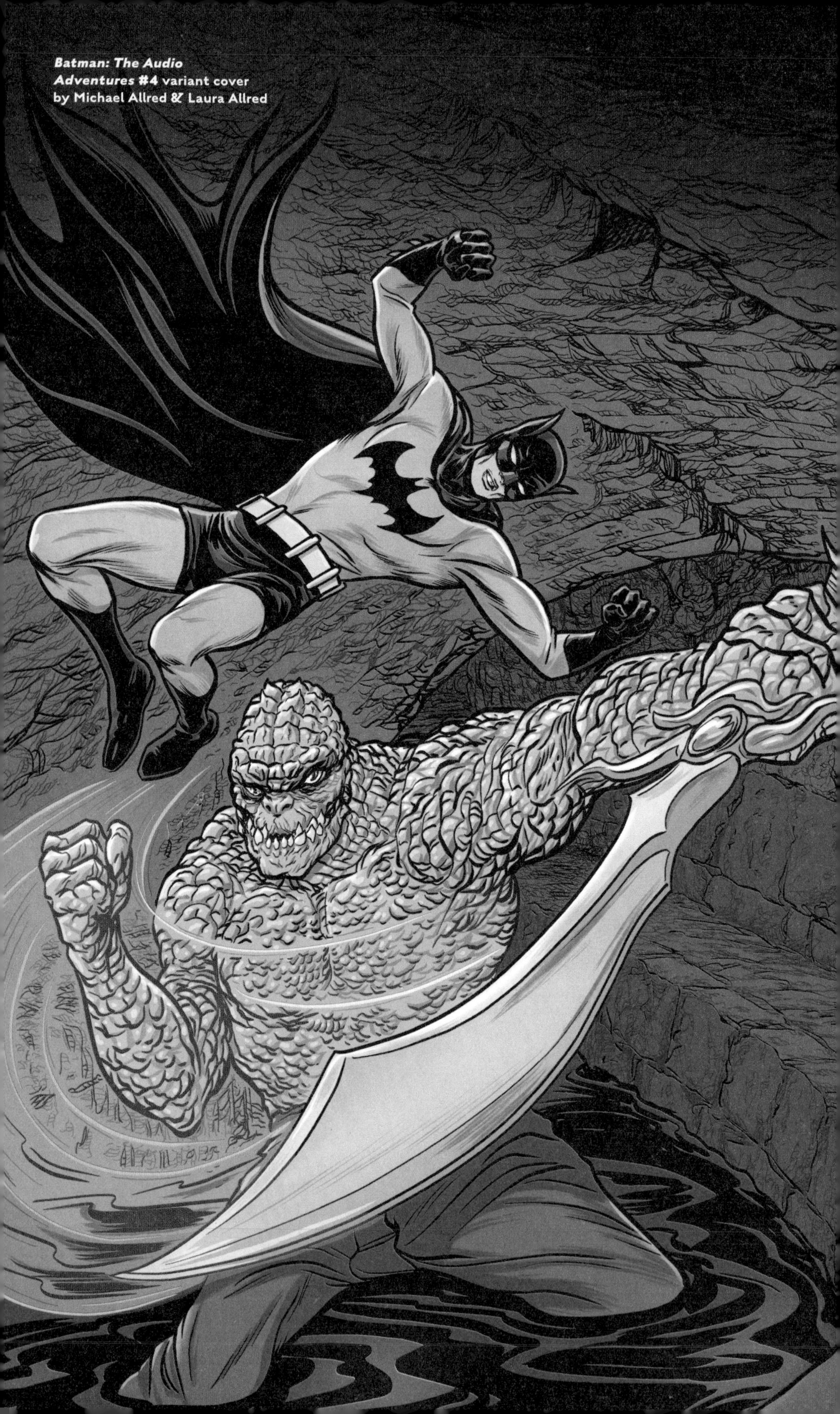

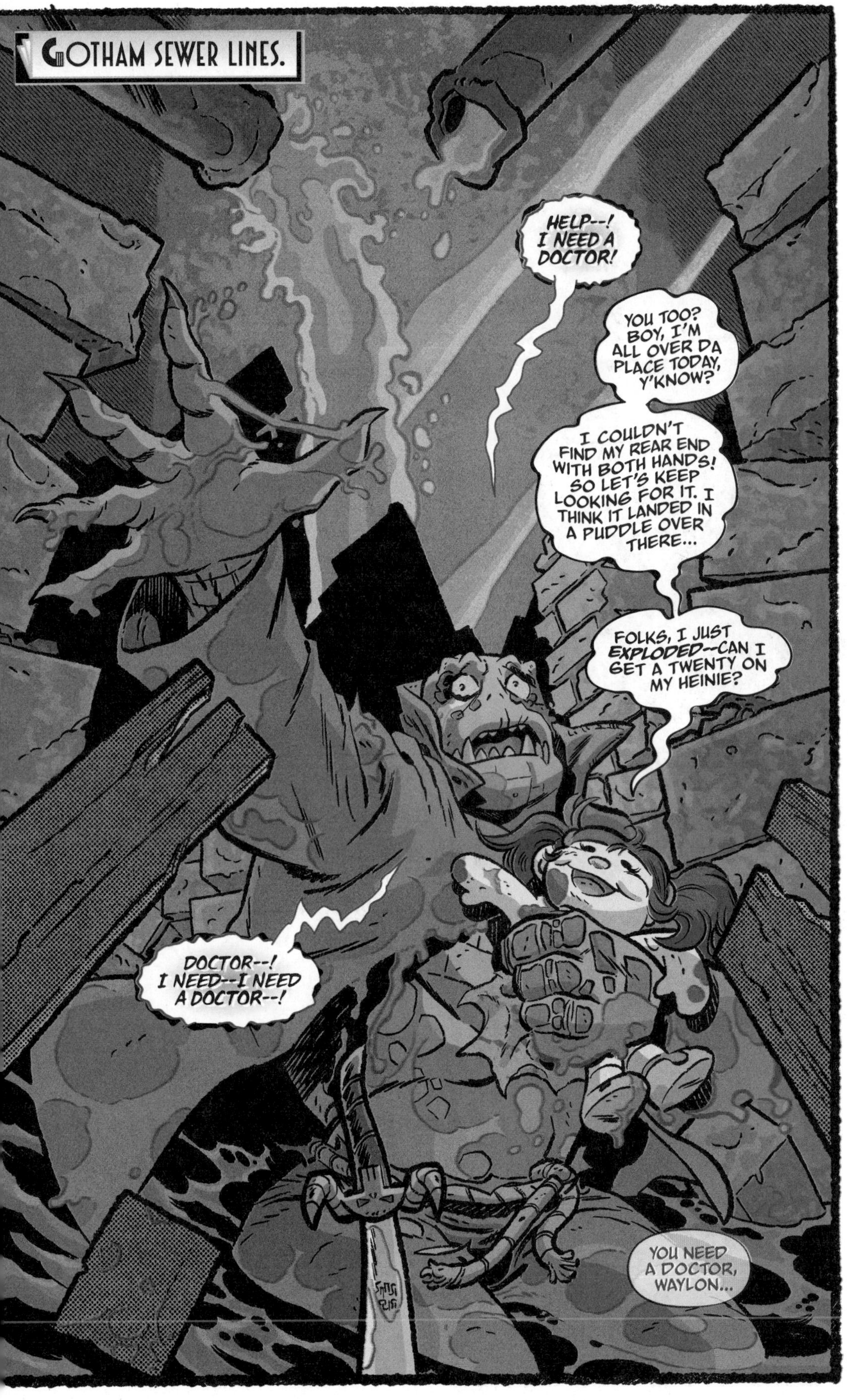
GOTHAM SEWER LINES.
HELP--! I NEED A DOCTOR!
YOU TOO? BOY, I'M ALL OVER DA PLACE TODAY, Y'KNOW?
I COULDN'T FIND MY REAR END WITH BOTH HANDS! SO LET'S KEEP LOOKING FOR IT. I THINK IT LANDED IN A PUDDLE OVER THERE...
FOLKS, I JUST EXPLODED--CAN I GET A TWENTY ON MY HEINIE?
DOCTOR--! I NEED--I NEED A DOCTOR--!
YOU NEED A DOCTOR, WAYLON...

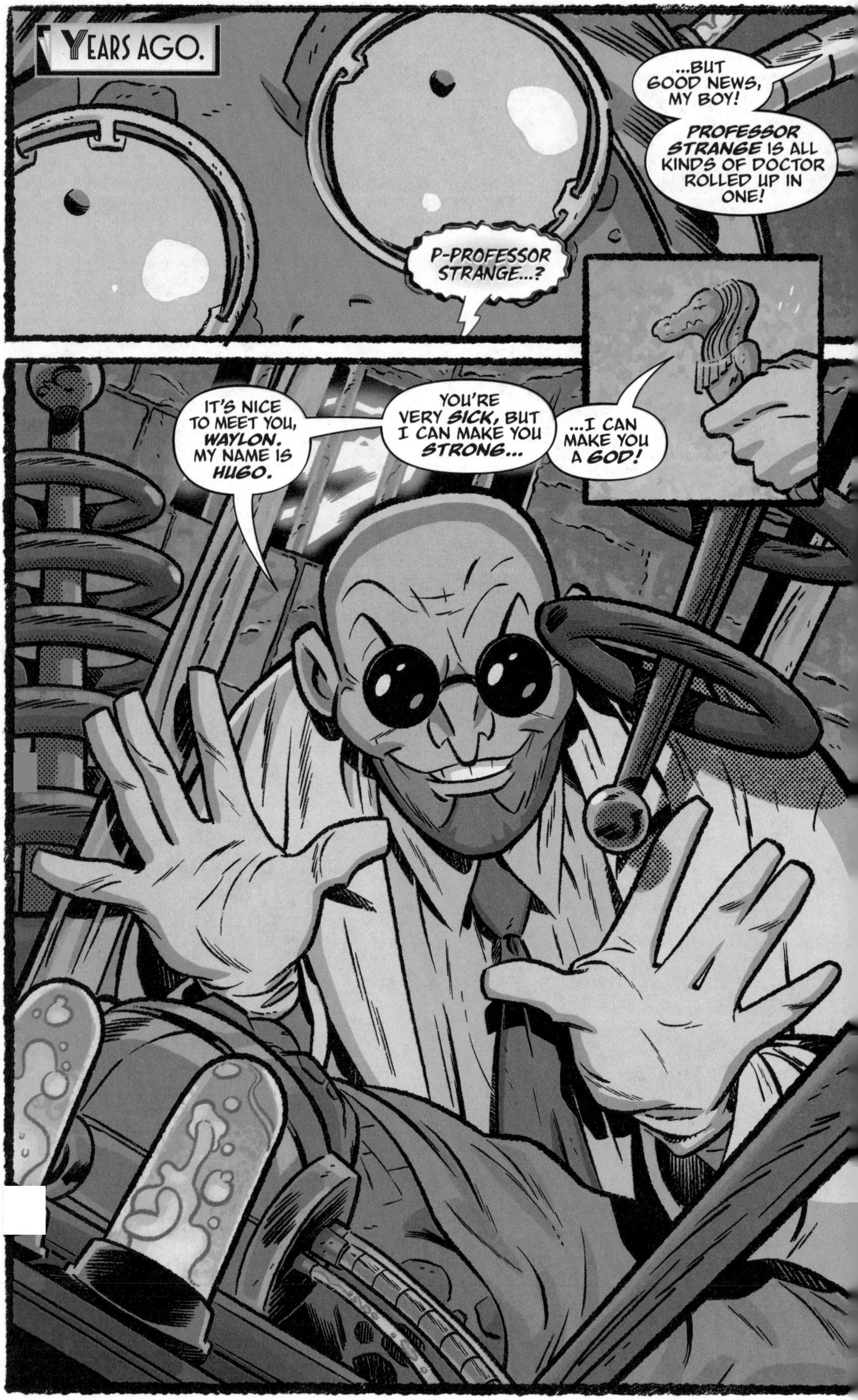
YEARS AGO.
P-PROFESSOR STRANGE...?
...BUT GOOD NEWS, MY BOY!
PROFESSOR STRANGE IS ALL KINDS OF DOCTOR ROLLED UP IN ONE!
IT'S NICE TO MEET YOU, WAYLON. MY NAME IS HUGO.
YOU'RE VERY SICK, BUT I CAN MAKE YOU STRONG...
...I CAN MAKE YOU A GOD!

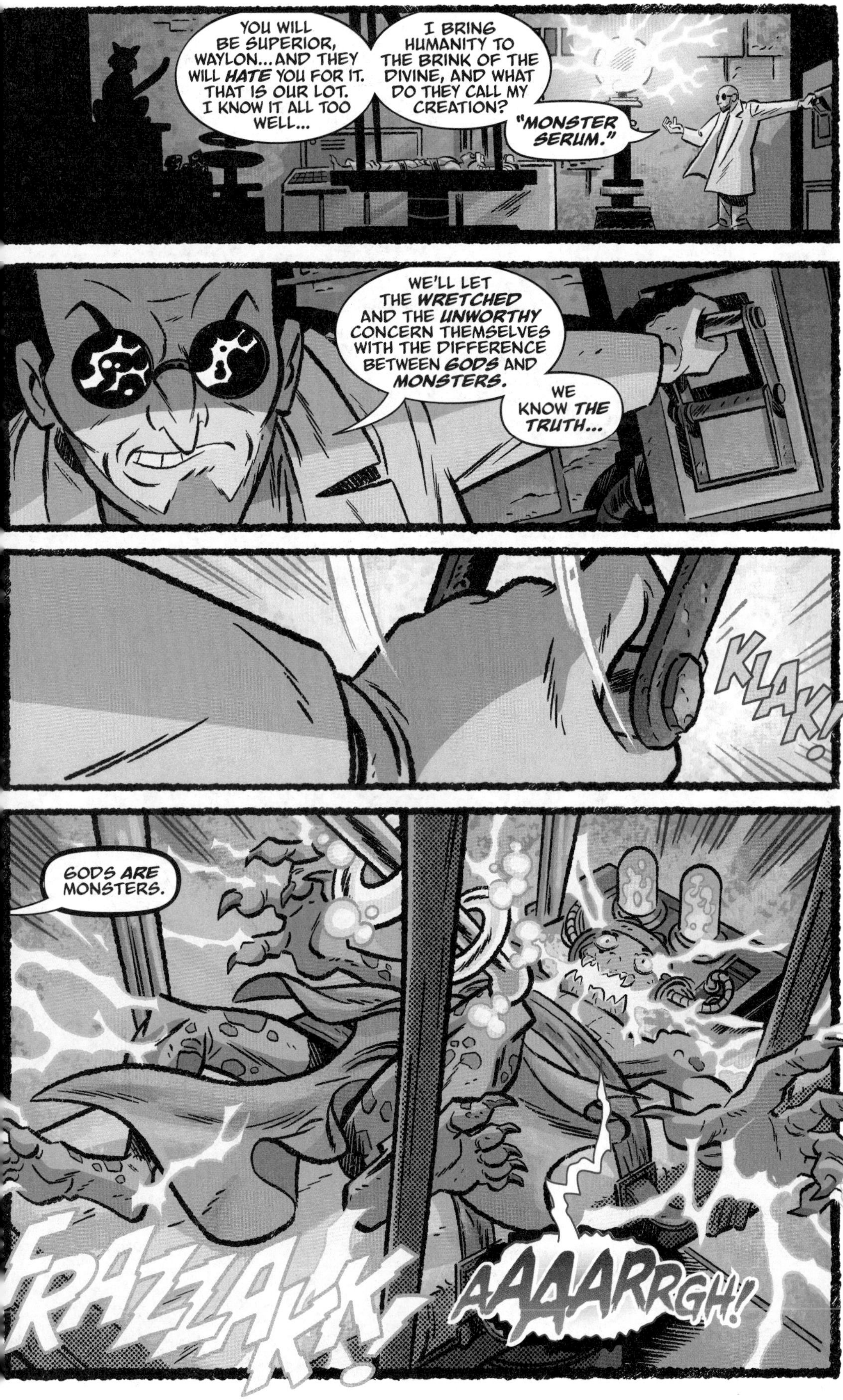
YOU WILL BE SUPERIOR, WAYLON... AND THEY WILL HATE YOU FOR IT. THAT IS OUR LOT. I KNOW IT ALL TOO WELL...
I BRING HUMANITY TO THE BRINK OF THE DIVINE, AND WHAT DO THEY CALL MY CREATION?
"MONSTER SERUM."
WE'LL LET THE WRETCHED AND THE UNWORTHY CONCERN THEMSELVES WITH THE DIFFERENCE BETWEEN GODS AND MONSTERS.
WE KNOW THE TRUTH...
KLAK!
GODS ARE MONSTERS.
FRAZZLAKK!
AAAARRGH!

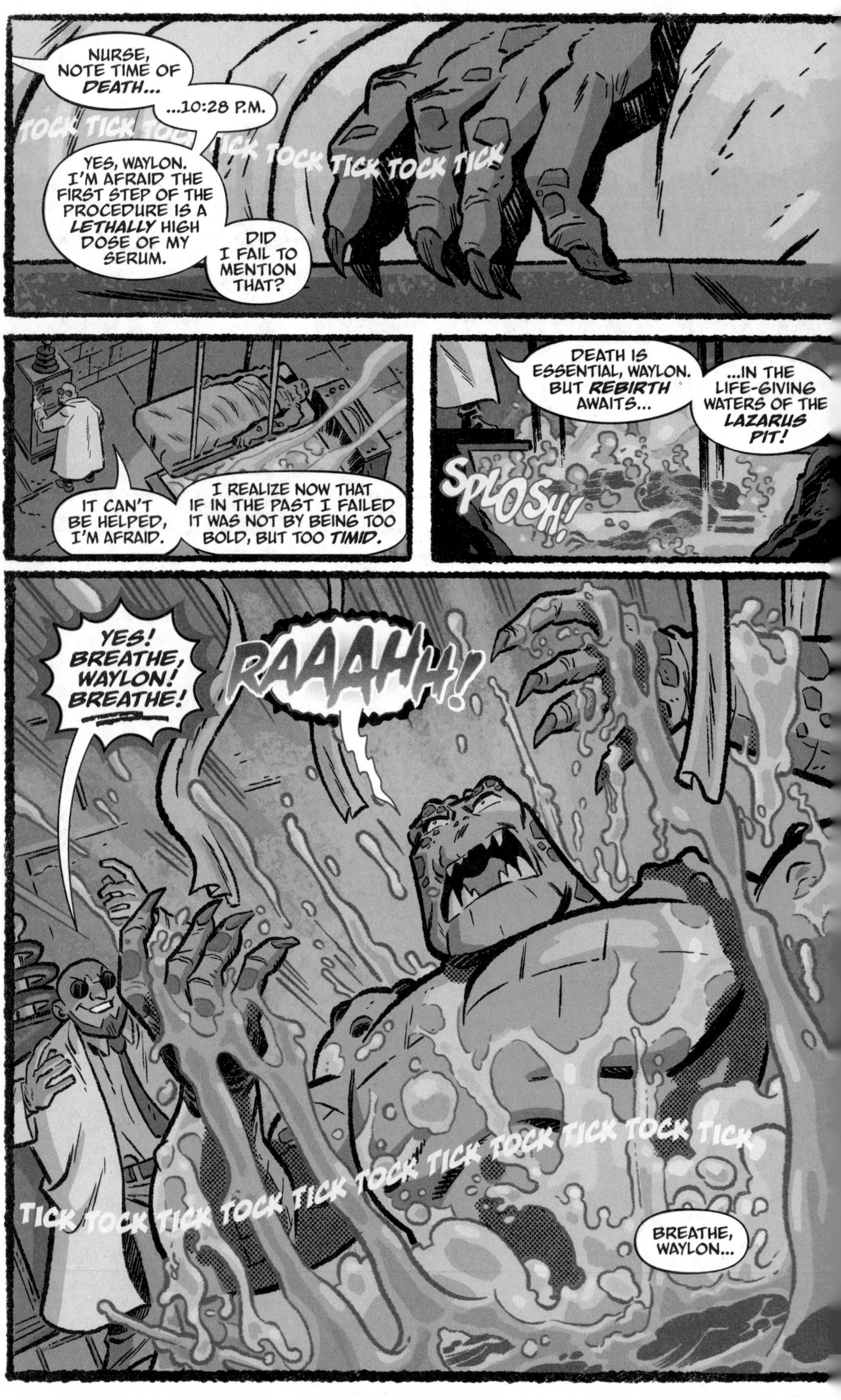
NURSE, NOTE TIME OF DEATH...
...10:28 P.M.
TOCK TICK TOCK TICK TOCK TICK TOCK TICK
YES, WAYLON. I'M AFRAID THE FIRST STEP OF THE PROCEDURE IS A LETHALLY HIGH DOSE OF MY SERUM.
DID I FAIL TO MENTION THAT?
IT CAN'T BE HELPED, I'M AFRAID.
I REALIZE NOW THAT IF IN THE PAST I FAILED IT WAS NOT BY BEING TOO BOLD, BUT TOO TIMID.
DEATH IS ESSENTIAL, WAYLON. BUT REBIRTH AWAITS...
...IN THE LIFE-GIVING WATERS OF THE LAZARUS PIT!
SPLOSH!
YES! BREATHE, WAYLON! BREATHE!
RAAAHH!
TICK TOCK TICK TOCK TICK TOCK TICK TOCK TICK TOCK TICK
BREATHE, WAYLON...

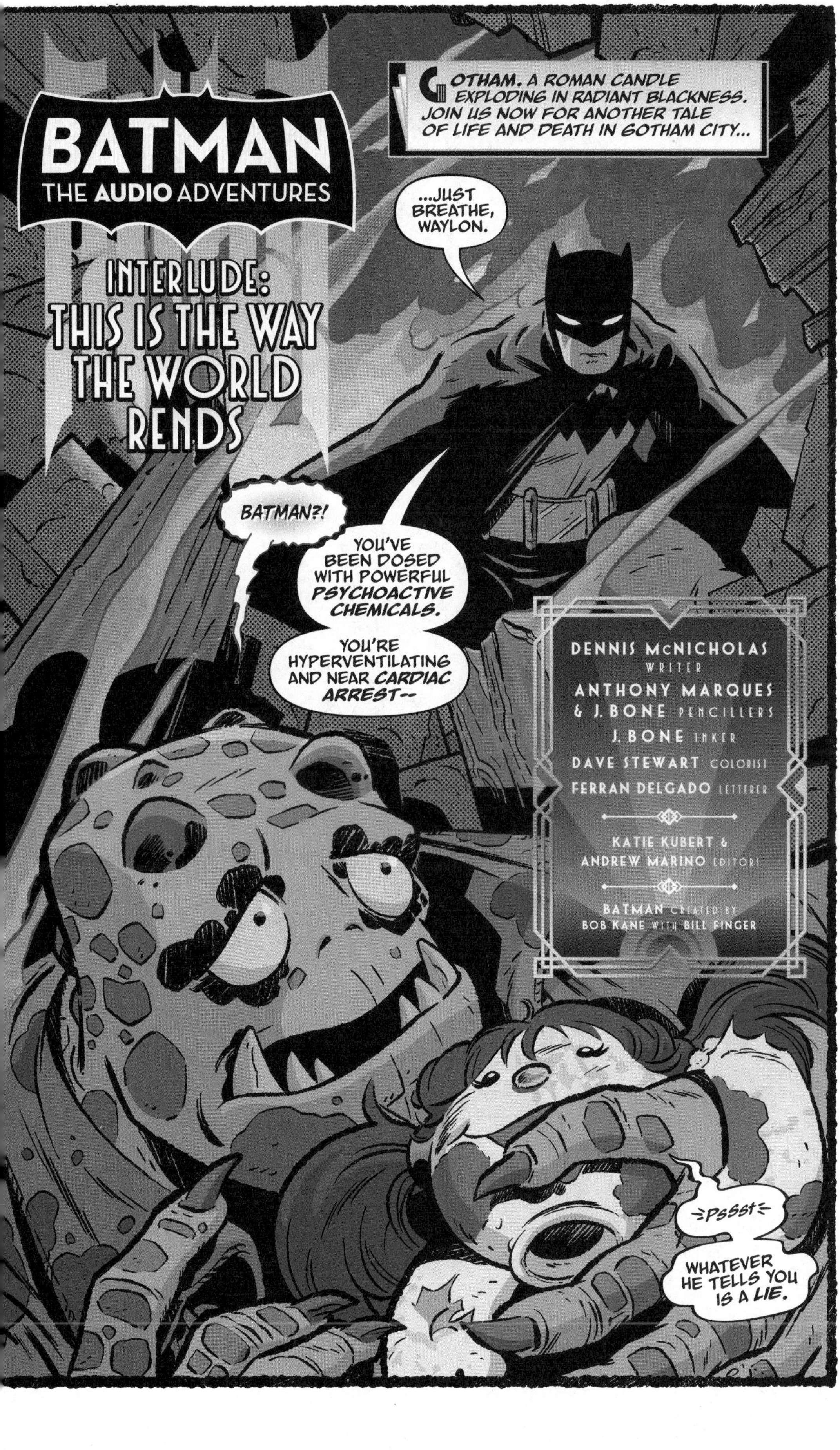
BATMAN
THE AUDIO ADVENTURES
INTERLUDE: THIS IS THE WAY THE WORLD RENDS
GOTHAM. A ROMAN CANDLE EXPLODING IN RADIANT BLACKNESS. JOIN US NOW FOR ANOTHER TALE OF LIFE AND DEATH IN GOTHAM CITY...
...JUST BREATHE, WAYLON.
BATMAN?!
YOU'VE BEEN DOSED WITH POWERFUL PSYCHOACTIVE CHEMICALS.
YOU'RE HYPERVENTILATING AND NEAR CARDIAC ARREST--
DENNIS McNICHOLAS WRITER
ANTHONY MARQUES & J. BONE PENCILLERS
J. BONE INKER
DAVE STEWART COLORIST
FERRAN DELGADO LETTERER
KATIE KUBERT & ANDREW MARINO EDITORS
BATMAN CREATED BY BOB KANE WITH BILL FINGER
=PSSST=
WHATEVER HE TELLS YOU IS A LIE.

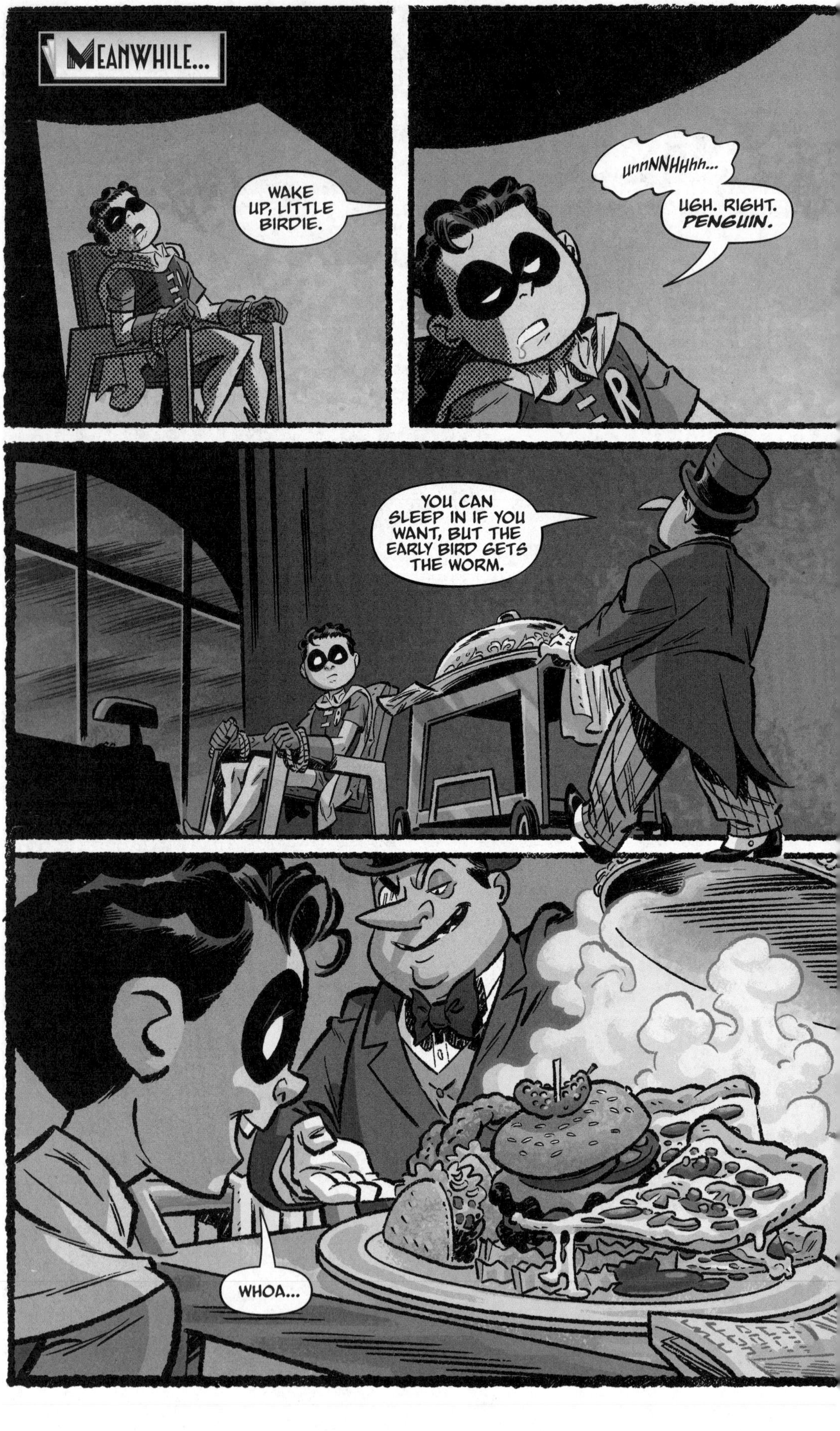
MEANWHILE...
WAKE UP, LITTLE BIRDIE.
unnNNHhhh...
UGH. RIGHT. PENGUIN.
YOU CAN SLEEP IN IF YOU WANT, BUT THE EARLY BIRD GETS THE WORM.
WHOA...

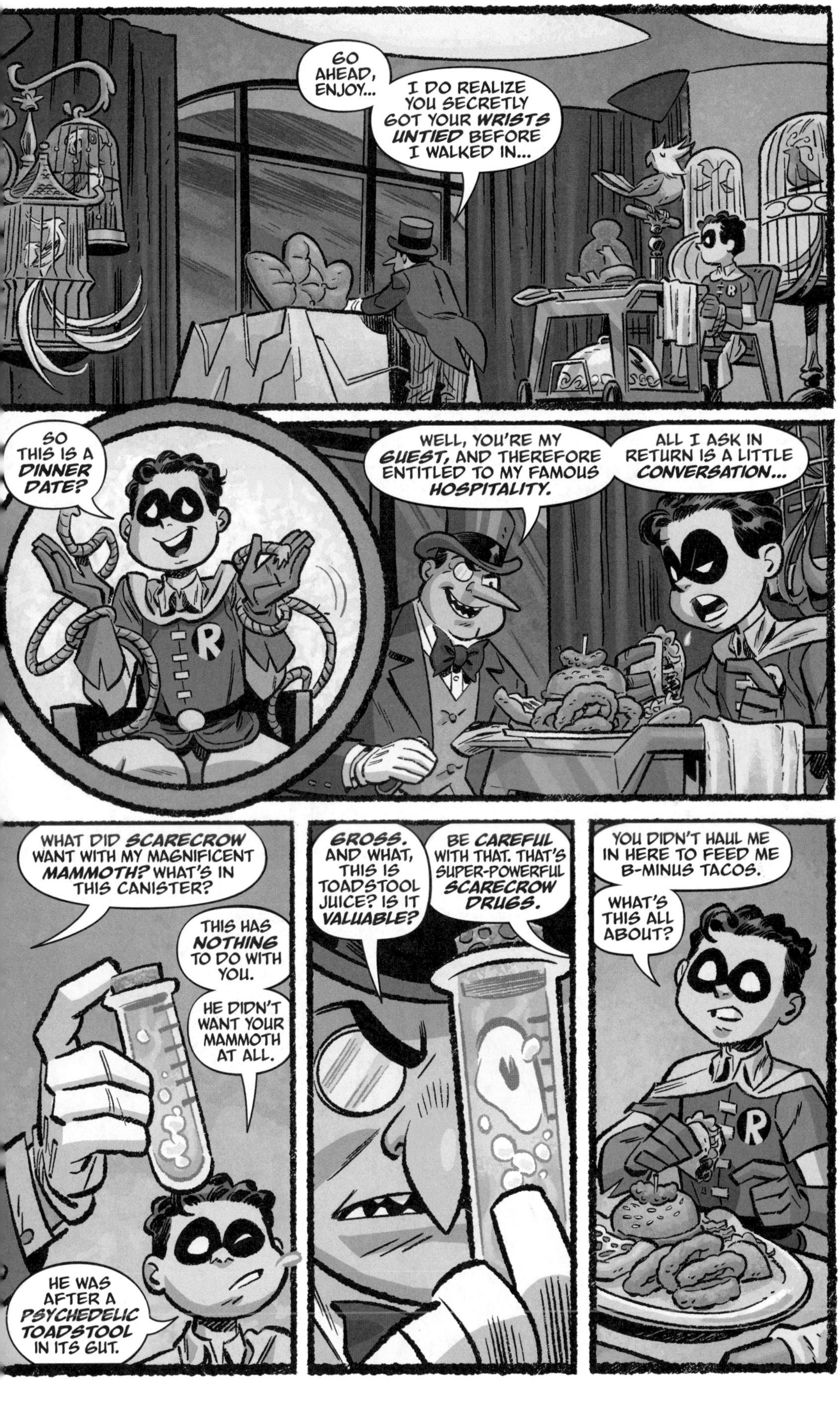
GO AHEAD, ENJOY...
I DO REALIZE YOU SECRETLY GOT YOUR WRISTS UNTIED BEFORE I WALKED IN...
SO THIS IS A DINNER DATE?
WELL, YOU'RE MY GUEST, AND THEREFORE ENTITLED TO MY FAMOUS HOSPITALITY.
ALL I ASK IN RETURN IS A LITTLE CONVERSATION...
WHAT DID SCARECROW WANT WITH MY MAGNIFICENT MAMMOTH? WHAT'S IN THIS CANISTER?
THIS HAS NOTHING TO DO WITH YOU.
HE DIDN'T WANT YOUR MAMMOTH AT ALL.
HE WAS AFTER A PSYCHEDELIC TOADSTOOL IN ITS GUT.
GROSS. AND WHAT, THIS IS TOADSTOOL JUICE? IS IT VALUABLE?
BE CAREFUL WITH THAT. THAT'S SUPER-POWERFUL SCARECROW DRUGS.
YOU DIDN'T HAUL ME IN HERE TO FEED ME B-MINUS TACOS.
WHAT'S THIS ALL ABOUT?

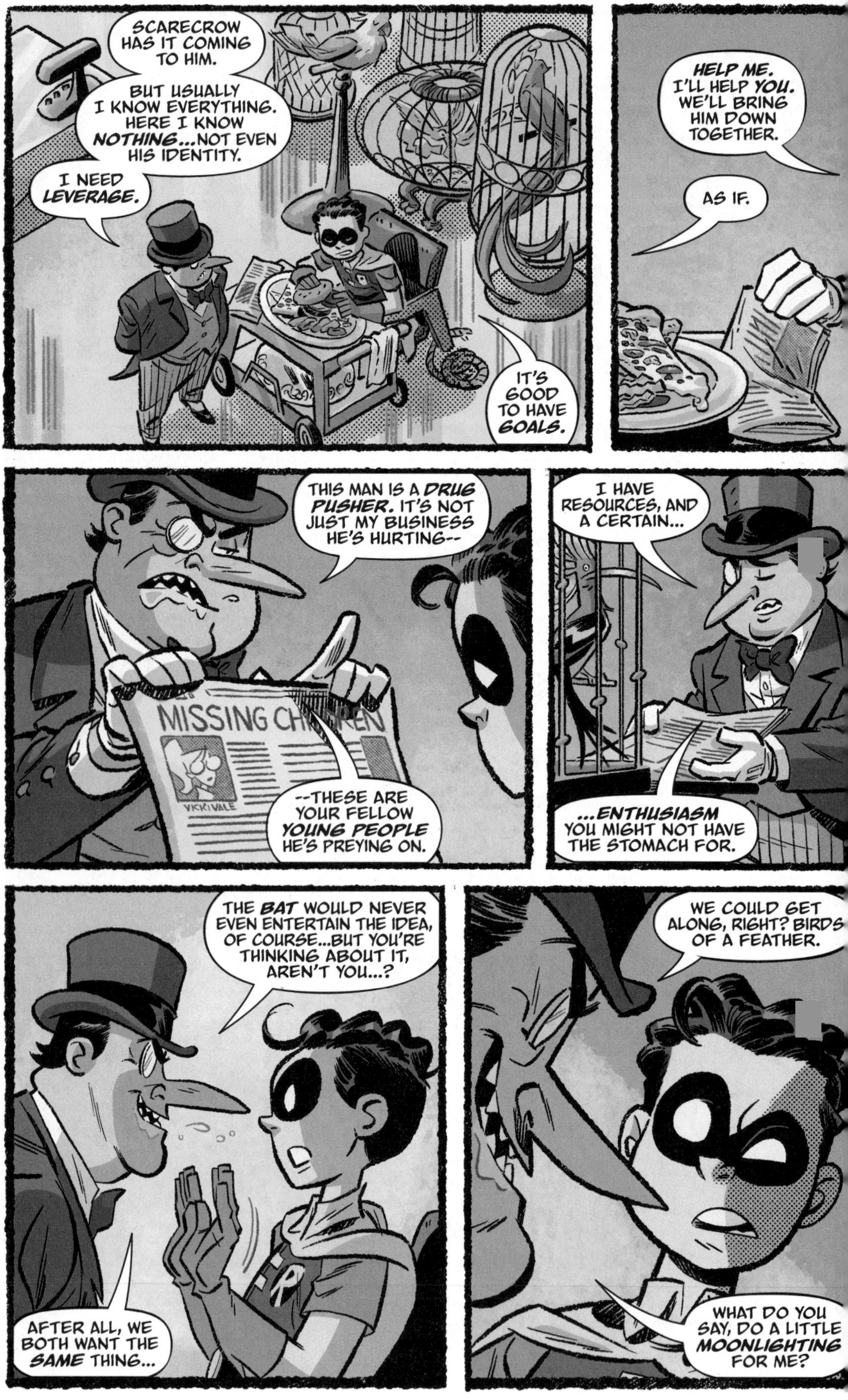
SCARECROW HAS IT COMING TO HIM.
BUT USUALLY I KNOW EVERYTHING. HERE I KNOW NOTHING...NOT EVEN HIS IDENTITY.
I NEED LEVERAGE.
IT'S GOOD TO HAVE GOALS.
HELP ME. I'LL HELP YOU. WE'LL BRING HIM DOWN TOGETHER.
AS IF.
THIS MAN IS A DRUG PUSHER. IT'S NOT JUST MY BUSINESS HE'S HURTING--
MISSING CHILDREN
VIKKI VALE
--THESE ARE YOUR FELLOW YOUNG PEOPLE HE'S PREYING ON.
I HAVE RESOURCES, AND A CERTAIN...
...ENTHUSIASM YOU MIGHT NOT HAVE THE STOMACH FOR.
THE BAT WOULD NEVER EVEN ENTERTAIN THE IDEA, OF COURSE...BUT YOU'RE THINKING ABOUT IT, AREN'T YOU...?
AFTER ALL, WE BOTH WANT THE SAME THING...
WE COULD GET ALONG, RIGHT? BIRDS OF A FEATHER.
WHAT DO YOU SAY, DO A LITTLE MOONLIGHTING FOR ME?

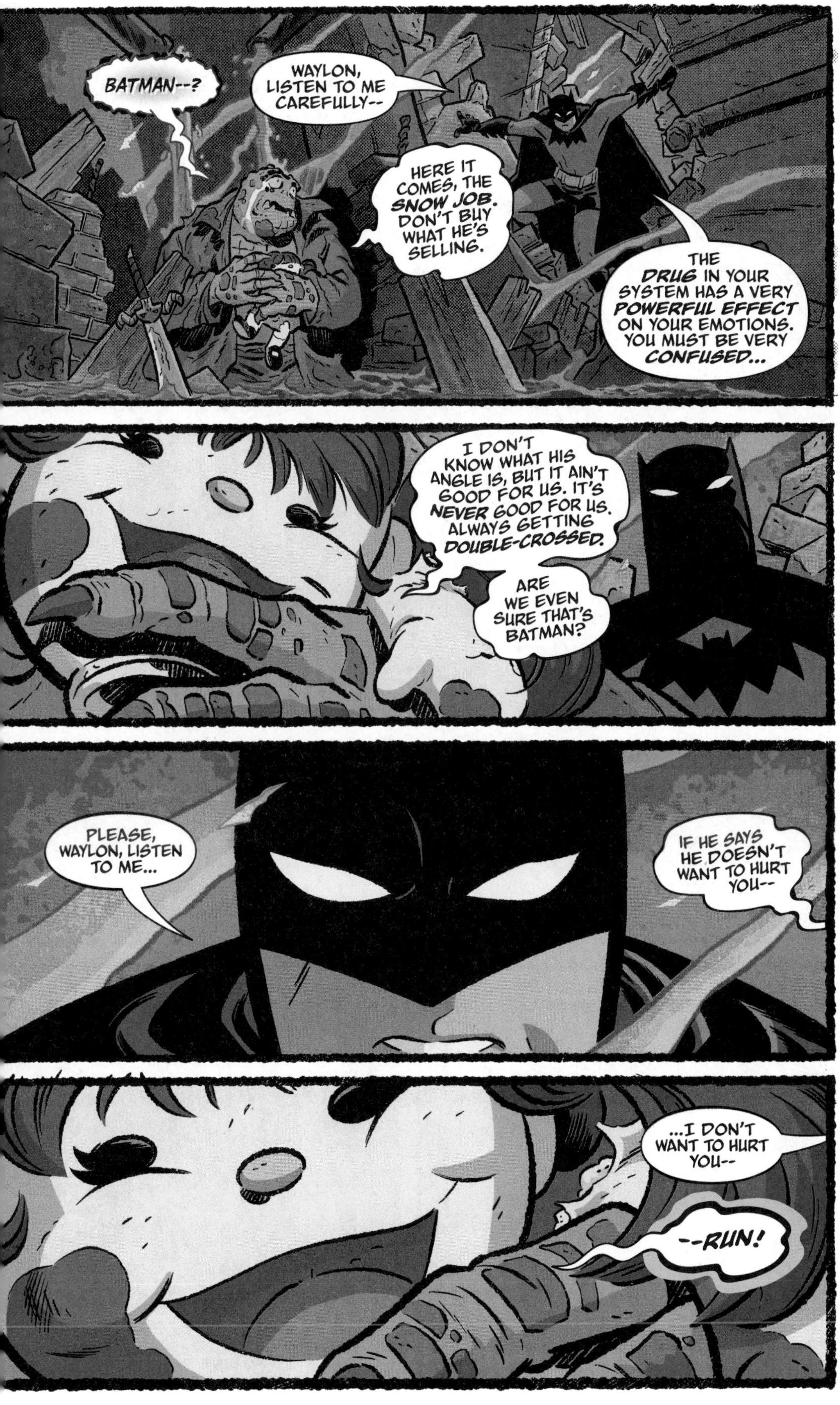
BATMAN--?
WAYLON, LISTEN TO ME CAREFULLY--
HERE IT COMES, THE SNOW JOB. DON'T BUY WHAT HE'S SELLING.
THE DRUG IN YOUR SYSTEM HAS A VERY POWERFUL EFFECT ON YOUR EMOTIONS. YOU MUST BE VERY CONFUSED...
I DON'T KNOW WHAT HIS ANGLE IS, BUT IT AIN'T GOOD FOR US. IT'S NEVER GOOD FOR US. ALWAYS GETTING DOUBLE-CROSSED.
ARE WE EVEN SURE THAT'S BATMAN?
PLEASE, WAYLON, LISTEN TO ME...
IF HE SAYS HE DOESN'T WANT TO HURT YOU--
...I DON'T WANT TO HURT YOU--
--RUN!

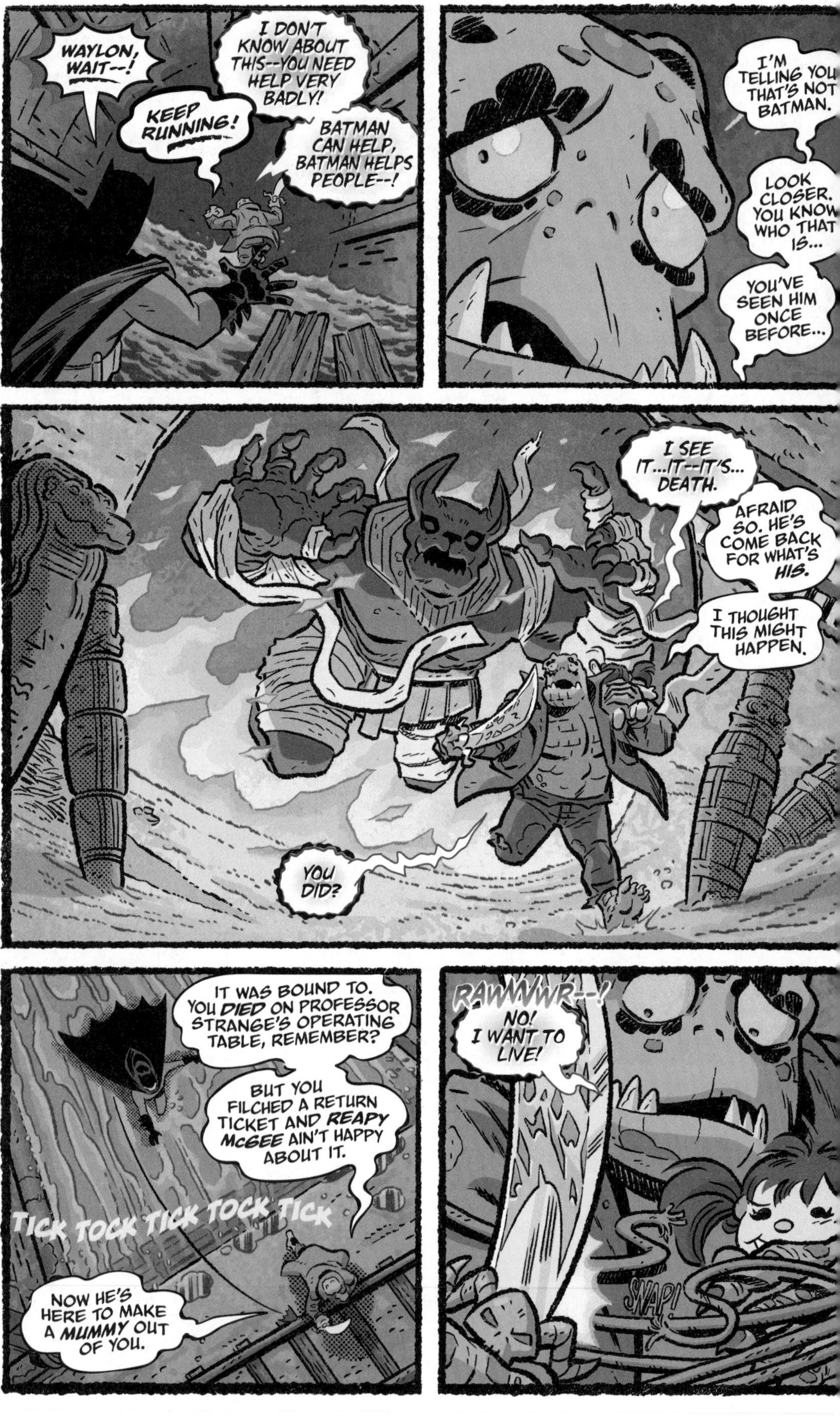
WAYLON, WAIT--!
KEEP RUNNING!
I DON'T KNOW ABOUT THIS--YOU NEED HELP VERY BADLY!
BATMAN CAN HELP, BATMAN HELPS PEOPLE--!
I'M TELLING YOU THAT'S NOT BATMAN.
LOOK CLOSER. YOU KNOW WHO THAT IS...
YOU'VE SEEN HIM ONCE BEFORE...
I SEE IT...IT--IT'S... DEATH.
AFRAID SO. HE'S COME BACK FOR WHAT'S HIS.
I THOUGHT THIS MIGHT HAPPEN.
YOU DID?
IT WAS BOUND TO. YOU DIED ON PROFESSOR STRANGE'S OPERATING TABLE, REMEMBER?
BUT YOU FILCHED A RETURN TICKET AND REAPY McGEE AIN'T HAPPY ABOUT IT.
TICK TOCK TICK TOCK TICK
NOW HE'S HERE TO MAKE A MUMMY OUT OF YOU.
RAWWWR--!
NO! I WANT TO LIVE!
SNAP!

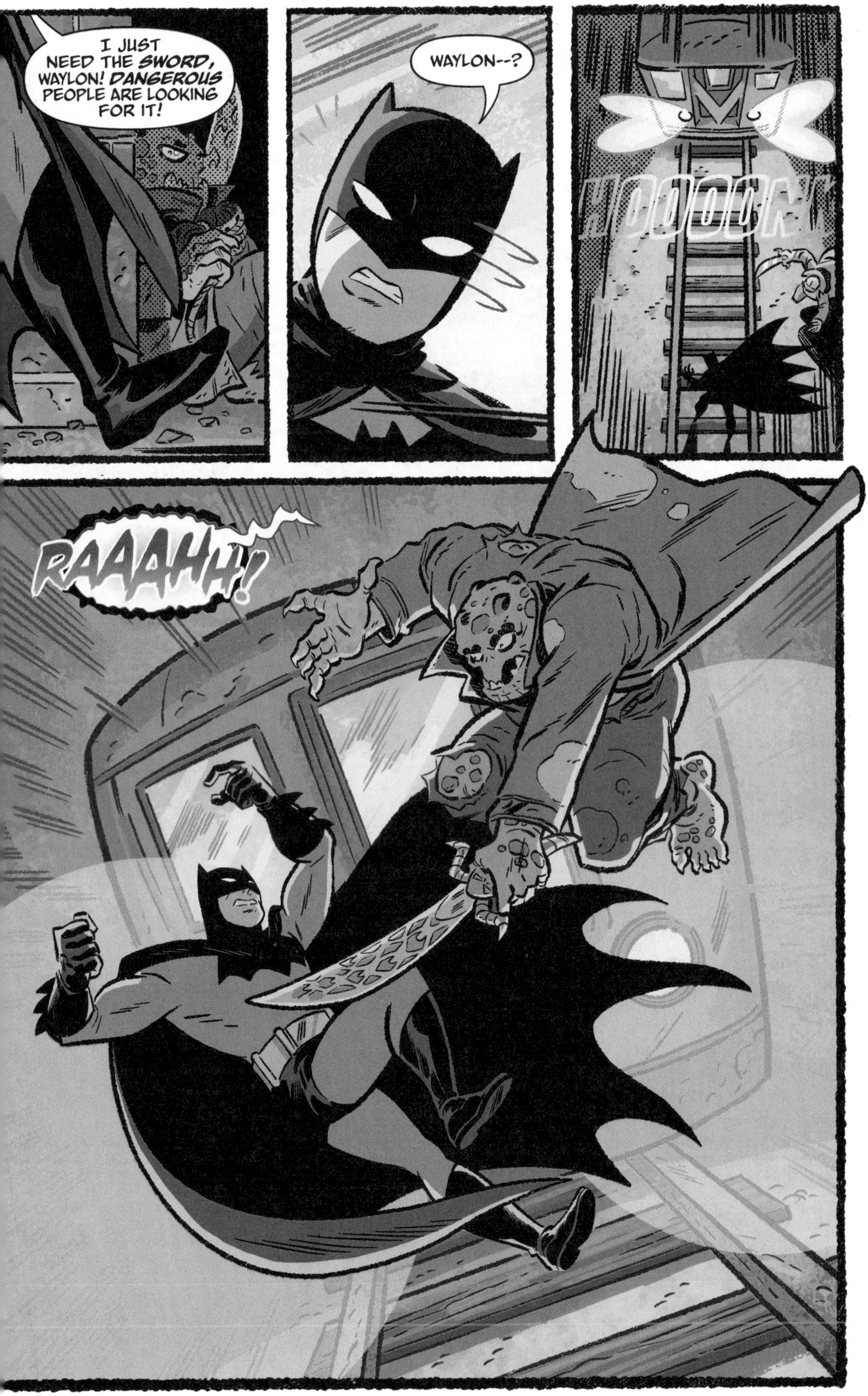
I JUST NEED THE SWORD, WAYLON! DANGEROUS PEOPLE ARE LOOKING FOR IT!
WAYLON--?
HOOOOONK!
RAAAHH!

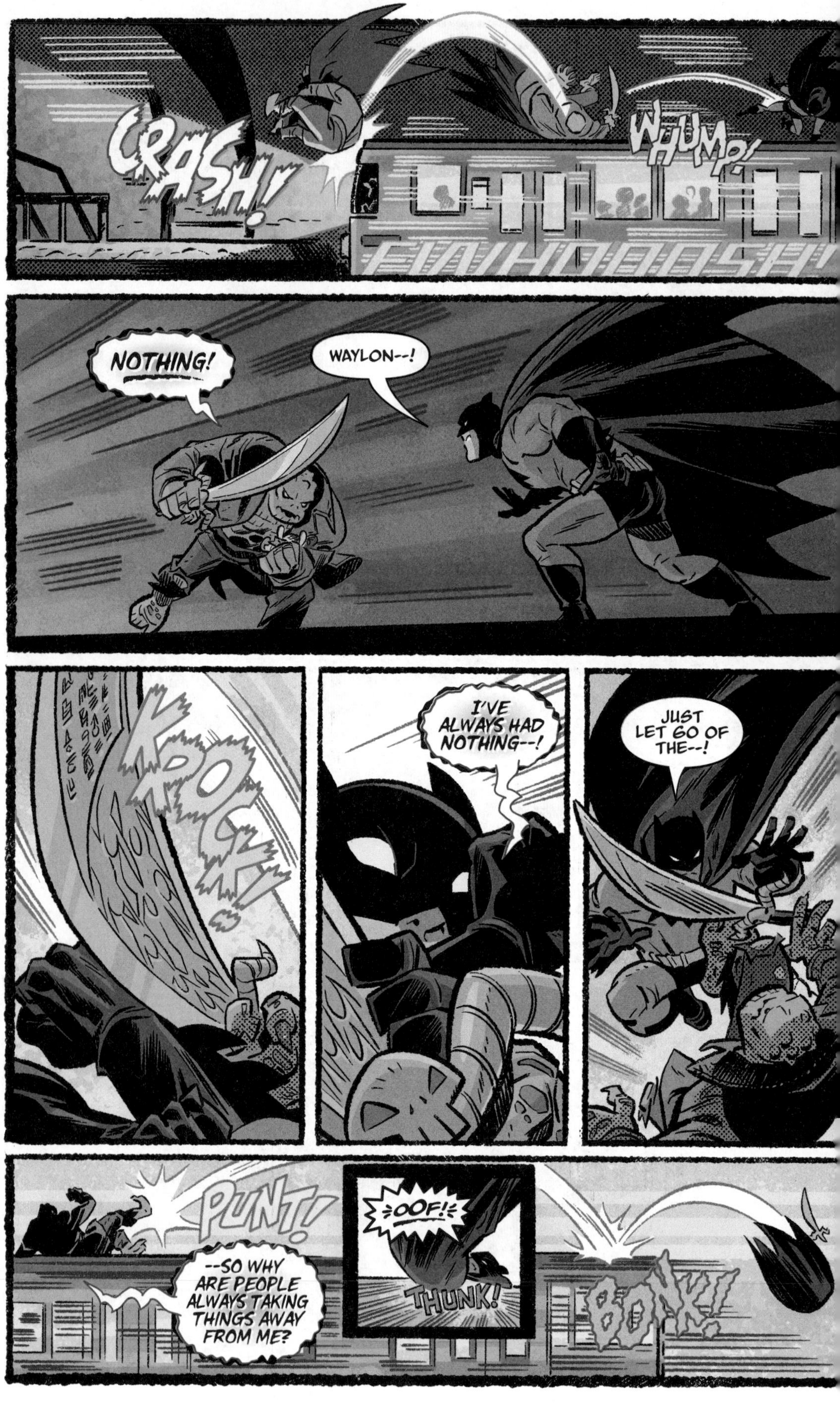
CRASH!
WHUMP!
FWHOOOSH!
NOTHING!
WAYLON--!
KROCK!
I'VE ALWAYS HAD NOTHING--!
JUST LET GO OF THE--!
PUNT!
--SO WHY ARE PEOPLE ALWAYS TAKING THINGS AWAY FROM ME?
OOF!
THUNK!
BONK!

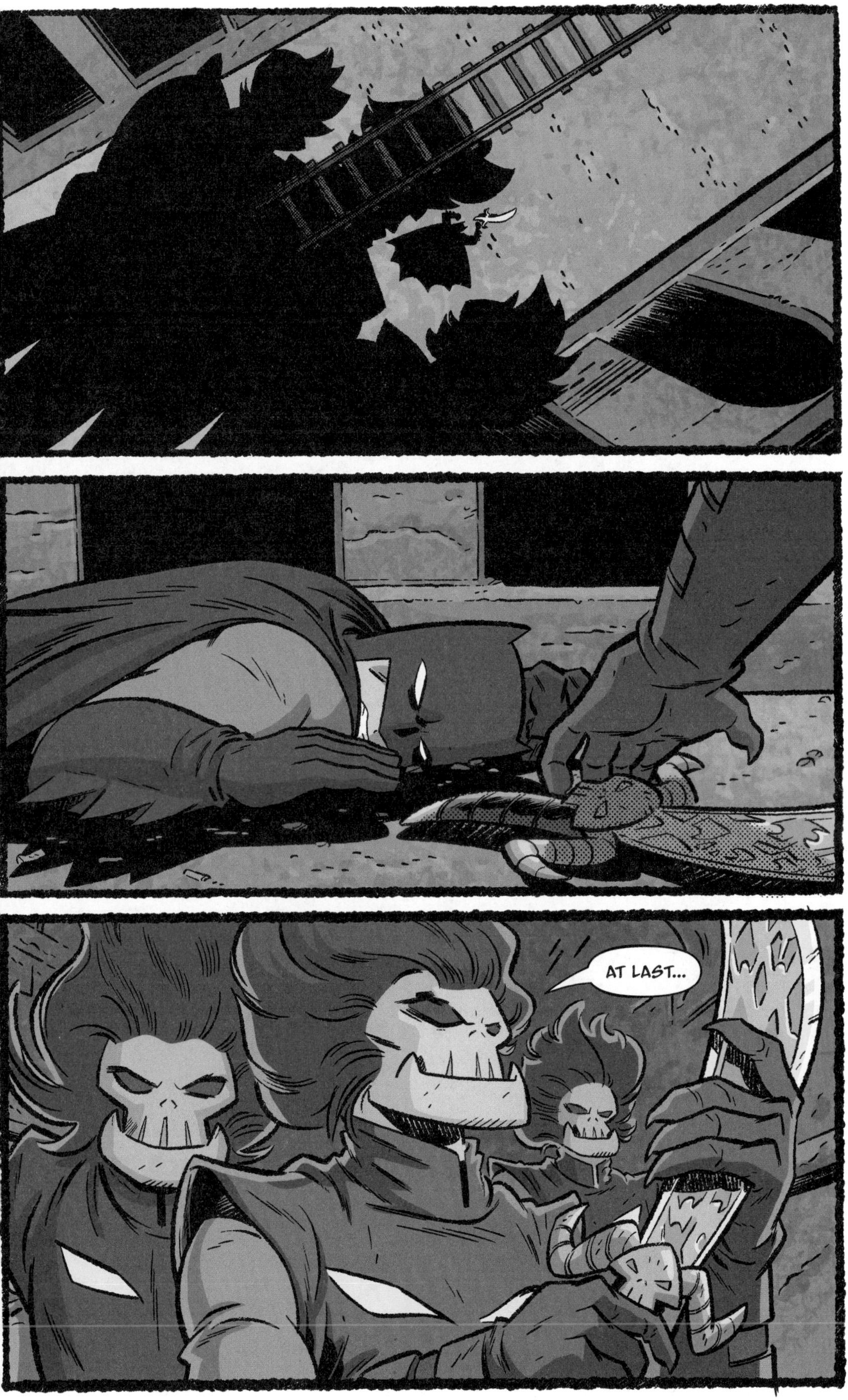
AT LAST...

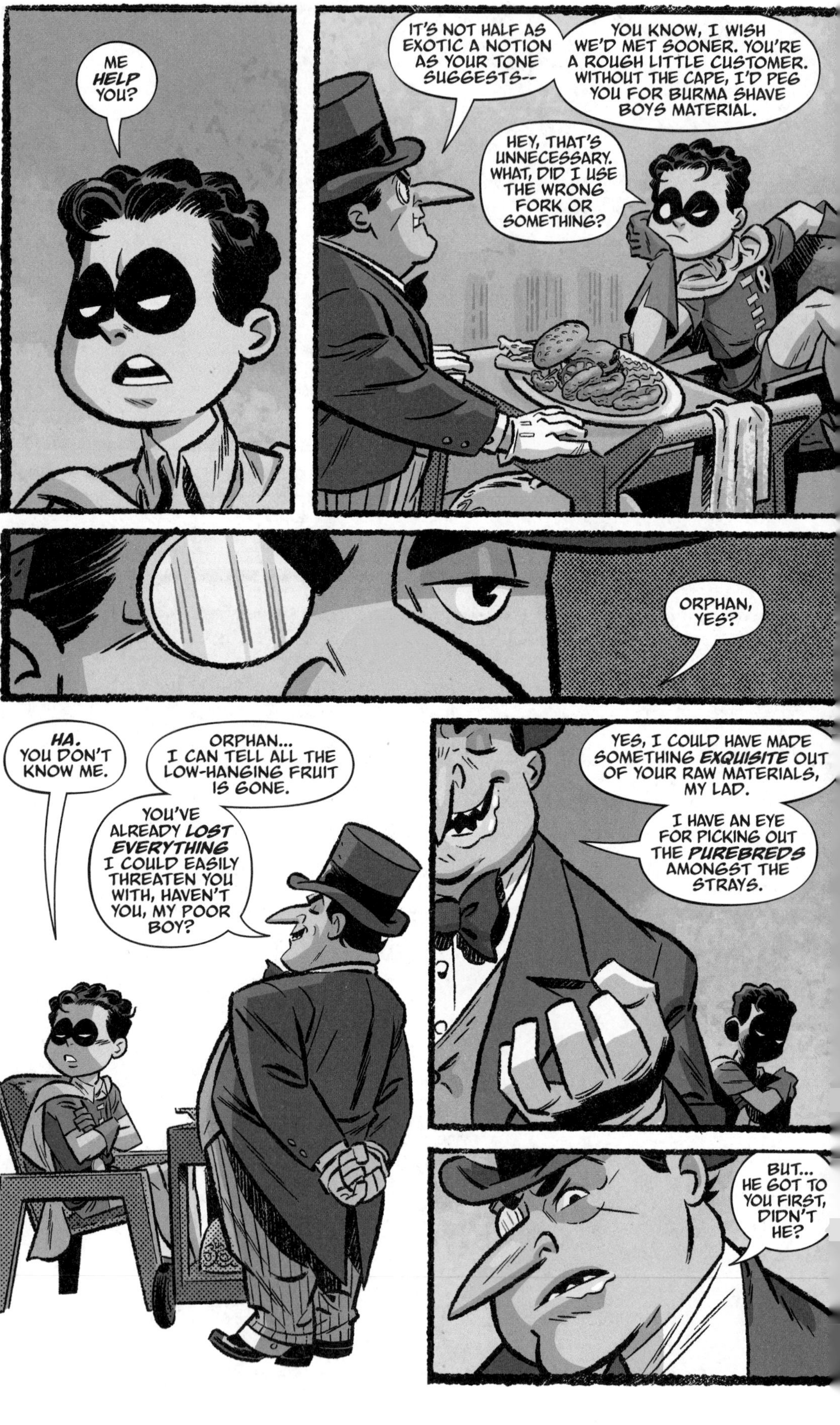
ME HELP YOU?
IT'S NOT HALF AS EXOTIC A NOTION AS YOUR TONE SUGGESTS--
YOU KNOW, I WISH WE'D MET SOONER. YOU'RE A ROUGH LITTLE CUSTOMER. WITHOUT THE CAPE, I'D PEG YOU FOR BURMA SHAVE BOYS MATERIAL.
HEY, THAT'S UNNECESSARY. WHAT, DID I USE THE WRONG FORK OR SOMETHING?
ORPHAN, YES?
HA. YOU DON'T KNOW ME.
ORPHAN... I CAN TELL ALL THE LOW-HANGING FRUIT IS GONE.
YOU'VE ALREADY LOST EVERYTHING I COULD EASILY THREATEN YOU WITH, HAVEN'T YOU, MY POOR BOY?
YES, I COULD HAVE MADE SOMETHING EXQUISITE OUT OF YOUR RAW MATERIALS, MY LAD.
I HAVE AN EYE FOR PICKING OUT THE PUREBREDS AMONGST THE STRAYS.
BUT... HE GOT TO YOU FIRST, DIDN'T HE?

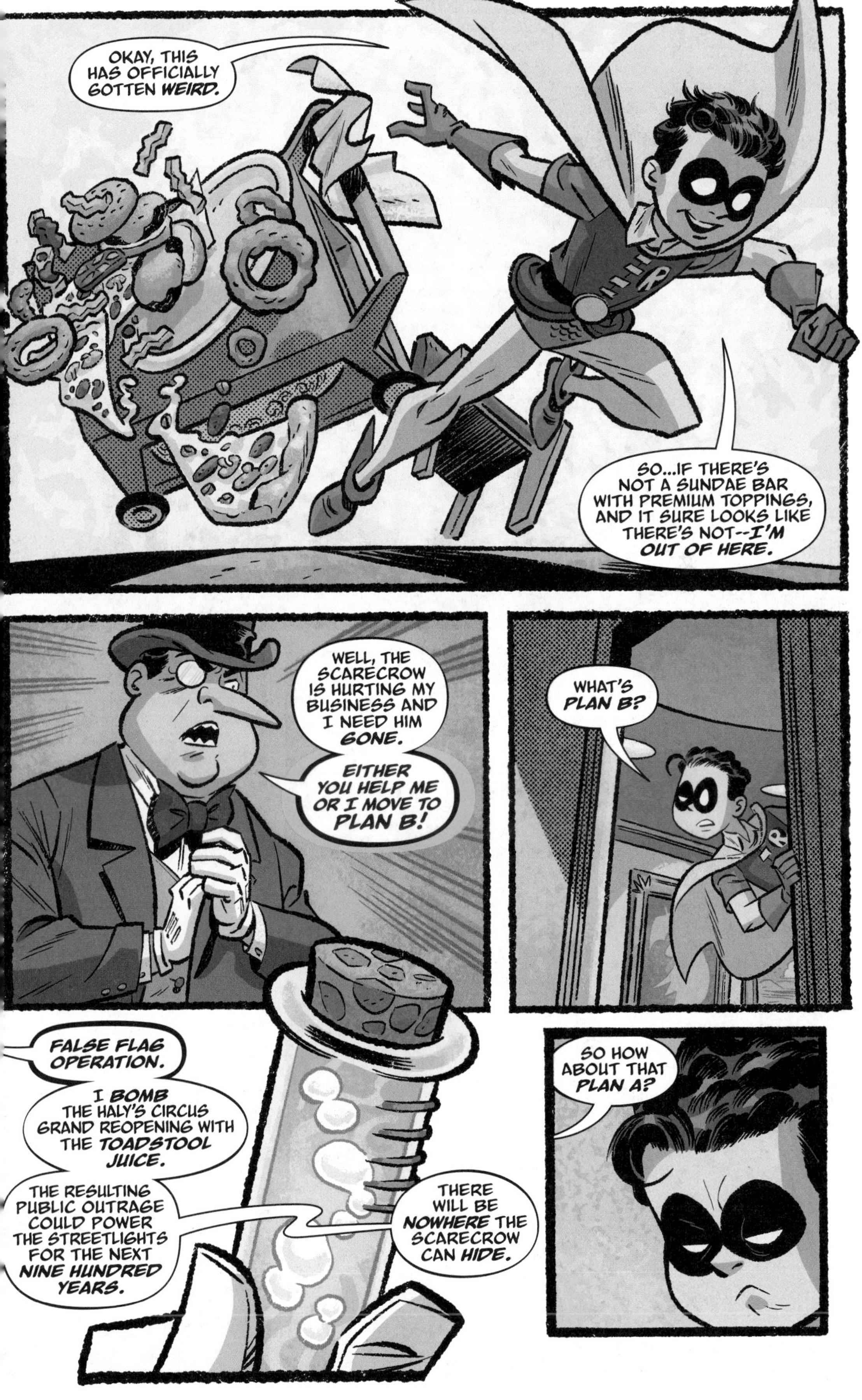
OKAY, THIS HAS OFFICIALLY GOTTEN WEIRD.
SO...IF THERE'S NOT A SUNDAE BAR WITH PREMIUM TOPPINGS, AND IT SURE LOOKS LIKE THERE'S NOT--I'M OUT OF HERE.
WELL, THE SCARECROW IS HURTING MY BUSINESS AND I NEED HIM GONE.
EITHER YOU HELP ME OR I MOVE TO PLAN B!
WHAT'S PLAN B?
FALSE FLAG OPERATION.
I BOMB THE HALY'S CIRCUS GRAND REOPENING WITH THE TOADSTOOL JUICE.
THE RESULTING PUBLIC OUTRAGE COULD POWER THE STREETLIGHTS FOR THE NEXT NINE HUNDRED YEARS.
THERE WILL BE NOWHERE THE SCARECROW CAN HIDE.
SO HOW ABOUT THAT PLAN A?

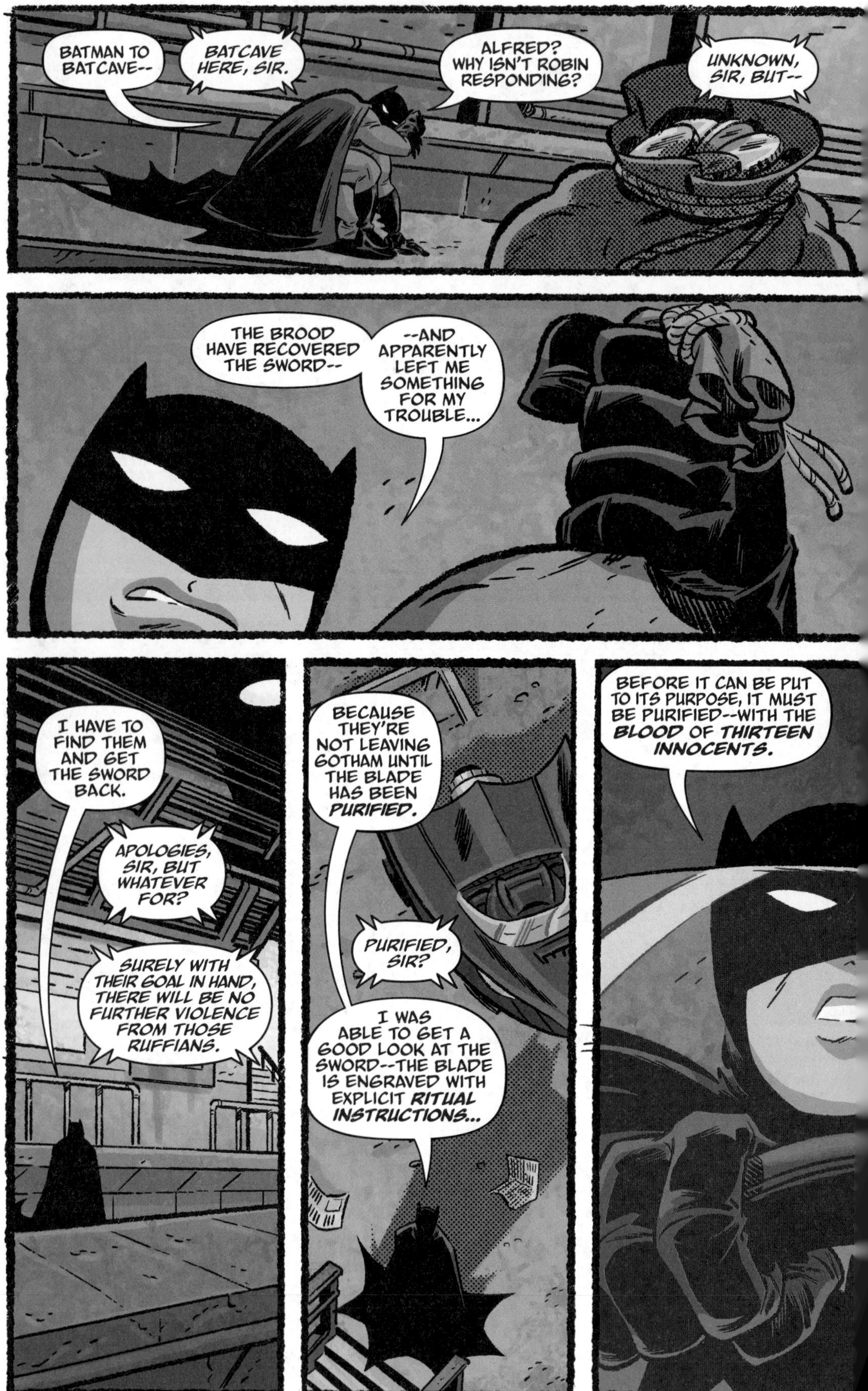
BATMAN TO BATCAVE--
BATCAVE HERE, SIR.
ALFRED? WHY ISN'T ROBIN RESPONDING?
UNKNOWN, SIR, BUT--
THE BROOD HAVE RECOVERED THE SWORD--
--AND APPARENTLY LEFT ME SOMETHING FOR MY TROUBLE...
I HAVE TO FIND THEM AND GET THE SWORD BACK.
APOLOGIES, SIR, BUT WHATEVER FOR?
SURELY WITH THEIR GOAL IN HAND, THERE WILL BE NO FURTHER VIOLENCE FROM THOSE RUFFIANS.
BECAUSE THEY'RE NOT LEAVING GOTHAM UNTIL THE BLADE HAS BEEN PURIFIED.
PURIFIED, SIR?
I WAS ABLE TO GET A GOOD LOOK AT THE SWORD--THE BLADE IS ENGRAVED WITH EXPLICIT RITUAL INSTRUCTIONS...
BEFORE IT CAN BE PUT TO ITS PURPOSE, IT MUST BE PURIFIED--WITH THE BLOOD OF THIRTEEN INNOCENTS.

WE GOTTA GET YOU TO THE D-DOCTOR!
PLOK! PLOK!
YEAH? WHAT MAKES YA SAY THAT?
DON'T WORRY-- I KNOW WHERE HE IS! I'M TAKING YOU TO HIM--!
I DUNNO, BIG GUY. THIS MIGHT BE DA OFF-RAMP...
PLEASE, JUST HANG ON. STAY WITH ME! STAY WITH ME!
PLIP
THEN.
YOU CAN'T STAY WITH US.
BUT I'M NOT BETTER YET, PROFESSOR. I STILL FEEL SICK...
THE EXPERIMENT IS CONCLUDED, WAYLON.
BUT WHERE WILL I GO?

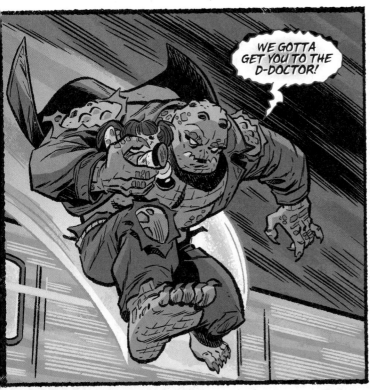

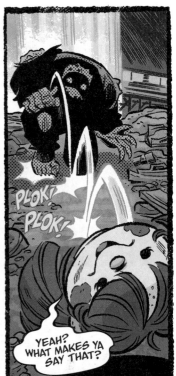

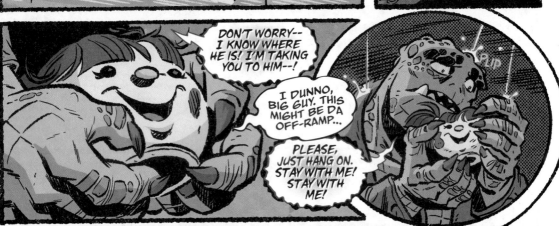

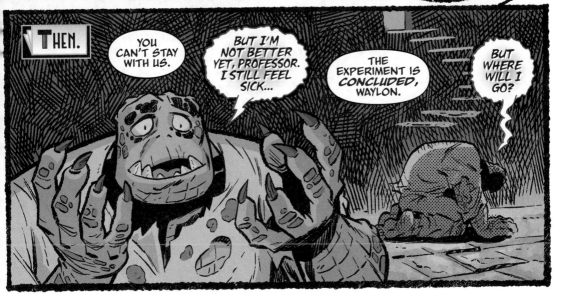

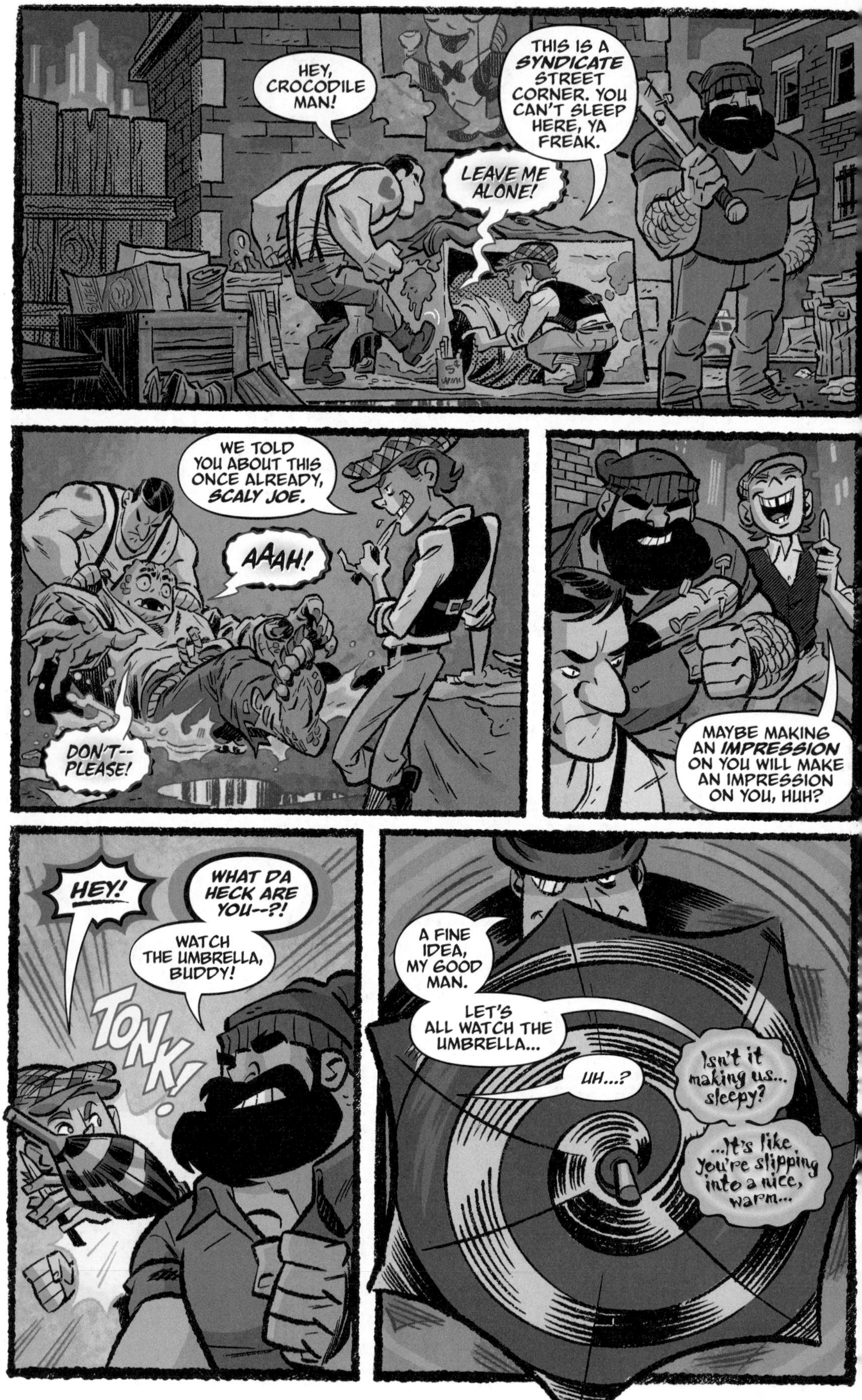
HEY, CROCODILE MAN!
THIS IS A SYNDICATE STREET CORNER. YOU CAN'T SLEEP HERE, YA FREAK.
LEAVE ME ALONE!
WE TOLD YOU ABOUT THIS ONCE ALREADY, SCALY JOE.
AAAH!
DON'T-- PLEASE!
MAYBE MAKING AN IMPRESSION ON YOU WILL MAKE AN IMPRESSION ON YOU, HUH?
HEY!
WHAT DA HECK ARE YOU--?!
WATCH THE UMBRELLA, BUDDY!
TONK!
A FINE IDEA, MY GOOD MAN.
LET'S ALL WATCH THE UMBRELLA...
UH...?
Isn't it making us... sleepy?
...It's like you're slipping into a nice, warm...

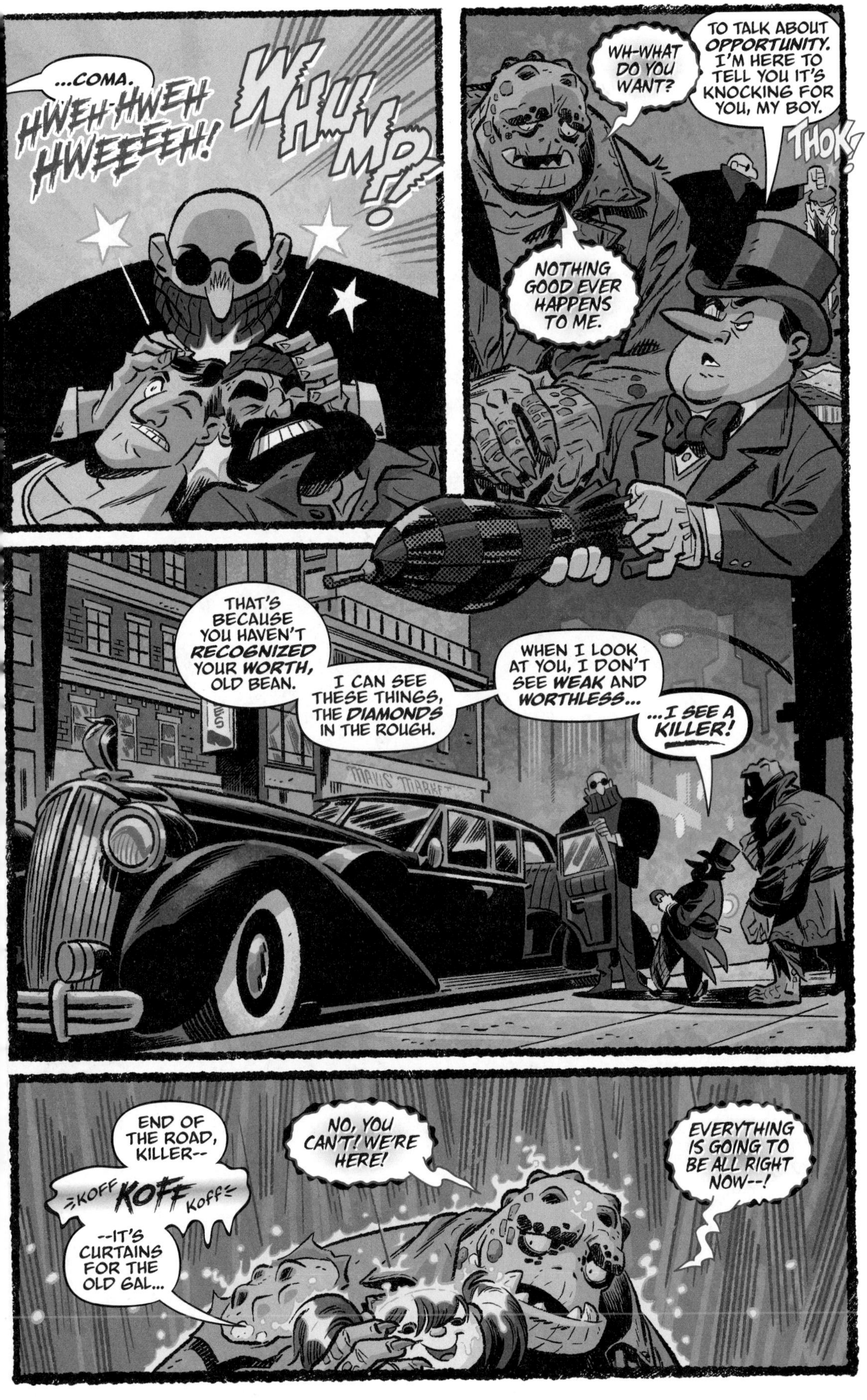
...COMA.
HWEH-HWEH HWEEEEH!
WHUMP!
WH-WHAT DO YOU WANT?
TO TALK ABOUT OPPORTUNITY. I'M HERE TO TELL YOU IT'S KNOCKING FOR YOU, MY BOY.
THOK!
NOTHING GOOD EVER HAPPENS TO ME.
THAT'S BECAUSE YOU HAVEN'T RECOGNIZED YOUR WORTH, OLD BEAN.
I CAN SEE THESE THINGS, THE DIAMONDS IN THE ROUGH.
WHEN I LOOK AT YOU, I DON'T SEE WEAK AND WORTHLESS...
...I SEE A KILLER!
MAVIS' MARKET
END OF THE ROAD, KILLER--
KOFF KOFF KOFF
--IT'S CURTAINS FOR THE OLD GAL...
NO, YOU CAN'T! WE'RE HERE!
EVERYTHING IS GOING TO BE ALL RIGHT NOW--!

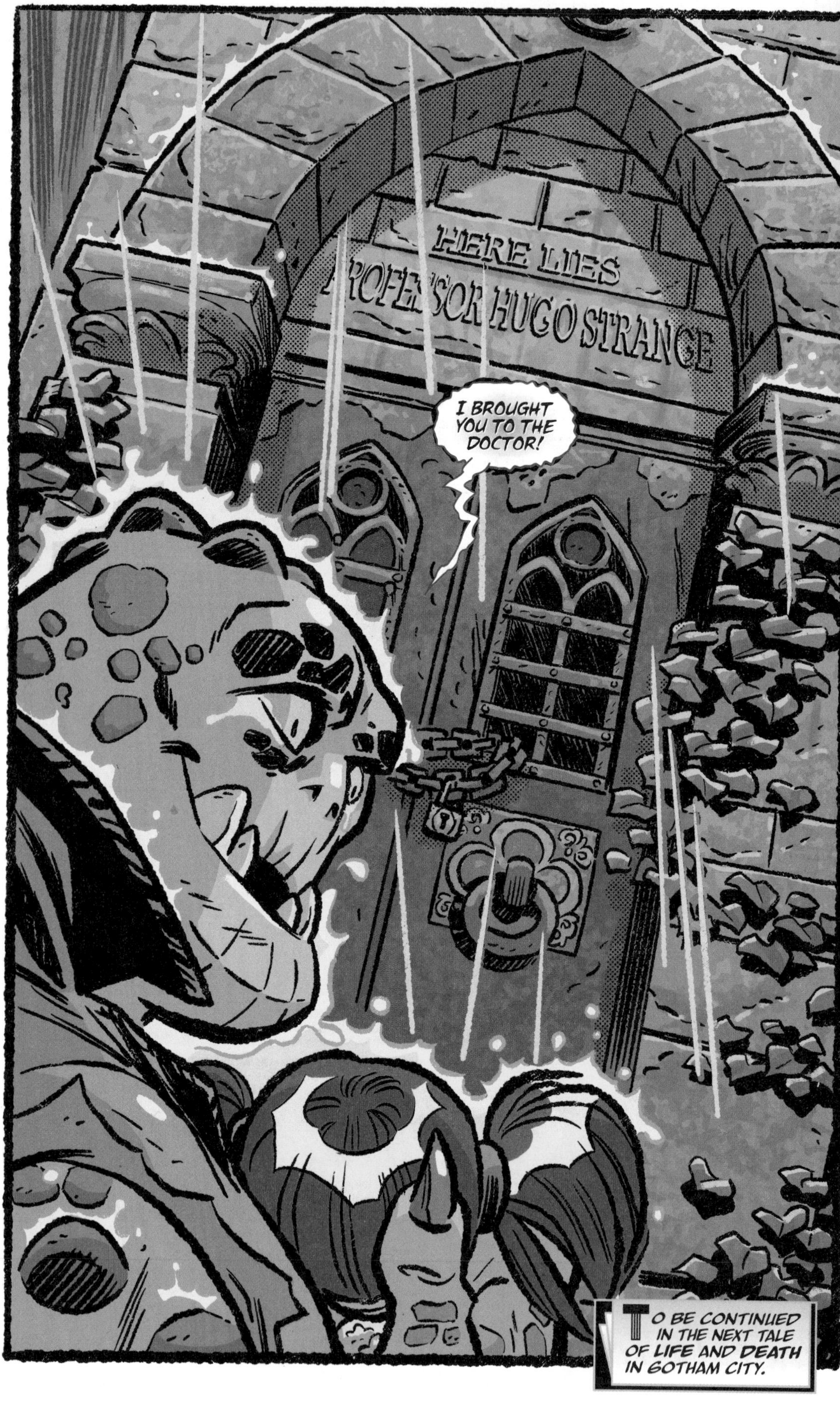
HERE LIES
PROFESSOR HUGO STRANGE
I BROUGHT YOU TO THE DOCTOR!
TO BE CONTINUED IN THE NEXT TALE OF LIFE AND DEATH IN GOTHAM CITY.

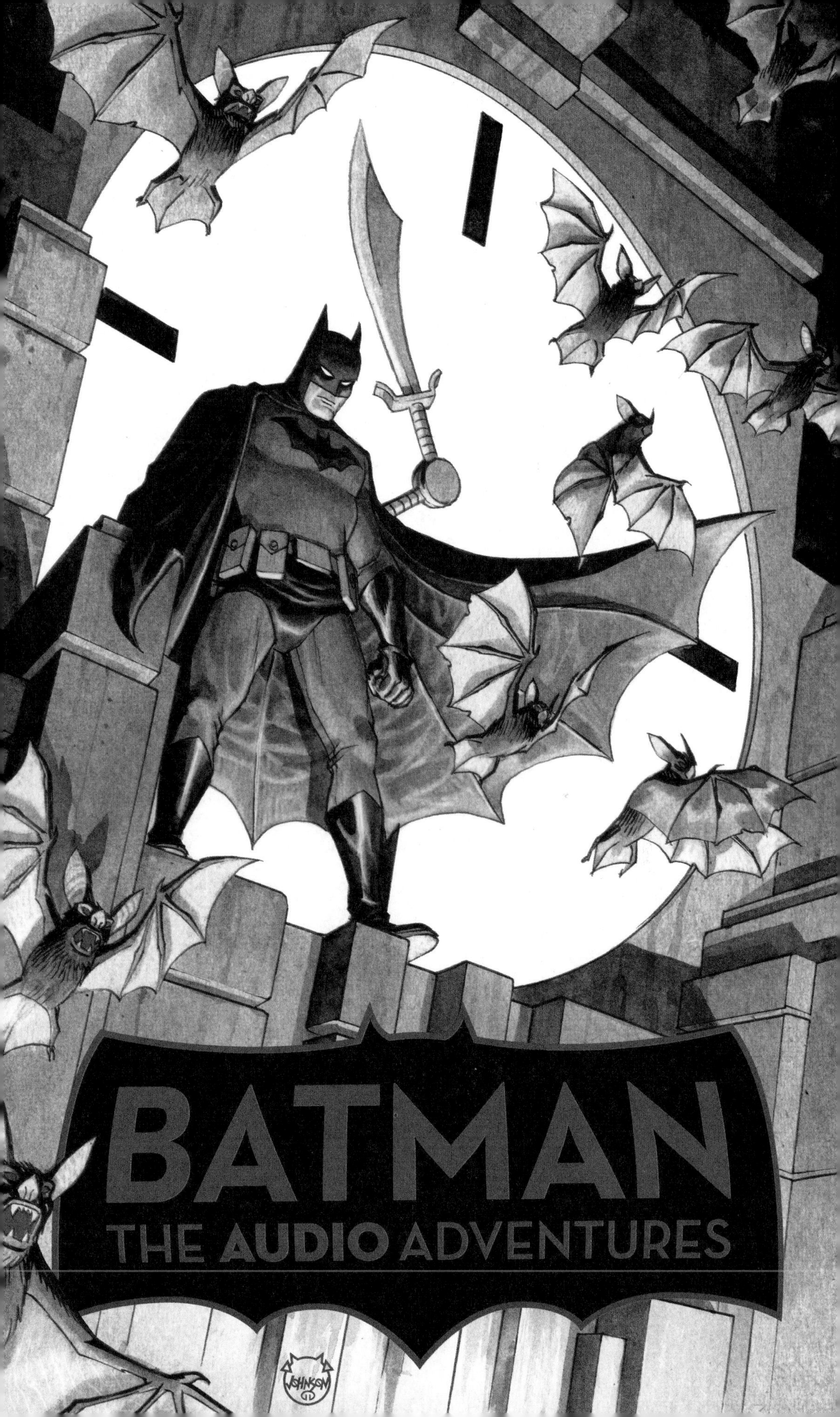
BATMAN
THE AUDIO ADVENTURES
JOHNSON

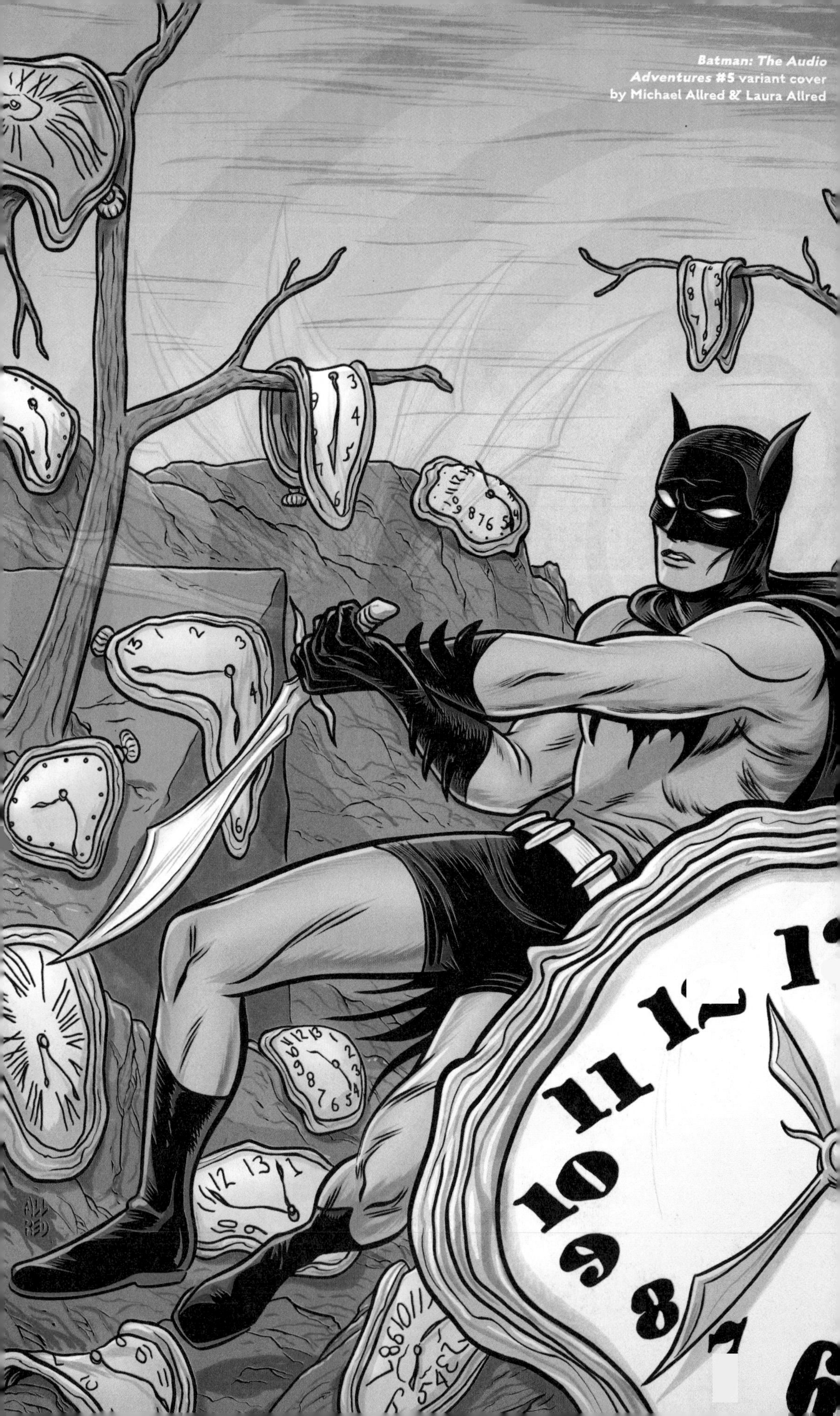

Batman: The Audio Adventures #5 variant cover by Michael Allred & Laura Allred

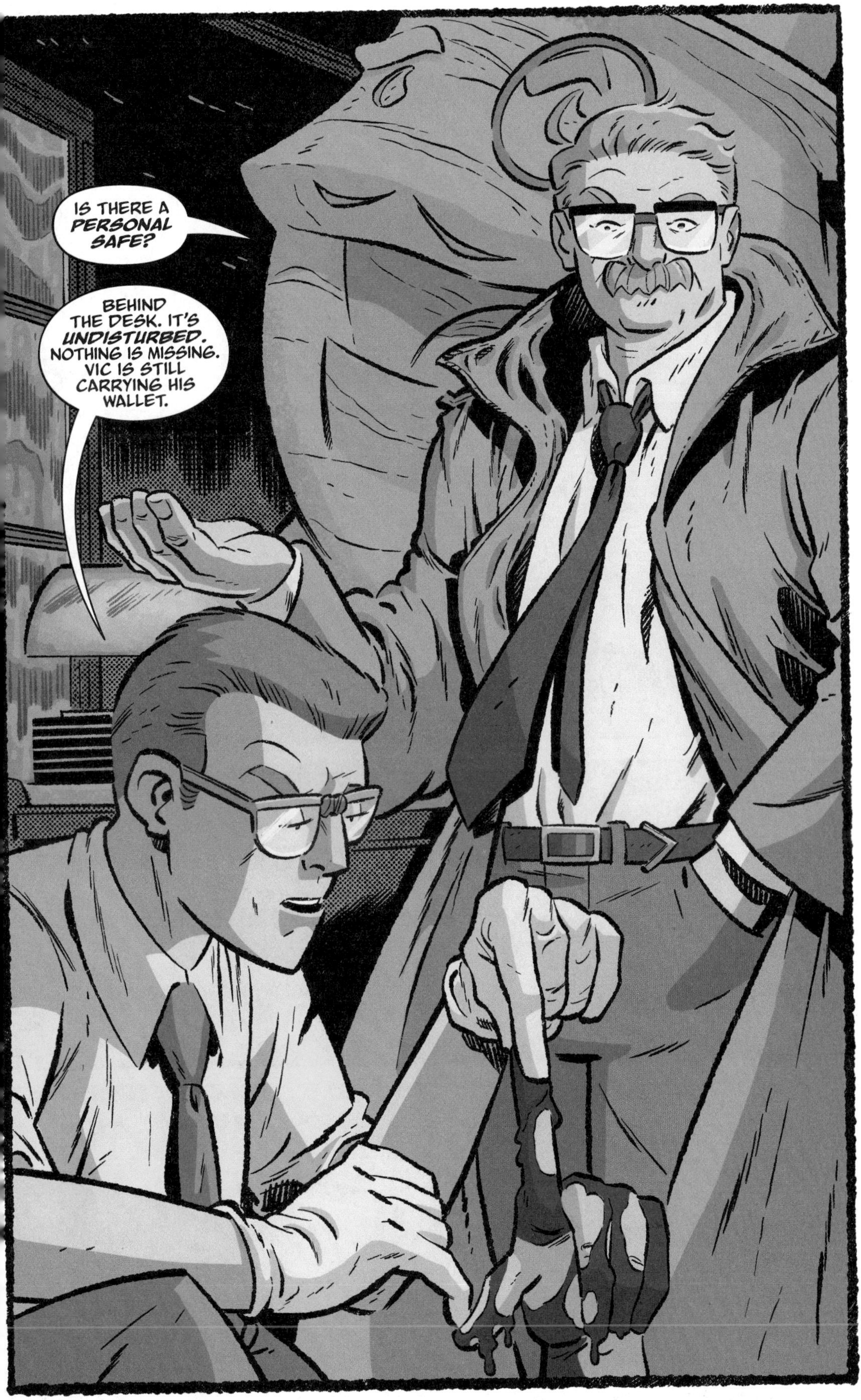
IS THERE A *PERSONAL* SAFE?
BEHIND THE DESK. IT'S *UNDISTURBED*. NOTHING IS MISSING. VIC IS STILL CARRYING HIS WALLET.

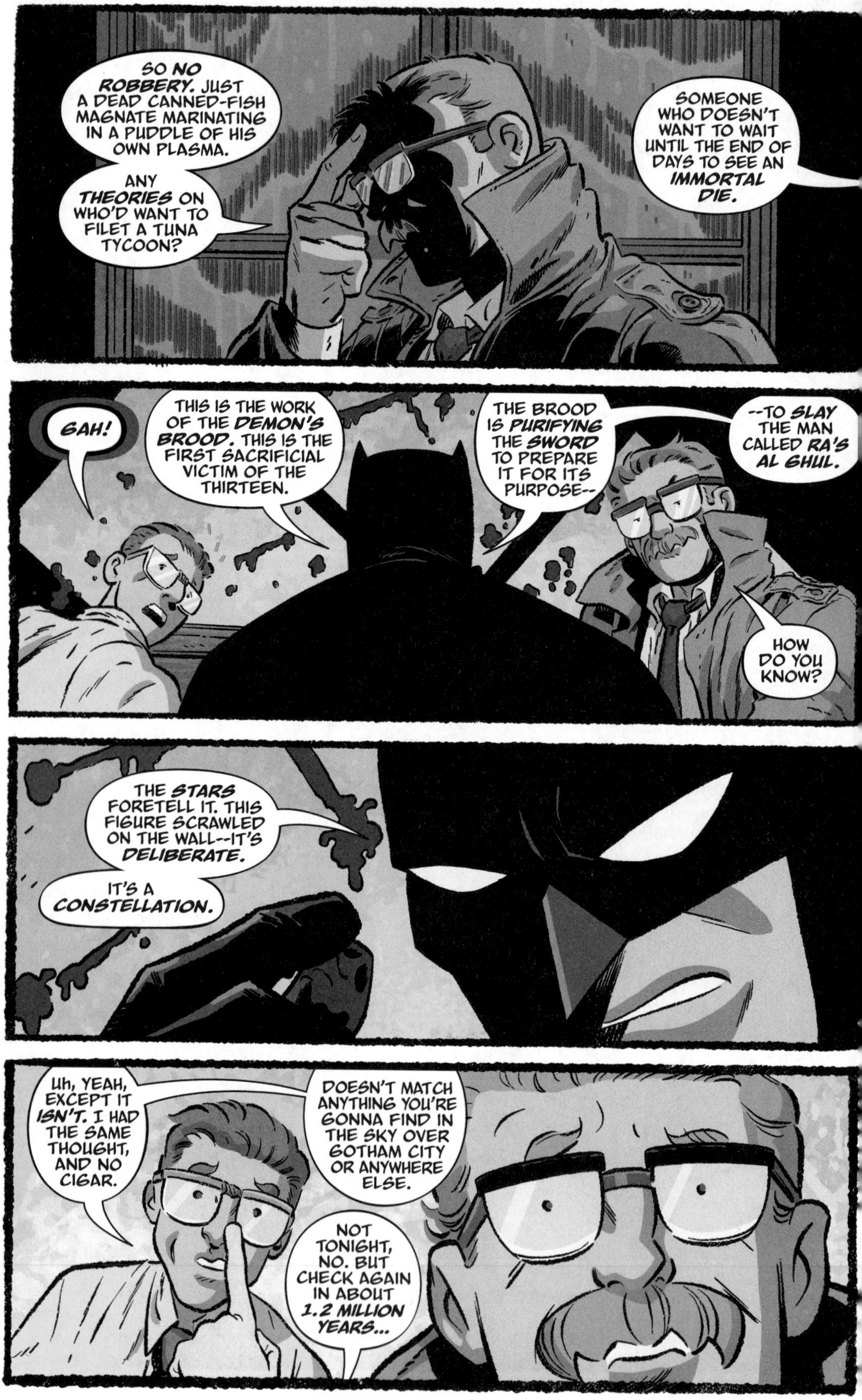
SO NO ROBBERY. JUST A DEAD CANNED-FISH MAGNATE MARINATING IN A PUDDLE OF HIS OWN PLASMA.
ANY THEORIES ON WHO'D WANT TO FILET A TUNA TYCOON?
SOMEONE WHO DOESN'T WANT TO WAIT UNTIL THE END OF DAYS TO SEE AN IMMORTAL DIE.
GAH!
THIS IS THE WORK OF THE DEMON'S BROOD. THIS IS THE FIRST SACRIFICIAL VICTIM OF THE THIRTEEN.
THE BROOD IS PURIFYING THE SWORD TO PREPARE IT FOR ITS PURPOSE--
--TO SLAY THE MAN CALLED RA'S AL GHUL.
HOW DO YOU KNOW?
THE STARS FORETELL IT. THIS FIGURE SCRAWLED ON THE WALL--IT'S DELIBERATE.
IT'S A CONSTELLATION.
UH, YEAH, EXCEPT IT ISN'T. I HAD THE SAME THOUGHT, AND NO CIGAR.
DOESN'T MATCH ANYTHING YOU'RE GONNA FIND IN THE SKY OVER GOTHAM CITY OR ANYWHERE ELSE.
NOT TONIGHT, NO. BUT CHECK AGAIN IN ABOUT 1.2 MILLION YEARS...

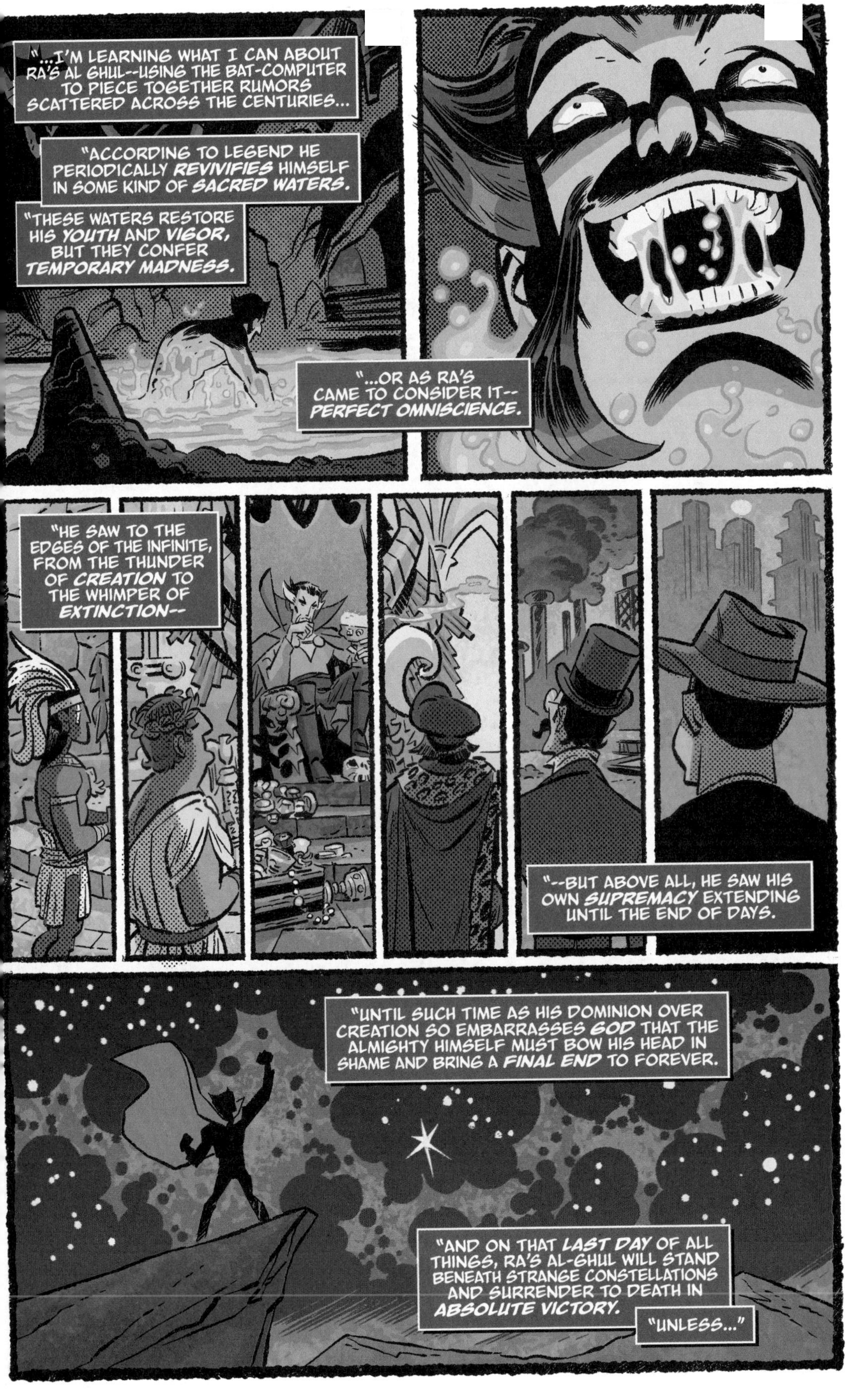
"...I'M LEARNING WHAT I CAN ABOUT RA'S AL GHUL--USING THE BAT-COMPUTER TO PIECE TOGETHER RUMORS SCATTERED ACROSS THE CENTURIES...
"ACCORDING TO LEGEND HE PERIODICALLY REVIVIFIES HIMSELF IN SOME KIND OF SACRED WATERS.
"THESE WATERS RESTORE HIS YOUTH AND VIGOR, BUT THEY CONFER TEMPORARY MADNESS.
"...OR AS RA'S CAME TO CONSIDER IT-- PERFECT OMNISCIENCE.
"HE SAW TO THE EDGES OF THE INFINITE, FROM THE THUNDER OF CREATION TO THE WHIMPER OF EXTINCTION--
"--BUT ABOVE ALL, HE SAW HIS OWN SUPREMACY EXTENDING UNTIL THE END OF DAYS.
"UNTIL SUCH TIME AS HIS DOMINION OVER CREATION SO EMBARRASSES GOD THAT THE ALMIGHTY HIMSELF MUST BOW HIS HEAD IN SHAME AND BRING A FINAL END TO FOREVER.
"AND ON THAT LAST DAY OF ALL THINGS, RA'S AL-GHUL WILL STAND BENEATH STRANGE CONSTELLATIONS AND SURRENDER TO DEATH IN ABSOLUTE VICTORY.
"UNLESS..."

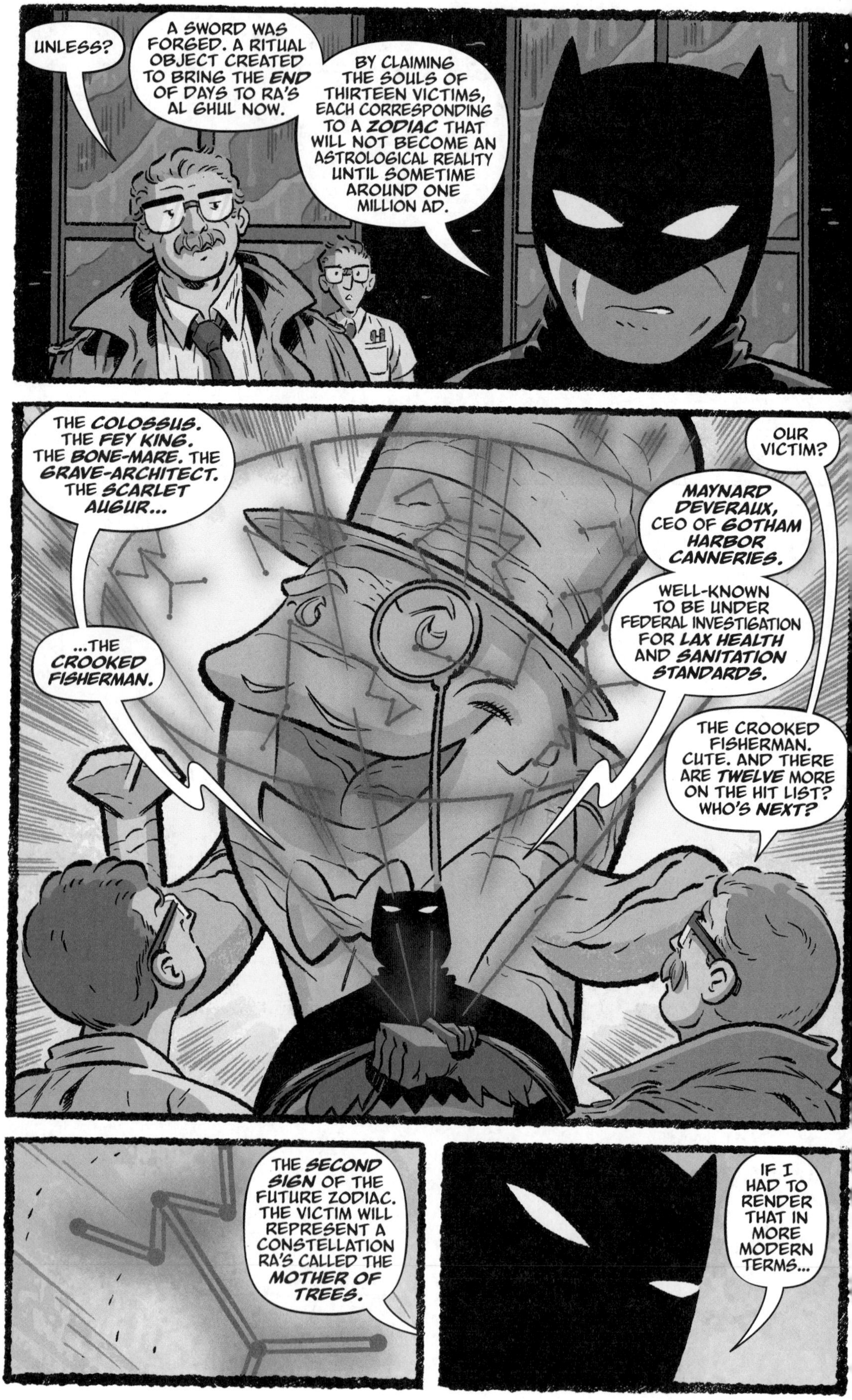

UNLESS?
A SWORD WAS FORGED. A RITUAL OBJECT CREATED TO BRING THE END OF DAYS TO RA'S AL GHUL NOW.
BY CLAIMING THE SOULS OF THIRTEEN VICTIMS, EACH CORRESPONDING TO A ZODIAC THAT WILL NOT BECOME AN ASTROLOGICAL REALITY UNTIL SOMETIME AROUND ONE MILLION AD.
THE COLOSSUS. THE FEY KING. THE BONE-MARE. THE GRAVE-ARCHITECT. THE SCARLET AUGUR...
...THE CROOKED FISHERMAN.
OUR VICTIM?
MAYNARD DEVERAUX, CEO OF GOTHAM HARBOR CANNERIES.
WELL-KNOWN TO BE UNDER FEDERAL INVESTIGATION FOR LAX HEALTH AND SANITATION STANDARDS.
THE CROOKED FISHERMAN. CUTE. AND THERE ARE TWELVE MORE ON THE HIT LIST? WHO'S NEXT?
THE SECOND SIGN OF THE FUTURE ZODIAC. THE VICTIM WILL REPRESENT A CONSTELLATION RA'S CALLED THE MOTHER OF TREES.
IF I HAD TO RENDER THAT IN MORE MODERN TERMS...

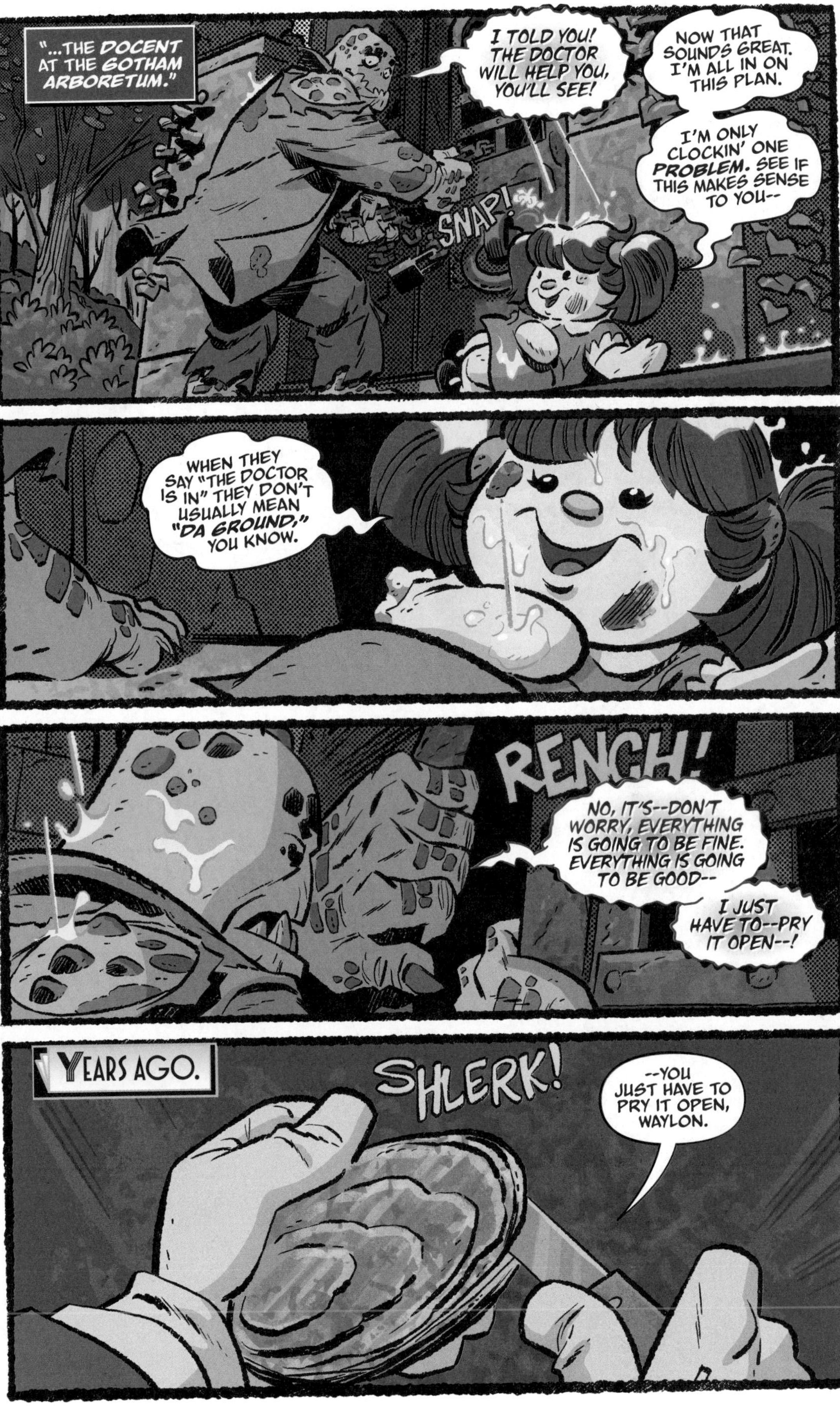
"...THE DOCENT AT THE GOTHAM ARBORETUM."
I TOLD YOU! THE DOCTOR WILL HELP YOU, YOU'LL SEE!
NOW THAT SOUNDS GREAT. I'M ALL IN ON THIS PLAN.
I'M ONLY CLOCKIN' ONE PROBLEM. SEE IF THIS MAKES SENSE TO YOU--
SNAP!
WHEN THEY SAY "THE DOCTOR IS IN" THEY DON'T USUALLY MEAN "DA GROUND," YOU KNOW.
RENCH!
NO, IT'S--DON'T WORRY, EVERYTHING IS GOING TO BE FINE. EVERYTHING IS GOING TO BE GOOD--
I JUST HAVE TO--PRY IT OPEN--!
YEARS AGO.
SHLERK!
--YOU JUST HAVE TO PRY IT OPEN, WAYLON.

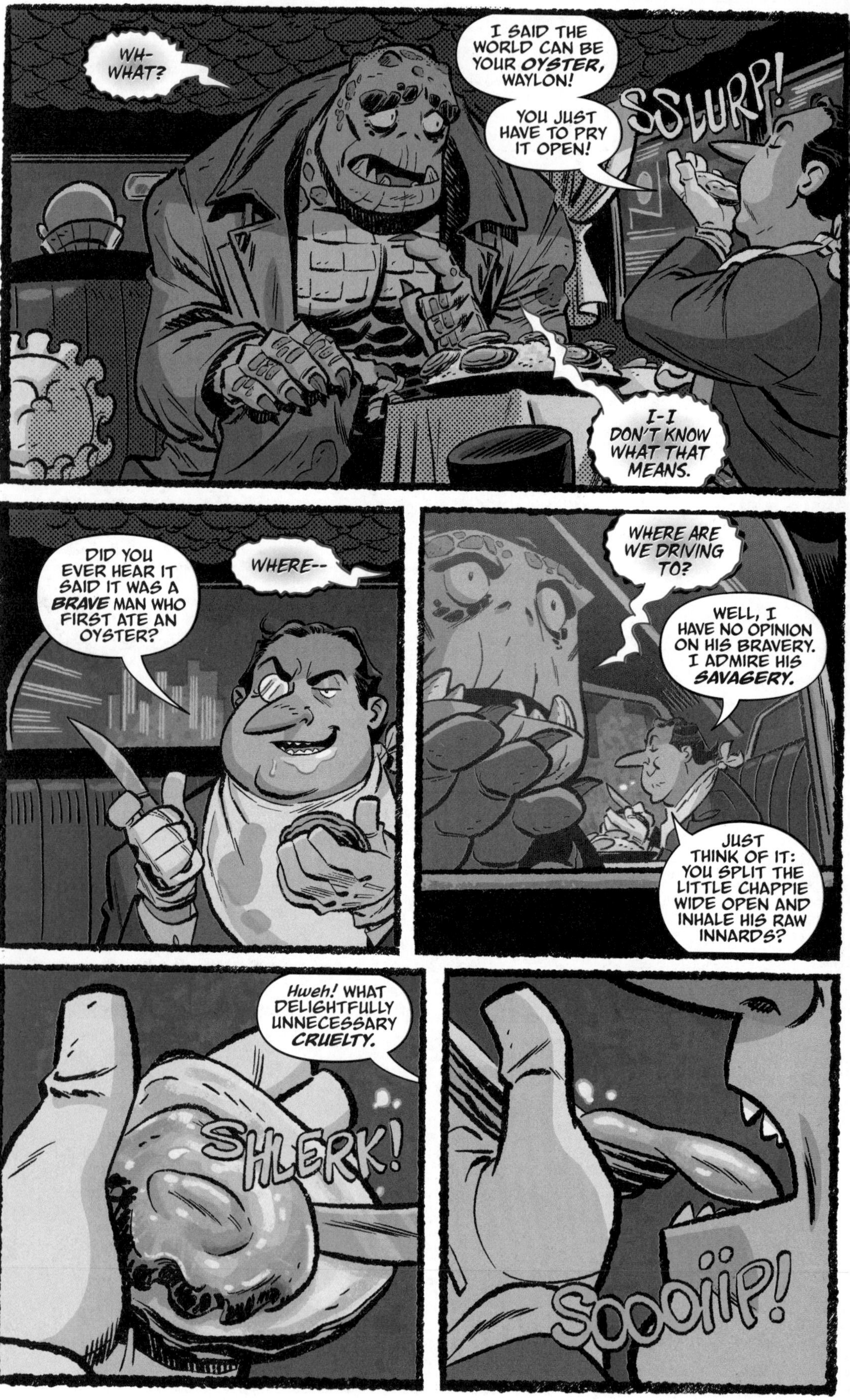
WH- WHAT?
I SAID THE WORLD CAN BE YOUR OYSTER, WAYLON!
YOU JUST HAVE TO PRY IT OPEN!
SSLURP!
I-I DON'T KNOW WHAT THAT MEANS.
DID YOU EVER HEAR IT SAID IT WAS A BRAVE MAN WHO FIRST ATE AN OYSTER?
WHERE--
WHERE ARE WE DRIVING TO?
WELL, I HAVE NO OPINION ON HIS BRAVERY. I ADMIRE HIS SAVAGERY.
JUST THINK OF IT: YOU SPLIT THE LITTLE CHAPPIE WIDE OPEN AND INHALE HIS RAW INNARDS?
Hweh! WHAT DELIGHTFULLY UNNECESSARY CRUELTY.
SHLERK!
SOOOÏIIP!

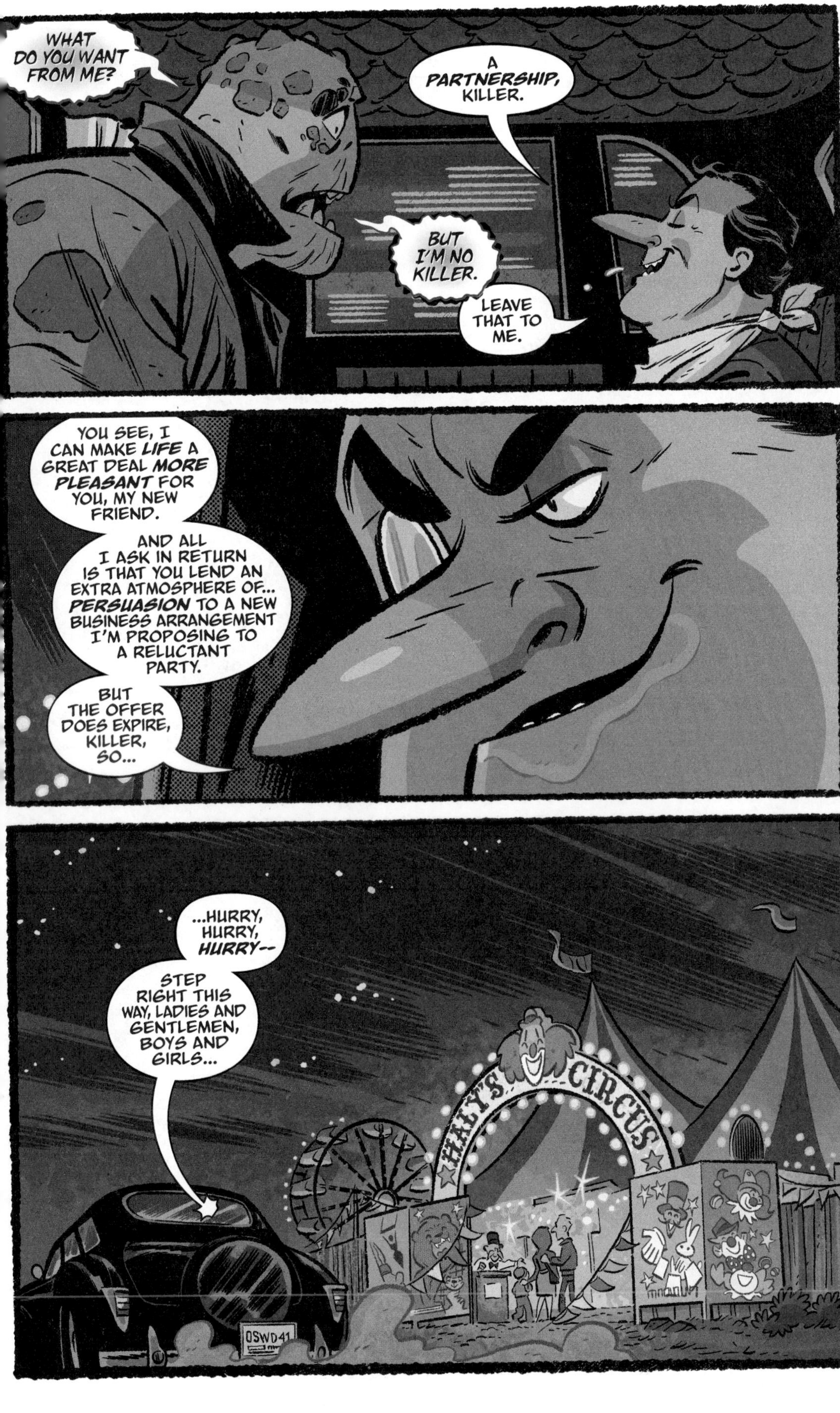
WHAT DO YOU WANT FROM ME?
A PARTNERSHIP, KILLER.
BUT I'M NO KILLER.
LEAVE THAT TO ME.
YOU SEE, I CAN MAKE LIFE A GREAT DEAL MORE PLEASANT FOR YOU, MY NEW FRIEND.
AND ALL I ASK IN RETURN IS THAT YOU LEND AN EXTRA ATMOSPHERE OF... PERSUASION TO A NEW BUSINESS ARRANGEMENT I'M PROPOSING TO A RELUCTANT PARTY.
BUT THE OFFER DOES EXPIRE, KILLER, SO...
...HURRY, HURRY, HURRY--
STEP RIGHT THIS WAY, LADIES AND GENTLEMEN, BOYS AND GIRLS...
HALY'S CIRCUS
OSWD41

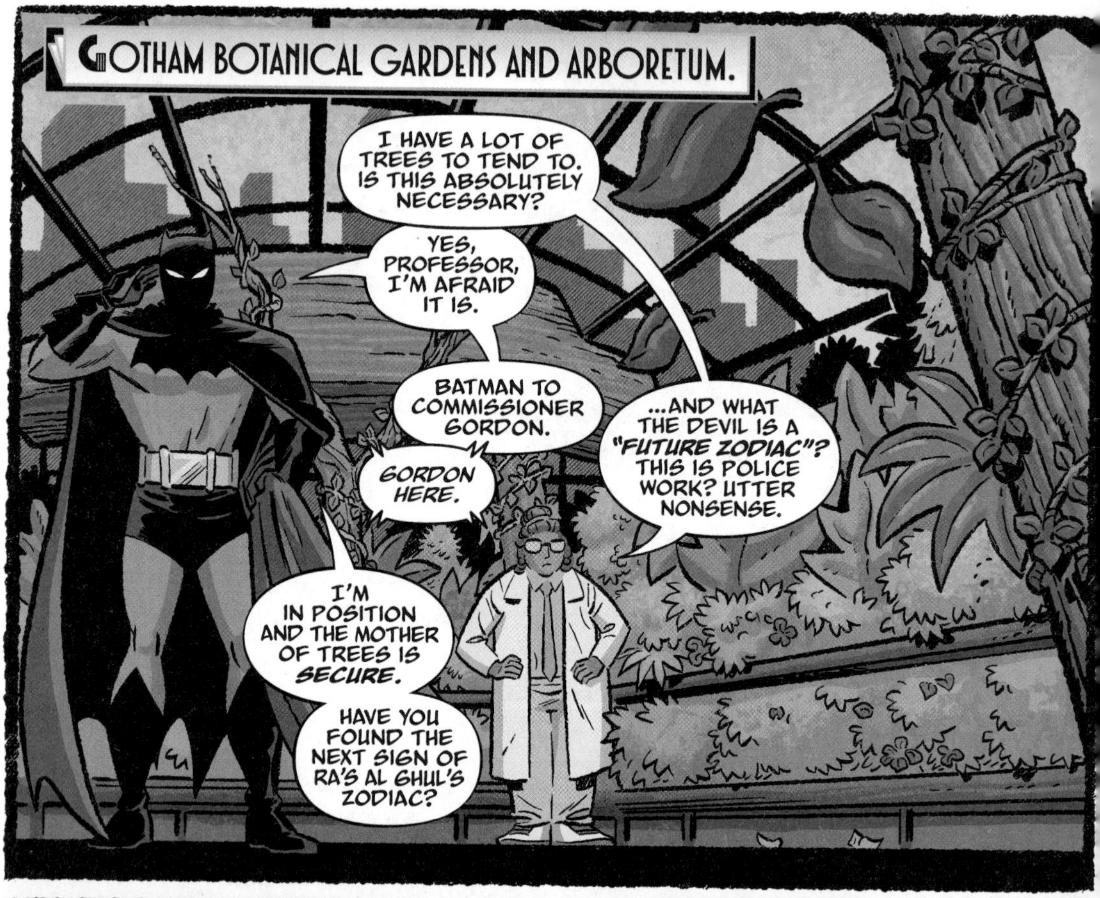
GOTHAM BOTANICAL GARDENS AND ARBORETUM.
I HAVE A LOT OF TREES TO TEND TO. IS THIS ABSOLUTELY NECESSARY?
YES, PROFESSOR, I'M AFRAID IT IS.
BATMAN TO COMMISSIONER GORDON.
GORDON HERE.
...AND WHAT THE DEVIL IS A "FUTURE ZODIAC"? THIS IS POLICE WORK? UTTER NONSENSE.
I'M IN POSITION AND THE MOTHER OF TREES IS SECURE.
HAVE YOU FOUND THE NEXT SIGN OF RA'S AL GHUL'S ZODIAC?

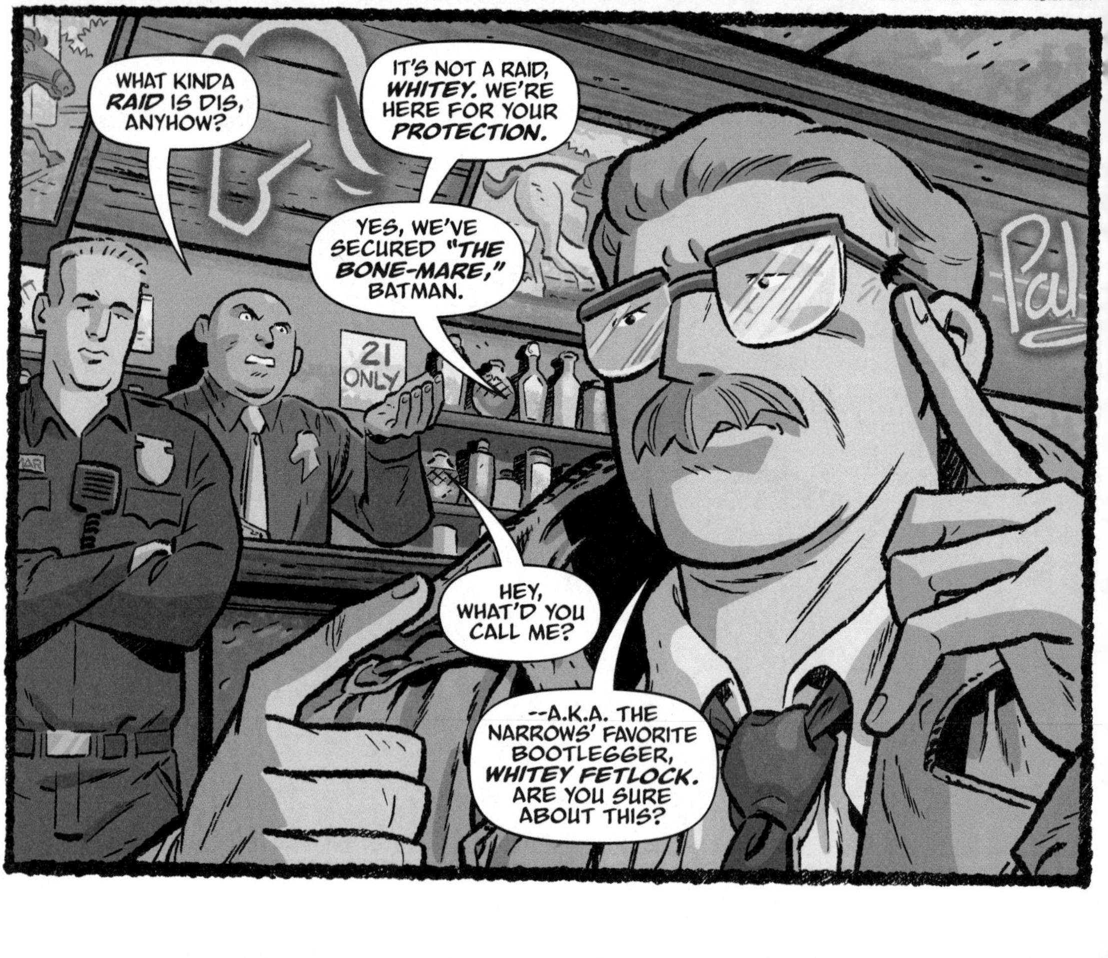
WHAT KINDA RAID IS DIS, ANYHOW?
IT'S NOT A RAID, WHITEY. WE'RE HERE FOR YOUR PROTECTION.
YES, WE'VE SECURED "THE BONE-MARE," BATMAN.
21 ONLY
HEY, WHAT'D YOU CALL ME?
--A.K.A. THE NARROWS' FAVORITE BOOTLEGGER, WHITEY FETLOCK. ARE YOU SURE ABOUT THIS?

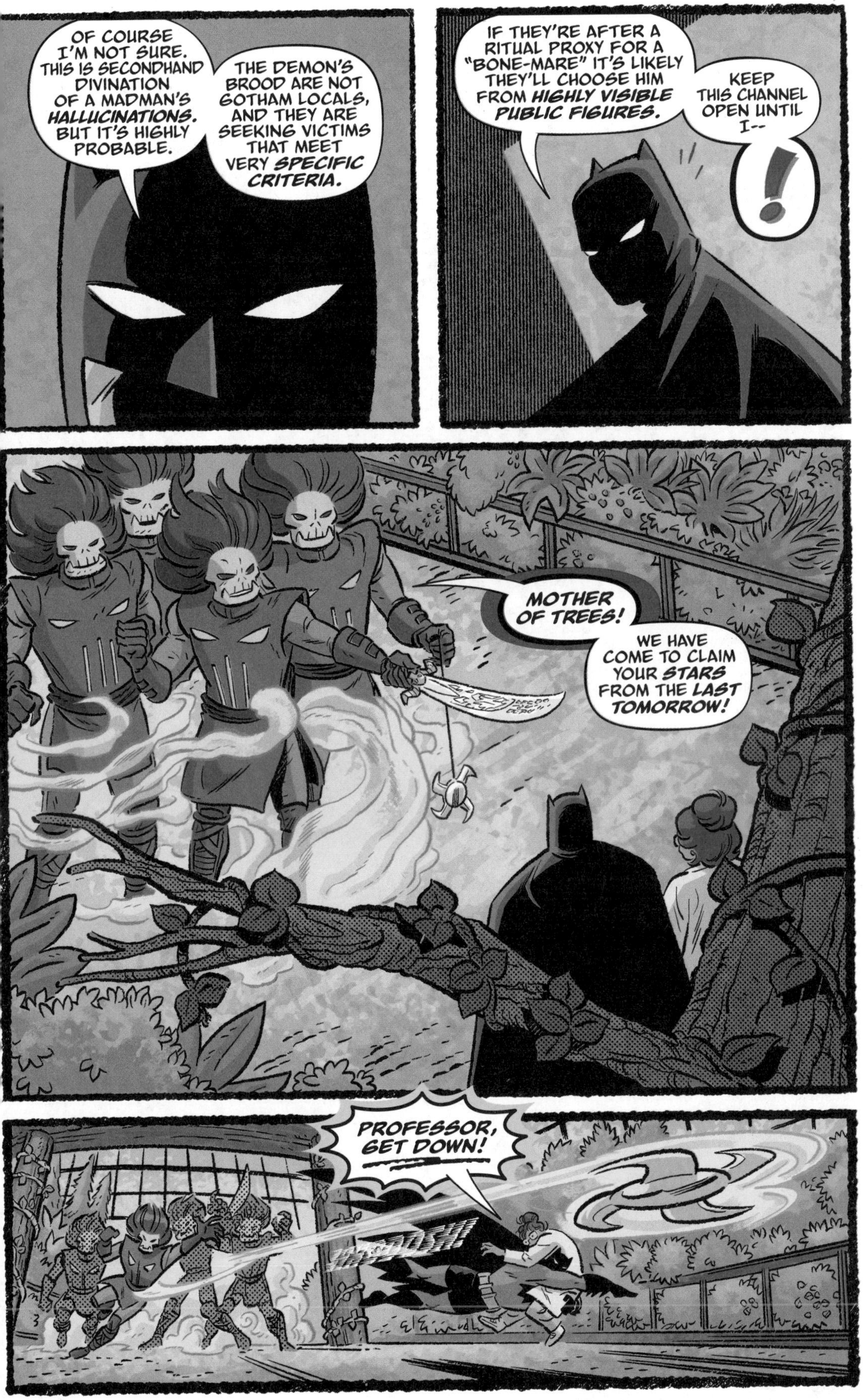

OF COURSE I'M NOT SURE. THIS IS SECONDHAND DIVINATION OF A MADMAN'S *HALLUCINATIONS*. BUT IT'S HIGHLY PROBABLE.
THE DEMON'S BROOD ARE NOT GOTHAM LOCALS, AND THEY ARE SEEKING VICTIMS THAT MEET VERY *SPECIFIC CRITERIA*.
IF THEY'RE AFTER A RITUAL PROXY FOR A "BONE-MARE" IT'S LIKELY THEY'LL CHOOSE HIM FROM *HIGHLY VISIBLE PUBLIC FIGURES*.
KEEP THIS CHANNEL OPEN UNTIL I--
!
MOTHER OF TREES!
WE HAVE COME TO CLAIM YOUR *STARS* FROM THE *LAST TOMORROW!*
PROFESSOR, GET DOWN!

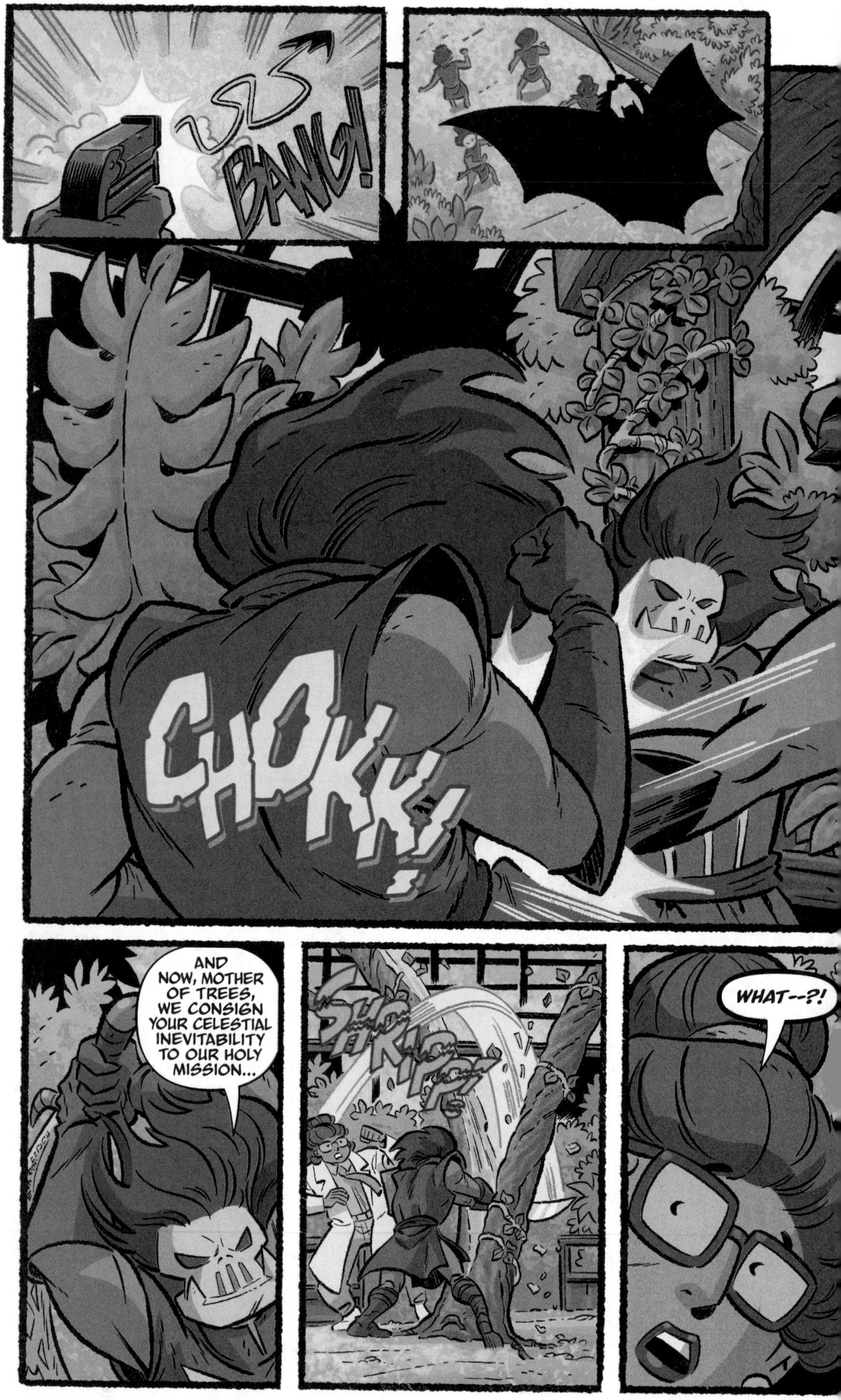
BANG!
CHOKK!
AND NOW, MOTHER OF TREES, WE CONSIGN YOUR CELESTIAL INEVITABILITY TO OUR HOLY MISSION...
SHRIPP!
WHAT--?!

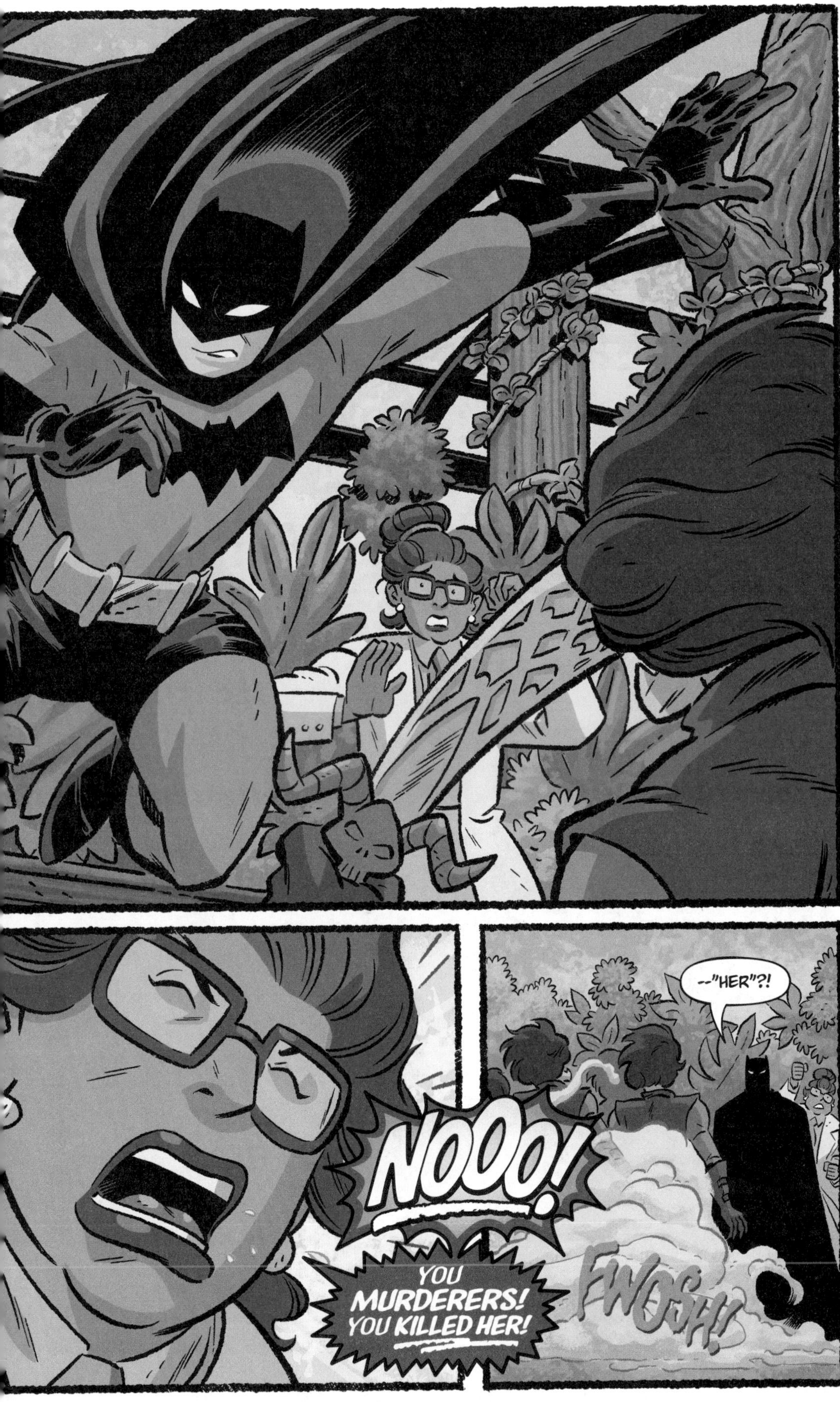
NOOO!
YOU MURDERERS! YOU KILLED HER!
--"HER"?!
FWOSH!

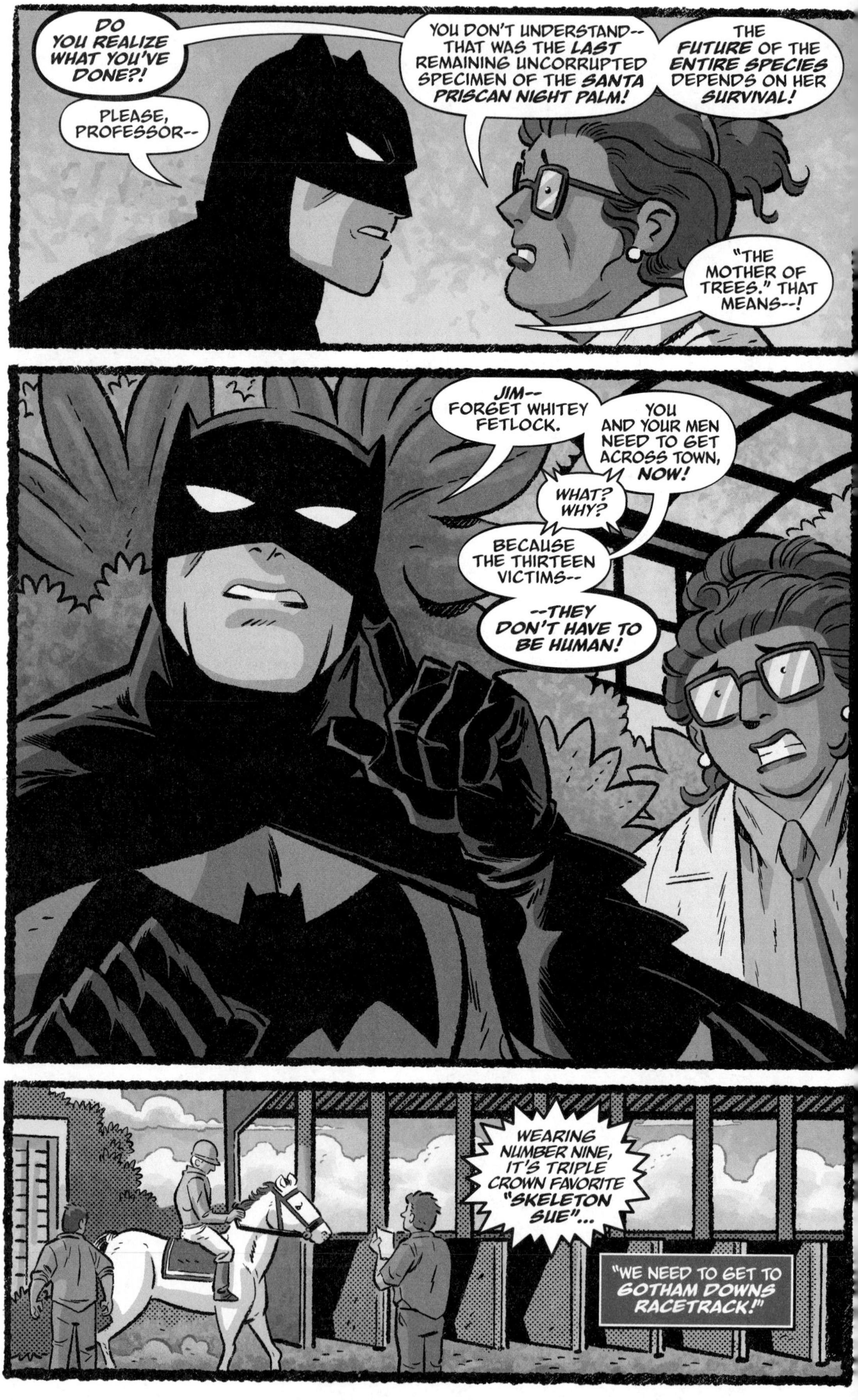
DO YOU REALIZE WHAT YOU'VE DONE?!
PLEASE, PROFESSOR--
YOU DON'T UNDERSTAND-- THAT WAS THE LAST REMAINING UNCORRUPTED SPECIMEN OF THE SANTA PRISCAN NIGHT PALM!
THE FUTURE OF THE ENTIRE SPECIES DEPENDS ON HER SURVIVAL!
"THE MOTHER OF TREES." THAT MEANS--!
JIM-- FORGET WHITEY FETLOCK.
YOU AND YOUR MEN NEED TO GET ACROSS TOWN, NOW!
WHAT? WHY?
BECAUSE THE THIRTEEN VICTIMS--
--THEY DON'T HAVE TO BE HUMAN!
WEARING NUMBER NINE, IT'S TRIPLE CROWN FAVORITE "SKELETON SUE"...
"WE NEED TO GET TO GOTHAM DOWNS RACETRACK!"

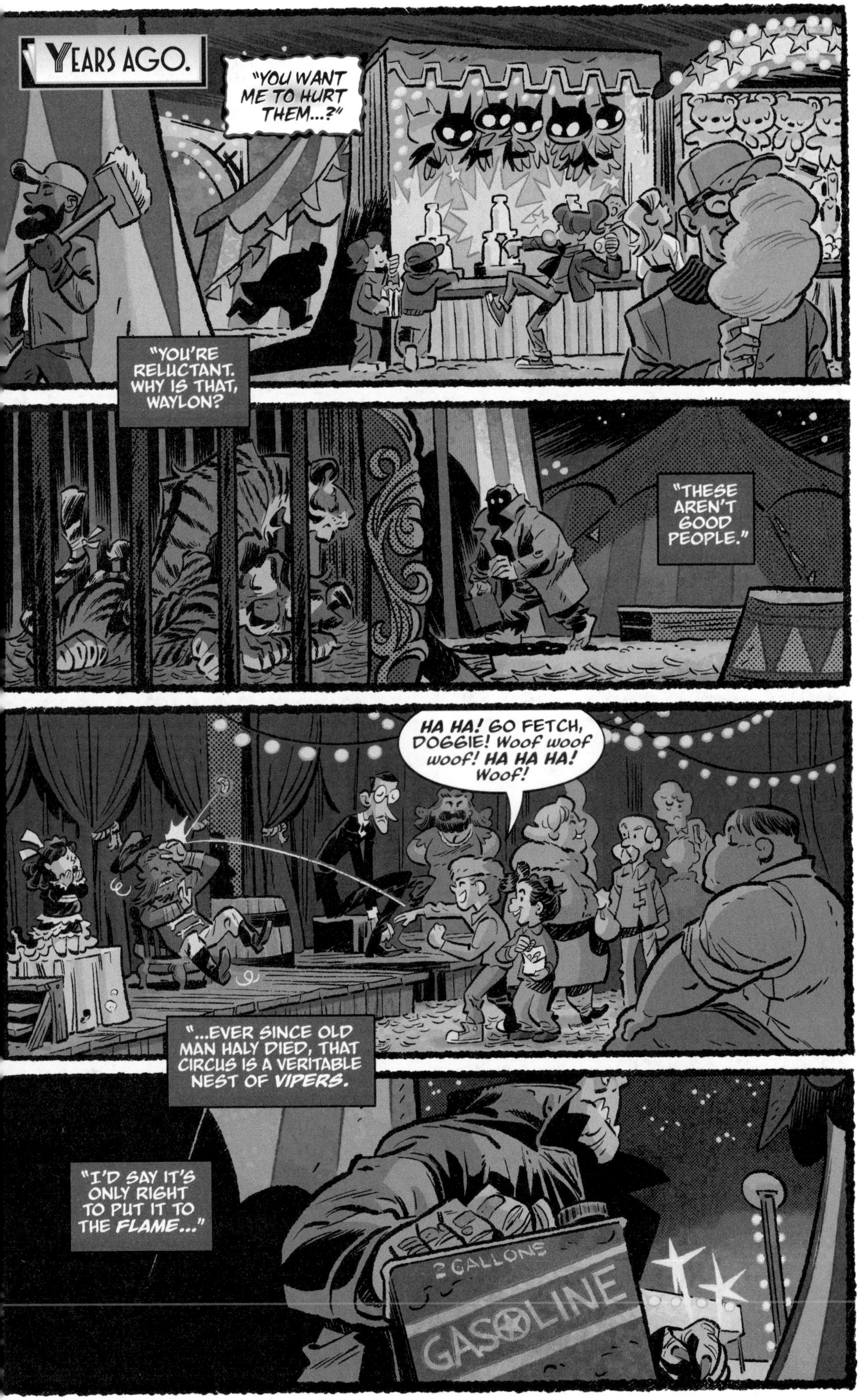

YEARS AGO.
"YOU WANT ME TO HURT THEM...?"
"YOU'RE RELUCTANT. WHY IS THAT, WAYLON?
"THESE AREN'T GOOD PEOPLE."
HA HA! GO FETCH, DOGGIE! Woof woof woof! HA HA HA! Woof!
"...EVER SINCE OLD MAN HALY DIED, THAT CIRCUS IS A VERITABLE NEST OF VIPERS.
"I'D SAY IT'S ONLY RIGHT TO PUT IT TO THE FLAME..."
2 GALLONS
GASOLINE

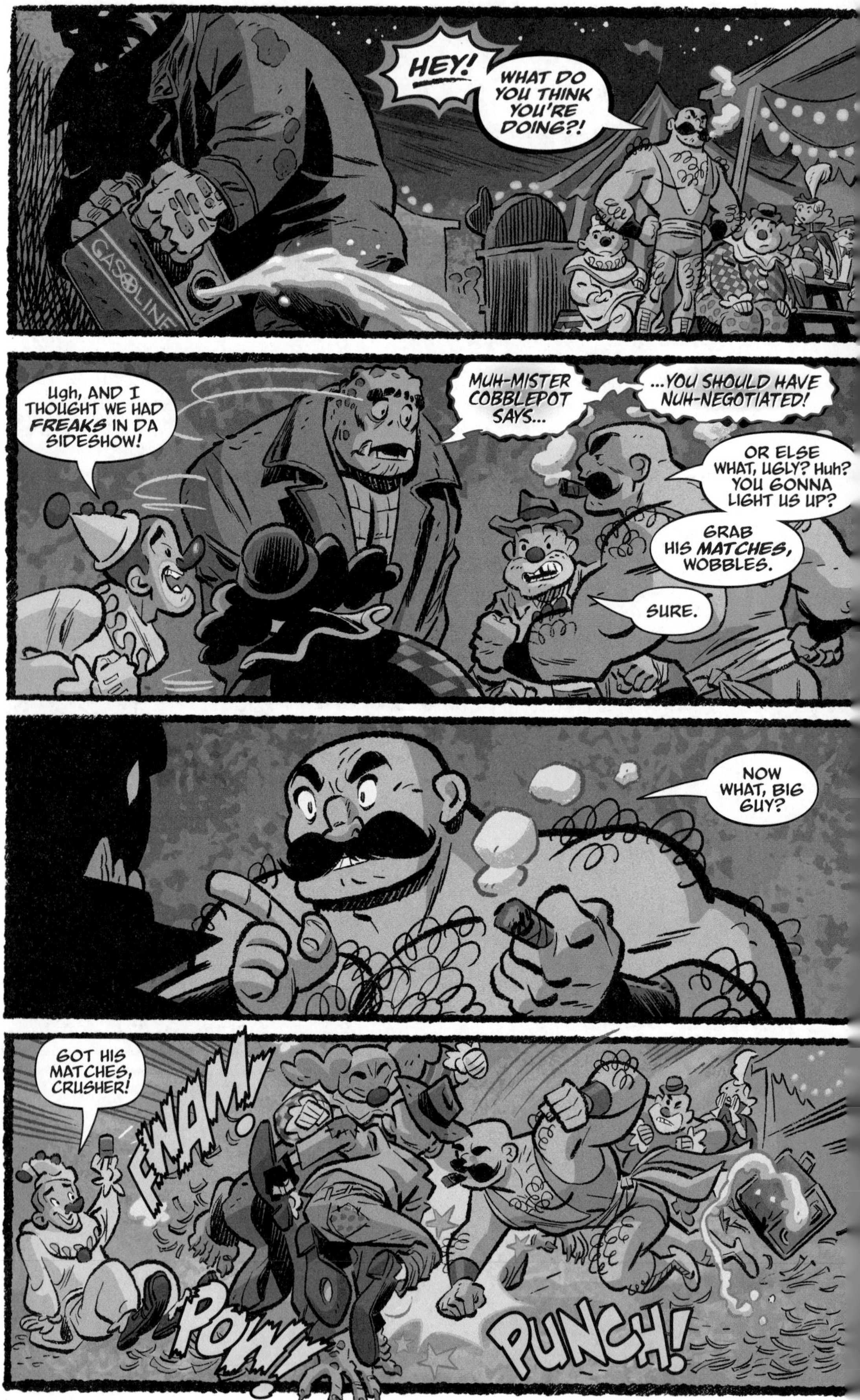
HEY!
WHAT DO YOU THINK YOU'RE DOING?!
GASOLINE
Ugh, AND I THOUGHT WE HAD FREAKS IN DA SIDESHOW!
MUH-MISTER COBBLEPOT SAYS...
...YOU SHOULD HAVE NUH-NEGOTIATED!
OR ELSE WHAT, UGLY? Huh? YOU GONNA LIGHT US UP?
GRAB HIS MATCHES, WOBBLES.
SURE.
NOW WHAT, BIG GUY?
GOT HIS MATCHES, CRUSHER!
FWAM!
POW!
PUNCH!

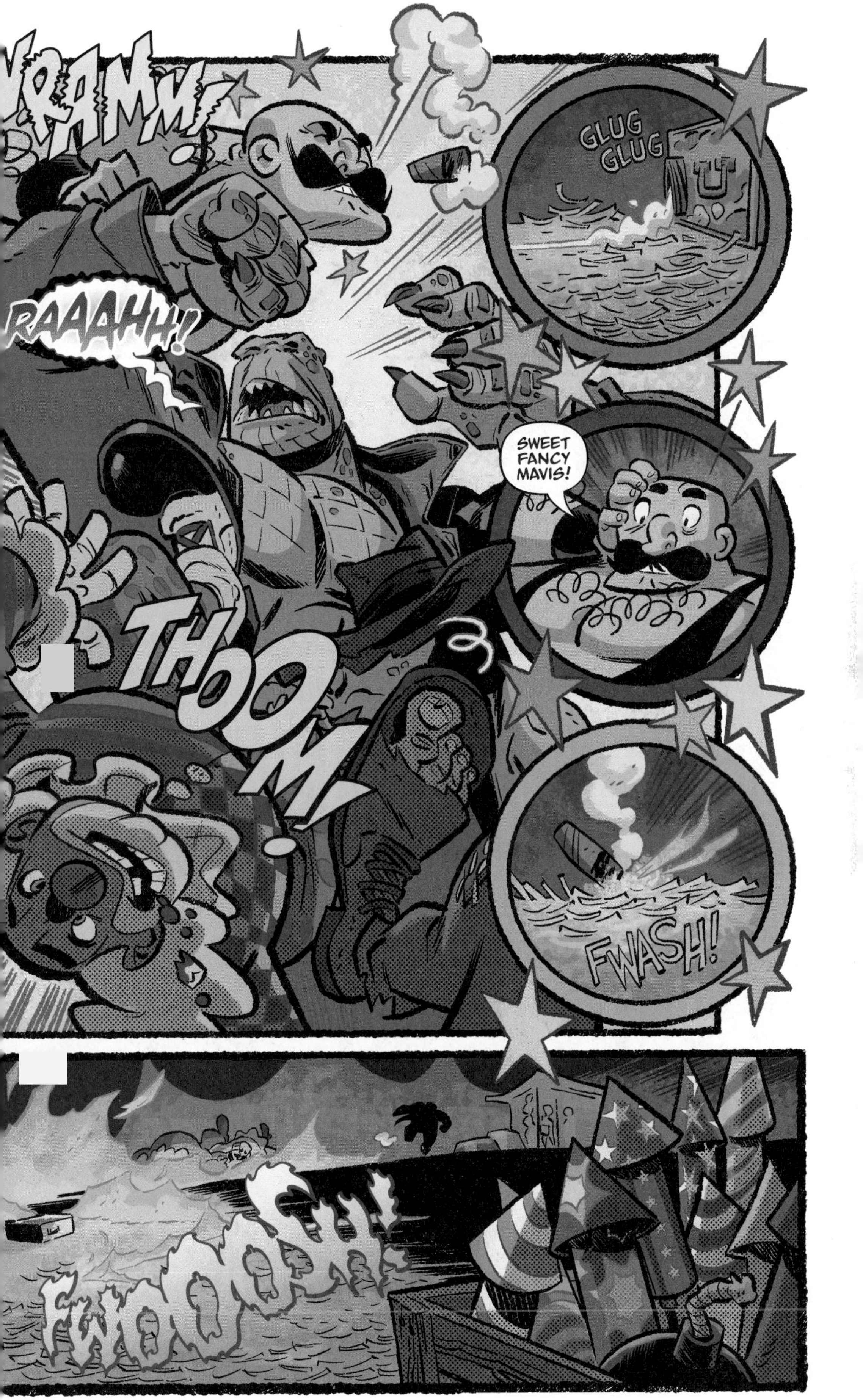

VRAMM!
GLUG GLUG
RAAAHH!
SWEET FANCY MAVIS!
THOOM!
FWASH!
FWOOOSH!

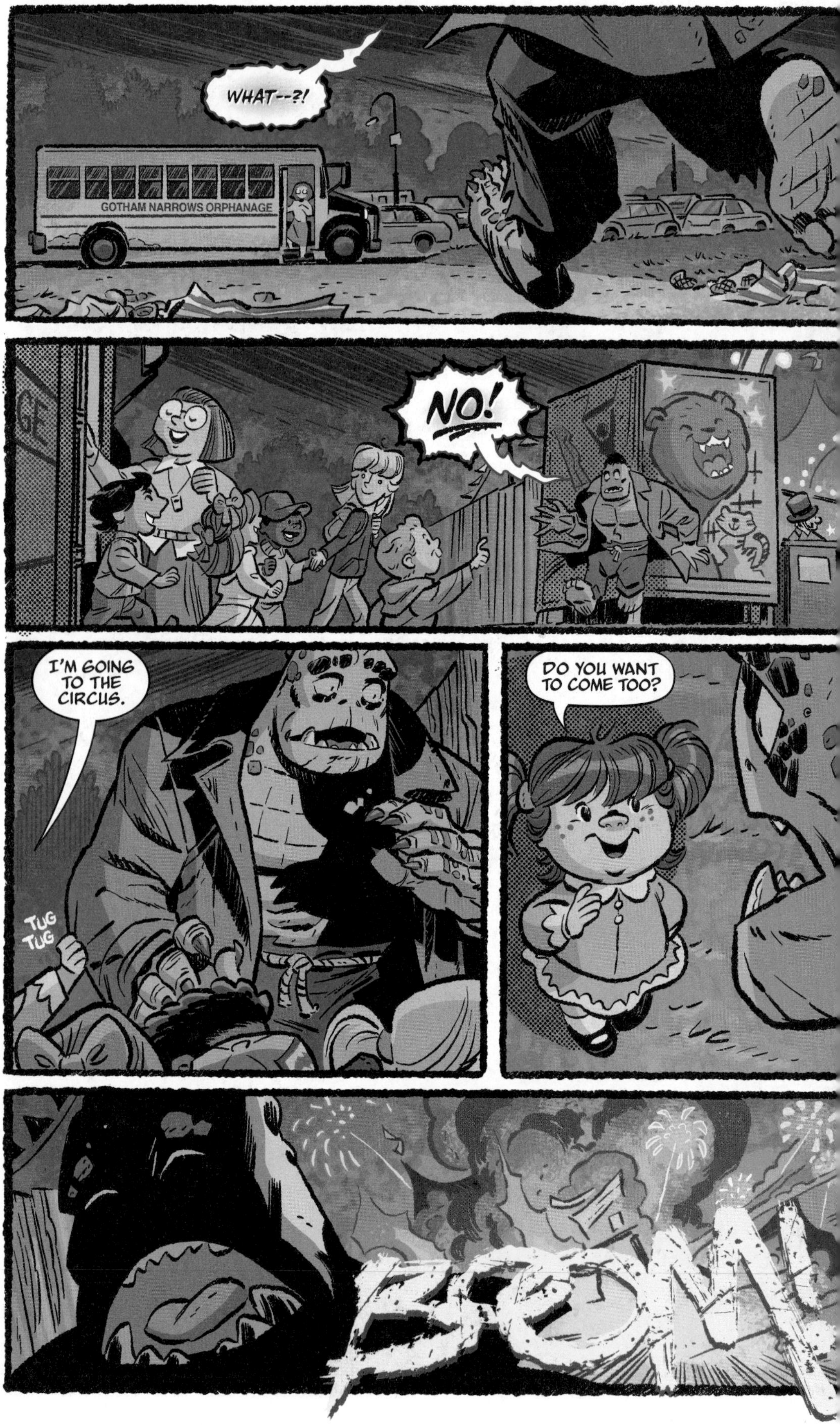
WHAT--?!
GOTHAM NARROWS ORPHANAGE
NO!
I'M GOING TO THE CIRCUS.
TUG TUG
DO YOU WANT TO COME TOO?

=Psssst=
HEY, BUDDY. YOU LOOK LIKE YOU JUST SAW A GHOST...
...ANY CHANCE IT'S THAT DEAD DOCTOR WE'RE LOOKIN' FOR?
NO. IT'S SOMETHING EVEN BETTER...
SAVE IT. I'M A GONER.
NO, PLEASE. STAY WITH ME JUST A LITTLE LONGER...
I CAN MAKE YOU STRONG! I CAN MAKE YOU LIVE AGAIN!
SHOOSH
MONOCLONAL STEROID SERUM

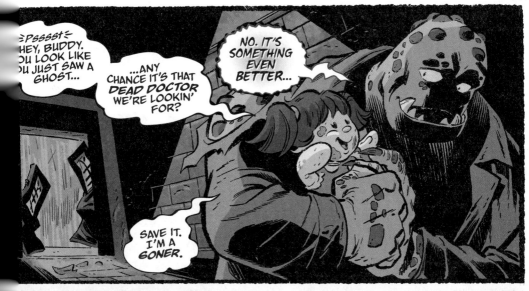

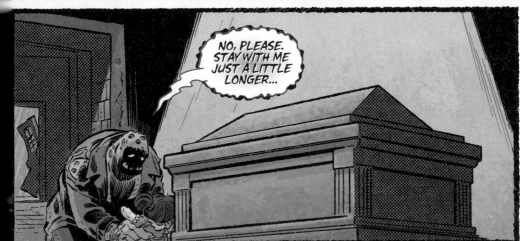

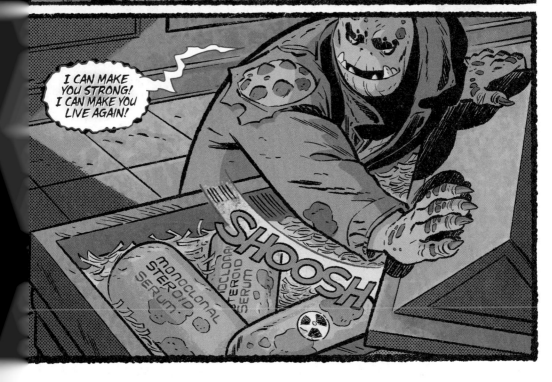

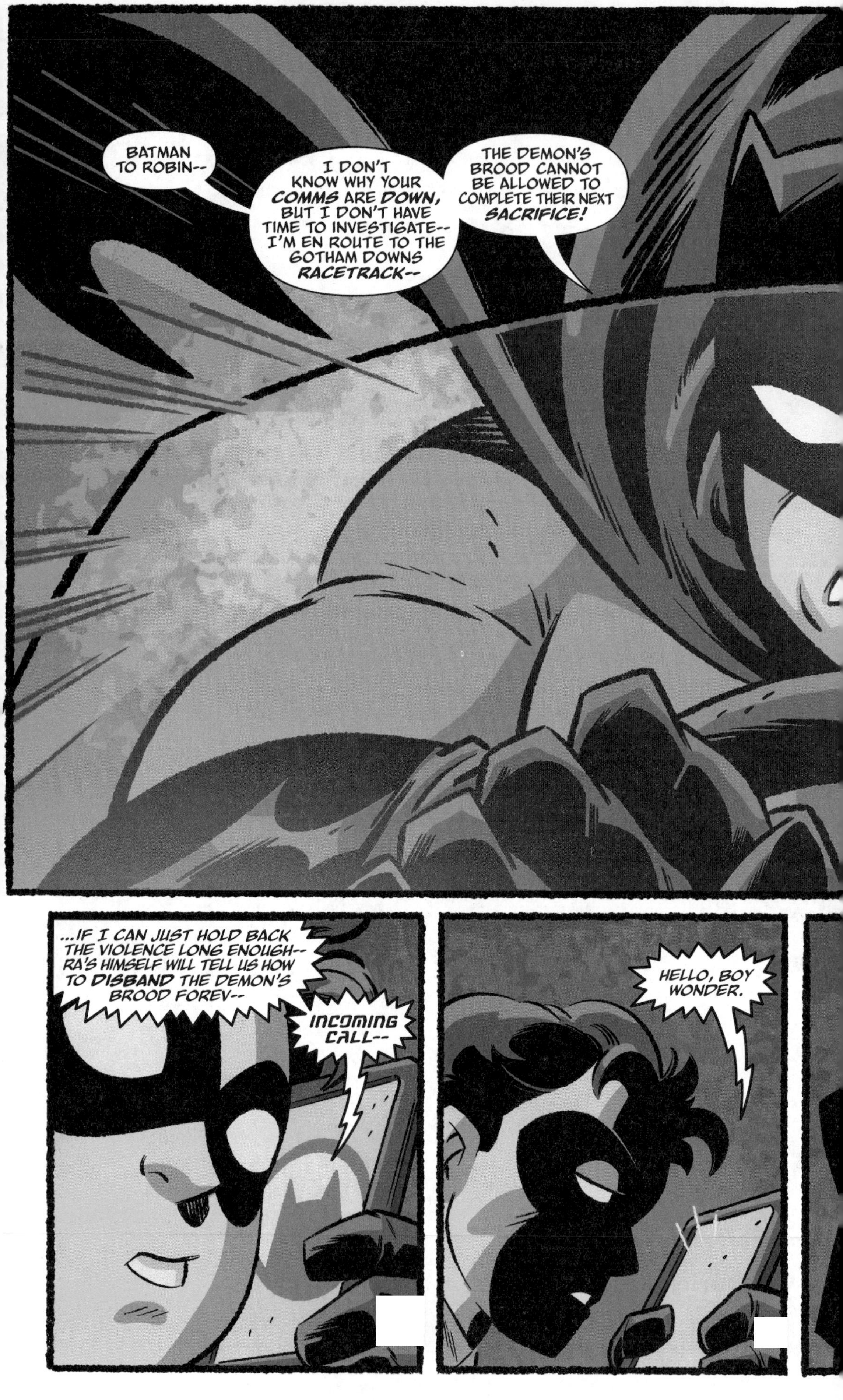
BATMAN TO ROBIN--
I DON'T KNOW WHY YOUR COMMS ARE DOWN, BUT I DON'T HAVE TIME TO INVESTIGATE-- I'M EN ROUTE TO THE GOTHAM DOWNS RACETRACK--
THE DEMON'S BROOD CANNOT BE ALLOWED TO COMPLETE THEIR NEXT SACRIFICE!
...IF I CAN JUST HOLD BACK THE VIOLENCE LONG ENOUGH-- RA'S HIMSELF WILL TELL US HOW TO DISBAND THE DEMON'S BROOD FOREV--
INCOMING CALL--
HELLO, BOY WONDER.

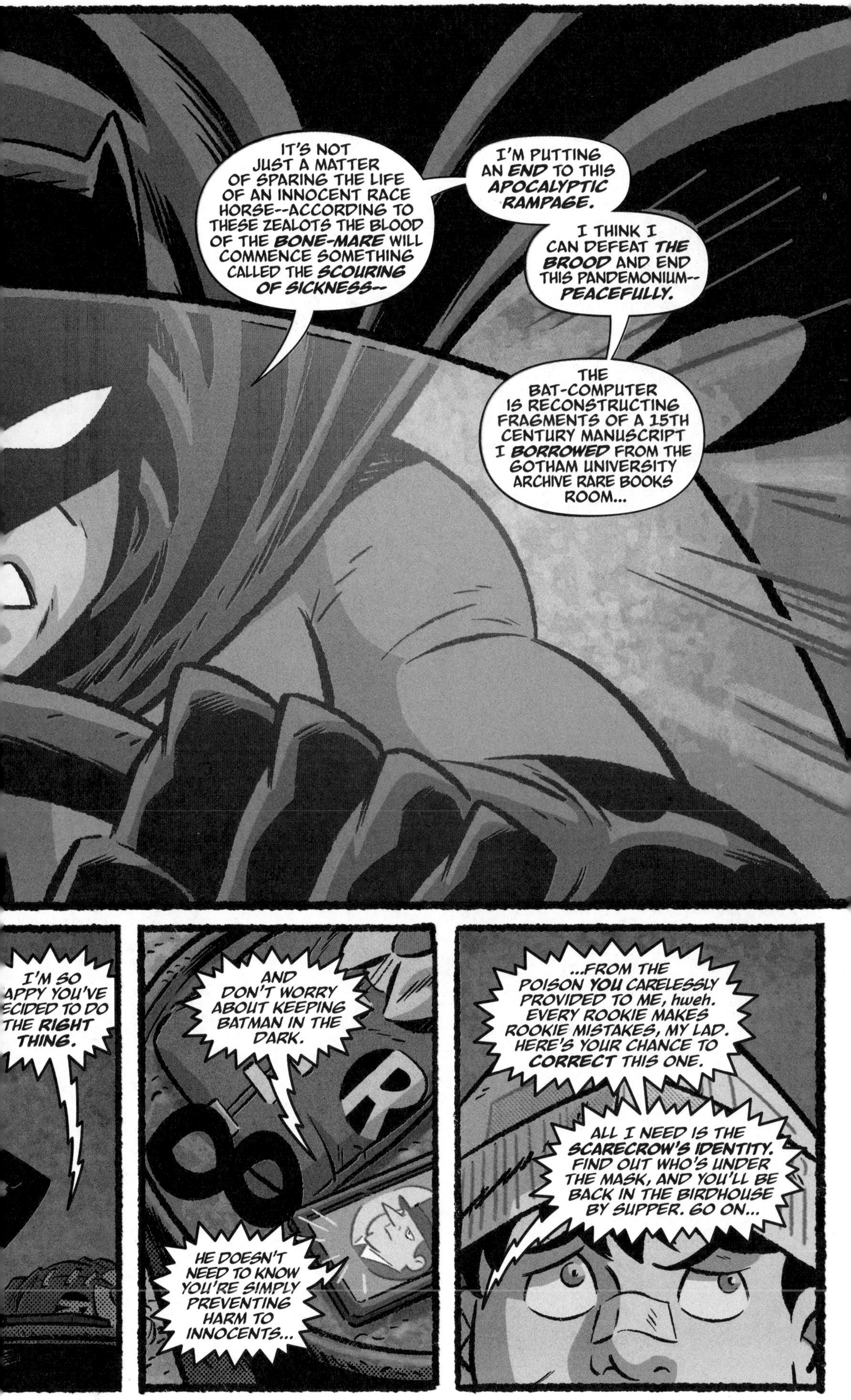
IT'S NOT JUST A MATTER OF SPARING THE LIFE OF AN INNOCENT RACE HORSE--ACCORDING TO THESE ZEALOTS THE BLOOD OF THE BONE-MARE WILL COMMENCE SOMETHING CALLED THE SCOURING OF SICKNESS--
I'M PUTTING AN END TO THIS APOCALYPTIC RAMPAGE.
I THINK I CAN DEFEAT THE BROOD AND END THIS PANDEMONIUM--PEACEFULLY.
THE BAT-COMPUTER IS RECONSTRUCTING FRAGMENTS OF A 15TH CENTURY MANUSCRIPT I BORROWED FROM THE GOTHAM UNIVERSITY ARCHIVE RARE BOOKS ROOM...
I'M SO APPY YOU'VE ECIDED TO DO THE RIGHT THING.
AND DON'T WORRY ABOUT KEEPING BATMAN IN THE DARK.
HE DOESN'T NEED TO KNOW YOU'RE SIMPLY PREVENTING HARM TO INNOCENTS...
...FROM THE POISON YOU CARELESSLY PROVIDED TO ME, hweh. EVERY ROOKIE MAKES ROOKIE MISTAKES, MY LAD. HERE'S YOUR CHANCE TO CORRECT THIS ONE.
ALL I NEED IS THE SCARECROW'S IDENTITY. FIND OUT WHO'S UNDER THE MASK, AND YOU'LL BE BACK IN THE BIRDHOUSE BY SUPPER. GO ON...

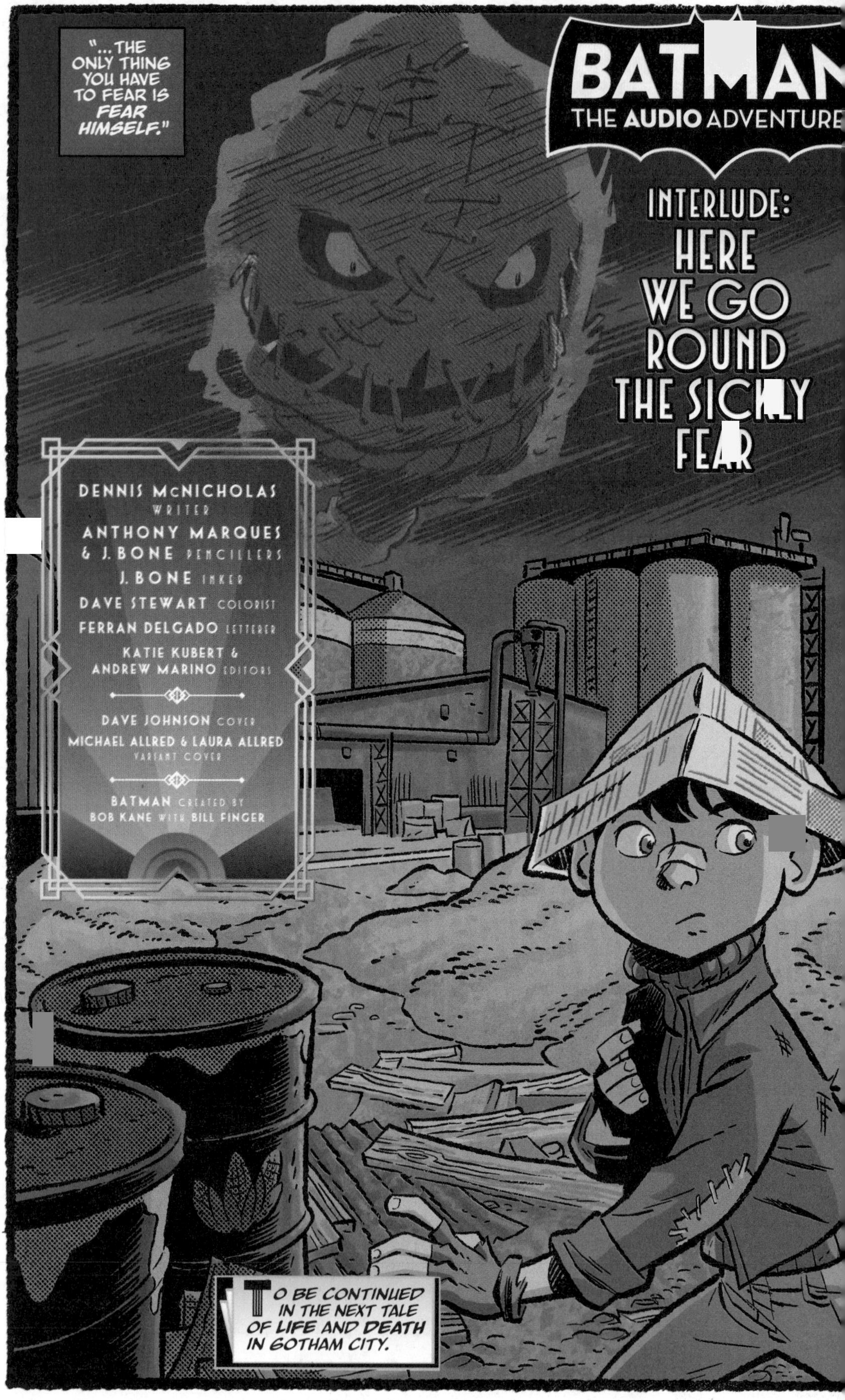
"...THE ONLY THING YOU HAVE TO FEAR IS *FEAR HIMSELF.*"
BATMAN
THE AUDIO ADVENTURES
INTERLUDE:
HERE WE GO ROUND THE SICKLY FEAR
DENNIS McNICHOLAS WRITER
ANTHONY MARQUES & J. BONE PENCILLERS
J. BONE INKER
DAVE STEWART COLORIST
FERRAN DELGADO LETTERER
KATIE KUBERT & ANDREW MARINO EDITORS
DAVE JOHNSON COVER
MICHAEL ALLRED & LAURA ALLRED VARIANT COVER
BATMAN CREATED BY BOB KANE WITH BILL FINGER
TO BE CONTINUED IN THE NEXT TALE OF *LIFE AND DEATH* IN GOTHAM CITY.

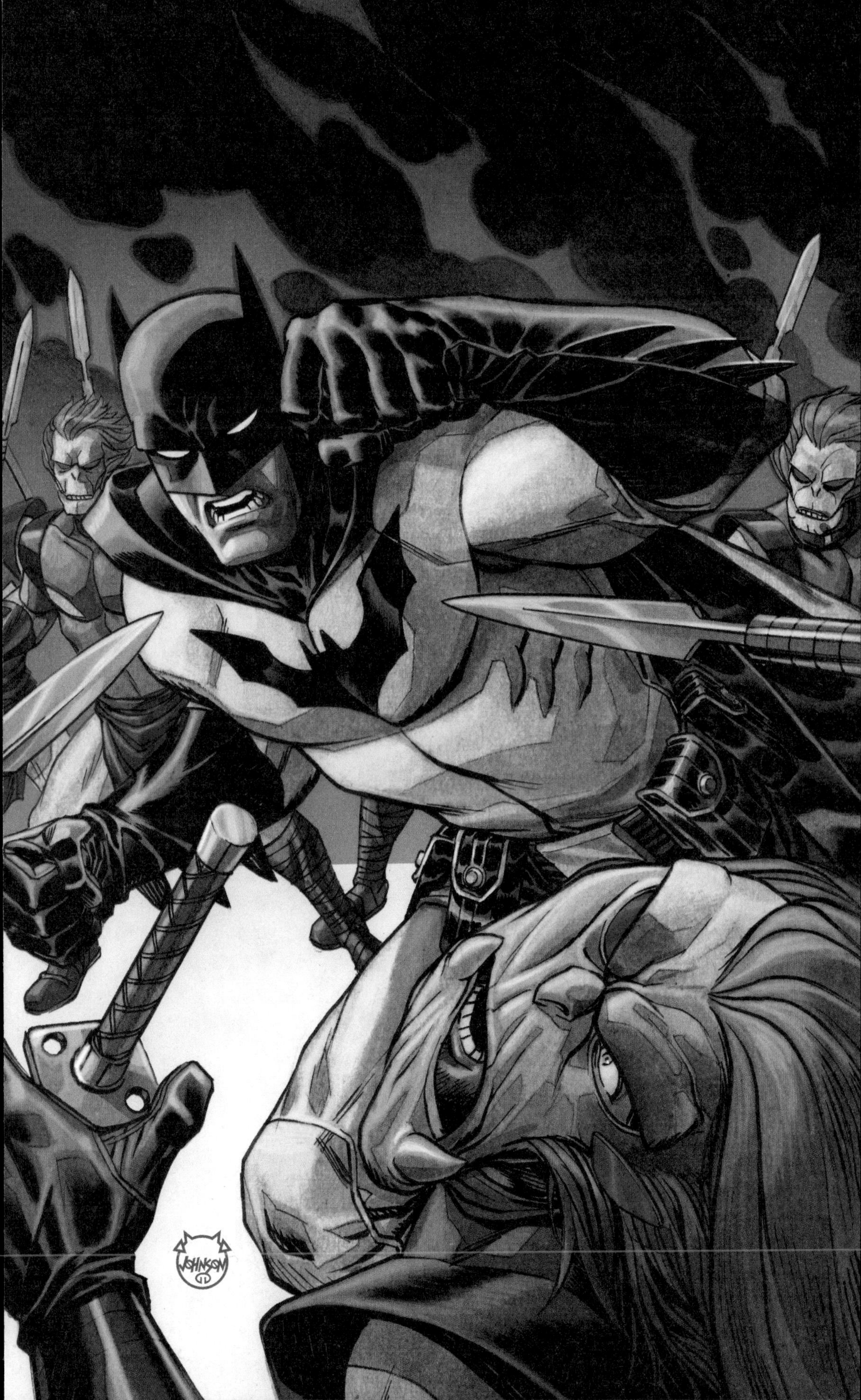
JOHNSON

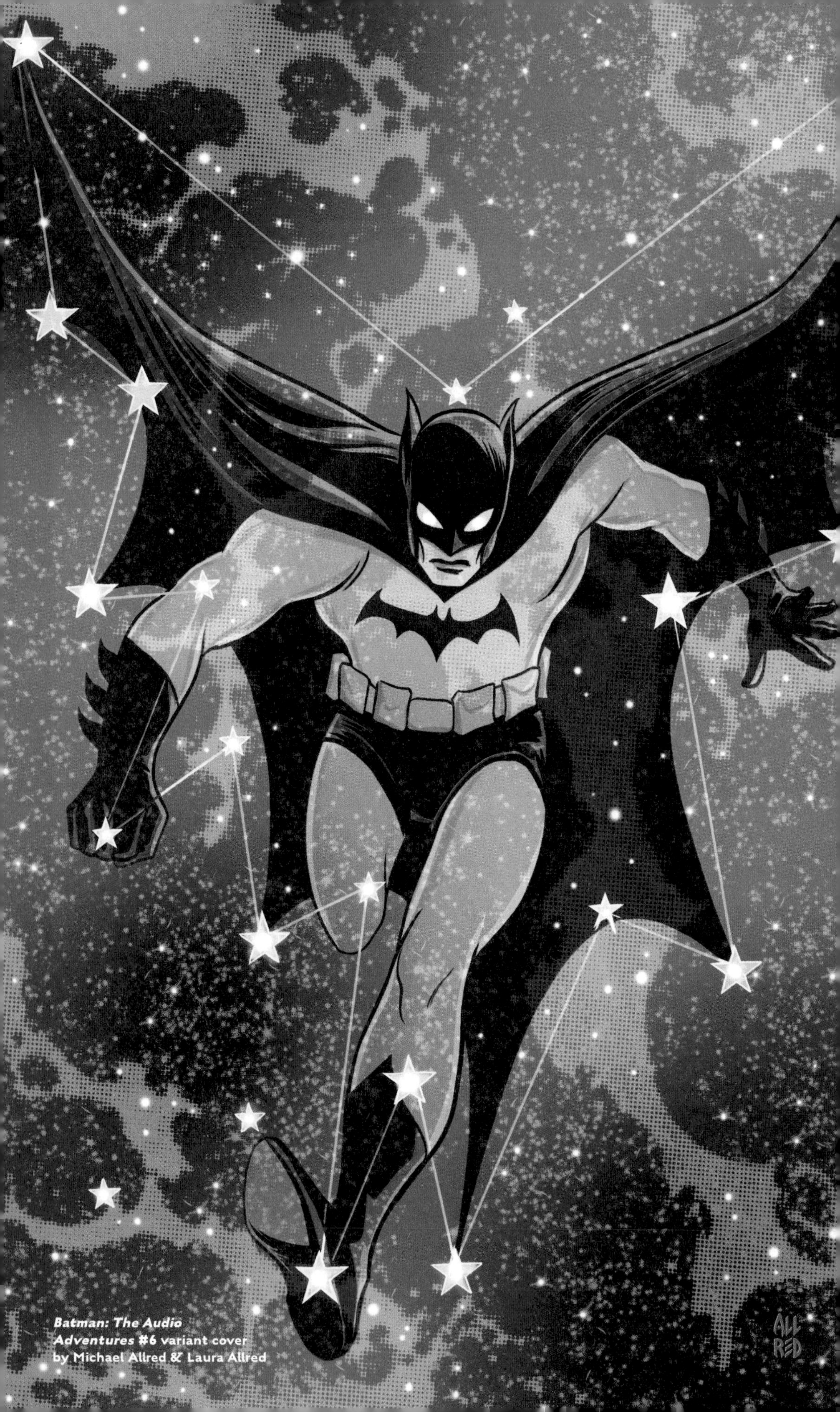
ALL
RED
Batman: The Audio Adventures #6 variant cover
by Michael Allred & Laura Allred

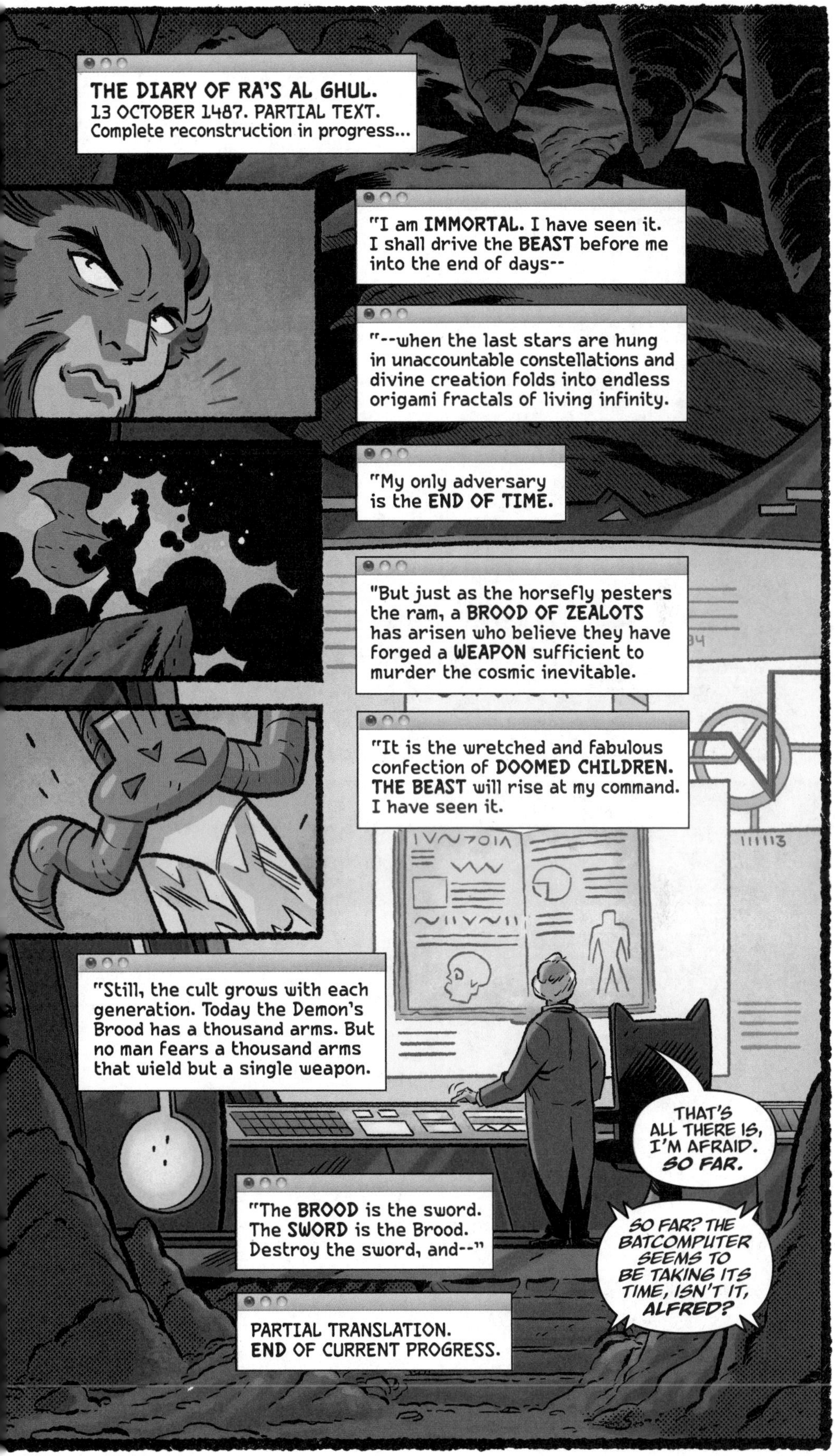
THE DIARY OF RA'S AL GHUL. 13 OCTOBER 1487. PARTIAL TEXT. Complete reconstruction in progress...
"I am IMMORTAL. I have seen it. I shall drive the BEAST before me into the end of days--
"--when the last stars are hung in unaccountable constellations and divine creation folds into endless origami fractals of living infinity.
"My only adversary is the END OF TIME.
"But just as the horsefly pesters the ram, a BROOD OF ZEALOTS has arisen who believe they have forged a WEAPON sufficient to murder the cosmic inevitable.
"It is the wretched and fabulous confection of DOOMED CHILDREN. THE BEAST will rise at my command. I have seen it.
"Still, the cult grows with each generation. Today the Demon's Brood has a thousand arms. But no man fears a thousand arms that wield but a single weapon.
THAT'S ALL THERE IS, I'M AFRAID. SO FAR.
"The BROOD is the sword. The SWORD is the Brood. Destroy the sword, and--"
SO FAR? THE BATCOMPUTER SEEMS TO BE TAKING ITS TIME, ISN'T IT, ALFRED?
PARTIAL TRANSLATION. END OF CURRENT PROGRESS.

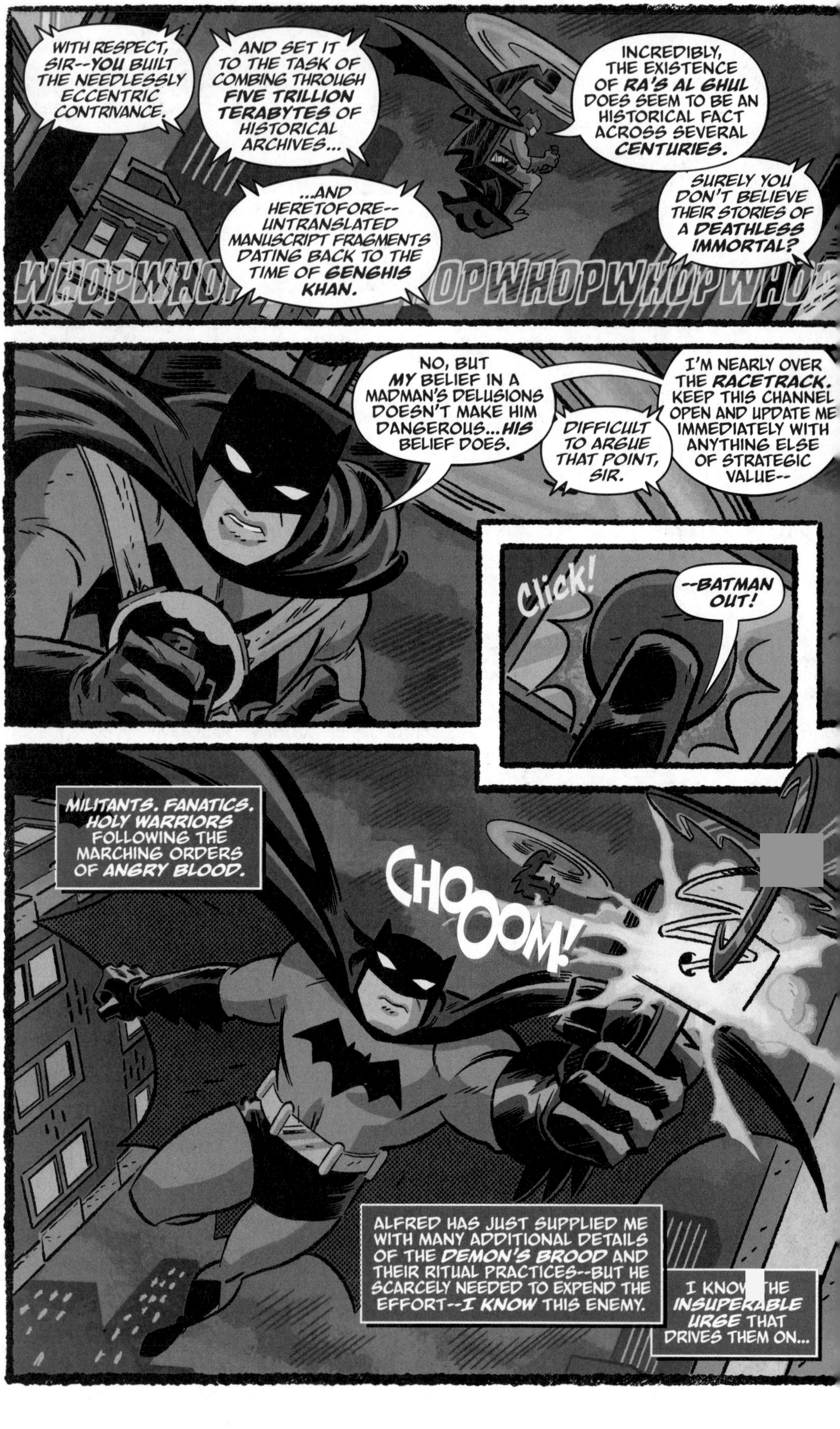

WITH RESPECT, SIR--YOU BUILT THE NEEDLESSLY ECCENTRIC CONTRIVANCE.
AND SET IT TO THE TASK OF COMBING THROUGH FIVE TRILLION TERABYTES OF HISTORICAL ARCHIVES...
...AND HERETOFORE--UNTRANSLATED MANUSCRIPT FRAGMENTS DATING BACK TO THE TIME OF GENGHIS KHAN.
INCREDIBLY, THE EXISTENCE OF RA'S AL GHUL DOES SEEM TO BE AN HISTORICAL FACT ACROSS SEVERAL CENTURIES.
SURELY YOU DON'T BELIEVE THEIR STORIES OF A DEATHLESS IMMORTAL?
WHOPWHO
OPWHOPWHOPWHOPWHO
NO, BUT MY BELIEF IN A MADMAN'S DELUSIONS DOESN'T MAKE HIM DANGEROUS...HIS BELIEF DOES.
DIFFICULT TO ARGUE THAT POINT, SIR.
I'M NEARLY OVER THE RACETRACK. KEEP THIS CHANNEL OPEN AND UPDATE ME IMMEDIATELY WITH ANYTHING ELSE OF STRATEGIC VALUE--
Click!
--BATMAN OUT!
MILITANTS. FANATICS. HOLY WARRIORS FOLLOWING THE MARCHING ORDERS OF ANGRY BLOOD.
CHOOOOM!
ALFRED HAS JUST SUPPLIED ME WITH MANY ADDITIONAL DETAILS OF THE DEMON'S BROOD AND THEIR RITUAL PRACTICES--BUT HE SCARCELY NEEDED TO EXPEND THE EFFORT--I KNOW THIS ENEMY.
I KNOW THE INSUPERABLE URGE THAT DRIVES THEM ON...

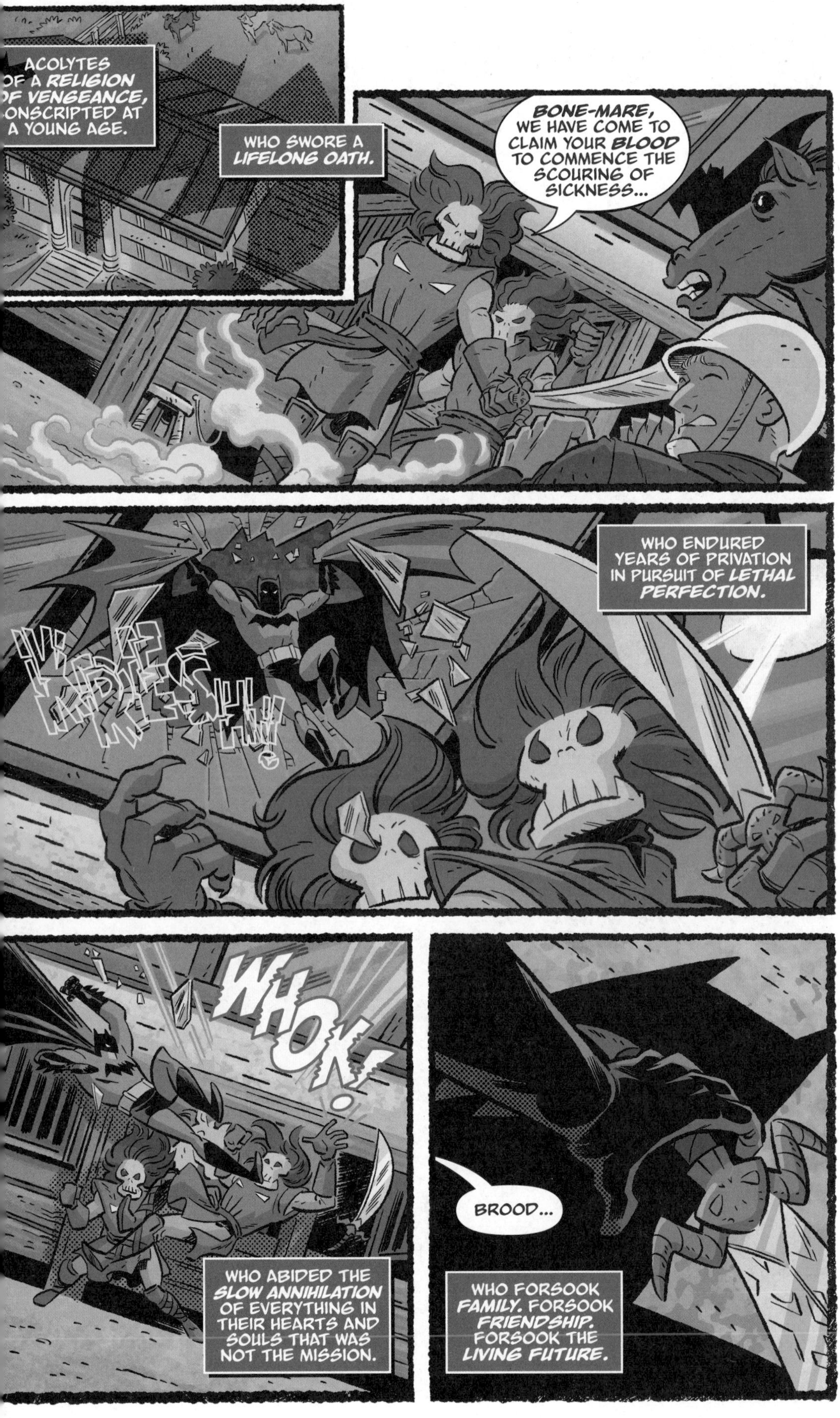
ACOLYTES OF A *RELIGION OF VENGEANCE*, CONSCRIPTED AT A YOUNG AGE.
WHO SWORE A *LIFELONG OATH.*
BONE-MARE, WE HAVE COME TO CLAIM YOUR *BLOOD* TO COMMENCE THE SCOURING OF SICKNESS...
WHO ENDURED YEARS OF PRIVATION IN PURSUIT OF *LETHAL PERFECTION.*
WHOK!
WHO ABIDED THE *SLOW ANNIHILATION* OF EVERYTHING IN THEIR HEARTS AND SOULS THAT WAS NOT THE MISSION.
BROOD...
WHO FORSOOK *FAMILY*. FORSOOK *FRIENDSHIP.* FORSOOK THE *LIVING FUTURE.*

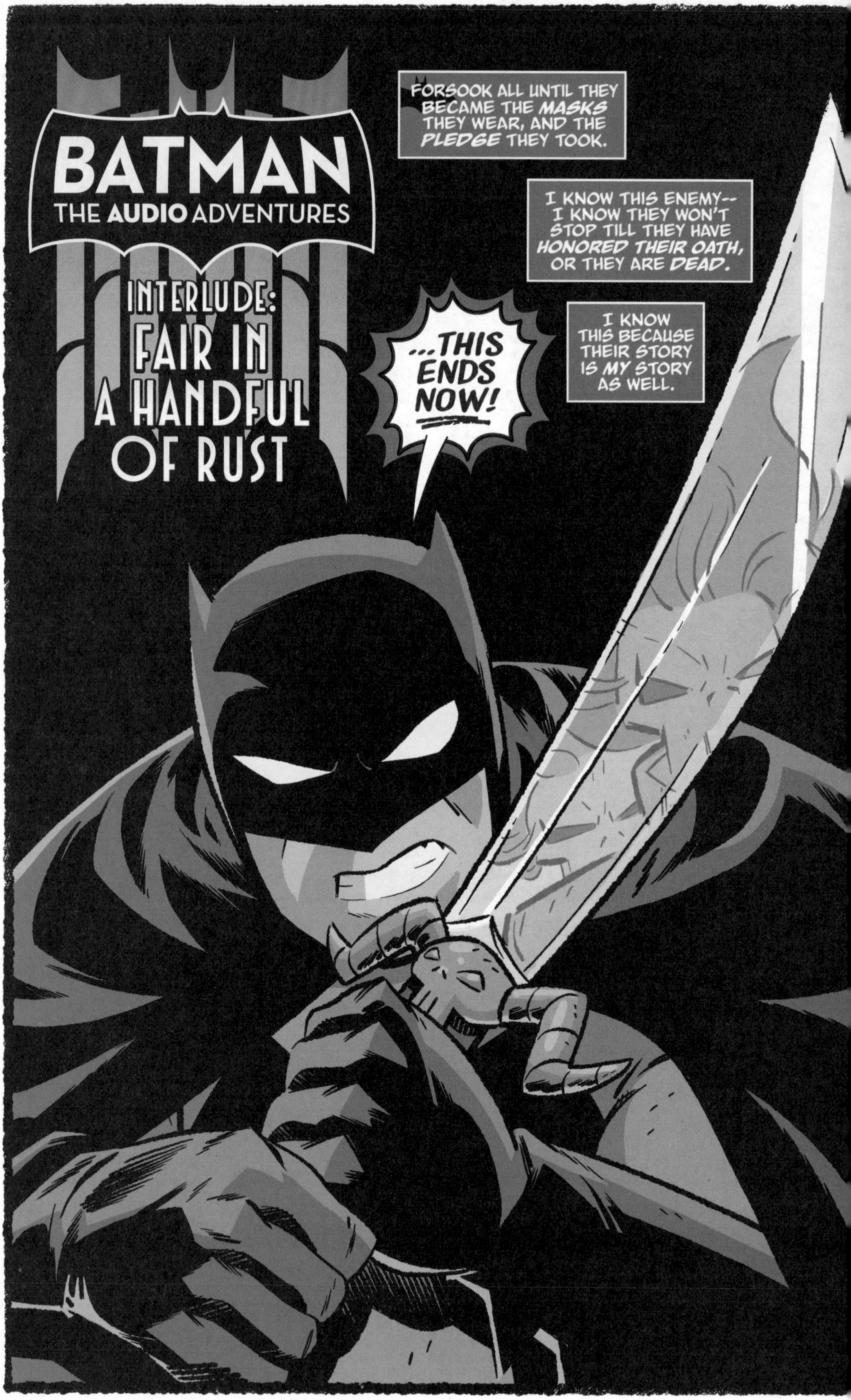

BATMAN
THE AUDIO ADVENTURES
INTERLUDE: FAIR IN A HANDFUL OF RUST
FORSOOK ALL UNTIL THEY BECAME THE MASKS THEY WEAR, AND THE PLEDGE THEY TOOK.
I KNOW THIS ENEMY-- I KNOW THEY WON'T STOP TILL THEY HAVE HONORED THEIR OATH, OR THEY ARE DEAD.
I KNOW THIS BECAUSE THEIR STORY IS MY STORY AS WELL.
...THIS ENDS NOW!

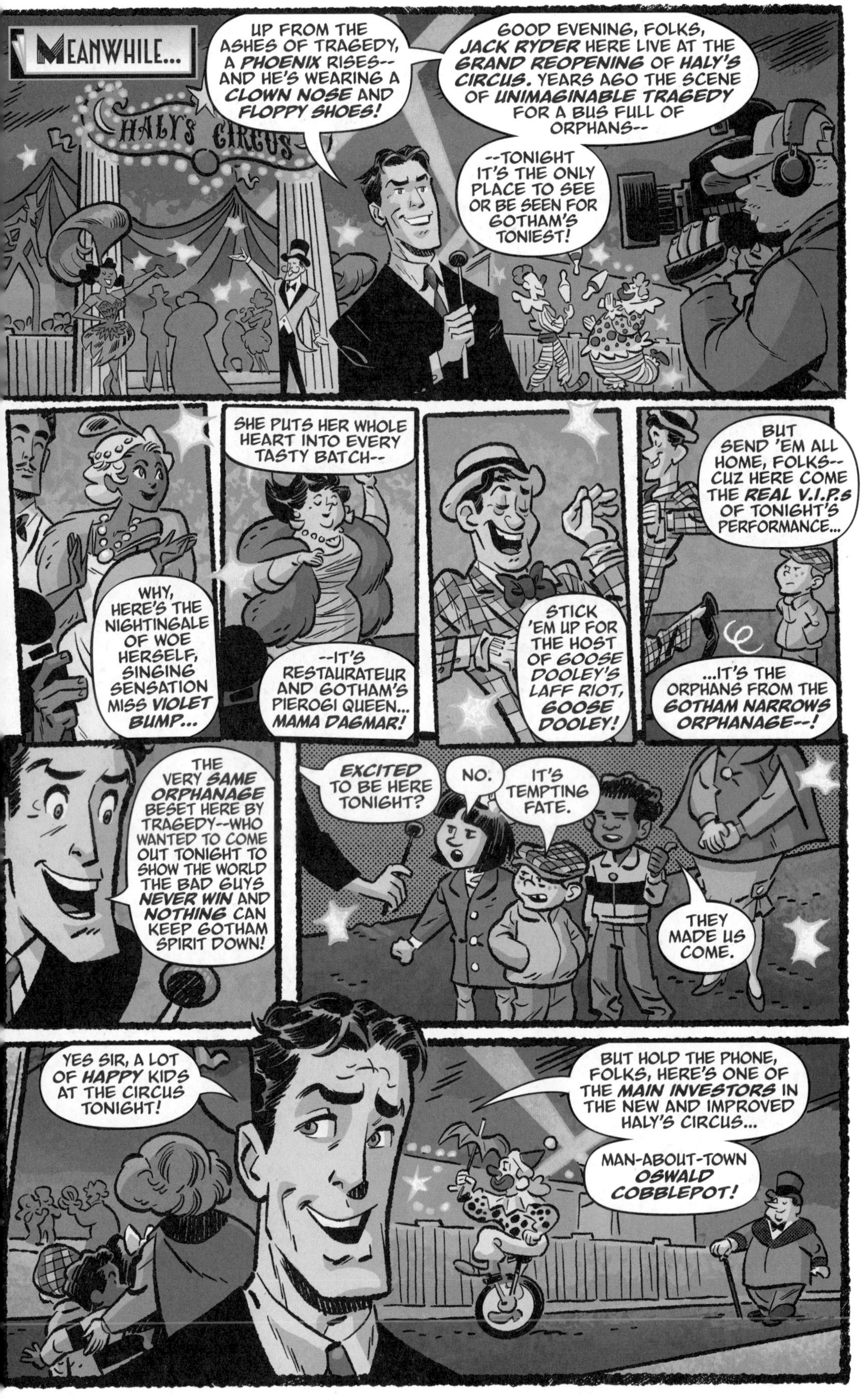
MEANWHILE...
UP FROM THE ASHES OF TRAGEDY, A PHOENIX RISES--AND HE'S WEARING A CLOWN NOSE AND FLOPPY SHOES!
GOOD EVENING, FOLKS, JACK RYDER HERE LIVE AT THE GRAND REOPENING OF HALY'S CIRCUS. YEARS AGO THE SCENE OF UNIMAGINABLE TRAGEDY FOR A BUS FULL OF ORPHANS--
--TONIGHT IT'S THE ONLY PLACE TO SEE OR BE SEEN FOR GOTHAM'S TONIEST!
HALY'S CIRCUS
WHY, HERE'S THE NIGHTINGALE OF WOE HERSELF, SINGING SENSATION MISS VIOLET BUMP...
SHE PUTS HER WHOLE HEART INTO EVERY TASTY BATCH--
--IT'S RESTAURATEUR AND GOTHAM'S PIEROGI QUEEN... MAMA DAGMAR!
STICK 'EM UP FOR THE HOST OF GOOSE DOOLEY'S LAFF RIOT, GOOSE DOOLEY!
BUT SEND 'EM ALL HOME, FOLKS--CUZ HERE COME THE REAL V.I.P.s OF TONIGHT'S PERFORMANCE...
...IT'S THE ORPHANS FROM THE GOTHAM NARROWS ORPHANAGE--!
THE VERY SAME ORPHANAGE BESET HERE BY TRAGEDY--WHO WANTED TO COME OUT TONIGHT TO SHOW THE WORLD THE BAD GUYS NEVER WIN AND NOTHING CAN KEEP GOTHAM SPIRIT DOWN!
EXCITED TO BE HERE TONIGHT?
NO.
IT'S TEMPTING FATE.
THEY MADE US COME.
YES SIR, A LOT OF HAPPY KIDS AT THE CIRCUS TONIGHT!
BUT HOLD THE PHONE, FOLKS, HERE'S ONE OF THE MAIN INVESTORS IN THE NEW AND IMPROVED HALY'S CIRCUS...
MAN-ABOUT-TOWN OSWALD COBBLEPOT!

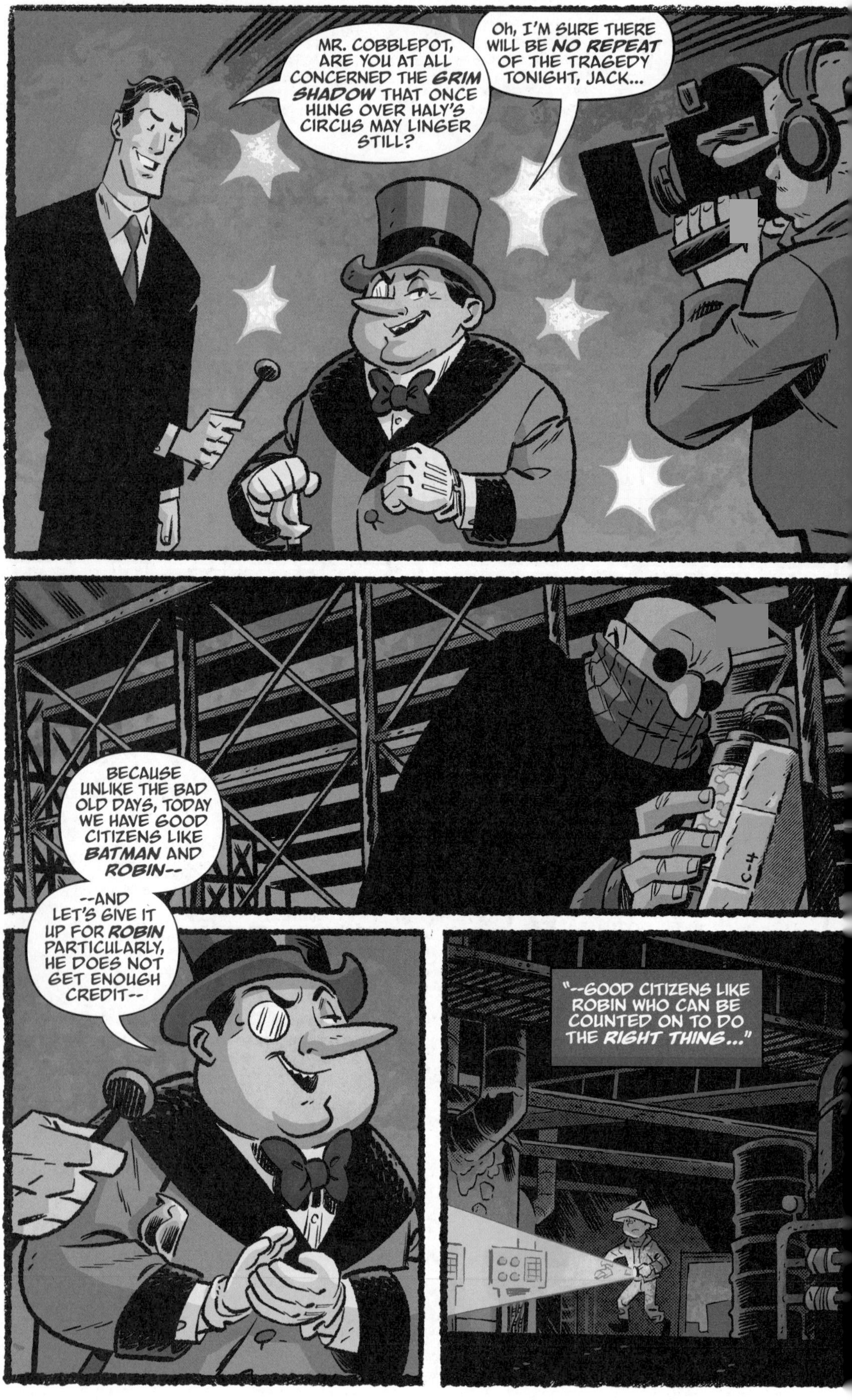
MR. COBBLEPOT, ARE YOU AT ALL CONCERNED THE *GRIM SHADOW* THAT ONCE HUNG OVER HALY'S CIRCUS MAY LINGER STILL?
Oh, I'M SURE THERE WILL BE *NO REPEAT* OF THE TRAGEDY TONIGHT, JACK...
BECAUSE UNLIKE THE BAD OLD DAYS, TODAY WE HAVE GOOD CITIZENS LIKE *BATMAN* AND *ROBIN*--
--AND LET'S GIVE IT UP FOR *ROBIN* PARTICULARLY, HE DOES NOT GET ENOUGH CREDIT--
"--GOOD CITIZENS LIKE ROBIN WHO CAN BE COUNTED ON TO DO THE *RIGHT THING*..."

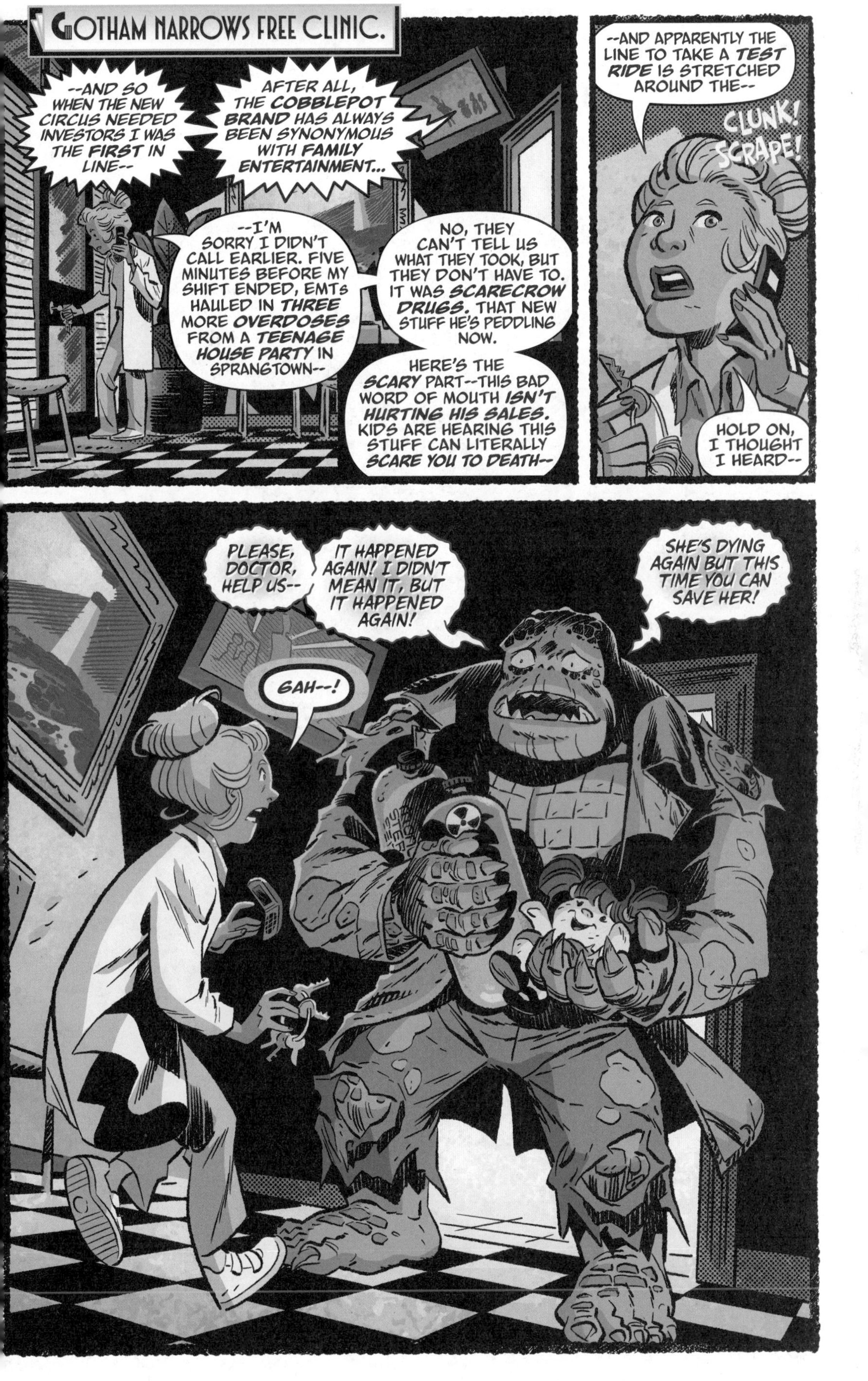
GOTHAM NARROWS FREE CLINIC.
--AND SO WHEN THE NEW CIRCUS NEEDED INVESTORS I WAS THE FIRST IN LINE--
AFTER ALL, THE COBBLEPOT BRAND HAS ALWAYS BEEN SYNONYMOUS WITH FAMILY ENTERTAINMENT...
--I'M SORRY I DIDN'T CALL EARLIER. FIVE MINUTES BEFORE MY SHIFT ENDED, EMTs HAULED IN THREE MORE OVERDOSES FROM A TEENAGE HOUSE PARTY IN SPRANGTOWN--
NO, THEY CAN'T TELL US WHAT THEY TOOK, BUT THEY DON'T HAVE TO. IT WAS SCARECROW DRUGS. THAT NEW STUFF HE'S PEDDLING NOW.
HERE'S THE SCARY PART--THIS BAD WORD OF MOUTH ISN'T HURTING HIS SALES. KIDS ARE HEARING THIS STUFF CAN LITERALLY SCARE YOU TO DEATH--
--AND APPARENTLY THE LINE TO TAKE A TEST RIDE IS STRETCHED AROUND THE--
CLUNK! SCRAPE!
HOLD ON, I THOUGHT I HEARD--
PLEASE, DOCTOR, HELP US--
IT HAPPENED AGAIN! I DIDN'T MEAN IT, BUT IT HAPPENED AGAIN!
SHE'S DYING AGAIN BUT THIS TIME YOU CAN SAVE HER!
GAH--!

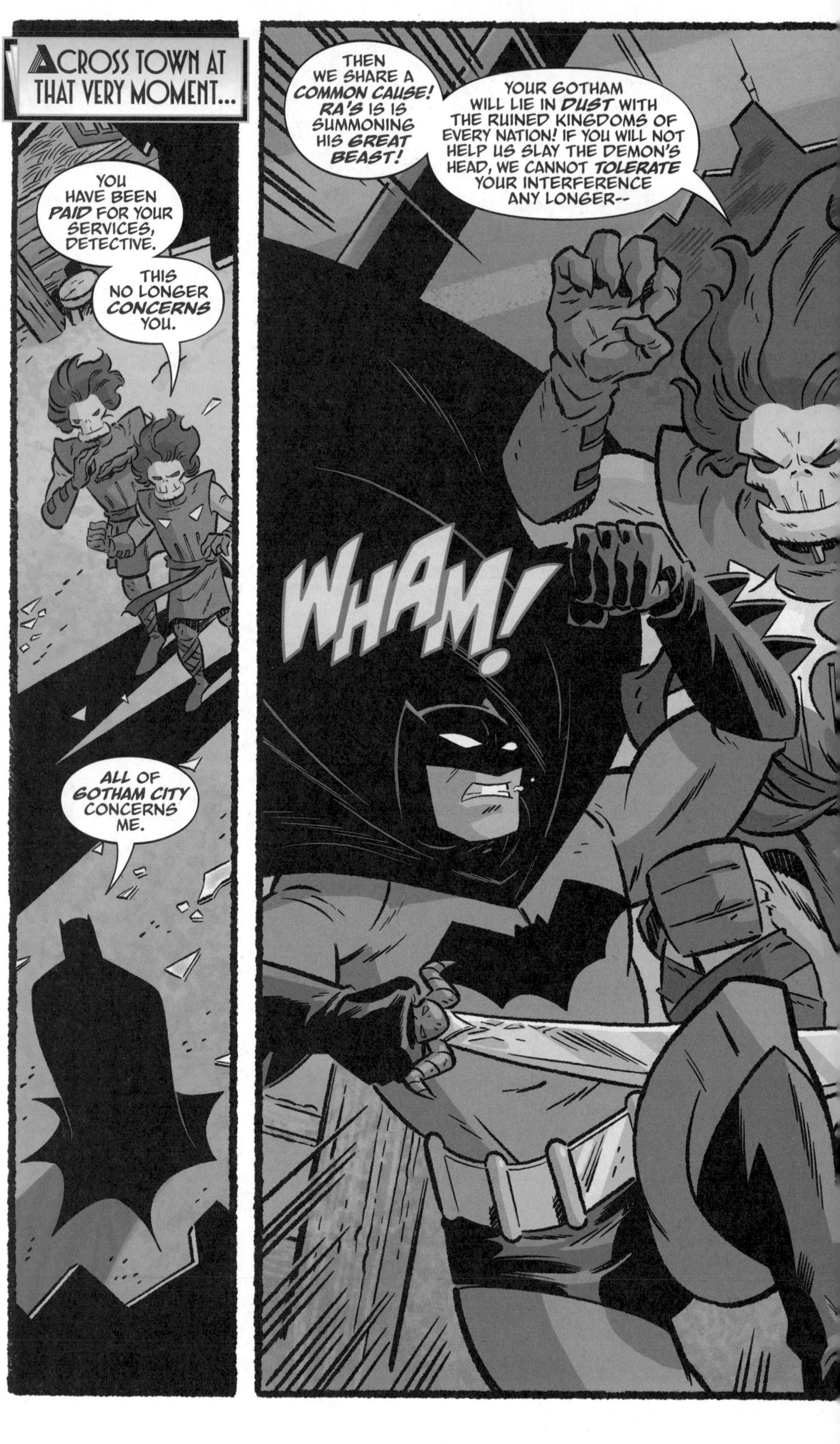

ACROSS TOWN AT THAT VERY MOMENT...
YOU HAVE BEEN PAID FOR YOUR SERVICES, DETECTIVE.
THIS NO LONGER CONCERNS YOU.
ALL OF GOTHAM CITY CONCERNS ME.
THEN WE SHARE A COMMON CAUSE! RA'S IS IS SUMMONING HIS GREAT BEAST!
YOUR GOTHAM WILL LIE IN DUST WITH THE RUINED KINGDOMS OF EVERY NATION! IF YOU WILL NOT HELP US SLAY THE DEMON'S HEAD, WE CANNOT TOLERATE YOUR INTERFERENCE ANY LONGER--
WHAM!

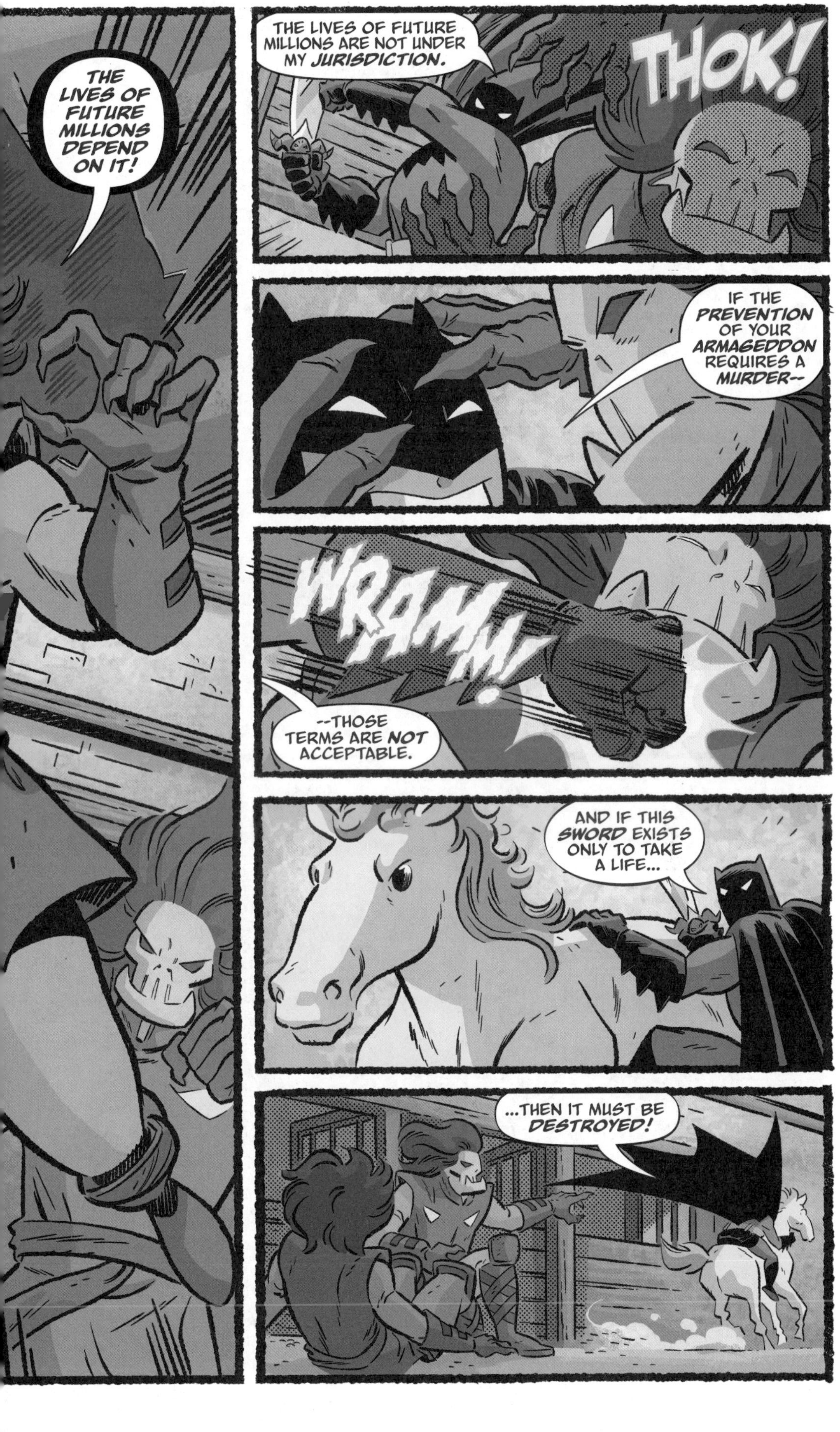
THE LIVES OF FUTURE MILLIONS DEPEND ON IT!
THE LIVES OF FUTURE MILLIONS ARE NOT UNDER MY JURISDICTION.
THOK!
IF THE PREVENTION OF YOUR ARMAGEDDON REQUIRES A MURDER--
WRAMM!
--THOSE TERMS ARE NOT ACCEPTABLE.
AND IF THIS SWORD EXISTS ONLY TO TAKE A LIFE...
...THEN IT MUST BE DESTROYED!

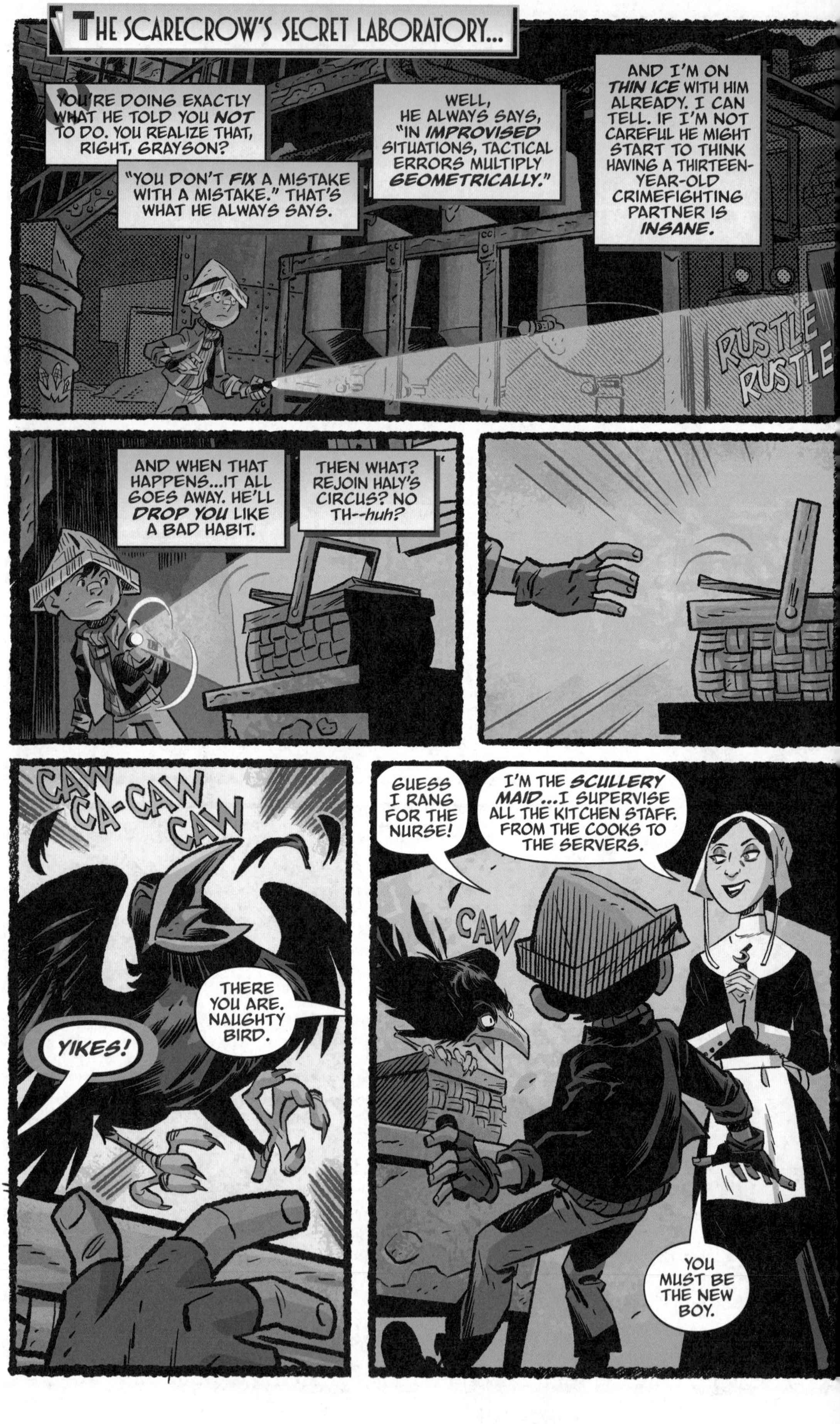
THE SCARECROW'S SECRET LABORATORY...
YOU'RE DOING EXACTLY WHAT HE TOLD YOU NOT TO DO. YOU REALIZE THAT, RIGHT, GRAYSON?
"YOU DON'T FIX A MISTAKE WITH A MISTAKE." THAT'S WHAT HE ALWAYS SAYS.
WELL, HE ALWAYS SAYS, "IN IMPROVISED SITUATIONS, TACTICAL ERRORS MULTIPLY GEOMETRICALLY."
AND I'M ON THIN ICE WITH HIM ALREADY. I CAN TELL. IF I'M NOT CAREFUL HE MIGHT START TO THINK HAVING A THIRTEEN-YEAR-OLD CRIMEFIGHTING PARTNER IS INSANE.
RUSTLE RUSTLE
AND WHEN THAT HAPPENS...IT ALL GOES AWAY. HE'LL DROP YOU LIKE A BAD HABIT.
THEN WHAT? REJOIN HALY'S CIRCUS? NO TH--huh?
CAW CA-CAW CAW
THERE YOU ARE. NAUGHTY BIRD.
YIKES!
GUESS I RANG FOR THE NURSE!
I'M THE SCULLERY MAID...I SUPERVISE ALL THE KITCHEN STAFF. FROM THE COOKS TO THE SERVERS.
CAW
YOU MUST BE THE NEW BOY.

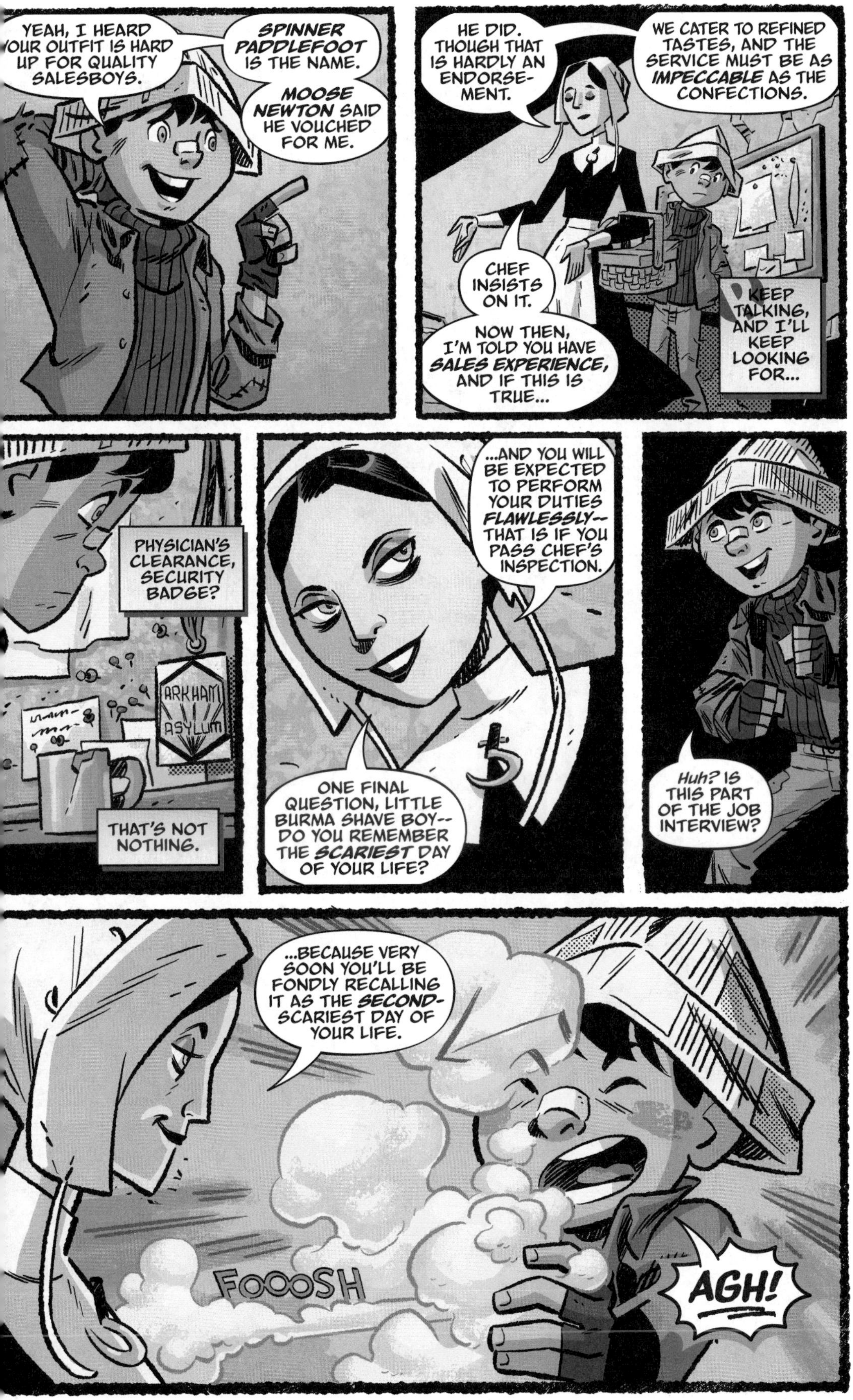
YEAH, I HEARD YOUR OUTFIT IS HARD UP FOR QUALITY SALESBOYS.
SPINNER PADDLEFOOT IS THE NAME.
MOOSE NEWTON SAID HE VOUCHED FOR ME.
HE DID. THOUGH THAT IS HARDLY AN ENDORSEMENT.
WE CATER TO REFINED TASTES, AND THE SERVICE MUST BE AS IMPECCABLE AS THE CONFECTIONS.
CHEF INSISTS ON IT.
NOW THEN, I'M TOLD YOU HAVE SALES EXPERIENCE, AND IF THIS IS TRUE...
KEEP TALKING, AND I'LL KEEP LOOKING FOR...
PHYSICIAN'S CLEARANCE, SECURITY BADGE?
ARKHAM ASYLUM
THAT'S NOT NOTHING.
...AND YOU WILL BE EXPECTED TO PERFORM YOUR DUTIES FLAWLESSLY-- THAT IS IF YOU PASS CHEF'S INSPECTION.
ONE FINAL QUESTION, LITTLE BURMA SHAVE BOY-- DO YOU REMEMBER THE SCARIEST DAY OF YOUR LIFE?
Huh? IS THIS PART OF THE JOB INTERVIEW?
...BECAUSE VERY SOON YOU'LL BE FONDLY RECALLING IT AS THE SECOND-SCARIEST DAY OF YOUR LIFE.
FOOOSH
AGH!

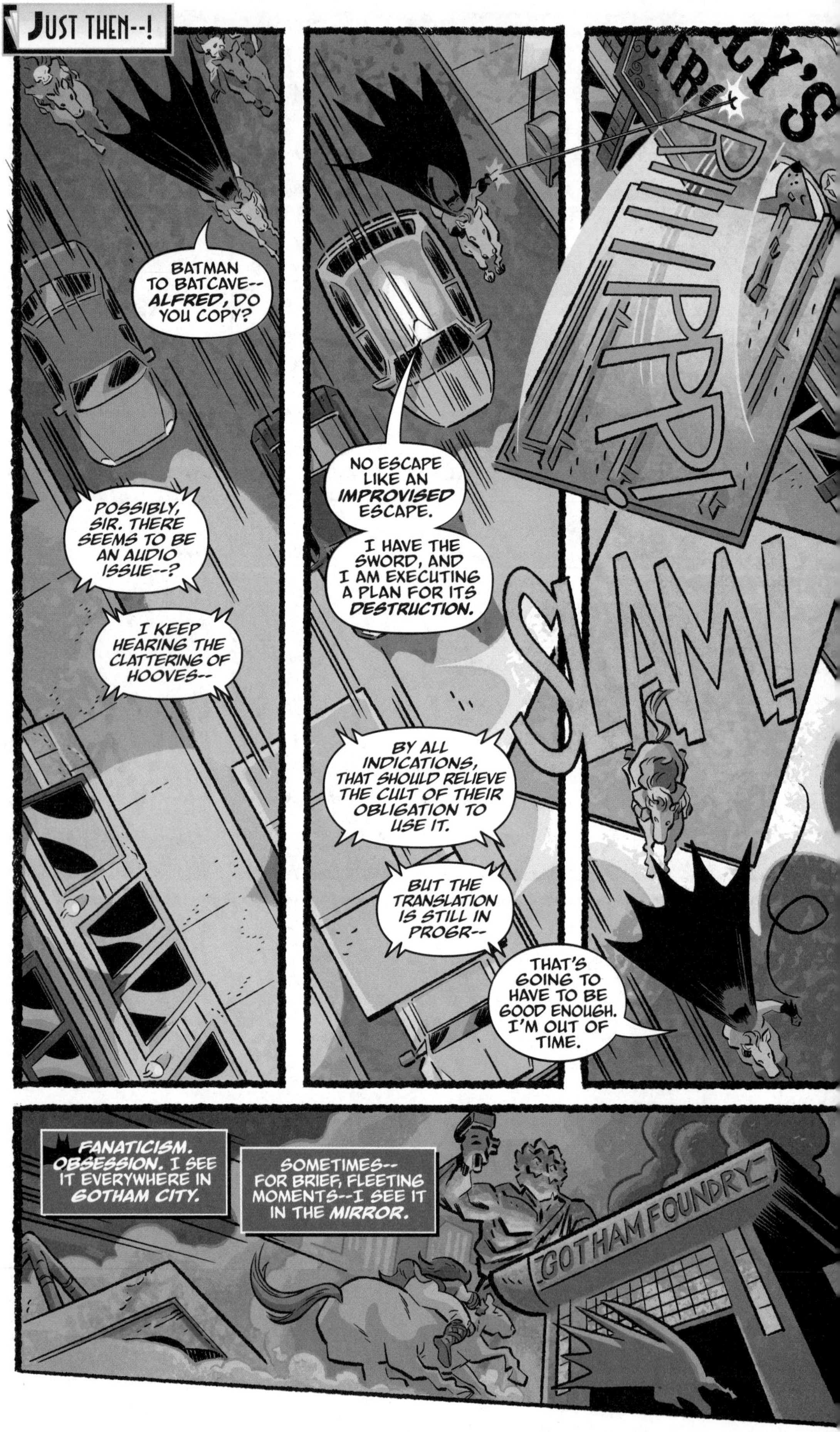

JUST THEN--!
BATMAN TO BATCAVE-- ALFRED, DO YOU COPY?
POSSIBLY, SIR. THERE SEEMS TO BE AN AUDIO ISSUE--?
I KEEP HEARING THE CLATTERING OF HOOVES--
NO ESCAPE LIKE AN IMPROVISED ESCAPE.
I HAVE THE SWORD, AND I AM EXECUTING A PLAN FOR ITS DESTRUCTION.
BY ALL INDICATIONS, THAT SHOULD RELIEVE THE CULT OF THEIR OBLIGATION TO USE IT.
BUT THE TRANSLATION IS STILL IN PROGR--
RIIIPPP!
SLAM!
THAT'S GOING TO HAVE TO BE GOOD ENOUGH. I'M OUT OF TIME.
FANATICISM. OBSESSION. I SEE IT EVERYWHERE IN GOTHAM CITY.
SOMETIMES-- FOR BRIEF, FLEETING MOMENTS--I SEE IT IN THE MIRROR.
GOTHAM FOUNDRY

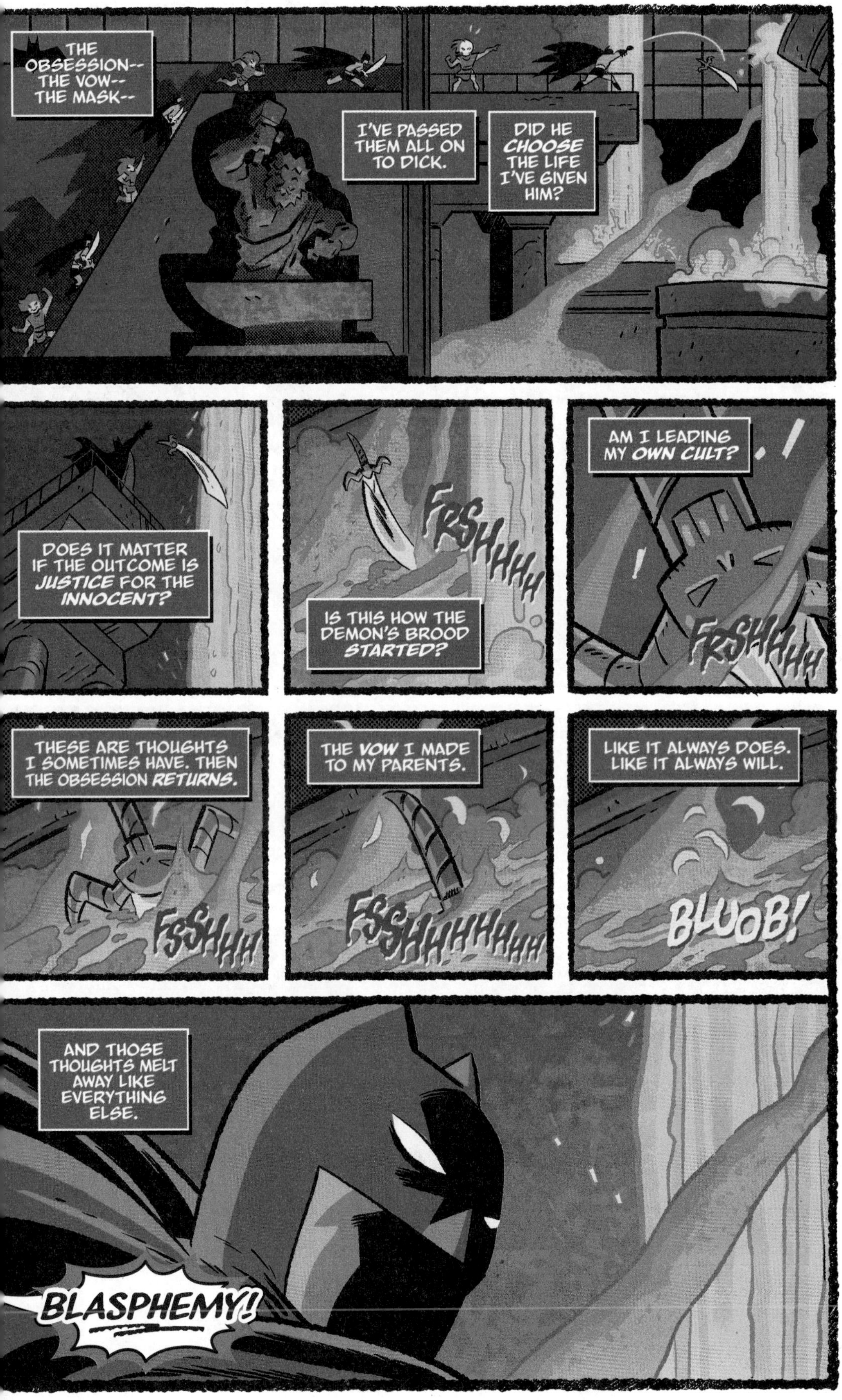
THE OBSESSION-- THE VOW-- THE MASK--
I'VE PASSED THEM ALL ON TO DICK.
DID HE CHOOSE THE LIFE I'VE GIVEN HIM?
DOES IT MATTER IF THE OUTCOME IS JUSTICE FOR THE INNOCENT?
FRSHHHH
IS THIS HOW THE DEMON'S BROOD STARTED?
AM I LEADING MY OWN CULT?
FRSHHHH
THESE ARE THOUGHTS I SOMETIMES HAVE. THEN THE OBSESSION RETURNS.
FSSHHH
THE VOW I MADE TO MY PARENTS.
FSSHHHHHHHH
LIKE IT ALWAYS DOES. LIKE IT ALWAYS WILL.
BLUOB!
AND THOSE THOUGHTS MELT AWAY LIKE EVERYTHING ELSE.
BLASPHEMY!

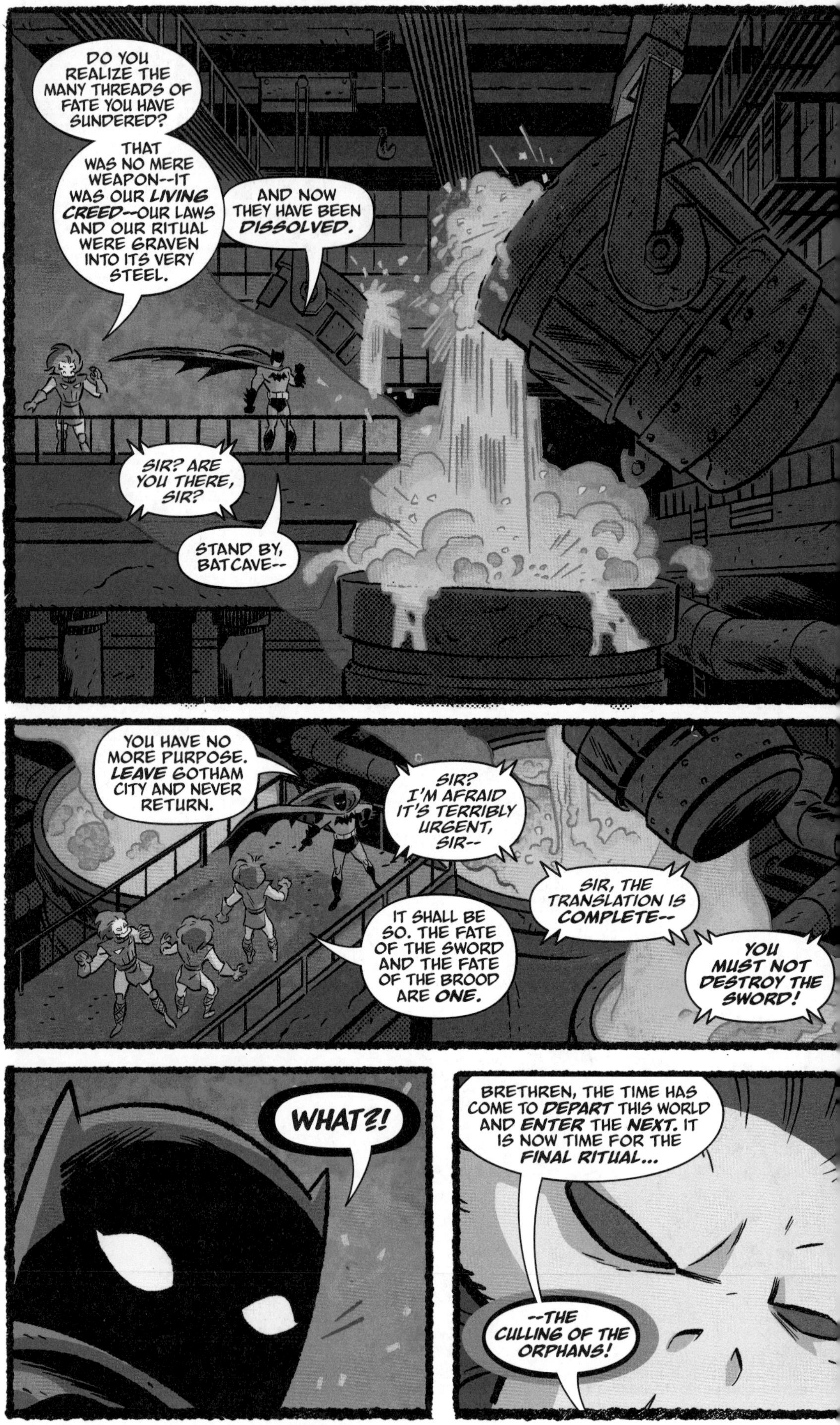
DO YOU REALIZE THE MANY THREADS OF FATE YOU HAVE SUNDERED?
THAT WAS NO MERE WEAPON--IT WAS OUR LIVING CREED--OUR LAWS AND OUR RITUAL WERE GRAVEN INTO ITS VERY STEEL.
AND NOW THEY HAVE BEEN DISSOLVED.
SIR? ARE YOU THERE, SIR?
STAND BY, BATCAVE--
YOU HAVE NO MORE PURPOSE. LEAVE GOTHAM CITY AND NEVER RETURN.
SIR? I'M AFRAID IT'S TERRIBLY URGENT, SIR--
IT SHALL BE SO. THE FATE OF THE SWORD AND THE FATE OF THE BROOD ARE ONE.
SIR, THE TRANSLATION IS COMPLETE--
YOU MUST NOT DESTROY THE SWORD!
WHAT?!
BRETHREN, THE TIME HAS COME TO DEPART THIS WORLD AND ENTER THE NEXT. IT IS NOW TIME FOR THE FINAL RITUAL...
--THE CULLING OF THE ORPHANS!

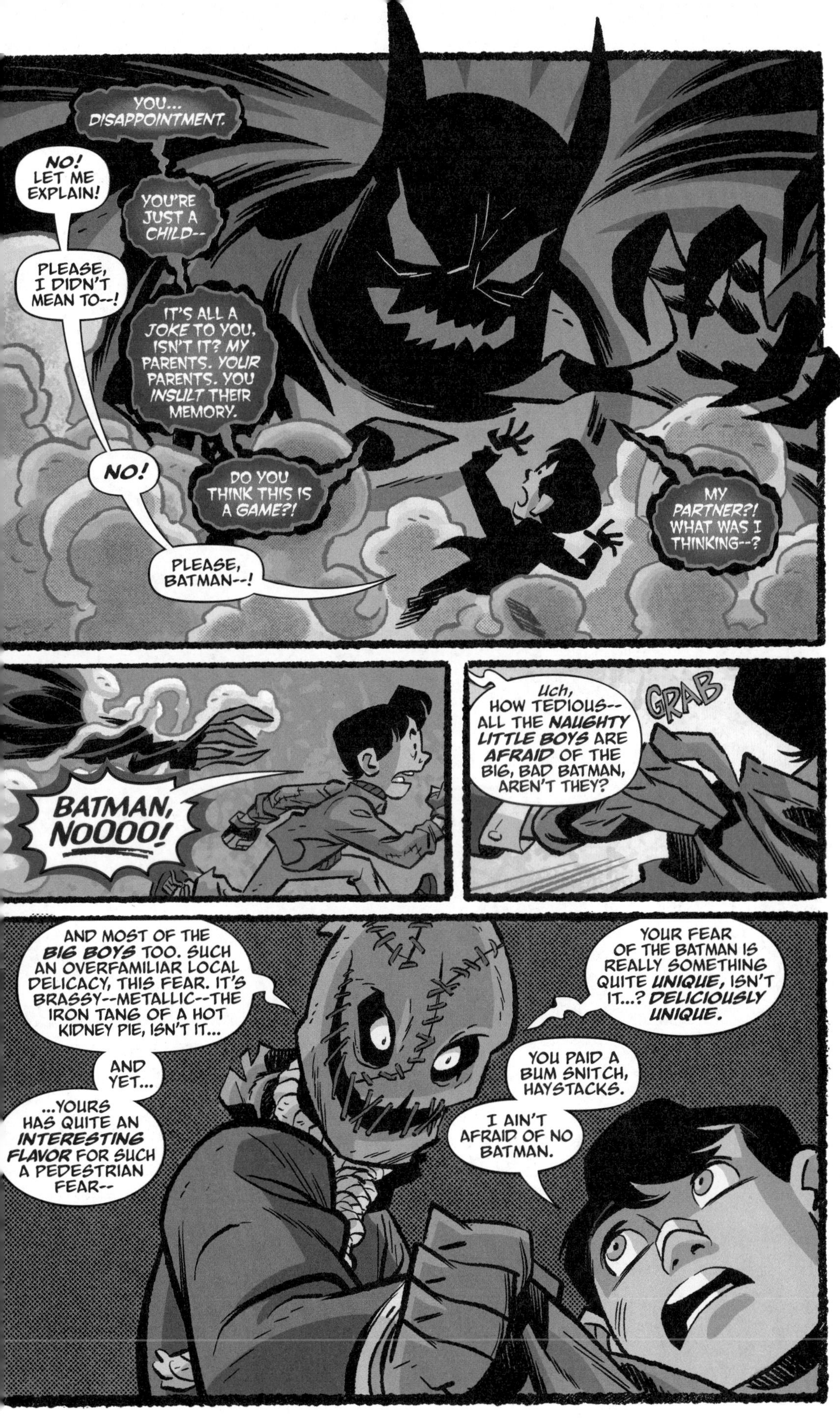
YOU... DISAPPOINTMENT.
NO! LET ME EXPLAIN!
YOU'RE JUST A CHILD--
PLEASE, I DIDN'T MEAN TO--!
IT'S ALL A JOKE TO YOU, ISN'T IT? MY PARENTS. YOUR PARENTS. YOU INSULT THEIR MEMORY.
NO!
DO YOU THINK THIS IS A GAME?!
MY PARTNER?! WHAT WAS I THINKING--?
PLEASE, BATMAN--!
BATMAN, NOOOO!
Uch, HOW TEDIOUS-- ALL THE NAUGHTY LITTLE BOYS ARE AFRAID OF THE BIG, BAD BATMAN, AREN'T THEY?
GRAB
AND MOST OF THE BIG BOYS TOO. SUCH AN OVERFAMILIAR LOCAL DELICACY, THIS FEAR. IT'S BRASSY--METALLIC--THE IRON TANG OF A HOT KIDNEY PIE, ISN'T IT...
AND YET...
...YOURS HAS QUITE AN INTERESTING FLAVOR FOR SUCH A PEDESTRIAN FEAR--
YOUR FEAR OF THE BATMAN IS REALLY SOMETHING QUITE UNIQUE, ISN'T IT...? DELICIOUSLY UNIQUE.
YOU PAID A BUM SNITCH, HAYSTACKS.
I AIN'T AFRAID OF NO BATMAN.

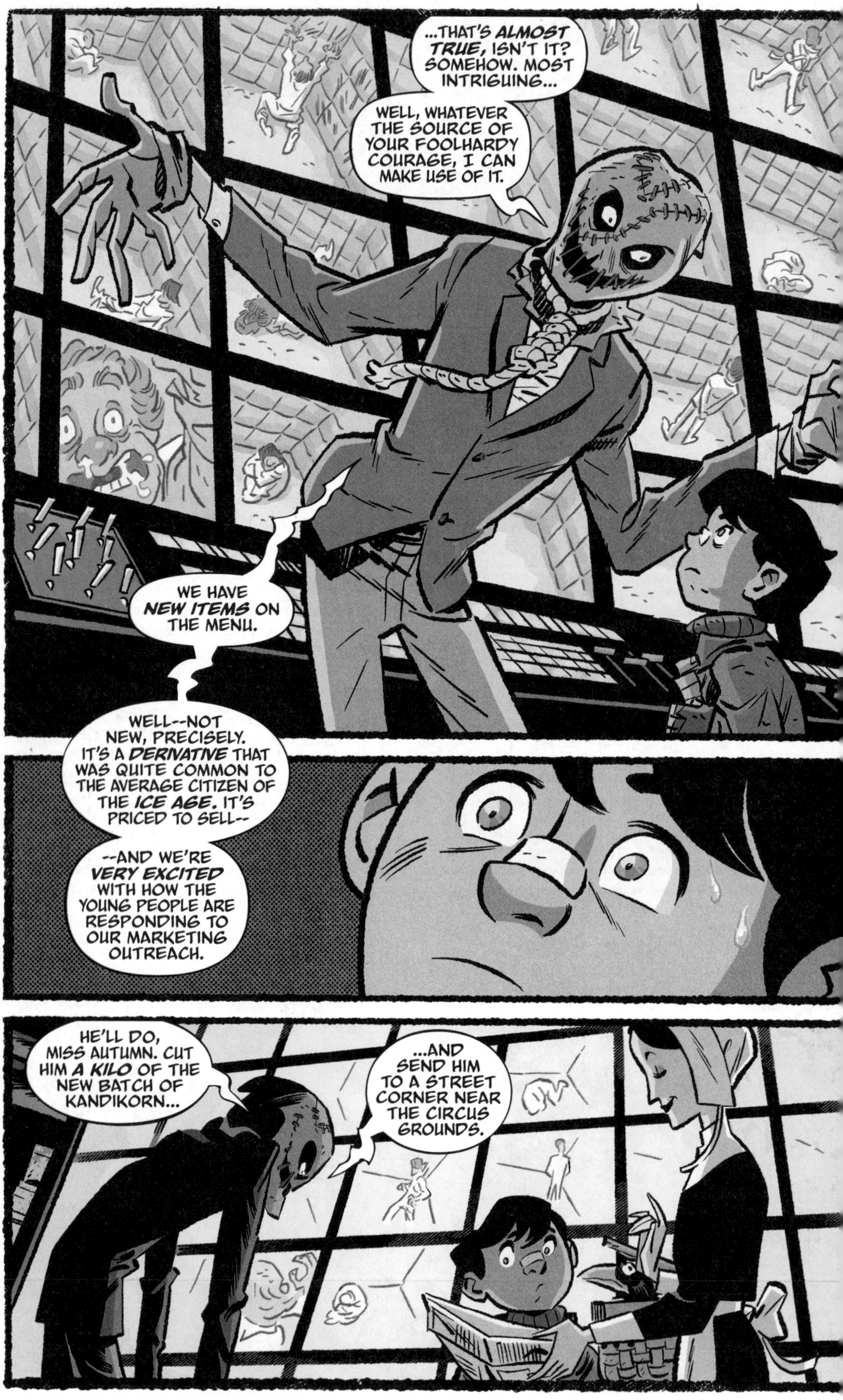
...THAT'S ALMOST TRUE, ISN'T IT? SOMEHOW. MOST INTRIGUING...
WELL, WHATEVER THE SOURCE OF YOUR FOOLHARDY COURAGE, I CAN MAKE USE OF IT.
WE HAVE NEW ITEMS ON THE MENU.
WELL--NOT NEW, PRECISELY. IT'S A DERIVATIVE THAT WAS QUITE COMMON TO THE AVERAGE CITIZEN OF THE ICE AGE. IT'S PRICED TO SELL--
--AND WE'RE VERY EXCITED WITH HOW THE YOUNG PEOPLE ARE RESPONDING TO OUR MARKETING OUTREACH.
HE'LL DO, MISS AUTUMN. CUT HIM A KILO OF THE NEW BATCH OF KANDIKORN...
...AND SEND HIM TO A STREET CORNER NEAR THE CIRCUS GROUNDS.

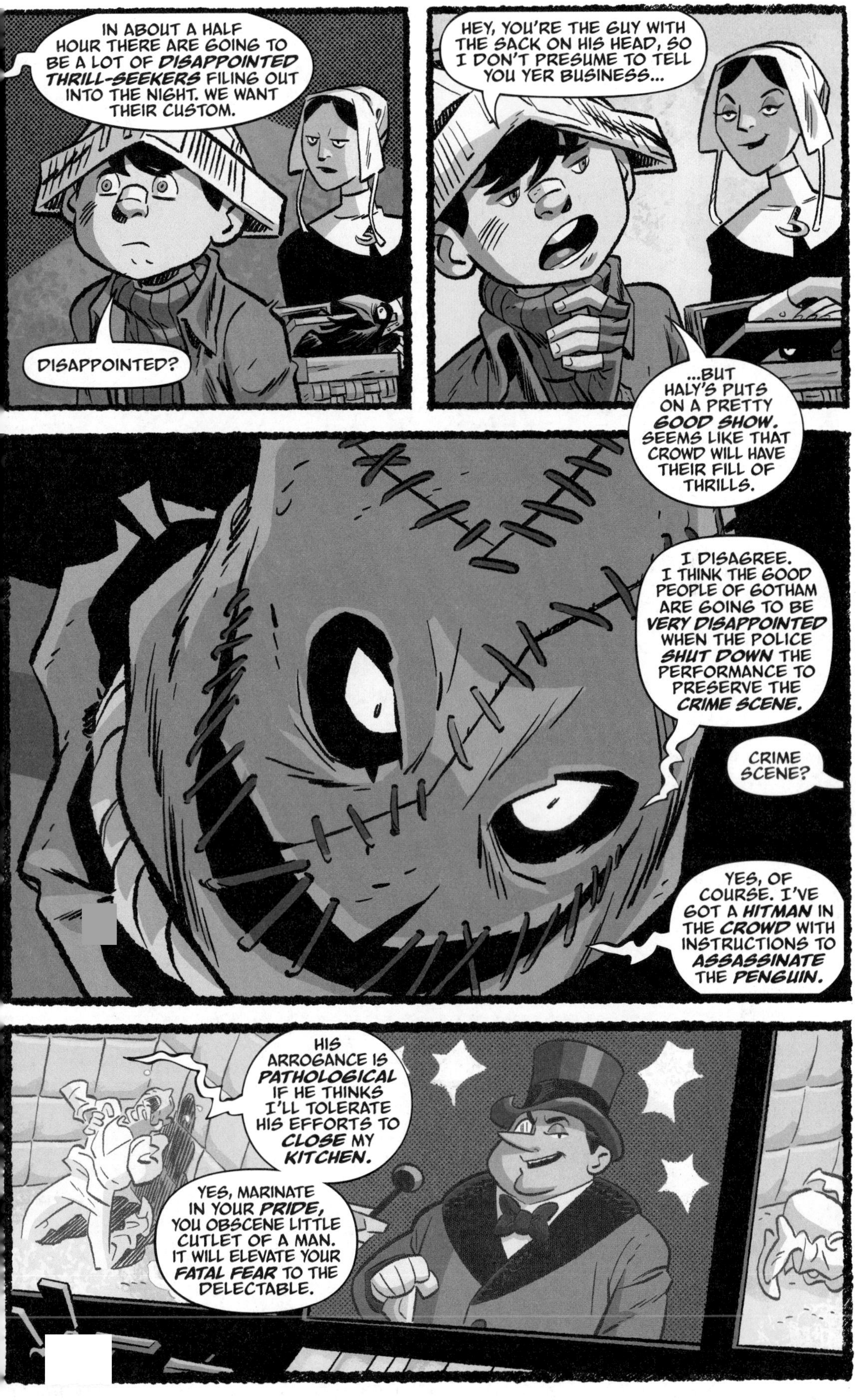
IN ABOUT A HALF HOUR THERE ARE GOING TO BE A LOT OF DISAPPOINTED THRILL-SEEKERS FILING OUT INTO THE NIGHT. WE WANT THEIR CUSTOM.
DISAPPOINTED?
HEY, YOU'RE THE GUY WITH THE SACK ON HIS HEAD, SO I DON'T PRESUME TO TELL YOU YER BUSINESS...
...BUT HALY'S PUTS ON A PRETTY GOOD SHOW. SEEMS LIKE THAT CROWD WILL HAVE THEIR FILL OF THRILLS.
I DISAGREE. I THINK THE GOOD PEOPLE OF GOTHAM ARE GOING TO BE VERY DISAPPOINTED WHEN THE POLICE SHUT DOWN THE PERFORMANCE TO PRESERVE THE CRIME SCENE.
CRIME SCENE?
YES, OF COURSE. I'VE GOT A HITMAN IN THE CROWD WITH INSTRUCTIONS TO ASSASSINATE THE PENGUIN.
HIS ARROGANCE IS PATHOLOGICAL IF HE THINKS I'LL TOLERATE HIS EFFORTS TO CLOSE MY KITCHEN.
YES, MARINATE IN YOUR PRIDE, YOU OBSCENE LITTLE CUTLET OF A MAN. IT WILL ELEVATE YOUR FATAL FEAR TO THE DELECTABLE.

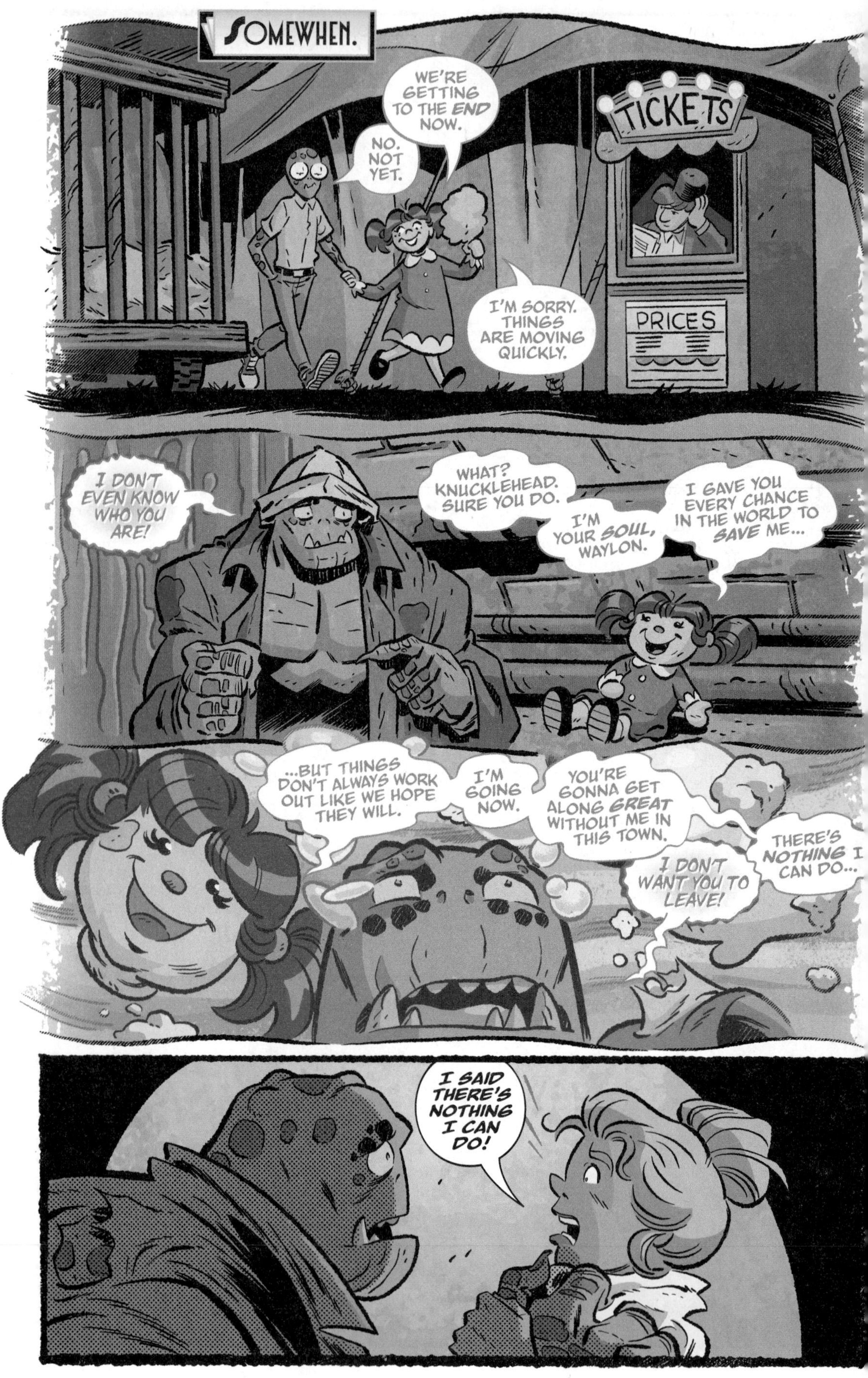
SOMEWHEN.
TICKETS
WE'RE GETTING TO THE END NOW.
NO. NOT YET.
I'M SORRY. THINGS ARE MOVING QUICKLY.
PRICES
I DON'T EVEN KNOW WHO YOU ARE!
WHAT? KNUCKLEHEAD. SURE YOU DO.
I'M YOUR SOUL, WAYLON.
I GAVE YOU EVERY CHANCE IN THE WORLD TO SAVE ME...
...BUT THINGS DON'T ALWAYS WORK OUT LIKE WE HOPE THEY WILL.
I'M GOING NOW.
YOU'RE GONNA GET ALONG GREAT WITHOUT ME IN THIS TOWN.
I DON'T WANT YOU TO LEAVE!
THERE'S NOTHING I CAN DO...
I SAID THERE'S NOTHING I CAN DO!

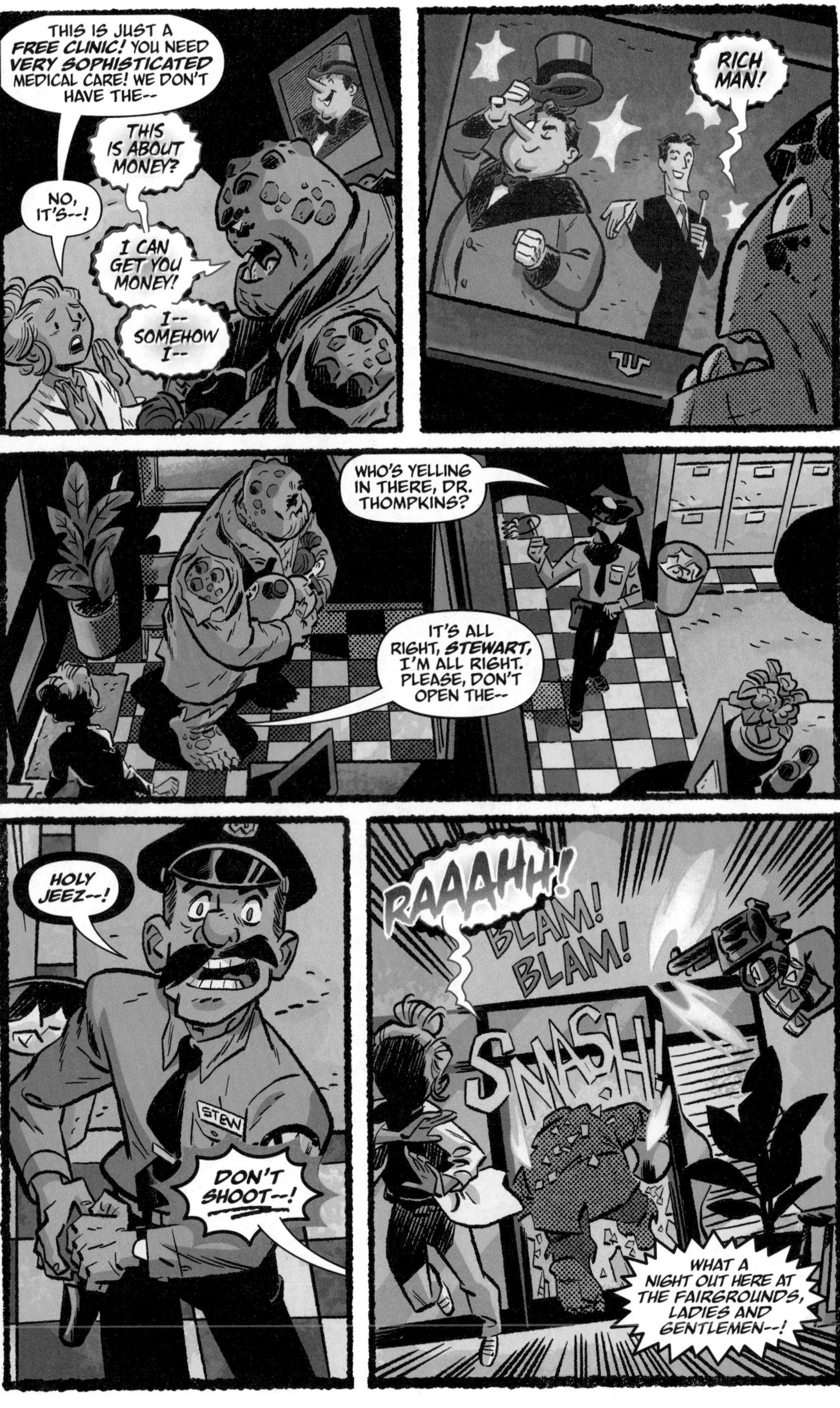
THIS IS JUST A FREE CLINIC! YOU NEED VERY SOPHISTICATED MEDICAL CARE! WE DON'T HAVE THE--
THIS IS ABOUT MONEY?
NO, IT'S--!
I CAN GET YOU MONEY!
I-- SOMEHOW I--
RICH MAN!
WHO'S YELLING IN THERE, DR. THOMPKINS?
IT'S ALL RIGHT, STEWART, I'M ALL RIGHT. PLEASE, DON'T OPEN THE--
HOLY JEEZ--!
STEW
DON'T SHOOT--!
RAAAHH!
BLAM! BLAM!
SMASH!
WHAT A NIGHT OUT HERE AT THE FAIRGROUNDS, LADIES AND GENTLEMEN--!

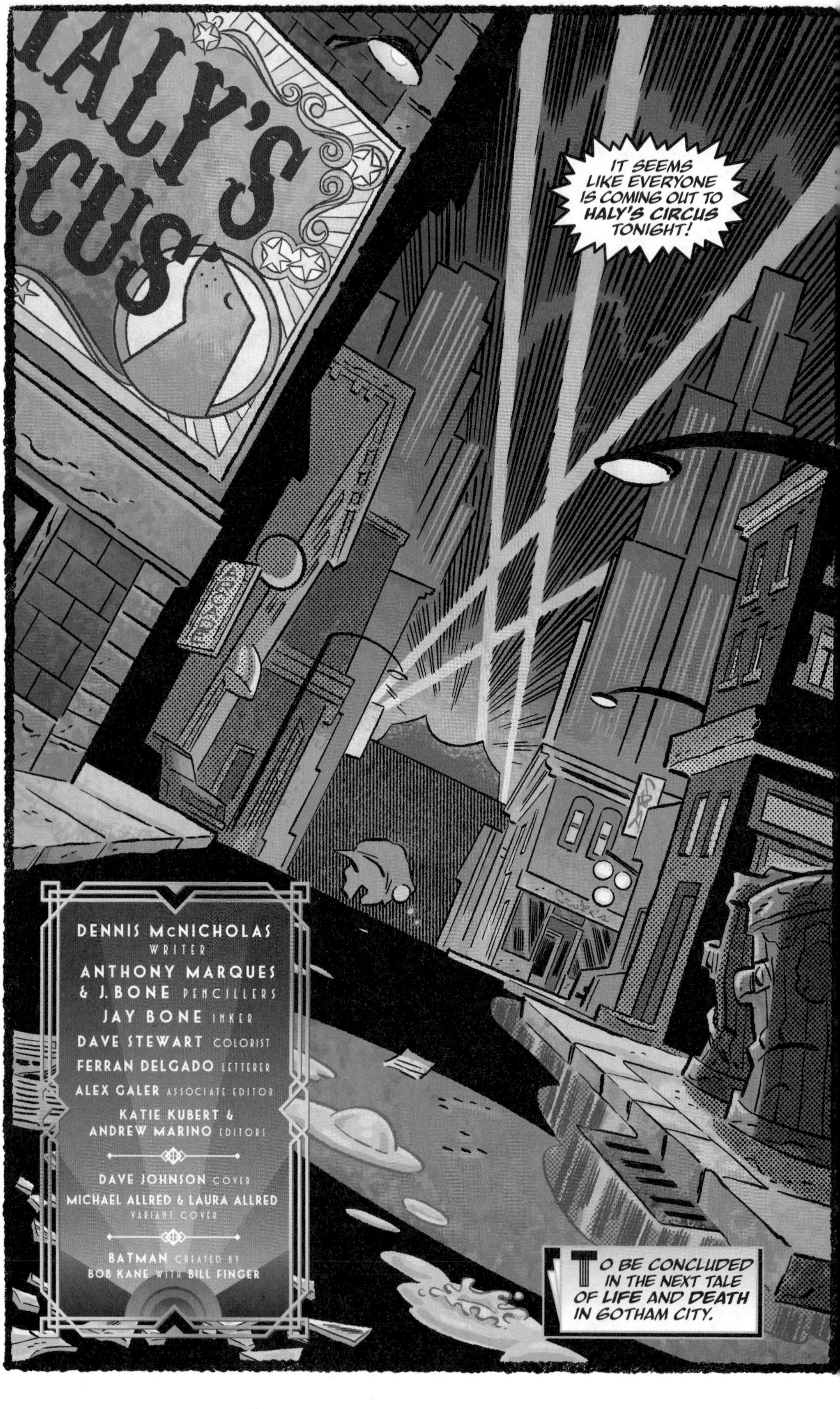
IT SEEMS LIKE EVERYONE IS COMING OUT TO HALY'S CIRCUS TONIGHT!
TO BE CONCLUDED IN THE NEXT TALE OF LIFE AND DEATH IN GOTHAM CITY.
DENNIS McNICHOLAS WRITER
ANTHONY MARQUES & J. BONE PENCILLERS
JAY BONE INKER
DAVE STEWART COLORIST
FERRAN DELGADO LETTERER
ALEX GALER ASSOCIATE EDITOR
KATIE KUBERT & ANDREW MARINO EDITORS
DAVE JOHNSON COVER
MICHAEL ALLRED & LAURA ALLRED VARIANT COVER
BATMAN CREATED BY BOB KANE WITH BILL FINGER

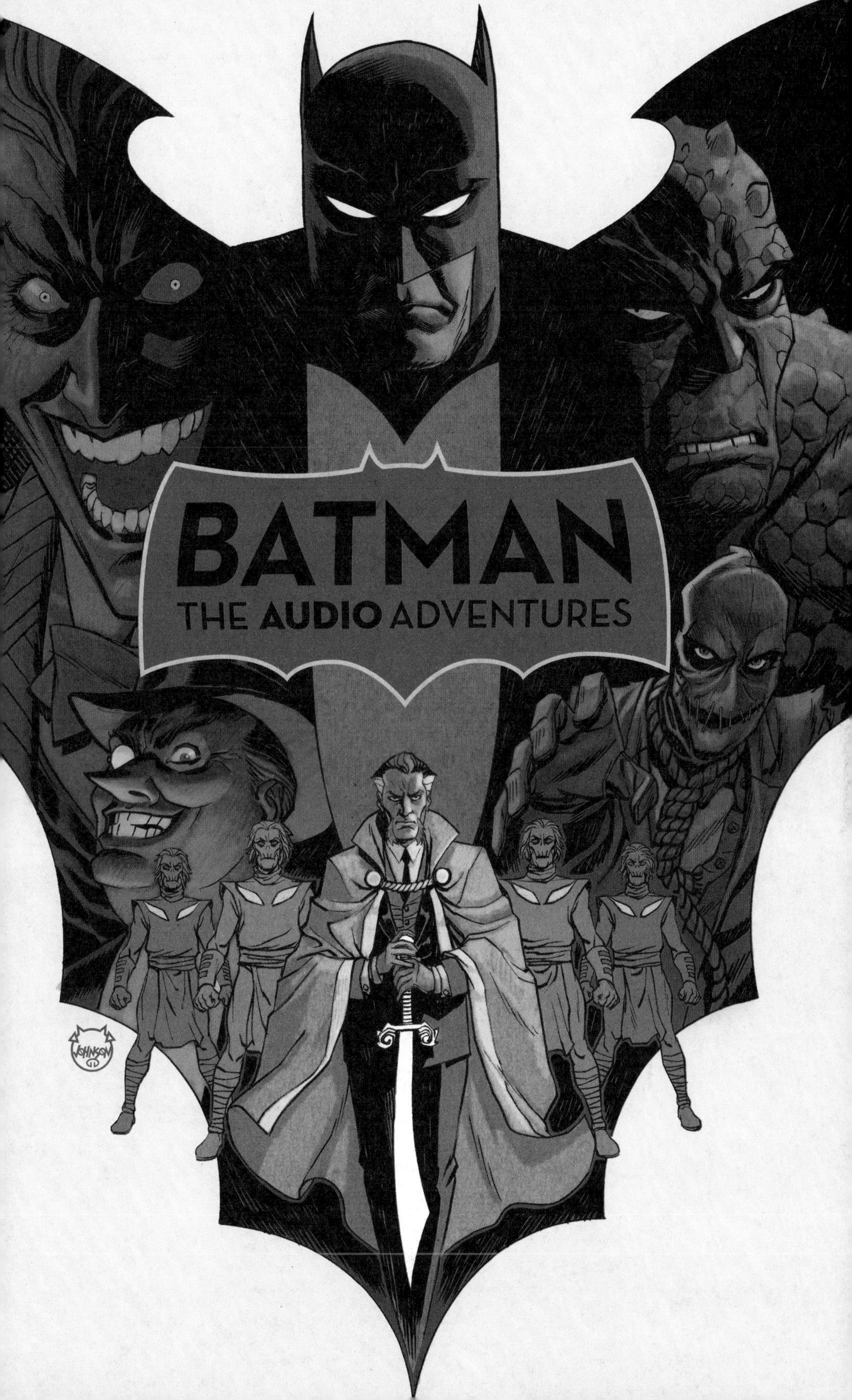
BATMAN
THE AUDIO ADVENTURES
JOHNSON

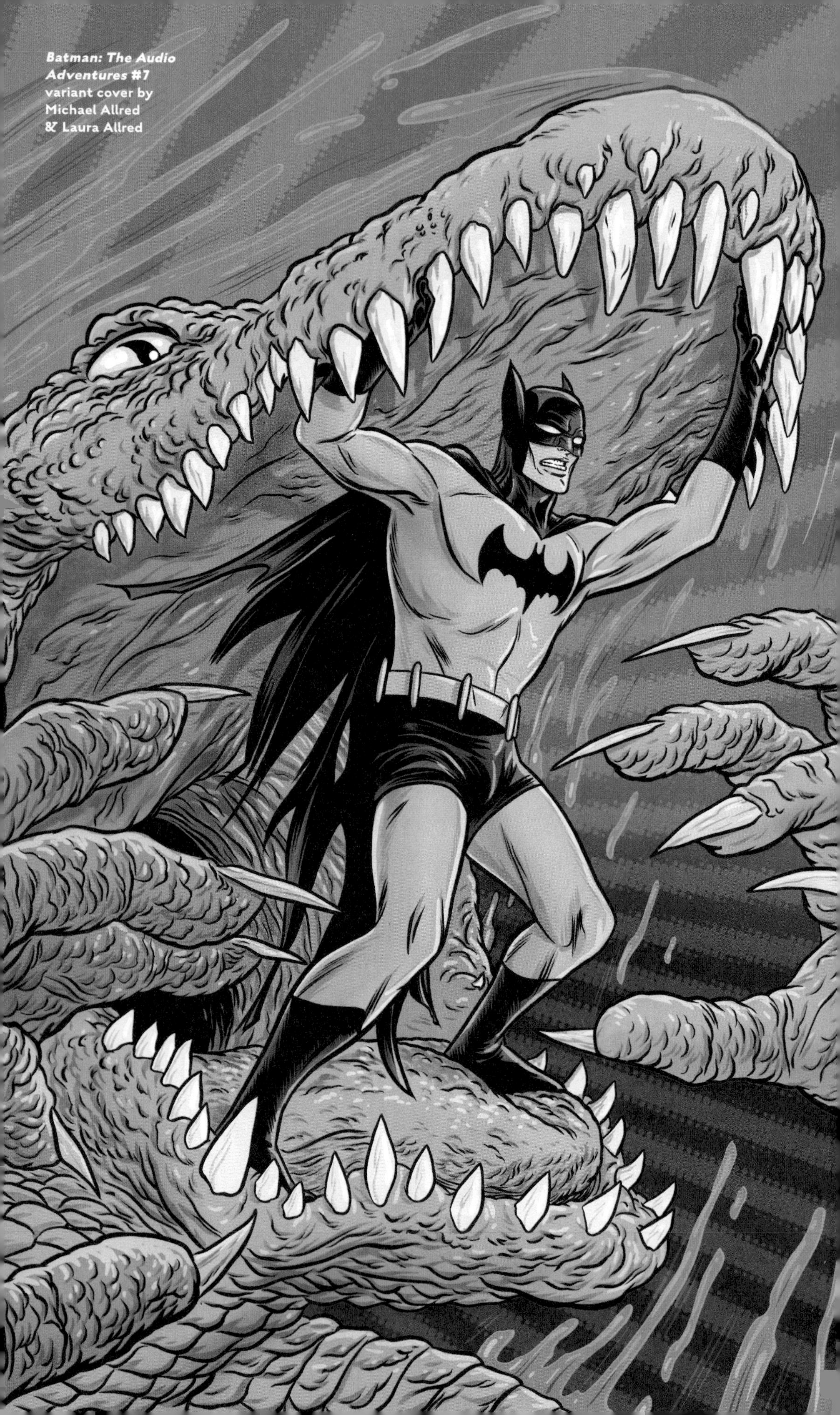

Batman: The Audio Adventures #7 variant cover by Michael Allred & Laura Allred

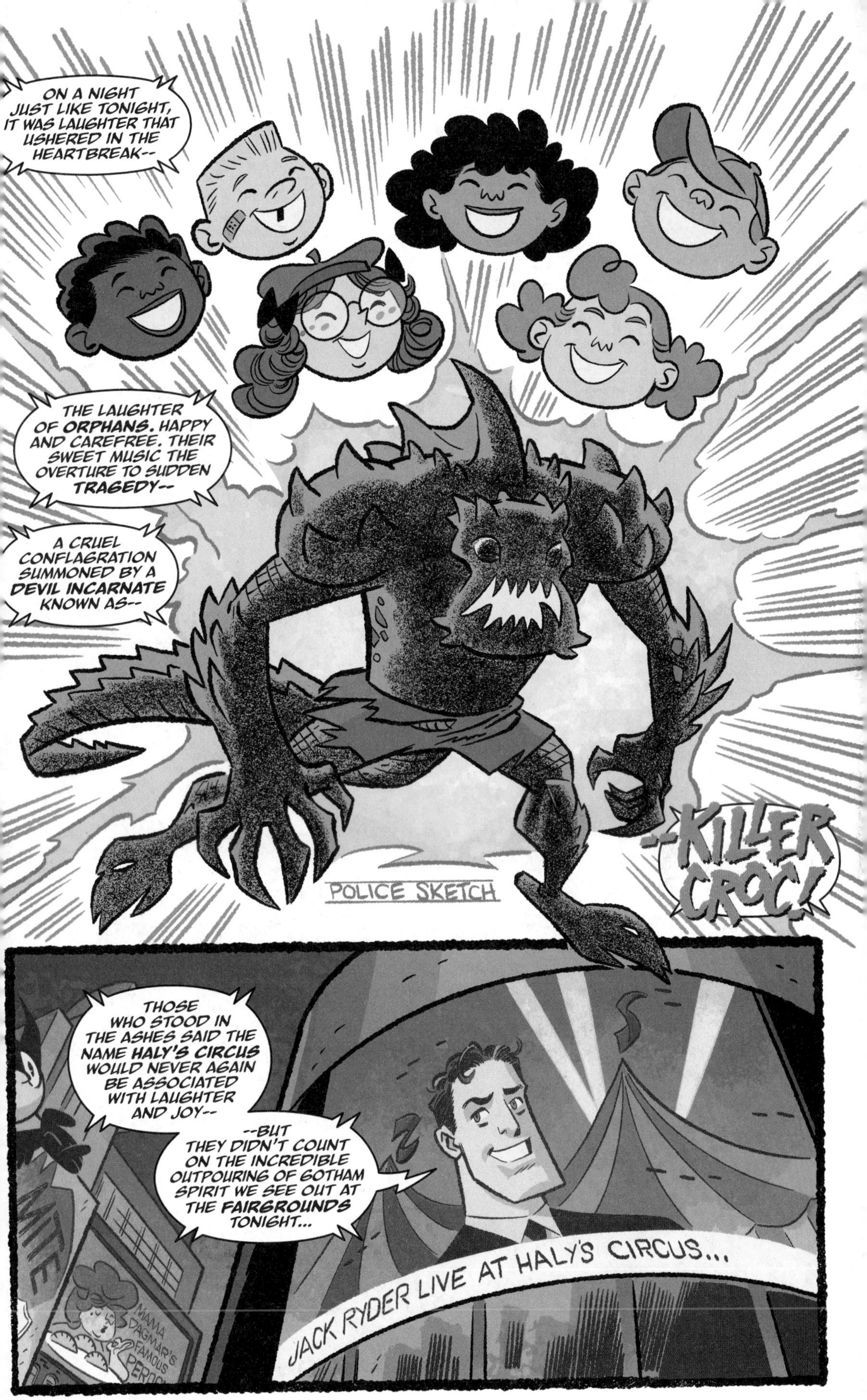
ON A NIGHT JUST LIKE TONIGHT, IT WAS LAUGHTER THAT USHERED IN THE HEARTBREAK--
THE LAUGHTER OF **ORPHANS.** HAPPY AND CAREFREE. THEIR SWEET MUSIC THE OVERTURE TO SUDDEN **TRAGEDY--**
A CRUEL CONFLAGRATION SUMMONED BY A **DEVIL INCARNATE** KNOWN AS--
POLICE SKETCH
--KILLER CROC!
THOSE WHO STOOD IN THE ASHES SAID THE NAME **HALY'S CIRCUS** WOULD NEVER AGAIN BE ASSOCIATED WITH LAUGHTER AND JOY--
--BUT THEY DIDN'T COUNT ON THE INCREDIBLE OUTPOURING OF GOTHAM SPIRIT WE SEE OUT AT THE **FAIRGROUNDS** TONIGHT...
JACK RYDER LIVE AT HALY'S CIRCUS...

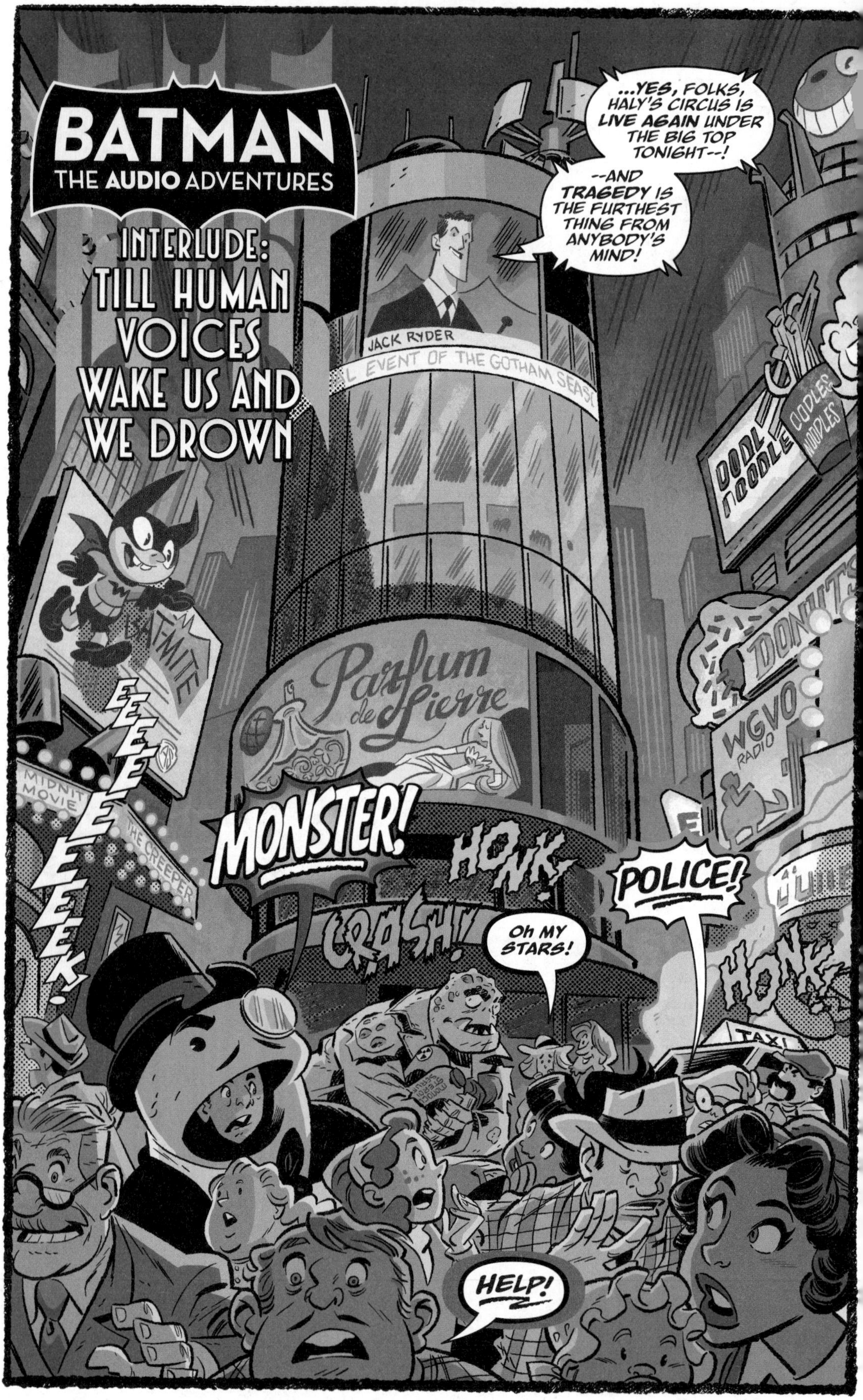
BATMAN
THE AUDIO ADVENTURES
INTERLUDE: TILL HUMAN VOICES WAKE US AND WE DROWN
...YES, FOLKS, HALY'S CIRCUS IS LIVE AGAIN UNDER THE BIG TOP TONIGHT--!
--AND TRAGEDY IS THE FURTHEST THING FROM ANYBODY'S MIND!
JACK RYDER
EVENT OF THE GOTHAM SEAS
Parfum de Pierre
EEEEEEEEEEEK!
MIDNIT MOVIE
THE CREEPER
MONSTER!
HONK
CRASH!
POLICE!
Oh MY STARS!
HONK
TAXI
WGVO RADIO
DONUTS
HELP!

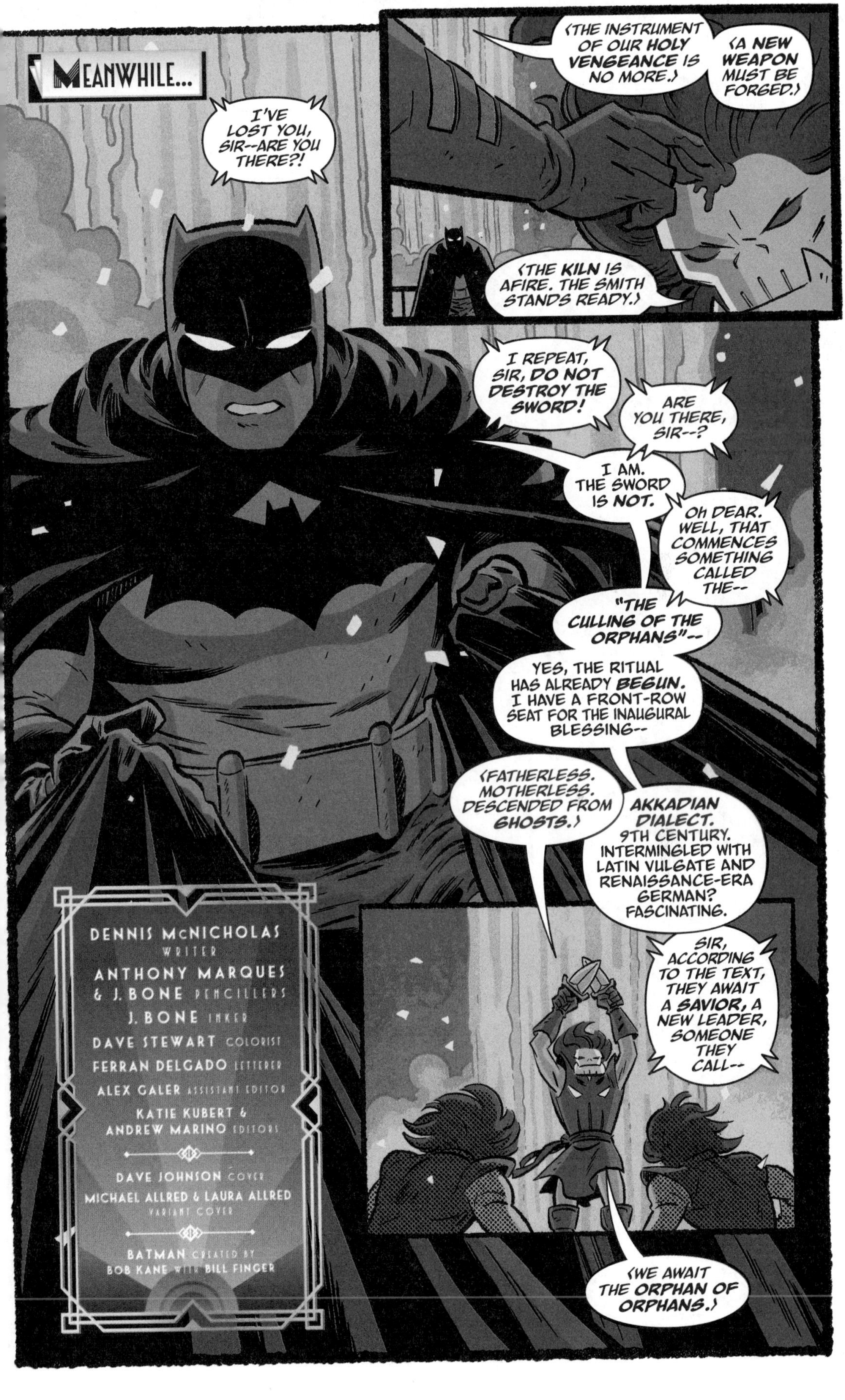
MEANWHILE...
I'VE LOST YOU, SIR--ARE YOU THERE?!
‹THE INSTRUMENT OF OUR HOLY VENGEANCE IS NO MORE.›
‹A NEW WEAPON MUST BE FORGED.›
‹THE KILN IS AFIRE. THE SMITH STANDS READY.›
I REPEAT, SIR, DO NOT DESTROY THE SWORD!
ARE YOU THERE, SIR--?
I AM. THE SWORD IS NOT.
Oh DEAR. WELL, THAT COMMENCES SOMETHING CALLED THE--
"THE CULLING OF THE ORPHANS"--
YES, THE RITUAL HAS ALREADY BEGUN. I HAVE A FRONT-ROW SEAT FOR THE INAUGURAL BLESSING--
‹FATHERLESS. MOTHERLESS. DESCENDED FROM GHOSTS.›
AKKADIAN DIALECT. 9TH CENTURY. INTERMINGLED WITH LATIN VULGATE AND RENAISSANCE-ERA GERMAN? FASCINATING.
SIR, ACCORDING TO THE TEXT, THEY AWAIT A SAVIOR, A NEW LEADER, SOMEONE THEY CALL--
‹WE AWAIT THE ORPHAN OF ORPHANS.›
DENNIS McNICHOLAS WRITER
ANTHONY MARQUES & J. BONE PENCILLERS
J. BONE INKER
DAVE STEWART COLORIST
FERRAN DELGADO LETTERER
ALEX GALER ASSISTANT EDITOR
KATIE KUBERT & ANDREW MARINO EDITORS
DAVE JOHNSON COVER
MICHAEL ALLRED & LAURA ALLRED VARIANT COVER
BATMAN CREATED BY BOB KANE WITH BILL FINGER

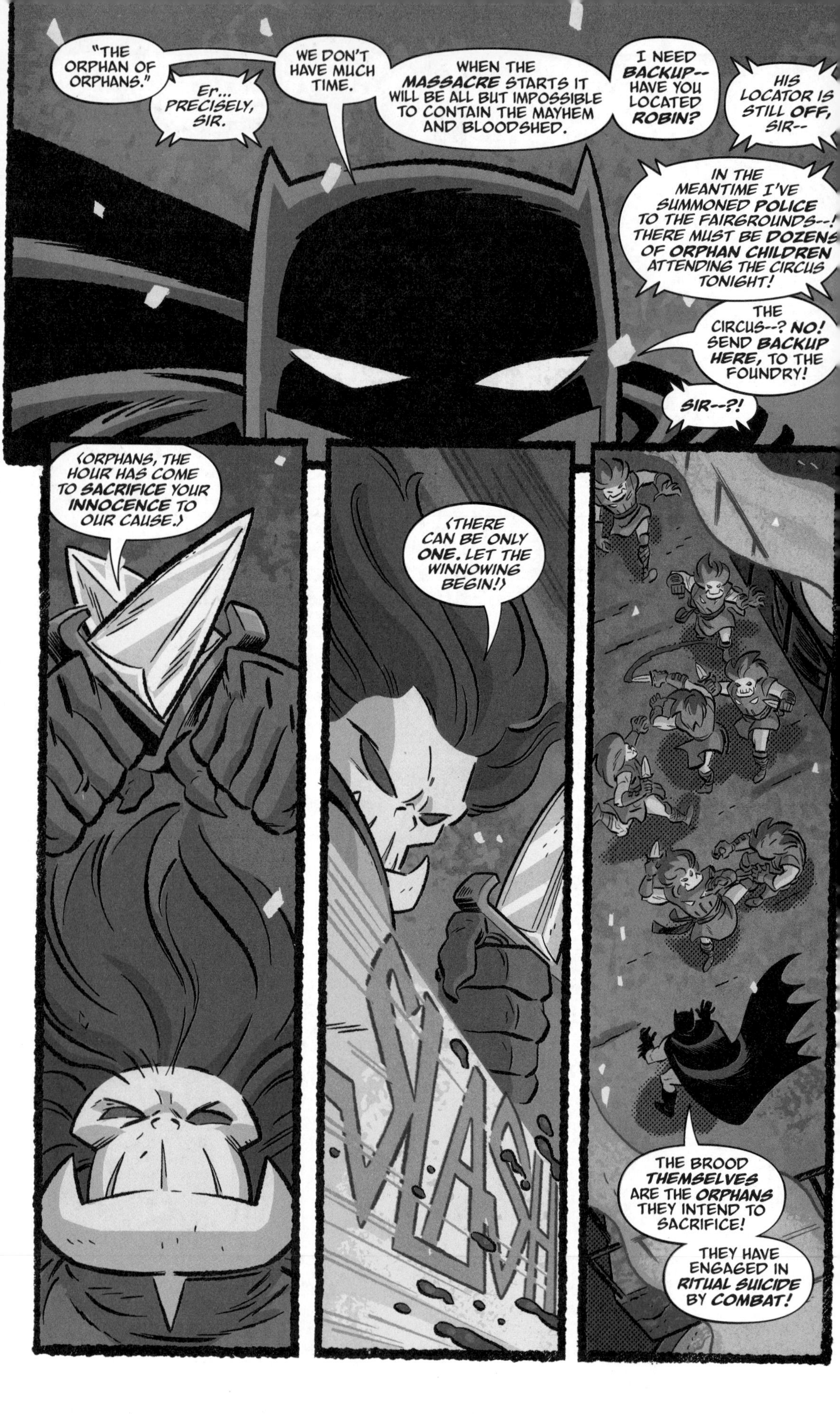

"THE ORPHAN OF ORPHANS."
Er... PRECISELY, SIR.
WE DON'T HAVE MUCH TIME.
WHEN THE MASSACRE STARTS IT WILL BE ALL BUT IMPOSSIBLE TO CONTAIN THE MAYHEM AND BLOODSHED.
I NEED BACKUP-- HAVE YOU LOCATED ROBIN?
HIS LOCATOR IS STILL OFF, SIR--
IN THE MEANTIME I'VE SUMMONED POLICE TO THE FAIRGROUNDS--! THERE MUST BE DOZENS OF ORPHAN CHILDREN ATTENDING THE CIRCUS TONIGHT!
THE CIRCUS--? NO! SEND BACKUP HERE, TO THE FOUNDRY!
SIR--?!
‹ORPHANS, THE HOUR HAS COME TO SACRIFICE YOUR INNOCENCE TO OUR CAUSE.›
‹THERE CAN BE ONLY ONE. LET THE WINNOWING BEGIN!›
SLASH
THE BROOD THEMSELVES ARE THE ORPHANS THEY INTEND TO SACRIFICE!
THEY HAVE ENGAGED IN RITUAL SUICIDE BY COMBAT!

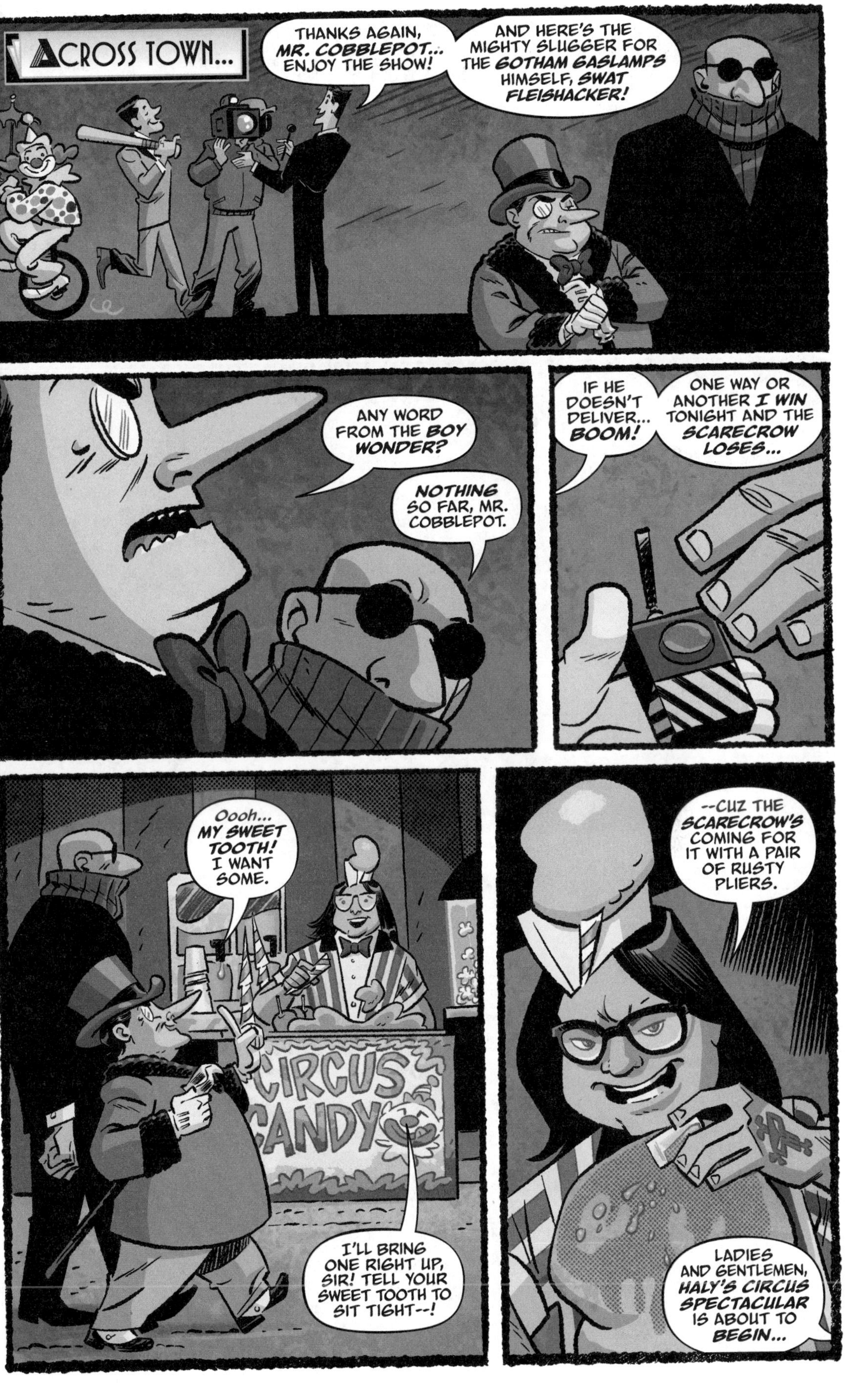
ACROSS TOWN...
THANKS AGAIN, MR. COBBLEPOT... ENJOY THE SHOW!
AND HERE'S THE MIGHTY SLUGGER FOR THE GOTHAM GASLAMPS HIMSELF, SWAT FLEISHACKER!
ANY WORD FROM THE BOY WONDER?
NOTHING SO FAR, MR. COBBLEPOT.
IF HE DOESN'T DELIVER... BOOM!
ONE WAY OR ANOTHER I WIN TONIGHT AND THE SCARECROW LOSES...
Oooh... MY SWEET TOOTH! I WANT SOME.
I'LL BRING ONE RIGHT UP, SIR! TELL YOUR SWEET TOOTH TO SIT TIGHT--!
CIRCUS CANDY
--CUZ THE SCARECROW'S COMING FOR IT WITH A PAIR OF RUSTY PLIERS.
LADIES AND GENTLEMEN, HALY'S CIRCUS SPECTACULAR IS ABOUT TO BEGIN...

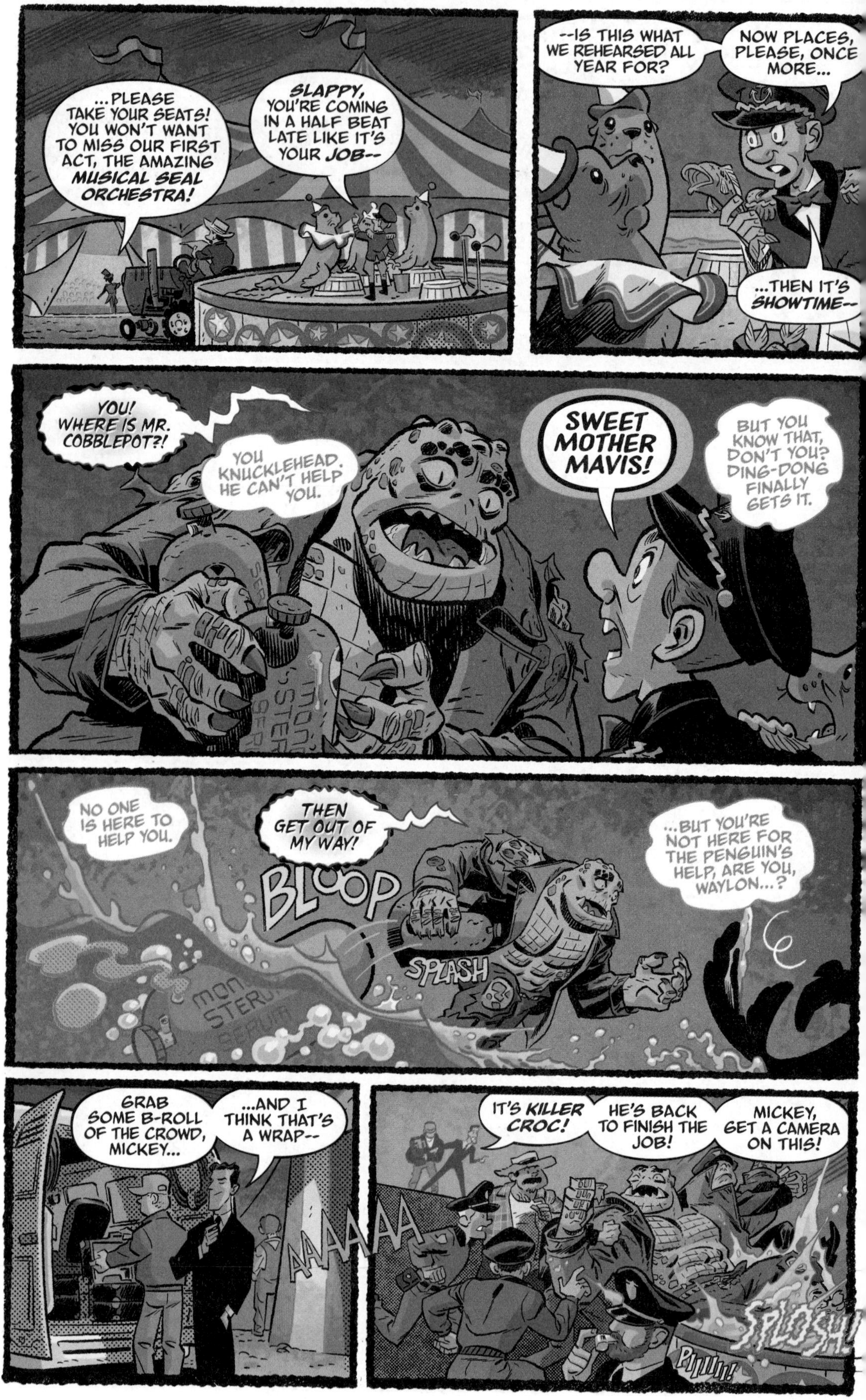
...PLEASE TAKE YOUR SEATS! YOU WON'T WANT TO MISS OUR FIRST ACT, THE AMAZING MUSICAL SEAL ORCHESTRA!
SLAPPY, YOU'RE COMING IN A HALF BEAT LATE LIKE IT'S YOUR JOB--
--IS THIS WHAT WE REHEARSED ALL YEAR FOR?
NOW PLACES, PLEASE, ONCE MORE...
...THEN IT'S SHOWTIME--
YOU! WHERE IS MR. COBBLEPOT?!
YOU KNUCKLEHEAD. HE CAN'T HELP YOU.
SWEET MOTHER MAVIS!
BUT YOU KNOW THAT, DON'T YOU? DING-DONG FINALLY GETS IT.
NO ONE IS HERE TO HELP YOU.
THEN GET OUT OF MY WAY!
BLOOP
SPLASH
...BUT YOU'RE NOT HERE FOR THE PENGUIN'S HELP, ARE YOU, WAYLON...?
GRAB SOME B-ROLL OF THE CROWD, MICKEY...
...AND I THINK THAT'S A WRAP--
AAAAAA
IT'S KILLER CROC!
HE'S BACK TO FINISH THE JOB!
MICKEY, GET A CAMERA ON THIS!
PIIIIII!

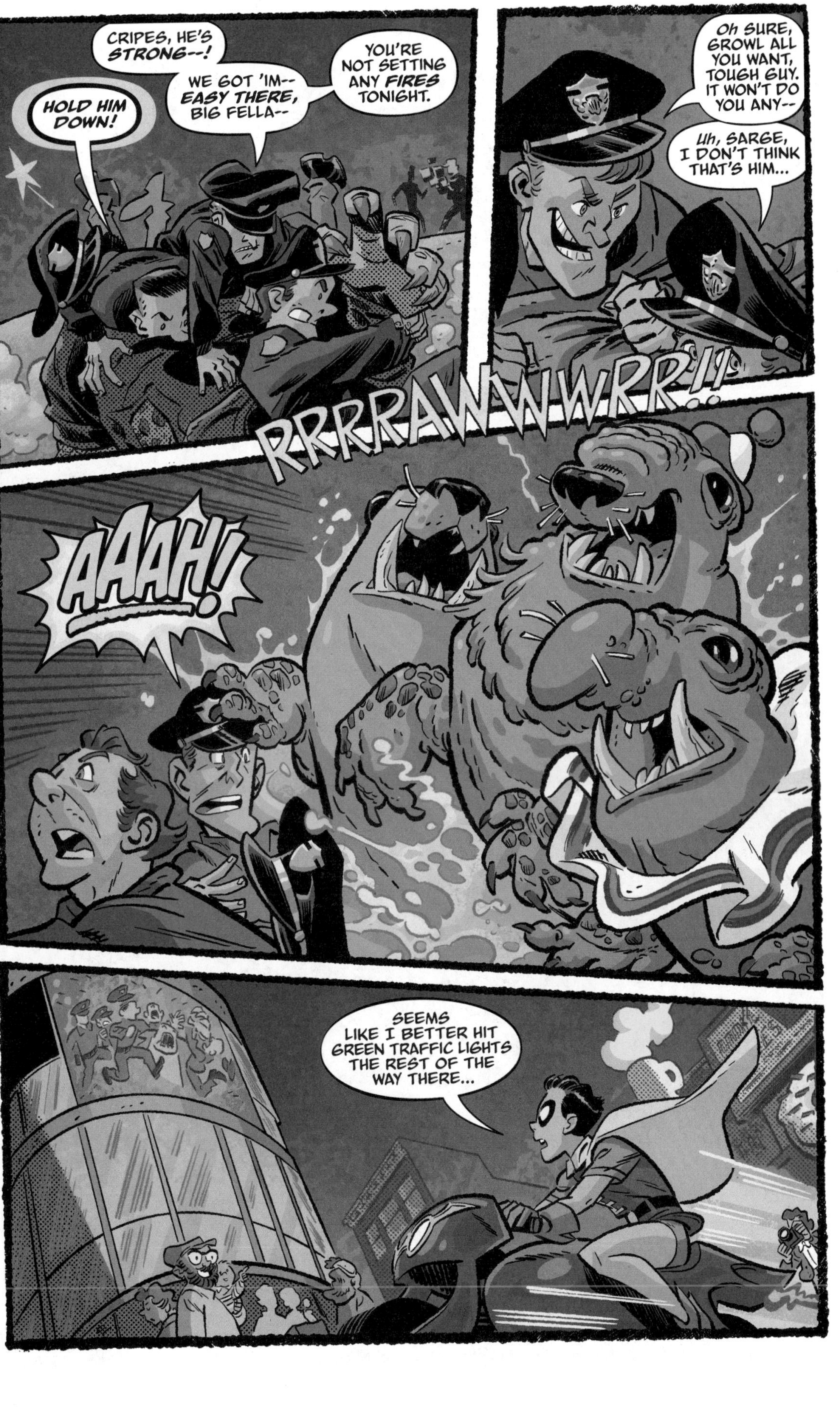
HOLD HIM DOWN!
CRIPES, HE'S STRONG--!
WE GOT 'IM-- EASY THERE, BIG FELLA--
YOU'RE NOT SETTING ANY FIRES TONIGHT.
Oh SURE, GROWL ALL YOU WANT, TOUGH GUY. IT WON'T DO YOU ANY--
Uh, SARGE, I DON'T THINK THAT'S HIM...
RRRRAWWWRR!!
AAAH!
SEEMS LIKE I BETTER HIT GREEN TRAFFIC LIGHTS THE REST OF THE WAY THERE...

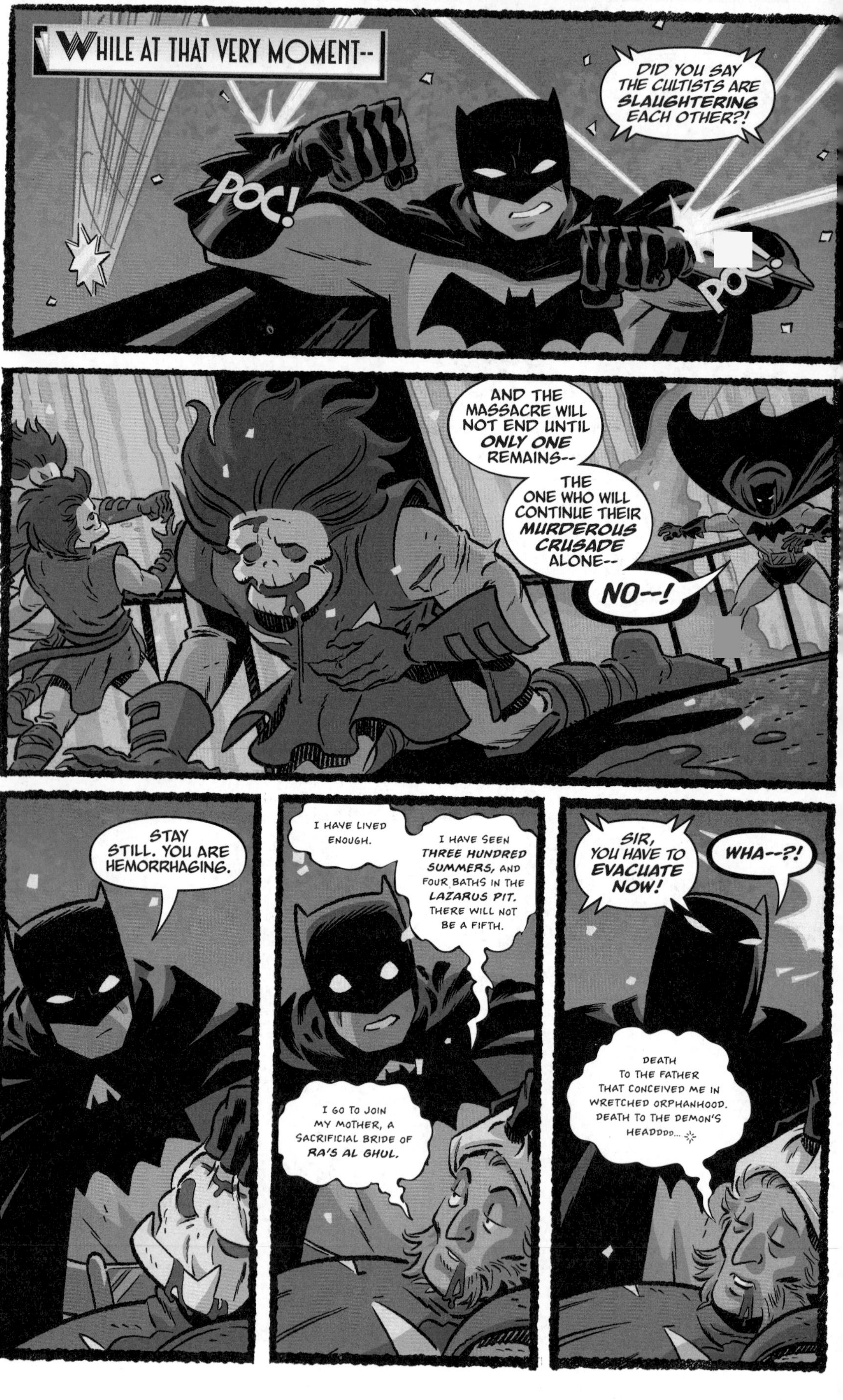
WHILE AT THAT VERY MOMENT--
DID YOU SAY THE CULTISTS ARE SLAUGHTERING EACH OTHER?!
POC!
POC!
AND THE MASSACRE WILL NOT END UNTIL ONLY ONE REMAINS--
THE ONE WHO WILL CONTINUE THEIR MURDEROUS CRUSADE ALONE--
NO--!
STAY STILL. YOU ARE HEMORRHAGING.
I HAVE LIVED ENOUGH.
I HAVE SEEN THREE HUNDRED SUMMERS, AND FOUR BATHS IN THE LAZARUS PIT. THERE WILL NOT BE A FIFTH.
I GO TO JOIN MY MOTHER, A SACRIFICIAL BRIDE OF RA'S AL GHUL.
SIR, YOU HAVE TO EVACUATE NOW!
WHA--?!
DEATH TO THE FATHER THAT CONCEIVED ME IN WRETCHED ORPHANHOOD. DEATH TO THE DEMON'S HEADDDD...

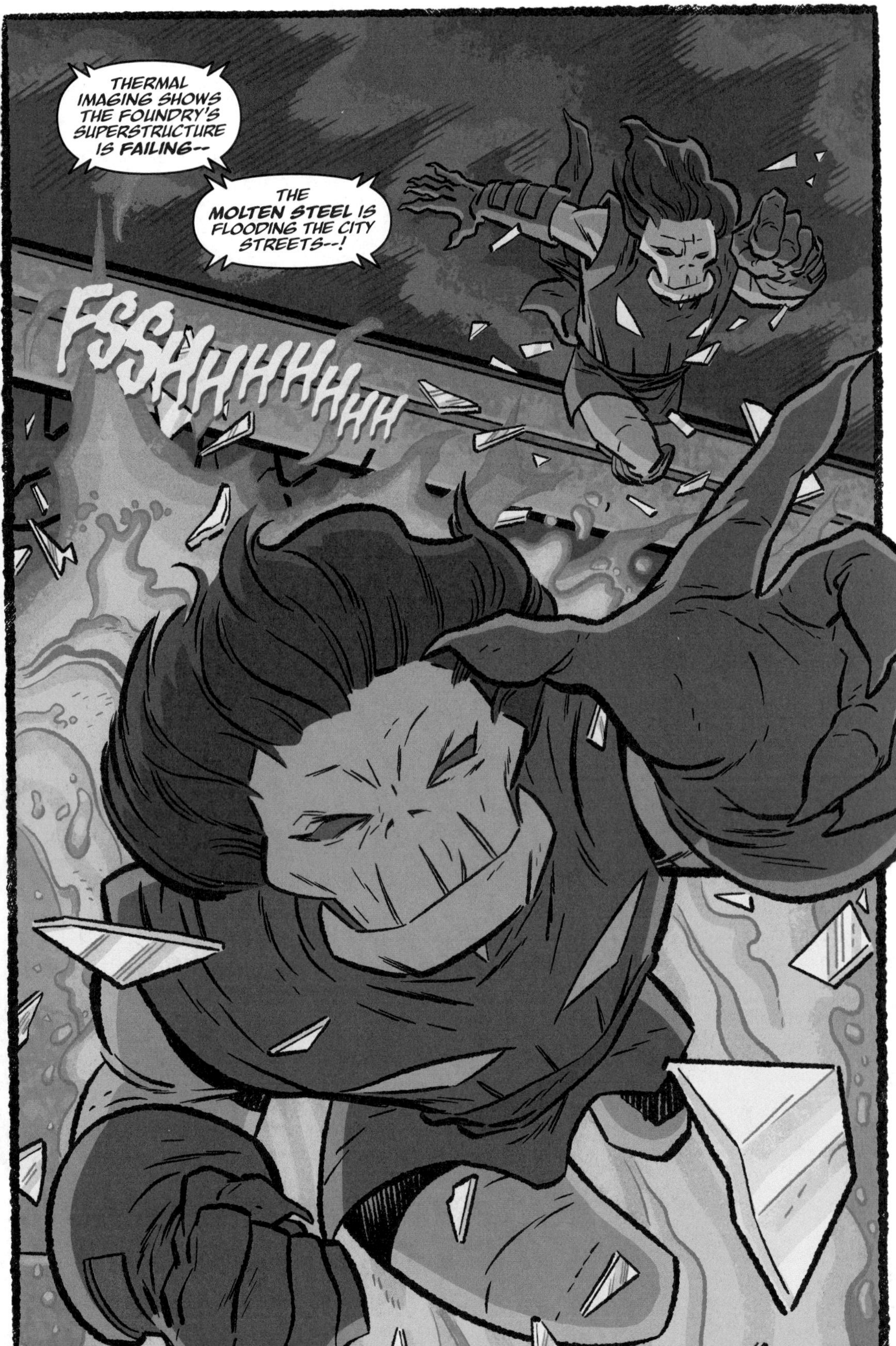
THERMAL IMAGING SHOWS THE FOUNDRY'S SUPERSTRUCTURE IS FAILING--
THE MOLTEN STEEL IS FLOODING THE CITY STREETS--!
FSSHHHHHHHH

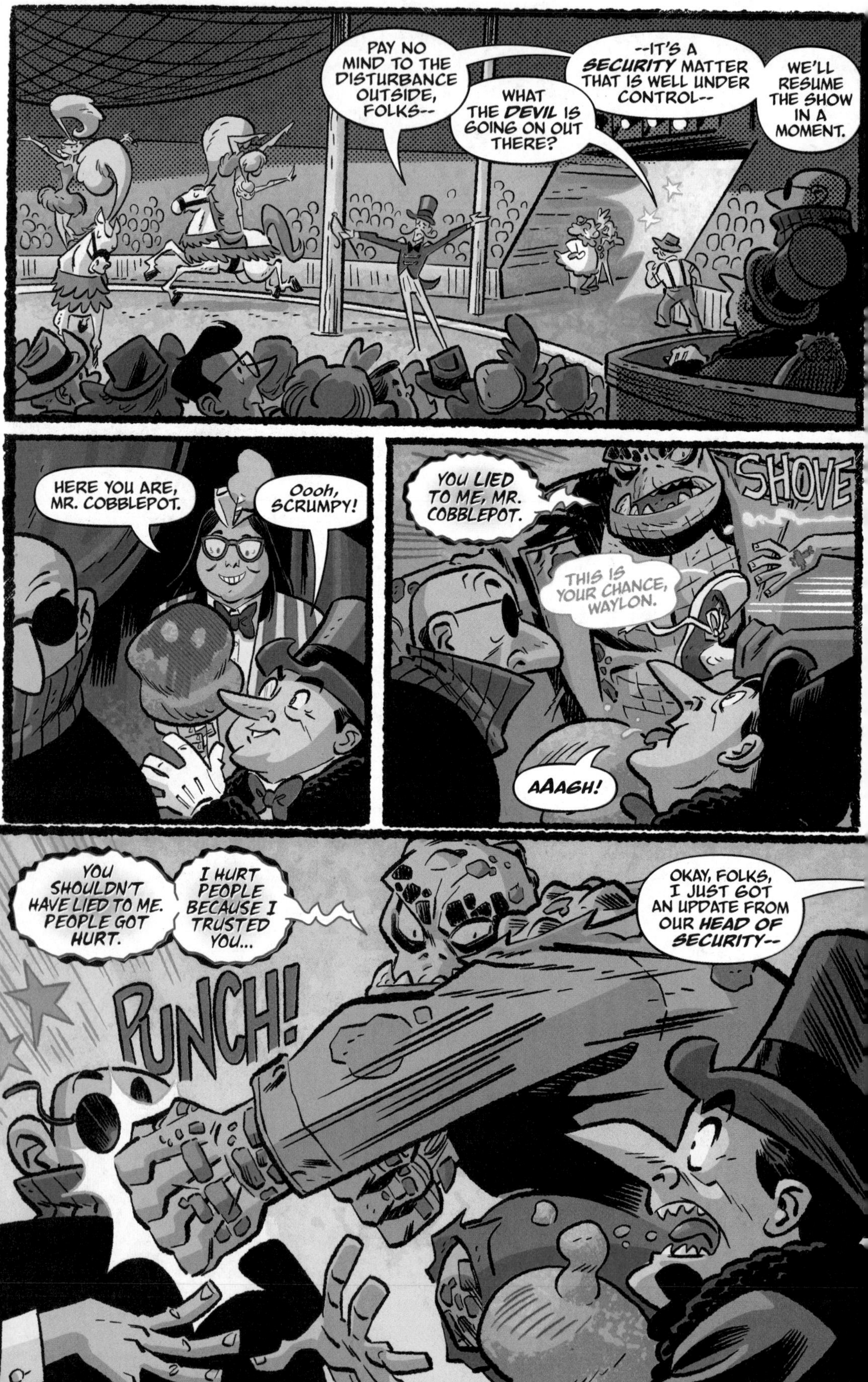
PAY NO MIND TO THE DISTURBANCE OUTSIDE, FOLKS--
WHAT THE DEVIL IS GOING ON OUT THERE?
--IT'S A SECURITY MATTER THAT IS WELL UNDER CONTROL--
WE'LL RESUME THE SHOW IN A MOMENT.
HERE YOU ARE, MR. COBBLEPOT.
Oooh, SCRUMPY!
YOU LIED TO ME, MR. COBBLEPOT.
SHOVE
THIS IS YOUR CHANCE, WAYLON.
AAAGH!
YOU SHOULDN'T HAVE LIED TO ME. PEOPLE GOT HURT.
I HURT PEOPLE BECAUSE I TRUSTED YOU...
OKAY, FOLKS, I JUST GOT AN UPDATE FROM OUR HEAD OF SECURITY--
PUNCH!

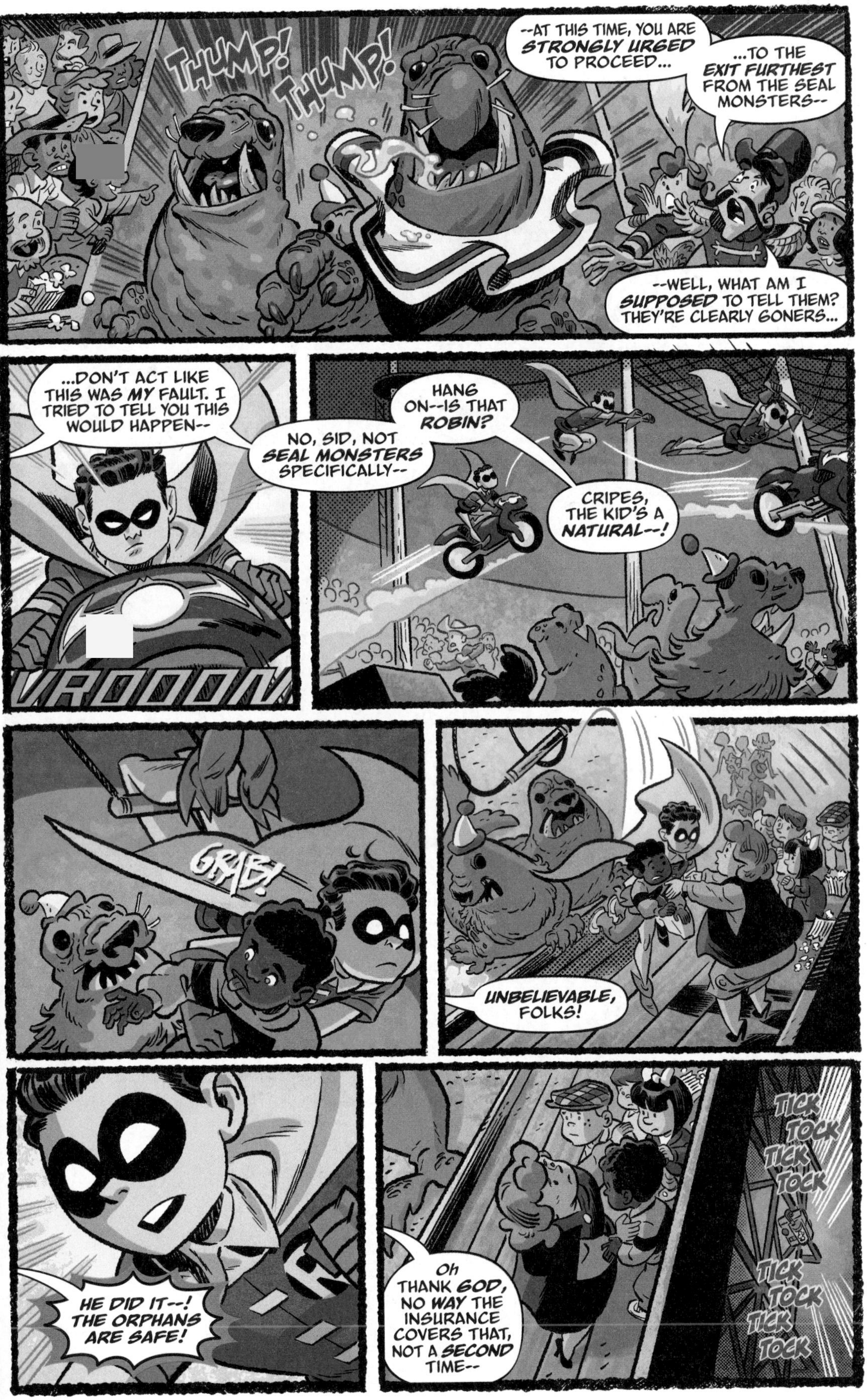
THUMP! THUMP!
--AT THIS TIME, YOU ARE STRONGLY URGED TO PROCEED...
...TO THE EXIT FURTHEST FROM THE SEAL MONSTERS--
--WELL, WHAT AM I SUPPOSED TO TELL THEM? THEY'RE CLEARLY GONERS...
...DON'T ACT LIKE THIS WAS MY FAULT. I TRIED TO TELL YOU THIS WOULD HAPPEN--
NO, SID, NOT SEAL MONSTERS SPECIFICALLY--
VROOOOM
HANG ON--IS THAT ROBIN?
CRIPES, THE KID'S A NATURAL--!
GRAB!
UNBELIEVABLE, FOLKS!
HE DID IT--! THE ORPHANS ARE SAFE!
Oh THANK GOD, NO WAY THE INSURANCE COVERS THAT, NOT A SECOND TIME--
TICK TOCK TICK TOCK
TICK TOCK TICK TOCK

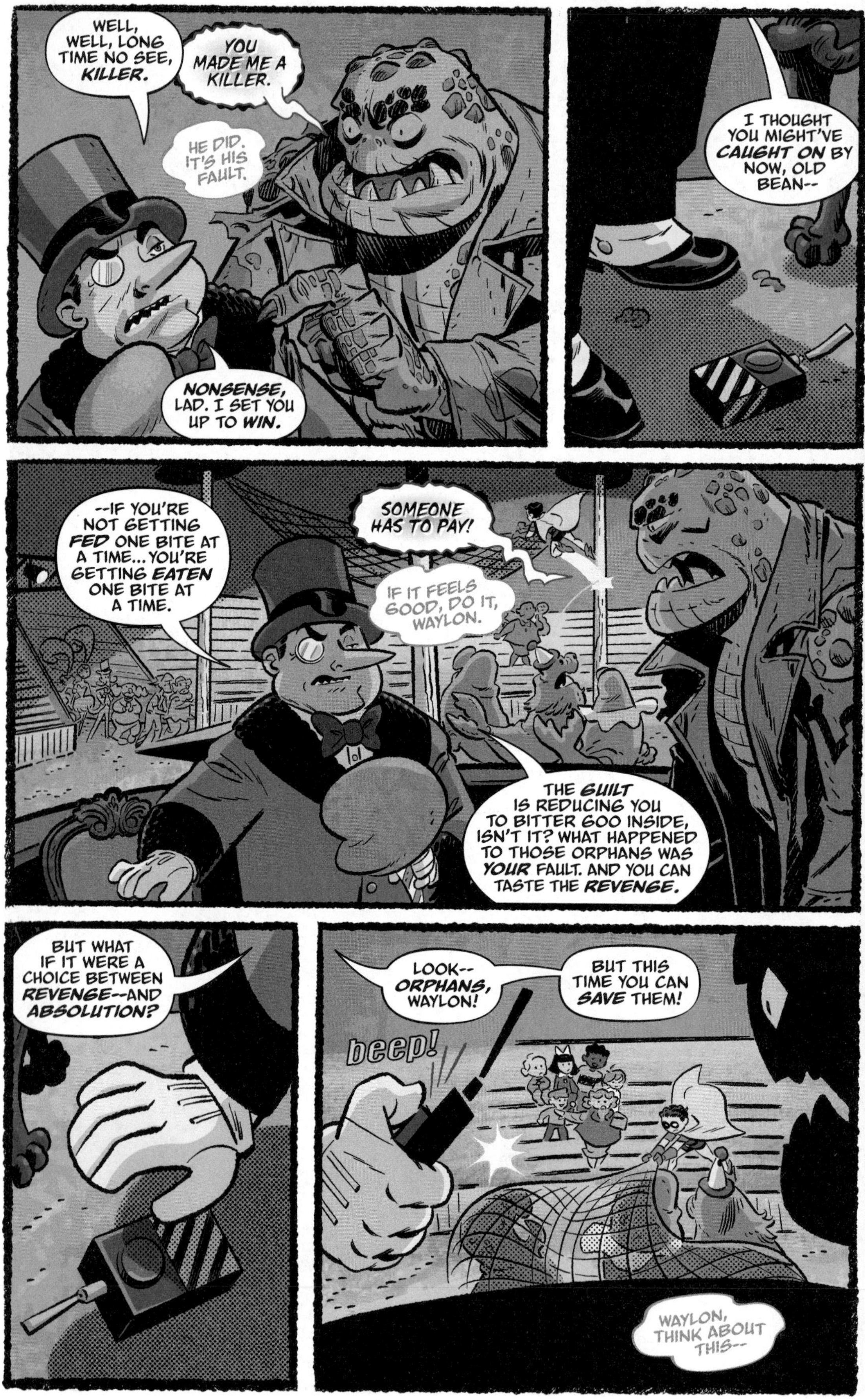
WELL, WELL, LONG TIME NO SEE, KILLER.
YOU MADE ME A KILLER.
HE DID. IT'S HIS FAULT.
NONSENSE, LAD. I SET YOU UP TO WIN.
I THOUGHT YOU MIGHT'VE CAUGHT ON BY NOW, OLD BEAN--
--IF YOU'RE NOT GETTING FED ONE BITE AT A TIME... YOU'RE GETTING EATEN ONE BITE AT A TIME.
SOMEONE HAS TO PAY!
IF IT FEELS GOOD, DO IT, WAYLON.
THE GUILT IS REDUCING YOU TO BITTER GOO INSIDE, ISN'T IT? WHAT HAPPENED TO THOSE ORPHANS WAS YOUR FAULT. AND YOU CAN TASTE THE REVENGE.
BUT WHAT IF IT WERE A CHOICE BETWEEN REVENGE--AND ABSOLUTION?
LOOK--ORPHANS, WAYLON!
BUT THIS TIME YOU CAN SAVE THEM!
beep!
WAYLON, THINK ABOUT THIS--

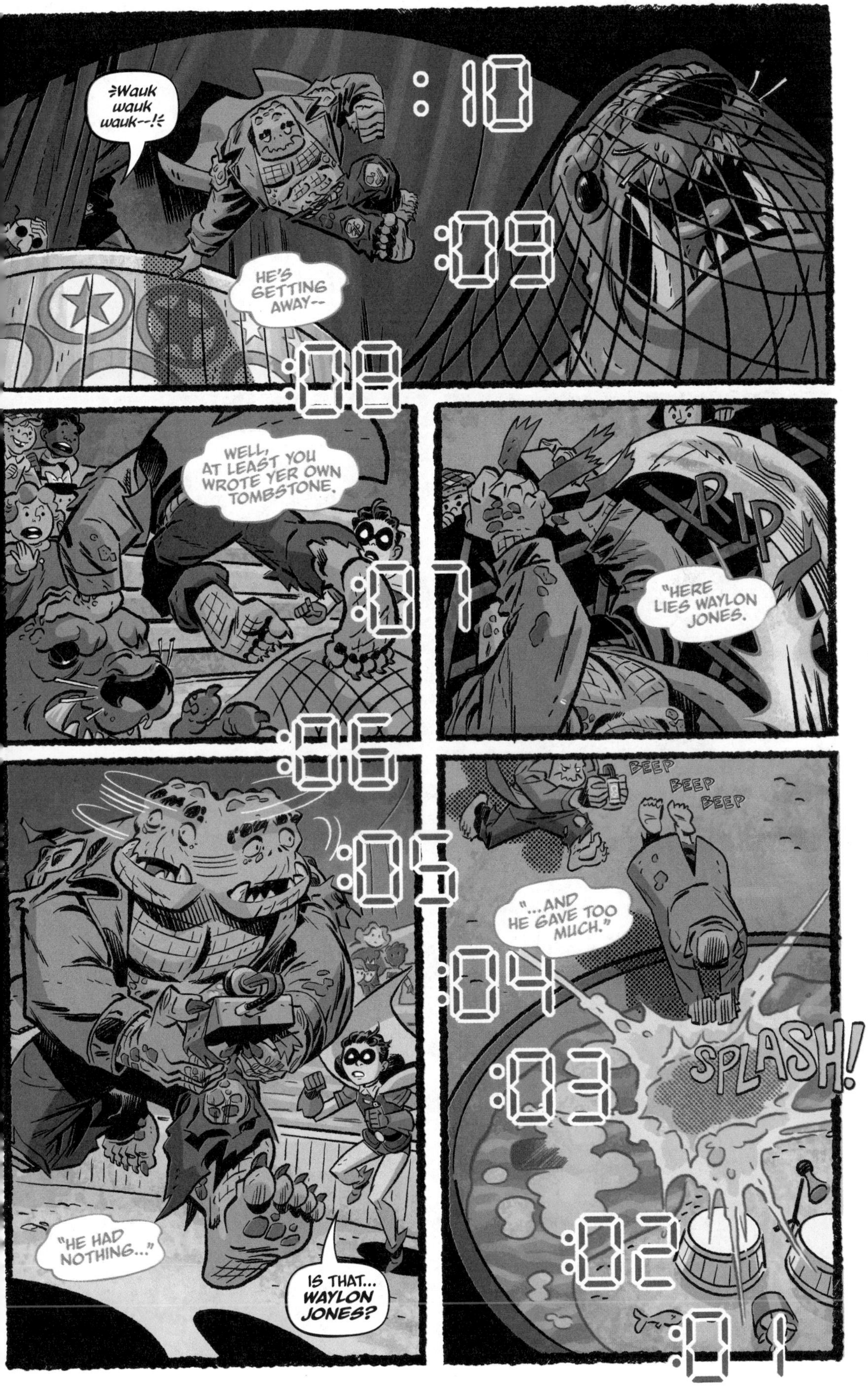

:10
≯Wauk wauk wauk--!≮
:09
HE'S GETTING AWAY--
:08
WELL, AT LEAST YOU WROTE YER OWN TOMBSTONE.
:07
RIP
"HERE LIES WAYLON JONES.
:06
:05
BEEP
BEEP
BEEP
"...AND HE GAVE TOO MUCH."
:04
:03
SPLASH!
"HE HAD NOTHING..."
IS THAT... WAYLON JONES?
:02
:01

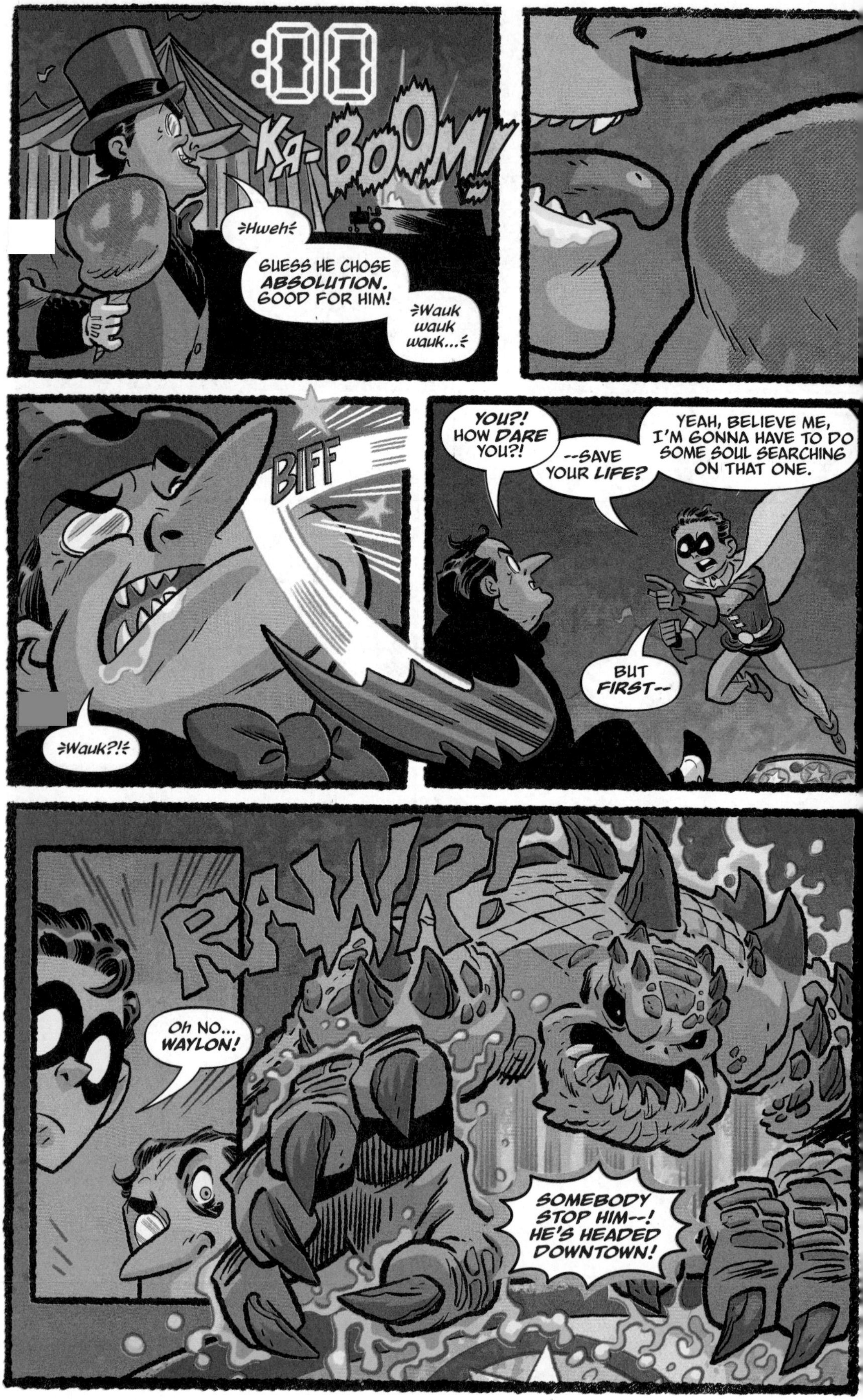
:00
KA-BOOM!
Hweh
GUESS HE CHOSE ABSOLUTION. GOOD FOR HIM!
Wauk wauk wauk...
BIFF
Wauk?!
YOU?! HOW DARE YOU?!
--SAVE YOUR LIFE?
YEAH, BELIEVE ME, I'M GONNA HAVE TO DO SOME SOUL SEARCHING ON THAT ONE.
BUT FIRST--
RAWR!
Oh NO... WAYLON!
SOMEBODY STOP HIM--! HE'S HEADED DOWNTOWN!

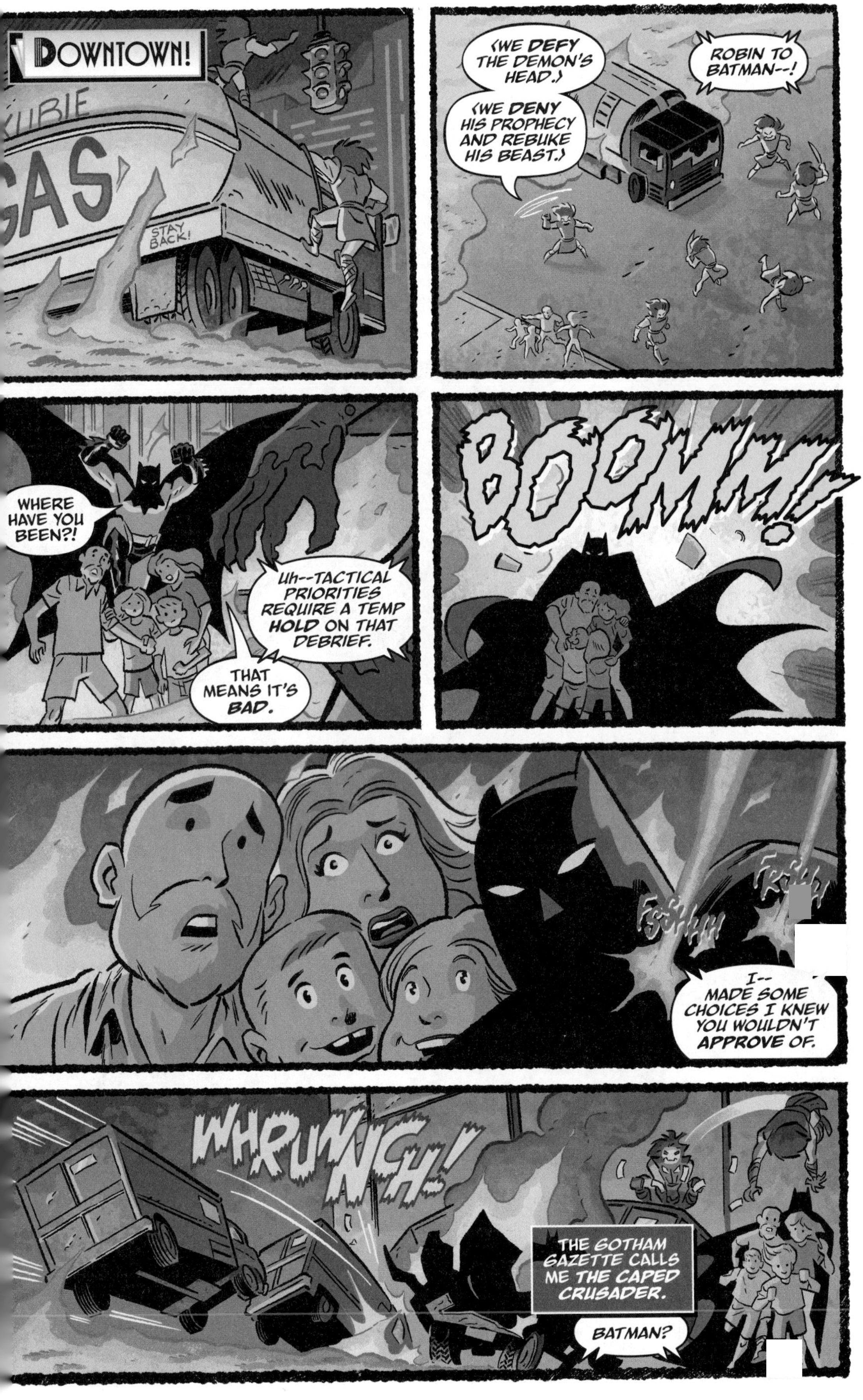
DOWNTOWN!
XUBIE
GAS
STAY BACK!
‹WE DEFY THE DEMON'S HEAD.›
‹WE DENY HIS PROPHECY AND REBUKE HIS BEAST.›
ROBIN TO BATMAN--!
WHERE HAVE YOU BEEN?!
Uh--TACTICAL PRIORITIES REQUIRE A TEMP HOLD ON THAT DEBRIEF.
THAT MEANS IT'S BAD.
BOOMM!
FSSHHH
I-- MADE SOME CHOICES I KNEW YOU WOULDN'T APPROVE OF.
WHRUNNCH!
THE GOTHAM GAZETTE CALLS ME THE CAPED CRUSADER.
BATMAN?

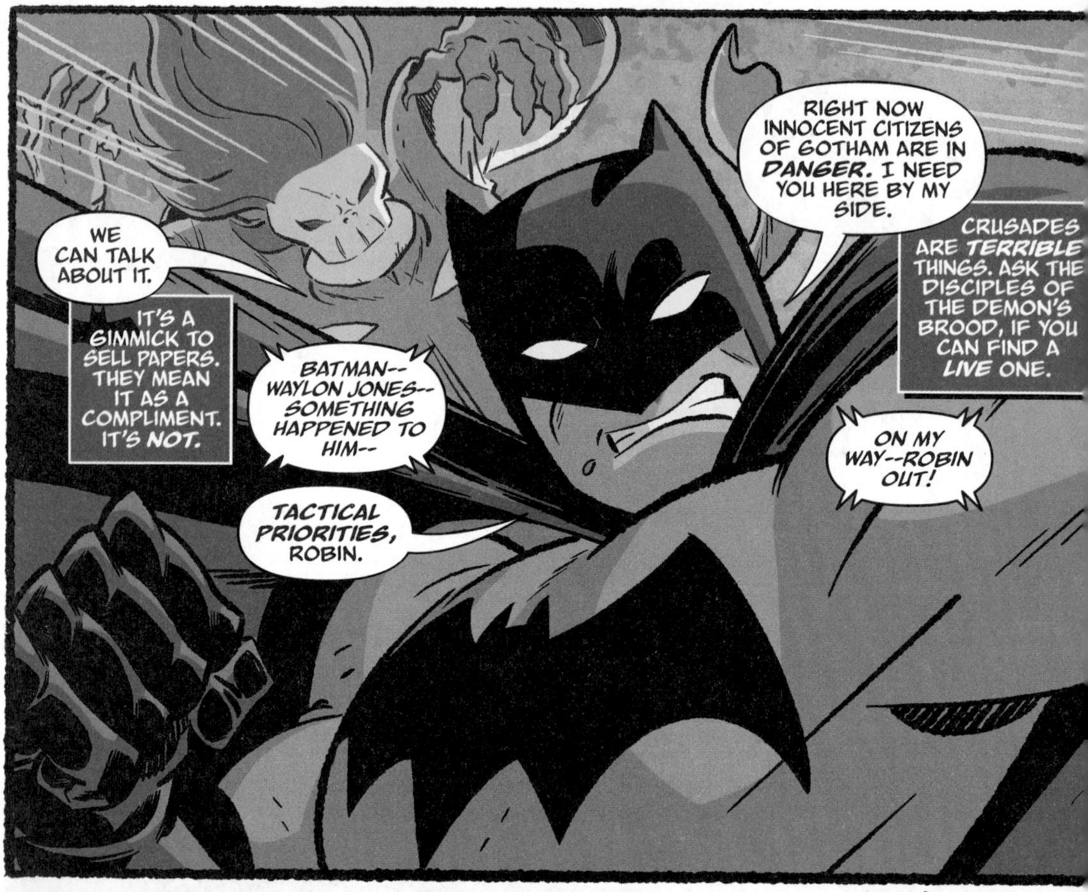
RIGHT NOW INNOCENT CITIZENS OF GOTHAM ARE IN DANGER. I NEED YOU HERE BY MY SIDE.
WE CAN TALK ABOUT IT.
CRUSADES ARE TERRIBLE THINGS. ASK THE DISCIPLES OF THE DEMON'S BROOD, IF YOU CAN FIND A LIVE ONE.
IT'S A GIMMICK TO SELL PAPERS. THEY MEAN IT AS A COMPLIMENT. IT'S NOT.
BATMAN--WAYLON JONES--SOMETHING HAPPENED TO HIM--
TACTICAL PRIORITIES, ROBIN.
ON MY WAY--ROBIN OUT!

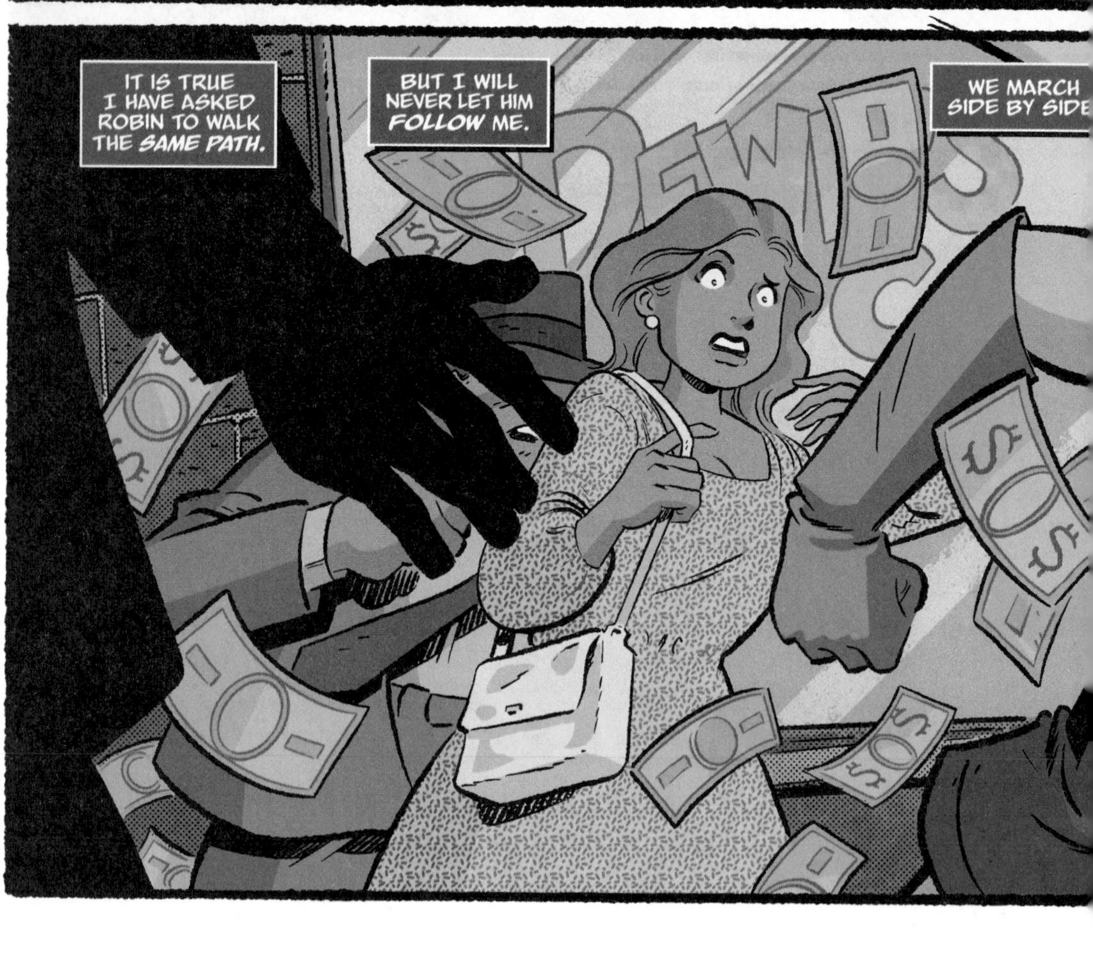
IT IS TRUE I HAVE ASKED ROBIN TO WALK THE SAME PATH.
BUT I WILL NEVER LET HIM FOLLOW ME.
WE MARCH SIDE BY SIDE

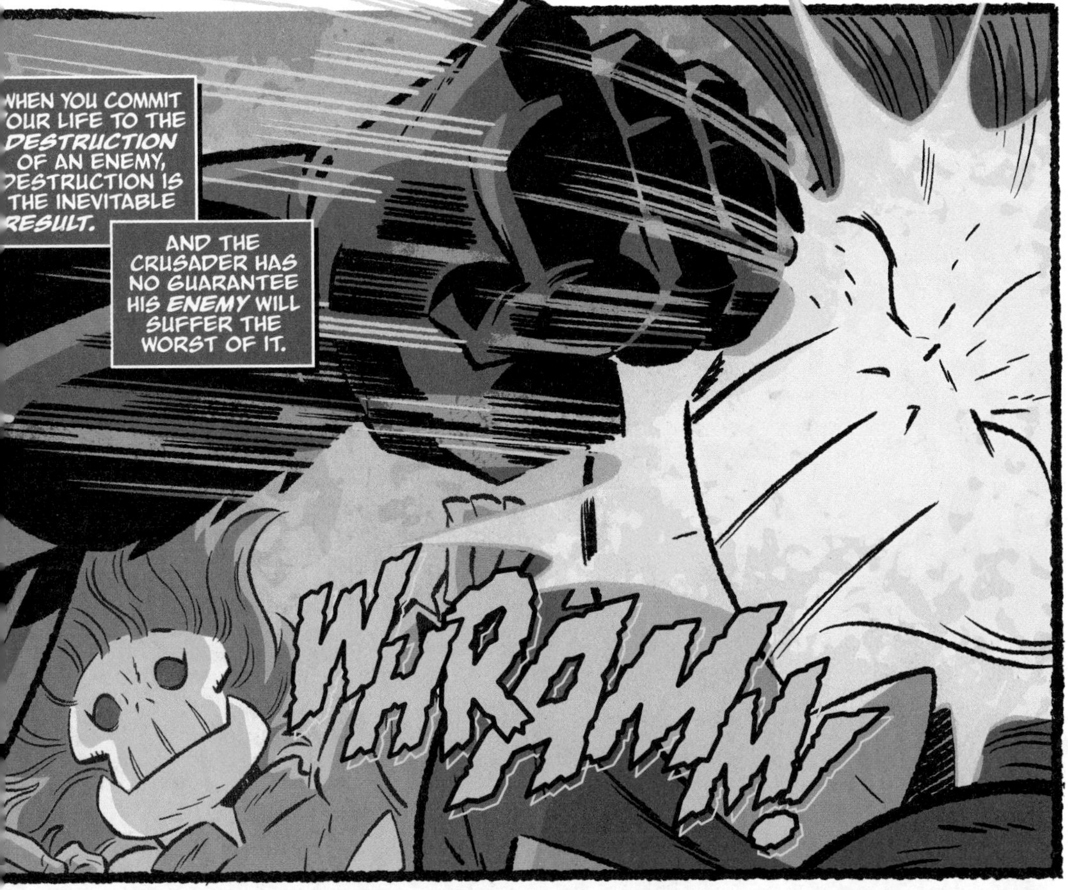
WHEN YOU COMMIT YOUR LIFE TO THE *DESTRUCTION* OF AN ENEMY, DESTRUCTION IS THE INEVITABLE *RESULT.*
AND THE CRUSADER HAS NO GUARANTEE HIS *ENEMY* WILL SUFFER THE WORST OF IT.
WHRAMM!

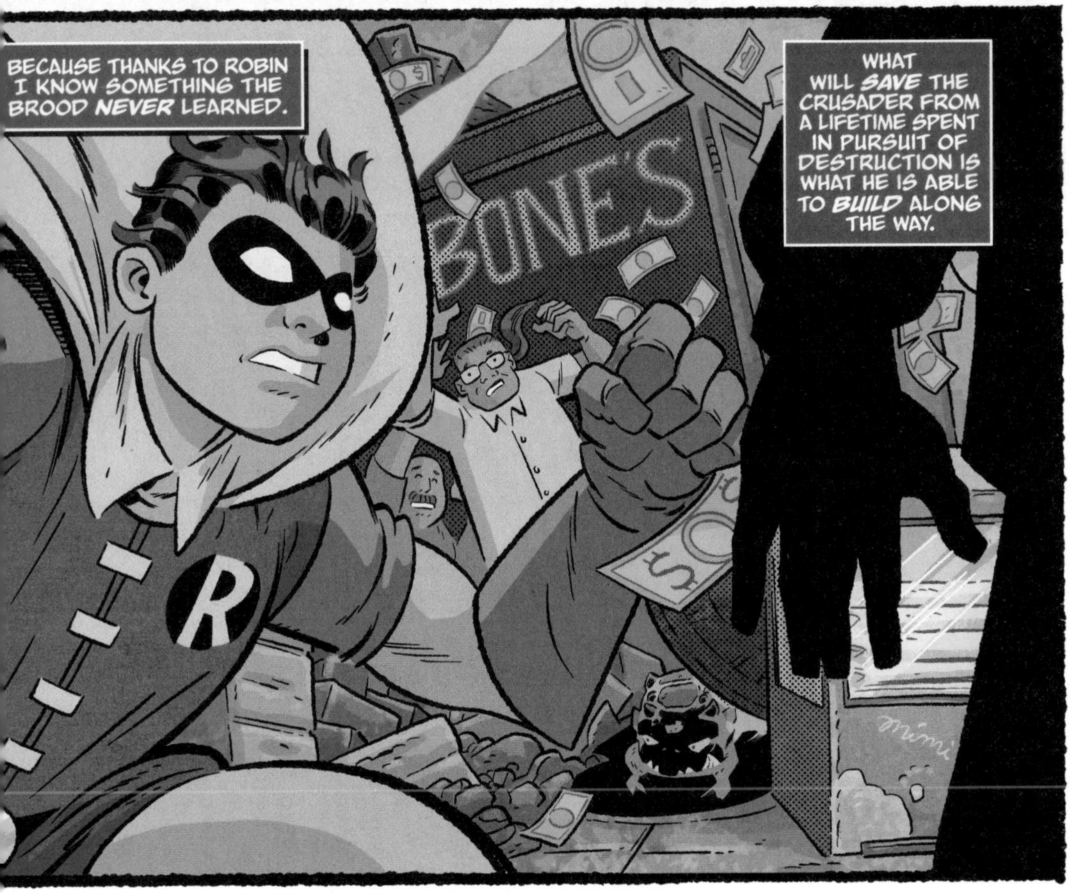
BECAUSE THANKS TO ROBIN I KNOW SOMETHING THE BROOD *NEVER* LEARNED.
WHAT WILL *SAVE* THE CRUSADER FROM A LIFETIME SPENT IN PURSUIT OF DESTRUCTION IS WHAT HE IS ABLE TO *BUILD* ALONG THE WAY.
BONE'S

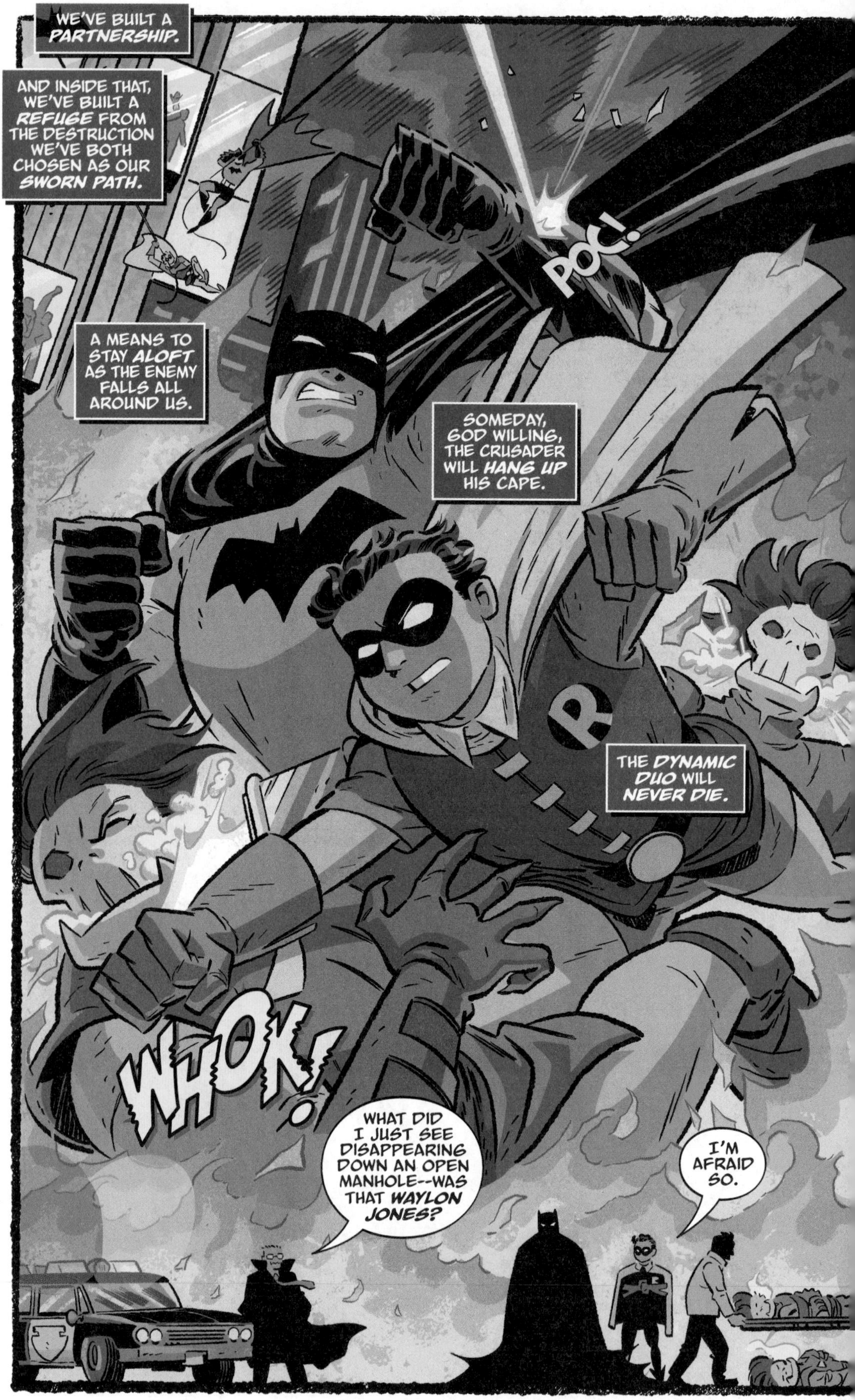
WE'VE BUILT A PARTNERSHIP.
AND INSIDE THAT, WE'VE BUILT A REFUGE FROM THE DESTRUCTION WE'VE BOTH CHOSEN AS OUR SWORN PATH.
POC!
A MEANS TO STAY ALOFT AS THE ENEMY FALLS ALL AROUND US.
SOMEDAY, GOD WILLING, THE CRUSADER WILL HANG UP HIS CAPE.
THE DYNAMIC DUO WILL NEVER DIE.
WHOK!
WHAT DID I JUST SEE DISAPPEARING DOWN AN OPEN MANHOLE--WAS THAT WAYLON JONES?
I'M AFRAID SO.

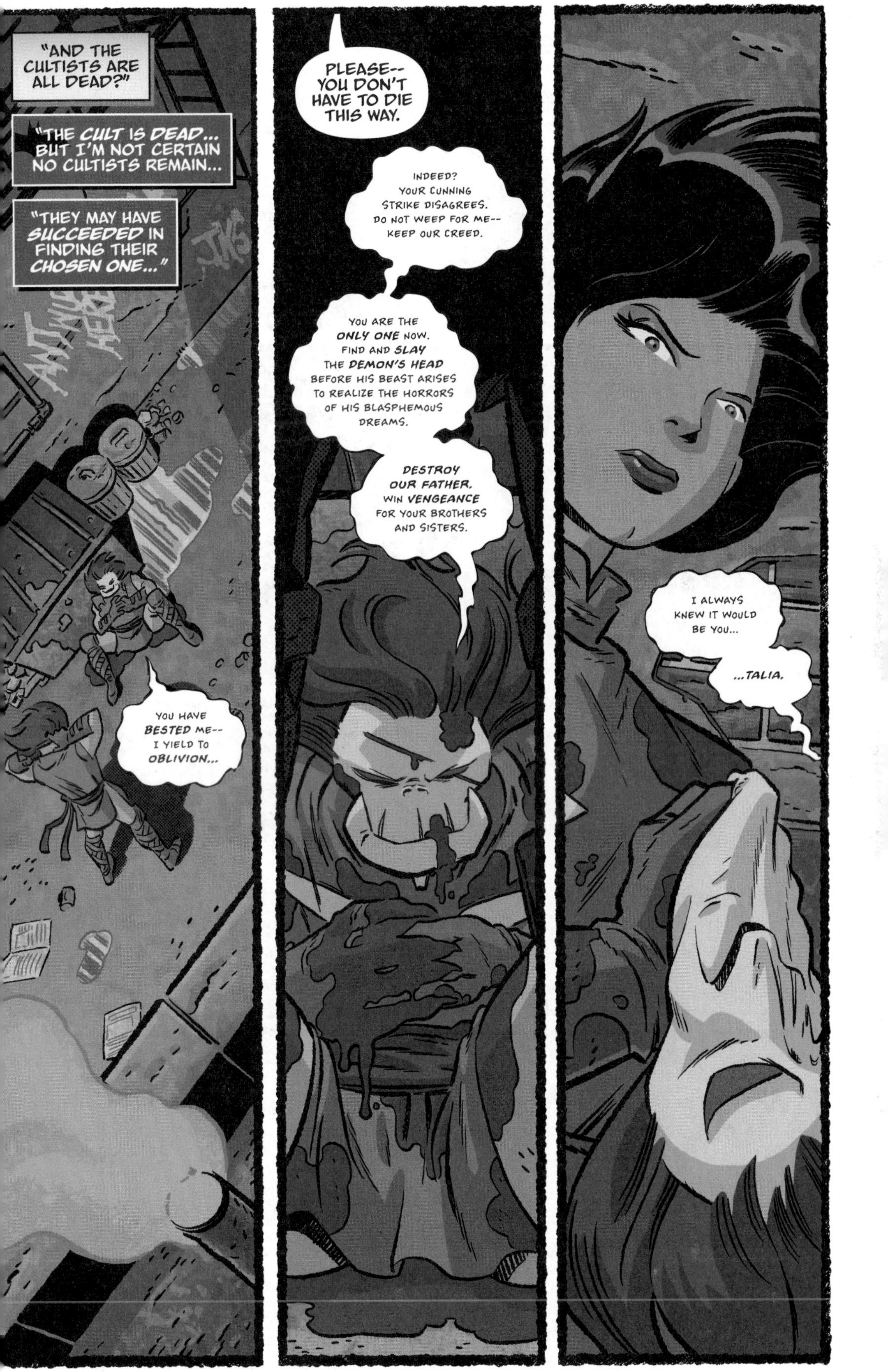
"AND THE CULTISTS ARE ALL DEAD?"
"THE CULT IS DEAD... BUT I'M NOT CERTAIN NO CULTISTS REMAIN...
"THEY MAY HAVE SUCCEEDED IN FINDING THEIR CHOSEN ONE..."
YOU HAVE BESTED ME-- I YIELD TO OBLIVION...
PLEASE-- YOU DON'T HAVE TO DIE THIS WAY.
INDEED? YOUR CUNNING STRIKE DISAGREES. DO NOT WEEP FOR ME-- KEEP OUR CREED.
YOU ARE THE ONLY ONE NOW. FIND AND SLAY THE DEMON'S HEAD BEFORE HIS BEAST ARISES TO REALIZE THE HORRORS OF HIS BLASPHEMOUS DREAMS.
DESTROY OUR FATHER. WIN VENGEANCE FOR YOUR BROTHERS AND SISTERS.
I ALWAYS KNEW IT WOULD BE YOU...
...TALIA.

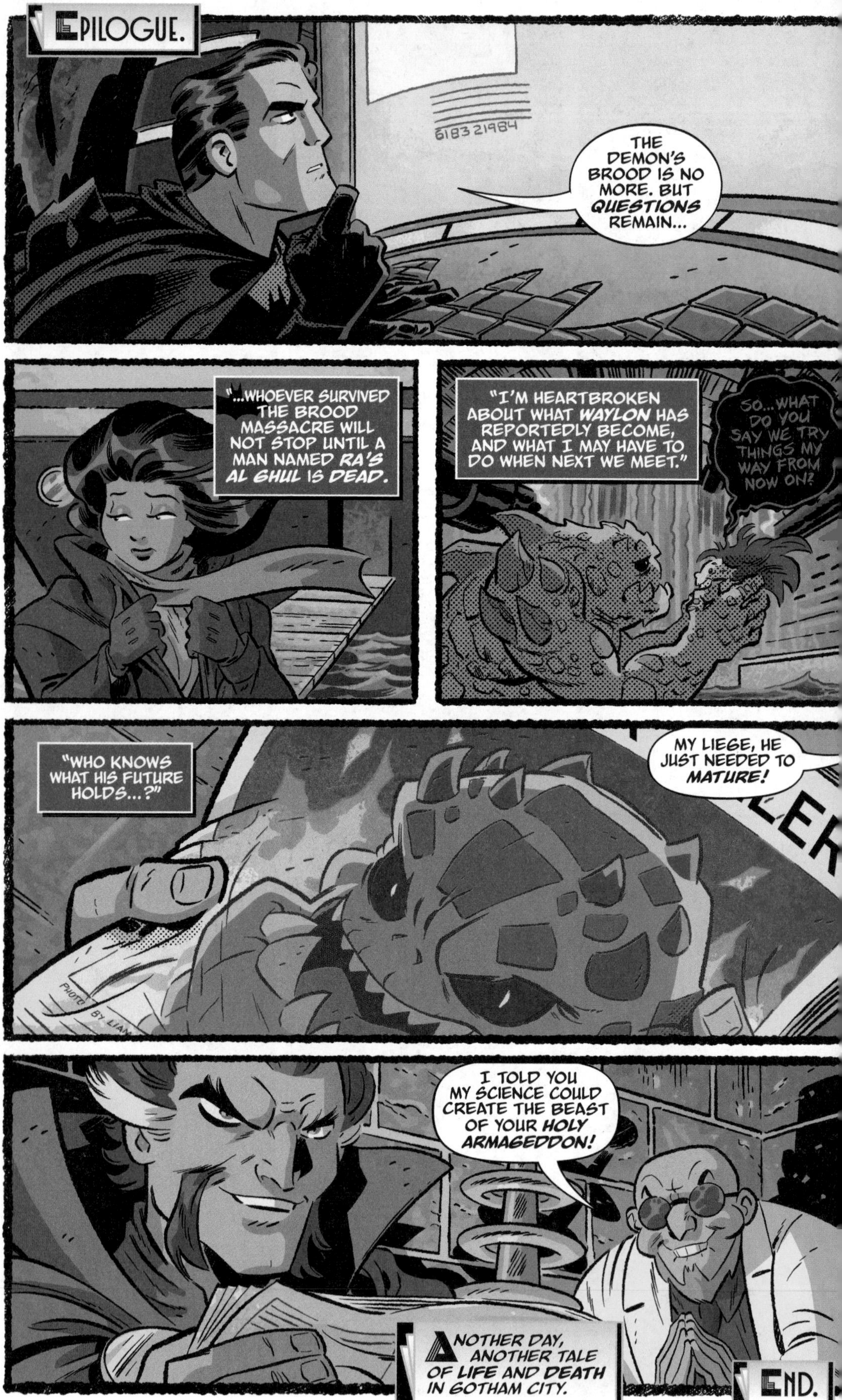
EPILOGUE.
6183 21984
THE DEMON'S BROOD IS NO MORE. BUT QUESTIONS REMAIN...
"...WHOEVER SURVIVED THE BROOD MASSACRE WILL NOT STOP UNTIL A MAN NAMED RA'S AL GHUL IS DEAD.
"I'M HEARTBROKEN ABOUT WHAT WAYLON HAS REPORTEDLY BECOME, AND WHAT I MAY HAVE TO DO WHEN NEXT WE MEET."
SO...WHAT DO YOU SAY WE TRY THINGS MY WAY FROM NOW ON?
"WHO KNOWS WHAT HIS FUTURE HOLDS...?"
MY LIEGE, HE JUST NEEDED TO MATURE!
I TOLD YOU MY SCIENCE COULD CREATE THE BEAST OF YOUR HOLY ARMAGEDDON!
ANOTHER DAY, ANOTHER TALE OF LIFE AND DEATH IN GOTHAM CITY.
END.

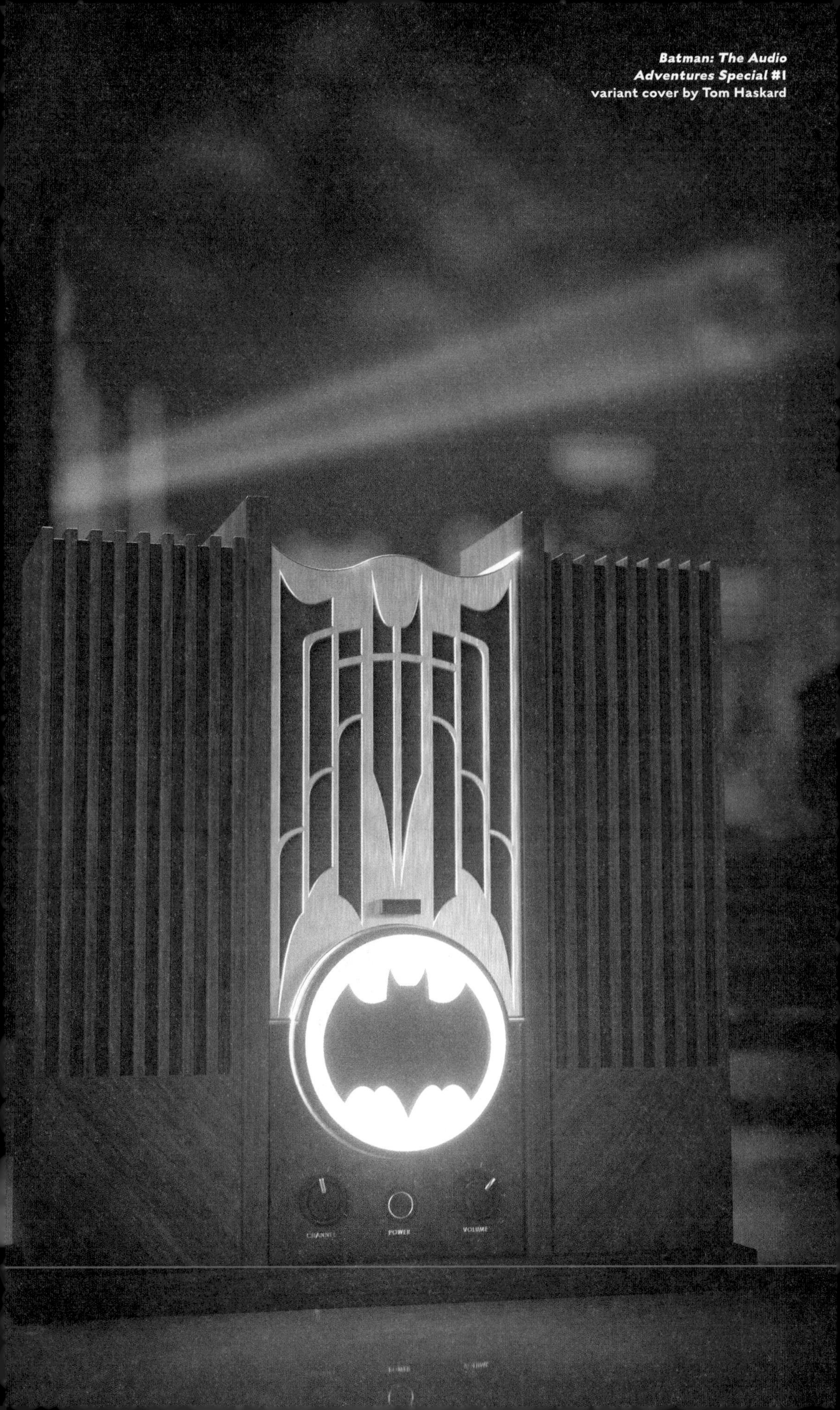
CHANNEL
POWER
VOLUME

Batman: The Audio Adventures Special #1
variant cover by Tom Haskard

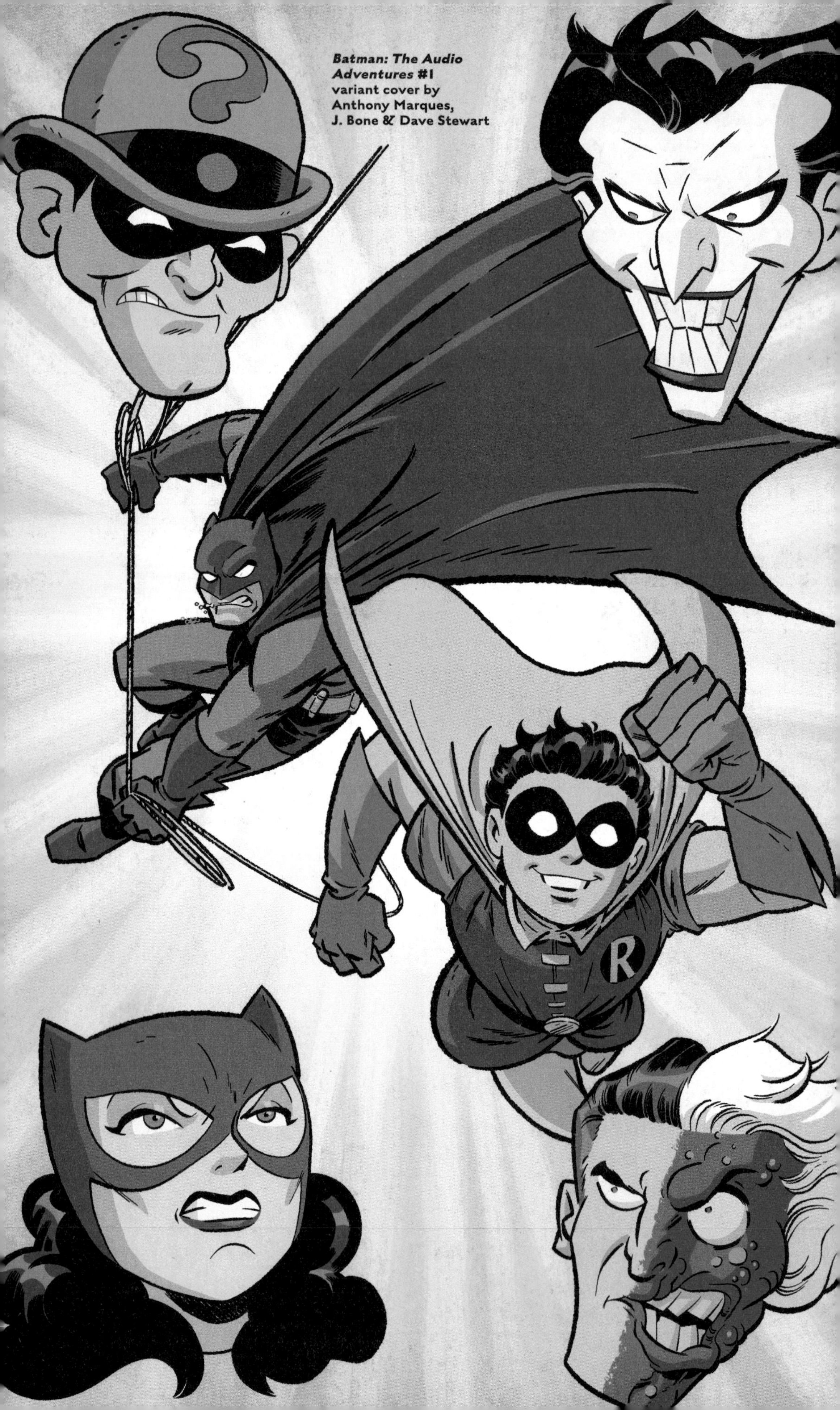

Batman: The Audio Adventures #1 variant cover by Anthony Marques, J. Bone & Dave Stewart

CHARACTER DESIGNS
by Anthony Marques, J. Bone & Dave Stewart

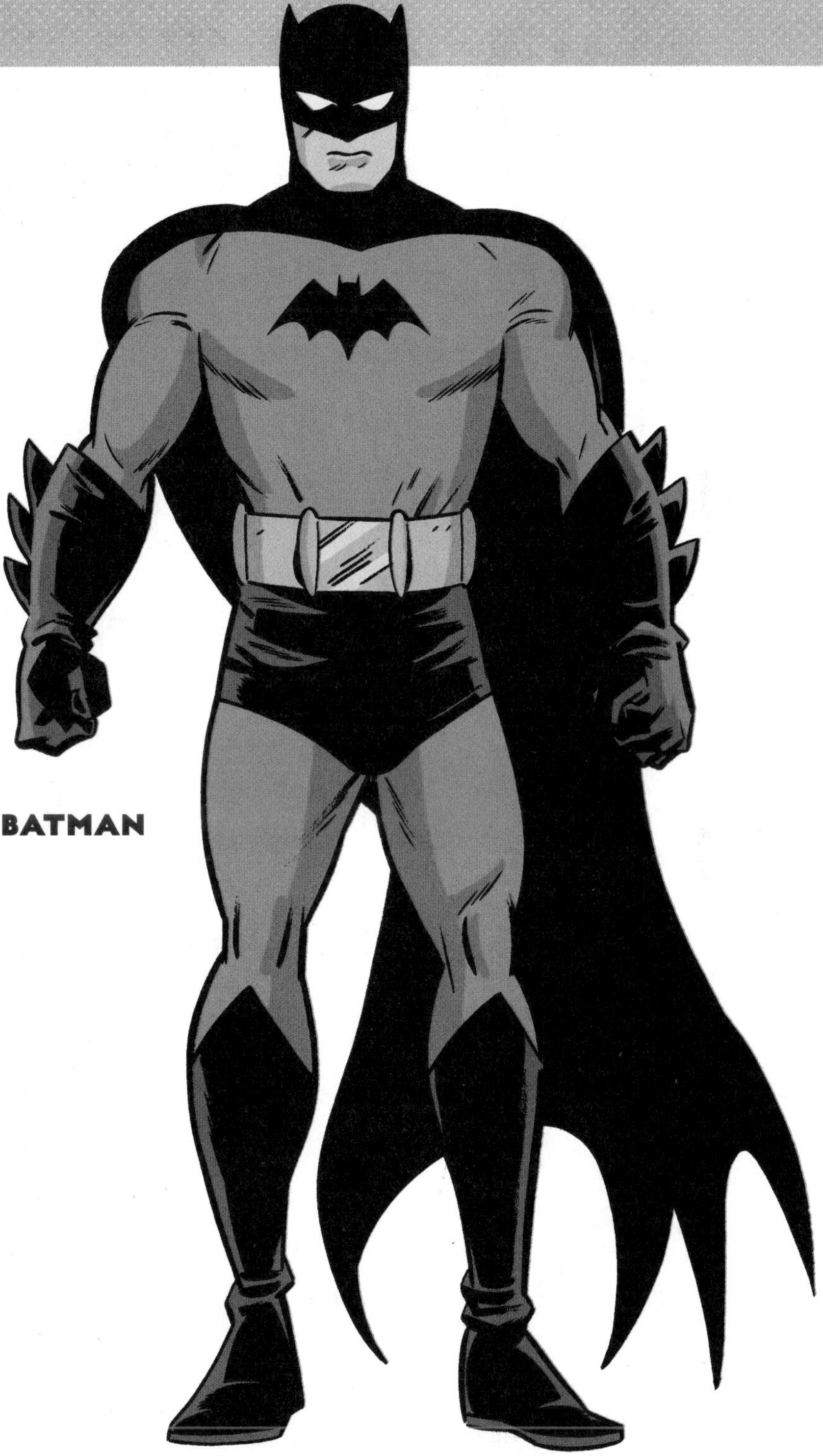

ANTHONY MARQUES
J-BONE 2021

BATMAN

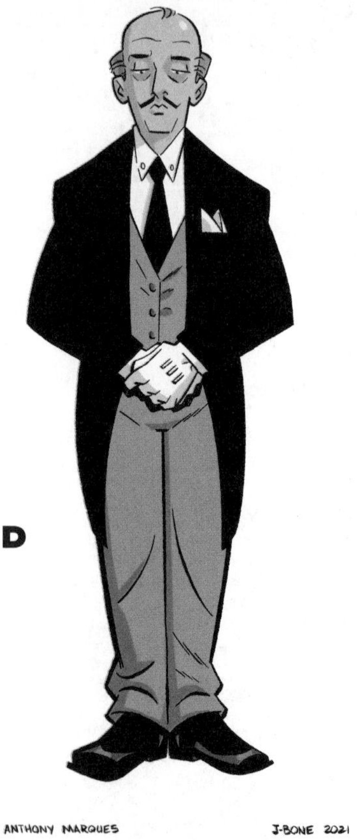
ANTHONY MARQUES
J-BONE 2021

ALFRED

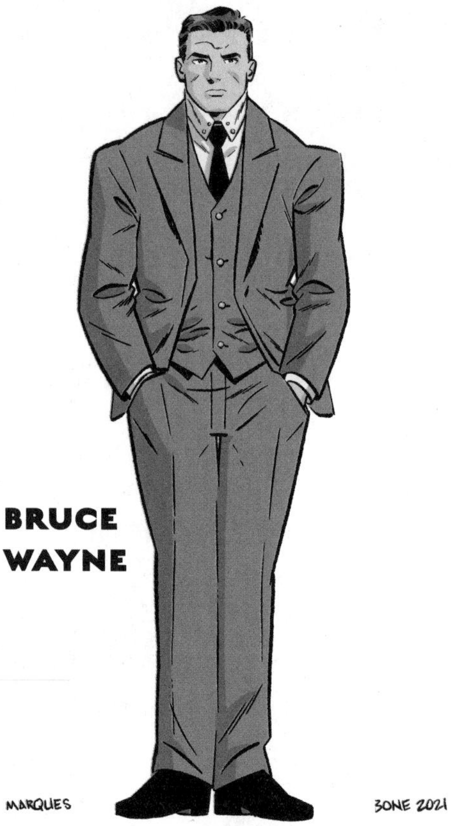
MARQUES
BONE 2021

BRUCE WAYNE

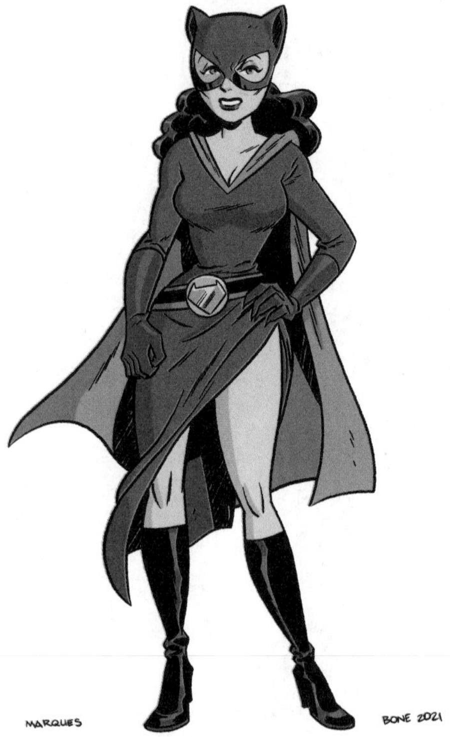
MARQUES
BONE 2021

CATWOMAN

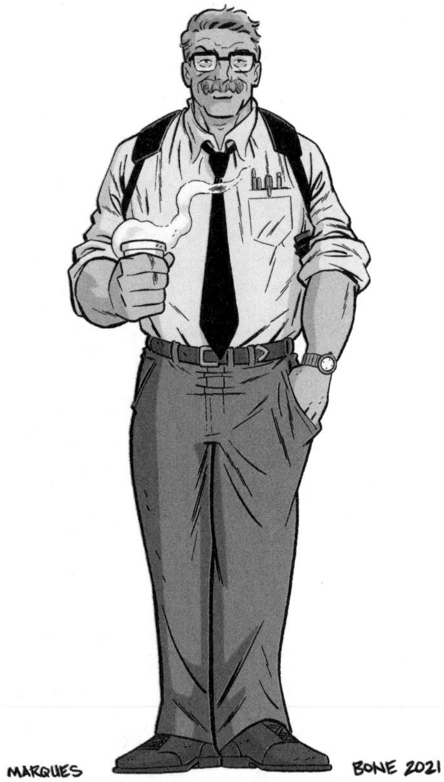
MARQUES
BONE 2021

COMMISSIONER GORDON

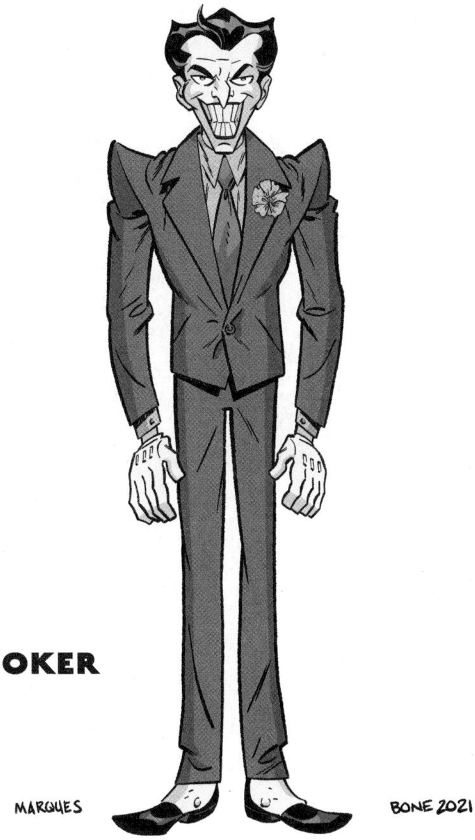
MARQUES
BONE 2021

JOKER

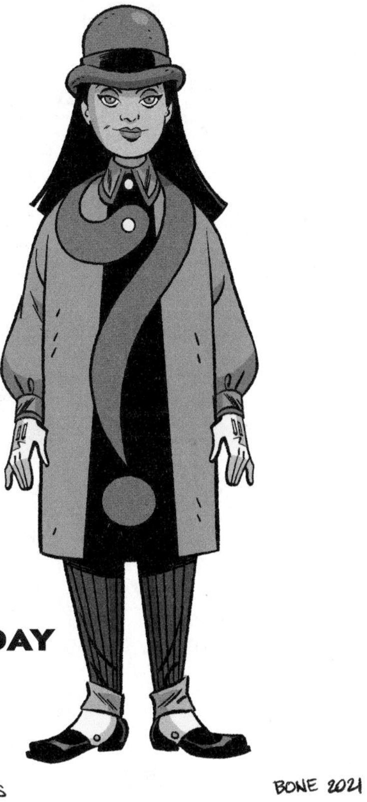
MARQUES
BONE 2021

MISS TUESDAY

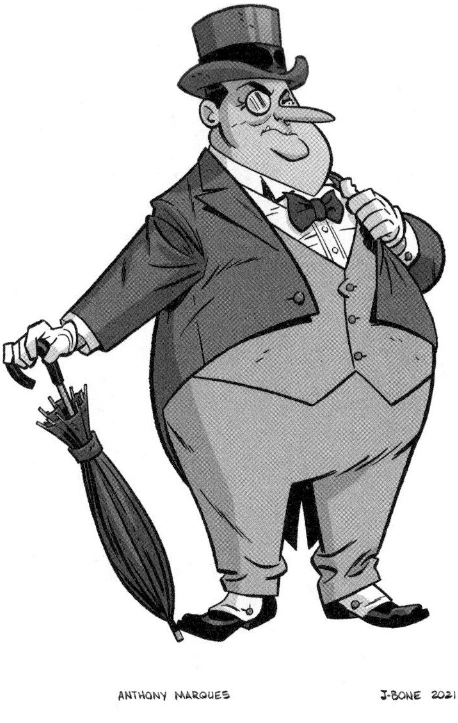
ANTHONY MARQUES
J-BONE 2021

PENGUIN

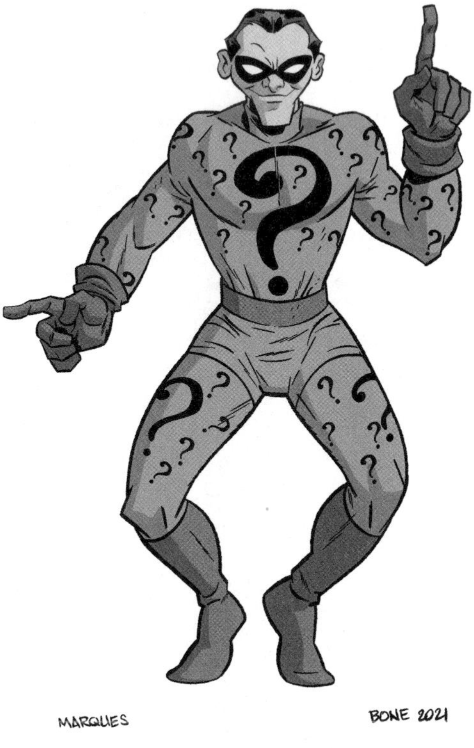
MARQUES
BONE 2021

RIDDLER

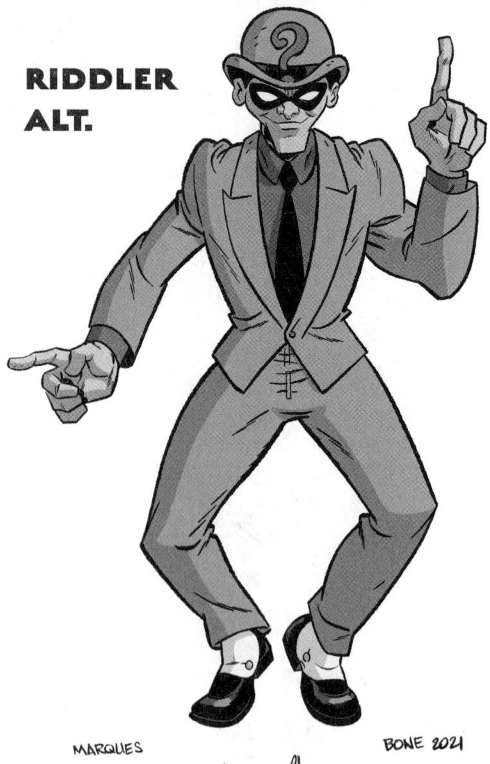
RIDDLER
ALT.
MARQUES
BONE 2021

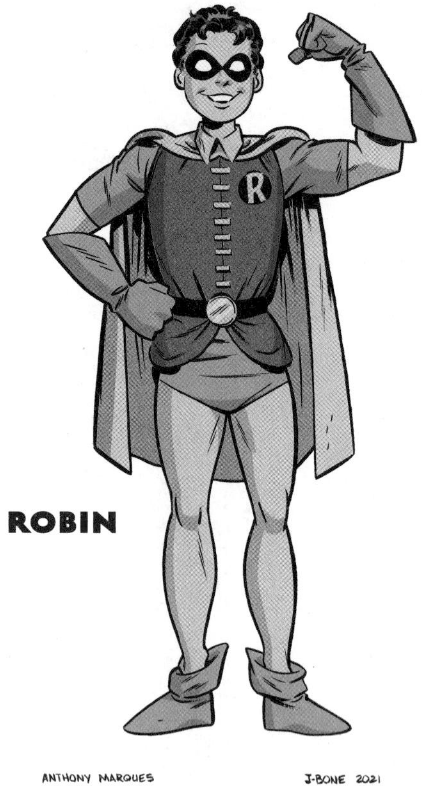
ROBIN
ANTHONY MARQUES
J-BONE 2021

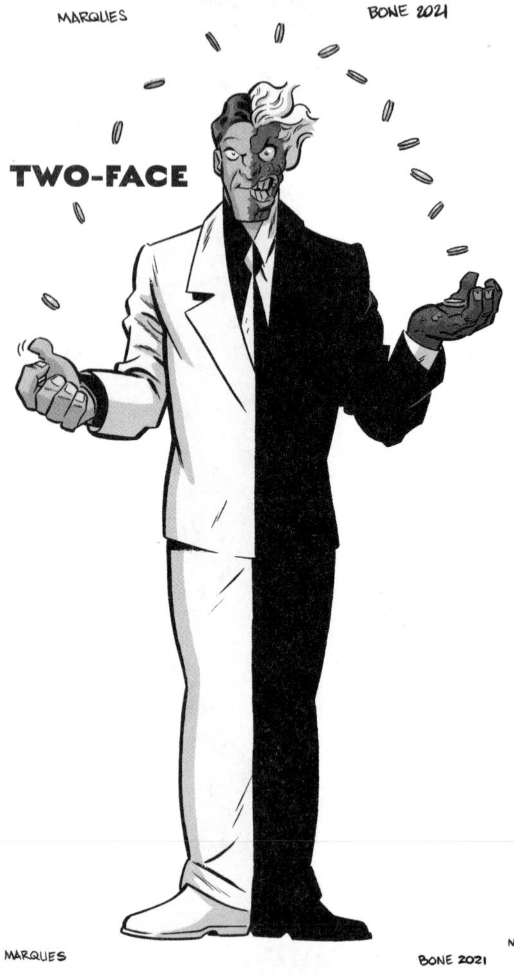
TWO-FACE
MARQUES
BONE 2021

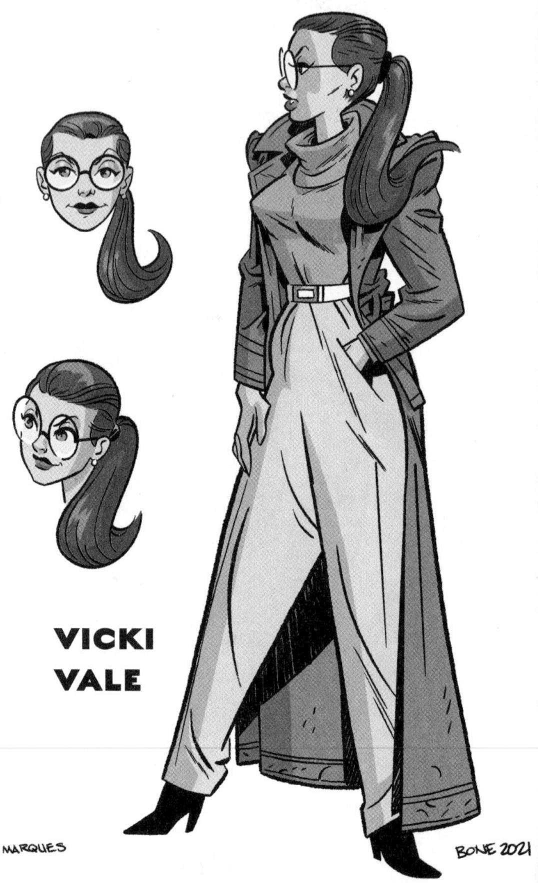
VICKI
VALE
MARQUES
BONE 2021

BATMAN VOL. 1: THE COURT OF OWLS (The New 52)

Batman has heard tales of Gotham City's Court of Owls: that the members of this powerful cabal are the true rulers of Gotham. The Dark Knight dismissed the stories as rumors and old wives' tales. Gotham was his city. Until now.

THE #1 NEW YORK TIMES BESTSELLER
THE NEW 52!
BATMAN
VOLUME 1
THE COURT OF OWLS
SCOTT SNYDER GREG CAPULLO JONATHAN GLAPION

Writer: **SCOTT SNYDER**
Artist: **GREG CAPULLO**
Price: **USA $16.99/CAN $19.99**
Format: **TR**
ISBN: **9781401235420**

BATMAN VOL. 2: THE CITY OF OWLS (The New 52)

For over a century, the Court of Owls has ruled Gotham City in secret—their reach inescapable, their power unstoppable. Until they battled the Batman.

THE #1 NEW YORK TIMES BEST-SELLING SERIES
THE NEW 52!
BATMAN
VOLUME 2
THE CITY OF OWLS
SCOTT SNYDER GREG CAPULLO JONATHAN GLAPION JAMES TYNION IV
RAFAEL ALBUQUERQUE JASON FABOK

Writer: **SCOTT SNYDER**
Artist: **GREG CAPULLO**
Price: **USA $16.99/CAN $19.99**
Format: **TR**
ISBN: **9781401232597**

BATMAN VOL. 1: THEIR DARK DESIGNS

Deathstroke, the world's greatest mercenary, is back in town under a new contract. As the Caped Crusader draws closer to uncovering the figure pulling the strings, the love of his life, Catwoman, holds the sinister secret in her claws. Can Batman pry it from her without tearing their relationship apart? And will it be enough to stop the coming plot against him?

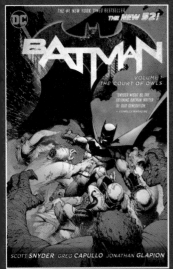

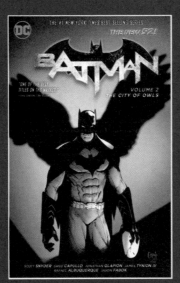

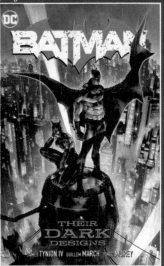

BATMAN
THEIR DARK DESIGNS
JAMES TYNION IV GUILLEM MARCH TOMEU MOREY

Writer: **JAMES TYNION IV**
Artist: **GUILLEM MARCH**
Price: **USA $24.99/CAN $33.99**
Format: **TR**
ISBN: **9781779508010**

BATMAN VOL. 1: I AM GOTHAM (Rebirth)

There are two new heroes in town with the powers of Superman and a devotion to preserving all that is good about this twisted city. But what happens if Gotham's new guardians go bad? What if they blame the Batman for the darkness that threatens to drown their city?

DC UNIVERSE REBIRTH
BATMAN
VOL. 1 I AM GOTHAM
TOM KING • DAVID FINCH

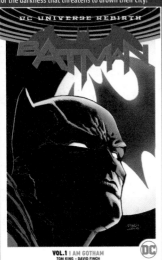

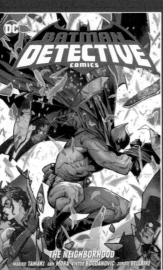

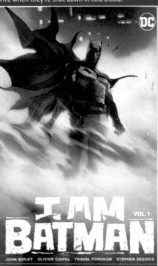

Writer: **TOM KING**
Artist: **DAVID FINCH**
Price: **USA $16.99/CAN $22.99**
Format: **TR**
ISBN: **9781401267773**

BATMAN: DETECTIVE COMICS VOL. 1: THE NEIGHBORHOOD

With the loss of his fortune and manor, the election of Mayor Nakano, and the growing anti-vigilante sentiment in Gotham, Bruce Wayne must rethink how to be Batman...or risk being left behind by his own city.

BATMAN
DETECTIVE
COMICS
THE NEIGHBORHOOD
MARIKO TAMAKI DAN MORA VIKTOR BOGDANOVIC JORDIE BELLAIRE

Writer: **MARIKO TAMAKI**
Artists: **DAN MORA and VIKTOR BOGDANOVIC**
Price: **USA $29.99/CAN $39.99**
Format: **HC**
ISBN: **9781779514226**

I AM BATMAN VOL. 1

Jace Fox thrusts himself into action when the Magistrate's crackdown on Alleytown begins! With his own Batsuit, Jace hits the streets to inspire and protect...but one Gotham vigilante pays the ultimate price when they're shot down in cold blood.

I AM BATMAN
VOL. 1
JOHN RIDLEY OLIVIER COIPEL TRAVEL FOREMAN STEPHEN SEGOVIA

Writer: **JOHN RIDLEY**
Artists: **OLIVIER COIPEL, TRAVEL FOREMAN, and STEPHEN SEGOVIA**
Price: **USA $24.99/CAN $33.99**
Format: **HC**

THE BATMAN WHO LAUGHS

Combining everything that makes the Caped Crusader a hero and the Clown Prince a killer, *The Batman Who Laughs* is the Dark Multiverse's deadliest criminal mastermind. Now he's come to Gotham to turn Bruce Wayne's home into an incubator for evil.

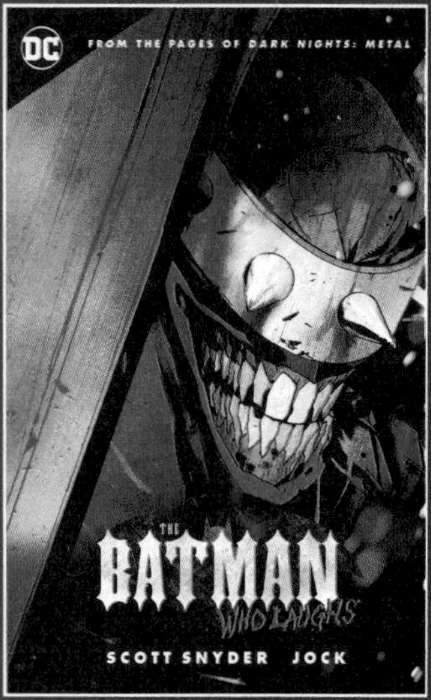
FROM THE PAGES OF DARK NIGHTS: METAL
THE BATMAN WHO LAUGHS
SCOTT SNYDER JOCK

Writer: **SCOTT SNYDER**
Artist: **JOCK**
Price: **USA $19.99/CAN $25.99**
Format: **TR**
ISBN: **9781779504463**

BATMAN: EARTH ONE

Batman is not a hero. He is just a man. Fallible, vulnerable, and angry. Writer Geoff Johns and artist Gary Frank reimagine a new mythology for the Dark Knight, where the familiar is no longer the expected.

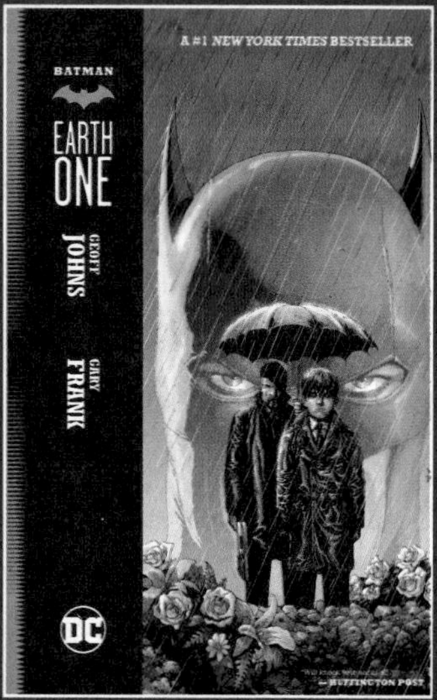
A #1 NEW YORK TIMES BESTSELLER
BATMAN
EARTH ONE
GEOFF JOHNS
GARY FRANK

Writer: **GEOFF JOHNS**
Artist: **GARY FRANK**
Price: **USA $14.99/CAN $17.99**
Format: **TR**
ISBN: **9781401232092**

BATMAN: THE ADVENTURES CONTINUE SEASON ONE

Picking up where *The Batman Adventures* left off, Batman comes face-to-face with a whole host of new adversaries and allies. Reunited visionary producers of *Batman: The Animated Series* Alan Burnett and Paul Dini show that Batman's adventures in Gotham always continue!

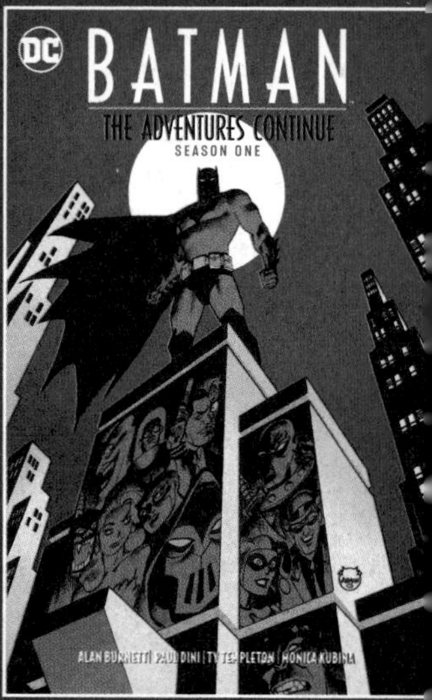
BATMAN
THE ADVENTURES CONTINUE
SEASON ONE

Writers: **ALAN BURNETT and PAUL DINI**
Artists: **TY TEMPLETON and MONICA KUBINA**
Price: **USA $19.99/CAN $25.99**
Format: **TR**
ISBN: **9781779507891**

BATMAN: KILLING TIME

Three villains, one Dark Knight, and a deadly heist gone wrong. Catwoman, the Riddler, and the Penguin join forces to pull off the greatest robbery in the history of Gotham City. And their prize? A mysterious and priceless artifact in the secret possession of Bruce Wayne!

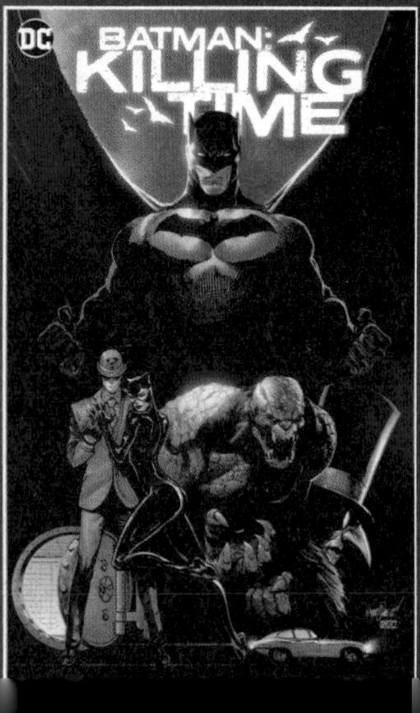
BATMAN: KILLING TIME

BATMAN '89

In 1989, moviegoers were amazed at the new vision of the Dark Knight brought to the screen by filmmaker Tim Burton, starring Michael Keaton as Batman and Jack Nicholson as The Joker. *Batman '89* is set in gothic Gotham City and features colorful villains including The Joker and Two-Face.

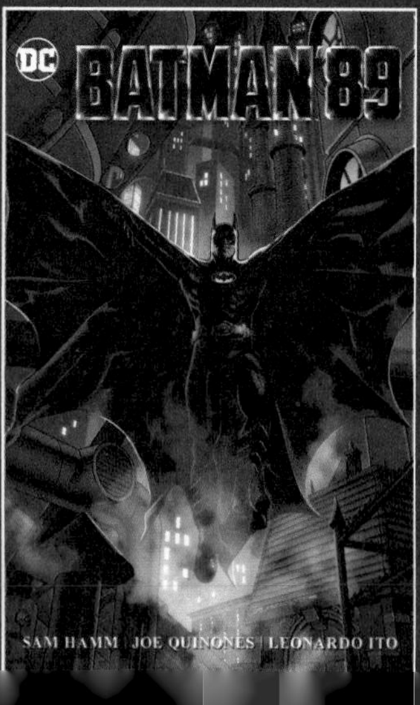
BATMAN '89
SAM HAMM | JOE QUINONES | LEONARDO ITO

ROBIN & BATMAN

Robin is just starting out at the side of Batman, struggling to find his own path from personal tragedy to being a superhero. The Eisner-winning superstar team of writer Jeff Lemire (*Sweet Tooth*) and artist Dustin Nguyen (*Batman*) unite for a three-issue limited series exploring the beginning of Dick Grayson's crime-fighting career.

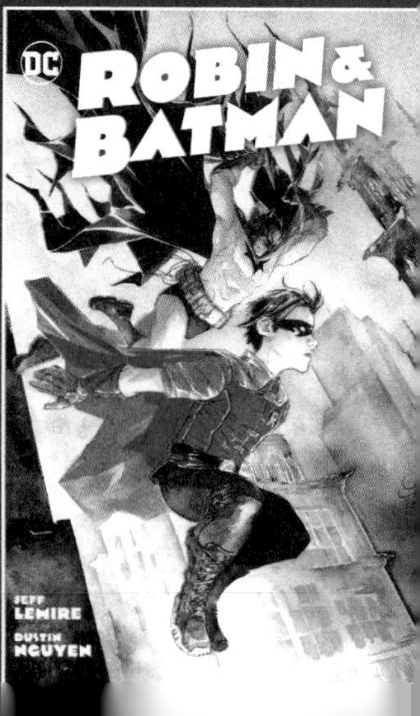
ROBIN & BATMAN
JEFF LEMIRE
DUSTIN NGUYEN